NETWORK CONVERGENCE

NETWORK CONVERGENCE

Ethernet Applications and Next Generation Packet Transport Architectures

VINOD JOSEPH and
SRINIVAS MULUGU

ELSEVIER

AMSTERDAM • BOSTON • HEIDELBERG • LONDON
NEW YORK • OXFORD • PARIS • SAN DIEGO
SAN FRANCISCO • SINGAPORE • SYDNEY • TOKYO
Morgan Kaufmann is an imprint of Elsevier

Publisher: *Steve Elliot*
Editorial Project Manager: *Kaitlin Herbert*
Project Manager: *Malathi Samayan*
Designer: *Mark Rogers*

Morgan Kaufmann is an imprint of Elsevier
225 Wyman Street, Waltham, MA 02451, USA

Library of Congress Cataloging-in-Publication Data
Joseph, Vinod.
  Network convergence : Ethernet applications and next generation packet transport architectures / Vinod Joseph, Srinivas Mulugu.
     pages cm
  Includes bibliographical references and index.
  ISBN 978-0-12-397877-6 (pbk.)
1. Ethernet (Local area network system) 2. Packet transport networks. 3. Computer network architectures. 4. Convergence (Telecommunication) 5. Internetworking (Telecommunication) I. Mulugu, Srinivas. II. Title.
  TK5105.383.J68 2013
  004.6–dc23
                                                                              2013025197

British Library Cataloguing-in-Publication Data
A catalogue record for this book is available from the British Library

ISBN: 978-0-12-397877-6

For information on all MK publications visit our website at
http://store.elsevier.com

Working together
to grow libraries in
developing countries

www.elsevier.com • www.bookaid.org

CONTENTS

INTRODUCTION

Over the years, Ethernet has become the de facto vehicle for deploying Internet communication transport infrastructures at the access, aggregation, and even the core aspects. Because of the simplicity, capacity for scalability, availability, and levels of integration that Ethernet offers across the various networking layers, it has been adopted widely across the industry. The objective of the book is to highlight the convergence of new developments, applications, and services that are emerging in Ethernet transport.

The book discusses various applications and services that can be deployed using Ethernet as a converged infrastructure linking multiple carrier and/or enterprise infrastructures. In the book we examine several services, such as MPLS Layer 3 VPNs, Point-to-Point and Multi-Point Ethernet over MPLS PWs, and provider backbone bridging, which is an option available for scaling Ethernet layer 2 services. We then move on to look at how MPLS can be used in all Ethernet access, aggregation, and core aspects to offer services such as mobility and still retain operational scale and control. We also examine MPLS-TP, a trend that is applicable in certain Ethernet access environments, before moving on to discuss how packet and optical layers can be integrated.

Please note that among all the graphics and figures appearing in this book, all symbols of routers and switches are purely generic to illustrate a device or concept. None of them represents any actual vendor. Some of the configuration templates provided are from actual vendors, such as Juniper, Cisco, and Alcatel-Lucent. This is to provide diversity and also help the reader relate to specific topics. It is by no means an endorsement of any vendors or their respective technologies.

Finally, this book is written by the two authors in their own capacities. It has no affiliation to any organizations they are directly or indirectly involved with.

DEPLOYING ETHERNET MULTI-POINT SERVICES USING VPLS

Introduction

In this chapter we take a look at virtual private LAN services (VPLS) and the various building blocks of deploying multipoint Ethernet services using VPLS.

Virtual Private LAN Service (VPLS)

Although our topic is VPLS, let us begin by taking a quick look at MPLS Layer 2 VPNs, also referred to as point-to-point services.

A point-to-point L2 VPN circuit, as defined by the pseudowire encapsulation edge to edge working group (PWE3) of the Internet Engineering Task Force (IETF), is a provider service that offers a point-to-point service infrastructure over an IP/MPLS packet switched network. The PWE3 working group describes mechanisms for delivering L2 VPN services across this kind of network. The basic reference model is shown in Figure 1.1.

A pseudowire (PW) is a connection between two provider edge (PE) devices, which connects two attachment circuits (ACs). An AC can be a Frame Relay DLCI, an ATM VPI/VCI, an Ethernet port, a VLAN, a HDLC, a PPP connection on a physical interface, a PPP session from an L2TP tunnel, an MPLS LSP, etc. During the setup of a PW, the two PE routers are configured or automatically exchange information about the service to be emulated so that later they know how to process packets coming from the other end. The PE routers use Targeted LDP (T-LDP) sessions for setting the PW. After a PW is set up between two PE routers, frames received by one PE from an AC are encapsulated and sent over the PW to the remote PE, where native frames are re-constructed and forwarded to the other CE.

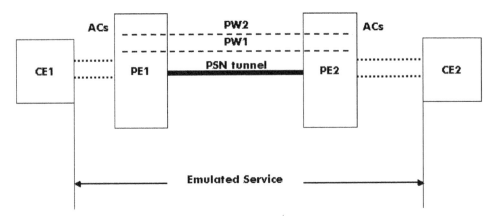

Figure 1.1

From a data-plane perspective, different PWs in the same packet-switched network (PSN) tunnel are identified using a multiplexing field. This multiplexing field is an MPLS label, and the encapsulation of the customer frames over these (MPLS) connections or PWs is defined by the PWE3 working group. PSN tunnels are implemented in the provider's network as MPLS LSPs (RSVP, LDP), or using IP-in-IP (GRE). Figure 1.2 shows the protocol stack in the core of the provider's network for Ethernet frames.

Ethernet is particularly appealing to enterprise networkers: It is mature, reliable, cheap, scalable, and well understood. Common networking practice is to connect local sites (subnets, floors, or buildings of a campus) with an Ethernet backbone switch, managing and scoping the network with layer 2 VLANs. So it comes as no surprise that such network operators would like to be able to connect sites across a wider area using the same Ethernet backbones. Nor is this interest new; as much as 15 years ago many local providers were offering metropolitan-area Ethernet services such as Transparent LAN Service (TLS), based on proprietary technologies, and LAN Emulation (LANE), based on ATM backbones. But such service offerings were not ideal for the provider due to factors such as dependency on a single vendor, for a proprietary TLS solution, and prohibitive complexity, for a LANE solution. As Ethernet technology itself advanced, permitting greater speeds at greater transmission distances, more recent metropolitan Ethernet offerings have been built around Ethernet switches. But these switch-based infrastructures have their own limitations, primarily lack of scalability due to the numeric limitations on VLAN IDs.

In recent years, VPLS has arisen as a practical, economical, and scalable alternative for creating metro Ethernet services. VPLS, in

Byte4	Byte3	Byte2	Byte1

CRC			
CRC			
Data			
Protocol ID		Source MAC address	
Source MAC address			
Destination MAC address			
Destination MAC address		MPLS VC Label	
MPLS VC Label		MPLS PSN Tunnel Label	
MPLS PSN Tunnel Label		Protocol ID	
Source MAC address			
Source MAC address		Destination MAC address	
Destination MAC address			

Figure 1.2

turn, has been made possible by the advent of MPLS, which has seen accelerating deployment in carrier and service provider networks beginning in the late 1990s. MPLS provides a means of creating virtual circuits, similar to Frame Relay DLCIs and ATM VCI/VPIs, over IP networks. Its appeal is its ability to eliminate Frame Relay and ATM infrastructures while moving the services provided by those infrastructures to an IP network, thereby reducing the overall capital and operational costs of the network. These MPLS virtual circuits—called label-switched paths (LSPs)—have for many years been used to provide Layer 3 IPv4 VPNs and Layer 2 point-to-point VPNs. More recently, the technology has been extended to support Layer 3 IPv6 VPNs, Layer 3 Multicast VPNs, and VPLS.

The advantage of VPLS for the service provider is in building on the capital and operational cost savings of an MPLS VPN network: a common IP/MPLS infrastructure with no Ethernet switches required to support the VPLS, and a common set of standards-based protocols to support all services, simplifying the management of the network. Supplying the desired service to the customer is a simple matter of installing and configuring the correct interface.

While the advantages of VPLS described here benefit the service provider, from the customer's perspective there is nothing to differentiate VPLS from any other metro Ethernet solution, beyond possibly having some of the provider's cost savings passed along as a less expensive service. However, service providers who add an inter-provider element to their VPLS offering, can differentiate themselves from competitors by providing their customers with an expanded "service footprint."

Figure 1.3 shows the VPLS reference model.

In Figure 1.3 an IP/MPLS backbone network (the packet-switched network, PSN) operated by a service provider offers a VPLS service to two VPN customers: an Orange customer and a Red

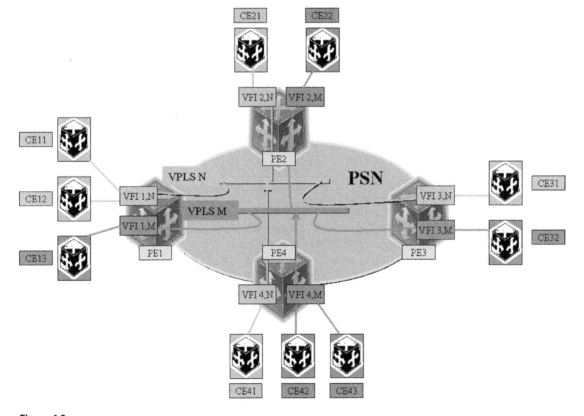

Figure 1.3

customer. Each customer has private sites that it wants to interconnect at the Ethernet layer. Customer sites are connected to the SP's backbone via attachment circuits (AC) between customer edge (CE) devices and provider edge (PE) devices. As such, a VPN can be represented by a collection of CE devices. In this illustration, the Orange L2VPN N consists of < CE11, CE12, CE21, CE31, CE41 > while the Red L2VPN M consists of < CE22, CE31, CE32, CE42, CE43 >.

As with all PE-based VPNs, with VPLS, the CE devices are unaffected by the service: a VPLS CE can be a standard router, or an Ethernet bridge or host. It is the PE device that implements VPLS-specific functions. Indeed, the PE device needs to implement a separate virtual forwarding instance (VFI)–also known as virtual switched instance (VSI), the equivalent of VRF tables for MPLS Layer 3 VPNs)–for every VPLS it is attached to. This VFI has physical direct interfaces to attached CE devices that belong to the VPLS, and virtual interfaces or pseudowires that are point-to-point connections to remote VFIs belonging to the same VPLS and located in other PE devices. These PWs are carried from one PE to another PE via PSN tunnels. From a data-plane perspective, different PWs in the same PSN tunnel are identified using a multiplexing field. This multiplexing field is an MPLS label. The encapsulation of the customer Ethernet frames over these MPLS connections or PWs is defined by the PWE3 working group. PSN tunnels are implemented in the provider's network as MPLS LSPs (RSVP, LDP) or using IP-in-IP (GRE). Figure 1.4 shows the protocol stack in the core of the provider's network.

A Draft-Rosen MVPN represents itself as an emulated LAN. Each MVPN has a logical PIM interface and will form an adjacency to every other PIM interface across PE routers within the same MVPN. This is illustrated in Figure 1.__.

Note that with VPLS, a full mesh of PSN tunnels between the network's PE devices is assumed, and for every VPLS instance there is a full mesh of pseudowires between the VFIs belonging to that VPLS. The IETF Layer 2 VPN working group has produced two separate VPLS standards,0 documented in RFC 4761 and RFC 4762 (see Kompella and Rekhter, Jan. 2007, and Lasserre and Kompella, Jan. 2007). These two RFCs define almost identical approaches with respect to the VPLS data plane, but they specify significantly different approaches to implementing the VPLS control planes.

VPLS Control Plane

The VPLS control plane has two primary functions: autodiscovery and signaling. Discovery refers to the process of finding all PE routers that participate in a given VPLS instance. A PE router can be

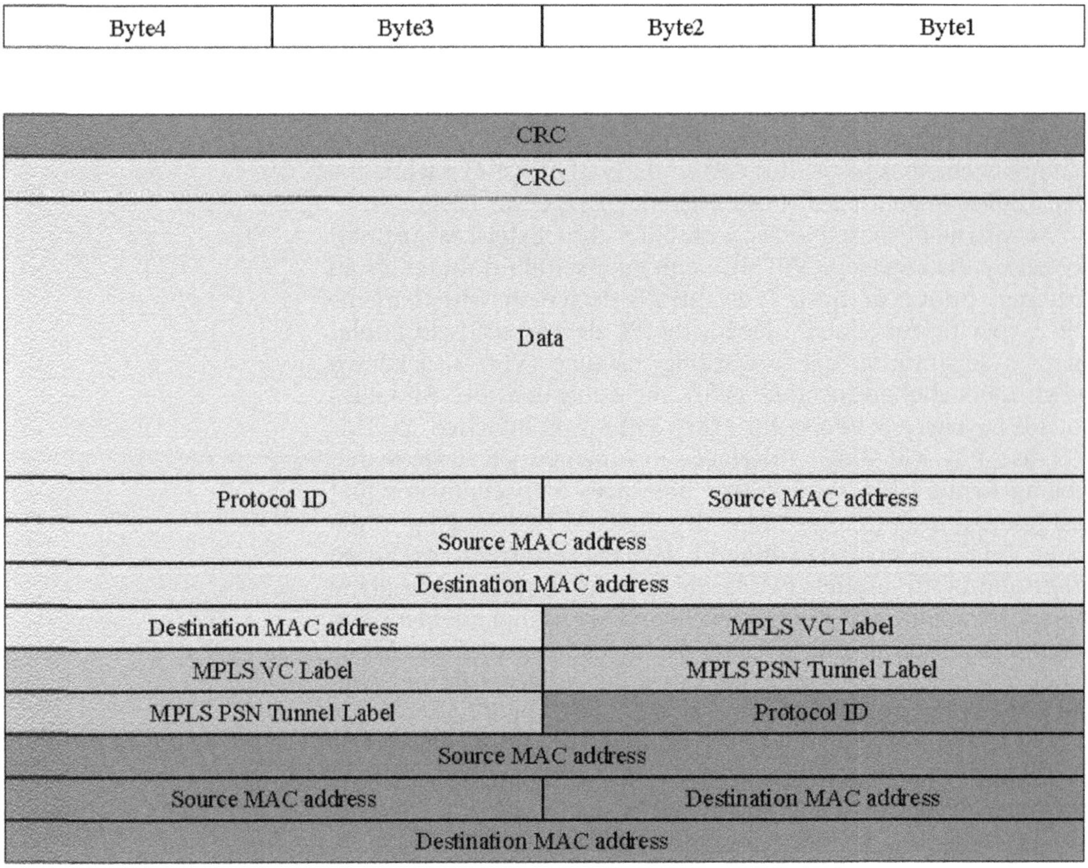

Byte4	Byte3	Byte2	Byte1

CRC			
CRC			
Data			
Protocol ID		Source MAC address	
Source MAC address			
Destination MAC address			
Destination MAC address		MPLS VC Label	
MPLS VC Label		MPLS PSN Tunnel Label	
MPLS PSN Tunnel Label		Protocol ID	
Source MAC address			
Source MAC address		Destination MAC address	
Destination MAC address			

Figure 1.4

configured with the identities of all the other PE routers in a given VPLS instance, or the PE router can use a protocol to discover the other PE routers. The latter method is called autodiscovery. After discovery occurs, each pair of PE routers in a VPLS network must be able to establish pseudowires to each other, and in the event of membership change, the PE router must be able to tear down the established pseudowires. This process is known as signaling. Signaling is also used to transmit certain characteristics of the pseudowire that a PE router sets up for a given VPLS.

BGP-VPLS Control Plane

The BGP-VPLS control plane, as defined by RFC 4761, is similar to that for Layer 2 and Layer 3 (see Kompella, Jan. 2006, and Rosen and Rekhter, Feb. 2006). It defines a means for a PE router to

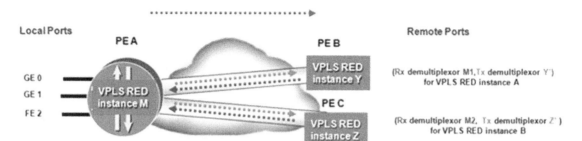

Auto-Discovery : PE-A Announces to other PEs (or RR) that it has VPLS Instance M for VPLS domain RED

Signaling : PE-A Announce to other PEs which demultiplexors (M1 & M2) should be used to send it traffic (Rx)

* **A VPLS Domain is a set of VPLS Instances.**
* **Each VPLS Instance consist of:**
    * Local Ports
    * Remote Ports
        * Each connects a VPLS Instance
        * Requires a set of pseudo-wires, one to send traffic and one to receive

Figure 1.5

discover which remote PE routers are members of a given VPLS (autodiscovery), and for a PE router to know which pseudowire label a given remote PE router will use when sending the data to the local PE router (signaling). With the BGP-VPLS control plane, BGP carries enough information to provide the autodiscovery and signaling functions simultaneously. See Figure 1.5.

The details for de-multiplexer fields will be discussed in the following sections. As in the BGP scheme for Layer 2 and Layer 3 VPNs, a route target is configured on each PE router for each VPLS present on the PE router. The route target is the same for a particular VPLS across all PE routers and is used to identify the VPLS instance to which an incoming BGP message pertains. For each VPLS on each PE router, an identifier, known as a site identifier, is configured. Each PE router involved in a particular VPLS must be configured with a unique site identifier. The site identifier is the same as the virtual edge identifier (VE ID) referred to in RFC 4761, which prescribes one VE ID per PE for each VPLS instance, irrespective of how many local ports belong to that VPLS. A label block is a set of de-multiplexer labels used to reach a given VPLS site within a set of remote sites. The PE router uses a label block to send a single common update message to establish a pseudowire with multiple PE routers, instead of having to send an individual

```
routing-instances vpnA {  // Configuration for VPN A
   instance-type vpls;       // vpls
   interface ge-0/0/0.0;  // multipoint Ethernet interface
   route-distinguisher 1234:5.6.7.8;
   route-target 1234:8765; // set Route Target to 1234:8765
   protocols {                     // PE-CE protocol
      vpls {
         site-range 20;
         site CE-A3 {
            site-identifier 3;
         }
      }
   }
}
```

Figure 1.6

message to each PE router. A number of illustrations in the following sections elaborate on this in greater detail.

Note: Each PE router creates a virtual connection table (VCT) per VPLS instance. The VCT is similar to the virtual forwarding instance (VFI) referred to earlier in this chapter). Hence the terms VCT and VFI are used interchangeably in this chapter.

Figure 1.6 shows a JUNOS Configuration snippet describing the basic setup of a BGP-based VPLS instance. The configuration here is exactly the same as the configuration for BGP/MPLS Layer 3 VPNs, with the exception of the keyword "VPLS" defined under the protocols hierarchy, which in the case of BGP/MPLS VPNs would BGP or OSPF or RIP, etc.

Figure 1.7 illustrates a two-site VPLS instance created between two PE routers clarifies the configuration statements provided above, and their relevance.

In Figure 1.7, PE2 allocates a label base of "2000" for a given VPLS instance: VPLS RED. PE3 uses label base "3000" for the same VPLS instance. The illustration that follows shows the role of the label base.

In Figure 1.8, PE2 has been allotted 3002 by PE3, as the inner label to be used to reach Site 3 on PE3. Similarly PE3 will use 2003 as the Inner label for reaching Site 2 on PE2. Another label would be used by each of the PE routers, if they needed to connect to another site within the same VPLS instance (VPLS RED) on another PE. The MPLS outer labels are also displayed in PE2's VFT (Label 640).

If more PE routers are added to VPLS instance RED, each of them uses different label. This is illustrated in Figure 1.9.

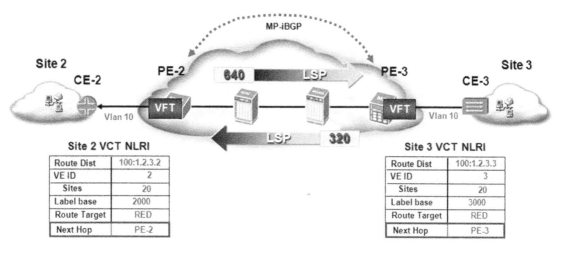

Site 2 VCT NLRI	
Route Dist	100:1.2.3.2
VE ID	2
Sites	20
Label base	2000
Route Target	RED
Next Hop	PE-2

Site 3 VCT NLRI	
Route Dist	100:1.2.3.3
VE ID	3
Sites	20
Label base	3000
Route Target	RED
Next Hop	PE-3

PE-PE VCT distribution using Multi-Protocol BGP (RFC 2858)
- Requires full-mesh MP-iBGP or Route Reflectors
- Route Distinguisher: "uniquifies" VCT information
- Route Target: determines VPN topology
- Analogous to CE-PE routes advertisements in RFC2547 VPNs
- One single LNRI advertisement per VPLS instance per PE is sufficient

Figure 1.7

In PE2's VFT, site-id "1" and site-id "15" have different MPLS outer and inner labels. This indicates that those sites belong to different PE routers. The same is the case with PE3.

LDP-VPLS Control Plane

In contrast to the BGP-VPLS control plane, the LDP-VPLS control plane provides only signaling but no autodiscovery (more on this in the following sections). In this control plane, LDP is used to signal the pseudowires that interconnect the VPLS instances of a given customer on the PE routers. The LDP signaling scheme for VPLS is similar to the LDP scheme for point-to-point Layer 2 connections (see Martini et al., Apr. 2006). In the absence of an autodiscovery mechanism, the identities of all the remote PE routers that are part of a VPLS instance must be configured on each PE router manually.

The virtual circuit identifier (VCID), which is in the point-to-point Layer 2 connection used to identify a specific pseudowire, is configured to be the same for a particular VPLS instance on all PE routers. Hence, the VCID enables a PE router to identify

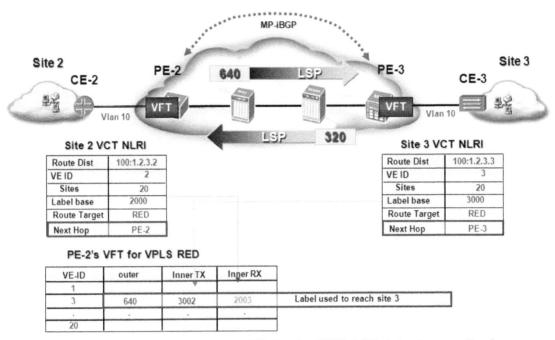

Site 2 VCT NLRI

Route Dist	100:1.2.3.2
VE ID	2
Sites	20
Label base	2000
Route Target	RED
Next Hop	PE-2

Site 3 VCT NLRI

Route Dist	100:1.2.3.3
VE ID	3
Sites	20
Label base	3000
Route Target	RED
Next Hop	PE-3

PE-2's VFT for VPLS RED

VE-ID	outer	Inner TX	Inner RX	
1				
3	640	3002	2003	Label used to reach site 3
.	.	.	.	
20				

▪ PE-2 receives BGP NLRI from PE-3's for RED VPLS instance site 3

Figure 1.8

the VPLS instance to which the LDP message refers. This is illustrated in Figure 1.10.

LDP-VPLS and BGP-VPLS Forwarding Planes

Forwarding plane procedures, at least for unicast and to some extent for multicast (which we will see later in this chapter), are the same for BGP-VPLS and LGP-VPLS. For each VPLS, a PE VPLS data plane functions as a learning bridge and supports all the standard bridge operations, such as MAC address learning, aging, and flooding. All the pseudowires established by BGP or LDP signaling and the local customer edge (CE) router ports of a VPLS instance constitute the logical ports of a bridge domain.

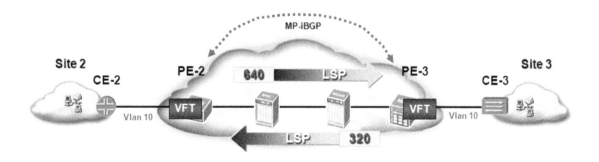

PE-2's VFT for VPLS RED

VE-ID	outer	Inner TX	Inner RX
1	600	5002	2001
3	640	3002	2003
.	.	.	.
15	670	9002	2020

PE-3's VFT for VPLS RED

VE-ID	outer	Inner TX	Inner RX
1	300	5003	3001
2	320	2003	3002
.	.	.	.
15	360	9003	3020

- A full mesh of pseudo-wires are set-up between all VPLS instances for VPLS RED

Figure 1.9

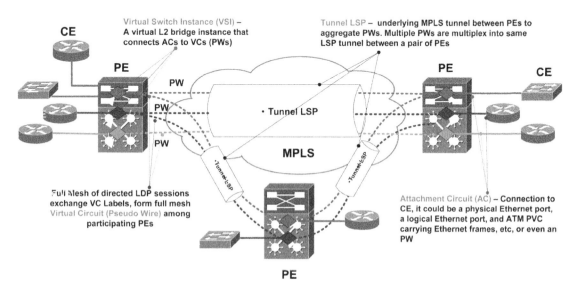

Virtual Switch Instance (VSI) – A virtual L2 bridge instance that connects ACs to VCs (PWs)

Tunnel LSP – underlying MPLS tunnel between PEs to aggregate PWs. Multiple PWs are multiplex into same LSP tunnel between a pair of PEs

Full Mesh of directed LDP sessions exchange VC Labels, form full mesh Virtual Circuit (Pseudo Wire) among participating PEs

Attachment Circuit (AC) – Connection to CE, it could be a physical Ethernet port, a logical Ethernet port, and ATM PVC carrying Ethernet frames, etc, or even an PW

Figure 1.10

A MAC forwarding table is created for each VPLS instance on a PE router. This table is populated using a source MAC address learning function and is used to forward unicast VPLS traffic based on the destination MAC address of the received frame. The control plane of VPLS does not need to advertise and distribute reachability information; it uses address learning of the standard bridge function in the data plane to provide reachability. Just like an Ethernet switch, the VPLS floods all the received Ethernet packets with unknown unicast addresses, broadcast addresses, and multicast addresses to all ports (i.e., all the ports and PWs associated with the VPLS instance.).

To forward a packet, a PE must be able to establish an MAC forwarding database (FDB). Different from the BGP/MPLS Layer 3 VPN that uses the route advertisement mechanism to establish a routing table in the control plane, the VPLS uses the standard bridge learning function to establish the FDB in the forwarding plane. The MAC address FDB is established by MAC address learning, which includes learning packets from UNI/Attachment Circuit and packets from PWs. The MAC address learning process has two parts:
- Remote MAC address learning associated with PWs connected to remote PE routers
- Local MAC address learning of the port directly connected to the user attachment circuit

The MAC learning process is shown in Figure 1.11. The process starts with a user having MAC address A and IP address "1.1.1.2" try to reach MAC address B connected to a remote PE. The ingress PE floods the packet across all PWs for the relevant VPLS instance (if the destination MAC address is unknown). In this case, one of the PE router responds to the ARP request originated by the sender's MAC address. The ingress PE builds its MAC database with the relevant MAC-Address-PW/Remote PE for future use. The illustration also shows that another PE router, in the same VPLS instance, also builds its MAC FDB with an entry for MAC A.

Autodiscovery for LDP-VPLS

The previous section discussed how LDP-based VPLS traditionally relied on manual and static configurations on all participating PE routers. For instance, if a new customer with 20 sites were to be provisioned in the network, each PE router would need to be configured with all the customer-specific details, such as the VC-ID, to facilitate creating a PW with each PE router. If a new customer site were later added to these initial 20 sites, all the PE routers would again need to be configured to identify this new site. The configuring has to be performed manually, which

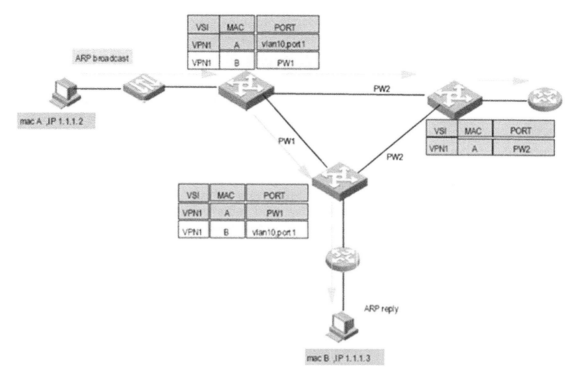

Figure 1.11

becomes an operational nightmare in a large carrier network, because of the large the number of touch-points involved in provisioning new sites or customers.

LDP-VPLS can now rely on BGP for autodiscovery (AD). BGP AD is a framework for automatically discovering, connecting, and maintaining the endpoints for a VPLS instance. It provides one-touch provisioning for LDP-VPLS where all the related PEs are discovered automatically. The service provider can use existing BGP policies to regulate the exchanges between PEs. The procedure does not require carriers to uproot their existing VPLS deployments and change the signaling protocol just to provide discovery functions.

The BGP protocol establishes neighbor relationships between configured peers. An OPEN message is sent after the completion of the three-way TCP handshake. This OPEN message contains information about the BGP peer sending the message, including the Autonomous System Number, BGP version, timer information, and operational parameters, including capabilities. The capabilities of a peer are exchanged using two numerical values, the address family identifier (AFI) and subsequent address family identifier (SAFI). These numbers are allocated by the Internet Assigned Numbers Authority (IANA). A peer that announces a capability AFI 65 (L2VPN) and SAFI 25 (BGP-VPLS) is indicating support for BGP AD. The complete list of AFI and SAFI allocations can be found at these URLS: "http://www.iana.org/assignments/address-family-numbers" and "http://www.iana.org/assignments/safi-namespace."

Following the establishment of the peer relationship, the discovery process begins as soon as a new VPLS service is provisioned on the PE. Two VPLS identifiers are used to indicate the VPLS membership and the individual VPLS instance:

1. VPLS-ID – membership information and a unique network-wide identifier. The same value is assigned for all VPLS switch/forwarding instances belonging to the same VPLS. It is encodable and carried as a BGP extended community in one of the following formats:
   - A two-octet AS-specific extended community
   - An IPv4 address-specific extended community
2. VSI-ID – a unique identifier for each VSI/VFI, built by linking a route distinguisher (RD) with a 4 bytes identifier (usually the system IP of the VPLS PE). It is encoded and carried as a BGP-VPLS NLRI: i.e., RD:IP.

To advertise this information BGP AD employs a simplified version of the BGP-VPLS NLRI, where just the RD and the next 4 bytes (VE ID and VE Block Offset) are used to identify the VPLS instance. There is no need for label block and label size fields, as T-LDP will take care of signaling the service labels later on. The resulting format of the BGP AD NLRI is very similar to the one used for BGP/MPLS Layer 3 VPNs, as depicted in Figure 1.12. The system IP may be used for the last 4 bytes of the VSI ID, further simplifying the addressing and the provisioning process.

Network layer reachability information (NLRI) is exchanged between BGP peers, indicating how to reach prefixes. With VPLS, the NLRI is used to tell PE peers how to reach the VSI, rather than specific prefixes. The advertisement includes the BGP next hop and a route target (RT). The BGP next hop indicates the VSI location and in the next step is used to determine which signaling session should be employed for PW signaling. The RT, also coded as

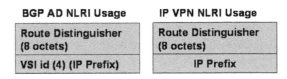

Figure 1.12

an extended community, can be used to build a VPLS full mesh or an H-VPLS hierarchy, using BGP import/export policies. BGP is only used to discover VPN endpoints and exchange reachability information. It is not used to signal the PW labels. This task remains the responsibility of targeted-LDP (T-LDP).

Exploring the topic of T-LDP further: Two LDP FEC elements are defined in RFC 4447 (PW Setup and Maintenance Using LDP). The original PWid FEC element 128 (0x80) employs a 32-bit field to identify the virtual circuit ID and was used extensively in early VPLS deployments. The simple format is easy to understand, but it does not provide the required structure for the BGP autodiscovery function. To support BGP AD and other new applications, a new Layer 2 FEC Element, the generalized PWid FEC element 129 (0x81) is required.[1]

The generalized PWid FEC element has been designed for autodiscovery applications. It provides a field, the Address Group Identifier (AGI), that can be used to signal membership information, for example, VPLS id in the VPLS case. Separate address fields are provided for the source and target endpoints, called, respectively, Source Attachment Individual Identifier (SAII) and Target Attachment Individual Identifier (TAII). These are the VSI id for the two instances to be connected through the signaled PW.

The format for FEC 129 is depicted in Figure 1.13.

Each FEC field is designed as a sub-TLV equipped with its own type and length, providing support for new applications. To accommodate the BGP AD information model, the following FEC formats are used:

- AGI (type 1), which is identical in format and content with the BGP extended community attribute used to carry the VPLS-ID value
- Source AII (type 1), a 4-bytes value destined to carry the local VSI-id (outgoing NLRI minus the RD)
- Target AII (type 1), a 4-bytes value destined to carry the remote VSI-id (incoming NLRI minus the RD)

BGP is responsible for discovering the location of VSIs that share the same VPLS membership. LDP protocol is responsible for setting up the PW infrastructure between the related VSIs by exchanging service-specific labels between them. Once the local VPLS information is provisioned in the PE, the related PEs participating in the same VPLS are identified through BGP AD exchanges. A list of far-end PEs is generated and will trigger LDP-specific functions: such as the creation, if required, of

---

[1] More detailed information for each FEC can be found in sections 5.2 (0x80) and 5.3 (0x81) of RFC 4447.

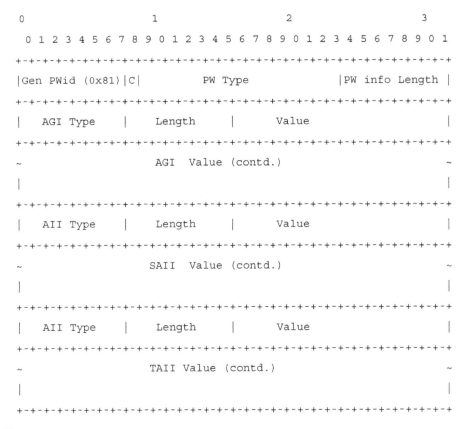

Figure 1.13

T-LDP sessions needed by these PEs and the exchange of service-specific VPN labels. The steps for the BGP AD process and the LDP session establishment and label exchange are shown in Figure 1.14.

Implementations allow for PWs that are provisioned and auto-discovered manually to coexist in the same VPLS instance, that is, both FEC 128 and FEC 129 are supported. This allows autodiscovery to be introduced gradually into an existing VPLS deployment. Still, since FEC 128 and 129 represent different addressing schemes, it is important to make sure that just one of them is used at any point in time between the same two VPLS instances. Otherwise both PWs may become active, causing a loop that might cause the service to malfunction. Hence it is recommended to disable the FEC 128 PW in a portion of the network as soon as the FEC 129 addressing scheme is introduced there. Alternatively, a Layer 2 protocol such as RSTP may be used during the migration provide additional protection against operational errors.

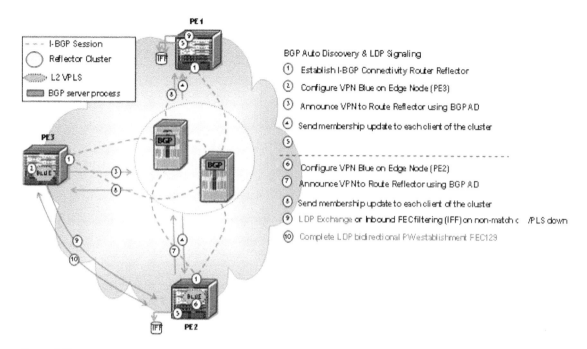

Figure 1.14

Autodiscovery for LDP-VPLS – Implementation Details

This section looks at details of implementation to understand the concepts just discussed. For this purpose we are using a TiMOS (Alcatel-Lucent) specific configuration only. We are not illustrating other vendor implementations (JUNOS or Cisco IOS/XR), since the objective of this section is simply to examine the level of configuration detail required for BGP AD.

Based on Figure 1.15, let's assume PE6 was previously configured with VPLS 100, as indicated by the configuration lines in the upper right. The BGP AD process will commence after PE134 is configured with the VPLS 100 instance shown in the upper left, a simple, basic BGP AD configuration. The minimum requirement for enabling BGP AD on a VPLS instance is configuring the VPLS-id and pointing to a pw-template.

In many cases VPLS connectivity is based on a PW mesh. To reduce the configuration requirement, the BGP values can be automatically generated using the vpls-id and the PE router-id. By default, the lower six bytes of the vpls-id are used to generate the RD and the RT values. The VSI-id value is generated from the PE router-id. All of these parameters are configurable and can be coded to suit the customer's requirements and to build different

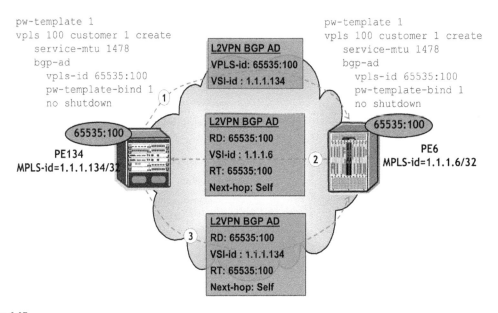

Figure 1.15

topologies. In the configuration above, a VPLS instance named "Customer 1" with a service-identifier of "100" is created. BGP AD is configured along with the VPLS-ID for this instance, which is configured as "65535:100." This is similar to the RD in the context of a BGP/MPLS VPN. The MTU SIZE is also set to 1478 bytes.

The command "PW-Template" is defined under the top level `service` command and specifies whether to use an automatically generated service distribution path (SDP). By definition, an SDP acts as a logical way of directing traffic from one PE to another through a uni-directional service tunnel.

A SDP originating on one node terminates at a destination node, which then directs incoming traffic to the correct egress service access point (SAP), as it is known in TiMOS, or UNI. The easiest way to refer to an SDP is to consider it as the equivalent of a PW. An SDP can be automatically created using a PW-Template or by manual configuration, wherein each VPLS customer/instance is associated with a given SDP. Two types of SDPs can be used in a VPLS deployment:

- Spoke SDP: Flooded traffic received on the spoke SDP is replicated on all ports within the same VPLS instance, with split horizon assumed.
- Mesh SDP: Flooded traffic received on any mesh SDP is replicated to all ports within the same VPLS instance, with the exception of not being forwarded on any mesh SDP.

```
PERs6>config>service# pw-template 1 create
 - [no] pw-template <policy-id> [use-provisioned-sdp]

 <policy-id>          : [1..2147483647]
 <use-provisioned-s*> : keyword


 [no] accounting-pol* - Configure accounting-policy to be used
 [no] collect-stats   - Enable/disable statistics collection
 [no] disable-aging   - Enable/disable aging of MAC addresses
 [no] disable-learni* - Enable/disable learning of new MAC addresses
 [no] discard-unknow* - Enable/disable discarding of frames with unknown
                        source MAC address
      egress          + Spoke SDP binding egress configuration
      igmp-snooping   + Configure IGMP snooping parameters
      ingress         + Spoke SDP binding ingress configuration
 [no] limit-mac-move  - Configure mac move
 [no] mac-pinning     - Enable/disable MAC address pinning on this spoke
SDP
 [no] max-nbr-mac-ad* - Configure the maximum number of MAC entries in
the FDB
                        from this SDP
 [no] split-horizon-* + Configure a split horizon group
      vc-type         - Configure VC type
 [no] vlan-vc-tag     - Configure VLAN VC tag
```

Figure 1.16 Commands for PW Binding

SDP deployment is discussed further in subsequent sections.

Now we will look at some commands: The command given in Figure 1.16 provides the set of parameters required for establishing the PW binding described in the sections that follow.

A pw-template-bind command configured within the VPLS service under the bgp-ad subcommand is a pointer to the pw-template that should be used. If a VPLS service does not specify an import-rt list, then that binding applies to all route targets accepted by that VPLS. The pw-template-bind command can select a different template on a per import-rt basis. Further, it is possible to specify pw-templates for some route targets with a VPLS service and use the single pw-template-bind command to address all unspecified but accepted imported targets. In the configuration shown above, the pw-template-bind 1, binds template 1 with a set of given characteristics to a particular VPLS instance. The various command options are given in Figure 1.17.

It is important understand the significancc of the split horizon group used by the pw-template. Traditionally, when a VPLS instance was created manually, the PWs were automatically

```
PERs6>config>service>vpls>bgp-ad# pw-template-bind
  -   pw-template-bind  <policy-id>  [split-horizon-group  <group-name>]
[import-rt
    {ext-community, ...(upto 5 max)}]
  - no pw-template-bind <policy-id>

 <policy-id>           :  [1..2147483647]
 <group-name>          :  [32 chars max]
 <ext-community>         :  target:{<ip-addr:comm-val>|<as-number:ext-comm-
val>}

                      ip-addr     - a.b.c.d
                      comm-val    - [0..65535]
                      as-number   - [1..65535]
                      ext-comm-val - [0..4294967295]
```

Figure 1.17 Options for the PW-Template Command

placed in a common split horizon group to prevent forwarding between the PWs in the VPLS instances. This prevented loops that would have otherwise occurred in the Layer 2 service. However, with a VPLS service using BGP autodiscover, the service provider has the option of associating the autodiscovered PWs with a split horizon group to control the forwarding between PWs.

Once the VPN endpoints have been discovered using BGP, T-LDP is triggered. The T-LDP session between the PEs is established when one does not exist. The Far-End IP address required for the T-LDP identification is gleaned from the BGP AD next hop information. The pw-template and pw-template-bind configuration statements are used to establish the automatic SDP or to map to the appropriate SDP (if a PW is already established between two PE routers and a new site is coming up on one of these PEs). The FEC 129 content is built using the following values:

- AGI from the locally configured VPLS-id
- The SAII from the locally configured VSI-id
- The TAII from the VSI-id contained in the last 4 bytes of the received BGP NLRI

The illustration in Figure 1.18 shows in detail the different phases of the LDP signaling path, after BGP AD is complete. It also shows how some fields can be autogenerated when they are not specified in the configuration.

Now to check a few operational commands as given in Figure 1.19: The first command displays the LDP peering relationships that have been established. The type of adjacency is displayed in the Adj Type column. In this case the type is Both, meaning link and targeted sessions have been successfully established.

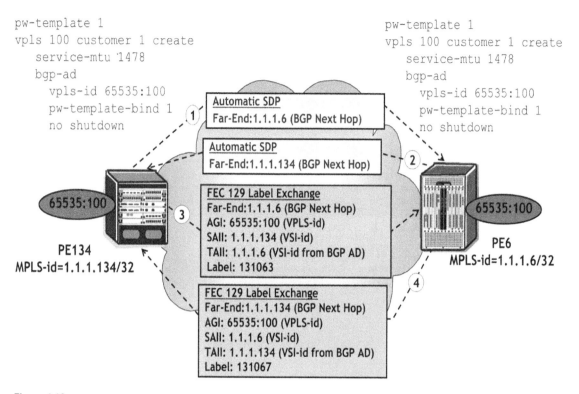

```
pw-template 1                        pw-template 1
vpls 100 customer 1 create           vpls 100 customer 1 create
  service-mtu 1478                      service-mtu 1478
  bgp-ad                               bgp-ad
    vpls-id 65535:100                    vpls-id 65535:100
    pw-template-bind 1                   pw-template-bind 1
    no shutdown                          no shutdown
```

Figure 1.18

```
PE6# show router ldp session
===============================================================================
LDP Sessions
===============================================================================
Peer LDP Id        Adj Type    State        Msg Sent   Msg Recv   Up Time
-------------------------------------------------------------------------------
1.1.1.134:0        Both        Established  21482      21482      0d 15:38:44
-------------------------------------------------------------------------------
No. of Sessions: 1
===============================================================================
```

Figure 1.19 Verifying the LDP Session

The second command, in Figure 1.20, shows the specific LDP service label information broken up according to its FEC element type, either 128 or 129. The information for FEC element 129 includes the AGI, SAII, and TAII. The SDP-ID is a number assigned to the PW or SDP between the two PE routers for the given VPLS instance.

To further understand specific topologies and their implementations in regard to BGP AD, we will consider several use cases in later sections of this chapter.

```
PE# show router ldp bindings fec-type services
================================================================================
LDP LSR ID: 1.1.1.6
================================================================================
Legend: U - Label In Use, N - Label Not In Use, W - Label Withdrawn
        S - Status Signaled Up,  D - Status Signaled Down
        E - Epipe Service, V - VPLS Service, M - Mirror Service
        A - Apipe Service, F - Fpipe Service, I - IES Service, R - VPRN service
        P - Ipipe Service, C - Cpipe Service
        TLV - (Type, Length: Value)
================================================================================
LDP Service FEC 128 Bindings
================================================================================
Type   VCId       SvcId     SDPId  Peer           IngLbl  EgrLbl  LMTU  RMTU
--------------------------------------------------------------------------------
No Matching Entries Found

================================================================================
LDP Service FEC 129 Bindings
================================================================================
AGI                               SAII             TAII
Type           SvcId     SDPId  Peer           IngLbl  EgrLbl  LMTU  RMTU
--------------------------------------------------------------------------------
65535:100                         1.1.1.6          1.1.1.134
V-Eth          100       17406  1.1.1.134      131063U 131067S 1464  1464
--------------------------------------------------------------------------------
No. of FEC 129s: 1
================================================================================
```

Figure 1.20 Verifying LDP Bindings

Characteristics of LDP-VPLS

To enable VPLS, all PE routers connected to common VPLS customers must be able to exchange VPLS signaling information. As the number of PE routers in the network increases, scaling this signaling component of the VPLS control plane becomes essential.

For LDP-VPLS signaling, VPLS signaling information is exchanged by setting up a full mesh of targeted LDP sessions between each pair of PE routers that have at least one VPLS in common. A brief description of T-LDP (Targeted LDP) is provided below.

Normally, LDP sessions are set up between directly connected LSRs. In a network in which the IGP routes need to be labeled this is sufficient, because the label switching of packets is hop per hop—if the label bindings are advertised hop per hop for the IGP routes, the LSPs are set up. However, in cases where LSRs are not directly connected, for example, with VPLS or Layer 3

VPN services,, a remote or targeted LDP session is needed. Targeted LDP sessions are different because during the discovery phase, hellos are unicast to the LDP peer rather than multicast.

As the size of the VPLS network grows, the number of LDP targeted sessions increases exponentially on the order of $O(N^2)$, where N is the number of LDP-VPLS PE routers in the network. Maintenance of all these LDP sessions creates an additional load on the control plane of PE routers in the VPLS network. The operational challenge resulting from the $O(N^2)$ increase in LDP sessions becomes even more noticeable when a service provider authenticates the sessions using Message Digest 5 (MD5) because MD5 keys must be configured on each end of every LDP session. Adding a new PE router or deleting an existing one becomes a cumbersome task because the configuration on each PE router in the network must be modified. An illustration of the full-mesh problem in LDP-VPLS is provided in Figure 1.21.

To address the control plane scaling issues in using a Flat-VPLS model as illustrated above, a hierarchy can be defined within the VPLS domain. This method of creating a hierarchy is known as H-VPLS (Hierarchical VPLS). H-VPLS tries to mitigate the full-mesh requirement by creating a two-level hierarchy of hub and spoke devices. Using an H-VPLS model, a service provider can deploy MTUs (multi-tenant units) in a multi-tenant building, with each enterprise in the beginning potentially belonging to a different VPLS VPN. The service provider then needs to aggregate the MTU traffic towards the PE device in the central office or point of presence (POP).

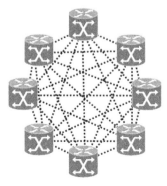

- Potential signaling overhead
- Full PW mesh from the edge
- Packet replication done at the edge

Figure 1.21

A traditional MTU is an Ethernet device that supports all Layer 2 switching functions, including the normal bridging functions of learning and replication on all of its ports. It is typically dedicated to one enterprise. It is also technically possible to extend the VPLS functionality to the MTUs. In this case, the MTUs act like PE devices, leading to a large number of MTUs participating in the VPLS. In a network with numerous PEs/MTUs, this leads to scalability limitations in terms of the number of PWs to be maintained. Here H-VPLS can be used to introduce a hierarchy, eliminating the need for a full mesh of PWs among all participating devices. Hierarchy is achieved by augmenting the base VPLS core mesh of PE-to-PE PWs (referred to as hub PWs) with access PWs (called spoke PWs) to form a two-tier hierarchical VPLS model, as shown in Figure 1.22.

In the illustration, the term VB stands for Virtual Bridge. Two VPLS customers are hosted on the same PE router, which acts as a virtual bridge for both customers. Spoke PWs are created between the MTUs and the PE routers. The hub PW is the PWs between PE routers in the core. These are typically mesh SDPs.

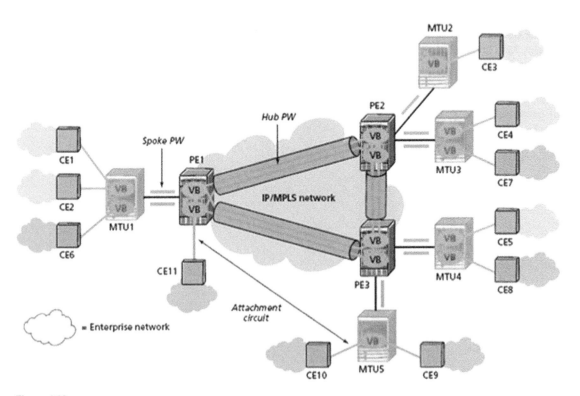

Figure 1.22

H-VPLS offers certain operational advantages by centralizing major functions (e.g., VPLS end-point autodiscovery, participating in a routed backbone, maintaining a full mesh of tunnel LSPs, and multiple full meshes of PWs) in the POP PE routers. This makes it possible to use lower-cost, low-maintenance MTU devices, thereby reducing the overall capital expenditure and operating expenses, since typically there are an order of magnitude more MTU devices than PE routers. Another operational advantage offered by H-VPLS along with BGP AD, is centralized provisioning, which means fewer elements to touch when upleveling service for a customer. Adding a new MTU device requires some configuration of the local PE router but does not require any signaling to other PE routers or MTU devices, thereby simplifying the provisioning process.

In H-VPLS, a CE is attached to an MTU through an attachment circuit. An AC from a specific customer is associated (by configuration) with a virtual bridge dedicated to that customer within the considered MTU. An AC may be a physical or a virtual LAN (VLAN) tagged logical port. In the basic scenario, an MTU has one uplink to a PE. This uplink contains one spoke PW (spoke SDP) for each VPLS served by the MTU. The end points of this spoke PW are an MTU and a PE. As in the illustration above, the uplink between MTU1 and PE1 carries two PWs because MTU1 has two VPLS customers attached.

Use Cases for LDP-VPLS and BGP AD

Full-Mesh VPLS

The full mesh is likely the most common VPLS topology deployed today. It provides a full mesh of direct connections among all nodes in a VPLS. It is also the simplest to configure for BGP AD. This provides a logical starting point on which other configurations can build. In the diagram in Figure 1.23, BGP AD is used to connect MTUs1, PERs4, and MTUs2 in a full mesh. The VPLS service VPN200 instantiated on the three nodes.

The BGP AD configuration on all three nodes participating in VPN 200 is very similar. The service difference is the port on which the access port or UNI (referred to as SAP in TiMOS) is configured. Therefore only the configuration for MTUs1 is presented in Figure 1.24.

The basic service display has been extended to include the BGP AD service information and any automatically generated SDP. See Figure 1.25.

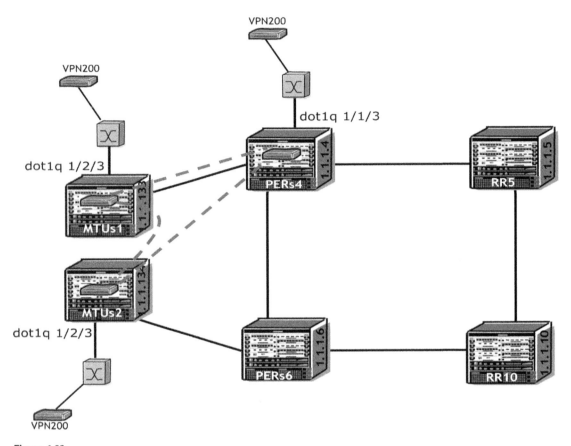

Figure 1.23

```
MTUs1
pw-template 1 create
    split-horizon-group "mesh"
    exit
exit
vpls 200 customer 1 create
    service-mtu 1478
    bgp-ad
        vpls-id 65535:200
        pw-template-bind 1
        no shutdown
    exit
    exit
    stp
      shutdown
    exit
    sap 1/2/3:200 create
    exit
    no shutdown
exit
```

Figure 1.24 BGP AD Configuration

```
MTUs1# show service id 200 base
===============================================================================
Service Basic Information
===============================================================================
Service Id          : 200              Vpn Id           : 0
Service Type        : VPLS
Customer Id         : 1
Last Status Change: 01/18/2008 06:19:22
Last Mgmt Change  : 01/18/2008 08:05:51
Admin State         : Up               Oper State       : Up
MTU                 : 1478             Def. Mesh VC Id  : 200
SAP Count           : 1                SDP Bind Count   : 2
Snd Flush on Fail : Disabled           Host Conn Verify : Disabled
Def. Gateway IP   : None
Def. Gateway MAC  : None
-------------------------------------------------------------------------------
BGP Auto-discovery Information
-------------------------------------------------------------------------------
Admin State         : Up               Vpls Id          : 65535:200
Route Dist          : 65535:200        Prefix           : 1.1.1.133 -> vsi-id
Rte-Target Import : None               Rte-Target Export : None
L2-Auto-Bind Plcy : 1                  L2-Auto-Bind SHG  : None
Vsi-Import          : None
Vsi-Export          : None
-------------------------------------------------------------------------------
Service Access & Destination Points
-------------------------------------------------------------------------------
Identifier                             Type     AdmMTU  OprMTU  Adm  Opr
-------------------------------------------------------------------------------
sap:1/2/3:200                          q-tag    1518    1518    Up   Up
sdp:17406:4294967295 SB(1.1.1.4)       BgpAd    0       1492    Up   Up
sdp:17407:4294967295 SB(1.1.1.134)     BgpAd    0       1492    Up   Up
-------------------------------------------------------------------------------
[<sap-id>] indicates a Managed SAP
===============================================================================
```

Figure 1.25 Checking the Service

The standard SDP show commands are used to view the relationship of the service to the SDP, regardless of whether they were created automatically, following the BGP AD process, or manually. See Figure 1.26.

The LDP binding command has been extended to include the Generic PWid FEC Element 129 (0x81). This display includes all the LDP specific attributes for the VPLS instance, including the AGI, SAII, and TAII signaling options. See Figure 1.27.

Specific L2VPN AD routes are stored in the BGP RIB IN and RIB OUT tables. MTUs1 receives two L2VPN AD routes for VPN 200 for PERs4, one advertised from each route reflector. Only one of these will be actively used. To determine the L2VPN AD routes advertised from MTUs1 (RIB OUT), the local loopback address is used as the prefix. See Figure 1.28.

```
MTUs1# show service sdp-using
===============================================================================
SDP Using
===============================================================================
SvcId       SdpId               Type    Far End        Opr S* I.Label  E.Label
-------------------------------------------------------------------------------
200         17406:4294967295    BgpAd   1.1.1.4        Up     131064   131063
200         17407:4294967295    BgpAd   1.1.1.134      Up     131063   131064
-------------------------------------------------------------------------------
Number of SDPs : 2
-------------------------------------------------------------------------------
===============================================================================
* indicates that the corresponding row element may have been truncated.
```

Figure 1.26 Checking the SDP

```
MTUs1# show router ldp bindings service-id 200
===============================================================================
LDP LSR ID: 1.1.1.133
===============================================================================
Legend: U - Label In Use, N - Label Not In Use, W - Label Withdrawn
        S - Status Signaled Up,  D - Status Signaled Down
        E - Epipe Service, V - VPLS Service, M - Mirror Service
        A - Apipe Service, F - Fpipe Service, I - IES Service, R - VPRN service
        P - Ipipe Service, C - Cpipe Service
        TLV - (Type, Length: Value)
===============================================================================
LDP Service FEC 128 Bindings
===============================================================================

===============================================================================
LDP Service FEC 129 Bindings
===============================================================================
AGI                             SAII                TAII
Type          SvcId     SDPId   Peer                IngLbl  EgrLbl  LMTU  RMTU
-------------------------------------------------------------------------------
65535:200                       1.1.1.133           1.1.1.4
V-Eth         200       17406   1.1.1.4             131064U 131063S 1464  1464

65535:200                       1.1.1.133           1.1.1.134
V-Eth         200       17407   1.1.1.134           131063U 131064S 1464  1464
-------------------------------------------------------------------------------
No. of FEC 129s: 2
===============================================================================
===============================================================================
```

Figure 1.27 LDP Specific Attributes

Mixed FEC 128 and FEC 129 Configurations

Numerous cases may require carriers to mix manually configured endpoint environments with discovered Layer 2 services using BGP AD. Some of these may include:

```
*A:MTUs1# show router bgp routes l2-vpn 1.1.1.4/32 hunt → Remote PE
===============================================================================
BGP Router ID : 1.1.1.133          AS : 65535    Local AS : 65535
===============================================================================
Legend -
Status codes  : u - used, s - suppressed, h - history, d - decayed, * - valid
Origin codes  : i - IGP, e - EGP, ? - incomplete, > - best


===============================================================================
BGP L2VPN-AD Routes
===============================================================================
-------------------------------------------------------------------------------
RIB In Entries
-------------------------------------------------------------------------------
Network        : 1.1.1.4/32
Nexthop        : 1.1.1.4
Route Dist.    : 65535:200
From           : 1.1.1.10
Res. Nexthop   : 0.0.0.0
Local Pref.    : 100               Interface Name : NotAvailable
Aggregator AS  : None              Aggregator     : None
Atomic Aggr.   : Not Atomic        MED            : 0
Community      : target:65535:200  l2-vpn:65535:200
Cluster        : 1.1.1.5
Originator Id  : 1.1.1.4           Peer Router Id : 1.1.1.10
Flags          : Used  Valid  Best  IGP
AS-Path        : No As-Path

Network        : 1.1.1.4/32
Nexthop        : 1.1.1.4
Route Dist.    : 65535:200
From           : 1.1.1.5
Res. Nexthop   : 0.0.0.0
Local Pref.    : 100               Interface Name : NotAvailable
Aggregator AS  : None              Aggregator     : None
Atomic Aggr.   : Not Atomic        MED            : 0
Community      : target:65535:200  l2-vpn:65535:200
Cluster        : 1.1.1.5
Originator Id  : 1.1.1.4           Peer Router Id : 1.1.1.5
Flags          : Valid  IGP
AS-Path        : No As-Path


-------------------------------------------------------------------------------
RIB Out Entries
-------------------------------------------------------------------------------
```

Figure 1.28 Checking the L2VPN Routes

- H-VPLS solutions where the carrier does not want to deploy BGP to the edge nodes but still wants the benefits of MPLS to the edge
- Mixed operational models used by different operational bodies inside the same carrier
- During a migration from manually provisioned services to a discovered operational model

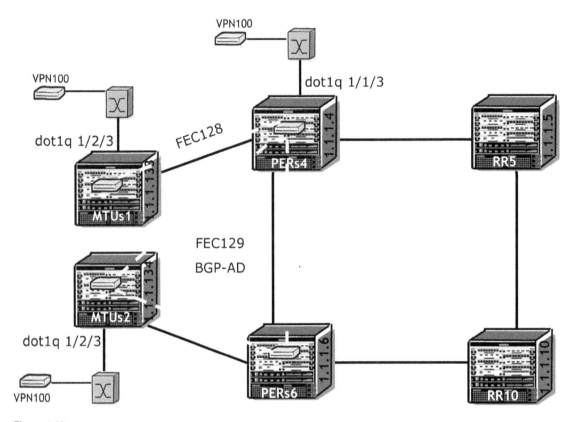

Figure 1.29

Let us look at the case study in Figure 1.29.

In this example, VPN 100 uses the H-VPLS solution. Manually configured PWs connect the MTU nodes to the PE nodes, and BGP AD is used to build the full mesh between the PE-rs nodes. PERs4 contains both the PWid FEC Element 128 (0x80) and the Generalized PWid FEC Element 129 (0x81). MTUs1 uses the standard configuration for a VPLS, including the SDP and the service definition. See Figure 1.30.

As stated earlier, PERs4 includes the manual service configuration for VPN 100 facing MTUs1 and for BGP AD facing the other nodes in the full mesh. The standard configuration for the FEC-128-only node (MTUs1), is highlighted in red in Figure 1.31.

The other two nodes participating in the VPN 100 full mesh only require BGP AD. Here PERs6, PERs4, and MTUs2 have a full mesh of PW among them, and MTUs1 is only connected to PERs4. See Figure 1.32.

```
MTUs1
sdp 14 mpls create ---→ SDP config
    far-end 1.1.1.4 → Remote PE
    ldp -→ T-LDP enabled
    keep-alive
      shutdown
    exit
    no shutdown
exit
vpls 100 customer 1 create
    service-mtu 1478
    stp
        shutdown
    exit
    sap 1/2/3:100 create
    exit
    spoke-sdp 14:100 create
    exit
      no shutdown
exit
```

Figure 1.30 MTU Configuration

```
PERs4
sdp 41 mpls create
    far-end 1.1.1.133
    ldp
    keep-alive
        shutdown
    exit
    no shutdown
exit
pw-template 1 create
    split-horizon-group "mesh"
    exit
exit
vpls 100 customer 1 create
    service-mtu 1478
    bgp-ad
        vpls-id 65535:100
        pw-template-bind 1
    no shutdown
    exit
    stp
      shutdown
    exit
    sap 1/1/3:100 create
    exit
    spoke-sdp 41:100 create
    exit
    no shutdown
exit
```

Figure 1.31 PERs Configuration

Now to look at some operational commands: The basic service display command has been extended to include the BGP AD service information and any automatically generated SDP. See Figure 1.33.

```
MTUs2                                      PERs6
pw-template 1 create                       pw template 1 create
    split-horizon-group "mesh"                 split-horizon-group "mesh"
    exit                                       exit
exit                                       exit
vpls 100 customer 1 create                 vpls 100 customer 1 create
    service-mtu 1478                           service-mtu 1478
    bgp-ad                                     bgp-ad
        vpls-id 65535:100                          vpls-id 65535:100
        pw-template-bind 1                         pw-template-bind 1
        no shutdown                                no shutdown
    exit                                       exit
     stp                                       stp
      shutdown                                  shutdown
    exit                                       exit
    sap 1/2/3:100 create                       no shutdown
    exit                                   exit
    no shutdown
exit
```

Figure 1.32 MTU and PERs Configurations

```
PERs-4# show service id 100 base
===================================================================
Service Basic Information
===================================================================
Service Id         : 100          Vpn Id            : 0
Service Type       : VPLS
Customer Id        : 1
Last Status Change : 01/18/2008 09:06:45
Last Mgmt Change   : 01/18/2008 09:08:15
Admin State        : Up           Oper State        : Up
MTU                : 1478         Def. Mesh VC Id   : 100
SAP Count          : 1            SDP Bind Count    : 3
Snd Flush on Fail  : Disabled     Host Conn Verify  : Disabled
Def. Gateway IP    : None
Def. Gateway MAC   : None



-------------------------------------------------------------------
BGP Auto-discovery Information
-------------------------------------------------------------------
Admin State        : Up           Vpls Id           : 65535:100
Route Dist         : 65535:100    Prefix            : 1.1.1.4
Rte-Target Import  : None         Rte-Target Export : None
L2-Auto-Bind Plcy  : 1            L2-Auto-Bind SHG  : None
Vsi-Import         : None
Vsi-Export         : None



-------------------------------------------------------------------
Service Access & Destination Points
-------------------------------------------------------------------
Identifier                          Type      AdmMTU  OprMTU  Adm  Opr
-------------------------------------------------------------------
sap:1/1/3:100                       q-tag     1518    1518    Up   Up
sdp:41:100 S(1.1.1.133)             n/a       0       1492    Up   Up
sdp:17405:4294967295 SB(1.1.1.6)    BgpAd     0       1556    Up   Up
sdp:17407:4294967294 SB(1.1.1.134)  BgpAd     0       1556    Up   Up
-------------------------------------------------------------------
[<sap-id>] indicates a Managed SAP
===================================================================
```

Figure 1.33 Checking the Service ID

```
PERs-4# show service sdp-using
===============================================================================
SDP Using
===============================================================================
SvcId       SdpId              Type     Far End       Opr S* I.Label  E.Label
-------------------------------------------------------------------------------
100         41:100             Spoke    1.1.1.133     Up     131062   131065
100         17405:4294967295   BgpAd    1.1.1.6       Up     131060   131064
100         17407:4294967294   BgpAd    1.1.1.134     Up     131061   131063
-------------------------------------------------------------------------------
Number of SDPs : 3
-------------------------------------------------------------------------------
```

Figure 1.34 Checking the SDP

The standard SDP show commands are used to view the relationship of the service to the SDP, regardless of whether they were created automatically, following the BGP AD process, or manually. See Figure 1.34.

The LDP binding command has been extended to include the Generic PWid FEC Element 129 (0x81). This display includes all the LDP specific attributes for the VPLS instance, including the AGI, SAII, and TAII signaling options. See Figure 1.35.

H-VPLS Configurations

As VPLS networks expand, some carriers deploy H-VPLS as a hierarchical solution model. In this case MTUs nodes single homed to one PE node can make use of BGP AD to automatically discover the VPN memberships. Membership is derived from the configured VPLS-id. The corresponding topology is built based on import and export route targets. H-VPLS topologies require each PE-rs to export and import a unique route target to and from the MTUs nodes it is responsible for. This means a PE-rs node is required to import and export two different route targets, one for all the MTUs nodes connected to it and one for the full mesh connecting it to other PE-rs nodes. The PE-rs nodes must map the two different route targets to different pw-templates configured at the service level. The MTUs PWs must be able to switch between themselves, the SAPs, and the mesh. The PWs that form the mesh can only forward to SAPs and MTUs PWs, not to other mesh PWs. The illustration in Figure 1.36 shows the import and export requirements for the H-VPLS solution. See also Figures 1.37, 1.38, and 1.39.

The PE router being a hub for the MTUs devices in the metro domain and having fully meshed PWs between other PEs in the core is configured with an export policy that adds two RTs. One

```
PERs-4# show router ldp bindings service-id 100
===============================================================================
LDP LSR ID: 1.1.1.4
===============================================================================
Legend: U - Label In Use, N - Label Not In Use, W - Label Withdrawn
        S - Status Signaled Up,  D - Status Signaled Down
        E - Epipe Service, V - VPLS Service, M - Mirror Service
        A - Apipe Service, F - Fpipe Service, I - IES Service, R - VPRN service
        P - Ipipe Service, C - Cpipe Service
        TLV - (Type, Length: Value)
===============================================================================
LDP Service FEC 128 Bindings
===============================================================================
Type    VCId        SvcId      SDPId  Peer            IngLbl  EgrLbl  LMTU  RMTU
-------------------------------------------------------------------------------
V-Eth   100         100        41     1.1.1.133       131062U 131065S 1464  1464
-------------------------------------------------------------------------------
No. of VC Labels: 1


===============================================================================
LDP Service FEC 129 Bindings
===============================================================================
AGI                                   SAII            TAII
Type                SvcId      SDPId  Peer            IngLbl  EgrLbl  LMTU  RMTU
-------------------------------------------------------------------------------
65535:100                             1.1.1.4         1.1.1.6
V-Eth               100        17405  1.1.1.6         131060U 131064S 1464  1464

65535:100                             1.1.1.4         1.1.1.134
V-Eth               100        17407  1.1.1.134       131061U 131063S 1464  1464

-------------------------------------------------------------------------------
No. of FEC 129s: 2
===============================================================================
```

Figure 1.35 Checking LDP Bindings

RT is imported by the MTUs acting as spoke sites, and the other is imported by PEs acting as hub sites for their respective metro domains consisting of MTUs's. PERs4 is further configured (see Figure 1.40) appropriate import and export policies, and also associates a mesh SDP to other PEs (PERs6) and a spoke SDP to MTUs1. It is important to remember that flooded traffic from MTUs1 (using a spoke SDP) will be flooded to PERs6 via the mesh SDP. Similarly, traffic from PERs6 received via a mesh SDP will be flooded to MTUs1 via the spoke SDP. This ensures that MTUs1 learns about the MAC address behind MTUs2 only via PERs4 and therefore only has a single PW/SDP to PERs4. Traffic between MTUs1 and MTUs2 is switched via PERs4. This achieves a "reduction in the number of PWs between devices using a hierarchy."

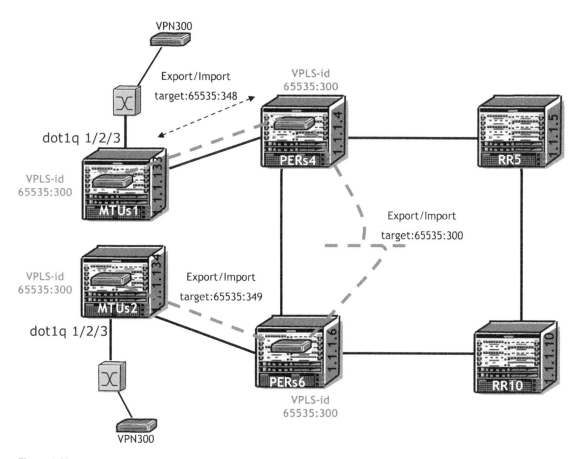

Figure 1.36

```
MTUs1
pw-template 2 create
exit
vpls 300 customer 1 create
     service-mtu 1478
     bgp-ad
        vpls-id 65535:300
        route-target export target:65535:348 import target:65535:348
        pw-template-bind 2
        no shutdown
     exit
     stp
       shutdown
     exit
     sap 1/2/3:300 create
     exit
     no shutdown
exit
```

Figure 1.37 MTU Configuration

```
MTUs2
pw-template 2 create
exit
vpls 300 customer 1 create
     service-mtu 1478
     bgp-ad
        vpls-id 65535:300
        route-target export target:65535:349 import target:65535:349
        pw-template-bind 2
        no shutdown
     exit
     stp
        shutdown
     exit
     sap 1/2/3:300 create
     exit
     no shutdown
exit
```

Figure 1.38 MTU Configuration

The display output for VPN 300 is from the perspective of PERs4. No SDP connection between PERs4 and MTUs2 is displayed. Similarly, there is no connection between MTUs1 and PERs6. Since there are no common import/export between these pairs of nodes, there is no automatically established SDP. See Figures 1.41 and 1.42.

Taking a slightly different approach, we can explore the L2VPN routes advertised from PERs4 (RIB OUT from IP address 1.1.1.4/32). PERs4 sends L2VPN AD routes to each route reflector server. Each of those route reflectors propagates that information to all of its I-BGP clients. Each of the receiving client's I-BGP peers determines whether or not to accept the L2VPN route, based on match VPLS-id and a corresponding import route target. To determine the L2VPN routes received by PERs4 from other peers (RIB IN), the specific remote peers /32 prefix is used. PERs4 imports and exports two route targets: 65535:348, which corresponds to MTUs1, and 65535:300, which corresponds to the full mesh to which PERs6 belongs. However, since BGP reflects information to all peers equally, all BGP peers would receive these advertisements—in this case, one from each route reflector. However, only those specifically configured with the VPLS-id and matching import route target would install the routes and trigger complimentary actions, like T-LDP sessions and service label exchanges. See Figure 1.43.

Hub and Spoke VPLS Configurations

Carriers can also use hub and spoke models to use their network resources to the best advantage. These types of solutions appear to the customer as full-mesh solutions. In the following

PERs4
```
Router Policy Configuration
---------------------------
community "mesh-300" members "target:65535:300"
community "h-vpls300" members "target:65535:300" "target:65535:348"
community "spoke-300" members "target:65535:348"
policy-statement "h-vpls300-exp"
    entry 10
        action accept
            community add "h-vpls300"
        exit
    exit
exit
policy-statement "h-vpls300-imp"
    entry 10
      from
            community "mesh-300"
      exit
      action accept
      exit
    exit
    entry 20
        from
            community "spoke-300"
        exit
        action accept
        exit
    exit
exit

Service Configuration
---------------------
pw-template 1 create
    split-horizon-group "mesh"
    exit
exit
    pw-template 2 create
    exit

vpls 300 customer 1 create
    service-mtu 1478
    bgp-ad
        vsi-export "h-vpls300-exp"
        vsi-import "h-vpls300-imp"
        vpls-id 65535:300
        pw-template-bind 1 import-rt "target:65535:300"
        pw-template-bind 2 import-rt "target:65535:348"
        no shutdown
    exit
    split-horizon-group "mesh" create
    exit
    stp
       shutdown
    exit
    no shutdown
exit
```

Figure 1.39 PERs Configuration

PERs6
Router Policy Configuration

```
community "mesh-300" members "target:65535:300"
community "h-vpls300" members "target:65535:300" "target:65535:349"
community "spoke-300" members "target:65535:34"
policy-statement "h-vpls300-exp"
    entry 10
        action accept
            community add "h-vpls300"
        exit
    exit
exit
policy-statement "h-vpls300-imp"
    entry 10
      from
            community "mesh-300"
      exit
      action accept
      exit
    exit
    entry 20
        from
            community "spoke-300"
        exit
        action accept
        exit
    exit
exit

Service Configuration
--------------------
pw-template 1 create
    split-horizon-group "mesh"
    exit
exit
pw-template 2 create
exit
vpls 300 customer 1 create
    service-mtu 1478
    bgp-ad
        vsi-export "h-vpls300-exp"
        vsi-import "h-vpls300-imp"
        vpls-id 65535:300
        pw-template-bind 1 import-rt "target:65535:300"
        pw-template-bind 2 import-rt "target:65535:349"
        no shutdown
    exit
    split-horizon-group "mesh" create
    exit
    stp
       shutdown
    exit
    no shutdown
  exit
```

Figure 1.40 PERs Configuration

```
PERs-4# show service id 300 base
===============================================================================
Service Basic Information
===============================================================================
Service Id          : 300               Vpn Id             : 0
Service Type        : VPLS
Customer Id         : 1
Last Status Change: 01/18/2008 09:15:59
Last Mgmt Change    : 01/18/2008 09:19:01
Admin State         : Up                Oper State         : Up
MTU                 : 1478              Def. Mesh VC Id    : 300
SAP Count           : 0                 SDP Bind Count     : 2
Snd Flush on Fail : Disabled            Host Conn Verify   : Disabled
Def. Gateway IP     : None
Def. Gateway MAC    : None


-------------------------------------------------------------------------------
BGP Auto-discovery Information
-------------------------------------------------------------------------------
Admin State         : Up                Vpls Id            : 65535:300
Route Dist          : 65535:300         Prefix             : 1.1.1.4
Rte-Target Import : None                Rte-Target Export : None
L2-Auto-Bind Plcy : 1                   L2-Auto-Bind SHG   : None
Vsi-Import          : h-vpls300-imp
Vsi-Export          : h-vpls300-exp
-------------------------------------------------------------------------------
Service Access & Destination Points
-------------------------------------------------------------------------------
Identifier                         Type      AdmMTU  OprMTU  Adm  Opr
-------------------------------------------------------------------------------
sdp:17405:4294967294 SB(1.1.1.6)   BgpAd     0       1556    Up   Up
sdp:17406:4294967294 SB(1.1.1.133) BgpAd     0       1492    Up   Up
===============================================================================


PERs-4# show service sdp-using
===============================================================================
SDP Using
===============================================================================
SvcId      SdpId           Type    Far End      Opr S* I.Label  E.Label
-------------------------------------------------------------------------------
300        17405:4294967294 BgpAd  1.1.1.6      Up     131058   131062
300        17406:4294967294 BgpAd  1.1.1.133    Up     131059   131062
-------------------------------------------------------------------------------
Number of SDPs : 2
-------------------------------------------------------------------------------
===============================================================================
* indicates that the corresponding row element may have been truncated.
```

Figure 1.41 Checking the Service

```
PERs-4# show router ldp bindings service-id 300
===============================================================================
LDP LSR ID: 1.1.1.4
===============================================================================
Legend: U - Label In Use, N - Label Not In Use, W - Label Withdrawn
        S - Status Signaled Up,  D - Status Signaled Down
        E - Epipe Service, V - VPLS Service, M - Mirror Service
        A - Apipe Service, F - Fpipe Service, I - IES Service, R - VPRN service
        P - Ipipe Service, C - Cpipe Service
        TLV - (Type, Length: Value)
===============================================================================
LDP Service FEC 128 Bindings
===============================================================================
Type    VCId        SvcId    SDPId  Peer           IngLbl  EgrLbl  LMTU  RMTU
-------------------------------------------------------------------------------
No Matching Entries Found
===============================================================================


===============================================================================
LDP Service FEC 129 Bindings
===============================================================================
AGI                            SAII                 TAII
Type               SvcId    SDPId  Peer             IngLbl  EgrLbl  LMTU  RMTU
-------------------------------------------------------------------------------
65535:300                          1.1.1.4               1.1.1.6
V-Eth              300      17405  1.1.1.6          131058U 131062S 1464  1464

65535:300                          1.1.1.4               1.1.1.133
V-Eth              300      17406  1.1.1.133        131059U 131062S 1464  1464


-------------------------------------------------------------------------------
No. of FEC 129s: 2
===============================================================================
```

Figure 1.42 Checking the LDP Bindings

backhaul case, the carrier can select different PE nodes to switch traffic rather than building direct logical connections. For example, all CPEs connections to the same PE can communicate directly. However, the different PEs would communicate through a central hub PE, rather than building a logical full mesh, thus emulating an H-VPLS model.

In Figure 1.44, MTUs1 and MTUs2 are logically connected to PERs4 via PWs (spoke SDPs), even though MTUs2 is physically connected to PERs6. Therefore both the MTUs's would learn about other sites (MAC addresses) only via PERs4. This is also the case for any sites connected via PERs6. Similarly, traffic forwarding would also be via PERs4 only.

```
PERs-4# show router bgp routes l2-vpn 1.1.1.4/32 hunt
===============================================================================
 BGP Router ID : 1.1.1.4          AS : 65535    Local AS : 65535
===============================================================================
 Legend -
 Status codes  : u - used, s - suppressed, h - history, d - decayed, * - valid
 Origin codes  : i - IGP, e - EGP, ? - incomplete, > - best


===============================================================================
BGP L2VPN-AD Routes
===============================================================================
-------------------------------------------------------------------------------
RIB Out Entries
-------------------------------------------------------------------------------
Network        : 1.1.1.4/32
Nexthop        : 1.1.1.4
Route Dist.    : 65535:300
To             : 1.1.1.10
Res. Nexthop   : n/a
Local Pref.    : 100                 Interface Name : NotAvailable
Aggregator AS  : None                Aggregator     : None
Atomic Aggr.   : Not Atomic          MED            : 0
Community      : target:65535:300  target:65535:348  l2-vpn:65535:300
Cluster        : No Cluster Members
Originator Id  : None                Peer Router Id : 1.1.1.10
Origin         : IGP
AS-Path        : No As-Path

Network        : 1.1.1.4/32
Nexthop        : 1.1.1.4
Route Dist.    : 65535:300
To             : 1.1.1.5
Res. Nexthop   : n/a
Local Pref.    : 100                 Interface Name : NotAvailable
Aggregator AS  : None                Aggregator     : None
Atomic Aggr.   : Not Atomic          MED            : 0
Community      : target:65535:300  target:65535:348  l2-vpn:65535:300
Cluster        : No Cluster Members
Originator Id  : None                Peer Router Id : 1.1.1.5
Origin         : IGP
AS-Path        : No As-Path


-------------------------------------------------------------------------------
RIB In Entries
-------------------------------------------------------------------------------
```

Figure 1.43 Checking the BGP Routes

The configurations are presented in Figures 1.45 and 1.46.

Many different models can be constructed with router targets and router policy. BGP AD does not hamper the ability to build these topologies. There are discovered connections between

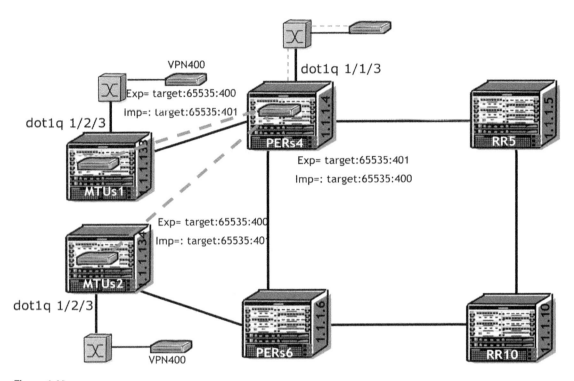

Figure 1.44

MTUs1

```
pw-template 2 create
exit
vpls 400 customer 1 create
    service-mtu 1478
    bgp-ad
        vpls-id 65535:400
        route-target export target:65535:400 import target:65535:401
        pw-template-bind 2
        no shutdown
    exit
    stp
        shutdown
    exit
    sap 1/2/3:400 create
    exit
    no shutdown
exit
```

Figure 1.45 MTU Configuration

MTUs2

```
pw-template 2 create
exit
vpls 400 customer 1 create
    service-mtu 1478
    bgp-ad
        vpls-id 65535:400
        route-target export target:65535:400 import target:65535:401
        pw-template-bind 2
        no shutdown
    exit
    stp
      shutdown
    exit
    sap 1/2/3:400 create
    exit
    no shutdown
exit
```

PERs4

```
pw-template 2 create
exit
vpls 400 customer 1 create
    service-mtu 1478
    bgp-ad
        vpls-id 65535:400
        route-target export target:65535:401 import target:65535:400
        pw-template-bind 2
        no shutdown
    exit
    stp
       shutdown
    exit
    sap 1/1/3:400 create
    exit
    no shutdown
exit
```

Figure 1.46 MTU Configuration

PERs4 and the two MTU nodes. The MTUs nodes do not connect directly because each one only imports the route target exported by the hub, i.e., "65535:401." The various operational commands are given in Figures 1.47, 1.48, 1.49, and 1.50.

```
PERs-4# show service id 400 base
==================================================================================
Service Basic Information
==================================================================================
Service Id         : 400          Vpn Id            : 0
Service Type       : VPLS
Customer Id        : 1
Last Status Change : 01/23/2008 13:43:30
Last Mgmt Change   : 01/23/2008 14:16:22
Admin State        : Up           Oper State        : Up
MTU                : 1478         Def. Mesh VC Id   : 400
SAP Count          : 2            SDP Bind Count    : 2
Snd Flush on Fail  : Disabled     Host Conn Verify  : Disabled
Def. Gateway IP    : None
Def. Gateway MAC   : None


----------------------------------------------------------------------------------
BGP Auto-discovery Information
----------------------------------------------------------------------------------
Admin State        : Up           Vpls Id           : 65535:400
Route Dist         : 65535:400    Prefix            : 1.1.1.4
Rte-Target Import  : 65535:400    Rte-Target Export : 65535:401
L2-Auto-Bind Plcy  : 2            L2-Auto-Bind SHG  : None
Vsi-Import         : None
Vsi-Export         : None


----------------------------------------------------------------------------------
Service Access & Destination Points
----------------------------------------------------------------------------------
Identifier                         Type     AdmMTU   OprMTU   Adm   Opr
----------------------------------------------------------------------------------
sap:1/1/3:400                      q-tag    1518     1518     Up    Up
sdp:17406:4294967295 SB(1.1.1.133) BgpAd    0        1492     Up    Up
sdp:17407:4294967295 SB(1.1.1.134) BgpAd    0        1556     Up    Up
----------------------------------------------------------------------------------
[<sap-id>] indicates a Managed SAP
==================================================================================
```

Figure 1.47 Checking the Service ID

```
PERs-4# show service sdp-using
==================================================================================
SDP Using
==================================================================================
SvcId      SdpId            Type    Far End       Opr S* I.Label  E.Label
----------------------------------------------------------------------------------
400        17406:4294967295 BgpAd   1.1.1.133     Up     131065   131065
400        17407:4294967295 BgpAd   1.1.1.134     Up     131063   131070
----------------------------------------------------------------------------------
Number of SDPs : 2
----------------------------------------------------------------------------------
==================================================================================
* indicates that the corresponding row element may have been truncated.
```

Figure 1.48 Checking the SDP

```
PERs-4# show router ldp bindings service-id 400
===============================================================================
LDP LSR ID: 1.1.1.4
===============================================================================
Legend: U - Label In Use, N - Label Not In Use, W - Label Withdrawn
        S - Status Signaled Up,  D - Status Signaled Down
        E - Epipe Service, V - VPLS Service, M - Mirror Service
        A - Apipe Service, F - Fpipe Service, I - IES Service, R - VPRN service
        P - Ipipe Service, C - Cpipe Service
        TLV - (Type, Length: Value)
===============================================================================
LDP Service FEC 128 Bindings
===============================================================================
Type    VCId       SvcId     SDPId  Peer            IngLbl EgrLbl LMTU  RMTU
-------------------------------------------------------------------------------
No Matching Entries Found
===============================================================================


===============================================================================
LDP Service FEC 129 Bindings
===============================================================================
AGI                            SAII            TAII
Type           SvcId     SDPId Peer            IngLbl EgrLbl LMTU  RMTU
-------------------------------------------------------------------------------
65535:400                      1.1.1.4         1.1.1.133
V-Eth          400       17406 1.1.1.133       131065U 131065S 1464  1464

65535:400                      1.1.1.4         1.1.1.134
V-Eth          400       17407 1.1.1.134       131063U 131070S 1464  1464

-------------------------------------------------------------------------------
No. of FEC 129s: 2
===============================================================================
```

Figure 1.49 Checking the LDP Bindings

The L2VPN routes received by PERs4 from other peers (RIB IN) are determined using the specific remote peers /32 prefix. PERs4, the hub, imports the route target 65535:400, which is being exported by all the spokes. In Figure 1.51 we can see which L2VPN routes were received from MTUs1.

A point to remember about H-VPLS is that even though it is an attempt to scale the control plane by reducing the number of LDP-based PWs that need to be created in the network, this could potentially create scaling problems on the PE devices, if those devices are acting as hub sites). As an example, even if the PE router does not host any VPLS sites for a given instance, it still has to maintain state information and MAC tables for the customer in order to offload burden from the MTU devices. Therefore a solution to address a control plane scaling issue can now

```
PERs-4# show router bgp routes l2-vpn 1.1.1.4/32 hunt
===============================================================================
 BGP Router ID : 1.1.1.4          AS : 65535    Local AS : 65535
===============================================================================
 Legend -
 Status codes  : u - used, s - suppressed, h - history, d - decayed, * - valid
 Origin codes  : i - IGP, e - EGP, ? - incomplete, > - best


===============================================================================
BGP L2VPN-AD Routes
===============================================================================
-------------------------------------------------------------------------------
RIB In Entries
-------------------------------------------------------------------------------


-------------------------------------------------------------------------------
RIB Out Entries
-------------------------------------------------------------------------------
Network        : 1.1.1.4/32
Nexthop        : 1.1.1.4
Route Dist.    : 65535:400
To             : 1.1.1.5
Res. Nexthop   : n/a
Local Pref.    : 100               Interface Name : NotAvailable
Aggregator AS  : None              Aggregator     : None
Atomic Aggr.   : Not Atomic        MED            : 0
Community      : target:65535:401  l2-vpn:65535:400
Cluster        : No Cluster Members
Originator Id  : None              Peer Router Id : 1.1.1.5
Origin         : IGP
AS-Path        : No As-Path

Network        : 1.1.1.4/32
Nexthop        : 1.1.1.4
Route Dist.    : 65535:400
To             : 1.1.1.10
Res. Nexthop   : n/a
Local Pref.    : 100               Interface Name : NotAvailable
Aggregator AS  : None              Aggregator     : None
Atomic Aggr.   : Not Atomic        MED            : 0
Community      : target:65535:401  l2-vpn:65535:400
Cluster        : No Cluster Members
Originator Id  : None              Peer Router Id : 1.1.1.10
Origin         : IGP
AS-Path        : No As-Path
-------------------------------------------------------------------------------
Routes : 2
===============================================================================
```

Figure 1.50 Checking the L2VPN Routes

```
*A:PERs-4# show router bgp routes l2-vpn 1.1.1.133/32 hunt
===============================================================================
BGP Router ID : 1.1.1.4          AS : 65535    Local AS : 65535
===============================================================================
Legend -
Status codes  : u - used, s - suppressed, h - history, d - decayed, * - valid
Origin codes  : i - IGP, e - EGP, ? - incomplete, > - best


===============================================================================
BGP L2VPN-AD Routes
===============================================================================
-------------------------------------------------------------------------------
RIB In Entries
-------------------------------------------------------------------------------
Network        : 1.1.1.133/32
Nexthop        : 1.1.1.133
Route Dist.    : 65535:400
From           : 1.1.1.10
Res. Nexthop   : 0.0.0.0
Local Pref.    : 100                Interface Name : NotAvailable
Aggregator AS  : None               Aggregator     : None
Atomic Aggr.   : Not Atomic         MED            : 0
Community      : target:65535:400  l2-vpn:65535:400
Cluster        : 1.1.1.5
Originator Id  : 1.1.1.133          Peer Router Id : 1.1.1.10
Flags          : Used  Valid  Best  IGP
AS-Path        : No As-Path

Network        : 1.1.1.133/32
Nexthop        : 1.1.1.133
Route Dist.    : 65535:400
From           : 1.1.1.5
Res. Nexthop   : 0.0.0.0
Local Pref.    : 100                Interface Name : NotAvailable
Aggregator AS  : None               Aggregator     : None
Atomic Aggr.   : Not Atomic         MED            : 0
Community      : target:65535:400  l2-vpn:65535:400
Cluster        : 1.1.1.5
Originator Id  : 1.1.1.133          Peer Router Id : 1.1.1.5
Flags          : Valid  IGP
AS-Path        : No As-Path


-------------------------------------------------------------------------------
RIB Out Entries
-------------------------------------------------------------------------------
-------------------------------------------------------------------------------
Routes : 2
===============================================================================
```

Figure 1.51 Checking the BGP Routes

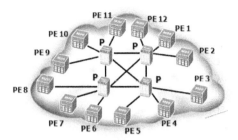

- **The 12x12 mesh of PEs has become a 4x4 mesh of Ps**
- **However, each P router needs to learn 3 times as many MACs, and also has to be VPLS-aware, and do traffic replication for flooding and broadcast**
  - This is especially bad as P routers should have no VPN state!

Figure 1.52

potentially affect the data plane scalability. In certain topologies, even MPLS provider routers would need to act as hub sites. This is true when the MTU devices act only as Layer 2 switches and the PE routers host VPLS instances. See the illustration in Figure 1.52 to understand this further.

LDP-BGP VPLS Interworking

Currently, both LDP-VPLS and BGP-VPLS are widely deployed in service provider networks. Two key business drivers for LDP-BGP VPLS interworking are the need to extend the VPLS networks—and therefore to also be able to scale them.

Scaling the VPLS Network

As the VPLS network expands, the LDP-VPLS control plane does impose certain scalability concerns as discussed in the earlier sections. In comparison, the BGP-VPLS control plane more easily enables the VPLS network to scale to support new VPLS customers and to include more sites for existing VPLS customers. One option for scaling the VPLS network, when there is an existing LDP-VPLS deployment, is to abandon the LDP-VPLS control plane entirely and transition the VPLS network to the BGP-VPLS control plane. However, this approach may not be feasible for a number of reasons, two of which are:

- Legacy PE routers may not support a BGP signaling mechanism, and for financial reasons, replacing the existing PE routers may not be a viable option.

- Operating overhead and possible disruption to the VPLS network for existing customers may not justify this transition.

Another option for scaling VPLS when there is an existing LDP-VPLS deployment is to cap the existing LDP-VPLS deployment and to expand the VPLS network using the BGP control plane. With this approach, the LDP- and BGP-VPLS control planes, including the signaling mechanisms, must coexist in the network, which requires some interworking between the two control plane mechanisms.

To be able to offer a regional or national VPLS network, service providers are seeking scalable ways to extend the reach of VPLS beyond a single LDP-VPLS metro domain. One mechanism is the use of BGP-VPLS in the Wide Area Network (WAN) to interconnect multiple LDP-VPLS metro domains. This approach requires a new inter-domain technique, since the existing defined solutions for multiple ASs require that all domains run the same signaling protocol. One of the critical requirements for such a deployment model is ensuring that the existing PE routers in the metro domains that are running the LDP-VPLS control plane do not require any changes or upgrades. A second requirement is the extension of VPLS without significant additional load on the control plane of the LDP-VPLS PE routers in the metro network. LDP-BGP VPLS interworking meets the above requirements and enables service providers to use a single protocol, BGP, in the WAN to offer multiple MPLS VPN services, including VPLS and Layer 2 and Layer 3 VPNs. Moreover, because a single protocol is used, provisioning the system can provide operating efficiency.

With basic LDP-BGP VPLS interworking, newly added PE routers in the network support both the LDP and BGP control planes, including the corresponding signaling mechanisms required. These new PE routers use the BGP-VPLS control plane when communicating with each other, and use the LDP-VPLS control plane to communicate with the existing PE routers, which run LDP-VPLS.

This deployment model facilitates expansion of existing VPLS customer sites, enabling a service provider to add new sites to BGP-VPLS PE routers while keeping the existing sites unchanged on the LDP-VPLS PE routers. A key feature of this interworking mechanism is that no changes are made to the currently defined LDP-VPLS control plane (RFC 4762; see Lasserre and Kompella, Jan. 2007). The LDP-VPLS-only routers continue to communicate using the LDP-VPLS control plane. From their perspective, the newly added BGP-VPLS PE routers are simply LDP-VPLS PE routers. The BGP-VPLS routers, on the other hand, use both the

BGP-VPLS and LDP-VPLS control planes. They use the BGP-VPLS control plane among themselves for autodiscovery and for signaling, establishing an internal BGP (IBGP) session among themselves or via a route reflector. They also use LDP-VPLS signaling to communicate with the LDP-VPLS-only routers, establishing LDP sessions with the existing PE routers. For all VPLS customers that have sites on only the existing LDP-VPLS PE routers or the newly added BGP-VPLS PE routers, VPLS is set up using a single control plane and a single signaling protocol.

The LDP-BGP VPLS model employs two groups of PE routers. All PE routers in the first group run only the LDP-VPLS control plane among themselves, whereas all PE routers in the second group run only the BGP-VPLS control plane among themselves. These two groups are interconnected through a single PE router, referred to as the interworking PE router, which runs both LDP-VPLS and BGP-VPLS control planes. The illustration in Figure 1.53 shows how the LDP-VPLS network is expanded using the BGP control plane in a scalable model.

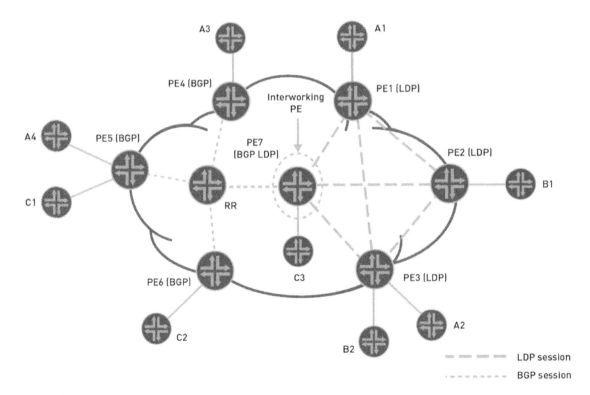

Figure 1.53

In this illustration, the PE1, PE2, and PE3 routers are existing PE routers supporting only the LDP-VPLS control plane. The newly added PE routers (PE4, PE5, and PE6) support the BGP-VPLS control plane. The PE7 router is the interworking PE router, supporting both LDP and BGP control planes and the interworking between them. While the existing LDP-VPLS PE routers and the newly added BGP-VPLS PE routers are isolated into two groups, the PE7 router is part of both groups and plays the vital role of interconnecting them.

For example, VPLS Customer A has multiple sites in both the LDP- and BGP-VPLS groups. Customer A's sites A1 and A2 are connected to the LDP PE routers, and sites A3 and A4 are connected to the BGP PE routers. PE7 router provides the LDP-BGP VPLS interworking function and stitches together the pseudowires created by the signaling components of the two different control planes. PE routers in the BGP-VPLS group are provisioned only for the BGP-VPLS control plane. From their perspective, the interworking PE router (PE7) is a standard BGP-VPLS peer, and they are unaware of the PE routers in the LDP-VPLS group. Legacy PE routers in the LDP-VPLS group are provisioned only for the LDP-VPLS control plane. From their perspective, the interworking PE router (PE7) is a standard LDP-VPLS peer, and they are unaware of the PE routers in the BGP-VPLS group.

Containing all the existing LDP-VPLS PE routers in a single group caps the LDP-VPLS deployment and allows network expansion to occur in the BGP-VPLS group without creating additional control plane or data plane overhead on existing LDP-VPLS PE routers. This eliminates a fundamental problem with the previous method: that all BGP-VPLS PE routers had to also operate in the LDP-VPLS control plane. However, in some network designs, containing all the LDP-VPLS PE routers in a single group may not be feasible because of geographical limitations or other administrative reasons. In such environments, multiple groups of PE routers can be running the LDP-VPLS control plane and a single group of PE routers can be running the BGP-VPLS control plane, which interconnects all the LDP-VPLS control plane groups through multiple interworking PE routers.

Interconnecting multiple metro networks using BGP-VPLS is the most efficient and scalable way to extend VPLS beyond the metro network. The illustration in Figure 1.54 shows how basic inter-domain LDP-BGP VPLS interworking techniques can be expanded to interconnect multiple LDP-VPLS domains using the BGP-VPLS control plane in the WAN. The existing PE routers in domains Metro X and Metro Y are not aware that the border routers C-ASBR1 and C-ASBR2 are extending their domain reach using the BGP-VPLS control plane in the WAN.

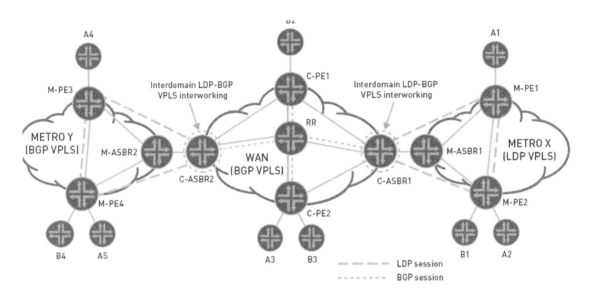

Figure 1.54

The basic LDP-BGP VPLS interworking method requires minimal configuration changes on the existing LDP-VPLS PE routers. However, new PE routers added as part of the network expansion must support both LDP-VPLS and BGP-VPLS. The support provided by the new PE routers is essential for basic LDP-BGP VPLS interworking to succeed. Because the new PE routers support both LDP-VPLS and BGP-VPLS, they can establish pseudowires using both the LDP and BGP signaling mechanisms. These pseudowires can be created for VPLS customers with sites attached to both existing LDP-VPLS routers and the newly added BGP-VPLS routers. A full mesh of pseudowires is created between the existing LDP-VPLS PE routers and the newly added BGP-VPLS PE router. As a result, data plane operations on all PE routers adhere to the split-horizon forwarding rule, and the VPLS traffic is not switched between pseudowires. Additionally, no changes are required to the existing LDP or BGP control plane procedures themselves.

Case Study – Connecting LDP- and BGP-VPLS Metro Domains

Let us look at a sample case study of two metro domains, one using LDP-VPLS and the other using BGP-VPLS, being interconnected via a BGP-VPLS interworking PE, as shown in Figure 1.55.

The configurations required to enable this are based on JUNOS.

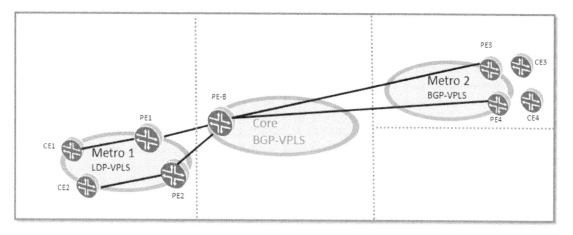

Figure 1.55

```
interfaces {
ge-1/2/1 {
  unit 0 {
    family inet {
    address 10.12.31.1/24;
    }
  }
}
}
    }
```

Figure 1.56 Router CE3 Configuration

We start with the CE router configuration. The only configuration needed here is the interface and IP subnet details. See Figure 1.56.

Router PE3 is configured for VPLS by configuring BGP, MPLS, OSPF, and LDP. (These protocols are the basis for most Layer 2 VPN-related applications, including VPLS.) The configuration includes the signaling statement at the [edit protocols bgp group *group-name* family l2vpn] hierarchy level.

Looking at this in more detail: The command "encapsulation VPLS" is used on Ethernet CE-facing interfaces that have VPLS enabled and are supposed to accept packets carrying standard Tag Protocol ID (TPID) values. If the interface needs to accept VLAN (Tagged) packets, then encapsulation "vlan-vpls" is to be used. The family "vpls" statement enables the interface with the VPLS address family. The statement "family l2vpn signaling" enables BGP signaling for VPLS. All services (L2VPN, L3VPN, VPLS, etc) are configured under the routing-instances hierarchy.

In this case, a VPLS instance named "ABCCORP" is configured along with the RD and VRF targets. BGP-VPLS relies on route targets for discovery and the association of a remote PE to an instance. The same procedure is used as in BGP/MPLS VPNs. The "site-range" defines the number of sites that can exist in a VPLS instance. The site-name is a generic name and can be used to identify the site. The site-id configured on each PE needs to be unique per VPLS domain. Each site within a given PE participating in the same VPLS instance needs a unique site-id as well. See Figure 1.57.

Router PE4's configuration would identical to PE3's, except for its unique site-id, RD, and RT, so there is no need to illustrate it.

The key element in this system, the interconnect PE router, PE-B, is configured to connect the BGP and LGP-VPLS domains. Its configuration has two portions, both defined under the VPLS instance "ABCCORP." The first portion is router PE-B's participation in the BGP-VPLS domain, the second portion is its participation within the LDP-VPLS domain. The command "vpls-id" identifies the virtual circuit identifier used for the VPLS routing instance. This statement is part of the configuration to enable LDP signaling for VPLS. The VPLS-ID needs to be the same for all PE routers for the same VPLS instance, and therefore needs to be globally unique.

A bit of recap here: We have seen that a single VPLS routing instance can encompass one set of PE routers that use BGP for signaling and another set of PE routers that use LDP for signaling. Within each set, all of the PE routers are fully meshed in both the control and data planes and have a bidirectional pseudowire to each of the other routers in the set. However, the BGP-signaled routers cannot be directly connected to the LDP-signaled routers. This where the interconnect/border PE router comes in.

In the control plane, each fully meshed set of PE routers in a VPLS routing instance is called a PE router mesh group. The border PE router must be reachable by and have bidirectional pseudowires to all of the PE routers that are a part of the VPLS routing instance, both the LDP-signaled and the BGP-signaled routers. To configure LDP-BGP interworking for VPLS, the mesh group statement is included in the VPLS routing instance configuration of the PE border router, as illustrated in the configuration below. The "neighbor" statement identifies each LDP-VPLS PE statically and builds PWs to each of them.

You can configure multiple mesh groups to map each fully-meshed LDP-signaled or BGP-signaled VPLS domain to a mesh group. In the data-plane, the border router maintains a common MAC table used to forward traffic between the LDP-signaled and

```
[edit]
interfaces {
so-0/2/1 {
 unit 0 {
   family inet {
     address 10.12.100.10/30;
 }
   family mpls;
}
so-0/2/2 {
   unit 0 {
     family inet {
       address 10.12.100.21/30;
}
   family mpls;
   }
}
ge-1/3/1 { ----------> CE Facing interface
encapsulation ethernet-vpls; ->
unit 0 {
   family vpls;
   }
 }
}
   }
protocols {
mpls {
 interface all;
}
bgp {
 log-updown;
   group int {
   type internal;
   local-address 10.255.170.96;
   family l2vpn {
   signaling;
}
 neighbor 10.255.170.98;
 neighbor 10.255.170.102;
}
}
ospf {
 area 0.0.0.0 {
 interface so-0/2/1.0;
 interface so-0/2/2.0;
 interface lo0.0 {
 passive;
 }
}
   }
```

Figure 1.57 Router PE3 Configuration

Continued

```
ldp {
  interface so-0/2/1.0;
  interface so-0/2/2.0;
}
}
routing-instances {
ABCCORP {
  instance-type vpls;
  interface ge-1/3/1.0;
  route-distinguisher 10.255.170.96:1;
  vrf-target target:1:2;
  protocols {
   vpls {
     site-range 10;
     site 1 {
       site-identifier 3;
     }
    }
   }
  }

     }

ge-1/2/1 {
   unit 0 {
    family inet {
    address 10.12.31.1/24;
   }
  }
 }

     }
```

Figure 1.57, cont'd

BGP-signaled mesh groups. When forwarding any VPLS traffic received over a PE router's pseudowire, the border router assures that traffic is not forwarded back to the PE routers that are in same mesh group as the originating PE router.

Consider, for instance, a situation where two LDP-meshed groups are configured, each mesh group having its own set of PE routers that are fully meshed with each other and with the interconnect PE router at the control plane. If a CE connected to, let us say, LDP-VPLS Mesh-Group1 sends a frame whose destination MAC address is on LDP-VPLS Mesh-Group2, the ingress PE router will receive the frame and perform a MAC address lookup. The MAC address will not be in its MAC table and so it will flood the frame to the other PEs in LDP-VPLS Mesh-Group1, which, from its perspective, are the only members of the VPLS network. When the interconnect PE receives the data, it won't find the MAC address in its MAC table and so it will flood the frame to all the BGP-VPLS PE routers and LDP-VPLS PE routers in Mesh-Group2, but not back to Mesh-Group1. The PE routers will then perform a MAC-table lookup and flood the data to their CE routers. See Figure 1.58.

Now let us move on to the configurations of the LDP PE routers, beginning with PE1. The configuration does not include any BGP-specific statements or any mesh group definitions. Only the "vpls-id" and "neighbor" statements are used. Router PEB is also configured to participate in the LDP-VPLS instance. See Figure 1.59. PE2's configuration is identical to that of PE1, and hence is not illustrated.

The command in Figure 1.60 can be used to validate and verify the BGP and LDP interworking state on PEB.

```
[edit]

interfaces {
fe-0/0/3 {
 unit 0 {
   family inet {
   address 10.12.100.13/30;
 }
   family mpls;
 }
}
t1-0/1/2 {
 unit 0 {
   family inet {
   address 10.12.100.1/30;
 }
   family mpls;
 }
}
t1-0/1/3 {
 unit 0 {
   family inet {
     address 10.12.100.5/30;
 }
   family mpls;
 }
}
so-0/2/2 {
 unit 0 {
   family inet {
     address 10.12.100.9/30;
 }
```

Figure 1.58 Router PEB Configuration

Continued

```
      family mpls;
    }
  }
}
protocols {
mpls {
   interface all;
}
bgp {
 log-updown;
 group int {
   type internal;
   local-address 10.255.170.98;
   family l2vpn {
     signaling;
 }
   neighbor 10.255.170.96;
   neighbor 10.255.170.102;
 }
}
ospf {
   area 0.0.0.0 {
     interface t1-0/1/2.0;
     interface t1-0/1/3.0;
     interface so-0/2/2.0;
     interface fe-0/0/3.0;
     interface lo0.0 {
       passive;
     }
   }
 }
ldp {
 interface fe-0/0/3.0;
 interface t1-0/1/2.0;
 interface t1-0/1/3.0;
 interface so-0/2/2.0;
 interface lo0.0;
 }
 }
routing-instances {
ABCCORP {
 instance-type vpls;
  route-distinguisher 10.255.170.98:1;
  vrf-target target:1:2;
  protocols {
   vpls {
   site-range 10;
    site 1 {
     site-identifier 1;
 }
   vpls-id 101;
     mesh-group ldp-1 {
      neighbor 10.255.170.106;
      neighbor 10.255.170.104;
   }
  }
 }
 }
 }
    }
```

Figure 1.58, cont'd

```
[edit]
  interfaces {
  fe-0/0/3 {
   encapsulation ethernet-vpls;
    unit 0 {
    family vpls;
   }
  }
}
t1-0/1/0 {
  unit 0 {
   family inet {
   address 10.12.100.2/30;
  }
   family mpls;
  }
}
t1-1/1/1 {
  unit 0 {
   family inet {
   address 10.12.100.17/30;
  }
   family mpls;
  }
}
   }
protocols {
mpls {
 interface all;
}
ospf {
 area 0.0.0.0 {
  interface t1-0/1/0.0;
  interface t1-1/1/1.0;
  interface lo0.0 {
  passive;
  }
 }
}
ldp {
  interface t1-0/1/0.0;
  interface t1-1/1/1.0;
  interface lo0.0;
}
}
routing-instances {
ABCCORP {
instance-type vpls;
interface fe-0/0/3.0;
  protocols {
   vpls {
    vpls-id 101;
    neighbor 10.255.170.98;
    neighbor 10.255.170.104;

  }
 }
}
   }
```

Figure 1.59 Router PE1 Configuration

```
user@B>show vpls connections
Layer-2 VPN connections:

Legend for connection status (St)
EI -- encapsulation invalid      NC -- interface encapsulation not CCC/TCC/VPLS
EM -- encapsulation mismatch     WE -- interface and instance encaps not same
VC-Dn -- Virtual circuit down    NP -- interface hardware not present
CM -- control-word mismatch      -> -- only outbound connection is up
CN -- circuit not provisioned    <- -- only inbound connection is up
OR -- out of range               Up -- operational
OL -- no outgoing label          Dn -- down
LD -- local site signaled down   CF -- call admission control failure
RD -- remote site signaled down  SC -- local and remote site ID collision LN --
local site not designated  LM -- local site ID not minimum designated RN --
remote site not designated RM -- remote site ID not minimum designated XX --
unknown connection status  IL -- no incoming label
MM -- MTU mismatch               MI -- Mesh-Group ID not availble

Legend for interface status
Up -- operational
Dn -- down

Instance: v1
BGP-VPLS State
  Local site: 1 (1)
    connection-site      Type  St    Time last up        # Up trans
    3                    rmt   Up    Jan 21 16:38:47 2011           1
      Local interface: vt-0/3/0.1048834, Status: Up, Encapsulation: VPLS
        Description: Intf - vpls v1 local site 1 remote site 3
      Remote PE: 10.255.170.96, Negotiated control-word: No
      Incoming label: 800258, Outgoing label: 800000
    4                    rmt   Up    Jan 21 16:38:54 2011           1
      Local interface: vt-0/3/0.1048835, Status: Up, Encapsulation: VPLS
        Description: Intf - vpls v1 local site 1 remote site 4
      Remote PE: 10.255.170.102, Negotiated control-word: No
      Incoming label: 800259, Outgoing label: 800000
LDP-VPLS State
VPLS-id: 101
  Mesh-group connections: m1
    Neighbor                   Type  St    Time last up        # Up trans
    10.255.170.104(vpls-id 101) rmt Up     Jan 21 16:38:40 2011           1
      Local interface: vt-0/3/0.1048833, Status: Up, Encapsulation: ETHERNET
        Description: Intf - vpls v1 neighbor 10.255.170.104 vpls-id 101
      Remote PE: 10.255.170.104, Negotiated control-word: No
      Incoming label: 800001, Outgoing label: 800000
    10.255.170.106(vpls-id 101) rmt Up     Jan 21 16:38:39 2011           1
      Local interface: vt-0/3/0.1048832, Status: Up, Encapsulation: ETHERNET
        Description: Intf - vpls v1 neighbor 10.255.170.106 vpls-id 101
      Remote PE: 10.255.170.106, Negotiated control-word: No
      Incoming label: 800000, Outgoing label: 800000
```

Figure 1.60 Verifying the BGP and LDP Interworking

Multicast Traffic in VPLS

In each VPLS routing instance, it is possible to configure a dedicated point-to-multipoint (P2MP) LSP to carry all unknown unicast, broadcast, and multicast traffic. Enabling this feature increases the efficiency of the network because duplicate copies of flooded traffic do not have to be created for each PE router in the VPLS routing instance.

Figure 1.61 shows how flooded traffic reaches PE routers in a VPLS routing instance when a P2MP LSP is not configured for flooding. In this diagram, PE1 needs to forward 100 Mbps of multicast traffic. Since there are three recipient PE routers (PE2, PE3, and PE4), PE1 creates three copies of traffic, which now becomes 300 Mbps in bandwidth. P1 also sends 200 Mbps of traffic towards P2, since PE2 and PE3 are behind P2, and sends one copy (100 Mbps) towards PE4. Finally, P2 sends the traffic (a copy each) to the receivers, PE2 and PE3.

In a large network with high volumes of multicast, unknown unicast/broadcast traffic this can be a very costly affair, since the bandwidth consumption is so high.

In contrast, if the VPLS instance is configured to use a P2MP LSP, the ingress PE router creates a single copy of the unknown traffic that needs to be flooded, and each node in the P2MP LSP path creates a single copy for its respective branch nodes. This applies throughout the network. As illustrated in Figure 1.62, this means a huge reduction in bandwidth utilization and offers significant cost savings to the operator.

Let us take a look at some sample configurations, based on JUNOS in Figure 1.63. In the first configuration, a P2MP label-switched template has been associated with the VPLS instance.

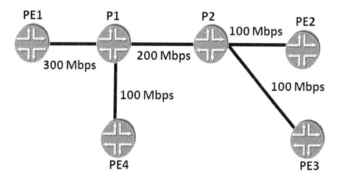

Figure 1.61

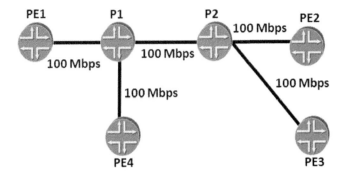

Figure 1.62

```
[edit]
routing-instances {
    GOLD {
      instance-type vpls;
       interface ge-1/0/0.1;
       route-distinguisher 1.1.1.1:1;
        provider-tunnel {
          rsvp-te {
             label-switched-path-template {
                vpls-GOLD-p2mp-template;
        }
      }
    }
        vrf-target target:65000:1;
        protocols {
          vpls {
          site-range 8;
           site CE1 {
              site-identifier 1;
        }
      }
     }
    }
}
protocols {
mpls {
  label-switched-path vpls-GOLD-p2mp-template {
    template;
    link-protection;
     p2mp;
  }
interface all;
interface fxp0.0 {
  disable;
  }
  }
}
```

Figure 1.63 VPLS P2MP Configuration

```
admin@PEA# show route table GOLD.l2vpn.0 extensive
GOLD.l2vpn.0: 5 destinations, 5 routes (5 active, 0 holddown, 0
hidden)
1.1.1.1:1:1:1/96 (1 entry, 1 announced)
*BGP    Preference: 170/-65536
Route Distinguisher: 1.1.1.1:1
PMSI: Flags 0:RSVP-
TE:label[0:0:0]:Session_13[1.1.1.1:0:9519:1.1.1.1]
Next hop type: Indirect
Next-hop reference count: 4
Source: 7.7.7.7
Protocol next hop: 1.1.1.1
Indirect next hop: 2 no-forward
State: <Secondary Active Int Ext>
Local AS: 65000 Peer AS: 65000
Age: 2:30:44 Metric2: 1
Task: BGP_65000.7.7.7.7+179
Announcement bits (1): 0-GOLD-l2vpn
AS path: I (Originator) Cluster list: 7.7.7.7
AS path: Originator ID: 1.1.1.1
Communities: target:65000:1 Layer2-info: encaps:VPLS, control
flags:, mtu: 0, site
preference: 65535
Import Accepted
Label-base: 262145, range: 8
Localpref: 65535
Router ID: 7.7.7.7
Primary Routing Table bgp.l2vpn.0
Indirect next hops: 1
Protocol next hop: 1.1.1.1 Metric: 3
Indirect next hop: 2 no-forward
Indirect path forwarding next hops: 1
Next hop type: Router
Next hop: 10.10.8.2 via xe-0/1/0.0 weight 0x1
1.1.1.1/32 Originating RIB: inet.3
Metric: 3 Node path count: 1
Forwarding nexthops: 1
Nexthop: 10.10.8.2 via xe-0/1/0.0
[Output Truncated]
```

Figure 1.64 BGP Information for Participating PE Routers

The configurations in Figures 1.64 and 1.65 show commands for viewing the association of the P2MP LSP with the VPLS instance. The first command displays the BGP table with all the route information for PE routers that are part of the same VPLS instance. The second command shows details of the VPLS instance.

```
admin@PEA# show vpls connections extensive
...
Instance: GOLD
Local site: CE3 (3)
Number of local interfaces: 1
Number of local interfaces up: 1
IRB interface present: no
ge-1/0/0.1
lsi.1048832 1 Intf - vpls GOLD local site 3 remote site 1
lsi.1048833 2 Intf - vpls GOLD local site 3 remote site 2
Interface flags: VC-Down
lsi.1048834 5 Intf - vpls GOLD local site 3 remote site 5
Interface flags: VC-Down
Label-base Offset Range Preference
262145 1 8 65535
connection-site Type St Time last up # Up trans
1 rmt Up Nov 16 11:22:01 2010 1
Remote PE: 1.1.1.1, Negotiated control-word: No
Incoming label: 262145, Outgoing label: 262147
Local interface: lsi.1048832, Status: Up, Encapsulation: VPLS
Description: Intf - vpls GOLD local site 3 remote site 1
RSVP-TE P2MP lsp:
Egress branch LSP: 3.3.3.3:1.1.1.1:1:vpls:GOLD, State: Up
Connection History:
Nov 16 11:22:54 2009 PE route changed
Nov 16 11:22:01 2009 status update timer
Nov 16 11:22:01 2009 PE route changed
Nov 16 11:22:01 2009 Out lbl Update 262147
Nov 16 11:22:01 2009 In lbl Update 262145
Nov 16 11:22:01 2009 loc intf up lsi.1048832
3 rmt RN
5 rmt RD
Ingress RSVP-TE P2MP LSP: vpls-GOLD, Flood next-hop ID: 616
```

Figure 1.65 VPLS Instance Information

Selective Trees for Multicast in VPLS

One of the issues that needs to be addressed when creating a P2MP tree in the context of VPLS is how to handle multicast flooding, which still delivers traffic to PE routers that do not have any interested receivers. The solution is to use Inclusive P-Tunnels. While the present model does offer extremely significant bandwidth savings, the need for more optimal multicast delivery always exists.

The Internet draft "draft-ietf-l2vpn-vpls-mcast-08.txt" specifies procedures for delivering multicast traffic for VPLS, including the use of selective trees. Some passages from the draft are quoted here:

Once a PE decides to bind a set of VPLSes or customer multicast groups to an Inclusive P-Multicast tree or a Selective P-Multicast tree, it needs to announce this binding to other PEs in the network.

This procedure is referred to as Inclusive P-Multicast tree or Selective P-Multicast tree binding distribution and is performed using BGP.

If an Inclusive P-Multicast tree is used to instantiate the provider tunnel for VPLS multicast on the PE, the advertising PE MUST advertise the type and the identity of the P-Multicast tree in the PMSI Tunnel attribute.

Selective trees provide a PE the ability to create separate P-Multicast trees for certain < C-S, C-G> streams. The source PE, that originates the Selective tree, and the egress PEs, MUST use the Selective tree for the < C-S, C-G> streams that are mapped to it. This may require the source and egress PEs to switch to the Selective tree from an Inclusive tree if they were already using an Inclusive tree for the < C-S, C-G> streams mapped to the Selective tree. Once a source PE decides to setup an Selective tree, it MUST announce the mapping of the < C-S, C-G> streams (which may be in different VPLSes) that are mapped to the tree to the other PEs using BGP. After the egress PEs receive the announcement they set up their forwarding path to receive traffic on the Selective tree if they have one or more receivers interested in the < C-S, C-G> streams mapped to the tree. Setting up the forwarding path requires setting up the de-multiplexing forwarding entries based on the top MPLS label (if there is no inner label) or the inner label (if present). The egress PEs MAY perform this switch to the Selective tree once the advertisement from the ingress PE is received or wait for a preconfigured timer to do so, after receiving the advertisement, when the P2MP LSP protocol is mLDP. When the P2MP LSP protocol is P2MP RSVP-TE an egress PE MUST perform this switch to the Selective tree only after the advertisement from the ingress PE is received and the RSVP-TE P2MP LSP has been setup to the egress PE. This switch MAY be done after waiting for a preconfigured timer after these two steps have been accomplished. A source PE MUST use the following approach to decide when to start transmitting data on the Selective tree, if it was already using an Inclusive tree. A certain pre-configured delay after advertising the < C-S, C-G> streams mapped to an Selective tree, the source PE begins to send traffic on the Selective tree. At this point it stops to send traffic for the < C-S, C-G> streams, that are mapped on the Selective tree, on the Inclusive tree. This traffic is instead transmitted on a Selective tree.

The infrastructure to deliver multicast traffic using selective trees described by the draft is very similar to the Next-Gen MVPN framework and relies on the same BGP procedures for creating the control plane infrastructure. VPLS PEs rely on PIM/IGMP snooping on the PE-CE interfaces to build multicast state information.

Inter-Provider VPLS

Inter-provider VPLS makes it possible for a service provider to serve an entirely new set of customers, such as international businesses who have sites spread over a very large geographic area and are served by multiple ISPs. By establishing VPLS partnerships with other service providers outside of the service provider's own service region, the footprint of the provider's own VPLS offering is expanded. These partnerships can be negotiated based on known customer needs or on projected customer bases in the shared regions. For the customer, the inter-provider peering is transparent; each of the customer's sites still appears to be connected to a shared Ethernet switch. Inter-provider VPLS also opens a potential new source of revenue for carriers with large regional or global MPLS networks by providing a wide-area VPLS backbone for regional or local VPLS service providers. For both metro Ethernet providers wanting to develop direct VPLS partnerships with other metro Ethernet providers and carrier wanting to provide a VPLS backbone to metro Ethernet providers, creating an inter-provider VPLS network requires underlying protocols that allow VPLS to span one or multiple autonomous system boundaries.

Discovery

A PE is configured to know what VPLS sites, or instances, it is connected to. But for each of its configured VPLS instances, it must have some way of knowing which PEs are a part of the same VPLS instance. That is, if a PE has a local interface connected to VPLS 1, it must know which other PEs have interfaces to VPLS 1. Thus the final requirement for a practical VPLS implementation is discovery.

When LDP is used as the VPLS signaling protocol, no discovery mechanism is supported within the protocol itself. Each PE must be individually configured with the identities of all other PEs belonging to each VPLS instance, and every time an instance is changed (a PE is added or deleted, or an entire instance is added or deleted) each PE must be reconfigured. Touching each PE for every change quickly becomes operationally prohibitive for a commercially viable VPLS offering, and it can also significantly increase the potential for configuration errors in the network.

Several mechanisms have been proposed for autodiscovery in LDP-based VPLS networks, using a centralized database system accessed through DNS or RADIUS. However such solutions, by adding more protocols and procedures to the system, increase the complexity and risk. MP-BGP, on the other hand, enables auto-discovery as a part of its VPLS procedures. The same protocol can be used for both signaling and autodiscovery, reducing complexity while at the same time simplifying changes to VPLS instances.

The previous section ended with an example of how implementing VPLS with MP-BGP is preferable to implementing with LDP: MP-BGP offers a means of performing autodiscovery to simplify the management of VPLS instances without requiring the addition of new protocols and procedures, and LDP does not. But there are many more reasons for using MP-BGP to implement VPLS. This section shows why MP-BGP VPLS is the superior solution for large-scale VPLS deployments, even within a single Autonomous System (AS); for inter-provider VPLS, it is the only practical solution.

Common Inter-AS Procedures

As we have seen in the previous sections, BGP-based VPLS is preferable to LDP-based VPLS for any serious service offering because of its autodiscovery capabilities, its ability to support multiple services, and its superior scalability. These qualities hold when the VPLS service offering spans only a single AS. But when a commercially viable VPLS offering must span multiple ASs, BGP-based VPLS is no longer merely the best solution; it is the only practical solution.

The fundamental role of BGP is, after all, inter-AS routing. The autodiscovery, the multiprotocol (and hence multiservice) support, and the practical scaling capabilities of MP-BGP can therefore be easily extended across AS boundaries. Further, using a single group of common procedures means that engineers do not have to design a separate logical infrastructure for interprovider VPLS, and that operations personnel are not burdened with additional complexity (and risk). Specifically, BGP-based VPLS supports the same three inter-AS design options as do Layer 3 BGP/MPLS VPNs. These three options are referred to throughout the industry as Options A, B, and C.

Option A

Option A is the perhaps simplest of the three inter-AS design options to implement, but it is also the least scalable. Essentially, the routers connecting two ASs—the autonomous system boundary routers (ASBRs)—see themselves as PEs and their peers in the neighboring AS as CEs. In the illustration in Figure 1.66, for

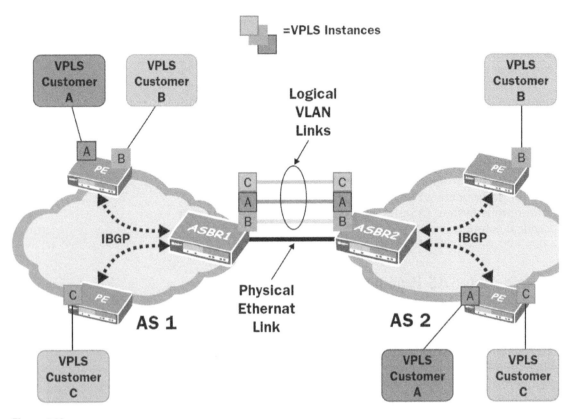

Figure 1.66

example, ASBR1 sees itself as a PE and sees ASBR2 as a connected CE; conversely, ASBR2 sees itself as a PE and sees ASBR1 as a connected CE.

This relationship means that the connecting medium between the ASBRs must be Ethernet, which can be a limiting factor: ASBRs must be co-located or at least geographically close enough to accommodate the distance limitations of a physical Ethernet link. On the other hand, Option A is the only option that does not require an LSP between the two ASs, which might be a consideration should the operators of the two ASs wish to completely isolate their MPLS topologies from each other. The key limiting factor of Option A, however, is the fact that the ASBRs are, for all practical purposes, PEs. This breaks the desired VPLS model in four respects:

- There is no single LSP between the edge PEs. Instead, in each AS the edge PEs connect to the ASBRs, which decapsulate the frames from MPLS and forward them to the peer ASBR via native Ethernet, where the frames are re-encapsulated in MPLS and forwarded to their destination.

- Since the ASBRs are PEs, they maintain VPLS state. Specifically, they must perform learning and record MAC addresses and ports, which limits the number of VPLS instances they can support. The growth of the inter-AS VPLS service is then subject to the same limitations.
- For each VPLS instance on the ASBRs, a separate VLAN instance must be established between the ASBRs. For example, if there are 100 VPLS instances, 100 separate VLANs between the ASBRs must be established and maintained.
- Because the logical relationship on each side of the AS boundary is that of a PE to a CE, the ASBRs on each side must be configured as PEs. The autodiscovery capability of BGP-based VPLS is lost, and operational overhead increases accordingly.

Option B

Option B eliminates the maintenance of VPLS state in the ASBRs. A single EBGP session between the ASBRs signals VPLS, and VPLS traffic can be carried on a single LSP between the ASBRs. No PE functions such as MAC learning and VPLS state maintenance are required in Option B, making it much more scalable than Option A. See Figure 1.67.

Option C

Option C moves the EBGP session endpoints from the ASBRs to the PEs themselves, using multihop EBGP. This option is considered the most scalable of the three because no VPLS-related configuration is required on the ASBRs at all. The VPLS topology between ASs remains the same as it is within a single AS: All "VPLS intelligence" is in the PEs connecting VPLS sites, and the network core is "VPLS unaware." Option C can be made even more scalable by leveraging BGP's route reflector capabilities. Rather than establish multihop EBGP sessions between individual PEs, the sessions can be established between route reflectors. This accords the same scaling benefits in inter-AS VPLS as in single-AS VPLS that uses route reflectors. See Figure 1.68.

While Option C is the most scalable, many operators prefer Option B because it has the same "feel" as other inter-AS peering arrangements and allows them to apply the same policies. What is most important, however, is that BGP-based VPLS offers design options not available with LDP-based VPLS, and unlike LDP-based VPLS, it offers the ability to build an inter-AS solution that is practical for a commercial VPLS offering.

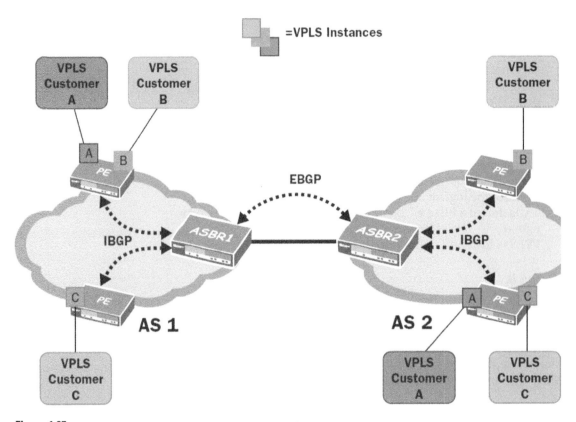

Figure 1.67

Conclusion

In this chapter we took a look at the various models for building VPLS infrastructures and the mechanisms for addressing various requirements. A clear point to remember here is that LDP-VPLS raises two issues that need to be addressed: the control plane state in terms of number of LDP sessions needed, and the forwarding state (MAC information) that needs to be accommodated, on all devices. On the contrary, BGP-VPLS can scale extremely well by reducing the control plane state information through BGP RR hierarchies and hence reducing the number of sessions between VPLS peers. One of the options for reducing the forwarding state information is discussed in the next chapter.

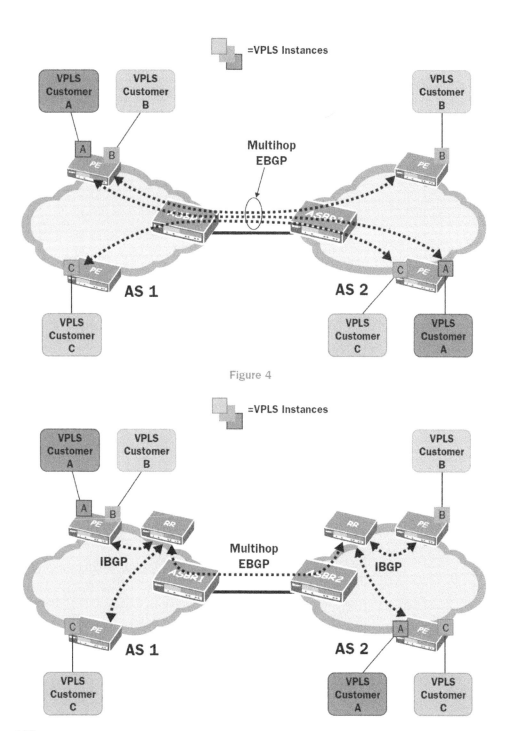

Figure 4

Figure 1.68

2

UNDERSTANDING ADVANCED MPLS LAYER 3 VPN SERVICES

Introduction

The previous chapter discussed the building blocks of deploying Ethernet-based multipoint services. In this chapter we look at the deployment scenarios of MPLS Layer 3 VPNs.

MPLS Layer 3 VPNs

RFC 2547bis defines a mechanism that allows service providers to use their IP backbone to provide VPN services to their customers. RFC 2547bis VPNs are also known as BGP/MPLS VPNs because BGP is used to distribute VPN routing information across the provider's backbone and because MPLS is used to forward VPN traffic from one VPN site to another.

The primary objectives of this approach are as follows:
- Make the service very simple for customers to use even if they lack experience in IP routing
- Make the service very scalable and flexible to facilitate large-scale deployment
- Allow the policies used to create a VPN to be implemented by the service provider alone, or by the service provider working together with the customer
- Allow the service provider to deliver a critical value-added service that galvanizes customer loyalty

Network Components

In the context of RFC 2547bis, a VPN is a collection of policies, and these policies control connectivity among a set of sites. A customer site is connected to the service provider network by one or more ports, where the service provider associates each port with a

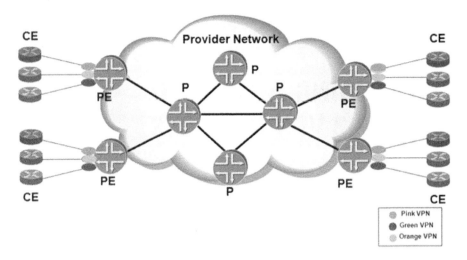

Figure 2.1

VPN routing table. In RFC 2547bis terms, the VPN routing table is called a VPN routing and forwarding (VRF) table.

Figure 2.1 illustrates the fundamental building blocks of a BGP/MPLS VPN.

Customer Edge (CE) Routers

A customer edge (CE) device provides customer access to the service provider network over a data link to one or more provider edge (PE) routers. While the CE device can be a host or a Layer 2 switch, typically the CE device is an IP router that establishes an adjacency with its directly connected PE routers. After the adjacency is established, the CE router advertises the site's local VPN routes to the PE router and learns remote VPN routes from the PE router.

Provider Edge (PE) Routers

PE routers exchange routing information with CE routers using static routing, RIPv2, OSPF, or EBGP. While a PE router maintains VPN routing information, it is only required to maintain VPN routes for those VPNs to which it is directly attached. This design enhances the scalability of the RFC 2547bis model because it eliminates the need for PE routers to maintain all of the service provider's VPN routes.

Each PE router maintains a VRF for each of its directly connected sites. Each customer connection (such as Frame Relay PVC, ATM PVC, and VLAN) is mapped to a specific VRF. Thus, it is a port on the PE router and not a site that is associated with a VRF. Note that multiple ports on a PE router can be associated with a single VRF. It is the ability of PE routers to maintain multiple forwarding tables that supports the per-VPN segregation of routing information.

After learning local VPN routes from CE routers, a PE router exchanges VPN routing information with other PE routers using IBGP. PE routers can maintain IBGP sessions to route reflectors as an alternative to a full mesh of IBGP sessions. Deploying multiple route reflectors enhances the scalability of the RFC 2547bis model because it eliminates the need for any single network component to maintain all VPN routes.

Finally, when using MPLS to forward VPN data traffic across the provider's backbone, the ingress PE router functions as the ingress LSR and the egress PE router functions as the egress LSR.

Provider (P) Routers

A provider (P) router is any router in the provider's network that does not attach to CE devices. P routers function as MPLS transit LSRs when forwarding VPN data traffic between PE routers. Since traffic is forwarded across the MPLS backbone using a two-layer label stack, P routers are only required to maintain routes to the provider's PE routers; they are not required to maintain specific VPN routing information for each customer site.

Operational Model

Two fundamental traffic flows occur in a BGP/MPLS VPN:
- A control flow that is used for VPN route distribution and label switched path (LSP) establishment
- A data flow that is used to forward customer data traffic

Sample Network Topology

Figure 2.2 provides a sample network topology where a single service provider delivers a BGP/MPLS VPN service to several customers. In this network there are two PE routers connected to four different customer sites.

The inter-site connectivity can be described by the following policies:
- Any host in site 1 can communicate with any host in Site 2.
- Any host in site 2 can communicate with any host in Site 1.
- Any host in site 3 can communicate with any host in Site 4.
- Any host in site 4 can communicate with any host in Site 3.

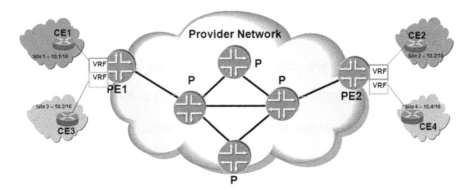

Figure 2.2

Control Flow

In a BGP/MPLS VPN, the control flow consists of two subflows:
- The first control subflow is responsible for the exchange of routing information between the CE and PE routers at the edges of the provider's backbone and between the PE routers across the provider's backbone.
- The second control subflow is responsible for the establishment of LSPs across the provider's backbone between PE routers.

In the example in Figure 2, PE1 is configured to associate VRF Green with the interface or subinterface over which it learns routes from CE1. When CE1 advertises the route for prefix 10.1/16 to PE1, PE1 installs a local route to 10.1/16 in VRF Green. PE1 advertises the route for 10.1/16 to PE2 using IBGP. Before advertising the route, PE1 selects an MPLS label (for this example, 222) to advertise with the route and assigns its loopback address as the BGP next hop for the route.

RFC 2547bis supports overlapping address spaces (private addressing as defined in RFC 1918) by the use of route distinguishers (RDs) and the VPN-IPv4 address family. RFC 2547bis constrains the distribution of routing information among PE routers by the use of route filtering based on BGP extended community attributes (route targets). When PE2 receives PE1's route advertisement, it determines if it should install the route to prefix 10.1/16 into VRF Green by performing route filtering based on the BGP extended community attributes carried with the route. If PE2 decides to install the route in VRF Green, it then advertises the route to prefix 10.1/16 to CE2. The same process is followed for VRF Orange.

LSP Establishment

In order to use MPLS to forward VPN traffic across the provider's backbone, MPLS LSPs must be established between the PE router that learns the route and the PE router that advertises the route. See Figure 2.3.

MPLS LSPs can be established and maintained across the service provider's network using either Label Distribution Protocol (LDP) or Resource Reservation Protocol (RSVP). The provider uses RSVP if it wants to MPLS Fast Reroute for ~50 ms convergence in the case of link/node failures in the provider network. RSVP LSPs also offer the option to either assign bandwidth to the LSP or use Traffic Engineering, a technique used to select an explicit path for the LSP within the network. RSVP-based LSPs support specific quality of service (QoS) guarantees and/or specific traffic engineering objectives. It is also possible to use both LDP and RSVP LSPs—LDP for basic MPLS forwarding and RSVP for Traffic Engineering—and Fast Reroute, depending on the network architecture.

When both LDP-based and RSVP-based LSPs exist between a pair of PE routers, the ingress label switching router (LSR) selects the RSVP-based LSP instead of the LDP-based LSP. This is due to the fact that RSVP LSPs have a higher preference than their LDP counterparts. This model supports the incremental configuration of RSV-based LSPs across the service provider's backbone.

Data Flow

Figure 2.4 shows the flow of VPN data traffic across the service provider's backbone from one customer site to another customer site.

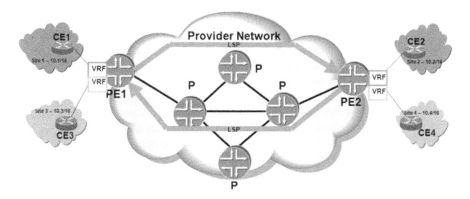

Figure 2.3

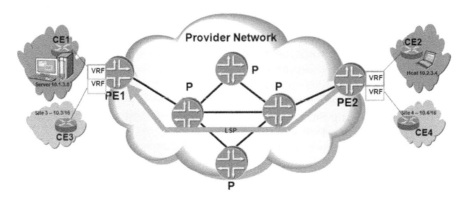

Figure 2.4

Assume that Host 10.2.3.4 at Site 2 wants to communicate with Server 10.1.3.8 at Site 1. Host 10.2.3.4 forwards all data packets for Server 10.1.3.8 to its default gateway. When a packet arrives at CE2, it performs a longest-match route lookup and forwards the IPv4 packet to PE2. PE2 receives the packet, performs a route lookup in VRF Green, and obtains the following information:

- The MPLS label that was advertised by PE 1 with the route (label = 222)
- The BGP next hop for the route (the loopback address of PE1)
- The outgoing subinterface for the LSP from PE2 to PE1
- The initial MPLS label for the LSP from PE2 to PE1

User traffic is forwarded from PE2 to PE1 using MPLS with a label stack containing two labels. For this data flow, PE2 is the ingress LSR for the LSP and PE1 is the egress LSR for the LSP. Before transmitting a packet, PE2 pushes the label 222 onto the label stack, making it the bottom (or inner) label. This label is originally installed in VRF Green when PE2 receives PE1's IBGP advertisement for the route to 10.1/16. Next, PE2 pushes the label associated with the LDP or RSVP-based LSP to PE1 (the route's BGP next hop) onto the label stack, making it the top (or outer) label. After creating the label stack, PE2 forwards the MPLS packet on the outgoing interface to the first P router along the LSP from PE2 to PE1. P routers switch packets across the core of the provider's backbone network based on the top label, which is exchanged using LDP/RSVP. The penultimate router to PE1 pops the top label (exposing the bottom or inner label) and forwards the packet to PE1.

When PE1 receives the packet, it pops the label, creating a native IPv4 packet. PE1 uses the bottom label (222) to identify the directly attached CE that is the next hop to 10.1/16. Finally,

PE1 forwards the native IPv4 packet to CE, which forwards the packet to Server 10.1.3.8 at Site 1.

Benefits of BGP/MPLS VPNs

The major objective of BGP/MPLS VPNs is to simplify network operations for customers while allowing the service provider to offer scalable, revenue-generating, value-added services. BGP/MPLS VPNs offers many benefits, including the following:

- There are no constraints on the address plan used by each VPN customer. The customer can use either globally unique or private IP address spaces. From the service provider's perspective, different customers can have overlapping address spaces.
- The CE router at each customer site does not directly exchange routing information with other CE routers. Customers do not have to deal with inter-site routing issues because inter-site routing issues are the responsibility of the service provider.
- VPN customers do not have a backbone or a virtual backbone to administer. Thus customers do not need management access to PE or P routers.
- Providers do not have a separate backbone or virtual backbone to administer for each customer VPN. Thus providers do not require management access to CE routers.
- The policies that determine whether a specific site is a member of a particular VPN are the policies of the customer. The administrative model for RFC 2547bis VPNs allows customer policies to be implemented by the provider alone or by the service provider working together with the customer.
- The VPN can span multiple service providers.
- Without the use of cryptographic techniques, security is equivalent to that supported by existing Layer 2 (ATM or Frame Relay) backbone networks.
- Service providers can use a common infrastructure to deliver both VPN and Internet connectivity services.
- Flexible and scalable QoS for customer VPN services is supported through the use of the experimental bits in the MPLS shim header or by the use of traffic engineered LSPs (signaled by RSVP).
- The RFC 2547bis model is link layer (Layer 2) independent.

Challenges and Solutions

RFC 2547bis uses several mechanisms to enhance the scalability of the approach and solve specific VPN operational issues. These issues include the following:

- Supporting overlapping customer address spaces
- Constraining network connectivity
- Maintaining updated VPN routing information
- Conserving backbone bandwidth and PE router packet processing resources
- Overlapping customer address spaces

VPN customers often manage their own networks and use the RFC 1918 private address space. If customers do not use globally unique IP addresses, the same 32-bit IPv4 address can be used to identify different systems in different VPNs. The result can be routing difficulties because BGP assumes that each IPv4 address it carries is globally unique. To solve this problem, BGP/MPLS VPNs support a mechanism that converts non-unique IP addresses into globally unique addresses by combining the use of the VPN-IPv4 address family with the deployment of Multiprotocol BGP Extensions (MP-BGP).

The VPN-IPv4 Address Family

One challenge posed by overlapping address spaces is that if conventional BGP sees two different routes to the same IPv4 address prefix (where the prefix is assigned to systems in different VPNs), BGP treats the prefixes as if they are equivalent and installs only one route. As a result, the other system is unreachable. Eliminating this problem requires a mechanism that allows BGP to disambiguate the prefixes so that it is possible to install two completely different routes to that address, one for each VPN. RFC 2547bis supports this capability by defining the VPN-IPv4 address family.

A VPN-IPv4 address is a 12-byte quantity composed of an 8-byte RD followed by a 4-byte IPv4 address prefix. See Figure 2.5.

The 8-byte RD is composed of a 2-byte Type field and a 6-byte Value field. The Type field determines the lengths of the Value field's two subfields (Administrator and Assigned Number), as

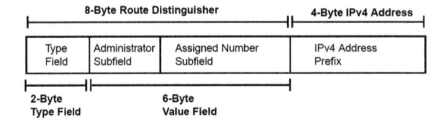

Figure 2.5

well as the semantics of the Administrator field. Currently, two values are defined for the Type field: 0 and 1.

- For Type 0, the Administrator subfield contains 2 bytes, and the Assigned Number subfield contains 4 bytes. The Administrator subfield holds an autonomous system number (ASN). The use of an ASN from the private ASN space is strongly discouraged. The Assigned Number subfield holds a value from the numbering space administered by the service provider who offers the VPN service and to which the ASN has been assigned.

- For Type 1, the Administrator subfield contains 4 bytes and the Assigned Number subfield contains 2 bytes. The Administrator subfield holds an IPv4 address. The use of an IP address from the private IP address space is strongly discouraged. The Assigned Number subfield holds a value from the numbering space administered by the service provider that offers the VPN service and to which the ASN has been assigned. A configuration option for Type 1 RDs is to use the loopback address of the PE router that originates the route for the 4-byte Administrator subfield and to select a number that is local to that PE router for the 2-byte Assigned Number subfield.

When configuring RDs on PE routers, RFC 2547bis does not require that all the routes within a VPN use the same RD; in fact, each VRF within a VPN can use its own RD. However, the service provider must ensure that each RD is globally unique. For this reason, using the private ASN space or the private IP address space when defining RDs is strongly discouraged. Using the public ASN space or the public IP address space guarantees that each RD is globally unique. Globally unique RDs provide a mechanism that allows each service provider to administer its own address space and create globally unique VPN-IPv4 addresses without conflicting with the RD assignments made by other service providers.

The use of globally unique RDs supports the following:

- The creation of distinct routes to a common IPv4 prefix
- The creation of multiple globally unique routes to the same system
- The use of policy to decide which packets use which route

Finally, the following points help to avoid confusion concerning how VPN-IPv4 addresses are used in a BGP/MPLS VPN:

- VPN-IPv4 addresses are used only within the service provider network.
- VPN customers are not aware of the use of VPN-IPv4 addresses.
- VPN-IPv4 addresses are carried only in routing protocols that run across the provider's backbone.

- VPN-IPv4 addresses are not carried in the packet headers of VPN data traffic as it crosses the provider's backbone.

Multiprotocol BGP Extensions

Another limitation of using conventional BGP4 to support BGP/MPLS VPNs is that it was originally designed to carry routing information only for the IPv4 address family. Realizing this limitation, the IETF is working to standardize the Multiprotocol Extensions for BGP4. These extensions were originally defined in RFC 2283 (February 1998) and later updated in RFC 2858 (June 2000). The extensions allow BGP4 to carry routing information for multiple Network Layer protocols (IPv6, IPX, VPN-IPv4, etc.). Therefore, to deploy BGP/MPLS VPNs and support the distribution of VPN-IPv4 routes, PE routers are required to support the MP-BGP extensions and not just conventional BGP.

RFC 2547bis requires that BGP capabilities negotiations take place before VPN-IPv4 routing information is exchanged to ensure that the BGP peers are both capable of processing the VPN-IPv4 address family. Note that the MP-BGP extensions are backwards compatible, so a router that supports these extensions can still inter-operate with a router that does not support these extensions, using conventional BGP4 (however, conventional BGP4 does not support RFC 2547bis VPNs).

Other Challenges and Solutions

Assuming a routing table does not contain a default route, a basic assumption of IP routing is that if the route to a specific network is not installed in a router's forwarding table, the network is unreachable from that router. By constraining the flow of routing information, service providers can efficiently control the flow of customer VPN data traffic. The BGP/MPLS VPN model constrains the flow of routing information using two mechanisms:

- Multiple forwarding tables
- BGP extended community attributes

Multiple Forwarding Tables

Each PE router maintains one or more per-site forwarding tables known as VRFs. When a PE router is configured, each of its VRFs is associated with one or more ports (interfaces/subinterfaces) on the PE router that connects directly to the service provider's customers. If a given site contains hosts that are members of multiple VPNs, the VRF associated with the customer site contains routes for all VPNs of which the site is a member.

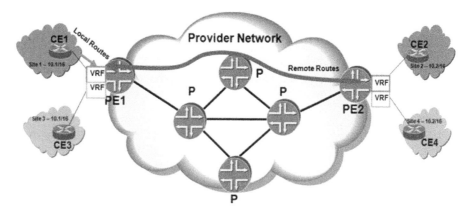

Figure 2.6

When receiving an outbound customer data packet from a directly attached CE router, the PE router performs a route lookup in the VRF associated with that site. The specific VRF is determined by the subinterface over which the data packet is received. Support for multiple forwarding tables makes it easy for the PE router to provide the per-VPN segregation of routing information. See Figure 2.6.

- PE1 learns Site 1's VPN Green routes from CE1 and installs them into VRF Green.
- Remote routes are learned via MP-IBGP from other PE routers that are directly connected to sites with hosts that are members of VPN Green. PE1 learns Site 2's VPN Red routes from CE2 and installs them into VRF Green. The import of remote routes into VRF Green is managed by the use of BGP extended community route target attributes.
- Local VPN Orange routes at Site 4 and remote VPN Orange routes at Site 3 are not associated with VPN Green and are not imported into VRF Green.

A number of benefits are derived from having PE routers support multiple forwarding tables:

- Different VPN sites served by the same PE router can use overlapping address spaces.
- Selection of the specific forwarding table for data traffic is determined by policy (the mapping of a router subinterface to a VRF), and not by the user content of the packet.
- Multiple forwarding tables prevent communication between sites that have no VPNs in common.
- Scalability is enhanced because PE routers are not required to maintain a dedicated VRF for all of the VPNs supported by the

provider's network. Each PE router is only required to maintain a VRF for each of its directly connected sites.

- Finally, the backbone network can support multiple different routes to the same system where the route for a specific packet is determined by the site from which the packet enters the provider's backbone.

BGP Extended Community Attributes

The distribution of VPN routing information is constrained through the use of BGP extended community attributes. Extended community attributes are carried in BGP messages as attributes of the route. They identify the route as belonging to a specific collection of routes, all of which are treated the same with respect to routing policy. Each BGP extended community must be globally unique (it contains either a public IP address or an ASN) and can be used by only one VPN. However, a given customer VPN can make use of multiple globally unique BGP extended communities to help control the distribution of routing information.

BGP/MPLS VPNs use 32-bit BGP extended community attributes instead of conventional 16-bit BGP community attributes. The use of 32-bit extended community attributes enhances scalability because it allows a single service provider to support a maximum of 2^{32} communities (not just 2^{16}). Since each community attribute contains the provider's globally unique autonomous system (AS) number, the service provider can control local assignment while also maintaining the global uniqueness of that assignment.

RFC 2547bis VPNs can use up to three different types of BGP extended community attributes:

- The route target attribute identifies a collection of sites (VRFs) to which a PE router distributes routes. A PE router uses this attribute to constrain the import of remote routes into its VRFs.
- The VPN-of-origin attribute identifies a collection of sites and establishes the associated route as coming from one of the sites in that set.
- The site-of-origin attribute identifies the specific site from which a PE router learns a route. It is encoded as a route origin extended community attribute, which can be used to prevent routing loops.

Operational Model

Before distributing local routes to other PE routers, the ingress PE router attaches a route target attribute to each route learned from directly connected sites. The route target attached to the route is based on the value of the VRFs configured export target policy. This approach provides a tremendous amount of flexibility in the way that a PE router can assign a route target attribute to a route.

- The ingress PE router can be configured to assign a single route target attribute to all routes learned from a given site.
- The ingress PE router can be configured to assign one route target attribute to a set of routes learned from a site and other route target attributes to other sets of routes learned from a site.
- If the CE router communicates with the PE router via EBGP, the CE router can specify one or more route targets for each route. This approach shifts the control of implementing VPN policies from the service provider to the customer.

Before installing remote routes that have been distributed by another PE router, each VRF on an egress PE router is configured with an import target policy. A PE router can only install a VPN-IPv4 route in a VRF if the route target attribute carried with the route matches one of the PE router VRFs import targets.

This approach allows a service provider to use a single mechanism to support VPN customers who have a wide range of inter-site connectivity policies. By careful configuration of export target and import target policies, service providers can construct different types of VPN topologies. The mechanisms that implement the VPN topologies can be completely restricted to the service provider so VPN customers are not aware of this process.

BGP/MPLS VPN Topologies

In this section, we take a look at the various topologies that can be created for the customer network by virtue of establishing policies in route population within a given VRF table.

Full-Mesh VPN Topology

Assume that Corporation Green (VPN Green) wants its BGP/MPLS VPN service provider to create a VPN that supports full-mesh site connectivity. Each Corporation Green site can send traffic directly to another Corporation Green site, but sites of Corporation Orange (VPN Orange) receiving BGP/MPLS VPN service from the same service provider cannot send traffic to or receive traffic from Corporation Green sites. See Figure 2.7.

Each Corporation Green site is associated with VRF Green on its PE router. A single globally unique route target (Green) is configured for each VRF Green as both the import target and the

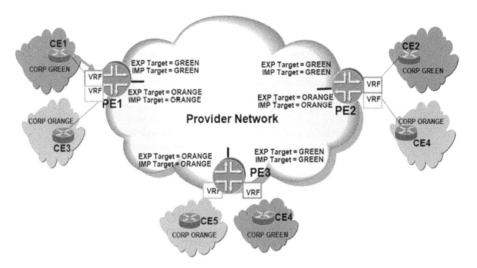

Figure 2.7

export target. This route target (Green) is not assigned to any other VRF as the import or the export target. The result is full-mesh connectivity among Corporation Green sites. The same applies to Corporation Orange sites.

Hub and Spoke VPN Topology

Let us assume that Corporation Green wants its BGP/MPLS VPN service provider to create a VPN that supports hub and spoke site connectivity. The inter-site connectivity for Corporation Green can be described by the following policies:

- Site 1 can communicate directly with Site 5 but not directly with Site 2. If Site 1 wants to communicate with Site 2, it must sent traffic by way of Site 5.
- Site 2 can communicate directly with Site 5 but not directly with Site 1. If Site 2 wants to communicate with Site 1, it must sent traffic by way of Site 5.
- Site 5 can communicate directly with Site 1 and Site 2.

Of course, privacy requires that Corporation Green sites and Corporation Orange sites cannot send traffic to or receive traffic from each other.

A hub and spoke topology is created using two globally unique route target values: hub and spoke. See Figure 2.8.

- The hub site's VRF is configured with an export target (hub) and an import target (spoke). The VRF at the hub site distributes all of the routes in its VRF with a hub attribute that causes

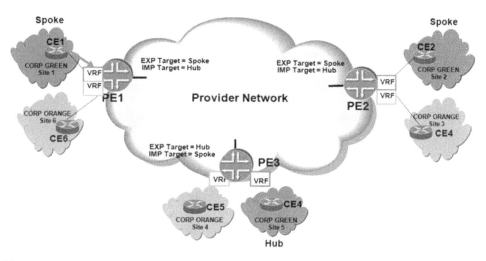

Figure 2.8

the routes to be imported by the spoke sites. The VRF at the hub site imports all remote routes with a spoke attribute.

- Conversely, the VRF at each spoke site is configured with an export target (spoke) and an import target (hub). The VRF at each spoke site distributes its routes with a spoke attribute, which causes the routes to be imported by the hub site but dropped by other spoke sites. The VRF at a spoke site imports only routes with a hub attribute, which causes its VRF to be populated only with routes advertised by the hub site.

Maintaining Updated VPN Routing Information

When the configuration of a PE router is changed by creating a new VRF or by adding one or more new import target policies to an existing VRF, the PE router might need to obtain VPN-IPv4 routes that it previously discarded. The speed of delivering updated routing information can present a problem with conventional BGP4 because it is a stateful protocol and does not support the exchange of route refresh request messages and the subsequent re-advertisement of routes. Once BGP peers synchronize their routing tables, they do not exchange routing information until there is a change in that routing information.

A solution to this design feature is provided by the BGP route refresh capability. During the establishment of an MP-IBGP session, a BGP speaker that wants to receive a route refresh message from its peer or route reflector advertises the BGP route refresh capability using a BGP capabilities advertisement. The BGP route refresh capability states that a BGP speaker can send a route refresh message to a peer or route reflector only if it has received a route refresh capabilities advertisement from that peer or route reflector. Whenever the configuration of a PE router is changed, the PE router can request the retransmission of routing information from its MP-IBGP peers to obtain routing information it previously discarded. When the routes are re-advertised, the updated import target policy is applied as the PE router populates its VRFs.

Backbone B/W and PE Router Packet Processing Resources

During the process of populating its VRFs, a BGP speaker often receives and then filters unwanted routes from peers based on each VRF's import target policy. Since the generation, transmission, and processing of routing updates consumes backbone bandwidth and router packet processing resources, these assets can be conserved by eliminating the transmission of unnecessary routing updates.

The number of BGP routing updates can be reduced by enabling BGP cooperative route filtering capability. During the establishment of the MP-IBGP session, a BGP speaker that wants to send or receive outbound route filters (ORFs) to or from its peer or route reflector advertises the cooperative route filtering capability using a BGP capabilities advertisement. The BGP speaker sends its peer a set of ORFs that are expressed in terms of BGP communities. The ORF entries are carried in BGP route refresh messages. The peer applies the received ORFs in addition to its locally configured export target policy, to constrain and filter outbound routing updates to the BGP speaker. Note that a BGP peer might or might not honor the ORFs received from a BGP speaker. By implementing this mechanism, BGP cooperative route filtering can be used to conserve service provider backbone bandwidth and PE router packet processing resources.

Case Study

Assume a single service provider has an IP/MPLS backbone to deliver BGP/MPLS VPN services to different enterprises. There are three PE routers in the network connected to seven customer sites. See Figure 2.9.

The following policies describe the desired inter-site connectivity for this case study:

Any host in site 1 can communicate with any host in Site 4.

Any host in site 2 can communicate with any host in Site 5.

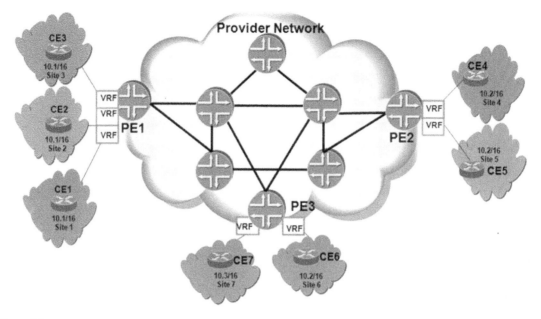

Figure 2.9

Any host in site 3 can communicate with any host in site 6 and Site 7.

Any host in site 4 can communicate with any host in Site 1.

Any host in site 5 can communicate with any host in Site 2.

Any host in site 6 can communicate with any host in site 3 and Site 7.

Any host in site 7 can communicate with any host in site 3 and Site 6.

In this example, the service provider uses RSVP to establish LSPs across its backbone as shown in Figure 2.10. The label displayed at the ingress of each LSP is the label that the PE router associates with the route that it uses to forward traffic to the remote PE router.

See Figure 2.11 for a generic configuration for PE1.

See Figure 2.12 for a generic configuration for PE2.

See Figure 2.13 for a generic configuration for PE3.

Distribution of VPN Routing Information

Before a customer site can forward VPN traffic to a remote site, VPN routing information must be distributed from each customer site across the backbone to other customer sites.

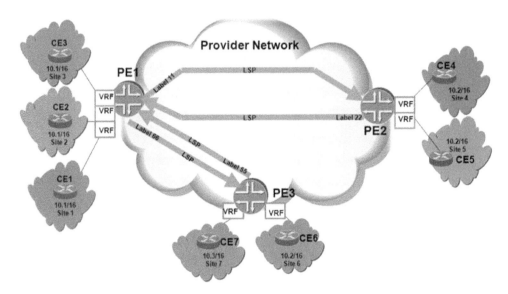

Figure 2.10

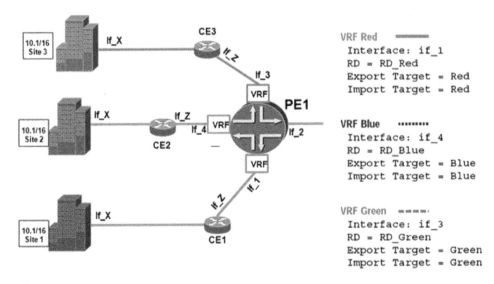

Figure 2.11

CE Router to Ingress PE Route Distribution

The CE router advertises IPv4 route prefixes to its PE router. There are several mechanisms that a PE router can use to learn routes from each of its directly connected CE routers:

- Static routing
- Running an IGP (RIPv2, OSPF, for example) with the CE router
- Establishing an EBGP connection with the CE router

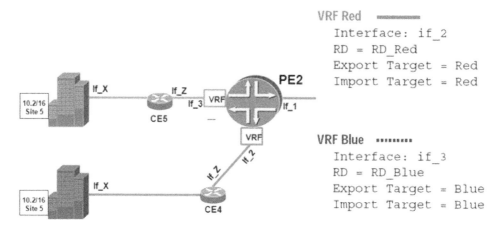

Figure 2.12

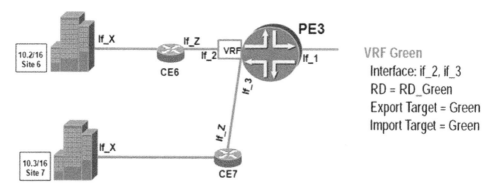

Figure 2.13

In the CE-to-ingress-PE flow of routing information, the PE router performs a number of functions. It creates and maintains a VRF for each of its directly connected sites. Note that in this example, PE 3 is configured to associate multiple sites (Site 6 and Site 7) with a single VRF. The PE checks all routes against the locally configured import policy for the routing protocol running between the PE router and the CE router. If the route passes the import policy, the prefix is installed in the VRF as an IPv4 route. The PE must be careful that the routes that it learns from each CE (via an IGP connection) are not leaked into the provider's backbone IGP. Before advertising a route, the PE assigns an MPLS label to the route.

Router PE1

Getting back to the case study: Assume that PE1 assigns the label 1001 to the routes learned from Site 1, the label 1002 to routes learned from Site 2, and the label 1003 to routes learned from Site 3. PE1 installs three MPLS routes such that when a packet with the label 1001, 1002, or 1003 is received from the backbone, it can simply pop the label and forward the IPv4 packet directly to CE1, CE2, or CE3, based on the packet's label. See Figure 2.14.

As a result of these operations, the VRFs in PE1 contain the following local routes, as shown in Figure 2.15.

Router PE2

Let us also say that PE2 assigns the label 1004 to routes learned from Site 4 and the label 1005 to routes learned from Site 5. PE2 installs two MPLS routes such that when a packet with the label 1004 or 1005 is received from the backbone, it can simply pop

```
MPLS Forwarding Table  (PE 1)

 Input                                    Output
Interface      Label       Action       Interface
   If_2        1001         Pop           if_1
   If_2        1002         Pop           if_4
   If_2        1003         Pop           if_3
```

Figure 2.14

```
VRF Red
                  BGP                    Bottom    Top
Destination     Next-Hop   Interface     Label    Label
10.1/16          Direct       if_1        1001       -


VRF Blue
                  BGP                    Bottom    Top
Destination     Next-Hop   Interface     Label    Label
10.1/16          Direct       if_4        1002       -


VRF Green
                  BGP                    Bottom    Top
Destination     Next-Hop   Interface     Label    Label
10.1/16          Direct       if_3        1003       -
```

Figure 2.15

```
MPLS Forwarding Table (PE 2)

    Input                           Output
Interface    Label    Action    Interface
   If_1      1004      Pop        if_2
   If_1      1005      Pop        if_3
```

Figure 2.16

```
VRF Red
                     BGP                    Bottom   Top
Destination       Next-Hop   Interface     Label    Label
10.2/16            Direct       if_2        1004      -


VRF Blue
                     BGP                    Bottom   Top
Destination       Next-Hop   Interface     Label    Label
10.2/16            Direct       if_3        1005      -
```

Figure 2.17

the label and send the IPv4 packet directly to CE4 or CE5, based on the packet's label. See Figure 2.16.

As a result of these operations, the VRFs in PE2 contain the following local routes as shown in Figure 2.17.

Router PE3

Assume that PE3 assigns the label 1006 to routes learned from Site 6 and the label 1007 to routes learned from Site 7. PE3 installs two MPLS routes such that when a packet with a label 1006 or 1007 is received from the backbone, it can simply pop the label and forward the IPv4 packet directly to CE6 or CE7, based on the packet's label. See Figure 2.18.

As a result of these operations, the VRFs in PE3 contain the local routes seen in Figure 2.19.

```
MPLS Forwarding Table (PE 3)

   Input                                    Output
Interface    Label      Action           Interface
   If_1       1006        Pop                if_2
   If_1       1007        Pop                if_3
```

Figure 2.18

```
VRF Green
                      BGP                    Bottom    Top
Destination        Next-Hop   Interface     Label     Label
10.2/16             Direct       if_2        1006       -
10.3/16             Direct       if_3        1007       -
```

Figure 2.19

Ingress PE to Egress PE Route Distribution across the Backbone

Ingress PE routers use MP-IBGP to distribute routes received from directly connected sites to egress PE routers. PE routers are required to maintain an MP-IBGP mesh or use route reflectors to ensure that routing information can be distributed to all PE routers. Before the ingress PE router distributes local VPN routes to its MP-IBGP peers, it converts each IPv4 prefix into a VPN-IPv4 prefix, using the RDs configured for the VRF that contains the route. The advertisement for each route contains the following:

- The VPN-IPv4 address prefix for the route.
- A BGP next hop that contains the loopback address of the ingress PE router. The address is encoded as a VPN-IPv4 address with a RD=0, since MP-BGP requires that the next hop be a member of the same address family as the route being advertised.
- The MPLS label that was assigned to the route by the ingress PE router when it learned the local route from the directly attached CE router.
- A route target attribute based on the locally configured export target policy for the VRF containing the local route. Recall that all of the PE routers in this example have been configured to assign a route target=Red when advertising VPN

Red routes, a route target=Blue when advertising VPN Blue routes, and a route target=Green when advertising VPN Green routes.

- Optionally, the site-of-origin attribute could be encoded as a route origin extended community.

When an ingress PE router advertises its local VPN-IPv4 routes to its MP-IBGP peers, it can either send all of the routes in its VRFs to all of its MP-IBGP peers or construct a distinct advertisement for each peer that excludes the specific VPN routes it does not share with a given peer. This is accomplished by the use of ORFs that allow a BGP speaker to announce to its peer or route reflector the set of routes that can be imported into one or more VRFs maintained by the PE router.

When an egress PE router receives a VPN-IPv4 route from a peer, it compares the route to all of the VRF import policies for all of the VPNs that are directly attached to the egress PE router. If the route target carried with the route matches the import target policy of at least one of the egress PE's VRFs, the VPN-IPv4 route is installed in its VPN_IPv4 routing table.

The VPN routing table contains all routes that satisfy the import policy of at least one of the egress PE router's VRFs. This table is the only one that relies on the RD to disambiguate routes because it contains all of the routes from all of the VPNs directly connected to the given PE router. The routes in this table should be globally unique because overlapping IPv4 addresses will have been assigned globally unique RDs. BGP path selection occurs in this table before routes are exported to their target VRF.

Note that user errors when configuring RDs can cause VPN-IPv4 routes in this table to have the same structure when they should be different. If this situation occurs, the BGP path selection is executed and only one of these routes is installed in its VRF. For this reason, RFC 2547bis recommends the use of globally unique public ASNs and IPv4 addresses when a service provider defines its RDs, which is critical if the BGP/MPLS VPN spans multiple service providers. The best route is selected for each VPN-IPv4 prefix and, based on the route target stored with the route, installed in the target VRF as an IPv4 route.

Ingress PE Route Advertisements

This section describes how the ingress PE routers in this case study advertise their local routes across the service provider's backbone to egress PE routers. Let us look at the Route Advertisements of routers PE1, PE2, and PE3. See Figure 2.20.

PE2

```
Destination = RD_Red:10.2/16
Label = 1004
BGP Next Hop = PE 2
Route Target = Red

Destination = RD_Blue:10.2/16
Label = 1005
BGP Next Hop = PE 2
Route Target = Blue
```

PE1

```
Destination = RD_Red:10.1/16
Label = 1001
BGP Next Hop = PE 1
Route Target = Red

Destination = RD_Blue:10.1/16
Label = 1002
BGP Next Hop = PE 1
Route Target = Blue

Destination = RD_Green:10.1/16
Label = 1003
BGP Next Hop = PE 1
Route Target = Green
```

PE3

```
Destination = RD_Green:10.2/16
Label = 1006
BGP Next Hop = PE 3
Route Target = Green

Destination = RD_Green:10.3/16
Label = 1007
BGP Next Hop = PE 3
Route Target = Green
```

Figure 2.20

Egress PE Route Installation

This section describes how the egress PE routers in this case study filter and then install remote routes received from ingress PE routers. See Figure 2.21.

Figure 2.22 shows the various VRF tables that get created and populated on the three PE routers in this case study.

Egress PE Router to CE Route Distribution

If the egress PE router installs a route in the VRF to route packets received from a directly connected CE router, the PE router can distribute that route to the CE router. There are several mechanisms that a CE router can use to learn VPN routes from its directly connected PE router.

- Run an IGP (RIPv2, OSPF) with the PE router
- Establish an EBGP connection with the PE router
- Have the PE-to-CE routing protocol distribute a default route pointing to the PE router
- Configure the CE with a static default route pointing to the PE router

PE1

```
Destination = RD_Red:10.2/16
Label = 1004
BGP Next Hop = PE 2
Route Target = Red
```

```
Destination = RD_Blue:10.2/16
Label = 1005
BGP Next Hop = PE 2
Route Target = Blue
```

```
Destination = RD_Green:10.2/16
Label = 1006
BGP Next Hop = PE 3
Route Target = Green


Destination = RD_Green:10.3/16
Label = 1007
BGP Next Hop = PE 3
Route Target = Green
```

PE2

```
Destination = RD_Red:10.1/16
Label = 1001
BGP Next Hop = PE 1
Route Target = Red
```

```
Destination = RS_Blue:10.1/16
Label = 1002
BGP Next Hop = PE 1
Route Target = Blue
```

PE3

```
Destination = RD_Green:10.1/16
Label = 1003
BGP Next Hop = PE 1
Route Target = Green
```

Figure 2.21

PE1

VRF Red

Destination	BGP Next-Hop	Interface	Bottom Label	Top Label
10.1/16	Direct	if_1	1001	-
10.2/16	PE-2	if_2	1004	11

VRF Blue

Destination	BGP Next-Hop	Interface	Bottom Label	Top Label
10.1/16	Direct	if_4	1002	-
10.2/16	PE-2	if_2	1005	11

VRF Green

Destination	BGP Next-Hop	Interface	Bottom Label	Top Label
10.1/16	Direct	if_3	1003	-
10.2/16	PE-3	if_2	1006	11
10.3/16	PE-3	if_2	1007	66

PE2

VRF Red

Destination	BGP Next-Hop	Interface	Bottom Label	Top Label
10.1/16	PE-1	if_1	1001	22
10.2/16	Direct	if_2	1004	

VRF Blue

Destination	BGP Next-Hop	Interface	Bottom Label	Top Label
10.1/16	PE_1	if_1	1002	22
10.2/16	Direct	if_2	1005	-

PE3

VRF Green

Destination	BGP Next-Hop	Interface	Bottom Label	Top Label
10.1/16	PE-1	if_1	1003	55
10.2/16	Direct	if_2	1006	-
10.3/16	Direct	if_3	1007	-

Figure 2.22

```
CE 1 Routing Table
Destination      Next-Hop     Interface
10.1/16          Direct       if_x
10.2/16          PE 1         if_z

CE 2 Routing Table
Destination      Next-Hop     Interface
10.1/16          Direct       if_x
10.2/16          PE 1         if_z

CE 3 Routing Table
Destination      Next-Hop     Interface
10.1/16          Direct       if_x
10.2/16          PE 1         if_z
10.3/16          PE 1         if_z

CE 4 Routing Table
Destination      Next-Hop     Interface
10.1/16          PE 2         if_z
10.2/16          Direct       if_x

CE 5 Routing Table
Destination      Next-Hop     Interface
10.1/16          PE 2         if_z
10.2/16          Direct       if_x

CE 6 Routing Table
Destination      Next-Hop     Interface
10.1/16          PE 3         if_z
10.2/16          Direct       if_x
10.3/16          PE 3         if_z

CE 7 Routing Table
Destination      Next-Hop     Interface
10.1/16          PE 3         if_z
10.2/16          PE 3         if_z
10.3/16          Direct       if_x
```

Figure 2.23

Figure 2.23 shows the contents of the CE routing tables after all routes are distributed from the egress PE routers to CE routers.

Forwarding Customer VPN Traffic across the BGP/MPLS Backbone

Transmitting customer traffic from one VPN site to another VPN site involves a number of different forwarding decisions:
- The source CE router to ingress PE router forwarding decision
- The ingress PE router forwarding decision
- The forwarding decision at each P router
- The egress PE router to destination CE router forwarding decision

We will look at these one by one.

Source CE Router to Ingress PE Router Forwarding

When a CE router receives an outbound IPv4 data packet from a system in its site, the CE router performs a traditional longest-match route lookup and forwards the native IPv4 packet to its directly attached PE router.

Ingress PE Router Forwarding

When a PE router receives an IPv4 data packet from a CE router, the PE router performs a route lookup in the VRF for the site, based on the packet's incoming subinterface. The packet's destination address is matched against the IPv4 prefix. If a match is found in the VRF, the route lookup returns a next hop and an outgoing sub-interface. If the packet's outgoing subinterface is associated with the same VRF as the incoming packet, the next hop is either another CE device located at the same site or a CE from a different directly connected site that is a member of the same VPN. Recall that a single VRF in a PE router maintains the routes from all directly connected sites of a given VPN.

If the packet's outgoing subinterface and incoming subinter-face are associated with two different VRFs, they are directly attached sites that have at least one VPN in common and each site has a separate forwarding table. To forward the packet, it might be necessary to lookup the packet's destination address in the VRF associated with the outgoing interface.

If the packet's outgoing subinterface is not associated with a VRF, then the packet must travel at least one hop across the provider's backbone to reach a remote PE router. If the packet must cross the provider's backbone, then it has two next hops: a BGP next hop and an IGP next hop:

- The BGP next hop is the ingress PE router that initially advertises the VPN-IPv4 route. The BGP next hop assigns and distributes a label with the route via MP-IBGP that it subsequently uses to identify the directly connected site that advertised the route. The PE router pushes this label onto the packet's label stack, and it becomes the bottom (or inner) label.
- The IGP next hop is the first hop in the LPS to the BGP next hop. The IGP next hop will have assigned a label (via LDP or RSVP) for the LSP that leads to the BGP next-hop router. This label is pushed onto the packet's label stack and becomes the top (or outer) label. In this case, the PE router that receives the packet from the CE and creates the label stack is the ingress LSR, and the BGP next hop is the egress LSR for the LSP across the service provider's network. If the BGP next hop and the IGP next hop are the same routers, and if penultimate hop popping is used, the packet can be transmitted with only the BGP-supplied bottom (or inner) label.

P   Router Forwarding

The MPLS backbone switches the labeled packet, swapping the top label at each hop until it reaches the penultimate router to the PE router to which the packet is sent. At the penultimate router, the top label is popped and the packet is sent to the target PE router.

PE Router to Destination CE Router Forwarding

When the PE router receives the packet, it looks for a matching MPLS route (label, subinterface) for the bottom label. If there is a match, the bottom label is popped and a native IPv4 packet is sent directly to the CE router associated with the label. Note that the VRF for the directly connected site does not have to be consulted. A snapshot of the process is given in Figure 2.24.

Actual VPN Forwarding Based on the Case Study

Let us assume that Host 10.1.2.3 at Site 1 wants to transmit a packet to Server 10.2.9.3 at Site 4, based on the case study just described. Figure 2.25 provides a detailed deep-dive.

When the native IPv4 packet arrives at CE1, it performs a longest-match route lookup in its IP forwarding table. The entry in CE1's forwarding table that best matches the packet's destination address is seen in Figure 2.26.

As a result of this lookup, CE1 forwards the native IPv4 packet to PE1. PE1 receives the native IPv4 packet on the CE interface. Since all packets that arrive on the given interface are associated with VRF RED, PE1 performs a longest-match route lookup in VRF RED. The entry in VRF RED that best matches the packet's destination address is shown in Figure 2.27.

Since the packet's outgoing subinterface (if_2) is not associated with a local VRF, the packet must travel at least one hop across the provider's MPLS backbone. PE1 creates an MPLS header for the

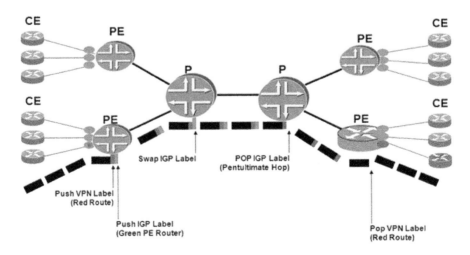

Figure 2.24

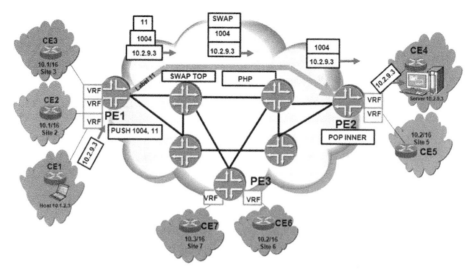

Figure 2.25

Destination	Next-Hop	Interface
10.2/16	PE 1	if_z

Figure 2.26

Destination	BGP Next-Hop	Interface	Bottom Label	Top Label
10.2/16	PE 2	if_2	1004	11

Figure 2.27

packet and then pushes the label 1004 (assigned by PE2 when it originally advertised the route to 10.2/16) onto the packet's label stack, making it the bottom label. PE1 then pushes the first label (11) for the LSP from PE1 to PE2 onto the packet's label stack, making it the top label. The packet is then forwarded to the first transit router in the LSP from PE1 to PE2. The MPLS backbone switches the labeled packet along the LSP, swapping the top label at each hop, until it reaches the penultimate router to PE2. At the penultimate router, the top label is popped and the packet with a single label (1004) is sent to PE2. When PE2 receives the labeled packet on if_1, it performs an exact match lookup in its MPLS forwarding table. The entry in the MPLS forwarding table that matches the packet's label is shown in Figure 2.28.

```
Input                              Output
Interface    Label    Action    Interface
   if_1       1004      Pop        if_2
```

Figure 2.28

```
Destination    Next-Hop    Interface
10.2/16         Direct        if_x
```

Figure 2.29

As a result of this lookup, PE2 pops the label and forwards the native IPv4 packet over if_2 to CE4. When the native IPv4 packet arrives at CE4, it performs a longest-match route lookup in its IP forwarding table. The entry in CE4's forwarding table that best matches the packet's destination address is shown in Figure 2.29.

Finally, as a result of this lookup, CE4 forwards the packet to Server 10.2.9.3 at Site 4.

Conclusion

The following list summarizes some of the important aspects of the operation of a BGP/MPLS VPN that help in achieving scalability for operations:

- A BGP/MPLS VPN is not constructed as an overlay network that sits on top of the service provider's network. Hence, the n-squared scalability issues typically associated with the overlay model do not exist.
- If there are multiple attachments between a customer site and a PE router, all of the attachments are mapped to a single forwarding table to conserve PE router resources.
- Overlapping address spaces are supported, thus allowing customers to efficiently use the private IP address space.
- PE routers are required to maintain VPN routes, but only for those VPNs to which they are directly attached.
- Route targets constrain the distribution of routing information, making policy enforcement easy. Also, PE routers do not maintain routes to remote CE routers, only to other PE routers.
- P routers do not maintain any VPN routing information because a two-level label stack is used.
- No single system in the provider's backbone is required to maintain routing information for all of the VPNs supported by the service provider.
- Network management is simplified because service providers do not have a backbone or virtual backbone to administer for each customer VPN.

- RDs are structured to ensure that every service provider can administer its own numbering space and create globally unique RDs that do not conflict with the RDs assigned by any other service provider.
- ORFs reduce the amount of routing information distributed across the provider's backbone and conserve PE router packet processing resources.
- The challenge of maintaining a full mesh of MP-IBGP connections is eliminated through the use of route reflectors.
- Route reflectors are the only systems in the network required to maintain VPN routing information for sites to which they are not directly connected. Segmented route reflection enhances scalability because no single route reflector has to maintain routing information for all VPN-IPv4 routes deployed across the provider's network.
- RSVP-based-traffic-engineered LSPs optimize connectivity between PE routers.

MPLS Layer 3 Inter-AS VPNs

The MPLS VPN inter-AS feature provides a method of interconnecting VPNs between different MPLS VPN service providers. This allows a customer's sites to exist on several carrier networks (Autonomous Systems) with seamless VPN connectivity between these sites.

Section 10 of RFC 4364 (which obsoletes RFC 2547bis) defines three options that provide MPLS VPN connectivity between different carrier networks, as follows:

- Option A – Back-to-Back VRF connections
- Option B – VPNv4 route distribution between ASBRs
- Option C – VPNv4 route distribution between route reflectors in each AS

The following paragraphs are excerpts from Section 10 of "draft-ietf-l3vpn-rfc2547bis-01.txt" describing the three solutions. We use Cisco IOS configuration snippets for illustrating each of the inter-AS options in detail.

Option A – Back-to-Back VRF Connections

In Option A, a PE router in one AS attaches directly to a PE router in another. The two PE routers are attached by multiple sub-interfaces, at least one for each of the VPNs whose routes need pass from AS to AS. Each PE router will treat the other as if it were a CE router. That is, the PE routers associate each such sub-interface with a VRF and use a dynamic routing protocol to distribute unlabeled IPv4 addresses to each other (eBGP is preferred).

This is a very simple procedure that does not require any exchange of labels. However, it is the least scalable of the solutions, as a VRF and a sub-interface must be provisioned for every customer that requires an inter-AS service, as shown in Figure 2.30.

Option B – VPNv4 Routes Distribution between ASBRs

In Option B, illustrated in Figure 2.31, the AS border routers (ASBR) peer with each other using an eBGP session. The ASBR also performs the function of a PE router and therefore peers with every other PE router in their AS. However, the ASBR does not hold any VRFs; rather, it holds all or a subset (those that need to be passed to the other AS) of the VPVv4 routes from every other PE router. The VPNv4 routes are kept unique in the ASBR by use of the route distinguisher.

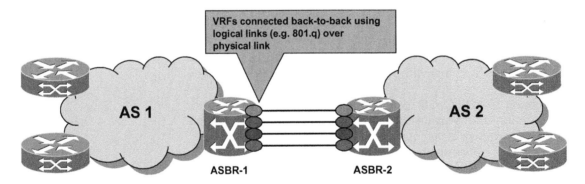

Figure 2.30

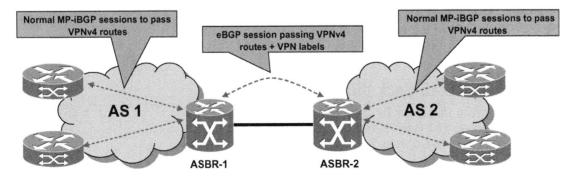

Figure 2.31

The ASBR can control which VPNv4 routes it accepts through the use of route targets. The ABSR then exchanges the VPNv4 routes, plus the associated VPN label with the other ASBR using eBGP. This procedure requires more coordination between carriers so that eBGP peering and the route targets will be accepted.

This solution is quite scalable, as a single eBGP peer will carry all customer VPNv4 routes across the AS boundary. A slight drawback is that the ASBR must carry the routes of all VPNv4 routes for this AS to egress to the neighbor AS.

Option C – VPNv4 Route Distribution between RRs

In Option C, illustrated in Figure 2.32, VPNv4 routes are neither maintained nor distributed by the ASBRs. The ASBR only requires knowledge of all the PE router loopback addresses. The ASBR uses eBGP to distribute the PE router loopback addresses to the neighbor AS. Therefore, each ASBR will learn the loopback routes to all the PE routers in the other AS that have customers requiring the inter-AS service. The ASBR can then redistribute these loopbacks into its own AS (providing a view of the PE routers in the other AS), thereby providing direct next hop access to the PE routers between ASs.

The other option is for the ASBR to change the next hop to itself. Therefore any VPNv4 routes destined to the other AS would use a next hop of the local ASBR. The VPNv4 routes are then exchanged between the ASs using route reflectors (RR). Since the RRs already hold the VPNv4 routes, there is no need for the ASBR to hold them, as is the case in Option B. Option C is the most

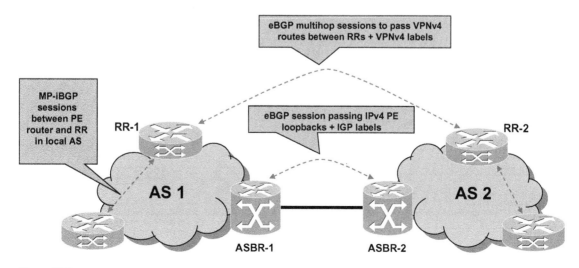

Figure 2.32

scalable of all options; however, it does require a greater level of trust between carriers, as IGP routes are being exchanged.

Option B

This section details the operation of Option B of inter-AS connectivity, where the VPNv4 routes are exchanged directly between the AS boundary routers. The test scenario consists of two separate MPLS VPN networks (AS200 and AS300) that distribute VPN routes between each other. There are two inter-AS (eBGP) connections between the ASBRs: the primary path and the backup path. VPN traffic will normally travel over the primary inter-AS path and switch over to the backup path in the event of a failure.

Test Setup

Figure 2.33 shows the test environment for the Option B scenario.

The following points summarize the test setup that is the basis for the operational examples:

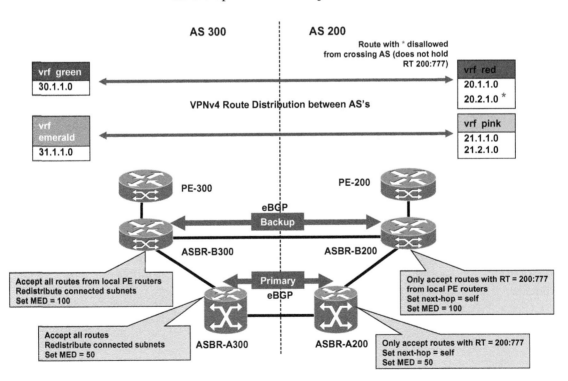

Figure 2.33

- There are two BGP Autonomous systems, AS 200 and AS 300.
- AS 200 has three routers:
  1. ASBR-A200, acting as the primary ASBR
  2. ASBR-B200, acting both the backup ASBR and a P router
  3. PE-200, acting as a PE which has two VRFs: Red and Pink
     - AS 300 has three routers:
  1. ASBR-A300, acting as the primary ASBR
  2. ASBR-B300, acting both the backup ASBR and a P router
  3. PE-300, acting as a PE which has two VRFs: Green and Emerald
     - The primary eBGP session applies a MED (Multi-Exit Discriminator) value of 50 to all routes distributed between ABSR-A200 and ABSR-A300.
     - The backup eBGP session applies a MED value of 100 to all routes distributed between ABSR-B200 and ABSR-B300; therefore the primary session's routes are given preference.
     - PE-200 and PE-300 have two iBGP sessions, one to each of their respective ASBRs to exchange VPNv4 routing information.[1]
     - As discussed in [1] there are two methods to distribute the next hop for VPNv4 routes between ASBRs:
  1. Next-Hop-Self Method: changing next hop to that of the local ASBR for all VPNv4 routes learned from the other ASBR
  2. Redistribute Connected Subnets Method: redistributing the next hop address of the remote ASBR into the local IGP using "redistribute connected subnets" command; i.e., the next hop is not changed when the VPNv4 routes are redistributed into the local AS
     - To demonstrate each method, the ASBRs in AS200 change the next hop to themselves for all VPNv4 routes learned, while the ASBRs in AS300 redistribute the host route (next hop) of the AS200 ASBRs.
     - The ASBRs in AS200 will only distribute routes across the AS boundary if the locally learned VPNv4 route holds 200:777 as one of its route targets / extended community strings. This has a couple of advantages: it minimizes the amount of memory necessary on the ASBRs and it provides control over which VPNv4 routes the remote AS can see.

---

[1] It is most likely that in a large network, route-reflectors would be responsible for the VPN route distribution.

- The ASBRs in AS300 have been configured to accept all VPNv4 routes learned locally and pass them to AS200.
- Routes will be exported/imported between VRFs Red and Green, and between VRF Pink and Emerald across the inter-AS boundary. That is, there is a corresponding route target import for the remote VRF's route target export.
- The VRFs Red and Pink are configured to export an additional route target of 200:777 so the local ASBRs will accept the VPNv4 routes. VRF Red uses a route-map to set the additional route target, while VRF Pink uses the standard route target export command. The difference between these methods is that with VRF Red it is possible to select individual prefixes to be distributed to the remote AS. In the test example, route target 200:777 is set only on prefix 20.1.1.0, thereby denying 20.2.1.0 from being seen by the remote-AS. With VRF Pink, all route prefixes are distributed to the remote AS because they are all exported with 200:777.
- To make it easier to visually distinguish label allocations in each AS, the AS300 label allocations start as 160, while AS200 label allocations start at 16.
- All VRF routes from AS200 are in the 20.0.0.0 – 21.0.0.0 range, and all VRF routes from AS300 are in the 30.0.0.0 – 31.0.0.0 range.

Figure 2.34 shows the logical layout of the test network. Several loopback addresses are used to generate prefixes within the various VRFs.

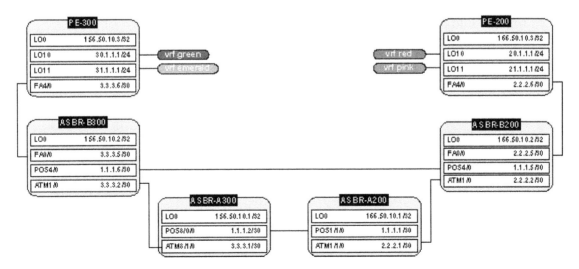

Figure 2.34

Option B Inter-AS Operation

The following sections describe the operation of the next-hop-self and the redistribute connected subnets methods. The values for the IP addresses, VPN, and IGP labels are based on the actual values allocated in the test setup.

VPNv4 Route Distribution

This section describes the steps taken to distribute the VPNv4 routes between the autonomous systems via the ASBRs using the next-hop-self method and the redistribute connected subnets method.

Next-Hop-Self Method Figure 2.35 shows the various steps taken to distribute the VPNv4 route 300:1:30.1.1.0 from AS300 to AS200 using the next-hop-self method. The example below shows the VPNv4 route distribution using the primary path only. However, the backup path is identical in operation.

- The VPNv4 route 300:1:30.1.1.0 is allocated the BGP label of {161} by PE-300. The BGP next hop is set to the PE-300 loopback 156.50.10.3.
- ASBR-A300 receives the VPNv4 update via an MP-iBGP session from PE-300.
- ASBR-A300 then allocates a new BGP local label {164} for the VPNv4 route and sets the BGP next hop to its interface

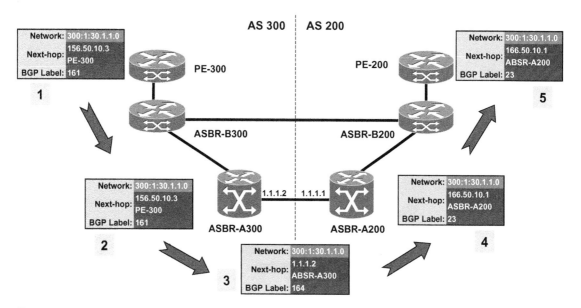

Figure 2.35

1.1.1.2. The BGP VPNv4 table for the route will show 164/161 as the labels being used for the route (refer to Figure 2.53).

- ASBR-A200 receives the VPNv4 update via the MP-eBGP session from ASBR-A300. Since next-hop-self is set to the PE neighbor PE-200, a new BGP local label {23} will be allocated and the next hop will be set to the loopback 166.50.10.1. The BGP VPNv4 table for the route will show 23/164 as the labels being used for the route.
- PE-200 receives the VPNv4 routes and inserts it into VRF Red. PE-200 will then use the BGP label {23} and the appropriate IGP label for next-hop 166.50.10.1 to get to 30.1.1.0.

Redistribute Connected Subnets Method Figure 2.36 shows the various steps taken to distribute the VPNv4 route 200:1:20.1.1.0 between the two ASs using the redistribute connected subnets method The example in the figure only shows the VPNv4 route distribution using the primary path. However, the backup path is identical in operation.

- The VPNv4 route 200:1:20.1.1.0 is allocated the BGP label of {29} by PE-200. The BGP next hop is set to PE-200 loopback 166.50.1.3.
- ASBR-A200 receives the VPNv4 update via an MP-iBGP session from PE-200. It will then check to see if the VPNv4 route holds

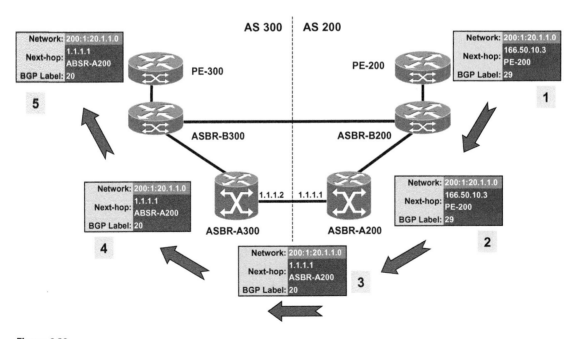

Figure 2.36

the extended community attribute 200:777. If it doesn't it will ignore the update.

- ASBR-A200 then allocates a new BGP local label {20} for the VPNv4 route and sets the BGP next hop to its interface 1.1.1.1. The BGP VPNv4 table for the route will show 20/29 as the labels being used for the route (refer to Figure 2.49).
- ASBR-A300 receives the VPNv4 update via the MP-eBGP session from ASBR-A200. The next-hop and the BGP label will be received and distributed without change to PE-300. The BGP VPNv4 table for the route will show notag/20 as the labels being used for the route (refer to Figure 2.55).
- PE-300 receives the VPNv4 routes and inserts it into VRF Green. PE-300 will then use BGP label **{20}** and the appropriate IGP label for next-hop 1.1.1.1 to get to 20.1.1.0.

Label Switch Path Forwarding

This section describes the steps taken to forward the labelled packet across the LSP between the autonomous systems via the ASBRs using the next-hop-self method and the redistribute connected subnets method.

Next-Hop-Self Method Figure 2.37 gives an example of the various labels that get pushed, swapped, and popped on the stack as a packet makes its way from PE-200 for a host in destination **30.1.1.0** using the next-hop-self method.

- PE-200 receives an incoming frame from a CE destined for a host in 30.1.1.0. It will push the BGP label {23} onto the stack for the next hop ASBR-A200. The IGP label {16} (provided by ASBR-B200) is then pushed onto the stack to forward the frame to 166.50.10.1.
- ASBR-B200 receives the labeled frame (note that ASBR-B200 is also a P router in this example). Since ASBR-B200 is the penultimate hop to ASBR-A200, the IGP label is removed.
- ASBR-A200 receives the frame with just the BGP label.
- ASBR-A200 then looks up its LFIB for the corresponding VPNv4 prefix entry and swaps {23} with {164}. The frame is forwarded across the inter-AS link with a single level stack consisting of the BGP label.
- ASBR-A300 receives the labeled frame, and replaces {164} with PE-300's BGP label {161} for the prefix 30.1.1.0. The IGP label {162} is then pushed onto the stack (provided by ASBR-B300) to forward the frame to 166.
- ASBR-B300 receives the labeled frame and removes the IGP label, since it is the penultimate hop.

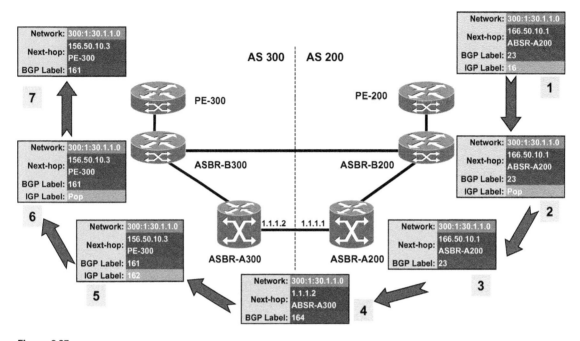

Figure 2.37

- PE-300 receives the frame with the BGP label, removes the label, and forwards it to the appropriate CE.

Redistribute Connected Subnets Method Figure 2.38 gives an example of the various labels that get pushed, swapped, and popped on the stack as a packet makes its way from PE-300 for a host in destination 20.1.1.0 using the redistribute connected subnets method.
- PE-300 receives an incoming frame from a CE destined for a host in 20.1.1.0. It will push the BGP label {20} onto the stack for the next hop ASBR-A200. The IGP label {166} (provided by ASBR-B300) is then pushed onto the stack to forward the frame to 1.1.1.1.
- ASBR-B300 receives the labeled frame (note that ASBR-B300 is also a P router in this example). ASBR-B300 swaps IGP label {166} for {160}.
- ASBR-A300 receives the frame and pops the IGP label, as it is the penultimate hop to ASBR-A200.
- ASBR-A300 forwards the frame (BGP label unchanged) to ASBR-A200 across the inter-AS link. Notice that there is only one label in the stack.

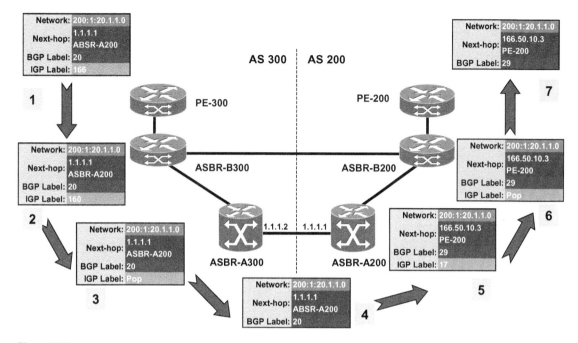

Figure 2.38

- ASBR-A200 receives the frame then looks up its LFIB for the corresponding VPNv4 prefix entry and swaps the BGP label {20} with {29}. The IGP label {17} is pushed onto the stack that corresponds to PE-200's next hop address.
- ASBR-B200 receives the labeled frame, and pops {17}.
- PE-200 receives the frame with the BGP label only, removes the label, and forwards it to the appropriate CE.

Configuration Analysis

This section describes the various outputs from various show commands and how they relate among the different routers for inter-AS Option B. Each of the relevant routers as well as various tables, such as CEF, BGP VPNv4 and LFIB, is examined.

Router PE-200

This section describes the outputs from PE-200 in AS 200.

VPN Routing and Forwarding (VRF) Tables As discussed above, PE-200 originates VPN routes in the Red and Pink VRFs. VRF Red imports all the routes from VRF Green (AS300), and VRF Pink imports all routes from VRF Emerald (AS300).

```
PE-200#show ip route vrf red
Codes: C - connected, S - static, I - IGRP, R - RIP, M - mobile, B - BGP
       D - EIGRP, EX - EIGRP external, O - OSPF, IA - OSPF inter area
       N1 - OSPF NSSA external type 1, N2 - OSPF NSSA external type 2
       E1 - OSPF external type 1, E2 - OSPF external type 2, E - EGP
       i - IS-IS, L1 - IS-IS level-1, L2 - IS-IS level-2, ia - IS-IS inter area
       * - candidate default, U   per-user static route, o - ODR
       P - periodic downloaded static route

Gateway of last resort is not set

     20.0.0.0/24 is subnetted, 2 subnets
C       20.1.1.0 is directly connected, Loopback10
S       20.2.1.0 [1/0] via 20.1.1.2, Loopback10
     30.0.0.0/24 is subnetted, 1 subnets
B       30.1.1.0 [200/50] via 166.50.10.1, 00:06:31
```

Figure 2.39 VRF Red on PE-200

```
PE-200#show ip route vrf pink
Codes: C - connected, S - static, I - IGRP, R - RIP, M - mobile, B - BGP
       D - EIGRP, EX - EIGRP external, O - OSPF, IA - OSPF inter area
       N1 - OSPF NSSA external type 1, N2 - OSPF NSSA external type 2
       E1 - OSPF external type 1, E2 - OSPF external type 2, E - EGP
       i - IS-IS, L1 - IS-IS level-1, L2 - IS-IS level-2, ia - IS-IS inter area
       * - candidate default, U - per-user static route, o - ODR
       P - periodic downloaded static route

Gateway of last resort is not set

     21.0.0.0/24 is subnetted, 2 subnets
C       21.1.1.0 is directly connected, Loopback11
S       21.2.1.0 [1/0] via 21.1.1.2, Loopback11
     31.0.0.0/24 is subnetted, 1 subnets
B       31.1.1.0 [200/50] via 166.50.10.1, 00:06:36
```

Figure 2.40 VRF Pink on PE-200

Figure 2.39 and Figure 2.40 show the various show output commands.

VRF Red has imported the route 30.1.1.0 from VRF Green with the next hop of ASBR-A200 (166.50.10.1). This is correct, as ASBR-A200 set the BGP next hop to itself for all routes coming from AS300. The same can be seen for VRF Pink, which has imported 31.1.1.0 via 166.50.10.1.

BGP VPNv4 Table The BGP path selection process for imported routes chose ASBR-A200 (MED = 50) as the next hop because the MED had a lower value than that of ASBR-B200 (MED = 100). This can be seen in Figure 2.41.

The metric for 30.1.1.0 and 31.1.1.0 is 50; thus when the import process runs, it will select these routes to import into the Red and

```
PE-200#show ip bgp vpnv4 all
BGP table version is 207, local router ID is 166.50.10.3
Status codes: s suppressed, d damped, h history, * valid, > best, i -
internal
Origin codes: i - IGP, e - EGP, ? - incomplete

   Network           Next Hop           Metric LocPrf Weight Path
Route Distinguisher: 200:1 (default for vrf red)
*> 20.1.1.0/24       0.0.0.0                 0          32768 ?
*> 20.2.1.0/24       20.1.1.2                0          32768 ?
*>i30.1.1.0/24       166.50.10.1            50    100       0 300 ?
Route Distinguisher: 200:2 (default for vrf pink)
*> 21.1.1.0/24       0.0.0.0                 0          32768 ?
*> 21.2.1.0/24       21.1.1.2                0          32768 ?
*>i31.1.1.0/24       166.50.10.1            50    100       0 300 ?
Route Distinguisher: 300:1
*>i30.1.1.0/24       166.50.10.1            50    100       0 300 ?
* i                  166.50.10.2           100    100       0 300 ?
Route Distinguisher: 300:2
*>i31.1.1.0/24       166.50.10.1            50    100       0 300 ?
* i                  166.50.10.2           100    100       0 300 ?
```

Figure 2.41 BGP VPNv4 table on PE-200

Pink VRFs. Note that the prefixes 30.1.1.0 and 31.1.1.1 are dupli-
cated when installing into the appropriate VRF.

CEF Table Figure 2.42 shows the detail CEF entries for the
imported prefixes from AS300. Label {16} is common to both prefixes and is the IGP label to get to the BGP next hop of ASBR-A200
(166.50.10.1). This corresponds to the outgoing tag entry for prefix
166.50.10.1 in Figure 2.43 for PE-200.

```
PE-200#show ip cef vrf red 30.1.1.1
30.1.1.0/24, version 44, cached adjacency 2.2.2.5
0 packets, 0 bytes
  tag information set
    local tag: VPN-route-head
    fast tag rewrite with Fa4/0, 2.2.2.5, labels imposed: {16 23}
  via 166.50.10.1, 0 dependencies, recursive
    next hop 2.2.2.5, FastEthernet4/0 via 166.50.10.1/32
    valid cached adjacency
    tag rewrite with Fa4/0, 2.2.2.5, labels imposed: {16 23}

PE-200#show ip cef vrf pink 31.1.1.1
31.1.1.0/24, version 57, cached adjacency 2.2.2.5
0 packets, 0 bytes
  tag information set
    local tag: VPN-route-head
    fast tag rewrite with Fa4/0, 2.2.2.5, labels imposed: {16 22}
  via 166.50.10.1, 0 dependencies, recursive
    next hop 2.2.2.5, FastEthernet4/0 via 166.50.10.1/32
    valid cached adjacency
    tag rewrite with Fa4/0, 2.2.2.5, labels imposed: {16 22}
```

Figure 2.42 CEF Table for VRF Entries in PE-200

The BGP VPNv4 labels {22} and {23}, are labels allocated by ASBR-A200 for the incoming routes 31.1.1.1 and 30.1.1.1, respectively, from AS300. This can be seen from ASBR-A200's LFIB table in in a later section.

Label Forwarding Information Base (LFIB) Figure 2.43 shows the Label Forwarding Information Base (LFIB), which is discussed later. PE-200 has allocated labels 29, 31, 35, and 36 for each of the prefixes in the two VRF tables (Red and Pink). As a side note, the word "aggregate" means that if a frame arrives with this label, then do a second lookup in the routing information base for that VRF to get a more specific route.

Exporting Routes As mentioned previously, VRF Red uses a route-map to select which prefixes are permitted across the inter-AS link, while VRF Pink allows all prefixes across. This is accomplished using the configuration shown in Figure 2.44. VRF Pink is fairly standard, so we shall concentrate on the VRF Red configuration.

```
PE-200#show tag forwarding
Local  Outgoing    Prefix          Bytes tag  Outgoing   Next Hop
tag    tag or VC   or Tunnel Id    switched   interface
26     Pop tag     2.2.2.0/30      0          Fa4/0      2.2.2.5
27     16          166.50.10.1/32  0          Fa4/0      2.2.2.5
28     Pop tag     166.50.10.2/32  0          Fa4/0      2.2.2.5
29     Aggregate   20.1.1.0/24[V]  74838608
31     Aggregate   20.2.1.0/24[V]  0
35     Aggregate   21.1.1.0/24[V]  505461166
36     Aggregate   21.2.1.0/24[V]  1040
```

Figure 2.43 LFIB on PE-200

```
ip vrf pink
 rd 200:2
 route-target export 200:2
 route-target export 200:777
 route-target import 200:2
 route-target import 300:2
!
ip vrf red
 rd 200:1
 export map OUT-INTER-AS
 route-target export 200:1
 route-target import 200:1
 route-target import 300:1

access-list 10 permit 20.1.1.0 0.0.0.55
route-map OUT-INTER-AS permit 10
 match ip address 10
 set extcommunity rt  200:777 additive
```

Figure 2.44 VRF Configuration on PE-200

In VRF Red, only routes beginning with the prefix 20.1.1.0 are allowed through to AS300. The additive keyword says to append this route target to the existing list of route targets. In the case of VRF Red, 200:777 will be appended to the existing 200:1 route target from the export command. The absence of the additive keyword overwrites any existing route targets.[2]

Figure 2.45 shows the detail VPNv4 prefix entries for VRF Red. Prefix 20.2.1.0 does not hold RT 200:777 due to the route-map. Prefix 20.1.1.0 holds both route targets; therefore it will be allowed across the AS boundary and also be available for any remote VRF importing RT 200:1. Note that these prefixes are advertised to both AS200 ABSRs (166.50.10.1 and 166.50.10.2).

ASBRs in AS200

The two ASBRs in AS200 are almost identical in configuration except for the MED attribute. Therefore we shall discussion mainly to ASBR-A200.

Next-Hop-Self Method The ASBRs in AS200 use the next-hop-self method to distribute VPNv4 routes (see configlet in Figure 2.50). This means every remote VPNv4 route received will have its next hop changed to 166.50.10.1 (ASBR-A200) or 166.50.10.2 (ASBR-B200), as is evident in the output listings for PE-200 in Figure 2.41. See 0 for further information on the BGP configuration.

```
PE-200#show ip bgp vpnv4 all 20.1.1.0
BGP routing table entry for 200:1:20.1.1.0/24, version 10
Paths: (1 available, best #1, table red)
  Advertised to non peer-group peers:
  166.50.10.1 166.50.10.2
  Local
    0.0.0.0 from 0.0.0.0 (166.50.10.3)
      Origin incomplete, metric 0, localpref 100, weight 32768, valid,
sourced,t
      Extended Community: RT:200:1 RT:200:777

PE-200#show ip bgp vpnv4 all 20.2.1.0
BGP routing table entry for 200:1:20.2.1.0/24, version 11
Paths: (1 available, best #1, table red)
  Advertised to non peer-group peers:
  166.50.10.1 166.50.10.2
  Local
    20.1.1.2 from 0.0.0.0 (166.50.10.3)
      Origin incomplete, metric 0, localpref 100, weight 32768, valid,
sourced,t
      Extended Community: RT:200:1
```

Figure 2.45 VPNv4 Detail Entries on PE-200

---

[2] In older versions of IOS, additive was the default behavior (as the keyword did not exist, I think).

Label Forwarding Information Base (LFIB) On the ASBR, there is a new class of LFIB entry called a VPNv4 entry, which consists of the route distinguisher plus the IPv4 prefix. This is necessary since there may or may not be any VRFs defined on an ASBR,[3] but there must be some way of creating an LFIB entry for forwarding a prefix that is not associated with a VRF. See [2] Section 2.1, for further explanation of this.

As can be seen in Figure 2.46, there are five VPNv4 LFIB entries in ASBR-A200. Three entries are from VRFs in the local AS (those RDs that begin with 200), and two entries are from the remote AS 300 (those whose RDs begin with 300).

The LFIB will always hold VPNv4 routes that originate from VRFs in the local AS (subject to BGP route-map policies). The decision whether to install LFIB entries for remote AS VPNv4 routes (and hence allocate a local tag for those entries) depends on whether the next-hop-self is configured locally on the neighbor command to the remote ASBR.

Since next-hop-self is configured on ASBR-A200, a local label will be allocated for the VPNv4 route for each VPNv4 route received from ASBR-A300, plus the iBGP next hop will be set to 166.50.10.1. These local BGP VPNv4 labels are distributed to PEs in AS200 and will be used by PEs to forward traffic towards the remote AS 300 VRF.

Therefore when next-hop-self is used, extra memory is taken up in the form of LFIB entries. This can be seen in Figure 2.42. The BGP VPNv4 labels {**23**} {**22**} used in the CEF table of PE-200

```
ASBR-A200#show tag forwarding
Local   Outgoing    Prefix            Bytes tag   Outgoing    Next Hop
tag     tag or VC   or Tunnel Id      switched    interface
16      Pop tag     2.2.2.4/30        0           AT1/0/0     2.2.2.2
17      Pop tag     166.50.10.2/32    0           AT1/0/0     2.2.2.2
18      17          166.50.10.3/32    0           AT1/0/0     2.2.2.2
19      Pop tag     1.1.1.2/32        0           PO1/1/0     point2point
20      17          200:1:20.1.1.0/24  \
                                      14957460    AT1/0/0     2.2.2.2
21      17          200:2:21.1.1.0/24  \
                                      42839366    AT1/0/0     2.2.2.2
22      165         300:2:31.1.1.0/24  \
                                      0           PO1/1/0     point2point
23      164         300:1:30.1.1.0/24  \
                                      0           PO1/1/0     point2point
24      17          200:2:21.2.1.0/24  \
                                      0           AT1/0/0     2.2.2.2
```

Figure 2.46 LFIB on ASBR-A200

[3]It is recommended that an inter-AS ASBR be limited to just exchanging eBGP VPNv4 routes, not holding a local VRFs table for scalability and performance.

to get to 300:1:30.1.1.0 and 300:2:31.1.1.0 correspond to the local labels in the ASBR-A200 LFIB.

Outgoing Tags/Labels

VPNv4 LFIB Entries to Remote AS There is an outgoing label for each VPNv4 entry in the LFIB. If this VPNv4 entry is derived from the remote AS (i.e., it originated from a VRF in AS300), then the outgoing tag will be the value of the local tag allocated by the remote ASBR. For example, in Figure 2.47, the outgoing labels {164} and {165} are used for 300:1:30.1.1.0 and 300:2:31.1.1.0. These correspond directly to the local labels allocated by ASBR-A300 in Figure 2.53.

It is important to note that packets transferred on the Inter_AS link (between the ASBRs) have only a single label (the BGP VPNv4 one) pushed onto the stack. There is no need for two labels IGP + VPN.

VPNv4 LFIB Entries from VRFs in Local PEs In Figure 2.46, the outgoing label in the LFIB for a prefix derived from a local AS VRF shows the IGP label {17} to PE-200. Looking at the detail entries for the three local VPNv4 in Figure 2.48,[4] we can see that two labels will be pushed on to the stack; the IGP label {17} to get to PE-200 and {29}, {35}, or {36} to identify the VPN route. The BGP VPNv4 labels match the LFIB entries for PE-200 in Figure 2.43.

Note that if this ASBR is the penultimate hop for the VPNv4 entries (like ASNR-B200 is to PE200), then the outgoing tag entry consists of the BGP VPNv4 label. Therefore the outgoing label shown in the "show tag for" output is always the topmost one in the stack.

```
ASBR-A200#show tag for detail
Local   Outgoing     Prefix          Bytes tag  Outgoing    Next Hop
tag     tag or VC    or Tunnel Id    switched   interface
<output suppressed>
22      165          300:2:31.1.1.0/24    \
                                      0          PO1/1/0     point2point
        MAC/Encaps=4/8, MTU=4470, Tag Stack{165}
        0F008847 000A5000
        No output feature configured
23      164          300:1:30.1.1.0/24    \
                                      0          PO1/1/0     point2point
        MAC/Encaps=4/8, MTU=4470, Tag Stack{164}
        0F008847 000A4000
        No output feature configured
```

Figure 2.47 Remote AS VPNv4 LFIB Entries on ASBR-A200

---

[4]The "show tag forwarding detail" command did not support specifying an individual VPNv4 address in the IOS 12.1(5)T8. Therefore all entries were displayed and unrelated output was removed.

```
ASBR-A200#show tag for detail
Local   Outgoing     Prefix          Bytes tag   Outgoing    Next Hop
tag     tag or VC    or Tunnel Id    switched    interface
<output suppressed>
20      17           200:1:20.1.1.0/24    \
                                     14957460    AT1/0/0     2.2.2.2
        MAC/Encaps=12/20, MTU=4466, Tag Stack{17 29}
        00010000AAAA030000008847 000110000001D000
        No output feature configured
21      17           200:2:21.1.1.0/24    \
                                     42839366    AT1/0/0     2.2.2.2
        MAC/Encaps=12/20, MTU=4466, Tag Stack{17 35}
        00010000AAAA030000008847 0001100000023000
        No output feature configured
24      17           200:2:21.2.1.0/24    \
                                     0           AT1/0/0     2.2.2.2
        MAC/Encaps=12/20, MTU=4466, Tag Stack{17 36}
        00010000AAAA030000008847 0001100000024000
        No output feature configured
```

Figure 2.48 Local AS VPNv4 LFIB Entries on ASBR-A200

BGP VPNv4 Table Figure 2.49 shows the BGP VPNv4 labels for all the VPNv4 (remote and local) routes held in ASBR-A200. As next-hop-self is configured on ASBR-A200, there is a corresponding "In tag" allocated for the remote routes. For example, the route 30.1.1.0/24 has been advertised by ASBR-A300 with the label {164}. ASBR-A200 changes this label to {23} (because it becomes the BGP next hop) and then advertises {23} to all relevant Pes.

BGP Configuration Figure 2.50 shows the BGP configlet for ASBR-A200 (the backup ASBR-B200 is similar). For all VPNv4 routes distributed to ASBR-A300 (1.1.1.2), the BGP MED metric is set to 50 via the **"SETMETRIC"** route-map.

The "next-hop-self" is required for every PE in AS200 so that VPNv4 routes from the remote AS300 are seen as coming from ASBR-A200.

ABSR-A200 will only hold VPNv4 routes from the local PE, if extended community 200:777 is set. This is done via the

```
ASBR-A200#show ip bgp vpnv4 all tags
     Network          Next Hop      In tag/Out tag
Route Distinguisher: 200:1
     20.1.1.0/24      166.50.10.3    20/29
Route Distinguisher: 200:2
     21.1.1.0/24      166.50.10.3    21/35
     21.2.1.0/24      166.50.10.3    24/36
Route Distinguisher: 300:1
     30.1.1.0/24      1.1.1.2        23/164
Route Distinguisher: 300:2
     31.1.1.0/24      1.1.1.2        22/165
```

Figure 2.49 BGP VPNv4 Labels on ASBR-A200

```
address-family vpnv4
 neighbor 1.1.1.2 activate
 neighbor 1.1.1.2 send-community extended
 neighbor 1.1.1.2 route-map SETMETRIC out
 neighbor 166.50.10.3 activate
 neighbor 166.50.10.3 next-hop-self
 neighbor 166.50.10.3 send-community extended
 neighbor 166.50.10.3 route-map INTER-AS in
 exit-address-family
!
ip extcommunity-list 10 permit rt 200:777
!
access-list 1 permit any
route-map SETMETRIC permit 10
 match ip address 1
 set metric 50
!
route-map INTER-AS permit 10
 match extcommunity 10
```

Figure 2.50 BGP Configlet for ASBR-A200

"INTER-AS" route map. This would be applied to every PE neighbor.

ASBRs in AS300

The two ASBR in AS300 are almost identical in configuration except for the MED attribute. Therefore we shall limit our discussion mainly to ASBR-A300.

Redistribute Connected Subnets Method The ASBRs in AS300 uses the redistribute connected subnets method to distribute VPNv4 routes. In other words, the BGP next-hop is not changed for remote VPNv4 routes and will remain that of ASBR-A200, which is 1.1.1.1 (the interface address). Therefore the PEs in AS300 must have visibility of 1.1.1.1 in their IGP routing table. This address appears as a host or /32 route in the IGP so that an LSP (Label Switch Path) can be setup between the PE and the remote ASBR. (See [2] Section 2.2 for further details.)

To accomplish this, BGP will install a /32 connected neighbor route for any VPNv4 eBGP sessions. This is shown in Figure 2.51 as route 1.1.1.1/32. Note that the backup ABSR-B200 is shown as 1.1.1.5/32. All PEs in AS300 will have these /32 routes distributed to them via the "redistribute connected subnets" command in OSPF shown in Figure 2.52.

Label Forwarding Information Base By using **redistribute connected subnets** the ASBR-A300 does not have to keep remote VPNv4 entries in its LFIB. Therefore the only VPNv4 LFIB entries seen in Figure 2.53 are the ones that originated from PE-300. Local labels {164} and {165} are distributed, as previously discussed, to ASBR-A200. The label {162} is the outgoing label for the LSP to

```
ABSR-A300#show ip route
<output suppressed>

     1.0.0.0/8 is variably subnetted, 4 subnets, 2 masks
C       1.1.1.1/32 is directly connected, POS8/1/0
C       1.1.1.0/30 is directly connected, POS8/1/0
O E2    1.1.1.5/32 [110/20] via 3.3.3.2, 21:52:10, ATM8/0/0
O E2    1.1.1.4/30 [110/20] via 3.3.3.2, 21:52:10, ATM8/0/0
     3.0.0.0/30 is subnetted, 2 subnets
C       3.3.3.0 is directly connected, ATM8/0/0
O       3.3.3.4 [110/2] via 3.3.3.2, 21:52:10, ATM8/0/0
     156.50.0.0/32 is subnetted, 3 subnets
C       156.50.10.1 is directly connected, Loopback0
O       156.50.10.2 [110/2] via 3.3.3.2, 21:52:11, ATM8/0/0
O       156.50.10.3 [110/3] via 3.3.3.2, 21:52:11, ATM8/0/0
```

Figure 2.51 Routing Table on ASBR-A300

```
router ospf 300
 log-adjacency-changes
 redistribute connected subnets
 network 3.3.3.0 0.0.0.3 area 0
 network 156.50.10.0 0.0.0.255 area 0
```

Figure 2.52 OSPF Configlet for ASBR-A300

```
ASBR-A300#show tag forwarding
Local  Outgoing     Prefix           Bytes tag  Outgoing   Next Hop
tag    tag or VC    or Tunnel Id     switched   interface
160    Pop tag      1.1.1.1/32       15793536   PO8/1/0    point2point
161    Pop tag      3.3.3.4/30       0          AT8/0/0    3.3.3.2
162    Pop tag      156.50.10.2/32   0          AT8/0/0    3.3.3.2
163    162          156.50.10.3/32   0          AT8/0/0    3.3.3.2
164    162          300:1:30.1.1.0/24  \
                                       0        AT8/0/0    3.3.3.2
165    162          300:2:31.1.1.0/24  \
                                       0        AT8/0/0    3.3.3.2
166    Pop tag      1.1.1.4/30       0          AT8/0/0    3.3.3.2
167    161          1.1.1.5/32       0          AT8/0/0    3.3.3.2
```

Figure 2.53 LFIB on ASBR-A300

PE-300 (156.50.10.3) that originated the VPNv4 routes (it is not the label for the VPNv4 routes).

The VPNv4 labels allocated by PE-300 are shown in Figure 2.54. The labels {161} and {160} represent each of the VPNv4 routes originating from PE-300, while label {162} on the top of the stack is the IGP label.

BGP VPNv4 Table Figure 2.55 shows the BGP VPNv4 table for ASBR-A300. Since no change is made to the BGP next hop, no local

```
ABSR-A300#show tag for detail
Local  Outgoing    Prefix              Bytes tag  Outgoing    Next Hop
tag    tag or VC   or Tunnel Id        switched   interface
164    162         300:1:30.1.1.0/24    \
Local  Outgoing    Prefix              Bytes tag  Outgoing    Next Hop
tag    tag or VC   or Tunnel Id        switched   interface
                                        0          AT8/0/0    3.3.3.2
       MAC/Encaps=12/20, MTU=4466, Tag Stack{162 161}
       00010000AAAA030000008847 000A2000000A1000
       No output feature configured
165    162         300:2:31.1.1.0/24    \
                                        0          AT8/0/0    3.3.3.2
       MAC/Encaps=12/20, MTU=4466, Tag Stack{162 160}
       00010000AAAA030000008847 000A2000000A0000
       No output feature configured
```

Figure 2.54 VPNv4 LFIB Entries on ASBR-A300

```
ASBR-A300#show ip bgp vpnv4 all tags
    Network           Next Hop       In tag/Out tag
Route Distinguisher: 200:1
    20.1.1.0/24       1.1.1.1           notag/20
Route Distinguisher: 200:2
    21.1.1.0/24       1.1.1.1           notag/21
    21.2.1.0/24       1.1.1.1           notag/24
Route Distinguisher: 300:1
    30.1.1.0/24       156.50.10.3       164/161
Route Distinguisher: 300:2
    31.1.1.0/24       156.50.10.3       165/160
```

Figure 2.55 BGP VPNv4 Labels on ASBR-A300

tag is allocated for the three VPNVv4 routes received from ASBR-A200 (1.1.1.1). The BGP information (routes and outgoing labels, route-targets, etc.) are propagated as is to PE-300. Therefore, PE-300 will use BGP VPNv4 labels {20}, {21}, and {24} and the next hop of ASBR-A200's interface (1.1.1.1) to reach the remote routes.

Router PE-300

This section describes the outputs from PE-300 in AS300.

VPN Routing and Forwarding (VRF) Tables PE-300 originates VPN routes in the Green and Emerald VRFs. VRF Green imports all routes from VRF **red**, and VRF Emerald imports all routes from VRF Pink.

As Figure 2.56 and Figure 2.57 show, all the imported routes from AS200 have ASBR-A200 (1.1.1.1) as their next hop, since we are using the redistribute connected subnets method. As discussed in the PE-200 section, the BGP path selection process chose the next hop as 1.1.1.1, the metric (MED) lower than that of the routes coming from the backup ABSR-B200 (1.1.1.5).

```
PE-300#show ip route vrf green
Codes: C - connected, S - static, I - IGRP, R - RIP, M - mobile, B - BGP
       D - EIGRP, EX - EIGRP external, O - OSPF, IA - OSPF inter area
       N1 - OSPF NSSA external type 1, N2 - OSPF NSSA external type 2
       E1 - OSPF external type 1, E2 - OSPF external type 2, E - EGP
       i - IS-IS, L1 - IS-IS level-1, L2 - IS-IS level-2, ia - IS-IS inter
area
       * - candidate default, U - per-user static route, o - ODR
       P - periodic downloaded static route

Gateway of last resort is not set

     20.0.0.0/24 is subnetted, 1 subnets
B       20.1.1.0 [200/50] via 1.1.1.1, 1d19h
     30.0.0.0/24 is subnetted, 1 subnets
C       30.1.1.0 is directly connected, Loopback10
```

Figure 2.56 VRF Green on PE-300

```
PE-300#show ip route vrf emerald
Codes: C - connected, S - static, I - IGRP, R - RIP, M - mobile, B - BGP
       D - EIGRP, EX - EIGRP external, O - OSPF, IA - OSPF inter area
       N1 - OSPF NSSA external type 1, N2 - OSPF NSSA external type 2
       E1 - OSPF external type 1, E2 - OSPF external type 2, E - EGP
       i - IS-IS, L1 - IS-IS level-1, L2 - IS-IS level-2, ia - IS-IS inter
area
       * - candidate default, U - per-user static route, o - ODR
       P - periodic downloaded static route

Gateway of last resort is not set

     21.0.0.0/24 is subnetted, 2 subnets
B       21.1.1.0 [200/50] via 1.1.1.1, 1d19h
B       21.2.1.0 [200/50] via 1.1.1.1, 1d19h
     31.0.0.0/24 is subnetted, 1 subnets
C       31.1.1.0 is directly connected, Loopback11
```

Figure 2.57 VRF Emerald on PE-300

IGP (Global) Routing Table Figure 2.58 shows the global routing table for PE-300. Routes to both of the AS200 ASBRs have been installed as /32 entries. These routes and their corresponding labels (shown in Figure 2.60) are used as the IGP label for all VPNv4 routes imported from AS200.

CEF Table Figure 2.59 shows the detail entries for the imported VPN routes into the Green and Emerald VRFs. These VPN routes use {166} as the IGP label, which is the BGP next hop of ASBR-A200 (1.1.1.1). This can be confirmed in Figure 2.60, which shows the LFIB table. The BGP VPNv4 labels {20}, {21}, and {24} are the local labels that were assigned for the routes by ASBR-200.

```
PE-300#show ip route
<output suppressed>

     1.0.0.0/8 is variably subnetted, 4 subnets, 2 masks
O E2    1.1.1.1/32 [110/20] via 3.3.3.5, 1d20h, FastEthernet4/0
O E2    1.1.1.0/30 [110/20] via 3.3.3.5, 1d20h, FastEthernet4/0
O E2    1.1.1.5/32 [110/20] via 3.3.3.5, 1d20h, FastEthernet4/0
O E2    1.1.1.4/30 [110/20] via 3.3.3.5, 1d20h, FastEthernet4/0
     3.0.0.0/30 is subnetted, 2 subnets
O       3.3.3.0 [110/2] via 3.3.3.5, 1d20h, FastEthernet4/0
C       3.3.3.4 is directly connected, FastEthernet4/0
     156.50.0.0/32 is subnetted, 3 subnets
O       156.50.10.1 [110/3] via 3.3.3.5, 1d20h, FastEthernet4/0
O       156.50.10.2 [110/2] via 3.3.3.5, 1d20h, FastEthernet4/0
C       156.50.10.3 is directly connected, Loopback0
```

Figure 2.58 Routing Table on PE-300

```
PE-300#show ip cef vrf green detail
20.1.1.0/24, version 5, cached adjacency 3.3.3.5
0 packets, 0 bytes
  tag information set
    local tag: VPN-route-head
    fast tag rewrite with Fa4/0, 3.3.3.5, labels imposed: {166 20}
  via 1.1.1.1, 0 dependencies, recursive
    next hop 3.3.3.5, FastEthernet4/0 via 1.1.1.1/32
    valid cached adjacency
    tag rewrite with Fa4/0, 3.3.3.5, labels imposed: {166 20}

PE-300#show ip cef vrf emerald detail
21.1.1.0/24, version 6, cached adjacency 3.3.3.5
0 packets, 0 bytes
  tag information set
    local tag: VPN-route-head
    fast tag rewrite with Fa4/0, 3.3.3.5, labels imposed: {166 21}
  via 1.1.1.1, 0 dependencies, recursive
    next hop 3.3.3.5, FastEthernet4/0 via 1.1.1.1/32
    valid cached adjacency
    tag rewrite with Fa4/0, 3.3.3.5, labels imposed: {166 21}
21.2.1.0/24, version 7, cached adjacency 3.3.3.5
0 packets, 0 bytes
  tag information set
    local tag: VPN-route-head
    fast tag rewrite with Fa4/0, 3.3.3.5, labels imposed: {166 24}
  via 1.1.1.1, 0 dependencies, recursive
    next hop 3.3.3.5, FastEthernet4/0 via 1.1.1.1/32
    valid cached adjacency
    tag rewrite with Fa4/0, 3.3.3.5, labels imposed: {166 24}
```

Figure 2.59 CEF Table for VRF Entries in PE-300

```
PE-300#show tag forwarding
Local  Outgoing     Prefix         Bytes tag  Outgoing    Next Hop
tag    tag or VC    or Tunnel Id   switched   interface
160    Aggregate    31.1.1.0/24[V]  0
161    Aggregate    30.1.1.0/24[V]  0
162    Pop tag      3.3.3.0/30      0          Fa4/0       3.3.3.5
163    160          156.50.10.1/32  0          Fa4/0       3.3.3.5
164    Pop tag      156.50.10.2/32  0          Fa4/0       3.3.3.5
165    165          1.1.1.0/30      0          Fa4/0       3.3.3.5
166    166          1.1.1.1/32      0          Fa4/0       3.3.3.5
167    Pop tag      1.1.1.4/30      0          Fa4/0       3.3.3.5
168    161          1.1.1.5/32      0          Fa4/0       3.3.3.5
```

Figure 2.60 LFIB on PE-300

Label Forwarding Information Base Figure 2.60 shows the labels allocated by PE-300 for IGP and locally originated VRF routes.

Backup Path Check

This section verifies that the backup path works correctly if the primary path fails. A simple test was carried out with traffic originating from PE300 and traveling to PE200.

Under normal circumstances, all traffic between the ASs travels along the primary eBGP path, circuit addresses 1.1.1.1 – 1.1.1.2, which is verified in Figure 2.61.

The primary interface was shut down on ASBR-A200 to simulate a simple failure. The test was done several times. and it took between 16 and 24 seconds for the VPNv4 routes to be redistributed to select the backup path. The BGP scan timers were modified to provide the faster convergence. Refer to section 0 for configuration details and also [3], page 255, for a detailed discussion of VPN convergence.

Figure 2.62 shows the debug output for the new BGP label allocations, once the backup path was selected on PE-300. The labels {26}, {25}, and {24} are the BGP VPNv4 labels allocated by ASBR-B200 for the three AS200 VPN routes imported by PE-300.

```
PE-300#trace vrf green 20.1.1.1

Type escape sequence to abort.
Tracing the route to 20.1.1.1

  1 3.3.3.5 4 msec 4 msec 0 msec
  2 3.3.3.1 4 msec 4 msec 0 msec
  3 1.1.1.1 4 msec 4 msec 0 msec  ← ASBR-A200 primary
  4 2.2.2.2 4 msec 0 msec 4 msec
  5 20.1.1.1 0 msec *  0 msec
```

Figure 2.61 Trace Route on Primary Path

```
PE-300#
5d22h: vpn: tag_vpn_find_route_tags: 300:2:21.2.1.0 intag=vpn-route, outtag=26
5d22h: vpn: tag_vpn_find_route_tags: 300:2:21.1.1.0 intag=vpn-route, outtag=25
5d22h: vpn: tag_vpn_find_route_tags: 300:1:20.1.1.0 intag=vpn-route, outtag=24
```

Figure 2.62 VPN Labels after Switch to Backup BGP Path

```
ASBR-B200#show tag forwarding
Local  Outgoing    Prefix              Bytes tag   Outgoing    Next Hop
tag    tag or VC   or Tunnel Id        switched    interface
16     Pop tag     166.50.10.1/32      58203698    AT3/0       2.2.2.1
17     Pop tag     166.50.10.3/32      58165440    Fa0/0       2.2.2.6
18     Pop tag     1.1.1.6/32          0           PO4/0       point2point
21     168         300:2:31.1.1.0/24   \
                                       0           PO4/0       point2point
22     167         300:1:30.1.1.0/24   \
                                       0           PO4/0       point2point
24     29          200:1:20.1.1.0/24   \
                                       60047676    Fa0/0       2.2.2.6
25     35          200:2:21.1.1.0/24   \
                                       463102380   Fa0/0       2.2.2.6
26     36          200:2:21.2.1.0/24   \
                                       0           Fa0/0       2.2.2.6
```

Figure 2.63 LFIB on ASBR-B200 (Backup ASBR)

```
PE-300#trace vrf green 20.1.1.1

Type escape sequence to abort.
Tracing the route to 20.1.1.1

  1 3.3.3.5 0 msec 4 msec 0 msec
  2 1.1.1.5 0 msec 0 msec 4 msec  ← ASBR-B200 backup
  3 20.1.1.1 0 msec *  0 msec
```

Figure 2.64 Trace Route on Backup Path

Figure 2.63 shows the tag forwarding table on ASBR-B200 hold-ing the three VPNv4 routes, which originated on PE-200, and the labels {24}, {25}, and {26} allocated by ASBR-B200.

Figure 2.64 shows that all traffic between the PE-300 and PE-200 is now traveling on the backup path.

Load-Balancing across the Inter-AS Paths

This section discusses a simple method to load-balance VPNv4 prefixes across both inter-AS links, as opposed to sending all traf-fic over a primary path, while bandwidth on the backup path remains unused.

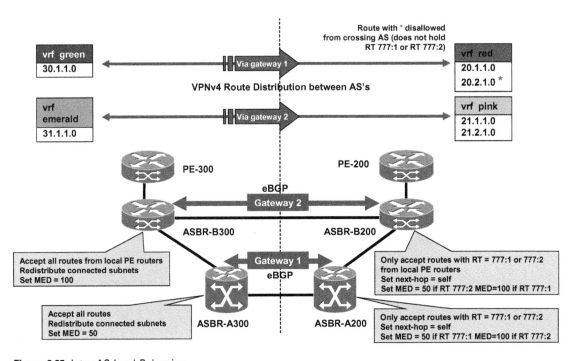

Figure 2.65 Inter-AS Load Balancing

Figure 2.65 shows the load balancing scenario and can be summarized as follows:

- The example was only configured on the AS200 side, although all ASs would be configured to match.
- In AS200 both inter-AS links are considered to carry some primary traffic and are called Gateway 1 (ASBR-A200) and Gateway 2 (ASBR-B200)
- The MED is set at each gateway, depending upon the route-target/extcommunity value on the VPNv4 route.
- If the route-target is 777:1, then Gateway 1 will be the primary with MED = 50 for that prefix while Gateway 2 will be the backup with MED = 100.
- If the route-target is 777:2, then Gateway 2 will take preference with MED = 50 for that prefix while Gateway 1 will be the backup with MED = 100.
- The gateways have both been configured to accept only VPNv4 routes that have the extcommunity attribute 777:1 or 777:2.
- The VRF routes in PE-200 have been configured as shown here. Therefore we should see the Red routes via 1.1.1.1 and the Pink routes via 1.1.1.5. See Figure 2.66.

VRF	Prefix	RT	Primary	Backup
Red	20.1.1.0	200:1 777:1	ASBR-A200 (1.1.1.1)	ASBR-B200 (1.1.1.5)
	20.2.1.0	200:1	Denied	Denied
Pink	21.1.1.0	200:2 777:2	ASBR-B200 (1.1.1.5)	ASBR-A200 (1.1.1.1)
	21.2.1.0	200:2 777:2	ASBR-B200 (1.1.1.5)	ASBR-A200 (1.1.1.1)

Figure 2.66

ASBR 200 Configurations

The configurations in the AS200 ASBRs have been modified as shown in Figure 2.67.

The INTER-AS route-map will cause the AS200 ASBRs to accept VPNv4 routes that hold the extcommunity attribute of 777:1 or 777:2. The VPNv4 routes will hold one or the other value, not both. Depending on which ASBR it is, the MED will be set appropriately, either 50 if it is chosen to be the primary or 100 if it is not chosen to be the primary.

PE-200 Configuration

The PE-200 configuration has been modified slightly so that all routes in VRF Pink have the route target 777:2, and hence will use ASBR-B200 as the primary path and ASBR-A200 as the backup path (from PE-300's perspective). The selected route via the

```
router bgp 200
...
address-family vpnv4
 neighbor 1.1.1.2 activate
 neighbor 1.1.1.2 send-community extended
 neighbor 1.1.1.2 route-map SETMETRIC out
 neighbor 166.50.10.3 activate
 neighbor 166.50.10.3 next-hop-self
 neighbor 166.50.10.3 send-community extended
 neighbor 166.50.10.3 route-map INTER-AS in
 exit-address-family
!
...
ip extcommunity-list 10 permit rt 777:1
ip extcommunity-list 11 permit rt 777:2
!
route-map SETMETRIC permit 10
 match extcommunity 10
 set metric 50             ← Metric is 100 on ASBR-B200
!
route-map SETMETRIC permit 11
 match extcommunity 11
 set metric 100            ← Metric is 50 on ASBR-B200
!
route-map INTER-AS permit 10
 match extcommunity 10 11
```

Figure 2.67 Modified Commands on ASBR-A200

```
ip vrf pink
 rd 200:2
 route-target export 200:2
 route-target export 777:2
 route-target import 200:2
 route-target import 300:2
 !
ip vrf red
 rd 200:1
 export map OUT-INTER-AS
 route-target export 200:1
 route-target import 200:1
 route-target import 300:1

access-list 10 permit 20.1.1.0 0.0.0.55
route-map OUT-INTER-AS permit 10
 match ip address 10
 set extcommunity rt  777:1 additive
 !
```

Figure 2.68 Modified Commands on PE-200

route-map in VRF Red will use ASBR-A200 as the primary path and ASBR-B200 as the backup path. See Figure 2.68.

PE-300 VPNv4 BGP Table

Figure 2.69 shows the BGP VPNv4 table on PE-300 after the VPNv4 routes from AS200 have been redistributed using the new route targets and MED values. As can be seen, the best routes have been chosen and imported into the Green and Emerald VRFs using the lower metric (MED), the next hop being either 1.1.1.1 or 1.1.1.5.

Configuration listings (Option B) are given in Figures 2.70, 2.71, and 2.72.

Option C

This section details the operation of Option C for inter-AS connectivity, where the VPNv4 routes are exchanged between route reflectors in each autonomous system. The BGP NLRI for the VPNv4 routes will also contain the IPv4 next hop (loopback) of the PE routers. The IPv4 routes of the PE router loopbacks are exchanged directly between the ASBR, with the associated label using eBGP and injected into the IGP of the remote AS. The test scenario is very similar to that used for Option B and consists of two separate MPLS VPN networks (AS200 and AS300) that distribute VPNv4 and IPv4 routes between each other. There is a single multi-hop eBGP session between the two RRs for exchange of VPNv4 routes plus their associated VPN labels. There is also a single eBGP connection between a pair of ASBRs for the exchange of

```
PE-300#show ip bgp vpnv4 all
BGP table version is 99, local router ID is 156.50.10.3
Status codes: s suppressed, d damped, h history, * valid, > best, i -
internal
Origin codes: i - IGP, e - EGP, ? - incomplete

     Network          Next Hop            Metric LocPrf Weight Path
  Route Distinguisher: 200:1
  *>i20.1.1.0/24      1.1.1.1                 50    100      0 200 ?
  *  i                1.1.1.5                100    100      0 200 ?
  Route Distinguisher: 200:2
  *  i21.1.1.0/24     1.1.1.1                100    100      0 200 ?
  *>i                1.1.1.5                 50    100      0 200 ?
  *  i21.2.1.0/24     1.1.1.1                100    100      0 200 ?
  *>i                1.1.1.5                 50    100      0 200 ?
  Route Distinguisher: 300:1 (default for vrf green)
  *>i20.1.1.0/24      1.1.1.1                 50    100      0 200 ? ← Via
  ASBR-A200
  *> 30.1.1.0/24      0.0.0.0                  0         32768 ?
  Route Distinguisher: 300:2 (default for vrf emerald)
  *>i21.1.1.0/24      1.1.1.5                 50    100      0 200 ? ← Via
  ASBR-B200
  *>i21.2.1.0/24      1.1.1.5                 50    100      0 200 ? ← Via
  ASBR-B200
  *> 31.1.1.0/24      0.0.0.0                  0         32768 ?
```

Figure 2.69 Load Balanced BGP VPNv4 Table on PE-300

IPv4 routes and their associated labels (this is also referred to as eBGP IPV4+Labels). These labels are the ones allocated to the IGP routers and are usually distributed by LDP inside the AS.

Option C Loopback Distribution Methods

Option C requires that the loopbacks of the local PE routers are known to the remote AS. This allows an LSP to be built between the PE routers for VPNv4 traffic to pass along.

There are two methods for distributing loopbacks in a remote AS:

- PE loopbacks of the other AS are advertised in the local AS via "IGP ROUTES" (redistributed from eBGP).
- PE loopbacks of the other AS are advertised in the local AS via "iBGP ROUTES."

IGP Routes Method

The IGP routes method can be summarized as follows:

- ASBRs need no VPN knowledge
- ASBRs exchange IPv4 routes+IGP labels via eBGP (these are the PE loopbacks)
- RRs exchange VPNv4 routes+VPN labels (these are the customer routes)
- RRs are peered via eBGP multi-hop

ABSR-A200	ABSR-A300

<pre>hostname ABSR-A200
!
interface Loopback0
 ip address 166.50.10.1 255.255.255.255
!
interface ATM1/0/0
 ip address 2.2.2.1 255.255.255.252
 ip route-cache distributed
 ip ospf network point-to-point
 no atm ilmi-keepalive
 pvc 1/102
  broadcast
  encapsulation aal5snap
  !
 tag-switching ip
!
interface POS1/1/0
 ip address 1.1.1.1 255.255.255.252
 ip route-cache distributed
 clock source internal
 pos ais-shut
 pos report lais
 pos report lrdi
!
router ospf 200
 log-adjacency-changes
 network 2.2.2.0 0.0.0.255 area 0
 network 166.50.10.0 0.0.0.255 area 0
!
router bgp 200
 no synchronization
 no bgp default ipv4-unicast
 no bgp default route-target filter
 bgp log-neighbor-changes
 neighbor 1.1.1.2 remote-as 300
 neighbor 166.50.10.3 remote-as 200
 neighbor 166.50.10.3 update-source Loopback0
 !
 address-family vpnv4
 neighbor 1.1.1.2 activate
 neighbor 1.1.1.2 send-community extended
 neighbor 1.1.1.2 route-map SETMETRIC out
 neighbor 166.50.10.3 activate
 neighbor 166.50.10.3 next-hop-self
 neighbor 166.50.10.3 send-community extended
 neighbor 166.50.10.3 route-map INTER-AS in
 exit-address-family
!
ip extcommunity-list 10 permit rt 200:777
!
access-list 1 permit any
route-map SETMETRIC permit 10
 match ip address 1
 set metric 50
!
route-map INTER-AS permit 10
 match extcommunity 10</pre>
	<pre>hostname ABSR-A300
	!
	tag-switching tag-range downstream 160 1000 0
	!
	interface Loopback0
	 ip address 156.50.10.1 255.255.255.255
	!
	interface ATM8/0/0
	 ip address 3.3.3.1 255.255.255.252
	 ip route-cache distributed
	 ip ospf network point-to-point
	 no atm ilmi-keepalive
	 pvc 1/102
	  broadcast
	  encapsulation aal5snap
	  !
	 tag-switching ip
	!
	interface POS8/1/0
	 ip address 1.1.1.2 255.255.255.252
	 ip route-cache distributed
	 pos ais-shut
	 pos report lais
	 pos report lrdi
	!
	interface GigabitEthernet10/0/0
	 no ip address
	 ip route-cache distributed
	 load-interval 30
	 shutdown
	 negotiation auto
	!
	router ospf 300
	 log-adjacency-changes
	 redistribute connected subnets
	 network 3.3.3.0 0.0.0.3 area 0
	 network 156.50.10.0 0.0.0.255 area 0
	!
	router bgp 300
	 no synchronization
	 no bgp default ipv4-unicast
	 no bgp default route-target filter
	 bgp log-neighbor-changes
	 neighbor 1.1.1.1 remote-as 200
	 neighbor 156.50.10.3 remote-as 300
	 neighbor 156.50.10.3 update-source Loopback0
	 !
	 address-family vpnv4
	 neighbor 1.1.1.1 activate
	 neighbor 1.1.1.1 send-community extended
	 neighbor 1.1.1.1 route-map SETMETRIC out
	 neighbor 156.50.10.3 activate
	 neighbor 156.50.10.3 send-community extended
	 bgp scan-time 10
	 bgp scan-time import 10
	 exit-address-family
	!
	access-list 1 permit any
	route-map SETMETRIC permit 10
	 match ip address 1
	 set metric 50</pre>

Figure 2.70

ASBR-B200	ASBR-B300
```hostname ABSR-B200```	```hostname ABSR-B300```

```
hostname ABSR-B200
!
interface Loopback0
 ip address 166.50.10.2 255.255.255.255
!
interface FastEthernet0/0
 ip address 2.2.2.5 255.255.255.252
 duplex full
 tag-switching ip
!
interface ATM3/0
 ip address 2.2.2.2 255.255.255.252
 ip ospf network point-to-point
 no atm ilmi-keepalive
 pvc 1/102
  broadcast
  encapsulation aal5snap
 !
 tag-switching ip
!
interface POS4/0
 ip address 1.1.1.5 255.255.255.252
 no ip route-cache cef
 clock source internal
!
interface FastEthernet6/0
 ip address 10.64.37.50 255.255.255.0
 duplex full
!
router ospf 200
 log-adjacency-changes
 network 2.2.2.0 0.0.0.255 area 0
 network 166.50.10.0 0.0.0.255 area 0
!
router bgp 200
 no synchronization
 no bgp default ipv4-unicast
 no bgp default route-target filter
 bgp log-neighbor-changes
 neighbor 1.1.1.6 remote-as 300
 neighbor 166.50.10.3 remote-as 200
 neighbor 166.50.10.3 update-source Loopback0
 !
 address-family vpnv4
 neighbor 1.1.1.6 activate
 neighbor 1.1.1.6 send-community extended
 neighbor 1.1.1.6 route-map SETMETRIC out
 neighbor 166.50.10.3 activate
 neighbor 166.50.10.3 next-hop-self
 neighbor 166.50.10.3 send-community extended
 neighbor 166.50.10.3 route-map INTER-AS in
 exit-address-family
!
ip extcommunity-list 10 permit rt 200:777
!
access-list 1 permit any
route-map SETMETRIC permit 10
 match ip address 1
 set metric 100
!
route-map INTER-AS permit 10
 match extcommunity 10
```

```
hostname ABSR-B300
!
interface Loopback0
 ip address 156.50.10.2 255.255.255.255
!
interface FastEthernet0/0
 ip address 3.3.3.5 255.255.255.252
 duplex full
 tag-switching ip
!
interface ATM3/0
 ip address 3.3.3.2 255.255.255.252
 ip ospf network point-to-point
 no atm ilmi-keepalive
 pvc 1/102
  broadcast
  encapsulation aal5snap
 !
 tag-switching ip
!
interface POS4/0
 ip address 1.1.1.6 255.255.255.252
 no ip route-cache cef
!
router ospf 300
 log-adjacency-changes
 redistribute connected subnets
 network 3.3.3.0 0.0.0.3 area 0
 network 3.3.3.4 0.0.0.3 area 0
 network 156.50.10.0 0.0.0.255 area 0
!
router bgp 300
 no synchronization
 no bgp default ipv4-unicast
 no bgp default route-target filter
 bgp log-neighbor-changes
 neighbor 1.1.1.5 remote-as 200
 neighbor 156.50.10.3 remote-as 300
 neighbor 156.50.10.3 update-source Loopback0
 !
 address-family vpnv4
 neighbor 1.1.1.5 activate
 neighbor 1.1.1.5 send-community extended
 neighbor 1.1.1.5 route-map SETMETRIC out
 neighbor 156.50.10.3 activate
 neighbor 156.50.10.3 send-community extended
 bgp scan-time 10
 bgp scan-time import 10
 exit-address-family
!
access-list 1 permit any
route-map SETMETRIC permit 10
 match ip address 1
 set metric 100
```

Figure 2.71

```
hostname PE-200                              hostname PE-300
!                                            !
ip vrf pink                                  ip vrf emerald
 rd 200:2                                     rd 300:2
 route-target export 200:2                    route-target export 300:2
 route-target export 200:777                  route-target import 300:2
 route-target import 200:2                    route-target import 200:2
 route-target import 300:2                   !
!                                            ip vrf green
ip vrf red                                    rd 300:1
 rd 200:1                                      route-target export 300:1
 export map OUT-INTER-AS                       route-target import 300:1
 route-target export 200:1                     route-target import 200:1
 route-target import 200:1                   ip cef
 route-target import 300:1                   tag-switching tag-range downstream 160 1000 0
ip cef                                       !
tag-switching tdp router-id Loopback0        interface Loopback0
!                                             ip address 156.50.10.3 255.255.255.255
interface Loopback0                          !
 ip address 166.50.10.3 255.255.255.255      interface Loopback10
!                                             ip vrf forwarding green
interface Loopback10                          ip address 30.1.1.1 255.255.255.0
 ip vrf forwarding red                       !
 ip address 20.1.1.1 255.255.255.0           interface Loopback11
!                                             ip vrf forwarding emerald
interface Loopback11                          ip address 31.1.1.1 255.255.255.0
 ip vrf forwarding pink                      !
 ip address 21.1.1.1 255.255.255.0           interface FastEthernet4/0
!                                             ip address 3.3.3.6 255.255.255.252
interface FastEthernet4/0                     duplex full
 ip address 2.2.2.6 255.255.255.252           tag-switching ip
 no ip route-cache cef                       !
 duplex full                                 router ospf 300
 tag-switching ip                             log-adjacency-changes
!                                             network 3.3.3.4 0.0.0.3 area 0
router ospf 200                               network 156.50.10.0 0.0.0.255 area 0
 log-adjacency-changes                       !
 network 2.2.2.0 0.0.0.255 area 0            router bgp 300
 network 166.50.10.0 0.0.0.255 area 0         no synchronization
!                                             no bgp default ipv4-unicast
router bgp 200                                bgp log-neighbor-changes
 no synchronization                           neighbor 156.50.10.1 remote-as 300
 no bgp default ipv4-unicast                  neighbor 156.50.10.1 update-source Loopback0
 bgp log-neighbor-changes                     neighbor 156.50.10.2 remote-as 300
 neighbor 166.50.10.1 remote-as 200           neighbor 156.50.10.2 update-source Loopback0
 neighbor 166.50.10.1 update-source Loopback0 !
 neighbor 166.50.10.2 remote-as 200          address-family ipv4 vrf green
 neighbor 166.50.10.2 update-source Loopback0 redistribute connected
 default-information originate                no auto-summary
 !                                            no synchronization
 address-family ipv4 vrf red                  exit-address-family
 redistribute connected                      !
 redistribute static                         address-family ipv4 vrf emerald
 no auto-summary                              redistribute connected
 no synchronization                           no auto-summary
 exit-address-family                          no synchronization
 !                                            exit-address-family
 address-family ipv4 vrf pink                !
 redistribute connected                      address-family vpnv4
 redistribute static                          neighbor 156.50.10.1 activate
 default-information originate                neighbor 156.50.10.1 send-community extended
 no auto-summary                              neighbor 156.50.10.2 activate
 no synchronization                           neighbor 156.50.10.2 send-community extended
 exit-address-family                          bgp scan-time 15
 !                                            bgp scan-time import 10
 address-family vpnv4                         exit-address-family
 neighbor 166.50.10.1 activate
 neighbor 166.50.10.1 send-community extended
 neighbor 166.50.10.2 activate
 neighbor 166.50.10.2 send-community extended
 default-information originate
 exit-address-family
!
ip route vrf red 20.2.1.0 255.255.255.0
Loopback10 20.1.1.2
ip route vrf pink 21.2.1.0 255.255.255.0
Loopback11 21.1.1.2
!
access-list 10 permit 20.1.1.0 0.0.0.55
route-map OUT-INTER-AS permit 10
 match ip address 10
 set extcommunity rt  200:777 additive
```

Figure 2.72

- RRs propagate the BGP next hop for VPNv4 routes unchanged (the RRs do not become next hop for the eBGP VPNv4 routes originating from the PE routers)
- Two labels are used:
  - one for the VPN
  - one for the PE loopback (like a regular MPLS-VPN)

Operation Figure 2.73 illustrates how the IGP routes method operates.

The operation of this method can be summarized as follows:

- Local PE routers (PE Loopbacks /32) are the next hops for locally originated VPNv4 routes.
- The local AS next-hop routes must be known in the remote AS.
- The loopback routes are known via the IGP in the remote AS.
- PE loopback routes are redistributed into eBGP on the ASBRs.
- On the remote AS, these loopback routes are redistributed from eBGP into the IGP.
- Each loopback route will have an associated IGP label.
- Route-maps are used on the redistribute command to filter these loopback routes.
- ASBRs need keyword "send-label" on the eBGP neighbor command.
- The label sent with the PE next-hop route is the local label that BGP retrieves from the TFIB for that route.
- Redistribution is from IGP into eBGP and vice versa.

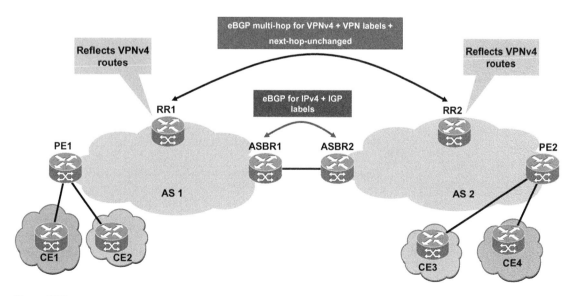

Figure 2.73

- Filtering is recommended to limit redistributed routes to the PE's next-hop routes.
- RRs need keyword "next-hop-unchanged" on the neighbor command to the eBGP multi-hop neighbor.
- The next hop of the VPNv4 routes needs to be kept to the next hop of the originating PE (normally, on a eBGP session, the next hop would be re-written).

Pros and Cons Some of the advantages and disadvantages of this method are as follows:
- Advantages
  - The ASBRs do not need to store VPNv4 routes.
  - The RRs already store VPNv4 routes.
  - IPv4 eBGP is only needed between ASBRs.
- Disadvantages
  - The PE next-hop routes must be advertised to other ASs into their IGP.
  - An element of trust between service providers is needed to allow distribution of loopbacks into each others ASs as well as peering between RRs.

BGP Routes Method

The BGP routes distribution method can be summarized as follows:
- ASBRs exchange IPv4 routes + labels via eBGP.
- PEs, RRs and ASBRs exchange IPv4 routes + labels via iBGP.
- RRs exchange VPNv4 routes + labels via multi-hop.
- RRs propagate the next hop unchanged.
- Three labels are used:
  - one for the VPN
  - one for destination PE (next hop)
  - one to get to the local ASBR
- Therefore three labels are used to get to destination AS, then two labels are used inside destination AS.

Operation Figure 2.74 illustrates how the BGP routes distribution method operates.
The operation of this method can be summarized as follows:
- Local PEs loopbacks are the next hop for VPNv4 routes in the remote AS.
- The next-hop routes (loopback) must be known in the other AS.
- These loopback routes should be propagated by BGP to all PEs in all ASs.

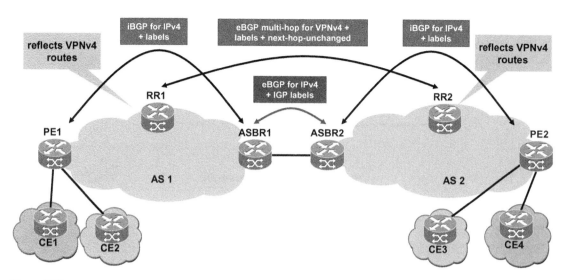

Figure 2.74

- In the local AS, these routes (+ label) must be advertised via iBGP to all PEs. ("iBGP+IPv4+label" is needed on all PEs, RRS and ASBRs.)

Pros and Cons Some of the advantages and disadvantages of this method are as follows:
- Advantages
  - Only PEs that participate in inter-AS need to know remote PE loopbacks.
    - (In the IGP method all routers in the local AS need to know.)
  - ASBRs do not need to store VPNv4 routes (and labels).
  - RRs already store VPNv4 routes.
- Disadvantages
  - PE next-hop routes must be advertised to other Ass.
    - "iBGP+IPv4+label" is needed between PEs, ASBRs. and RRs. (RRs need the "send-label" command towards the RR-clients and ASBRs towards the RRs.)

Option C Inter-AS Operation – IGP Routes Method

This section describes the operation of inter-AS using route reflectors to pass VPNv4 routes with the next hop unchanged. *The loopback addresses of remote PE routers are distributed within the local AS using the IGP (OSPF)*. The values given here for the IP addresses, VPN, and IGP labels are based on the actual values allocated in the test setup.

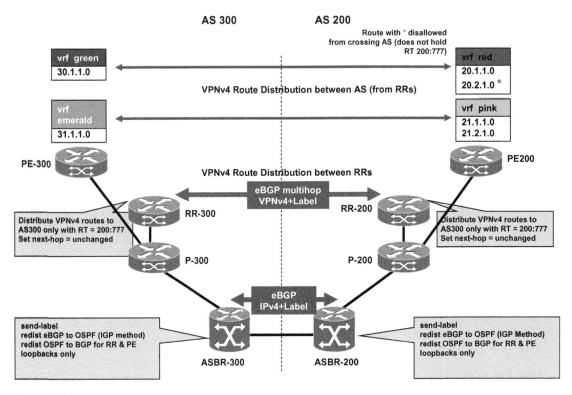

Figure 2.75

Test Setup

Figure 2.75 shows the test environment for the Option C scenario using the IGP to distribute the remote loopbacks within the local AS.

The following summarizes the test setup that was the basis for the operational examples:

- There are two BGP Autonomous Systems, AS200 and AS300, each running OSPF.
- AS 200 has four routers
  1. ASBR-200, acting as the primary ASBR
  2. P-200, acting as P router terminating the RR and the PE (note on the Option B example this router also was a backup ASBR - but it is not being used a such in this example)
  3. PE-200, acting as a PE which has two VRFs Red and Pink
  4. RR-200, which is the VPNv4 route reflector for AS200
     – AS 300 also has three routers;
  1. ASBR-A300, acting as the primary ASBR
  2. P-300, acting as P router terminating the RR and the PE

3. PE-300, acting as a PE which has two VRFs: Green and Emerald
4. RR-300, which is the route reflector for AS300
   - The ABSRs establish an eBGP session between each other to exchange the IPv4 prefixes of the loopbacks only for the route reflector and the PE router in their respective AS. The loopbacks of any other infrastructure devices do not need to be exchanged.
   - The ABSRs will re-distribute the received prefixes (loopbacks) from the other AS into the local OSPF process (IGP routes method). The IPv4 labels received via the eBGP session will also be inserted into the LFIB as the outgoing label for that prefix.
   - PE-200 and PE-300 have iBGP sessions to their respective RRs to exchange VPNv4 routing information from their VRFs.
   - RR-200 and RR-300 have an eBGP session established between them to pass the VPNv4 routes from the VRFs of their PE routers. This eBGP multi-hop session also passes the relevant VPN labels. The eBGP session is logically configured between the two RRs but physically passes across the ASBR interconnect. Peering connectivity is achieved between the RRs because the ASBRs pass the loopbacks of the RRs across the AS boundary.
   - Normally, when a route reflector passes routes over an eBGP session, the BGP next hop of the route (in this case, the PE loopback) is changed to that of the route reflector. In the Option C inter-AS scenario this is not desirable, as the RRs are not part of the forwarding plane; they are merely passing reachability information. Therefore the PE router loopbacks must be kept intact as the next-hop address for all VPNv4 routes. This is achieved by configuring the RRs to keep the next-hop information unchanged across the eBGP session.
   - The RRs in both ASs will only distribute routes across the eBGP session if the locally learned VPNv4 route holds 200:777 as one of its route targets/extended community strings. This has the advantage of providing some form of control over what VPNv4 routes the remote AS can see.
   - Routes will be exported/imported between VRF Red and Green and also between VRF Pink and Emerald across the inter-AS boundary. That is, there is a corresponding route target import for the remote VRF's route target export for these pairs of VRFs.

- All the VRFs are configured to export an additional route target of 200:777 so the local RRs will forward all VPNv4 routes in the VRF across the eBGP session. The exception is that VRF Red uses a route-map to set the route target 200:777, providing greater control over which prefixes are allowed across the inter-AS boundary. In this test example, much like the Option B example, we set only route target 200:777 on prefix 20.1.1.0, thereby denying 20.2.1.0 from being seen by the remote-AS. With the rest of the VRF, all route prefixes are distributed to the remote AS because they are all exported with 200:777.
- To make it easier to visually distinguish label allocations in each AS, the AS300 label allocations start as 160, while AS200 label allocations start at 16.
- All VRF routes from AS200 are in the 20.0.0.0 – 21.0.0.0 range and all VRF routes from AS300 are in the 30.0.0.0 – 31.0.0.0 range.

Figure 2.76 shows the logical layout of the test network. Several loopback addresses are used to generate prefixes within the various VRFs.

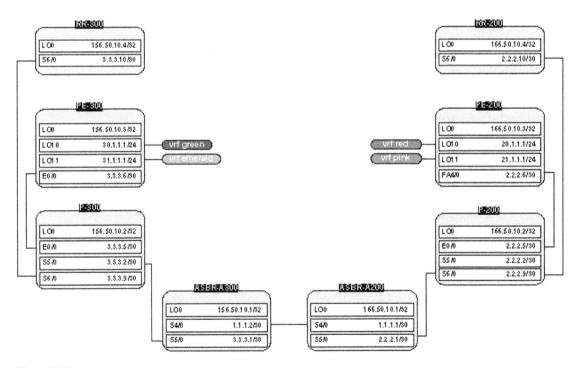

Figure 2.76

VPNv4 Route Distribution Process

Figure 2.77 shows the various steps taken to distribute the VPNv4 route **300:1:30.1.1.0** originating in VRF Green of PE-300 (AS300) to VRF Red of PE-200 (AS200). The steps involve several label distribution mechanisms:

- iBGP + VPNv4 + Label – used between the PE routers and local RRs to distribute VPNv4 information
- eBGP + VPNv4 + Label – used between the local and remote RRs to distribute information across the AS boundary
- eBGP + IPv4 + Label – used between ASBR to pass loopback addresses of relevant routers in local AS (RRs and PE routers)
- \LDP – used in the local AS to distribute labels for all the IGP routes
- The VPNv4 route 300:1:30.1.1.0 is allocated the BGP label of {165} by PE-300. The BGP next hop is set to the PE-300 loopback 156.50.10.3. The route and VPNv4 label is then distributed via an iBGP session to RR-300

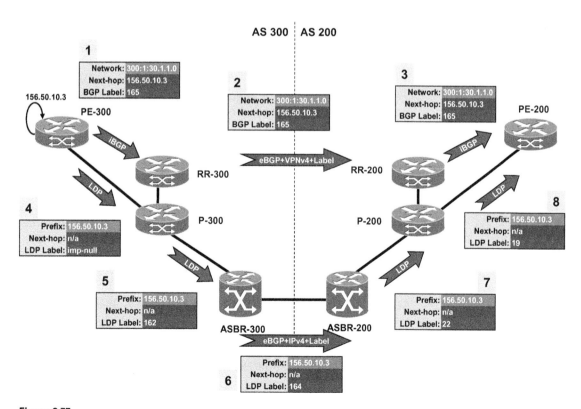

Figure 2.77

- RR-300 passes the VPNv4 route, label, route targets, and next hop (PE-300) unchanged to RR-200 via the eBGP session.
- When RR-200 receives the VPNv4 route, it will store it in its VPNV4 table. It is then reflected to all PE clients (in this case, PE-200). Therefore PE-200 will receive the reachability information for 300:1:30.1.1.0 exactly as PE-300 has sent it.
- To complete the connectivity, the loopback and label of PE-300 must be distributed into the AS200. PE-300 distributes its loopback (156.50.10.3) via OSPF plus an implicit null label via LDP to P-300.
- P-300 advertises label {162} towards ASBR-300 for 156.50.10.3
- When ASBR-300 receives the LDP binding for 156.50.10.3 it will update the LFIB with outgoing label {162} and also allocate the incoming label {164}. The route 156.50.10.3 and label {164} are then redistributed into eBGP and sent to ASBR-200.
- ASBR 200 will use label {164} across the AS boundary as the outgoing label to reach 156.50.10.3. The loopback 156.50.10.3 is then redistributed into OSPF, and an associated incoming label {22} is distributed by ASBR-200 to its upstream partner P-200.
- P-200 receives the loopback 156.50.10.3 via OSPF (it will also have the loopback for RR-300, but we have not shown this) plus the downstream label {22}. P-200 then provides PE-200 with the label {19} for loopback 156.50.10.3. At this point PE-200 has the VPNv4 route installed in its VRF, the BGP VPN label {165}, and the LDP label of the PE-300 {19}.

Label Switch Path Forwarding

This section describes the steps taken to forward traffic from PE-200 to PE-300 via the ASBRs. Figure 2.78 gives an example of the various labels that get pushed, swapped, and popped on the stack as a packet makes its way from PE-200 for a host in destination 30.1.1.0 on PE-300. Since the RRs are not used in the forwarding path, they are not shown in the example.

The forwarding path shown in Figure 2.78 is very straightforward compared to the Option B method, as no next hop self is required. The VPN label remains {165}, and the BGP next hop of 156.50.10.3 remains unchanged. The only slight difference from the Option B method is that two labels are used when forwarding traffic between the ASBRs (Step 3): the VPN and LDP labels (as in a normal forwarding situation within an AS).

While Option C is straightforward, it requires some trust between the AS providers to allow communication between the RRs as well as injection of loopbacks from each network.

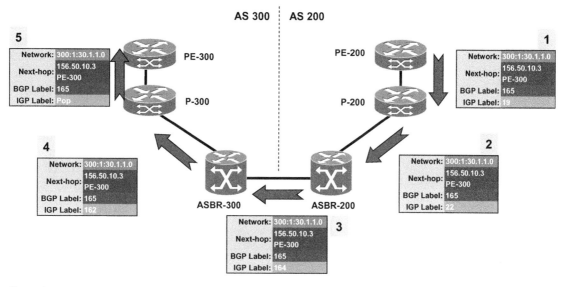

Figure 2.78

```
PE-200#trace  mpls ipv4 156.50.10.3/32 source 166.50.10.3
Tracing MPLS Label Switched Path to 156.50.10.3/32, timeout is 2 seconds

Codes: '!' - success, 'Q' - request not transmitted,
       '.' - timeout, 'U' - unreachable,
       'R' - downstream router but not target,
       'M' - malformed request

Type escape sequence to abort.
  0 2.2.2.6 MRU 1500 [Labels: 19 Exp: 0]
R 1 2.2.2.5 MRU 1500 [Labels: 22 Exp: 0] 180 ms
R 2 2.2.2.1 MRU 1500 [Labels: 164 Exp: 0] 76 ms
R 3 1.1.1.2 MRU 1500 [Labels: 162 Exp: 0] 188 ms
R 4 3.3.3.2 MRU 1504 [implicit-null] 120 ms
! 5 3.3.3.6 152 ms
```

Figure 2.79 Trace from PE-200 to PE-300

Figure 2.79 shows a trace of the LSP between PE-200 and PE-300.

Configuration Analysis

This section shows the relevant configurations and output to describe the operation of inter-AS Option C. The output focuses on the example in the previous sections of VPNv4 route 300:1:30.1.1.0 being distributed from PE-300 to PE-200 and the forwarding of VPN traffic from PE-200 towards PE-300 (156.50.10.3).

Router PE-200

VPN Routing and Forwarding (VRF) Tables Figure 2.80 shows the routing table on VRF Red. One important thing to note about this entry is that the VPNv4 route 30.1.1.0 imported from PE-300 has retained the next hop of PE-300, which is 156.50.10.3. In the Option B scenario, this entry would have been changed to one of the ASBRs, depending on whether next-hop-self was configured.

BGP VPNv4 Table Figure 2.81 shows the VPNv4 entry in the BGP table for 30.1.1.0. Note that the route was received from 166.50.10.4, which is RR-200 (which had received it from RR-300). The route also holds the extended community strings

```
PE-200#show ip route vrf red

Routing Table: red
Codes: C - connected, S - static, I - IGRP, R - RIP, M - mobile, B - BGP
       D - EIGRP, EX - EIGRP external, O - OSPF, IA - OSPF inter area
       N1 - OSPF NSSA external type 1, N2 - OSPF NSSA external type 2
       E1 - OSPF external type 1, E2 - OSPF external type 2, E - EGP
       i - IS-IS, su - IS-IS summary, L1 - IS-IS level-1, L2 - IS-IS level-2
       ia - IS-IS inter area, * - candidate default, U - per-user static route
       o - ODR

Gateway of last resort is not set

     20.0.0.0/24 is subnetted, 2 subnets
C       20.1.1.0 is directly connected, Loopback10
S       20.2.1.0 [1/0] via 20.1.1.2, Loopback10
     30.0.0.0/24 is subnetted, 1 subnets
B       30.1.1.0 [200/0] via 156.50.10.3, 19:36:23
```

Figure 2.80 VRF Red on PE-2000

```
PE-200#show ip bgp vpnv4 all 30.1.1.0
BGP routing table entry for 200:1:30.1.1.0/24, version 22
Paths: (1 available, best #1, table red)
  Not advertised to any peer
  300, imported path from 300:1:30.1.1.0/24
    156.50.10.3 (metric 1) from 166.50.10.4 (166.50.10.4)
      Origin incomplete, metric 0, localpref 100, valid, internal, best
      Extended Community: RT:200:777 RT:300:1,
      mpls labels in/out nolabel/165
BGP routing table entry for 300:1:30.1.1.0/24, version 21
Paths: (1 available, best #1, no table)
  Not advertised to any peer
  300
    156.50.10.3 (metric 1) from 166.50.10.4 (166.50.10.4)
      Origin incomplete, metric 0, localpref 100, valid, internal, best
      Extended Community: RT:200:777 RT:300:1,
      mpls labels in/out nolabel/165
```

Figure 2.81 BGP VPNv4 Table on PE-200

200:777, which allowed it to be distributed across the RR eBGP session between the two ASs, and 300:1, which allows it to be imported into VRF Red. Note also that the outbound label {165} and PE-300 next hop are also sent in the BGP update. This label and next hop remain unchanged throughout the network.

CEF Table Figure 2.82 shows the CEF entry for 30.1.1.0. As can be seen, VPN packets bound for 30.1.1.0 from PE-200 have {19 165} pushed onto the stack. Label {19} is derived from LDP via the ASBRs while label {165} is derived from BGP via the route reflectors.

Routing Table Figure 2.83 shows the routing table on PE-200. As can be seen, the loopbacks for RR-300 and PE-300 (156.50.10.x) appear as OSPF external routes, having been redistributed into the IGP from the BGP process in ASBR-200. The slight

```
PE-200#show ip cef vrf red 30.1.1.0
30.1.1.0/24, version 11, epoch 0, cached adjacency 2.2.2.5
0 packets, 0 bytes
   tag information set, all rewrites owned
      local tag: VPN route head
      fast tag rewrite with Et0/0, 2.2.2.5, tags imposed {19 165}
   via 156.50.10.3, 0 dependencies, recursive
      next hop 2.2.2.5, Ethernet0/0 via 156.50.10.3/32 (Default)
      valid cached adjacency
      tag rewrite with Et0/0, 2.2.2.5, tags imposed {19 165}
```

Figure 2.82 CEF Table for PE-200

```
PE-200#show ip route
Codes: C - connected, S - static, I - IGRP, R - RIP, M - mobile, B - BGP
       D - EIGRP, EX - EIGRP external, O - OSPF, IA - OSPF inter area
       N1 - OSPF NSSA external type 1, N2 - OSPF NSSA external type 2
       E1 - OSPF external type 1, E2 - OSPF external type 2, E - EGP
       i - IS-IS, su - IS-IS summary, L1 - IS-IS level-1, L2 - IS-IS level-2
       ia - IS-IS inter area, * - candidate default, U - per-user static
       o - ODR

Gateway of last resort is not set

     2.0.0.0/30 is subnetted, 3 subnets
O       2.2.2.0 [110/58] via 2.2.2.5, 1w4d, Ethernet0/0
C       2.2.2.4 is directly connected, Ethernet0/0
O       2.2.2.8 [110/58] via 2.2.2.5, 1w4d, Ethernet0/0
     156.50.0.0/32 is subnetted, 2 subnets
O E2    156.50.10.4 [110/1] via 2.2.2.5, 1w4d, Ethernet0/0
O E2    156.50.10.3 [110/1] via 2.2.2.5, 1w4d, Ethernet0/0
     166.50.0.0/32 is subnetted, 4 subnets
O       166.50.10.4 [110/59] via 2.2.2.5, 1w4d, Ethernet0/0
O       166.50.10.2 [110/11] via 2.2.2.5, 1w4d, Ethernet0/0
C       166.50.10.3 is directly connected, Loopback0
O       166.50.10.1 [110/59] via 2.2.2.5, 1w4d, Ethernet0/0
```

Figure 2.83 Routing Table on PE-200

disadvantage of redistributing the PE loopback into the IGP is that all routers in the AS will learn about that PE. The other option is to use BGP+Labels to distribute the loopbacks, which is explained in a later section.

Label Forwarding Information Base (LFIB) Figure 2.84 shows the LFIB on PE-200. Each of the loopbacks from AS300 is allocated a label in the normal manner, using LDP. Label {19} is the outgoing label for PE-200 (156.50.10.4) while label {20} has been allocated to RR-300. In practice, no labels are necessary for the route reflectors, as they are not part of the forwarding path for MPLS.

VRF Configuration The VRF configuration for PE-200 is unchanged from that shown in Figure 2.44 on page 116.

Route Reflector RR-200 The RR-200 route reflector peers with both RR-300, using eBGP, and PE-200, using iBGP. It passes the VPNv4 routes received from AS300 onwards to the client PE routers (in this case PE-200).

BGP VPNv4 Table The route reflectors do not need to MPLS (LDP is not activated), as they are not in the forwarding path. Nor do they have any VRFs configured. The RRs only hold the BGP VPNv4 table as shown in Figure 2.85.

In the example we can see that RR-200 holds six VPNv4 routes originating from PE-200 (next hop 166.50.10.3) or PE-300 in the other AS (156.50.10.3), as shown by the entries with Path 300.

Figure 2.86 shows the detailed entry for VPNv4 prefix 300:1:30.1.1.0. This prefix has been received from 156.50.10.4, which is RR-300 in the remote AS. The relevant community string has been passed, as well as the next hop of PE-300 and also the VPN label {**165**}.

OSPF and BGP Configuration Figure 2.87 shows the OSPF and BGP configurations for RR-200. There is no MPLS configured on

```
PE-200#sh tag for
Local   Outgoing     Prefix           Bytes tag   Outgoing    Next Hop
tag     tag or VC    or Tunnel Id     switched    interface
16      Pop tag      2.2.2.0/30       0           Et0/0       2.2.2.5
17      Pop tag      2.2.2.8/30       0           Et0/0       2.2.2.5
18      16           166.50.10.1/32   0           Et0/0       2.2.2.5
19      Pop tag      166.50.10.2/32   0           Et0/0       2.2.2.5
20      17           166.50.10.4/32   0           Et0/0       2.2.2.5
21      Aggregate    20.1.1.0/24[V]   1040
22      Aggregate    20.2.1.0/24[V]   0
23      Aggregate    21.1.1.0/24[V]   0
24      Aggregate    21.2.1.0/24[V]   0
25      19           156.50.10.3/32   0           Et0/0       2.2.2.5
26      20           156.50.10.4/32   0           Et0/0       2.2.2.5
```

Figure 2.84 LFIB for PE-200

```
RR-200#show ip bgp vpnv4 all
BGP table version is 13, local router ID is 166.50.10.4
Status codes: s suppressed, d damped, h history, * valid, > best, i -
internal,
               r RIB-failure, S Stale
Origin codes: i - IGP, e - EGP, ? - incomplete

    Network            Next Hop          Metric LocPrf Weight Path
Route Distinguisher: 200:1
*>i20.1.1.0/24       166.50.10.3            0    100      0 ?
*>i20.2.1.0/24       166.50.10.3            0    100      0 ?
Route Distinguisher: 200:2
*>i21.1.1.0/24       166.50.10.3            0    100      0 ?
*>i21.2.1.0/24       166.50.10.3            0    100      0 ?
Route Distinguisher: 300:1
*> 30.1.1.0/24       156.50.10.3                          0 300 ?
Route Distinguisher: 300:2
*> 31.1.1.0/24       156.50.10.3                          0 300 ?
```

Figure 2.85 BGP VPNv4 Table on RR-200

```
RR-200#show ip bgp vpnv4 all 30.1.1.0
BGP routing table entry for 300:1:30.1.1.0/24, version 13
Paths: (1 available, best #1, no table)
  Advertised to update-groups:
     1
  300
    156.50.10.3 (metric 1) from 156.50.10.4 (156.50.10.4)
      Origin incomplete, localpref 100, valid, external, best
      Extended Community: RT:200:777 RT:300:1,
      mpls labels in/out nolabel/165
```

Figure 2.86 VPNv4 Route Detail

any interface. The OSPF configuration to provide routing in the local AS is particularly simple.

The BGP configuration has two peers. One is an iBGP session to 166.50.10.3 (PE-200), while the other is an eBGP multi-hop session to 156.50.10.4 (RR-300). Under the VPNv4 address family the only thing that appears a little bit different is the presence of the "next-hop-unchanged" keyword on the neighbor command. This ensures that any VPNv4 routes sent from AS-200 to AS-300 will retain the next-hop address of the originating PE router. The route-map provides filtering capability so that no VPNv4 routes will be passed to the other AS unless they are holding the extended community 200:777 (previously added by the VRF route target).

ASBR 200 The ASBRs are only responsible for passing the loop-back addresses of the route reflectors and the relevant PE routers holding VPNv4 routes that need to cross the AS boundary. The RR loopbacks are necessary so that an eBGP peering session can be established between the RRs across the ABSR, while the PE router

```
router ospf 200
 log-adjacency-changes
 network 2.2.2.8 0.0.0.3 area 0
 network 166.50.10.0 0.0.0.255 area 0
!
router bgp 200
 no bgp default ipv4-unicast
 bgp log-neighbor-changes
 neighbor 156.50.10.4 remote-as 300
 neighbor 156.50.10.4 description RR-300
 neighbor 156.50.10.4 ebgp-multihop 10
 neighbor 156.50.10.4 update-source Loopback0
 neighbor 166.50.10.3 remote-as 200
 neighbor 166.50.10.3 description PE-200
 neighbor 166.50.10.3 update-source Loopback0
 !
 address-family vpnv4
 neighbor 156.50.10.4 activate
 neighbor 156.50.10.4 send-community extended
 neighbor 156.50.10.4 next-hop-unchanged
 neighbor 156.50.10.4 route-map INTER-AS out
 neighbor 166.50.10.3 activate
 neighbor 166.50.10.3 send-community extended
 neighbor 166.50.10.3 route-reflector-client
 exit-address-family
!

ip extcommunity-list 10 permit rt 200:777
!
route-map INTER-AS permit 10
 match extcommunity 10
```

Figure 2.87 PE-200 Configuration

loopbacks are necessary so that an MPLS LSP can be provisioned end-to-end between the PE routers (for VPN traffic).

BGP IPv4 Table The ASBRs do not carry any VPNv4 information, as is also the case in Option B. These ASBRs only contain the IPv4 addresses in the BGP table, as shown in Figure 2.88. Due to the filtering configured on the peering sessions, only the loopback addresses are maintained in the IPv4 table.

Figure 2.89 shows the LDP labels associated with the PE-300 loopback from AS300. As can be seen, there is an in and out label. The out label {164} was received from ASBR-300 and will be used as the topmost label for packet traveling across the ASBR interconnect towards PE-300. Label {22} is the in label LDP label advertised to upstream neighbors in AS200. So label {22} will be used by upstream neighbors in AS200 and then will be swapped with label {164} to go out across the ASBR connection.

Label Forwarding Information Base (LFIB) Figure 2.90 shows the LFIB for ASBR-200. The entry for 156.50.10.3 (PE-300) matches the in/out labels in the BGP IPv4 entry

```
ABSR-200#show ip bgp
BGP table version is 7, local router ID is 166.50.10.1
Status codes: s suppressed, d damped, h history, * valid, > best, i -
internal,
              r RIB-failure, S Stale
Origin codes: i - IGP, e - EGP, ? - incomplete

    Network           Next Hop          Metric LocPrf Weight Path
*>  156.50.10.3/32    1.1.1.2               59            0 300 ?
*>  156.50.10.4/32    1.1.1.2               97            0 300 ?
*>  166.50.10.3/32    2.2.2.2               59        32768 ?
*>  166.50.10.4/32    2.2.2.2               97        32768 ?
```

Figure 2.88 BGP IPv4 Table in ASBR 200

```
ABSR-200#show ip bgp 156.50.10.3
BGP routing table entry for 156.50.10.3/32, version 6
Paths: (1 available, best #1)
  Not advertised to any peer
  300
    1.1.1.2 from 1.1.1.2 (156.50.10.1)
      Origin incomplete, metric 59, localpref 100, valid, external, best,
      mpls labels in/out 22/164
```

Figure 2.89 IPv4 Labels in ASBR-200

```
ABSR-200#sh mpls for
Local  Outgoing    Prefix          Bytes tag  Outgoing    Next Hop
tag    tag or VC   or Tunnel Id    switched   interface
16     Pop tag     2.2.2.4/30      0          Se5/0       point2point
17     Pop tag     2.2.2.8/30      0          Se5/0       point2point
18     Pop tag     166.50.10.2/32  0          Se5/0       point2point
19     17          166.50.10.4/32  1152660    Se5/0       point2point
20     18          166.50.10.3/32  0          Se5/0       point2point
21     Pop tag     1.1.1.2/32      0          Se4/0       point2point
22     164         156.50.10.3/32  2272       Se4/0       point2point
23     163         156.50.10.4/32  1803850    Se4/0       point2point
```

Figure 2.90 LFIB on ASBR-200

ASBR Configuration Figure 2.91 shows the relevant configuration to enable BGP to send labels for IPv4 prefixes as well as redistribute those prefixes into the IGP (OSPF). The AS300-INBOUND route-map on OSPF will redistribute the prefixes received from BGP if they match the relevant loopback address from AS300 and have a label associated with that prefix.

The AS300-OUTBOUND route-map ensures that only the relevant loopbacks from AS200 are passed through to AS300. In addition, the "send-label" keyword on the neighbor command will include the LDP label for the associated prefix as part of the BGP update.

```
router ospf 200
 log-adjacency-changes
 redistribute bgp 200 subnets route-map AS300-INBOUND
 network 2.2.2.0 0.0.0.255 area 0
 network 166.50.10.0 0.0.0.255 area 0
!
router bgp 200
 no bgp default ipv4-unicast
 no bgp default route-target filter
 bgp log-neighbor-changes
 neighbor 1.1.1.2 remote-as 300
 !
 address-family ipv4
 redistribute ospf 200 route-map AS300-OUTBOUND
 neighbor 1.1.1.2 activate
 neighbor 1.1.1.2 send-label
 no auto-summary
 no synchronization
 exit-address-family
!
ip access-list standard AS200-Loopbacks
 permit 166.50.10.4
 permit 166.50.10.3
!
ip access-list standard AS300-Loopbacks
 permit 156.50.10.4
 permit 156.50.10.3
!
route-map AS300-OUTBOUND permit 10
 match ip address AS200-Loopbacks
!
route-map AS300-INBOUND permit 10
 match ip address AS300-Loopbacks
 match mpls-label
!
route-map INTER-AS permit 10
 match extcommunity 10
```

Figure 2.91 ASBR-200
Configuration

ASBR 300 The configurations and outputs on the AS300 side are very similar. The only thing that should be noted is the IPv4 BGP table for AS300.

BGP IPv4 Table Figure 2.92 shows the BGP IPv4 table for AS300. It looks similar to the BGP table on ASBR-200 in Figure 2.88 except that 156.50.x.x entries are local instead of from the remote AS.

The fact that 156.50.10.3/32 is a locally originated route affects the way the label entry appears in the BGP table, as shown in Figure 2.93

```
ABSR-300#sh ip bgp
BGP table version is 7, local router ID is 156.50.10.1
Status codes: s suppressed, d damped, h history, * valid, > best, i -
internal,
            r RIB-failure, S Stale
Origin codes: i - IGP, e - EGP, ? - incomplete

   Network          Next Hop          Metric LocPrf Weight Path
*> 156.50.10.3/32    3.3.3.2              59        32768 ?
*> 156.50.10.4/32    3.3.3.2              97        32768 ?
*> 166.50.10.3/32    1.1.1.1              59            0 200 ?
*> 166.50.10.4/32    1.1.1.1              97            0 200 ?
```

Figure 2.92 BGP IPv4 Table in ASBR-200

```
ABSR-A300#sh ip bgp 156.50.10.3
BGP routing table entry for 156.50.10.3/32, version 5
Paths: (1 available, best #1)
  Advertised to update-groups:
     1
  Local
     3.3.3.2 from 0.0.0.0 (156.50.10.1)
       Origin incomplete, metric 59, localpref 100, weight 32768, valid,
sourced, best,
       mpls labels in/out 164(from LDP)/nolabel
```

Figure 2.93 IPV4 Labels in ASBR-300

Notice that the entry only has an in label {164} and that it was derived from LDP. This label is forwarded across the iBGP IPv4 session towards ASBR-200.

Configuration listings (Option C - IGP Method) are shown in Figures 2.94, 2.95, and 2.96.

Option C Inter-AS Operation – BGP Routes Method

This section describes the operation of inter-AS using route reflectors to pass VPNv4 routes with the next hop unchanged, as with the IGP routes method. However, *the IPv4 loopback addresses of remote PE routers are distributed within the local AS using iBGP.* The values for the IP addresses, VPN, and IGP labels are based on the actual values allocated in the test setup.

The advantage of this method is that the loopback addresses of the remote AS are only distributed in the local AS to the routers that require them, namely, the PE routers with relevant VRFs and route reflectors. The core infrastructure routers (P routers) and PE routers that do not hold a VRF that needs InterAS VPN routes do not need to learn about the loopbacks addresses (hence they have no IPv4 BGP session).

ABSR-200	ABSR-300
hostname ABSR-200	hostname ABSR-300
!	!
ip cef	ip cef
!	mpls label range 160 1000
!	!
interface Loopback0	interface Loopback0
ip address 166.50.10.1 255.255.255.255	ip address 156.50.10.1 255.255.255.255
no ip directed-broadcast	no ip directed-broadcast
!	!
interface Serial4/0	interface Serial4/0
ip address 1.1.1.1 255.255.255.252	ip address 1.1.1.2 255.255.255.252
no ip directed-broadcast	no ip directed-broadcast
mpls bgp forwarding	mpls bgp forwarding
no fair-queue	no fair-queue
!	!
interface Serial5/0	interface Serial5/0
ip address 2.2.2.1 255.255.255.252	ip address 3.3.3.1 255.255.255.252
no ip directed-broadcast	no ip directed-broadcast
tag-switching ip	tag-switching ip
!	!
router ospf 200	router ospf 300
log-adjacency-changes	log-adjacency-changes
redistribute bgp 200 subnets route-map AS300-	redistribute static subnets
INBOUND	redistribute bgp 300 subnets route-map AS200-
network 2.2.2.0 0.0.0.255 area 0	INBOUND
network 166.50.10.0 0.0.0.255 area 0	network 3.3.3.0 0.0.0.255 area 0
!	network 156.50.10.0 0.0.0.255 area 0
router bgp 200	!
no bgp default ipv4-unicast	router bgp 300
no bgp default route-target filter	no bgp default ipv4-unicast
bgp log-neighbor-changes	bgp log-neighbor-changes
neighbor 1.1.1.2 remote-as 300	neighbor 1.1.1.1 remote-as 200
!	!
address-family ipv4	address-family ipv4
redistribute ospf 200 route-map AS300-OUTBOUND	redistribute ospf 300 route-map AS200-OUTBOUND
neighbor 1.1.1.2 activate	neighbor 1.1.1.1 activate
neighbor 1.1.1.2 send-label	neighbor 1.1.1.1 send-label
no auto-summary	no auto-summary
no synchronization	no synchronization
exit-address-family	exit-address-family
!	!
ip extcommunity-list 10 permit rt 200:777	ip access-list standard AS200-Loopbacks
!	permit 166.50.10.4
ip access-list standard AS200-Loopbacks	permit 166.50.10.3
permit 166.50.10.4	ip access-list standard AS300-Loopbacks
permit 166.50.10.3	permit 156.50.10.4
ip access-list standard AS300-Loopbacks	permit 156.50.10.3
permit 156.50.10.4	route-map AS200-OUTBOUND permit 10
permit 156.50.10.3	match ip address AS300-Loopbacks
access-list 1 permit any	!
route-map AS300-OUTBOUND permit 10	route-map AS200-INBOUND permit 10
match ip address AS200-Loopbacks	match ip address AS200-Loopbacks
!	match mpls-label
route-map AS300-INBOUND permit 10	
match ip address AS300-Loopbacks	
match mpls-label	
!	

Figure 2.94

RR-200	RR-300
```hostname RR-200```	```hostname RR-300```

```
hostname RR-200
!
interface Loopback0
 ip address 166.50.10.4 255.255.255.255
 no ip directed-broadcast
!
interface Serial6/0
 ip address 2.2.2.10 255.255.255.252
 no ip directed-broadcast
 no cdp enable
!
router ospf 200
 log-adjacency-changes
 network 2.2.2.8 0.0.0.3 area 0
 network 166.50.10.0 0.0.0.255 area 0
!
router bgp 200
 no bgp default ipv4-unicast
 bgp log-neighbor-changes
 neighbor 156.50.10.4 remote-as 300
 neighbor 156.50.10.4 description RR-300
 neighbor 156.50.10.4 ebgp-multihop 10
 neighbor 156.50.10.4 update-source Loopback0
 neighbor 166.50.10.3 remote-as 200
 neighbor 166.50.10.3 description PE-200
 neighbor 166.50.10.3 update-source Loopback0
 !
 address-family vpnv4
 neighbor 156.50.10.4 activate
 neighbor 156.50.10.4 send-community extended
 neighbor 156.50.10.4 next-hop-unchanged
 neighbor 156.50.10.4 route-map INTER-AS out
 neighbor 166.50.10.3 activate
 neighbor 166.50.10.3 send-community extended
 neighbor 166.50.10.3 route-reflector-client
 exit-address-family
!
ip extcommunity-list 10 permit rt 200:777
!
route-map INTER-AS permit 10
 match extcommunity 10
```

```
hostname RR-300
!
interface Loopback0
 ip address 156.50.10.4 255.255.255.255
 no ip directed-broadcast
!
interface Serial6/0
 ip address 3.3.3.10 255.255.255.252
 no ip directed-broadcast
 no cdp enable
!
router ospf 300
 log-adjacency-changes
 network 3.3.3.8 0.0.0.3 area 0
 network 156.50.10.0 0.0.0.255 area 0
!
router bgp 300
 no bgp default ipv4-unicast
 bgp log-neighbor-changes
 neighbor 156.50.10.3 remote-as 300
 neighbor 156.50.10.3 description PE-300
 neighbor 156.50.10.3 update-source Loopback0
 neighbor 166.50.10.4 remote-as 200
 neighbor 166.50.10.4 description RR-200
 neighbor 166.50.10.4 ebgp-multihop 10
 neighbor 166.50.10.4 update-source Loopback0
 !
 address-family vpnv4
 neighbor 156.50.10.3 activate
 neighbor 156.50.10.3 send-community extended
 neighbor 156.50.10.3 route-reflector-client
 neighbor 166.50.10.4 activate
 neighbor 166.50.10.4 send-community extended
 neighbor 166.50.10.4 next-hop-unchanged
 neighbor 166.50.10.4 route-map INTER-AS out
 exit-address-family
!
ip extcommunity-list 10 permit rt 200:777
!
route-map INTER-AS permit 10
 match extcommunity 10
```

Figure 2.95

Test Setup

Figure 2.97 shows the test environment for the Option C scenario using the BGP to distribute the remote loopbacks within the local AS.

The following summarizes the test setup that was the basis for the operational examples using the iBGP method to distribute IPv4 loopbacks within the local AS.

- There are two BGP Autonomous Systems, AS 200 and AS 300, each running OSPF.
- AS 200 has four routers:
  1. ASBR-200 acting as the primary ASBR
  2. P-200 acting as P router terminating the RR and the PE

| PE-200 | PE-300 |

```
hostname PE-200
!
ip cef
ip vrf pink
 rd 200:2
 route-target export 200:2
 route-target export 200:777
 route-target import 200:2
 route-target import 300:2
!
ip vrf red
 rd 200:1
 export map OUT-INTER-AS
 route-target export 200:1
 route-target import 200:1
 route-target import 300:1
!
tag-switching tdp router-id Loopback0
!
interface Loopback0
 ip address 166.50.10.3 255.255.255.255
 no ip directed-broadcast
!
interface Loopback10
 ip vrf forwarding red
 ip address 20.1.1.1 255.255.255.0
 no ip directed-broadcast
!
interface Loopback11
 ip vrf forwarding pink
 ip address 21.1.1.1 255.255.255.0
 no ip directed-broadcast
!
interface Ethernet0/0
 ip address 2.2.2.6 255.255.255.252
 no ip directed-broadcast
 tag-switching ip
!
router ospf 200
 log-adjacency-changes
 network 2.2.2.0 0.0.0.255 area 0
 network 166.50.10.0 0.0.0.255 area 0
!
router bgp 200
 no bgp default ipv4-unicast
 bgp log-neighbor-changes
 neighbor 166.50.10.4 remote-as 200
 neighbor 166.50.10.4 update-source Loopback0
 !
 address-family vpnv4
 neighbor 166.50.10.4 activate
 neighbor 166.50.10.4 send-community extended
 exit-address-family
 !
 address-family ipv4 vrf red
 redistribute connected
 redistribute static
 no auto-summary
 no synchronization
 exit-address-family
 !
 address-family ipv4 vrf pink
 redistribute connected
 redistribute static
 default-information originate
 no auto-summary
 no synchronization
 exit-address-family
!
ip route vrf pink 21.2.1.0 255.255.255.0
Loopback11 21.1.1.2
ip route vrf red 20.2.1.0 255.255.255.0
Loopback10 20.1.1.2
!
access-list 10 permit 20.1.1.0 0.0.0.55
route-map OUT-INTER-AS permit 10
 match ip address 10
 set extcommunity rt  200:777 additive
```

```
hostname PE-300
!
ip cef
ip vrf emerald
 rd 300:2
 route-target export 300:2
 route-target export 200:777
 route-target import 300:2
 route-target import 200:2
!
ip vrf green
 rd 300:1
 route-target export 300:1
 route-target export 200:777
 route-target import 300:1
 route-target import 200:1
!
mpls label range 160 1000
!
interface Loopback0
 ip address 156.50.10.3 255.255.255.255
 no ip directed-broadcast
!
interface Loopback10
 ip vrf forwarding green
 ip address 30.1.1.1 255.255.255.0
 no ip directed-broadcast
!
interface Loopback11
 ip vrf forwarding emerald
 ip address 31.1.1.1 255.255.255.0
 no ip directed-broadcast
!
interface Ethernet0/0
 ip address 3.3.3.6 255.255.255.252
 no ip directed-broadcast
 tag-switching ip
!
router ospf 300
 log-adjacency-changes
 network 3.3.3.0 0.0.0.255 area 0
 network 156.50.10.0 0.0.0.255 area 0
!
router bgp 300
 no bgp default ipv4-unicast
 bgp log-neighbor-changes
 neighbor 156.50.10.4 remote-as 300
 neighbor 156.50.10.4 update-source Loopback0
 !
 address-family vpnv4
 neighbor 156.50.10.4 activate
 neighbor 156.50.10.4 send-community extended
 bgp scan-time 15
 bgp scan-time import 10
 exit-address-family
 !
 address-family ipv4 vrf green
 redistribute connected
 no auto-summary
 no synchronization
 exit-address-family
 !
 address-family ipv4 vrf emerald
 redistribute connected
 no auto-summary
 no synchronization
 exit-address-family
```

Figure 2.96

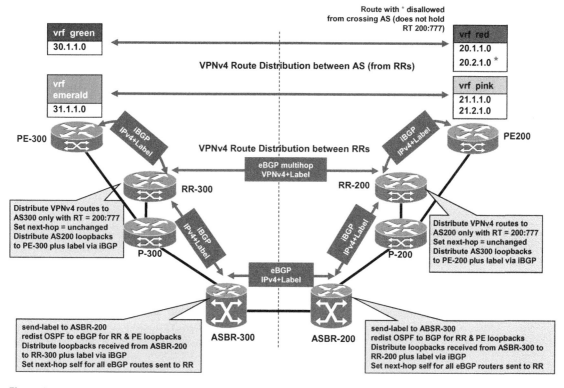

Figure 2.97

3. PE-200 acting as a PE which has two VRFs Red and Pink
4. RR-200 which is the VPNv4 route reflector for AS200
   – AS 300 also has three routers:
1. ASBR-A300 acting as the primary ASBR
2. P-300 acting as P router terminating the RR and the PE
3. PE-300 acting as a PE which has two VRFs Green and Emerald
4. RR-300 which is the route reflector for AS300
   – The ABSRs establish an eBGP session between each other to exchange the IPv4 prefixes of the loopbacks only for the route reflector and the PE router in their respective ASs. The loopbacks of any other infrastructure devices do not need to be exchanged.
   – The ABSRs DO NOT redistribute the received prefixes into the IGP. Instead, the ASBRs establish an iBGP session to the local router reflector. This session passes the IPv4 prefixes (loopbacks) plus the IPv4 labels received from the remote AS via the eBGP session. All routes sent to the RRs will have the next hop set to the

ASBR. This is so the remote ASBR address does not have to be learned in the local AS.

- PE-200 and PE-300 have iBGP sessions to their respective RRs to exchange VPNv4 routing information from their VRFs using the VPNv4 address family. In addition, they exchange IPv4 prefixes (loopbacks) using the IPv4 address family. It is this session that allows the local PE routers to learn of the loopback addresses of the relevant remote PE routers.

- RR-200 and RR-300 have a eBGP session established between them to pass the VPNv4 routes from the VRFs of their PE routers. This eBGP multi-hop session also passes the relevant VPN labels. The eBGP session is logically configured between the two RRs but physically passes across the ASBR interconnect. Peering connectivity is achieved between the RRs because the ASBRs pass the loopbacks of the RRs across the AS boundary via the eBGP session. Then they pass the received loopback address of the remote RR to the local RR over the iBGP session with the appropriate label.

- At no stage do the P routers P-300 and P-200 need to know about the loopback addresses of the remote PE routers or RRs. Therefore RR-200 and RR-300 must have MPLS enabled so an LSP can be made to the ASBR to access the remote RR. If MPLS was not enabled on the RR, then the BGP session would not activate, as the IP packets would black hole at the P routers.

- Normally when a route reflector passes routes over an eBGP session, the BGP next hop of the route (in this case, the PE loopback) would be changed to that of the route reflector. In the Option C InterAS scenario this is not desirable, as the RRs are not part of the forwarding plane; they are merely passing reachability information. Therefore the PE router loopbacks must be kept intact as the next-hop address for all VPNv4 routes. This is achieved by configuring the RRs to keep the next-hop information unchanged across the eBGP session.

- The RRs in both ASs will only distribute routes across the eBGP session if the locally learned VPNv4 route holds 200:777 as one of its route targets/extended community strings. This has the advantage of providing some form of control over which VPNv4 routes the remote AS can see.

- Routes will be exported/imported between VRF Red and Green and also between VRF Pink and Emerald across the inter-AS boundary. That is, there is a corresponding route target import for the remote VRF's route target export for these pairs of VRFs.

– All the VRFs are configured to export an additional route target of 200:777 so that the local RRs will forward all VPNv4 routes in the VRF across the eBGP session. The exception is that VRF Red uses a route-map to set the route target 200:777, providing greater control over which prefixes are allowed across the inter-AS boundary. In the test example, much like the Option B example, we set only route target 200:777 on prefix 20.1.1.0, thereby denying 20.2.1.0 from being seen by the remote AS. With the rest of the VRF all route prefixes are distributed to the remote AS because they are all exported with 200:777.

– To make it easier to visually distinguish label allocations in each AS, the AS300 label allocations start as 160, while AS200 label allocations start at 16.

– All VRF routes from AS200 are in the 20.0.0.0 – 21.0.0.0 range and all VRF routes from AS300 are in the 30.0.0.0 – 31.0.0.0 range.

Figure 2.98 shows the logical layout of the test network. Several loopback addresses are used to generate prefixes within the various VRFs.

VPNv4 Route Distribution Process

Figure 2.99 shows the various steps taken to distribute the VPNv4 route **300:1:30.1.1.0** originating in VRF Green of PE-300 from AS300 to AS200 to PE-200. The steps involve several label distribution mechanisms:

• iBGP + VPNv4 + Label – used between the PE routers and local RRs to distribute VPNv4 information.

• eBGP + VPNv4 + Label – used between the local and remote RRs to distribute information across the AS boundary.

• eBGP + IPv4 + Label – used between ASBR to pass loopback addresses of relevant routers in local AS (RRs and PE routers).

• iBGP + IPv4 + Label – used between RR and PE routers, and between RR and ASBR to distribute the loopback address and labels of the relevant routers in the remote AS. This avoids the infrastructure/core routers from needing to learn about the remote addresses.

• LDP – used in the local AS to distribute labels for all the IGP routes, including in this case the important labels for the ASBR loopbacks.

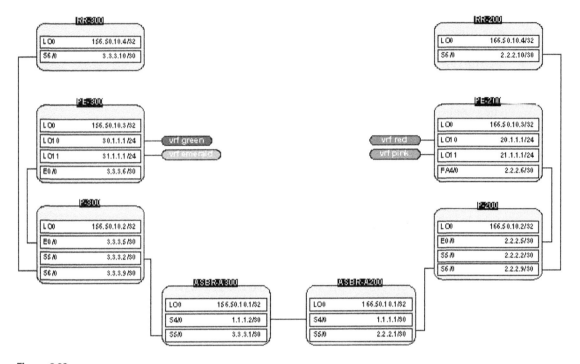

Figure 2.98

As can be seen in Figure 2.99, the sample process concentrates on providing the distribution and relevant connectivity for a route from PE-300 to PE-200. On the AS300 side, IGP routes use LDP to acquire a label. On the AS200 side, the remote IGP routes (PE and RR loopbacks) use eBGP distribute the labels.

• The VPNv4 route 300:1:30.1.1.0 is allocated the BGP label of {165} by PE-300. The BGP next hop is set to the PE-300 loopback 156.50.10.3. The route and VPNv4 label is then distributed via an iBGP session to RR-300 under the VPNv4 address family.

• RR-300 passes the VPNv4 route, label, route targets, and next hop (PE-300) unchanged to RR-200 via the eBGP session across the AS boundary. The session actually passes through the two ASBRs.

• When RR-200 receives the VPNv4 route, it stores it in its VPNV4 table. It is then reflected to all PE clients (in this case, PE-200). Therefore PE-200 receives the reachability information for 300:1:30.1.1.0 exactly as PE-300 has sent it. PE-200 uses label {165} as the bottom (VPN) label. The BGP next hop for the VPN route is 156.50.10.3; however, at this point PE-200 has not learned where 156.50.10.3 is and does not have an entry for it in its routing table. In the IGP routes method, PE-200

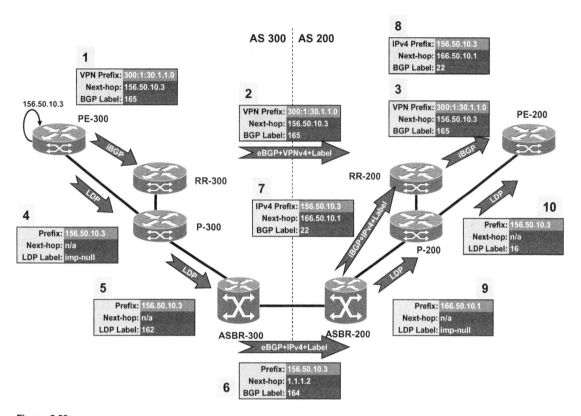

Figure 2.99

would have learned about 156.50.10.3 via OSPF, but that has been disabled in this scenario. PE-200 receive sinformation about 156.50.10.3 via the iBGP session from RR-200.

- In the local AS, PE-300 distributes its loopback (156.50.10.3) via OSPF with an implicit null label (POP) via LDP to P-300.
- P-300 advertises the LDP label {162} towards ASBR-300. This is the IN label P-300 uses for 156.50.10.3
- When ASBR-300 receives the LDP binding for 156.50.10.3, it updates the LFIB with outgoing label {162} and also allocates the incoming label {164}. The route 156.50.10.3 and label {164} are then redistributed from OSPF into eBGP and sent to ASBR-200. The BGP next hop of 156.50.10.3 will be 1.1.1.2, which is the interface address of ASBR-300.
- ASBR-200 will use label {164} across the AS boundary as the outgoing label to reach 156.50.10.3. At this point ASBR-200 will distribute 156.50.10.3 with an associated incoming label {22} to

RR-200 via the iBGP session using the IPv4 address family. The label {22} is the local label allocated by ASBR-200 for 156.50.10.3. An important thing to note is that "next-hop-self" is set on the iBGP session to RR-200; therefore the BGP prefix 156.50.10.3 will have its next hop changed from 1.1.1.2 to 166.50.10.1. Setting the next hop to ASBR-200 obviates the need to distribute the prefix 1.1.1.2 into AS200.

- RR-200 then reflects the received IPv4 route from ASBR-200 to PE-200. At this point, PE-200 has routing knowledge of how to get to PE-300 (156.50.10.3) using the BGP next hop of ASBR-200 (166.50.10.1). It also knows to push label {22} onto the stack for 156.50.10.3 and then LDP label {16} (seen in step 10) when passing traffic to PE-300.

- Now that PE-200 has the relevant routing knowledge for PE-300, the next step is to distribute the LDP labels to create an LSP to ASBR-200. ASBR-200 sends an implicit-null (POP) to P-200.

- P-200 (which has no knowledge of remote AS300 routes) allocates an IN label of {16}, which it passes to PE-200, and uses an OUT label of POP when sending traffic towards ASBR-200.

At the end of this process PE-200 has the three labels using the BGP routes method to send a VPN packet destined to the customer network 30.1.1.0 connected to PE-300, as shown in Figure 2.100. The LSP forwarding with the labels is discussed in the following section.

Label Switch Path Forwarding

This section describes the steps taken to forward traffic from PE-200 to PE-300 via the ASBRs using the various labels received via eBGP, iBGP and LDP. Figure 2.101 shows the labels that get pushed, swapped and popped on the stack as a packet makes its way from PE-200 for a host in destination 30.1.1.0 on PE-300. Since the RRs are not used in the forwarding path, they are not shown in the example.

- PE-200 pushes {16 22 165} on to the stack, with {16} being the top label. Label {16} is used to tunnel the packet over an LSP to ASBR-200. Because of this, no routers in the path between PE-200 and ASBR-200 need to know about the infrastructure address of AS300.

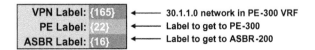

VPN Label: {165}	← 30.1.1.0 network in PE-300 VRF
PE Label: {22}	← Label to get to PE-300
ASBR Label: {16}	← Label to get to ASBR-200

Figure 2.100

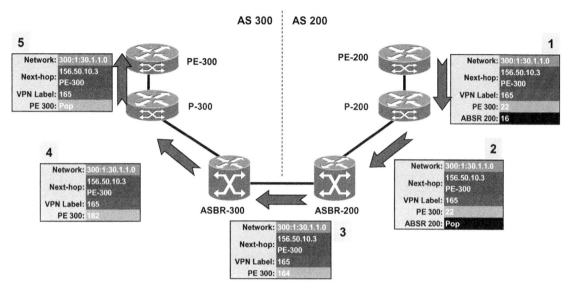

Figure 2.101

- At P-200 the top label {16} is popped and forwarded to ASBR-200. The POP function exposes the label {22}, which is the IN-label ASBR-200 allocated to the loopback of PE-300 (156.50.10.3)
- At ASBR-200 {22} is swapped with {164}, which was the label ASBR-200 received from ASBR-300 via the eBGP + IPV4 session.
- Once in the AS300 network, the packet is forwarded in the normal manner. At ASBR-300 {164} will be swapped with {162} which was received via LDP from P-300
- At P-300 {162} is popped, exposing the VPN label {165}, which is then processed and forwarded into the appropriate VPN by PE-300.

Figure 2.102 shows a trace of the LSP between PE-200 and PE-300. In the output we can see at sequence 0 2.2.2.6 (egress link address at PE-200) the two labels 16/22,[5] representing ASBR-200 and PE-300.[6] Line 1 is P-200 and shows that {16} is popped, exposing {22}. The U indicates that P-200 does not have a routing entry for 156.50.10.3 (see Figure 2.103). However, this is not an issue, as P-200 knows what interface to send the packet out to due to the contents of LFIB entry for {22}.

---

[5]Why the CEF format {16 22} was not used to display the labels remains a mystery.

[6]The VPN label is not used in the trace.

```
PE-200#trace mpls ipv4 156.50.10.3/32 source 166.50.10.3
Tracing MPLS Label Switched Path to 156.50.10.3/32, timeout is 2 seconds

Codes: '!' - success, 'Q' - request not transmitted,
       '.' - timeout, 'U' - unreachable,
       'R' - downstream router but not target,
       'M' - malformed request

Type escape sequence to abort.
  0 2.2.2.6 MRU 1496 [Labels: 16/22 Exp: 0/0]
U 1 2.2.2.5 MRU 1504 [Labels: 22 Exp: 0] 64 ms
R 2 2.2.2.1 MRU 1500 [Labels: 164 Exp: 0] 124 ms
R 3 1.1.1.2 MRU 1500 [Labels: 162 Exp: 0] 120 ms
. 4 *
! 5 3.3.3.6 136 ms
```

Figure 2.102 Trace from PE-200 to PE-300

Figure 2.103 LIB Entry on P-200 of PE-200

```
P-200#show mpls ldp bind 156.50.10.3 32
  tib entry: 156.50.10.3/32, rev 26(no route)
      remote binding: tsr: 166.50.10.1:0, tag: 22
```

Line 4 is of interest, as it has timed out. This entry represents P-300, which does not have any information about how to get back to 166.50.10.3, the source of the trace. Again this is because the core routers do not need to be aware of the infrastructure routes of the remote AS for the LSP to work.

Router PE-200 VPN

Routing and Forwarding (VRF) Tables Figure 2.104 shows the routing table on VRF Red, which is identical to what was used with the IGP routes method. The BGP next hop for the imported VPN route 30.1.1.0 remains 156.50.10.3 (PE-300).

BGP IPv4 Table Figure 2.105 shows the actual BGP entry for PE-300. As can be seen, label {22} has been sent, along with other network reachability information. Therefore PE-200 knows it must push {22} for any traffic leading to 30.1.1.0 in the VRF.

BGP VPNv4 Table Figure 2.106 shows the VPNv4 entry in the BGP table for 30.1.1.0. It is identical to the IGP routes method, as at this point nothing is different from when that method is used. The RRs use the eBGP+VPNv4+Labels session to pass the VPN route associated attributes. The VPN label remains {165}.

CEF Table Figure 2.107 shows the CEF entry for 30.1.1.0. This is where differences from the IGP routes method begin to show. As can be seen, VPN packets bound for 30.1.1.0 from PE-200 have {16 22 165} pushed onto the stack. Label {16} is derived from

```
PE-200#show ip route vrf red

Routing Table: red
Codes: C - connected, S - static, I - IGRP, R - RIP, M - mobile, B - BGP
       D - EIGRP, EX - EIGRP external, O - OSPF, IA - OSPF inter area
       N1 - OSPF NSSA external type 1, N2 - OSPF NSSA external type 2
       E1 - OSPF external type 1, E2 - OSPF external type 2, E - EGP
       i - IS-IS, su - IS-IS summary, L1 - IS-IS level-1, L2 - IS-IS level-2
       ia - IS-IS inter area, * - candidate default, U - per-user static
route
       o - ODR

Gateway of last resort is not set

     20.0.0.0/24 is subnetted, 2 subnets
C       20.1.1.0 is directly connected, Loopback10
S       20.2.1.0 [1/0] via 20.1.1.2, Loopback10
     30.0.0.0/24 is subnetted, 1 subnets
B       30.1.1.0 [200/0] via 156.50.10.3, 1d06h
```

Figure 2.104 VRF Red on PE-200

```
PE-200#show ip bgp 156.50.10.3
BGP routing table entry for 156.50.10.3/32, version 26
Paths: (1 available, best #1)
  Not advertised to any peer
  300
    166.50.10.1 (metric 59) from 166.50.10.4 (166.50.10.4)
      Origin incomplete, metric 59, localpref 100, valid, internal, best
      Originator: 166.50.10.1, Cluster list: 166.50.10.4,
      mpls labels in/out nolabel/22
```

Figure 2.105 BGP Entry for PE-300 on PE-200

```
PE-200#show ip bgp vpnv4 all 30.1.1.0
BGP routing table entry for 200:1:30.1.1.0/24, version 38
Paths: (1 available, best #1, table red)
  Not advertised to any peer
  300, imported path from 300:1:30.1.1.0/24
    156.50.10.3 (metric 59) from 166.50.10.4 (166.50.10.4)
      Origin incomplete, metric 0, localpref 100, valid, internal, best
      Extended Community: RT:200:777 RT:300:1,
      mpls labels in/out nolabel/165
BGP routing table entry for 300:1:30.1.1.0/24, version 36
Paths: (1 available, best #1, no table)
  Not advertised to any peer
  300
    156.50.10.3 (metric 59) from 166.50.10.4 (166.50.10.4)
      Origin incomplete, metric 0, localpref 100, valid, internal, best
      Extended Community: RT:200:777 RT:300:1,
      mpls labels in/out nolabel/165
```

Figure 2.106 BGP VPNv4 Table on PE-200

```
PE-200#show ip cef vrf red 30.1.1.0
30.1.1.0/24, version 13, epoch 0, cached adjacency 2.2.2.5
0 packets, 0 bytes
  tag information set, all rewrites owned
    local tag: VPN route head
    fast tag rewrite with Et0/0, 2.2.2.5, tags imposed {16 22 165}
  via 156.50.10.3, 0 dependencies, recursive
    next hop 2.2.2.5, Ethernet0/0 via 156.50.10.3/32 (Default)
    valid cached adjacency
    tag rewrite with Et0/0, 2.2.2.5, tags imposed {16 22 165}
```

Figure 2.107 CEF Table for PE-200

LDP identifying ASBR-200. Label {22} is derived from eBGP + IPv4 + Label originating from ASBR-200 (but received from RR-200) to identify the label to use for PE-300, while label {165} is derived from BGP via the route reflectors and identifies the VPN label.

Routing Table Figure 2.108 shows the routing table on PE-200. There are no OSPF external routes. Instead, the loopbacks for RR-300 and PE-300 (156.50.10.x) appear as BGP routes, having been distributed from ASBR-200 via RR-200. Note that the BGP next hop for both of these remote routes is 166.50.10.1 (ASBR-200).

The process is as follows:

- When PE-200 sends a packet to the VPN subnet 30.1.1.0, it uses the BGP next hop of PE-300 (see Figure 2.104).

```
PE-200#show ip route
Codes: C - connected, S - static, I - IGRP, R - RIP, M - mobile, B - BGP
       D - EIGRP, EX - EIGRP external, O - OSPF, IA - OSPF inter area
       N1 - OSPF NSSA external type 1, N2 - OSPF NSSA external type 2
       E1 - OSPF external type 1, E2 - OSPF external type 2, E - EGP
       i - IS-IS, su - IS-IS summary, L1 - IS-IS level-1, L2 - IS-IS level-2
       ia - IS-IS inter area, * - candidate default, U - per-user static
route
       o - ODR

Gateway of last resort is not set

     2.0.0.0/30 is subnetted, 3 subnets
O       2.2.2.0 [110/58] via 2.2.2.5, 5w6d, Ethernet0/0
C       2.2.2.4 is directly connected, Ethernet0/0
O       2.2.2.8 [110/58] via 2.2.2.5, 5w6d, Ethernet0/0
     156.50.0.0/32 is subnetted, 2 subnets
B       156.50.10.4 [200/97] via 166.50.10.1, 1d07h
B       156.50.10.3 [200/59] via 166.50.10.1, 1d07h
     166.50.0.0/32 is subnetted, 4 subnets
O       166.50.10.4 [110/59] via 2.2.2.5, 5w6d, Ethernet0/0
O       166.50.10.2 [110/11] via 2.2.2.5, 5w6d, Ethernet0/0
C       166.50.10.3 is directly connected, Loopback0
O       166.50.10.1 [110/59] via 2.2.2.5, 5w6d, Ethernet0/0
```

Figure 2.108 Routing Table on PE-200

- The rule is: if a route is derived from BGP, then the PE will look for the corresponding label for the BGP next hop and push it onto the stack (along with the VPN label).
- In this case there is a BGP next hop (156.50.10.3), which itself is a BGP route.
- Therefore we need to get the BGP next hop of 156.50.10.3, which happens to be 166.50.10.1 (ASBR-200).
- This label is then pushed onto the stack as well; hence the process ends up with three labels.
- In reality, the three labels are already set up by CEF; hence only a single CEF lookup is required to push all three labels onto the stack.

Label Forwarding Information Base (LFIB) Figure 2.109 shows the LFIB on PE-200. Note that there are no AS300 routes in the LFIB. However, RR-200 (166.50.10.4) does have an entry, which means it is using MPLS. In the IGP route method it did not need to use MPLS. The reason is explained in the next section.

VRF Configuration The VRF configuration for PE-200 is unchanged from that shown in Figure 2.44 on page 116.

Route Reflector RR-200 The RR-200 route reflector peers with RR-300 using eBGP, PE-200, and ABSR-200 using iBGP. It passes the VPNv4 routes received from AS300 onwards to the client PE routers (in this case PE-200). It also passes the remote IPv4 routes received from ASBR-200 to client PE routers. In this case. they are the loopbacks for PE-300 and RR-300 in AS300.

Label Forwarding Information Base (LFIB) The RRs must have MPLS enabled. This is different from the normal notion that RRs are routers-on-a-stick and do not lie in the forwarding path for MPLS traffic. Figure 2.110 shows the LFIB for RR-200. The only entries are for local IGP routes.

The reason MPLS is necessary is so that a path is available between RR-200 and RR-300 to form an eBGP session. Since P-

```
PE-200#sh tag for
Local  Outgoing    Prefix          Bytes tag  Outgoing   Next Hop
tag    tag or VC   or Tunnel Id    switched   interface
16     Pop tag     2.2.2.0/30      0          Et0/0      2.2.2.5
17     Pop tag     2.2.2.8/30      0          Et0/0      2.2.2.5
18     16          166.50.10.1/32  0          Et0/0      2.2.2.5
19     Pop tag     166.50.10.2/32  0          Et0/0      2.2.2.5
20     17          166.50.10.4/32  0          Et0/0      2.2.2.5
21     Aggregate   20.1.1.0/24[V]  9304
22     Aggregate   20.2.1.0/24[V]  0
23     Aggregate   21.1.1.0/24[V]  0
24     Aggregate   21.2.1.0/24[V]  0
```

Figure 2.109 LFIB for PE-200

```
RR-200#show tag for
Local  Outgoing    Prefix          Bytes tag  Outgoing    Next Hop
tag    tag or VC   or Tunnel Id    switched   interface
16     Pop tag     2.2.2.0/30      0          Se6/0       point2point
17     Pop tag     2.2.2.4/30      0          Se6/0       point2point
18     Pop tag     166.50.10.2/32  0          Se6/0       point2point
19     18          166.50.10.3/32  0          Se6/0       point2point
20     16          166.50.10.1/32  0          Se6/0       point2point
```

Figure 2.110 LFIB on RR-200

```
RR-200#show ip bgp ipv4 unicast
BGP table version is 7, local router ID is 166.50.10.4
Status codes: s suppressed, d damped, h history, * valid, > best, i -
internal,
            r RIB-failure, S Stale
Origin codes: i - IGP, e - EGP, ? - incomplete

   Network           Next Hop          Metric LocPrf Weight Path
*>i156.50.10.3/32   166.50.10.1            59    100      0 300 ?
*>i156.50.10.4/32   166.50.10.1            97    100      0 300 ?
```

Figure 2.111 BGP IPv4 Entries on RR-200

200 does not have any knowledge of the remote routes, RR-200 must use an LSP to get to ASBR-200 and then onwards to AS300.

BGP IPv4 Table Figure 2.111 shows the remote AS300 addresses learned from ASBR-200 (166.50.10.1) that have been installed into the BGP IPv4 table. For RR-200 to form an eBGP peering relationship with RR-300 it must first learn RR-300's loopback address (156.50.10.4), which it does via iBGP + IPv4 + Label from ASBR-200

Since ASBR-200 also passed the label for 156.50.10.4, as shown in Figure 2.112, it can set up the appropriate label stack {16 23} to form the eBGP peering.

CEF Table Figure 2.113 validates the label stack that will be imposed via CEF to form the eBGP peering session in order to receive the VPNv4 routes from RR-300.

```
RR-200#show ip bgp ipv4 unicast 156.50.10.4
BGP routing table entry for 156.50.10.4/32, version 3
Paths: (1 available, best #1)
  Advertised to update-groups:
     1
  300, (Received from a RR-client)
    166.50.10.1 (metric 97) from 166.50.10.1 (166.50.10.1)
      Origin incomplete, metric 97, localpref 100, valid, internal, best,
      mpls labels in/out nolabel/23
```

Figure 2.112 Label for RR-300

```
RR-200#show ip cef 156.50.10.4
156.50.10.4/32, version 17, epoch 0, cached adjacency to Serial6/0
0 packets, 0 bytes
  tag information set, all rewrites owned
    local tag: BGP route head
    fast tag rewrite with Se6/0, point2point, tags imposed {16 23}
  via 166.50.10.1, 0 dependencies, recursive
    next hop 2.2.2.9, Serial6/0 via 166.50.10.1/32 (Default)
    valid cached adjacency
    tag rewrite with Se6/0, point2point, tags imposed {16 23}
```

Figure 2.113 RR-300 CEF Table Entry

```
RR-200#show ip bgp vpnv4 all
BGP table version is 13, local router ID is 166.50.10.4
Status codes: s suppressed, d damped, h history, * valid, > best, i -
internal,
              r RIB-failure, S Stale
Origin codes: i - IGP, e - EGP, ? - incomplete

   Network          Next Hop        Metric LocPrf Weight Path
Route Distinguisher: 200:1
*>i20.1.1.0/24      166.50.10.3         0    100      0 ?
*>i20.2.1.0/24      166.50.10.3         0    100      0 ?
Route Distinguisher: 200:2
*>i21.1.1.0/24      166.50.10.3         0    100      0 ?
*>i21.2.1.0/24      166.50.10.3         0    100      0 ?
Route Distinguisher: 300:1
*> 30.1.1.0/24      156.50.10.3                       0 300 ?
Route Distinguisher: 300:2
*> 31.1.1.0/24      156.50.10.3                       0 300 ?
```

Figure 2.114 BGP VPNv4 Table on RR-200

BGP VPNv4 Table Now that the eBGP session has been established over an LSP to RR-300, the VPNv4 routes can be exchanged. Figure 2.114 shows that the VPNv4 table in RR-200 looks exactly like it did for the IGP routes method.

In the example we can see that RR-200 holds six VPNv4 routes originating from PE-200 (next hop 166.50.10.3) or PE-300 in the other AS (156.50.10.3), as shown by the entries with Path 300.

Figure 2.115 shows the detailed entry for VPNv4 prefix 300:1:30.1.1.0. This prefix has been received from 156.50.10.4, which is RR-300 in the remote AS. The relevant community string has been passed, as well as the next hop of PE-300 and also the VPN label {165}.

Configuration Figure 2.116 shows the relevant configuration for RR-200. MPLS configured is enabled on the interface facing P-200. The OSPF configuration to provide routing in the local AS is particularly simple.

```
RR-200#show ip bgp vpnv4 all 30.1.1.0
BGP routing table entry for 300:1:30.1.1.0/24, version 13
Paths: (1 available, best #1, no table)
  Advertised to update-groups:
     1
  300
    156.50.10.3 (metric 1) from 156.50.10.4 (156.50.10.4)
      Origin incomplete, localpref 100, valid, external, best
      Extended Community: RT:200:777 RT:300:1,
      mpls labels in/out nolabel/165
```

Figure 2.115 VPNv4
Route Detail

The BGP configuration has three peers:
- An iBGP session to 166.50.10.3 (PE-200) for IPv4 and VPNv4 addresses
- An iBGP session to 166.50.10.1 (ASBR-200) for IPv4 addresses
- An eBGP session to 156.50.10.4 (RR-300) for VPNv4 addresses

Two address families are defined for IPv4 and VPNv4 addresses. The IPv4 address family has PE-200 and ASBR-200 as member. The "send-label" keyword notifies the neighbor that this session has the capability to receive and send MPLS labels along with the IPv4 address. This keyword must appear at both neighbors for labels to be passed in the BGP update.

The VPNv4 address family allows VPN routes to be received from RR-300 and then reflected to PE-200. The route-map provides filtering capability so that no VPNv4 routes will be passed to the other AS unless they hold the extended community 200:777 (previously added by the VRF route target).

ASBR 200 The ASBRs are responsible for passing the loopback addresses of the route reflectors and of the relevant PE routers holding VPNv4 routes that need to cross the AS boundary. The RR loopbacks are necessary so that an eBGP peering session can be established between the RRs across the ABSR, while the PE router loopbacks are necessary so an MPLS LSP can be provisioned end-to-end between the PE routers (for VPN traffic).

BGP IPv4 Table The BGP table looks the same whether the BGP routes method or IGP routes method is used. The ASBRs do not carry any VPNv4 information, as would be the case in Option B. These ASBRs only contain the IPv4 addresses in the BGP table, as shown in Figure 2.117. Due to the filtering configured on the peering sessions, only the loopback addresses are maintained in the IPv4 table.

Figure 2.118 shows the LDP labels associated with the PE-300 loopback from AS300. As can be seen, there is an in and out label.

```
interface Serial6/0
 ip address 2.2.2.10 255.255.255.252
 no ip directed-broadcast
 tag-switching ip
 no cdp enable
!
router ospf 200
 log-adjacency-changes
 network 2.2.2.8 0.0.0.3 area 0
 network 166.50.10.0 0.0.0.255 area 0
!
router bgp 200
 no bgp default ipv4-unicast
 bgp log-neighbor-changes
 neighbor 156.50.10.4 remote-as 300
 neighbor 156.50.10.4 description RR-300
 neighbor 156.50.10.4 ebgp-multihop 10
 neighbor 156.50.10.4 update-source Loopback0
 neighbor 166.50.10.1 remote-as 200
 neighbor 166.50.10.1 description ASBR-200
 neighbor 166.50.10.1 update-source Loopback0
 neighbor 166.50.10.3 remote-as 200
 neighbor 166.50.10.3 description PE-200
 neighbor 166.50.10.3 update-source Loopback0
 !
 address-family ipv4
 neighbor 166.50.10.1 activate
 neighbor 166.50.10.1 route-reflector-client
 neighbor 166.50.10.1 send-label
 neighbor 166.50.10.3 activate
 neighbor 166.50.10.3 route-reflector-client
 neighbor 166.50.10.3 send-label
 no auto-summary
 no synchronization
 exit-address-family
 !
 address-family vpnv4
 neighbor 156.50.10.4 activate
 neighbor 156.50.10.4 send-community extended
 neighbor 156.50.10.4 next-hop-unchanged
 neighbor 156.50.10.4 route-map INTER-AS out
 neighbor 166.50.10.3 activate
 neighbor 166.50.10.3 send-community extended
 neighbor 166.50.10.3 route-reflector-client
 exit-address-family
!
ip classless
!
ip extcommunity-list 10 permit rt 200:777
!
no cdp run
route-map INTER-AS permit 10
 match extcommunity 10
```

Figure 2.116 RR-200 Configuration

```
ABSR-200#show ip bgp
BGP table version is 7, local router ID is 166.50.10.1
Status codes: s suppressed, d damped, h history, * valid, > best, i -
internal,
            r RIB-failure, S Stale
Origin codes: i - IGP, e - EGP, ? - incomplete

    Network          Next Hop         Metric LocPrf Weight Path
*> 156.50.10.3/32    1.1.1.2             59             0 300 ?
*> 156.50.10.4/32    1.1.1.2             97             0 300 ?
*> 166.50.10.3/32    2.2.2.2             59         32768 ?
*> 166.50.10.4/32    2.2.2.2             97         32768 ?
```

Figure 2.117 BGP IPv4 Table in ASBR 200

```
ABSR-200#show ip bgp 156.50.10.3
BGP routing table entry for 156.50.10.3/32, version 6
Paths: (1 available, best #1)
  Not advertised to any peer
  300
    1.1.1.2 from 1.1.1.2 (156.50.10.1)
      Origin incomplete, metric 59, localpref 100, valid, external, best,
      mpls labels in/out 22/164
```

Figure 2.118 IPv4 Labels in ASBR-200

The out label {164} was received from ASBR-300 and is used as the topmost label for packet traveling across the ASBR interconnect towards PE-300. Label {22} is the in label LDP label advertised to upstream neighbors in AS200. So label {22} will be used by upstream neighbours in AS200 and then will be swapped with label {164} to go out across the ASBR connection.

Label Forwarding Information Base (LFIB) Figure 2.119 shows the LFIB for ASBR-200. The entry for 156.50.10.3 (PE-300) matches the in/out labels in the BGP IPv4 entry. Again, the LFIB looks the same regardless of which route distribution method is used.

ASBR Configuration Figure 2.120 shows the relevant configuration to enable BGP to send labels for IPv4 prefixes to both ASBR-300 and RR-200. Notice that there is no redistribution of routes into OSPF, as the BGP routes method is being used.

Under the IPv4 address family, the AS300-OUTBOUND route-map ensures that only the relevant loopbacks from AS200 are passed through to AS300. In addition, each neighbor has a "send-label" keyword that will include the label for the associated prefix as part of the BGP update. Labels {22} and {23} (Figure 2.119) will be distributed with the remote AS300 routes to RR-200.

The last but still important part of the configuration is that the "next-hop-self" is set on any IPv4 prefixes distributed to RR-200

```
ABSR-200#sh mpls for
Local   Outgoing      Prefix           Bytes tag   Outgoing    Next Hop
tag     tag or VC     or Tunnel Id     switched    interface
16      Pop tag       2.2.2.4/30       0           Se5/0       point2point
17      Pop tag       2.2.2.8/30       0           Se5/0       point2point
18      Pop tag       166.50.10.2/32   0           Se5/0       point2point
19      17            166.50.10.4/32   1152660     Se5/0       point2point
20      18            166.50.10.3/32   0           Se5/0       point2point
21      Pop tag       1.1.1.2/32       0           Se4/0       point2point
22      164           156.50.10.3/32   2272        Se4/0       point2point
23      163           156.50.10.4/32   1803850     Se4/0       point2point
```

Figure 2.119 LFIB on ASBR-200

```
router ospf 200
 log-adjacency-changes
 redistribute bgp 200
 network 2.2.2.0 0.0.0.255 area 0
 network 166.50.10.0 0.0.0.255 area 0
!
router bgp 200
 no bgp default ipv4-unicast
 bgp log-neighbor-changes
 neighbor 1.1.1.2 remote-as 300
 neighbor 166.50.10.4 remote-as 200
 neighbor 166.50.10.4 update-source Loopback0
 !
 address-family ipv4
 redistribute ospf 200 route-map AS300-OUTBOUND
 neighbor 1.1.1.2 activate
 neighbor 1.1.1.2 send-label
 neighbor 166.50.10.4 activate
 neighbor 166.50.10.4 next-hop-self
 neighbor 166.50.10.4 send-label
 no auto-summary
 no synchronization
 exit-address-family
!
ip extcommunity-list 10 permit rt 200:777
!
ip access-list standard AS200-Loopbacks
 permit 166.50.10.4
 permit 166.50.10.3
ip access-list standard AS300-Loopbacks
 permit 156.50.10.4
 permit 156.50.10.3
access-list 1 permit any
route-map AS300-OUTBOUND permit 10
 match ip address AS200-Loopbacks
!
route-map AS300-INBOUND permit 10
 match ip address AS300-Loopbacks
 match mpls-label
!
route-map INTER-AS permit 10
 match extcommunity 10
!
```

Figure 2.120 ASBR-200 Configuration

(166.50.10.4). This is to ensure that a return path to AS300 will always be via ASBR-200 using an LSP. A similar configuration is done on the AS300 side.

Configuration listings (Option C – BGP Method) are given in Figures 2.121, 2.122, and 2.123.

Summary

Option A

- Option A is the simplest of all interconnects. However, it is not particularly scalable and should be limited to a small number of VRFs (in the 10s possibly to minimize operation complexity).
- A big advantage of Option A, however, is that VPN specific operations, such as rate limiting, can be done at the boundary point.

Option B

- Option B is most suitable when two service providers are under independent authoritative control. They only need to exchange VPNv4 routes and the boundary; therefore, the only touch required is between the ASBRs.
- Always configure inbound route-maps to filter only routes that need to be passed to the other AS. Not only does this conserve memory on both sides of the boundary, it also implements a simple form of security.
- Using next-hop-self requires an additional entry in the LFIB for each VPNv4 route (about 180) bytes. This is not likely to be an issue with routers with a lot of memory.
- If the service provider wishes to hide the inter-AS link, the next-hop-self method should be used; otherwise, use the redistribute connected subnets method.

Option C

- Option C requires some element of trust between the providers, as the RRs must peer with each other (they may not be the ASBRs and could be further into the network). Therefore it is most suitable where the Autonomous Systems being connected are under the same authoritative control, such as a service provider who wants to interconnect several different ASs it owns (this could be due to acquisitions or designating specific ASs for certain services, e.g., corporate versus public Internet).
- Two route distribution methods can be deployed to advertise remote IPv4 addresses:

ABSR-200	ABSR-300
| ```
hostname ABSR-A200
!
ip cef
!
interface Loopback0
 ip address 166.50.10.1 255.255.255.255
 no ip directed-broadcast
!
interface Serial4/0
 ip address 1.1.1.1 255.255.255.252
 no ip directed-broadcast
 mpls bgp forwarding
 no fair-queue
!
interface Serial5/0
 ip address 2.2.2.1 255.255.255.252
 no ip directed-broadcast
 tag-switching ip
!
router ospf 200
 log-adjacency-changes
 redistribute bgp 200
 network 2.2.2.0 0.0.0.255 area 0
 network 166.50.10.0 0.0.0.255 area 0
!
router bgp 200
 no bgp default ipv4-unicast
 bgp log-neighbor-changes
 neighbor 1.1.1.2 remote-as 300
 neighbor 166.50.10.4 remote-as 200
 neighbor 166.50.10.4 update-source Loopback0
 !
 address-family ipv4
 redistribute ospf 200 route-map AS300-OUTBOUND
 neighbor 1.1.1.2 activate
 neighbor 1.1.1.2 send-label
 neighbor 166.50.10.4 activate
 neighbor 166.50.10.4 next-hop-self
 neighbor 166.50.10.4 send-label
 no auto-summary
 no synchronization
 exit-address-family
!
ip access-list standard AS200-Loopbacks
 permit 166.50.10.4
 permit 166.50.10.3
ip access-list standard AS300-Loopbacks
 permit 156.50.10.4
 permit 156.50.10.3
access-list 1 permit any
route-map AS300-OUTBOUND permit 10
 match ip address AS200-Loopbacks
!
route-map AS300-INBOUND permit 10
 match ip address AS300-Loopbacks
 match mpls-label
``` | ```
hostname ABSR-A300
!
ip cef
mpls label range 160 1000
!
interface Loopback0
 ip address 156.50.10.1 255.255.255.255
 no ip directed-broadcast
!
interface Serial4/0
 ip address 1.1.1.2 255.255.255.252
 no ip directed-broadcast
 mpls bgp forwarding
 no fair-queue
!
interface Serial5/0
 ip address 3.3.3.1 255.255.255.252
 no ip directed-broadcast
 tag-switching ip
!
router ospf 300
 log-adjacency-changes
 redistribute bgp 300
 network 3.3.3.0 0.0.0.255 area 0
 network 156.50.10.0 0.0.0.255 area 0
!
router bgp 300
 no bgp default ipv4-unicast
 bgp log-neighbor-changes
 neighbor 1.1.1.1 remote-as 200
 neighbor 156.50.10.4 remote-as 300
 neighbor 156.50.10.4 update-source Loopback0
 !
 address-family ipv4
 redistribute ospf 300 route-map AS200-OUTBOUND
 neighbor 1.1.1.1 activate
 neighbor 1.1.1.1 send-label
 neighbor 156.50.10.4 activate
 neighbor 156.50.10.4 next-hop-self
 neighbor 156.50.10.4 send-label
 no auto-summary
 no synchronization
 exit-address-family
!
ip access-list standard AS200-Loopbacks
 permit 166.50.10.4
 permit 166.50.10.3
ip access-list standard AS300-Loopbacks
 permit 156.50.10.4
 permit 156.50.10.3
route-map AS200-OUTBOUND permit 10
 match ip address AS300-Loopbacks
!
route-map AS200-INBOUND permit 10
 match ip address AS200-Loopbacks
 match mpls-label
``` |

Figure 2.121

- The IGP route method requires all routes in the local AS to be aware of infrastructure routes in the remote AS.
- The BGP route method hides infrastructure routes to all local routers except the associated PE routers and route reflectors.

RR-200	RR-300

<pre>hostname RR-200
!
ip cef
!
interface Loopback0
 ip address 166.50.10.4 255.255.255.255
 no ip directed-broadcast
!
interface Serial6/0
 ip address 2.2.2.10 255.255.255.252
 no ip directed-broadcast
 tag-switching ip
 no cdp enable
!
router ospf 200
 log-adjacency-changes
 network 2.2.2.8 0.0.0.3 area 0
 network 166.50.10.0 0.0.0.255 area 0
!
router bgp 200
 no bgp default ipv4-unicast
 bgp log-neighbor-changes
 neighbor 156.50.10.4 remote-as 300
 neighbor 156.50.10.4 description RR-300
 neighbor 156.50.10.4 ebgp-multihop 10
 neighbor 156.50.10.4 update-source Loopback0
 neighbor 166.50.10.1 remote-as 200
 neighbor 166.50.10.1 description ASBR-200
 neighbor 166.50.10.1 update-source Loopback0
 neighbor 166.50.10.3 remote-as 200
 neighbor 166.50.10.3 description PE-200
 neighbor 166.50.10.3 update-source Loopback0
 !
 address-family ipv4
 neighbor 166.50.10.1 activate
 neighbor 166.50.10.1 route-reflector-client
 neighbor 166.50.10.1 send-label
 neighbor 166.50.10.3 activate
 neighbor 166.50.10.3 route-reflector-client
 neighbor 166.50.10.3 send-label
 no auto-summary
 no synchronization
 exit-address-family
 !
 address-family vpnv4
 neighbor 156.50.10.4 activate
 neighbor 156.50.10.4 send-community extended
 neighbor 156.50.10.4 next-hop-unchanged
 neighbor 156.50.10.4 route-map INTER-AS out
 neighbor 166.50.10.3 activate
 neighbor 166.50.10.3 send-community extended
 neighbor 166.50.10.3 route-reflector-client
 exit-address-family
!
ip extcommunity-list 10 permit rt 200:777
!
route-map INTER-AS permit 10
 match extcommunity 10</pre>
	<pre>hostname RR-300
	!
	ip cef
	!
	interface Loopback0
	 ip address 156.50.10.4 255.255.255.255
	 no ip directed-broadcast
	!
	interface Serial6/0
	 ip address 3.3.3.10 255.255.255.252
	 no ip directed-broadcast
	 tag-switching ip
	 no cdp enable
	!
	router ospf 300
	 log-adjacency-changes
	 network 3.3.3.4 0.0.0.3 area 0
	 network 3.3.3.8 0.0.0.3 area 0
	 network 156.50.10.0 0.0.0.255 area 0
	!
	router bgp 300
	 no bgp default ipv4-unicast
	 bgp log-neighbor-changes
	 neighbor 156.50.10.1 remote-as 300
	 neighbor 156.50.10.1 description ASBR-300
	 neighbor 156.50.10.1 update-source Loopback0
	 neighbor 156.50.10.3 remote-as 300
	 neighbor 156.50.10.3 description PE-300
	 neighbor 156.50.10.3 update-source Loopback0
	 neighbor 166.50.10.4 remote-as 200
	 neighbor 166.50.10.4 description RR-200
	 neighbor 166.50.10.4 ebgp-multihop 10
	 neighbor 166.50.10.4 update-source Loopback0
	 !
	 address-family ipv4
	 neighbor 156.50.10.1 activate
	 neighbor 156.50.10.1 send-label
	 neighbor 156.50.10.3 activate
	 neighbor 156.50.10.3 route-reflector-client
	 neighbor 156.50.10.3 send-label
	 no auto-summary
	 no synchronization
	 exit-address-family
	 !
	 address-family vpnv4
	 neighbor 156.50.10.3 activate
	 neighbor 156.50.10.3 send-community extended
	 neighbor 156.50.10.3 route-reflector-client
	 neighbor 166.50.10.4 activate
	 neighbor 166.50.10.4 send-community extended
	 neighbor 166.50.10.4 next-hop-unchanged
	 neighbor 166.50.10.4 route-map INTER-AS out
	 exit-address-family
	!
	ip extcommunity-list 10 permit rt 200:777
	!
	route-map INTER-AS permit 10
	 match extcommunity 10</pre>

Figure 2.122

PE-200	PE-300
| ```
hostname PE-200
!
ip cef
ip vrf pink
 rd 200:2
 route-target export 200:2
 route-target export 200:777
 route-target import 200:2
 route-target import 300:2
!
ip vrf red
 rd 200:1
 export map OUT-INTER-AS
 route-target export 200:1
 route-target import 200:1
 route-target import 300:1
!
tag-switching tdp router-id Loopback0
!
interface Loopback0
 ip address 166.50.10.3 255.255.255.255
 no ip directed-broadcast
!
interface Loopback10
 ip vrf forwarding red
 ip address 20.1.1.1 255.255.255.0
 no ip directed-broadcast
!
interface Loopback11
 ip vrf forwarding pink
 ip address 21.1.1.1 255.255.255.0
 no ip directed-broadcast
!
interface Ethernet0/0
 ip address 2.2.2.6 255.255.255.252
 no ip directed-broadcast
 tag-switching ip
!
router ospf 200
 log-adjacency-changes
 network 2.2.2.0 0.0.0.255 area 0
 network 166.50.10.0 0.0.0.255 area 0
!
router bgp 200
 no bgp default ipv4-unicast
 bgp log-neighbor-changes
 neighbor 166.50.10.4 remote-as 200
 neighbor 166.50.10.4 update-source Loopback0
 !
 address-family ipv4
 neighbor 166.50.10.4 activate
 neighbor 166.50.10.4 send-label
 default-information originate
 no auto-summary
 no synchronization
 exit-address-family
 !
 address-family vpnv4
 neighbor 166.50.10.4 activate
 neighbor 166.50.10.4 send-community extended
 exit-address-family
 !
 address-family ipv4 vrf red
 redistribute connected
 redistribute static
 no auto-summary
 no synchronization
 exit-address-family
 !
 address-family ipv4 vrf pink
 redistribute connected
 redistribute static
 default-information originate
 no auto-summary
 no synchronization
 exit-address-family
 !
 ip route vrf pink 21.2.1.0 255.255.255.0
 Loopback11 21.1.1.2
 ip route vrf red 20.2.1.0 255.255.255.0
 Loopback10 20.1.1.2
 !
 access-list 10 permit 20.1.1.0 0.0.0.55
 route-map OUT-INTER-AS permit 10
  match ip address 10
   set extcommunity rt  200:777 additive
``` | ```
hostname PE-300
!
ip cef
ip vrf emerald
 rd 300:2
 route-target export 300:2
 route-target export 200:777
 route-target import 300:2
 route-target import 200:2
!
ip vrf green
 rd 300:1
 route-target export 300:1
 route-target export 200:777
 route-target import 300:1
 route-target import 200:1
!
mpls label range 160 1000
!
interface Loopback0
 ip address 156.50.10.3 255.255.255.255
 no ip directed-broadcast
!
interface Loopback10
 ip vrf forwarding green
 ip address 30.1.1.1 255.255.255.0
 no ip directed-broadcast
!
interface Loopback11
 ip vrf forwarding emerald
 ip address 31.1.1.1 255.255.255.0
 no ip directed-broadcast
!
interface Ethernet0/0
 ip address 3.3.3.6 255.255.255.252
 no ip directed-broadcast
 tag-switching ip
!
router ospf 300
 log-adjacency-changes
 network 3.3.3.0 0.0.0.255 area 0
 network 156.50.10.0 0.0.0.255 area 0
!
router bgp 300
 no bgp default ipv4-unicast
 bgp log-neighbor-changes
 neighbor 156.50.10.4 remote-as 300
 neighbor 156.50.10.4 description RR-300
 neighbor 156.50.10.4 update-source Loopback0
 !
 address-family ipv4
 neighbor 156.50.10.4 activate
 neighbor 156.50.10.4 send-label
 no auto-summary
 no synchronization
 exit-address-family
 !
 address-family vpnv4
 neighbor 156.50.10.4 activate
 neighbor 156.50.10.4 send-community extended
 bgp scan-time 15
 bgp scan-time import 10
 exit-address-family
 !
 address-family ipv4 vrf green
 redistribute connected
 no auto-summary
 no synchronization
 exit-address-family
 !
 address-family ipv4 vrf emerald
 redistribute connected
 no auto-summary
 no synchronization
 exit-address-family
 !
``` |

Figure 2.123

- An advantage of Option C is that the route reflectors already carry all the VPN routes; therefore the ASBRs are limited to just passing the relevant IGP routes.

Advanced Next Generation Multicast over Layer 3 VPNs

This section examines how multicast can be delivered over MPLS Layer 3 VPNs. It focuses on using architecture called BGP Next Generation Multicast using MPLS as a transport vehicle.

NG-MVPN Control Plane

The Next Generation Multicast VPN (NG-MVPN) framework is based on the following Internet drafts:
- BGP encodings and procedures for multicast in BGP/MPLS VPNs (draft-ietf-l3vpn-2547bis-mcast-bgp)
- Multicast in BGP/MPLS VPNs (draft-ietf-l3vpn-2547bis-mcast)

The NG-MVPN control plane within the provider network is based on BGP signaling. In other words, BGP is used for exchanging both VPNv4 unicast and multicast information, thus replacing the need for PIM with the provider IP/MPLS network. The use of a single control plane protocol for all IP/MPLS-based services, such as IPv4 Internet prefixes, VPNv4 for both unicast and multicast, and IPv6, results in decreased operational overheads and also offers a simplified and converged control plane infrastructure. In the context of NG-MVPNs, BGP is used for the following functions:
- Autodiscovery of PE routers within a given NG-MVPN instance.
- Exchange of data plane (from this point onwards, the data plane is referred to as Provider-tunnel or P-tunnel) information between provider edge routers. In the context of NG-MVPN, details of the type and identifier of the tunnel used for transmitting C-MCAST traffic are advertised from the ingress PE to all relevant egress PE routers.
- Exchange of C-MCAST routing information. All joins from the customer domain (CE routers) are announced to the relevant PE routers within the context of a given NG-MVPN.

The introduction of the BGP control plane does not impose any restrictions in the customer multicast domain. CE routers continue to use PIM between the CE-PE links, as with Draft-Rosen. Therefore the introduction of NG-MVPNs or the migration of customers using Draft-Rosen to the NG-MVPN scheme (which is discussed in detail later in this chapter) does not warrant any re-design or changes to the customer infrastructure. A seamless migration for customer multicast infrastructures is one of the advantages NG-MVPN offers.

Regarding the BGP control plane, the 2547bis-mcast-bgp draft introduces a new BGP address family called MCAST-VPN for supporting NG-MVPN control plane operations. The new address family is assigned the subsequent address family identifier (SAFI) of 5 by IANA.

A PE router that participates in a BGP-based NG-MVPN network is required to send a BGP update message that contains an MCAST-VPN NLRI. An MCAST-VPN NLRI contains route type, length, and variable fields (illustrated in detail later in this chapter). The value of the variable field depends on the route type. Seven types of NG-MVPN BGP routes, also known as MVPN routes, are specified. The first five route types are called autodiscovery (AD) MVPN routes. This chapter also refers to Type 1-5 routes as non-C-multicast MVPN routes. Type 6 and Type 7 routes are called C-multicast MVPN routes.

Figure 2.124 provides details on the MVPN routes used.

Ingress and Egress PE routers

The term "ingress PE router" refers to a PE router which has an active C-MCAST source for a given NG-MVPN. Egress PE routers are referred also as leaf nodes, indicating that they are endpoints for a given C-MCAST traffic flow. One of the advantages of the NG-MVPN architecture is the ability to designate a PE router as a "Sender and Receiver" site or a "Receiver Only" site. The former indicates the specified PE router that can both originate and receive

Route	Definition
Type 1 Intra-AS I-PMSI AD	Originated by all PE routers and used for advertising and learning Intra-AS MVPN membership information.
Type 2 Inter-AS I-PMSI AD	Originated by NG-MVPN ASBR routers and used for advertising and learning inter-AS MVPN membership information.
Type 3 S-PMSI AD	Originated by Ingress PE routers and used for initiating a selective P-Tunnel for a given C-Source and C-Group multicast stream.
Type 4 Leaf AD	Originated by Egress PE routers in response to a Type 3 announcement. It used for indicating interest for a given C-Source and C-Group multicast stream.
Type 5 Source Active AD	Originated by a PE router (Ingress PE) when it learns about an active Multicast source. The Type 5 route is announced to all egress PEs that belong to a given NG-MVPN.
Type 6 Shared Tree Join	Originated by an egress PE when it receives a PIM Shared Tree join (C-*, C-G) from the CE device.
Type 7 Source Tree Join	Originated by an egress PE when it receives a Source Tree Join, or when it receives a Type 5 route announcement from an Ingress PE.

Figure 2.124

C-MCAST traffic, while the latter indicates a PE router that is only able to receive traffic. This is discussed further in later sections.

Provider Multicast Service Interface (PMSI)

A few of the BGP route types for NG-MVPNs named above include the term "PMSI." Let us discuss this concept in some detail, since it forms a key part of the MVPN architecture.

The NG-MVPN architecture uses a Provider Multicast Service Interface (PMSI) to simplify and generalize different options for the MVPN solution. PMSI distinguishes between services and the transport mechanism that support and realize the concept. When a PE gives a packet to PMSI, the underlying transport mechanisms, P-tunnels, deliver the packet to some or all of the other PEs. A PMSI is a conceptual "overlay" on the provider network with the following property: a PE in a given MVPN can give a packet to the PMSI, and the packet will be delivered to some or all of the other PEs in the MVPN, such that any PE receiving the packet can determine the MVPN to which the packet belongs. For instance, an ingress PE router may want to send C-MCAST traffic only to a given set of PE routers who express interest in the traffic, or send it to all PE routers that participate in a given MVPN whether they have interested receivers or not. This is achieved by attaching an appropriate PMSI attribute to the BGP routes.

The PMSI types are:
- Inclusive PMSI (I-PMSI)
- Selective PMSI (S-PMSI)

I-PMSI may be considered a unidirectional P2MP connection between an ingress PE and all egress PE routers. Therefore if a BGP route announcement (for example, a Type 1 BGP route used for autodiscovery) has an attached I-PMSI attribute, all traffic from the ingress PE router is delivered to every other PE router participating in a given NG-MVPN. This behavior can be compared to the operation of the Default MDT in a Draft-Rosen MVPN.

Selective PMSI (S-PMSI) may be considered a subset of the I-PMSI where a packet is delivered to a subset of PE routers participating in a given MVPN. This behavior can be compared to the Data MDT in Draft-Rosen.

The format of the PMSI Tunnel Attribute is displayed in Figure 2.125.

The Tunnel Type indicates the options available within the context of NG-MVPNs. Compared to Draft-Rosen, where PIM-GRE was the only option available for transport of multicast traffic, the NG-MVPN provides multiple options, including RSVP-TE, MLDP, and also traditional PIM GRE-based schemes as options for

Carried in BGP MCAST-VPN A-D route Updates to identify PMSI Tunnels

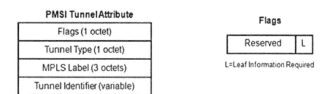

Tunnel Type: RSVP-TE P2MP, LDP P2MP, PIM-SSM, PIM-SM, PIM-BIDIR, Ingress Replication, LDP MP2MP

MPLS Label (high order 20 bits): the de-multiplexer value on aggregate trees (or zero)

Tunnel Identifier (format dependent on tunnel type):
    RSVP-TE: contents of SESSION object, < P2MP ID, Tunnel ID, Extended Tunnel ID >
    PIM: <sender IP address, P-multicast address>

Leaf information flag used to solicit Leaf auto-discovery routes for explicit tracking

    E.g. from remote PEs with interest in <C-S,C-G> when setting up an S-PMSI

Figure 2.125

provider tunnels (transport mechanisms). Each of these options will be discussed in subsequent sections.

The MPLS Label indicates the label assigned. It is always set to "zero", since both I-PMSI and S-PMSI tunnels always correspond to a single MVPN instance. MVPN differentiation is based on other values used in the BGP MVPN routes such as RD values, which uniquely identify a BGP/MPLS VPN.

The Tunnel Identifier uniquely identifies the P-tunnel. In this illustration we use RSVP-TE as an example for indicating the construct of a Tunnel Identifier.

Flag indicates whether the PMSI is an I-PMSI or an S-PMSI. A flag value of "0" indicates an I-PMSI, and "1" indicates an S-PMSI. In the case of an S-PMSI, interested leaf nodes need to identify themselves (similar to a Default MDT in Draft-Rosen); hence the only available flag is "Leaf Information Required." An example of an I-PMSI attribute attached to a BGP Type 1 route is provided in Figure 2.126.

Note: The discussion of NG_MVPN in this chapter focuses on the JUNOS CLI and related configurations and outputs. However the information provided here also applies other vendor implementations, since the JUNOS implementation completely adheres to the NG-MVPN IEFT draft. Other vendor implementations are covered in the subsequent chapters.

```
operator@PE1# run show route table FOO-MVPN.mvpn.0 detail
1:100:1:7.0.0.1/240 (1 entry, 1 announced)
*BGP      Preference: 170/-101
PMSI: Flags 0:RSVP-TE:label[0:0:0]:Session_13[7.0.0.1:0:28754:7.0.0.1]
[Output is Truncated]
```

Figure 2.126 I-PMSI Attribute

BGP MVPN Routes

Let us look at the various BGP MVPN routes in more detail to understand how they are used.

BGP Type 1 Autodiscovery Routes

Every NG-MVPN provider edge router advertises a BGP Type 1 route for each NG-MVPN hosted. For instance, if a PE router is connected to three NG-MVPN customer sites, three BGP Type 1 routes are created and announced to every NG-MVPN PE in the network. The format for a Type 1 AD route is illustrated in Figure 2.127.

The RD field indicates the route distinguisher, which is configured under the BGP/MPLS VPN, and is set to this value when the PE announces a Type 1 route. The field "Originating Router IP Address" is always set to the IPv4 loopback address of the originating PE router. Let us take a look at a sample output from a JUNOS-based PE router that displays a BGP Type 1 route. (See Figure 2.128.) In this example, there are three PE routers including the local PE router.

In the first entry "1:100:1:7.0.0.1/240," the entry "1"indicates a BGP Type 1 AD route type. The next part, 100:1, indicates the configured RD for the given BGP/MPLS NG-MVPN. "7.0.0.1" indicates the loopback IPv4 address of the PE. Finally, the field "BGP" indicates that this route was learned via BGP. The third entry in the illustration indicates that the local PE router with address "7.0.0.5" has created a Type 1 route entry for itself that is ready

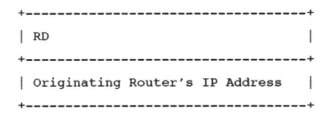

Figure 2.127

```
operator@PE1# run show route
1:100:1:7.0.0.1/240
                        *[BGP/170] 3d 02:04:45, localpref 100, from 7.0.0.1
                          AS path: I
                        > to 172.16.1.1 via ge-1/0/1.0, Push 300144
1:100:1:7.0.0.4/240
                        *[BGP/170] 5d 03:21:21, localpref 100, from 7.0.0.4
                          AS path: I
                        > to 172.16.1.1 via ge-1/0/1.0
1:100:1:7.0.0.5/240
                        *[MVPN/70] 5d 03:42:50, metric2 1
                          Indirect
[Output is Truncated]
```

Figure 2.128 BGP Type 1 AD Route

to be announced to other participating PE routers within the context of the same NG-MVPN instance. These concepts will become clearer as we progress through the following sections.

BGP Type 3 and Type 4 S-PMSI Routes

An ingress PE router signals a Type 3 BGP route for the creation of the S-PMSI. The creation of the S-PMSI is based on a variety of criteria, such as traffic thresholds (as used in Draft-Rosen Data MDT creation). Upon receiving the Type 3 BGP routes, egress PE routers with interested receivers respond to the announcement by advertising a Type 4 route. After this step, an ingress PE router creates the appropriate P-tunnel. Figure 2.129 shows the Type 3 and Type 4 routes on an ingress PE.

BGP Type 5 Source Active Routes

Type 5 routes carry information about active VPN sources and the groups to which they are transmitting data. These routes can

```
operator@PE1# run show route
3:100:1:32:192.168.1.9:32:236.1.1.1:7.0.0.1/240
        *MVPN    Preference: 70
                 Next hop type: Indirect
                 Next-hop reference count: 4
                 Protocol next hop: 7.0.0.1
                 Indirect next hop: 0 -

4:3:100:1:32:192.168.1.9:32:236.1.1.1:7.0.0.1:7.0.0.4/240
        *BGP     Preference: 170/-101
                 Next hop type: Indirect
                 Source: 7.0.0.4
                 Protocol next hop: 7.0.0.4
[Output is Truncated]
```

Figure 2.129 Type 3 and 4 Routes Displayed on the Ingress PE Router

be generated by any PE router that becomes aware of an active source. Type 5 routes apply only for PIM-SM (ASM) when inter-site source–tree-only mode is being used. A Type 5 route is illustrated in Figure 2.130 and Figure 2.131.

BGP Type 6 and Type 7 Routes

The C-multicast route exchange between PE routers refers to the propagation of C-joins from receiver PEs to sender PEs. In an NG-MVPN, C-joins are translated into (or encoded as) BGP C-multicast MVPN routes and advertised via BGP MCAST-VPN address family to the sender PEs. Two types of C-multicast MVPN routes are specified.

- Type 6 C-multicast routes are used in representing information contained in a shared tree (C-*, C-G) join.
- Type 7 C-multicast routes are used in representing information contained in a source tree (C-S, C-G) join.

NG-MVPN provides optimization in handling additional state information that is created in a shared tree environment, where every C-MCAST Source needs to register itself with the C-RP, and the receivers need to join the shared tree via the RP. Traffic flows initially over this shared tree, prior to moving to the SPT

```
operator@PE1# run show route
5:100:1:32:192.168.1.9:32:236.1.1.1/240 (1 entry, 1 announced)
        *PIM    Preference: 105
                Next hop type: Multicast (IPv4)
                State: <Active Int>
[Output is Truncated]
```

Figure 2.130 Type 5 Routes Displayed on the Ingress PE Router

```
operator@PE1# run show route
5:100:1:32:192.168.1.9:32:236.1.1.1/240 (1 entry, 1 announced)
        *BGP    Preference: 170/-101
                Next hop type: Indirect
                Next-hop reference count: 6
                Source: 7.0.0.1
                Protocol next hop: 7.0.0.1
                Indirect next hop: 2 no-forward
                State: <Secondary Active Int Ext>
                Local AS:    100 Peer AS:    100
                Localpref: 100
                Router ID: 7.0.0.1
[Output is Truncated]
```

Figure 2.131 Type 5 Routes Displayed on the Egress PE Router

or shortest path to the source. Prior to joining the SPT, the receivers send PRUNE messages to the RP to stop the traffic flowing through it for the group they have joined via the SPT. The RP further triggers another PRUNE towards the source, and now traffic flows via the source tree or SPT. This process increases the state information in the network, and causes additional complexity which adds no value, since traffic ends up flowing via the SPT eventually.

NG-MVPN by default provides a solution for this RPT to SPT switchover. Whenever an egress PE router generates a Type 6 BGP route for every PIM join (C-*, C-G) it receives from the customer multicast domain, it does not advertise this route to remote PE routers, unless it receives information of an active source by means of a Type 5 route. Sources by default do not register themselves with the RP; rather their locally connected router (CE device in the case of NG-MVPN) sends a unicast packet to the RP with the source's data packets encapsulated. In order for the PE routers to learn about active sources, two conditions need to be met.

- One of the PE routers needs to be designated as the customer RP.
- An MSDP session needs to be established between the PE router and customer RP.

It is only through one of the above procedures that a PE router (let's call it RP-PE) learns of an active source and generates a BGP Type 5 route. PE routers with interested receivers will generate a Type 7 route towards the ingress PE (not towards the RP) forming the SPT. A sample output taken from a PE router designated as a C-RP, with PIM register messages from a C-MCAST source is shown in Figure 2.132. A PIM Register message has been sent from a PE router with address "7.0.0.1" for a Source "192.168.1.9" at Group "235.1.1.12" to the RP at address "7.0.0.4".

Since the RP knows about an active source, a BGP Type 5 route will be originated. Figure 2.133 illustrates the format of a Type 5 route.

Figure 2.134 shows a real-life example.

A corresponding Type 7 route generated by the egress PE received at the engress PE is shown in Figure 2.135.

As we have seen, NG-MVPN's default mode of operation provides advantages. However, it requires that either the customer rendezvous point (C-RP) is located on a PE router or the Multicast Source Discovery Protocol (MSDP) is used between the C-RP and a PE router so the PE router can learn about active sources advertised by other PE routers.

```
operator@PE1# run show pim rps extensive instance NG-MVPN
Instance: PIM.NG-MVPN
RP: 7.0.0.4
Learned via: static configuration
Time Active: 01:59:32
Holdtime: 0

Register State for RP:
Group          Source          FirstHop        RP Address      State
235.1.1.1      192.168.1.9     7.0.0.1         7.0.0.4         Receive
[Output is Truncated]
```

Figure 2.132 PIM Register Messages Received by PE Acting as C-RP

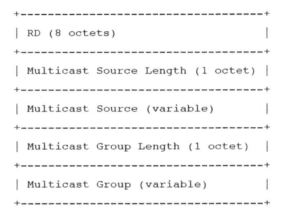

Figure 2.133

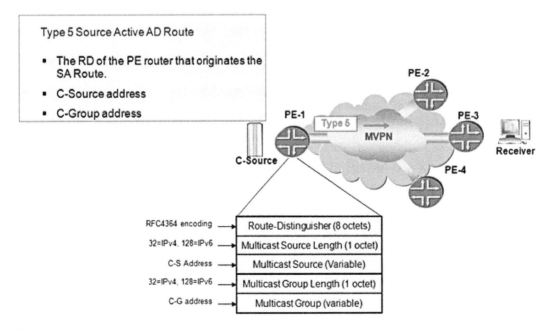

Figure 2.134

```
operator@PE1# run show route
7:100:1:100:32:192.168.1.9:32:235.1.1.1/240
*[PIM/105] 00:00:05
Multicast (IPv4)
[BGP/170] 00:00:05, localpref 100, from 7.0.0.4 ----------> Type 7 received
from Egress PE router PE2.
AS path: I
> to 172.16.1.5 via ge-4/0/0.0
[Output is Truncated]
```

Figure 2.135 Type 7 Route at the Ingress PE

If the default mode is not suitable for a given environment, RPT-SPT mode (also known as shared tree data distribution) can be configured, as documented in section 13 of the BGP-MVPN draft (draft-ietf-l3vpn-2547bis-mcast-bgp.txt). RPT-SPT mode supports the native PIM model of transmitting (*,G) messages from the receiver to the RP for inter-site shared tree join messages. This means that the Type 6 (*,G) routes get transmitted from one PE router to another. In RPT-SPT mode, the shared tree multicast routes are advertised from an egress PE router to the upstream router connected to the VPN site with the C-RP. The single-forwarder election is performed for the C-RP rather than for the source. The egress PE router takes the upstream hop to advertise the (*,G) and sends the Type 6 route towards the upstream PE router. After the data starts flowing on the RPT, the last-hop router switches to SPT mode, unless "spt-threshold infinity" statements are included in the configuration.

The switch to SPT mode is performed by PIM and not by MVPN type 5 and type 6 routes. After the last-hop router switches to SPT mode, the SPT (S,G) join messages follow the same rules as the SPT-only default mode.

The advantage of RPT-SPT mode is that it provides a method for PE routers to discover sources in the multicast VPN when the C-RP is located on the customer site instead of on a PE router. Because the shared C-tree is established between VPN sites, there is no need to run MSDP between the C-RP and the PE routers. RPT-SPT mode also enables egress PE routers to switch to receiving data from the PE connected to the source after the source information is learned, instead of receiving data from the RP. Let us look at an illustration of a Type 6 route. In Figure 2.136 we note the announcement of Type 6 routes from PE routers with C-MCAST (C-*, C-G) joins sent to the upstream

```
operator@PE1# run show route
6:100:1:100:32:8.0.0.4:32:237.1.1.1/240
                    *[PIM/105] 00:00:06
                       Multicast (IPv4)
                       [BGP/170] 00:00:06, localpref 100, from 7.0.0.5
                         AS path: I
                       > to 172.16.1.2 via ge-4/0/0.0
6:100:1:100:32:8.0.0.4:32:238.1.1.1/240
                    *[PIM/105] 00:00:06
                       Multicast (IPv4)
                       [BGP/170] 00:00:06, localpref 100, from 7.0.0.5
                         AS path: I
                       > to 172.16.1.2 via ge-4/0/0.0
6:100:1:100:32:8.0.0.4:32:239.1.1.2/240
                    *[PIM/105] 00:00:06
                       Multicast (IPv4)
                       [BGP/170] 00:00:06, localpref 100, from 7.0.0.5
                         AS path: I
                       > to 172.16.1.2 via ge-4/0/0.0
        [Output is Truncated]
```

Figure 2.136 Type 6 Routes Displayed on the PE Router Connected to the C-RP (CE)

PE (PE closest to the RP). These routes are further announced as PIM Joins towards the C-RP.

Customer Multicast Routing Information and Route Targets

Based on the details discussed in the previous sections, it is now clear that C-multicast MVPN routes (Type 6 and Type 7) are only useful to the PE router connected to the active C-S or C-RP. Therefore, C-multicast routes need to be installed only in the VRF table on the active sender PE for a given C-G in the case of SPT or Shortest Path Tree or in the PE router closest to the C-RP or acting as the C-RP in the case of RPT mode – where Type 6 routes are installed.

To accomplish this, "2547bis-mcast" proposes to attach a special dynamic RT to C-multicast MVPN routes, as illustrated in Figure 2.137.

The RT attached to C-multicast routes is also called "C-multicast import RT" and should not to be confused with rt-import used for importing unicast routing information. Note that C-multicast MVPN routes differ from other MVPN routes in one essential way: they carry a dynamic RT whose value depends on the identity of the active sender PE at a given time and may change if the active PE changes.

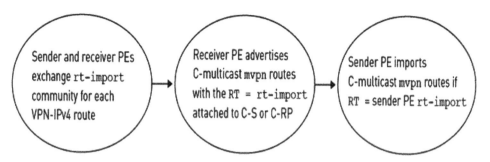

Figure 2.137

A PE router that receives a local C-join determines the identity of the active sender PE router by performing a unicast route lookup for the C-S or C-RP in the unicast VRF table. It chooses the appropriate upstream PE, also known as the active sender. After the active sender (upstream) PE is selected, the receiver PE constructs the C-multicast MVPN route corresponding to the local C-join. Once the C-multicast route is constructed, the receiver PE needs to attach the correct RT to this route targeting the active sender PE. As mentioned, each PE router creates a unique VRF route import (rt-import) community and attaches it to the VPN-IPv4 routes. When the receiver PE does a route lookup for C-S or C-RP, it can extract the value of the rt-import associated with this route and set the value of C-multicast import RT to the value of rt-import. On the active sender PE, C-multicast routes are imported only if they carry an RT whose value is the same as the rt-import that the sender PE generated. Figure 2.138 illustrates an output of this value, displayed on a sender PE.

In the output, the field "COMMUNITIES: TARGET: 7.0.0.1:5" indicates the import RT being set by the PE router with an IPv4 address of "7.0.0.1," and "5" is a random value chosen. Therefore any Type 6 or Type 7 route with this target attached will be accepted by the PE. Other PE routers receiving this route will ignore the route, since the import target does not match.

Let us also look at the fields set by the egress PE for this update. See Figure 2.139 and Figure 2.140.

Figure 2.141 shows the fields that constitute a C-MCAST route used in NG-MVPNs.

In Figure 2.141, we see that the Multicast source field is set to either C-Source or C-RP, depending on whether it is a source tree join or shared tree join. For a source tree join (Type 7 route), the source address is known by means of a type route announcement. Therefore this address is used in this field. On the other hand, a

```
operator@PE1# run show route
7:100:1:100:32:192.168.1.9:32:236.1.1.1/240 (2 entries, 2 announced)
                    BGP      Preference: 170/-101
                    Next hop type: Indirect
                    Next-hop reference count: 4
                    Source: 7.0.0.4
                    Protocol next hop: 7.0.0.4
                    Local AS:    100 Peer AS:    100
                    Age: 4:30        Metric2: 1
                    Task: BGP_100.7.0.0.4+51285
                    AS path: I
                    Communities: target:7.0.0.1:5
                    Import Accepted
                    Localpref: 100
                    Router ID: 7.0.0.4
        [Output is Truncated]
```

Figure 2.138 RT Import Community on the Ingress or Sender PE

```
operator@PE2# run show route
7:100:1:100:32:192.168.1.9:32:236.1.1.1/240 (2 entries, 2 announced)
*MVPN    Preference: 70
Next hop type: Multicast (IPv4), Next hop index: 1048575
Next-hop reference count: 19
Communities: target:7.0.0.1:5 ----→ Appropriate Target set
   [Output is Truncated]
```

Figure 2.139 RT Import Community on the Egress or Receiver PE

```
operator@PE1# run show route
6:100:1:100:32:8.0.0.4:32:230.1.1.1/240
                    BGP      Preference: 170/-101
                    Next hop type: Indirect
                    Next-hop reference count: 4
                    Source: 7.0.0.4
                    Protocol next hop: 7.0.0.4
                    Communities: target:7.0.0.1:5
                    Import Accepted
                    Localpref: 100
                    Router ID: 7.0.0.4
        [Output is Truncated]
```

Figure 2.140 Type 6 Route with the RT Import Community on the PE Closest to C-RP

Type 6 route does not know the source for a given group, so the RP address is entered in this field. Let us take another look at the Type 6 and Type 7 routes to make this clear. See Figure 2.142.

The address "8.0.0.4" indicated in the first line of the output is the address of a C-RP, since this is a shared tree join. The same field will have an IP sddress of the C-Source if it is a source tree join, in the case of a Type 7 route, as shown in Figure 2.143.

BGP Control Plane with MVPN Address Family

- Type of C-Multicast route (Shared/Source Tree Join)
- The RD of the route that advertises the multicast source into the VPN, or C-RP which is set to the Upstream PE router
- The multicast source AS
- C-Group address
- C-Source address or C-RP address
- The C-multicast route should also carry a Route Target Extended Community identifying the Selected Upstream Multicast Hop
- To remove (prune) itself from the C-multicast tree, the PE withdraws the corresponding BGP update (MP_UNREACH_NLRI)

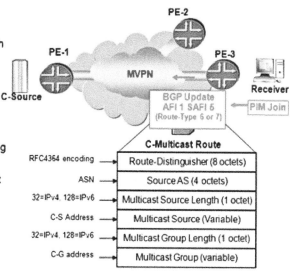

Figure 2.141

```
operator@PE2# run show route
6:100:1:100:32:8.0.0.4:32:230.1.1.1/240 (2 entries, 2 announced)
            BGP     Preference: 170/-101
            Next hop type: Indirect
            Next-hop reference count: 6
            Source: 7.0.0.1
            Protocol next hop: 7.0.0.1
            Local AS:    100 Peer AS:    100
            Age: 55         Metric2: 1
            Task: BGP_100.7.0.0.1+179
            Communities: target:7.0.0.4:5
            Import Accepted
            Localpref: 100
            Router ID: 7.0.0.1
      [Output is Truncated]
```

Figure 2.142 Type 6 Route with the Source Field Set to the C-RP

The address "192.168.1.9" indicated in the first line of the output is the address of a C-Source.

Putting the Building Blocks into Perspective

The points discussed regarding the steps involved in the BGP control plane for enabling multicast traffic flow within an

```
operator@PE2# run show route
7:100:1:100:32:192.168.1.9:32:230.1.1.1/240 (2 entries, 2 announced)
                BGP     Preference: 170/-101
                Next hop type: Indirect
                Next-hop reference count: 4
                Source: 7.0.0.1
                Protocol next hop: 7.0.0.1
                Indirect next hop: 2 no-forward
                State: <Secondary Int Ext>
                Inactive reason: Route Preference
                Local AS:   100 Peer AS:    100
                Age: 4:30       Metric2: 1
                AS path: I
                Communities: target:7.0.0.4:5
                Import Accepted
                Localpref: 100
                Router ID: 7.0.0.1
[Output is Truncated]
```

Figure 2.143 Type 7 Route with the Source Field Set to the C-Source

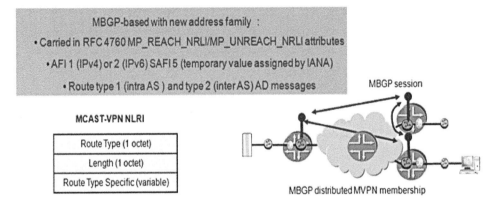

Figure 2.144

NG-MVPN are summarized in the following list. Illustrations are included for each task. See Figure 2.144 and Figure 2.145.

1. MVPN Membership and Autodiscovery
2. MVPN Membership and Autodiscovery+I-PMSI setup. The illustration uses PIM-SM as the P-tunnel, since other MPLS based P-tunnels, such as RSVP-TE, have not yet been discussed.

A PIM-SM P-tunnel uses an ASM group address (similar to default MDT in Draft Rosen), such as 239.1.1.1 which we have used above. A NG-MVPN with PIM-SM or PIM-SSM uses GRE encapsulation and is similar to Draft Rosen with the exception of using the superior BGP control plane. Some providers opt for

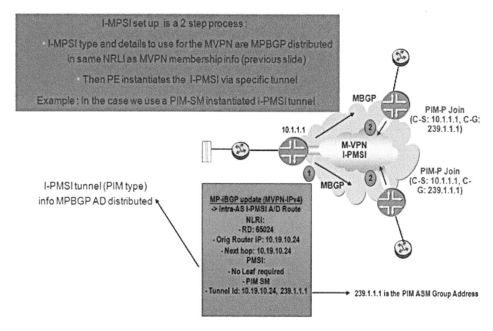

Figure 2.145

```
PMSI: 0:PIM-SM:label[0:0:0]:Sender10.1.1.1 Group 239.1.1.1
```
Figure 2.146

this model as a first step to migrate to NG-MVPNs, wherein the control plane is changed and the data plane is still preserved. It can be considered as an option for a phased migration. However the idea in this illustration is to demonstrate the setup of a BGP Type 1 route along with the I-PMSI setup.

I-PMSI field with a PIM-SM provider tunnel would look as shown in Figure 2.146.

1. Receivers come online and C-JOIN messages are sent to the receiver PE routers. The receiver PE routers perform a route lookup for C-S and C-RP, respectively, and extract the RD, rt-import, and src-as associated with each route. A PE with an interested receiver for a given group originates a Type 7 route upon receiving a Type 5 route, carrying RT information (value matching rt-import); a PE without an interested receiver creates a Type 6 route, but does not advertise it. See Figure 2.147.

2. Finally, the ingress PE compares the received Type 7 routes with the import-RT of itself, and, based on a match, the route is accepted and then passed onto the C-PIM infrastructure.

Route type 6 (share tree join), route type 7 (source tree join)

MCAST-VPN NLRI

| Route Type (1 octet) |
| Length (1 octet) |
| Route Type Specific (variable) |

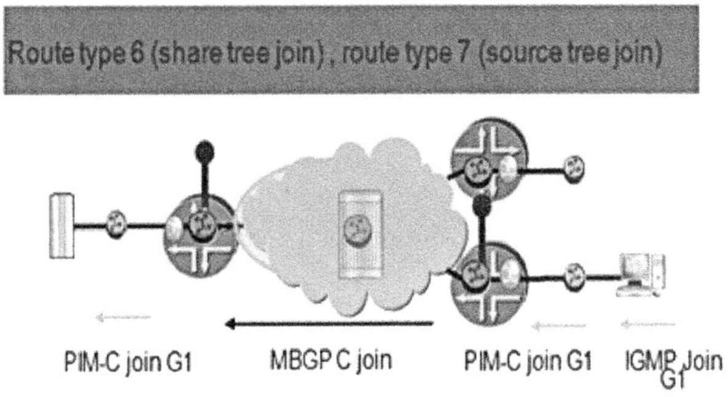

PIM-C join G1   MBGP C join   PIM-C join G1   IGMP Join G1

Figure 2.147

NG-MVPN Data Plane – Provider Tunnels

In this section, we move on to the data plane setup, where one of several supported options may be used for setting up provider tunnels in the network in order to facilitate C-MCAST traffic flows. The NG-MVPN framework currently provides support for the provider tunnels shown in Figure 2.148.

In theory, each NG-MVPN can be set up to use a different provider tunnel or data plane. However, this is unlikely, since operators prefer to use a single provider tunnel, much the way all unicast traffic uses a single data plane, such as RSVP-TE as an example. However the NG-MVPN framework permits an operator to use different data plane protocols for unicast traffic and for multicast traffic. P-tunnels are rooted at the ingress PE (sender), and receiver PEs join a given P-tunnel which signaled, based on either the NG-MVPN they belong to or C-MCAST receiver interest.

The sender PE goes through two steps when setting up the data plane. First, using the PMSI attribute, it advertises the P-tunnel it will be using via BGP using a Type 1 route. SEcond, it signals the

Tunnel Type 0 = No Tunnel Information is Present
Tunnel Type 1 = RSVP-TE Point-to-Multipoint LSP
Tunnel Type 2 = MLDP Point-to-Multipoint LSP
Tunnel Type 3 = PIM-Source Specific Multicast
Tunnel Type 4 = PIM-Sparse Mode Tree
Tunnel Type 5 = PIM-Bidirectional Tree
Tunnel Type 6 = Ingress Replication
Tunnel Type 7 = MLDP MP2MPLSP

Figure 2.148

tunnel, using whatever tunnel signaling protocol is configured for that VPN. This allows receiver PE routers to bind the tunnel that is being signaled to the VPN that imported the Type 1 intra-AS AD route. Binding a P-tunnel to a VRF table enables a receiver PE router to map the incoming traffic from the core network on the P-tunnel to the local target VRF table.

Point-to-Multipoint LSPs

In the illustration provided in the previous section, there was a reference to P2MP LSPs (point-to-multipoint LSPs). At the beginning of this chapter, we discussed the need for an MPLS-based transport for MVPN traffic, in contrast to using PIM GRE as an overlay. One of the key benefits we discussed was the need for a converged platform for all traffic types, multicast and unicast, which uses MPLS-based transport and a PIM free core. From an NG-MVPN point of view, there are two provider tunnel options that use MPLS as a transport mechanism: RSVP-TE and MLDP (Multicast LDP). All the other provider tunnels use GRE-based transport similar to Draft-Rosen, with the exception that the control plane is based on BGP (except ingress replication, which is discussed later in this chapter).

Figure 2.149 shows the hierarchy from an NG-MVPN BGP-based control plane with P2MP LSPs.

The signaling and setup of P2MP LSPs are discussed in the following sections.

MVPN Routing Tables in JUNOS

As mentioned earlier, at the time of this book's writing, NG-MVPNs are supported only on Juniper platforms. Therefore all of the applied examples of NG-MVPN in this chapter are focused on JUNOS. Hence it is important to understand the routing table infrastructure that JUNOS uses for NG-MVPN purposes. The components are shown in Figure 2.150.

RSVP-TE Provider Tunnels

In this section we move into the setup of provider tunnels and their signaling. RSVP-TE-based provider tunnels enable P2MP LSPs for an NG-MVPN, providing all the benefits of P2MP replication as discussed in the previous section. In addition, all standard RSVP-TE functionality, such as MPLS TE Fast Re-route (Only Link Protection), can be used for protecting both resource reservation and unicast and multicast traffic.

RSVP-TE P2MP LSPs can be used to signal both I-PMSI and S-PMSI tunnels. If a VPN is configured to use an inclusive P-tunnel, the sender PE signals one P2MP LSP for the VPN. If a

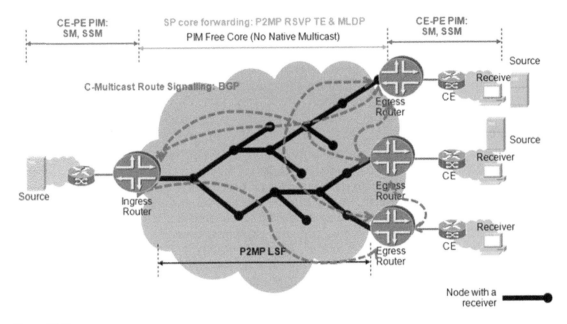

Figure 2.149

Automatically Generated Routing Table	Description
`bgp.l3vpn.0`	Populated with VPN-IPv4 routes received from remote PE routers via INET-VPN address family. The routes in the `bgp.l3vpn.0` table are in the form of `RD:IPv4-Address` and carry one or more `RT` communities. In an NG MVPN network, these routes also carry `rt-import` and `src-as` communities.
`bgp.mvpn.0`	Populated by mvpn routes (Type 1 – Type 7) received from remote PE routers via the MCAST-VPN address family. Routes in this table carry one or more `RT` communities.
`<routing-instance-name>.inet.0`	Populated by local and remote VPN unicast routes. The local VPN routes are typically learned from local CE routers via protocols like BGP, OSPF, and RIP, or via a static configuration. The remote VPN routes are imported from the `bgp.l3vpn.0` table if their `RT` matches one of the import `RT`s configured for the VPN. When remote VPN routes are imported from the `bgp.l3vpn.0` table, their `RD` is removed, leaving them as regular unicast IPv4 addresses.
`<routing-instance-name>.mvpn.0`	Populated by local and remote mvpn routes. The local mvpn routes are typically the locally originated routes, such as Type 1 intra-AS AD routes, or Type 7 C-multicast routes. The remote mvpn routes are imported from the `bgp.mvpn.0` table based on their `RT`. The import `RT` used for accepting mvpn routes into the `<routing-instance-name>.mvpn.0` table is different for C-multicast mvpn routes (Type 6 and Type 7) versus non-C-multicast mvpn routes (Type 1 – Type 5).

Figure 2.150

VPN is configured to use selective P-tunnels, the sender PE signals a P2MP LSP for each selective tunnel configured. Sender (ingress) PEs and receiver (egress) PEs play different roles in the P2MP LSP setup. Sender PEs are mainly responsible for initiating the parent P2MP LSP and the sub-LSPs associated with it. Receiver PEs are responsible for setting up states such that they can forward packets received over a sub-LSP to the correct VRF table (binding P-tunnel to the VRF).

Inclusive Tunnel P2MP LSP Setup

The P2MP LSP and associated sub-LSPs are signaled by the ingress PE router. The information about the P2MP LSP is advertised to egress PEs in the PMSI attribute via BGP. The ingress PE router signals P2MP sub-LSPs by originating P2MP RSVP PATH messages towards egress PE routers. The ingress PE learns the identity of the egress PEs from Type 1 routes installed in its < routing-instance-name >.mvpn.0 table. Each RSVP PATH message carries an S2L_Sub_LSP Object along with the P2MP Session Object. The S2L_Sub_LSP Object carries a 4-byte sub-LSP destination (egress) IP address. Sub-LSPs associated with a P2MP LSP can be signaled automatically by the system or via a static sub-LSP configuration. When they are automatically signaled, the system chooses a name for the P2MP LSP and each sub-LSP associated with it, using the following naming conventions:

P2MP LSP's naming convention: <ingress PE rid >:<a per VRF unique number >:mvpn:<routing-instance-name >

Sub-LSP's naming convention: < egress PE rid >:<ingress PE rid >:<a per VRF unique >:mvpn:<routing-instance-name >

Looking at the output in Figure 2.151, we notice the parent LSP and the two sub-LSPs that are created. The first sub-LSP is towards an egress PE router "7.0.0.5," and the next is to "7.0.0.4." The remaining fields identify the MVPN the sub-LSPs are associated with. Figure 2.152 further explains the parent LSP and sub-LSP.

The illustration shows a sub-LSP created from each ingress PE to an egress PE that belongs to the same MVPN. This is from the RSVP-TE signaling perspective.

Figure 2.153 shows the PATH and RESV messages being exchanged between the ingress and egress PE routers.

In this diagram three sub-LSPs are created from the ingress PE router. However, there is also a branch LSR in the form of a provider router. Referring back to the discussion in the previous section on P2MP LSPs, we note that the branch LSR creates the multiple copies (replication) of the same traffic stream to interested receiver PE routers. Therefore from a data plane perspective, we can expect the three sub-LSPs to merge into a single P2MP

```
operator@PE1-re0# run show mpls lsp p2mp
Ingress LSP: 1 sessions
P2MP name: 100:1:mvpn:FOO-MVPN, P2MP branch count: 2
To              From          State Rt P    ActivePath      LSPname
7.0.0.5         7.0.0.1       Up    0 *                     7.0.0.5:100:1:mvpn:FOO-MVPN
7.0.0.4         7.0.0.1       Up    0 *                     7.0.0.4:100:1:mvpn:FOO-MVPN
Total 2 displayed, Up 2, Down 0
```

Figure 2.151

A P2MP Tunnel

- Comprises one or more P2MP LSPs sharing same root and leaf nodes
- Supports resource reservation
- Unidirectional

S2L sub-LSP is one path of P2MP LSP
 − From the root node to a leaf node
A P2MP LSP comprises of multiple S2L sub-LSPs, one per leaf node

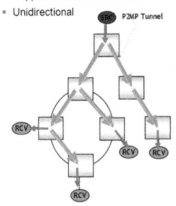

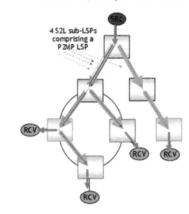

Figure 2.152

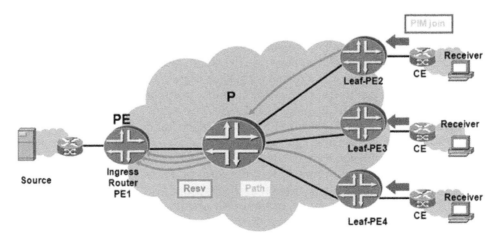

Figure 2.153

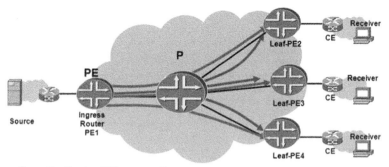

- From the Router "P"' perspective:
- Control Plane: 3 P2P sub-LSPs from the ingress to the leaves
- Data Plane: The 3 sub-LSP are merged into **one P2MP for replication**

Figure 2.154

RSVP-TE LSP. In that case, the ingress PE would send only one copy of the multicast stream, which would replicated to the three leaf nodes, by the branch LSR (router P).

This is illustrated in Figure 2.154.

Now let us consider the outputs of the RSVP-TE LSPs on both the ingress PE and the branch LSR (provider router). See Figure 2.155.

The ingress PE has signaled three RSVP-TE LSPs to the three egress PE routers as in the figure. In the outputs, we can see that each ingress LSP has an associated P2MP LSP name identifying the NG-MVPN configured on the ingress PE router. From an RSVP-TE signaling perspective, a total of three RSVP-TE Sub-LSPs are signaled as P2MP. The "Label out" values indicate the label allocated by the downstream LSR. In the figure, the output is the same for all the three LSPs,since the same branch LSR (provider router in the figure) connects to the three leaf nodes.

Now let us check the output on the provider router. See Figure 2.156.

From the output above we see the three LSP signaled from the ingress PE being displayed as P2MP LSPs on the provider router. The P-tunnel-NG-MVPN association is also displayed. The "Label OUT" field indicates the label announced by the egress PE routers for the SUB-LSP initiated by the ingress PE. In our case, we notice three labels announced by each of the egress PE routers (16, 18, & 17). A snapshot of the detailed S2L Sub-LSP signaling is provided in Figure 2.157.

Each egress PE router installs a forwarding entry in its "mpls forwarding table" for the label it has allocated for the sub-LSP.

```
operator@PE1# run show rsvp session extensive
Ingress RSVP: 3 sessions
4.4.4.4 ------------------------> PE2
  From: 1.1.1.1, LSPstate: Up, ActiveRoute: 0
  LSPname: 4.4.4.4:100:1:mvpn:FOO-MVPN, LSPpath: Primary
  P2MP LSPname: 100:1:mvpn:FOO-MVPN -------> P2MP LSP associated with MVPN
  Resv style: 1 SE, Label in: -, Label out: 300992
  Port number: sender 17 receiver 27121 protocol 0
  PATH rcvfrom: localclient
  Adspec: sent MTU 1500
  Path MTU: received 1500
  PATH sentto: 7.7.7.2 (ge-0/1/0.0) 31 pkts
  RESV rcvfrom: 7.7.7.2 (ge-0/1/0.0) 31 pkts
  Explct route: 7.7.7.2 14.14.14.2
  Record route: <self> 7.7.7.2 8.8.8.2 14.14.14.2

5.5.5.5 ------------------------> PE3
  From: 1.1.1.1, LSPstate: Up, ActiveRoute: 0
  LSPname: 5.5.5.5: 100:1:mvpn: FOO-MVPN, LSPpath: Primary
  P2MP LSPname: 100:1:mvpn: FOO-MVPN
  Resv style: 1 SE, Label in: -, Label out: 300992
  Port number: sender 17 receiver 27121 protocol 0
  PATH rcvfrom: localclient
  Adspec: sent MTU 1500
  Path MTU: received 1500
  PATH sentto: 7.7.7.2 (ge-0/1/0.0) 31 pkts
  RESV rcvfrom: 7.7.7.2 (ge-0/1/0.0) 32 pkts
  Explct route: 7.7.7.2 10.10.10.2
  Record route: <self> 7.7.7.2 10.10.10.2

6.6.6.6 ------------------------> PE4
  From: 1.1.1.1, LSPstate: Up, ActiveRoute: 0
  LSPname: 6.6.6.6: 100:1:mvpn: FOO-MVPN, LSPpath: Primary
  P2MP LSPname: 100:1:mvpn: FOO-MVPN
  Resv style: 1 SE, Label in: -, Label out: 300992
  Port number: sender 17 receiver 27121 protocol 0
  PATH rcvfrom: localclient
  Adspec: sent MTU 1500
  Path MTU: received 1500
  PATH sentto: 7.7.7.2 (ge-0/1/0.0) 31 pkts
  RESV rcvfrom: 7.7.7.2 (ge-0/1/0.0) 32 pkts
  Explct route: 7.7.7.2 8.8.8.2
  Record route: <self> 7.7.7.2 8.8.8.2
[Output Truncated]
```

Figure 2.155 RSVP-TE LSP Outputs on the Ingress PE Router

The MPLS label is installed with a POP operation, and the packet is passed on to the VRF table for a second route lookup. The second lookup on the egress PE is necessary for VPN multicast data packets to be processed inside the VRF table using normal C-PIM procedures. This is illustrated in Figure 2.158.

The Label "18" was announced by PE2 for the sub-LSP from the ingress PE, as verified in the output provided for the P router,

```
operator@P# run show mpls lsp p2mp extensive
P2MP name: 100:1:mvpn:FOO-MVPN, P2MP branch count: 2
5.5.5.5 ------------------------> PE2
   From: 1.1.1.1, LSPstate: Up, ActiveRoute: 0
   LSPname: 5.5.5.5:100:1:mvpn: FOO-MVPN, LSPpath: Primary
   P2MP LSPname: 100:1:mvpn: FOO-MVPN
   Resv style: 1 SE, Label in: 300992, Label out: 18
   Tspec: rate 0bps size 0bps peak Infbps m 20 M 1500
   Port number: sender 1 receiver 27121 protocol 0
   PATH rcvfrom: 7.7.7.1 (ge-0/2/1.0) 83 pkts
   Adspec: received MTU 1500 sent MTU 1500
   PATH sentto: 10.10.10.2 (ge-0/0/1.0) 83 pkts
   RESV rcvfrom: 10.10.10.2 (ge-0/0/1.0) 82 pkts
   Explct route: 10.10.10.2
   Record route: 7.7.7.1 <self> 10.10.10.2

4.4.4.4 ------------------------> PE2
   From: 1.1.1.1, LSPstate: Up, ActiveRoute: 0
   LSPname: 4.4.4.4:100:1:mvpn: FOO-MVPN, LSPpath: Primary
   P2MP LSPname: 100:1:mvpn: FOO-MVPN ------------------------> MVPN
   Resv style: 1 SE, Label in: 300992, Label out: 16
   Tspec: rate 0bps size 0bps peak Infbps m 20 M 1500
   Port number: sender 1 receiver 27121 protocol 0
   PATH rcvfrom: 7.7.7.1 (ge-0/2/1.0) 80 pkts
   Adspec: received MTU 1500 sent MTU 1500
   PATH sentto: 9.9.9.2 (ge-0/0/0.0) 81 pkts
   RESV rcvfrom: 9.9.9.2 (ge-0/0/0.0) 81 pkts
   Explct route: 9.9.9.2
   Record route: 7.7.7.1 <self> 9.9.9.2

6.6.6.6 ------------------------> PE2
   From: 1.1.1.1, LSPstate: Up, ActiveRoute: 0
   LSPname: 6.6.6.6:100:1:mvpn: FOO-MVPN, LSPpath: Primary
   P2MP LSPname: 100:1:mvpn: FOO-MVPN
   Resv style: 1 SE, Label in: 300992, Label out: 17
   Tspec: rate 0bps size 0bps peak Infbps m 20 M 1500
   Port number: sender 1 receiver 27121 protocol 0
   PATH rcvfrom: 7.7.7.1 (ge-0/2/1.0) 80 pkts
   Adspec: received MTU 1500 sent MTU 1500
   PATH sentto: 11.11.11.2 (ge-0/2/0.0) 81 pkts
   RESV rcvfrom: 11.11.11.2 (ge-0/2/0.0) 81 pkts
   Explct route: 11.11.11.2
   Record route: 7.7.7.1 <self> 11.11.11.2

Total 3 displayed, Up 3, Down 0
[Output Truncated]
```

Figure 2.156 Provider Router Outputs for the RSVP-TE P2MP LSP

indicated as "LABEL OUT" for the LSP terminating at PE2. In JUNOS, VPN multicast routing entries are stored in the < routing-instance-name >.inet.1 table, which is where the second route lookup occurs. In the example above, even though FOO-MVPN.inet.0 is listed as the routing table where the second lookup

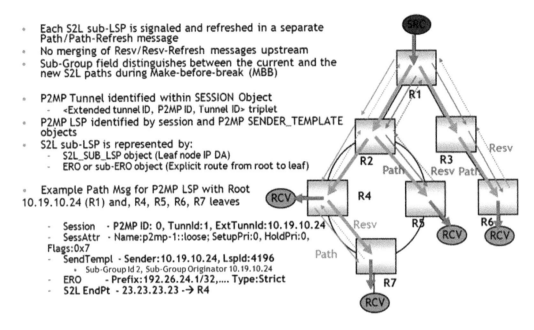

- Each S2L sub-LSP is signaled and refreshed in a separate Path/Path-Refresh message
- No merging of Resv/Resv-Refresh messages upstream
- Sub-Group field distinguishes between the current and the new S2L paths during Make-before-break (MBB)

- P2MP Tunnel identified within SESSION Object
  - <Extended tunnel ID, P2MP ID, Tunnel ID> triplet
- P2MP LSP identified by session and P2MP SENDER_TEMPLATE objects
- S2L sub-LSP is represented by:
  - S2L_SUB_LSP object (Leaf node IP DA)
  - ERO or sub-ERO object (Explicit route from root to leaf)

- Example Path Msg for P2MP LSP with Root 10.19.10.24 (R1) and, R4, R5, R6, R7 leaves

  - Session   · P2MP ID: 0, TunnId:1, ExtTunnId:10.19.10.24
  - SessAttr · Name:p2mp-1::loose; SetupPri:0, HoldPri:0, Flags:0x7
  - SendTempl - Sender:10.19.10.24, LspId:4196
    - Sub-Group Id 2, Sub-Group Originator 10.19.10.24
  - ERO   - Prefix:192.26.24.1/32,.... Type:Strict
  - S2L EndPt - 23.23.23.23 -→ R4

Figure 2.157

```
operator@PE2-re0# run show route table mpls label 18

mpls.0: 8 destinations, 8 routes (8 active, 0 holddown, 0 hidden)
+ = Active Route, - = Last Active, * = Both

18                       *[VPN/0] 00:16:48
                            to table FOO-MVPN.inet.0, Pop
     [Output Truncated]
```

Figure 2.158 Egress PE Output for the Label Entry – Router PE2

happens after the POP operation, internally the lookup is pointed to the FOO-MVPN.inet.1 table.

In Figure 2.159, PE2 contains the following VPN multicast forwarding entry, corresponding to the multicast routing entry for the local join: The upstream interface points to lsi.21, and the downstream interface (OIL) points to ge-4/0/2.1000 (towards local receivers). The upstream protocol is MVPN because the VPN multicast source is reachable via the NG-MVPN network. The lsi.21 interface is similar to the mt (GRE) interface used with PIM-based P-tunnels. The lsi.21 interface is used for removing the top MPLS header.

Since the top MPLS label used for the P2MP sub-LSP is tied to the VRF table on the egress PE routers, the penultimate-hop

```
operator@PE2# run show multicast route instance FOO-MVPN extensive
Family: INET
Group: 239.1.1.1
    Source: 192.168.1.9/32
    Upstream interface: lsi.21
    Downstream interface list:
        ge-4/0/2.100
    Session description: Administratively Scoped
    Statistics: 64 kBps, 762 pps, 356396 packets -> Traffic Statistics
    Next-hop ID: 1048577
    Upstream protocol: MVPN
    Route state: Active
    Forwarding state: Forwarding
    Cache lifetime/timeout: forever
    Wrong incoming interface notifications: 0
```

Figure 2.159 Checking the Multicast Forwarding Table

popping (PHP) operation must be disabled. PHP allows the pen-ultimate router (router before the egress PE) to remove the top MPLS label. PHP works well for VPN unicast data packets because they typically carry two MPLS labels: one for the VPN and one for the transport LSP. Once the LSP label is removed, unicast VPN packets still have a VPN label that can be used for determining the VPN to which the packets belong. VPN multicast data packets, on the other hand, carry only one MPLS label that is directly tied to the VPN. Therefore, the MPLS label carried by VPN multicast packets must be preserved until the packets reach the egress PE. Normally, PHP must be disabled through manual configuration. To simplify configuration, PHP is disabled by default on Juni-per PE routers when the protocol's "mvpn" statement is configured under the routing-instance hierarchy. It does not need to be disabled explicitly.

The details of P2MP data plane infrastructure have been discussed. The functions that each device in the P2MP infrastructure performs are summarized in Figure 2.160.

Figure 2.161 shows the nodes or devices within an NG-MVPN framework. Note that an ingress PE router may also be termed the root of a P2MP LSP.

An ingress PE will replicate only when it is a branch LSR by itself. As this diagram makes clear, the ingress PE has two physical paths to two branch LSRs, so it will replicate traffic across these two paths.

Label Allocation in RSVP-TE P2MP LSPs It is important to understand the label announcements and exchange between LSRs in a RSVP-TE P2MP LSP deployment. So far we have discussed the

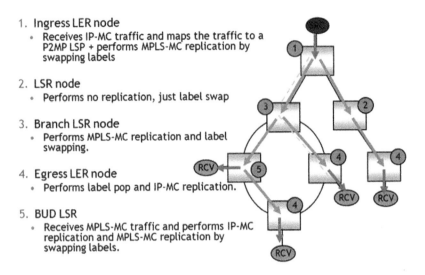

1. Ingress LER node
   - Receives IP-MC traffic and maps the traffic to a P2MP LSP + performs MPLS-MC replication by swapping labels

2. LSR node
   - Performs no replication, just label swap

3. Branch LSR node
   - Performs MPLS-MC replication and label swapping.

4. Egress LER node
   - Performs label pop and IP-MC replication.

5. BUD LSR
   - Receives MPLS-MC traffic and performs IP-MC replication and MPLS-MC replication by swapping labels.

Figure 2.160

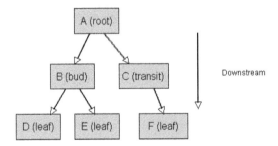

Figure 2.161

control plane operations, the P2MP LSP infrastructure from a replication standpoint, and the functions of each type of node in the P2MP data plane infrastructure. Now let us look at some simple examples to understand actual forwarding in more detail. The first step, of course, is the exchange of RSVP PATH messages from the ingress LSR to the egress LSRs. Even though this was discussed earlier, an illustration is provided in Figure 2.162 for the sake of completeness.

Upon receiving the PATH messages, egress PE routers respond with RESV messages with the appropriate labels for creating the P2MP LSP infrastructure, as illustrated in Figure 2.163.

Figure 2.164 shows traffic forwarding, along with label imposition and SWAP operations.

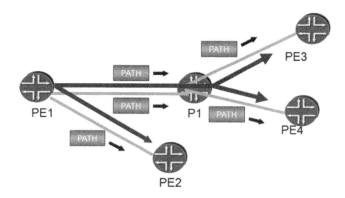

Head-end Router PE1 sends three path messages (one per destination)
    First PATH message: PE1 -> P1 -> PE3
    Second PATH message: PE1 -> P1 -> PE4
    Third PATH message: PE1 -> PE2

Figure 2.162

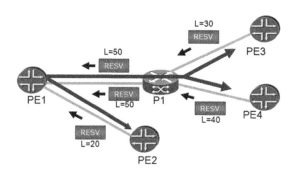

- PE3 advertises incoming "30", PE4 advertises "40" and PE2 advertises "20"
- Upon arrival of RESV from PE3 & PE4, P1 advertises incoming label "50" for the LSP destined for PE3 and PE4 – since it is a branch point.

Figure 2.163

In summary, the P2MP RSVP-TE is ingress-driven because it has initiated the tunnel setup. However, the label allocation is done by the egress PE routers, so in that sense it is downstream label allocation.

However, an MPLS LSR can also perform upstream label allocation, a technique is described in RFC 5331. An extract from this draft is given below:

When MPLS labels are upstream-assigned, the context of an MPLS label "L" is provided by the LSR that assigns the label and binds the

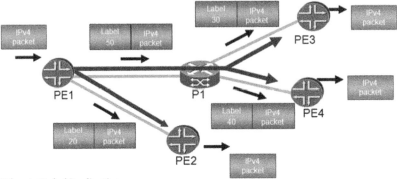

Mid-point Label Replication
- Advertise the same incoming label for LSP destined for PE3 and PE4
- This mechanism allows upstream LSR to perform label replication
Head-end Label Replication
- Sends one packet (outgoing label 50) for both LSP destined for PE3 and PE4

Figure 2.164

label to a "FEC F" for a label-switched path (LSP) LSP1. The LSR that assigns the label distributes the binding and context to an LSR "Lr" that then receives MPLS packets on LSP1 with label L. When Lr receives an MPLS packet on LSP1, it MUST be able to determine the context of this packet. An example of such a context is a tunnel over which MPLS packets on LSP1 may be received. In this case, the top label of the MPLS packet, after tunnel Decapsulation, is looked up in a label space that is specific to the root of the tunnel. This does imply that Lr be able to determine the tunnel over which the packet was received. Therefore, if the tunnel is an MPLS tunnel, penultimate-hop-popping (PHP) MUST be disabled for the tunnel.

This chapter does not discuss upstream label allocation, since the applications discussed in this book do not need this method of label allocation. The need for this scheme is discussed in the final chapter.

The Internet draft "draft-ietf-mpls-rsvp-upstream" also discusses upstream label allocation in the context of RSVP-TE, where upstream labels are allocated via RSVP-PATH messages.

Case Study for an RSVP-TE-based P2MP LSP – I-PMSI Setup

In this section, we take a look at the configurations required for creating Next Generation MVPNs based on BGP signaling using P2MP RSVP-TE LSPs. I-PMSI setup is also covered in this section. The topology given in Figure 2.165 is used for all illustrations in this section.

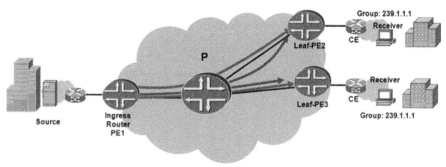

* The router "P" does not indicate a single Provider router, and indicates a Carrier Provider core, that may contain many devices. A single device is just given "ONLY" for illustrative reasons.

Figure 2.165

Configurations We have an ingress PE router (PE1) and two gress PE routers (PE2 and PE3) within a given NG-MVPN named "FOO-MVPN." Our customer FOO is a content provider who is distributing video feeds (traffic) to the two remote sites connected via PE2 and PE3. Therefore in our setup, PE1 is the sender site, and PE2 and PE3 are "receiver only" sites. Our configuration will focus on using RSVP-TE as the provider tunnel, and traffic will flow via an I-PMSI.

In Figure 2.166, only the relevant portions of the configuration are provided.

The first section of the configuration template enables the IGP, BGP, and MPLS traffic engineering. Note that the PE router uses LDP for unicast traffic, while we are also configuring RSVP-TE for multicast VPN traffic. As mentioned earlier in this chapter, this is a possible configuration option. In our example, RSVP-TE is chosen as the P-tunnel, since it offers features such as MPLS fast reroute protection, and bandwidth guarantees, which can be used by the P2MP Multicast LSPs.

RSVP-TE provider tunnels can be created in two ways: (1) using a static configuration wherein the P2MP LSP is established immediately even without an association with an MVPN instance; and (2) using a gynamic template which will be established if it is associated with an MVPN instance and membership information obtained. Dynamic LSP allows the constraints specified in the LSP template to be used for more than one MVPN, which reduces the configuration complexity. We use the dynamic template in all our examples.

The BGP configuration in the main instance (under protocols) is configured as the address family "inet-mvpn" in addition to "inet-vpn." The "inet-mvpn" address family allows PEs to

```
protocols {
    rsvp {
        interface ge-4/0/0.0;
        interface ge-0/1/0.0;
    }
    mpls {
        label-switched-path P2MP-RSVP-TE { -----> Dynamic Template
            template;
            p2mp; -------------> P2MP Flag
        }
        interface ge-4/0/0.0;
        interface ge-0/1/0.0;
    }
    bgp {
        group FOO {
            type internal;
            local-address 7.0.0.1;
            family inet-vpn {
                unicast;
            }
            family inet-mvpn {
                signaling;
            }
            neighbor 7.0.0.5 {
                peer-as 100;
            }
            neighbor 7.0.0.4 {
                peer-as 100;
            }
        }
    }
    ospf {
        traffic-engineering; ---> Enables MPLS Traffic Engineering
        area 0.0.0.0 {
            interface lo0.0 {
                passive;
            }
            interface ge-4/0/0.0 {
                interface-type p2p;
            }
            interface ge-0/1/0.0 {
                interface-type p2p;
            }
        }
    }
    ldp {
        interface ge-0/1/0.0;
        interface ge-4/0/0.0;
    }
}
routing-instances { ---------> MPLS Layer 3 VPN
 FOO-MVPN {
    instance-type vrf;
    interface ge-0/1/0.0; -----> PE-CE interface
    interface ge-4/0/1.0;
    interface lo0.1;
    route-distinguisher 100:1;
    provider-tunnel { -----> P-Tunnel Configuration
        rsvp-te { ------------------> RSVP-TE P2MP LSP
            label-switched-path-template { -> Uses the Dynamic Template
                P2MP-RSVP-TE;
            }
        }
    }
    vrf-target target:100:1;
    vrf-table-label;
    protocols {
        bgp { --------> PE-CE Routing uses BGP
```

Figure 2.166 Ingress PE Router Configuration – PE1

```
                        family inet {
                            unicast;
                        }
                        group peer {
                            type external;
                            peer-as 65005;
                            neighbor 192.168.1.9;
                            neighbor 192.168.1.17 {
                                peer-as 65010;
                            }
                        }
                    }
                    pim {  ------------> PIM towards the CE Domain
                        rp {
                            local {
                                address 7.0.0.1;
                            }
                        }
                        interface ge-4/0/1.0 {
                            mode sparse;
                            version 2;
                        }
                        interface lo0.1 {
                            mode sparse;
                            version 2;
                        }
                    }
                    mvpn;
                }
            }
        }
```

Figure 2.166, cont'd

enhance BGP capability in order to support multicast extensions that automatically discover MVPN membership information (autodiscovery) and exchange customer multicast routes without requiring full-mesh PIM adjacency among PE routers.

The "routing-instance" is the customer-specific VRF configuration for a given BGP/MPLS Layer 3 VPN. It is under this instance that customer-specific MVPN configurations are performed. Figure 2.166 depicts this in detail. The P-tunnel (RSVP-TE P2MP template) is associated with the routing instance for multicast transport. Then we configure PIM as the CE-PE multicast routing protocol. In our example, PE1 acts as the C-RP for the MVPN instance, so that configuration is also reflected.

The final step is to enable the "MVPN" protocol on the Layer 3 VPN service instance. This configuration is also used to set the policies in order to correctly identify and process various BGP advertisements for building the multicast routing table. An illustration is given in Figure 2.167.

```
mvpn {
  route-target {
    import-target {
      unicast;
      target target:100:1;
}
      export-target {
        unicast;
        target target:100:1;
    }
  }
}
...truncated...
```

Figure 2.167 MVPN Policies

However, if the import-target and export-target are the same, there is no need to explicitly configure the route targets for import and export as shown in Figure 2.167. Enabling the protocols MVPN in all the PE routers is sufficient. This is illustrated in our configuration template for PE1.

The configuration of the egress PE routers is exactly the same as for PE1, however the use of a provider tunnel is optional, since these PE routers are designated as "receiver only" PEs. In other words, they do not have any C-MCAST sources connected to their sites. See Figure 2.168 and Figure 2.169.

Now let us move on the configurations needed on the MPLS provider routers. Given in Figure 2.170 is a template for the provider core. The only sections required are the MPLS, and IGP configurations. No PIM or MVPN specific configurations are needed.

Validations In this section, we validate the functionality of the NG-MVPN by verifying the BGP control plane and the RSVP-TE-based data plane (only I-PMSI). Various commands are used to check the functionality at both the ingress and egress PE routers.

Validations at the Ingress PE router – PE1 Let us look at the ingress PE router first. We first check the autodiscovery process and the advertisements of BGP Type 1 routes. See Figure 2.171.

In the detailed output in Figure 2.172, we can verify that there are no PMSI attributes attached to the Type 1 announcement by the egress PE routers. Remember that we have not configured all the egress PE routers with an RSVP-TE provider tunnel for I-PMSI usage.

Next we check the P-tunnel information and the status of the P2MP LSP, which was configured under the NG-MVPN instance. The command in Figure 2.173 validates the P2MP

```
protocols {
    rsvp {
        interface so-4/1/0.0;
        interface ge-4/0/3.0;
        interface ge-4/0/0.0;
    }
    mpls {
        interface ge-4/0/0.0;
        interface ge-4/0/5.0;
        interface ge-4/0/3.0;
    }
    bgp {
        group FOO {
            type internal;
            local-address 7.0.0.4;
            family inet-vpn {
                unicast;
            }
            family inet-mvpn {
                signaling;
            }
            neighbor 7.0.0.5 {
                peer-as 100;
            }
            neighbor 7.0.0.1 {
                peer-as 100;
            }
        }
    }
    ospf {
        traffic-engineering;
        area 0.0.0.0 {
            interface lo0.0 {
                passive;
            }
            interface ge-4/0/0.0 {
                interface-type p2p;
            }
            interface ge-4/0/5.0 {
                interface-type p2p;
            }
            interface ge-4/0/3.0 {

                interface-type p2p;
            }
        }
    }
    ldp {
        interface ge-4/0/0.0;
        interface ge-4/0/3.0;
        interface ge-4/0/5.0;
    }
}
routing-instances {  ---------> MPLS Layer 3 VPN
FOO-MVPN {
        instance-type vrf;
        interface ge-4/0/2.100;
        interface lo0.1;
        route-distinguisher 100:1;
```

Figure 2.168 Egress PE Router Configuration – PE2

Continued

```
                vrf-target target:100:1;
                vrf-table-label;
                protocols {
                    bgp {
                        family inet {
                            unicast;
                        }
                        group peer {
                            type external;
                            peer-as 65003;
                            neighbor 192.168.1.1;
                        }
                    }
                    pim {
                        rp {
                            static {
                                address 7.0.0.1;  --→ PE1 is the C-RP
                            }
                        }
                        interface ge-4/0/2.100 {
                            mode sparse-dense;
                            version 2;
                        }
                        interface lo0.1 {
                            mode sparse-dense;
                            version 2;
                        }
                    }
                    mvpn;
                }
            }
        }
        [Output Truncated]
```

Figure 2.168, cont'd

```
                protocols {
                    rsvp {
                        interface ge-1/0/1.0;
                    }
                    mpls {
                        interface ge-1/0/1.0;
                        interface fe-1/1/0.0;
                    }
                    bgp {
                        group FOO {
                            type internal;
                            local-address 7.0.0.5;
                            family inet-vpn {
                                unicast;
                            }
                            family inet-mvpn {
                                signaling;
```

Figure 2.169 Egress PE Router Configuration – PE3

```
                }
                neighbor 7.0.0.4 {
                    peer-as 100;
                }
                neighbor 7.0.0.1 {
                    peer-as 100;
                }
            }
        }
        ospf {
            traffic-engineering;
            area 0.0.0.0 {
                interface ge-1/0/1.0 {
                    interface-type p2p;
                }
                interface lo0.0 {
                    passive;
                }
                interface fe-1/1/0.0;
            }
        }
        ldp {
            interface ge-1/0/1.0;
            interface fe-1/1/0.0;
        }
    }
    routing-instances { --------→ MPLS Layer 3 VPN
        FOO-MVPN {
            instance-type vrf;
            interface ge-1/0/2.0;
            interface lo0.1;
            route-distinguisher 100:1;
            vrf-target target:100:1;
            vrf-table-label;
            protocols {
                bgp {
                    family inet {
                        unicast;
                    }
                    group peer {
                        type external;
                        peer-as 65004;
                        neighbor 192.168.1.5;
                    }
                }
                pim {
                    rp {
                        static {
                            address 7.0.0.1;
                        }
                    }
                    interface ge-1/0/2.0 {
                        mode sparse-dense;
                        version 2;
                    }
                    interface lo0.1 {
                        mode sparse-dense;
                        version 2;
                    }
                }
                mvpn;
            }
        }
    }
}
```

Figure 2.169, cont'd

```
Protocols {
rsvp {
    interface ge-0/2/0.0;
    interface ge-0/0/0.0;
    interface ge-0/2/1.0;
    interface ge-0/0/1.0;
}
mpls {
    interface ge-0/2/0.0;
    interface ge-0/0/0.0;
    interface ge-0/2/1.0;
    interface ge-0/0/1.0;
}
ospf {
    traffic-engineering;
    area 0.0.0.0 {
        interface ge-0/2/0.0;
        interface ge-0/0/0.0;
        interface ge-0/2/1.0;
        interface ge-0/0/1.0;
        interface lo0.0;
    }
  }
}
```

Figure 2.170 MPLS Provider Router Configurations

```
operator@PE1# run show route table FOO-MVPN.mvpn.0
FOO-MVPN.mvpn.0: 3 destinations, 3 routes (3 active, 0 holddown, 0 hidden)
+ = Active Route, - = Last Active, * = Both

1:100:1:7.0.0.1/240    ---> Local Type 1 Route Generated
                  *[MVPN/70] 2d 06:46:56, metric2 1
                       Indirect
1:100:1:7.0.0.4/240                ---------> PE2
                  *[BGP/170] 00:01:14, localpref 100, from 7.0.0.4
                       AS path: I
                   > to 172.16.1.5 via ge-4/0/0.0
1:100:1:7.0.0.5/240             -------------> PE3
                  *[BGP/170] 00:01:14, localpref 100, from 7.0.0.5
                       AS path: I
                   > to 172.16.1.5 via ge-4/0/0.0, Push 299792
```

Figure 2.171 Checking for BGP Type 1 Route

LSP setup and indicates a branch count (leaf nodes or egress PEs) of two.

Moving on to more detailed output, we can check details on the P2MP LSP path, the label assignments, and the associated NG-MVPN for a given P2MP LSP. See Figure 2.174.

```
operator@PE1# run show route table FOO-MVPN.mvpn.0 detail
FOO-MVPN.mvpn.0: 4 destinations, 4 routes (4 active, 0 holddown, 0 hidden)
1:100:1:7.0.0.1/240 (1 entry, 1 announced)
*MVPN    Preference: 70
                    Next hop type: Indirect
                    Next-hop reference count: 3
                    Protocol next hop: 7.0.0.1
                    Indirect next hop: 0 -
                    State: <Active Int Ext>
                    Age: 2d 6:49:20          Metric2: 1
                    Task: mvpn global task
Announcement bits (3): 0-PIM.FOO-MVPN 1-mvpn global task 2-BGP RT
Background
                    AS path: I

1:100:1:7.0.0.4/240 (1 entry, 1 announced)
*BGP     Preference: 170/-101
                    Next hop type: Indirect
                    Next-hop reference count: 2
                    Source: 7.0.0.4
                    Protocol next hop: 7.0.0.4
                    Indirect next hop: 2 no-forward
                    State: <Secondary Active Int Ext>
                    Local AS:    100 Peer AS:    100
                    Age: 3:38        Metric2: 1
                    Task: BGP_100.7.0.0.4+51389
                    Announcement bits (2): 0-PIM.FOO-MVPN 1-mvpn global task
                    AS path: I
                    Communities: target:100:1
                    Import Accepted
                    Localpref: 100
                    Router ID: 7.0.0.4
                    Primary Routing Table bgp.mvpn.0

1:100:1:7.0.0.5/240 (1 entry, 1 announced)
*BGP     Preference: 170/-101
                    Next hop type: Indirect
                    Next-hop reference count: 2
                    Source: 7.0.0.5
                    Protocol next hop: 7.0.0.5
                    Indirect next hop: 2 no-forward
                    State: <Secondary Active Int Ext>
                    Local AS:    100 Peer AS:    100
                    Age: 3:38        Metric2: 1
                    Task: BGP_100.7.0.0.5+58906
                    Announcement bits (2): 0-PIM.FOO-MVPN 1-mvpn global task
                    AS path: I
                    Communities: target:100:1
                    Import Accepted
                    Localpref: 100
                    Router ID: 7.0.0.5
                    Primary Routing Table bgp.mvpn.0
```

Figure 2.172 Checking for BGP Type 1 Route – More Detailed Outputs

```
operator@PE1# run show mpls lsp p2mp
Ingress LSP: 1 sessions
P2MP name: 100:1:mvpn:FOO-MVPN, P2MP branch count: 2
To                 From           State Rt P    ActivePath       LSPname
7.0.0.5            7.0.0.1        Up     0 *    7.0.0.5:100:1:mvpn: FOO-MVPN
7.0.0.4            7.0.0.1        Up     0 *    7.0.0.4:100:1:mvpn: FOO-MVPN
Total 2 displayed, Up 2, Down 0
```

Figure 2.173 Checking the Status of the P2MP LSP

```
operator@PE1# run show rsvp session detail
Ingress RSVP: 2 sessions

7.0.0.5 ---------------------------------------→ To PE3
  From: 7.0.0.1, LSPstate: Up, ActiveRoute: 0
  LSPname: 7.0.0.5:100:1:mvpn:FOO-MVPN, LSPpath: Primary
  LSPtype: Dynamic Configured
  P2MP LSPname: 100:1:mvpn:FOO-MVPN --→ LSP to MVPN association details
  Suggested label received: -, Suggested label sent: -
  Recovery label received: -, Recovery label sent: 300096
  Resv style: 1 SE, Label in: -, Label out: 300096
  Time left:    -, Since: Sun Sep 19 17:29:18 2010
  Tspec: rate 0bps size 0bps peak Infbps m 20 M 1500
  Port number: sender 1 receiver 6834 protocol 0
  PATH rcvfrom: localclient
  Adspec: sent MTU 1500
  Path MTU: received 1500
  PATH sentto: 172.16.1.5 (ge-4/0/0.0) 35 pkts
  RESV rcvfrom: 172.16.1.5 (ge-4/0/0.0) 35 pkts
  Explct route: 172.16.1.5 172.16.1.2
  Record route: <self> 172.16.1.5 172.16.1.2

7.0.0.4 ---------------------------------------→ To PE2
  From: 7.0.0.1, LSPstate: Up, ActiveRoute: 0
  LSPname: 7.0.0.4:100:1:mvpn:FOO-MVPN, LSPpath: Primary
  LSPtype: Dynamic Configured
  P2MP LSPname: 100:1:mvpn:FOO-MVPN --→ LSP to MVPN association details
  Suggested label received: -, Suggested label sent: -
  Recovery label received: -, Recovery label sent: 37
  Resv style: 1 SE, Label in: -, Label out: 37
  Time left:    -, Since: Sun Sep 19 17:29:18 2010
  Tspec: rate 0bps size 0bps peak Infbps m 20 M 1500
  Port number: sender 1 receiver 6834 protocol 0
  PATH rcvfrom: localclient
  Adspec: sent MTU 1500
  Path MTU: received 1500
  PATH sentto: 172.16.1.5 (ge-4/0/0.0) 33 pkts
  RESV rcvfrom: 172.16.1.5 (ge-4/0/0.0) 39 pkts
  Explct route: 172.16.1.5
  Record route: <self> 172.16.1.5
 Total 2 displayed, Up 2, Down 0
```

Figure 2.174 Checking the Status of the P2MP LSP – Detailed Outputs

Now we can generate the video stream (multicast traffic) from the source, connected via PE1, towards the receivers connected to PE2 and PE3, respectively. Checking the MVPN routing table as displayed below indicates that the PE1 has generated a Type 5 route, and PE2 and PE3 have responded with Type 7 routes. See Figure 2.175.

Let us take a look at some detailed outputs of the same command verifying the MVPN routing table information on PE1.

```
operator@PE1# run show route table FOO-MVPN.mvpn.0

1:100:1:7.0.0.1/240
                      *[MVPN/70] 2d 09:37:05, metric2 1
                         Indirect
1:100:1:7.0.0.4/240
                      *[BGP/170] 02:34:30, localpref 100, from 7.0.0.4
                         AS path: I
                       > to 172.16.1.5 via ge-4/0/0.0
1:100:1:7.0.0.5/240
                      *[BGP/170] 02:34:18, localpref 100, from 7.0.0.5
                         AS path: I
                       > to 172.16.1.5 via ge-4/0/0.0, Push 299792
5:100:1:32:192.168.1.9:32:239.1.1.1/240  -> Originated by PE1
                      *[PIM/105] 00:00:03
                         Multicast (IPv4)
7:100:1:100:32:192.168.1.9:32:239.1.1.1/240
                    *[PIM/105] 00:00:03
                    Multicast (IPv4)
                    [BGP/170] 00:00:03, localpref 100, from 7.0.0.4
                    AS path: I
                     > to 172.16.1.5 via ge-4/0/0.0 -> Type 7 from PE2
                    [BGP/170] 00:00:03, localpref 100, from 7.0.0.5
                    AS path: I
                     > to 172.16.1.5 via ge-4/0/0.0, Push 299792 -> Type 7 from PE3
```

Figure 2.175 Checking the MVPN Routing Table for Type 5 and Type 7 Routes

Details on target communities and the status of the announced routes are displayed in Figure 2.176.

Having checked the control plane for the Type 5 and Type 7 routes, the next steps involve verifying the data plane – to ensure that traffic is being forwarded over the RSVP-TE P2MP LSPs. The output in Figure 2.177 shows traffic being forwarded via the LSP – The increments of packet and byte counters verify this.

This can be validated as follows:

Now we can check the multicast forwarding table for the MVPN instance. The forwarding table indicates the traffic being forwarded on a per C-MCAST-Source and C-MCAST-Group pair. The group we are interested in is "239.1.1.1." Our output in Figure 2.178 indeed indicates a multicast forwarding entry for this group, identified with a C-MCAST source and traffic forwarding details. The traffic is being forwarded, and the statistics indicate an incrementing packet count, while the route state is also in "ACTIVE."

Another useful command, shown in Figure 2.179, verifies the C-MCAST traffic flows and the appropriate P-tunnel and the type being used.

Let us also verify the PIM source information on PE1, which is designated as the C-RP. See Figure 2.180.

```
operator@PE1# run show route table FOO-MVPN.mvpn.0 detail
1:100:1:7.0.0.1/240 (1 entry, 1 announced)
        *MVPN   Preference: 70
                Next hop type: Indirect
                Next-hop reference count: 3
                Protocol next hop: 7.0.0.1
                Indirect next hop: 0 -
                State: <Active Int Ext>
                Age: 2d 9:37:36          Metric2: 1
                Task: mvpn global task
Announcement bits (3): 0-PIM.FOO-MVPN 1-mvpn global task 2-BGP RT
Background
                AS path: I

1:100:1:7.0.0.4/240 (1 entry, 1 announced)
        *BGP    Preference: 170/-101
                Next hop type: Indirect
                Next-hop reference count: 4
                Source: 7.0.0.4
                Protocol next hop: 7.0.0.4
                Indirect next hop: 2 no-forward
                State: <Secondary Active Int Ext>
                Local AS:    100 Peer AS:    100
                Age: 2:35:01    Metric2: 1
                Task: BGP_100.7.0.0.4+51389
                Announcement bits (2): 0-PIM. FOO-MVPN 1-mvpn global task
                AS path: I
                Communities: target:100:1
                Import Accepted
                Localpref: 100
                Router ID: 7.0.0.4
                Primary Routing Table bgp.mvpn.0

1:100:1:7.0.0.5/240 (1 entry, 1 announced)
        *BGP    Preference: 170/-101
                Next hop type: Indirect
                Next-hop reference count: 4
                Source: 7.0.0.5
                Protocol next hop: 7.0.0.5
                Indirect next hop: 2 no-forward
                State: <Secondary Active Int Ext>
                Local AS:    100 Peer AS:    100
                Age: 2:34:49    Metric2: 1
                Task: BGP_100.7.0.0.5+58906
                Announcement bits (2): 0-PIM. FOO-MVPN 1-mvpn global task
                AS path: I
                Communities: target:100:1
                Import Accepted
                Localpref: 100
                Router ID: 7.0.0.5
                Primary Routing Table bgp.mvpn.0

5:100:1:32:192.168.1.9:32:239.1.1.1/240 (1 entry, 1 announced)
        *PIM    Preference: 105
                Next hop type: Multicast (IPv4)
                Next-hop reference count: 4
```

Figure 2.176 Checking the MVPN Routing Table for Type 5 and Type 7 Routes – Detailed Outputs

```
                        State: <Active Int>
                        Age: 34
                        Task: PIM.FOO-MVPN
Announcement bits (3): 0-PIM. FOO-MVPN 1-mvpn global task 2-BGP RT
Background
                        AS path: I

7:100:1:100:32:192.168.1.9:32:239.1.1.1/240 (3 entries, 3 announced)
          *PIM         Preference: 105
                        Next hop type: Multicast (IPv4)
                        Next-hop reference count: 4
                        State: <Active Int>
                        Age: 34
                        Task: PIM. FOO-MVPN
                        Announcement bits (2): 0-PIM.FOO-MVPN 1-mvpn global task
                        AS path: I
                        Communities: no-advertise target:7.0.0.1:5
           BGP         Preference: 170/-101
                        Next hop type: Indirect
                        Next-hop reference count: 4
                        Source: 7.0.0.4
                        Protocol next hop: 7.0.0.4
                        Indirect next hop: 2 no-forward
                        State: <Secondary Int Ext>
                        Inactive reason: Route Preference
                        Local AS:    100 Peer AS:    100
                        Age: 34        Metric2: 1
                        Task: BGP_100.7.0.0.4+51389
                        Announcement bits (2): 0-PIM.FOO-MVPN 1-mvpn global task
                        AS path: I
                        Communities: target:7.0.0.1:5
                        Import Accepted
                        Localpref: 100
                        Router ID: 7.0.0.4
                        Primary Routing Table bgp.mvpn.0
           BGP         Preference: 170/-101
                        Next hop type: Indirect
                        Next-hop reference count: 4
                        Source: 7.0.0.5
                        Protocol next hop: 7.0.0.5
                        Indirect next hop: 2 no-forward
                        State: <Secondary NotBest Int Ext>
                        Inactive reason: Not Best in its group - Router ID
                        Local AS:    100 Peer AS:    100
                        Age: 34        Metric2: 1
                        Task: BGP_100.7.0.0.5+58906
                        Announcement bits (2): 0-PIM.FOO-MVPN 1-mvpn global task
                        AS path: I
                        Communities: target:7.0.0.1:5
                        Import Accepted
                        Localpref: 100
                        Router ID: 7.0.0.5
                        Primary Routing Table bgp.mvpn.0
```

Figure 2.176, cont'd

```
operator@PE1# run show rsvp session statistics
Ingress RSVP: 2 sessions
To       From    State Packets Bytes      LSPname
7.0.0.5 7.0.0.1   Up    689803 60702664 7.0.0.5:100:1:mvpn:FOO-MVPN
7.0.0.4 7.0.0.1   Up    689803 60702664 7.0.0.4:100:1:mvpn:FOO-MVPN
Total 2 displayed,Up 2, Down 0
```

Figure 2.177 Checking the P2MP RSVP-TE Statistics

```
operator@PE1# run show multicast route instance FOO-MVPN extensive
Family: INET
Group: 239.1.1.1
    Source: 192.168.1.9/32 ----> C-MCAST Source
    Upstream interface: ge-4/0/1.0 -> Interface towards the Source
    Session description: Administratively Scoped
    Statistics: 68 kBps, 813 pps, 1083247 packets -> Traffic forwarded
    Next-hop ID: 1048577
    Upstream protocol: MVPN
    Route state: Active
    Forwarding state: Forwarding -> In Active forwarding state
    Cache lifetime/timeout: forever
    Wrong incoming interface notifications: 0
```

Figure 2.178 Checking the P2MP RSVP-TE Statistics

```
operator@PE1# run show mvpn instance
MVPN instance:
Legend for provider tunnel
I-P-tnl -- inclusive provider tunnel S-P-tnl -- selective provider tunnel
Legend for c-multicast routes properties (Pr)
DS -- derived from (*, c-g)          RM -- remote VPN route
Instance : FOO-MVPN
  MVPN Mode : SPT-ONLY ----> Indicates SPT-Mode, and no RPT.
  Provider tunnel: I-P-tnl:RSVP-TE P2MP:7.0.0.1, 6834,7.0.0.1
  Neighbor                         I-P-tnl
  7.0.0.4
  7.0.0.5
  C-mcast IPv4 (S:G)         Ptnl                                St
  192.168.1.9/32:239.1.1.1/32   RSVP-TE P2MP:7.0.0.1, 6834,7.0.0.1   RM
```

Figure 2.179 Checking the P-Tunnel Information

Figure 2.180 Checking the P-Tunnel Information

```
operator@PE1# run show pim source instance FOO-MVPN detail
Instance: PIM.FOO-MVPN Family: INET
Source 192.168.1.9
    Prefix 192.168.1.8/30
    Upstream interface ge-4/0/1.0
    Active groups:239.1.1.1
```

Validations at Egress PE Router PE2 We can follow the same sequence of commands as in the previous section on each egress PE router to verify first the control plane and then the data plane infrastructure. The only difference between the ingress and egress PE routers from a MVPN routing table point of view is the Type 6 routes. PE routers generate Type 6 routers based on C-PIM joins. A Type 6 route is generated for each PIM join received via the CE router. In Figure 2.181, we notice a Type 6 route being generated for the group "239.1.1.1." The address "7.0.0.1" in the Type 6 route identifies the C-RP—in this case, ingress PE router PE1.

Using the "detail" keyword, we can validate key information such as the I-PMSI attribute attached by the ingress PE router. In the output in Figure 2.182, we notice a PMSI attribute with a P-tunnel type "RSVP-TE." However, the Type 1 announcement from PE3 does not have an attached I-PMSI attribute, since it is configured as a "receiver only" site, with no P-tunnel configuration.

In the next few figures, we check the multicast forwarding table and the PIM C-Join information received from locally connected CE routers. See Figure 2.183.

```
operator@PE2# run show route table FOO-MVPN.mvpn.0
1:100:1:7.0.0.1/240     ----→ PE1
                        *[BGP/170] 05:33:39, localpref 100, from 7.0.0.1
                          AS path: I
                        > to 172.16.1.6 via ge-4/0/3.0
1:100:1:7.0.0.4/240
                        *[MVPN/70] 05:16:47, metric2 1
                          Indirect
1:100:1:7.0.0.5/240     --------→ PE3
                        *[BGP/170] 05:16:34, localpref 100, from 7.0.0.5
                          AS path: I
                        > to 172.16.1.2 via ge-4/0/0.0
5:100:1:32:192.168.1.9:32:239.1.1.1/240 -→ Type 5 BGP route from PE1
                        *[BGP/170] 01:53:18, localpref 100, from 7.0.0.1
                          AS path: I
                        > to 172.16.1.6 via ge-4/0/3.0
6:100:1:100:32:7.0.0.1:32:239.1.1.1/240 --→ Type 6 based on PIM Joins
                        *[PIM/105] 05:33:39
                          Multicast (IPv4)
7:100:1:100:32:192.168.1.9:32:239.1.1.1/240--→ Type 7 originated by PE2
                        *[MVPN/70] 01:53:18, metric2 1
                          Multicast (IPv4)
                        [PIM/105] 01:53:18
                          Multicast (IPv4)
```

Figure 2.181 Checking for MVPN Routes

The output in Figure 2.184 provides information on the PIM joins received by the egress PE router. There are two entries here: shared tree join to the RP and source tree join to the 192.168.1.9 (C-MCAST source) sending traffic to the group "239.1.1.1."

In Figure 2.185 we check the P-tunnel information, the P2MP RSVP-TE LSP on which PE2 is a leaf node. Only 7.0.0.1 (PE1) has P-tunnel information, since it is the ingress PE.

Validations at Egress PE Router PE3 In Figure 2.186 we visit the outputs on PE3, which is the other egress PE router. The outputs are provided without explanation, since the information provided is exactly the same as in the previous section, for router PE2. See also Figures 2.187, 2.188, 2.189, and 2.190.

```
operator@PE2# run show route table FOO-MVPN.mvpn.0 detail
1:100:1:7.0.0.1/240 (1 entry, 1 announced)
*BGP     Preference: 170/-101
PMSI: Flags 0x0: Label[0:0:0]: RSVP-TE: Session_13[7.0.0.1:0:6834:7.0.0.1]
                Next hop type: Indirect
                Next-hop reference count: 4
                Source: 7.0.0.1
                Protocol next hop: 7.0.0.1
                Indirect next hop: 2 no-forward
                State: <Secondary Active Int Ext>
                Local AS:    100 Peer AS:    100
                Age: 5:47:09    Metric2: 1
                Task: BGP_100.7.0.0.1+179
                Announcement bits (2): 0-PIM.FOO-MVPN 1-mvpn global task
                AS path: I
                Communities: target:100:1
                Import Accepted
                Localpref: 100
                Router ID: 7.0.0.1
                Primary Routing Table bgp.mvpn.0

  1:100:1:7.0.0.4/240 (1 entry, 1 announced)
        *MVPN   Preference: 70
                Next hop type: Indirect
                Next-hop reference count: 3
                Protocol next hop: 7.0.0.4
                Indirect next hop: 0 -
                State: <Active Int Ext>
                Age: 5:30:17    Metric2: 1
                Task: mvpn global task
Announcement bits (3): 0-PIM.FOO-MVPN 1-mvpn global task 2-BGP RT
Background
                AS path: I

  1:100:1:7.0.0.5/240 (1 entry, 1 announced)
        *BGP    Preference: 170/-101
```

Figure 2.182 Checking for MVPN Routes – Detailed Outputs

```
                    Next hop type: Indirect
                    Next-hop reference count: 2
                    Source: 7.0.0.5
                    Protocol next hop: 7.0.0.5
                    Indirect next hop: 2 no-forward
                    State: <Secondary Active Int Ext>
                    Local AS:    100 Peer AS:    100
                    Age: 5:30:04    Metric2: 1
                    Task: BGP_100.7.0.0.5+179
                    Announcement bits (2): 0-PIM.FOO-MVPN 1-mvpn global task
                    AS path: I
                    Communities: target:100:1
                    Import Accepted
                    Localpref: 100
                    Router ID: 7.0.0.5
                    Primary Routing Table bgp.mvpn.0

    5:100:1:32:192.168.1.9:32:239.1.1.1/240 (1 entry, 1 announced)
            *BGP    Preference: 170/-101
                    Next hop type: Indirect
                    Next-hop reference count: 4
                    Source: 7.0.0.1
                    Protocol next hop: 7.0.0.1
                    Indirect next hop: 2 no-forward
                    State: <Secondary Active Int Ext>
                    Local AS:    100 Peer AS:    100
                    Age: 5 Metric2: 1
                    Task: BGP_100.7.0.0.1+179
                    Announcement bits (2): 0-PIM.FOO-MVPN 1-mvpn global task
                    AS path: I
                    Communities: target:100:1
                    Import Accepted
                    Localpref: 100
                    Router ID: 7.0.0.1
                    Primary Routing Table bgp.mvpn.0

    6:100:1:100:32:7.0.0.1:32:239.1.1.1/240 (1 entry, 1 announced)
            *PIM    Preference: 105
                    Next hop type: Multicast (IPv4), Next hop index: 1048577
                    Next-hop reference count: 16
                    State: <Active Int>
                    Age: 5:47:09
                    Task: PIM.FOO-MVPN
                    Announcement bits (2): 0-PIM.FOO-MVPN 1-mvpn global task
                    AS path: I
                    Communities: no-advertise target:7.0.0.1:5

    7:100:1:100:32:192.168.1.9:32:239.1.1.1/240 (2 entries, 2 announced)
            *MVPN   Preference: 70
                    Next hop type: Multicast (IPv4), Next hop index: 1048577
                    Next-hop reference count: 16
                    State: <Active Int Ext>
                    Age: 5 Metric2: 1
                    Task: mvpn global task
Announcement bits (3): 0-PIM.FOO-MVPN 1-mvpn global task 2-BGP RT
Background
                    AS path: I
                    Communities: target:7.0.0.1:5
            PIM     Preference: 105
                    Next hop type: Multicast (IPv4), Next hop index: 1048577
                    Next-hop reference count: 16
                    State: <Int>
                    Inactive reason: Route Preference
                    Age: 4
                    Task: PIM.FOO-MVPN
                    Announcement bits (2): 0-PIM.FOO-MVPN 1-mvpn global task
                    AS path: I
                    Communities: target:7.0.0.1:5
```

Figure 2.182, cont'd

```
operator@PE2# run show multicast route instance FOO-MVPN extensive
Family: INET
Group: 239.1.1.1
    Source: 192.168.1.9/32
    Upstream interface: lsi.21
    Downstream interface list:
        ge-4/0/2.100
    Session description: Administratively Scoped
    Statistics: 64 kBps, 762 pps, 356396 packets -→ Traffic Statistics
    Next-hop ID: 1048577
    Upstream protocol: MVPN
    Route state: Active
    Forwarding state: Forwarding
    Cache lifetime/timeout: forever
    Wrong incoming interface notifications: 0
```

Figure 2.183 Checking the Multicast Forwarding Table

```
operator@PE2# run show pim join instance FOO-MVPN extensive
Instance: PIM.FOO-MVPN Family: INET
R = Rendezvous Point Tree, S = Sparse, W = Wildcard
Group: 239.1.1.1 -----→ C-MCAST Group - Shared Tree Join
    Source: *
    RP: 7.0.0.1
    Flags: sparse,rptree,wildcard
    Upstream protcol: BGP
    Upstream interface: Through BGP
    Upstream neighbor: Through MVPN
    Upstream state: Join to RP
    Downstream neighbors:
        Interface: ge-4/0/2.100
            192.168.1.1 State: Join Flags: SRW Timeout: 184

Group: 239.1.1.1 -----→ C-MCAST Group - Source Tree Join
    Source: 192.168.1.9
    Flags: sparse
    Upstream protcol: BGP
    Upstream interface: Through BGP
    Upstream neighbor: Through MVPN
    Upstream state: None, Join to Source
    Keepalive timeout:
    Downstream neighbors:
        Interface: ge-4/0/2.100
            192.168.1.1 State: Join Flags: S Timeout: 184
```

Figure 2.184 Checking PIM
Joins from the CE

```
R = Rendezvous Point Tree, S = Sparse, W = Wildcard
```

Case Study for an RSVP-TE-Based P2MP LSP – S-PMSI Setup

In this section, we take a look at the actual configurations required for creating an S-PMSI for certain multicast groups. One of the advantages of an S-PMSI over an I-PMSI is the ability to have traffic forwarded to PE routers "ONLY" with interested

```
operator@PE2# run show mvpn instance
MVPN instance:
Legend for provider tunnel
I-P-tnl -- inclusive provider tunnel S-P-tnl -- selective provider tunnel
Legend for c-multicast routes properties (Pr)
DS -- derived from (*, c-g)          RM -- remote VPN route
Instance : FOO-MVPN
  MVPN Mode : SPT-ONLY
  Provider tunnel: I-P-tnl:invalid:
  Neighbor                           I-P-tnl
  7.0.0.1                            RSVP-TE P2MP:7.0.0.1, 6834,7.0.0.1
  7.0.0.5
  C-mcast IPv4 (S:G)        Ptnl                                St
  0.0.0.0/0:239.1.1.1/32
  192.168.1.9/32:239.1.1.1/32   RSVP-TE P2MP:7.0.0.1, 6834,7.0.0.1   DS
```

Figure 2.185 Checking the MVPN Instance for P-Tunnel Information

```
operator@PE3# run show route table FOO-MVPN.mvpn.0
1:100:1:7.0.0.1/240
                    *[BGP/170] 06:11:50, localpref 100, from 7.0.0.1
                      AS path: I
                    > to 172.16.1.1 via ge-1/0/1.0, Push 299856
1:100:1:7.0.0.4/240
                    *[BGP/170] 05:54:58, localpref 100, from 7.0.0.4
                      AS path: I
                    > to 172.16.1.1 via ge-1/0/1.0
1:100:1:7.0.0.5/240
                    *[MVPN/70] 05:54:45, metric2 1
                      Indirect
5:100:1:32:192.168.1.9:32:239.1.1.1/240
                    *[BGP/170] 00:24:46, localpref 100, from 7.0.0.1
                      AS path: I
                    > to 172.16.1.1 via ge-1/0/1.0, Push 299856
6:100:1:100:32:7.0.0.1:32:239.1.1.1/240
                    *[PIM/105] 03:21:37
                      Multicast (IPv4)
7:100:1:100:32:192.168.1.9:32:239.1.1.1/240
                    *[MVPN/70] 00:24:46, metric2 1
                      Multicast (IPv4)
                     [PIM/105] 00:24:45
                      Multicast (IPv4)
```

Figure 2.186 Checking for MVPN Routes

receivers. This is similar to the Data MDT functionality in the Draft-Rosen implementation. In this case study, we construct a scenario where PE2 is interested in receiving traffic for C-MCAST group "238.1.1.1." However, PE3 does not have any interested receivers for "238.1.1.1." Therefore the objective is to have traffic delivered over an S-PMSI to egress PE router PE2 only. Traffic to

```
operator@PE3# run show route table FOO-MVPN.mvpn.0 detail
1:100:1:7.0.0.1/240 (1 entry, 1 announced)
*BGP      Preference: 170/-101
PMSI: Flags 0x0: Label[0:0:0]: RSVP-TE: Session_13[7.0.0.1:0:6834:7.0.0.1]
                Next hop type: Indirect
                Next-hop reference count: 4
                Source: 7.0.0.1
                Protocol next hop: 7.0.0.1
                Indirect next hop: 2 no-forward
                State: <Secondary Active Int Ext>
                Local AS:    100 Peer AS:    100
                Age: 6:12:46    Metric2: 1
                Task: BGP_100.7.0.0.1+179
                Announcement bits (2): 0-PIM.FOO-MVPN 1-mvpn global task
                AS path: I
                Communities: target:100:1
                Import Accepted
                Localpref: 100
                Router ID: 7.0.0.1
                Primary Routing Table bgp.mvpn.0

1:100:1:7.0.0.4/240 (1 entry, 1 announced)
        *BGP      Preference: 170/-101
                Next hop type: Indirect
                Next-hop reference count: 2
                Source: 7.0.0.4
                Protocol next hop: 7.0.0.4
                Indirect next hop: 2 no-forward
                State: <Secondary Active Int Ext>
                Local AS:    100 Peer AS:    100
                Age: 5:55:54    Metric2: 1
                Task: BGP_100.7.0.0.4+63093
                Announcement bits (2): 0-PIM.FOO-MVPN 1-mvpn global task
                AS path: I
                Communities: target:100:1
                Import Accepted
                Localpref: 100
                Router ID: 7.0.0.4
                Primary Routing Table bgp.mvpn.0

1:100:1:7.0.0.5/240 (1 entry, 1 announced)
        *MVPN     Preference: 70
                Next hop type: Indirect
                Next-hop reference count: 3
                Protocol next hop: 7.0.0.5
                Indirect next hop: 0 -
                State: <Active Int Ext>
                Age: 5:55:41    Metric2: 1
                Task: mvpn global task
Announcement bits (3): 0-PIM.FOO-MVPN 1-mvpn global task 2-BGP RT
Background
                AS path: I

5:100:1:32:192.168.1.9:32:239.1.1.1/240 (1 entry, 1 announced)
        *BGP      Preference: 170/-101
                Next hop type: Indirect
                Next-hop reference count: 4
                Source: 7.0.0.1
                Protocol next hop: 7.0.0.1
                Indirect next hop: 2 no-forward
                State: <Secondary Active Int Ext>
                Local AS:    100 Peer AS:    100
                Age: 25:42     Metric2: 1
                Task: BGP_100.7.0.0.1+179
                Announcement bits (2): 0-PIM.FOO-MVPN 1-mvpn global task
                AS path: I
                Communities: target:100:1
                Import Accepted
```

Figure 2.187 Checking for MVPN Routes – Detailed Outputs

```
                         Localpref: 100
                         Router ID: 7.0.0.1
                         Primary Routing Table bgp.mvpn.0

     6:100:1:100:32:7.0.0.1:32:239.1.1.1/240 (1 entry, 1 announced)
              *PIM    Preference: 105
                      Next hop type: Multicast (IPv4), Next hop index: 1048577
                      Next-hop reference count: 14
                      State: <Active Int>
                      Age: 3:22:33
                      Task: PIM.FOO-MVPN
                      Announcement bits (2): 0-PIM.FOO-MVPN 1-mvpn global task
                      AS path: I
                      Communities: no-advertise target:7.0.0.1:5

     7:100:1:100:32:192.168.1.9:32:239.1.1.1/240 (2 entries, 2 announced)
              *MVPN   Preference: 70
                      Next hop type: Multicast (IPv4), Next hop index: 1048577
                      Next-hop reference count: 14
                      State: <Active Int Ext>
                      Age: 25:42      Metric2: 1
                      Task: mvpn global task
     Announcement bits (3): 0-PIM.FOO-MVPN 1-mvpn global task 2-BGP RT
     Background
                      AS path: I
                      Communities: target:7.0.0.1:5
               PIM    Preference: 105
                      Next hop type: Multicast (IPv4), Next hop index: 1048577
                      Next-hop reference count: 14
                      State: <Int>
                      Inactive reason: Route Preference
                      Age: 25:41
                      Task: PIM.FOO-MVPN
                      Announcement bits (2): 0-PIM.FOO-MVPN 1-mvpn global task
                      AS path: I
                      Communities: target:7.0.0.1:5
```

Figure 2.187, cont'd

```
     operator@PE3# run show multicast route instance FOO-MVPN extensive
     Family: INET
     Group: 239.1.1.1
         Source: 192.168.1.9/32
         Upstream interface: lsi.1
         Downstream interface list:
             ge-1/0/2.0
         Session description: Administratively Scoped
         Statistics: 67 kBps, 793 pps, 1467693 packets
         Next-hop ID: 1048577
         Upstream protocol: MVPN
         Route state: Active
         Forwarding state: Forwarding
         Cache lifetime/timeout: forever
         Wrong incoming interface notifications: 0
```

Figure 2.188 Checking the Multicast Forwarding Table

```
operator@PE3# run show pim join instance FOO-MVPN extensive
Instance: PIM.FOO-MVPN Family: INET
R = Rendezvous Point Tree, S = Sparse, W = Wildcard
Group: 239.1.1.1
    Source: *
    RP: 7.0.0.1
    Flags: sparse,rptree,wildcard
    Upstream protcol: BGP
    Upstream interface: Through BGP
    Upstream neighbor: Through MVPN
    Upstream state: Join to RP
    Downstream neighbors:
        Interface: ge-1/0/2.0
            192.168.1.5 State: Join Flags: SRW Timeout: 165

Group: 239.1.1.1
    Source: 192.168.1.9
    Flags: sparse
    Upstream protcol: BGP
    Upstream interface: Through BGP
    Upstream neighbor: Through MVPN
    Upstream state: None, Join to Source
    Keepalive timeout:
    Downstream neighbors:
    Interface: ge-1/0/2.0
        192.168.1.5 State: Join Flags: S Timeout: 165
R = Rendezvous Point Tree, S = Sparse, W = Wildcard
```

Figure 2.189 Checking PIM Joins from the CE

```
operator@PE3# run show mvpn instance
MVPN instance:
Legend for provider tunnel
I-P-tnl -- inclusive provider tunnel S-P-tnl -- selective provider tunnel
Legend for c-multicast routes properties (Pr)
DS -- derived from (*, c-g)          RM -- remote VPN route
Instance : FOO-MVPN
  MVPN Mode : SPT-ONLY
  Provider tunnel: I-P-tnl:invalid:
  Neighbor                          I-P-tnl
  7.0.0.1                           RSVP-TE P2MP:7.0.0.1, 6834,7.0.0.1
  7.0.0.4
  C-mcast IPv4 (S:G)        Ptnl                                St
  0.0.0.0/0:239.1.1.1/32
  192.168.1.9/32:239.1.1.1/32  RSVP-TE P2MP:7.0.0.1, 6834,7.0.0.1   DS
```

Figure 2.190 Checking the MVPN Instance for P-Tunnel Information

group "239.1.1.1" is to be delivered to both egress PE routers as usual.

The topology shown in Figure 2.191 is used for all illustrations in this section.

S-PMSI Configuration using a C-Source and C-Group Pair Let us review the configurations for ingress PE router PE1. The

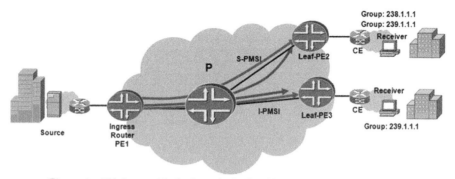

* The router "P" does not indicate a single Provider router, and indicates a
  Carrier Provider core, that may contain many devices. A single device is just
  given "ONLY" for illustrative reasons.

Figure 2.191

additional configuration for creating an S-PMSI for group
"238.1.1.1" is provided under the section "Selective" in the
routing-instance hierarchy. Only the routing-instance portion of
the configuration is provided in Figure 2.192.

A C-MCAST Source and C-MCAST Group for which we wish to
create an S-PMSI have been defined. In our configuration, PE2 has
an interested receiver for group "238.1.1.1"; therefore an S-PMSI is
created for source "192.168.1.9" transmitting to this group. Many
combinations and criteria can be defined under the S-PMSI hierarchy. Some of the key combinations that can be used are
discussed here.

The configuration for PE2 and PE3 remain unchanged, so they
are not provided here.

Validations In this section, we can validate the S-PMSI setup for
Group "238.1.1.1" and the existing I-PMSI infrastructure for
Group "239.1.1.1."

Validations at the Ingress PE router – PE1 Let us start by taking a
look at the ingress PE router, beginning with the MVPN routing
table. In Figure 2.193 we notice that PE1 has originated a Type 3
route for (Source: 192.168.1.9 and Group: 238.1.1.1) and received
a Type 4 announcement from PE2 (7.0.0.4) only, not from PE3.
Therefore the S-PMSI is only created between PE1 and PE2. However the I-PMSI setup for group "239.1.1.1" is still "UP" between
PE1 and PE2/PE3.

In Figure 2.194 we check the detailed outputs.

We can check the status of the multicast forwarding table on
ingress PE router PE1. In the output in Figure 2.195 we can see

```
routing-instances {
FOO-MVPN {
    instance-type vrf;
    interface ge-4/0/1.0;
    interface lo0.1;
    route-distinguisher 100:1;
    provider-tunnel {
        rsvp-te {
            label-switched-path-template {
                P2MP-RSVP-TE;
            }
        }
        selective { ----------> S-PMSI Configuration
            group 238.1.1.1/32 {
                source 192.168.1.9/32 {
                    rsvp-te {
                        label-switched-path-template {
                            P2MP-RSVP-TE;
                        }
                    }
                }
            }
        }
    }
    vrf-target target:100:1;
    vrf-table-label;
    protocols {
        bgp {
            family inet {
                unicast;
            }
            group peer {
                type external;
                peer-as 65005;
                neighbor 192.168.1.9;
                neighbor 192.168.1.17 {
                    peer-as 65010;
                }
            }
        }
        pim {
            rp {
                local {
                    address 7.0.0.1;
                }
            }
            interface ge-4/0/1.0 {
                mode sparse;
                version 2;
            }
            interface lo0.1 {
                mode sparse;
                version 2;
            }
        }
        mvpn;
    }
}
}
```

Figure 2.192 Ingress PE Router
Configuration – PE1

```
operator@PE1# run show route table FOO-MVPN.mvpn.0
FOO-MVPN.mvpn.0: 9 destinations, 12 routes (9 active, 0 holddown, 0 hidden)
+ = Active Route, - = Last Active, * = Both

1:100:1:7.0.0.1/240
                        *[MVPN/70] 00:15:22, metric2 1
                            Indirect
1:100:1:7.0.0.4/240
                        *[BGP/170] 00:14:51, localpref 100, from 7.0.0.4
                            AS path: I
                        > to 172.16.1.5 via ge-4/0/0.0
1:100:1:7.0.0.5/240
                        *[BGP/170] 00:14:51, localpref 100, from 7.0.0.5
                            AS path: I
                        > to 172.16.1.5 via ge-4/0/0.0, Push 299792
3:100:1:32:192.168.1.9:32:238.1.1.1:7.0.0.1/240              --> Type 3 Route
                        *[MVPN/70] 00:00:03, metric2 1
                            Indirect
4:3:100:1:32:192.168.1.9:32:238.1.1.1:7.0.0.1:7.0.0.4/240
                        *[BGP/170] 00:00:03, localpref 100, from 7.0.0.4
                            AS path: I --> Type 4 received from only PE2
                        > to 172.16.1.5 via ge-4/0/0.0
5:100:1:32:192.168.1.9:32:238.1.1.1/240
                        *[PIM/105] 00:00:03
                            Multicast (IPv4)
5:100:1:32:192.168.1.9:32:239.1.1.1/240
                        *[PIM/105] 00:00:06
                            Multicast (IPv4)
7:100:1:100:32:192.168.1.9:32:238.1.1.1/240
                        *[PIM/105] 00:00:03
                            Multicast (IPv4)
                        [BGP/170] 00:00:03, localpref 100, from 7.0.0.4
                            AS path: I
                        > to 172.16.1.5 via ge-4/0/0.0
7:100:1:100:32:192.168.1.9:32:239.1.1.1/240
                        *[PIM/105] 00:00:06
                            Multicast (IPv4)
                        [BGP/170] 00:00:06, localpref 100, from 7.0.0.4
                            AS path: I
                        > to 172.16.1.5 via ge-4/0/0.0
                        [BGP/170] 00:00:06, localpref 100, from 7.0.0.5
                            AS path: I
                        > to 172.16.1.5 via ge-4/0/0.0, Push 299792
```

Figure 2.193 Checking for BGP Routes

that the router is forwarding traffic for groups (238.1.1.1 and 239.1.1.1).

Let us also check the MVPN instance to verify whether the I-PMSI and S-PMSI have been correctly created for the configured groups, and their forwarding state. In the output in Figure 2.196, we indeed notice two P-tunnels. The first tunnel is indicated as "S-RSVP-TE" which is an S-PMSI, and the second one, "RSVP-TE," indicates an I-PMSI.

```
operator@PE1# run show route table FOO-MVPN.mvpn.0  detail
FOO-MVPN.mvpn.0: 9 destinations, 12 routes (9 active, 0 holddown, 0 hidden)
1:100:1:7.0.0.1/240 (1 entry, 1 announced)
        *MVPN   Preference: 70
                Next hop type: Indirect
                Next-hop reference count: 4
                Protocol next hop: 7.0.0.1
                Indirect next hop: 0 -
                State: <Active Int Ext>
                Age: 15:24       Metric2: 1
                Task: mvpn global task
Announcement bits (3): 0-PIM.FOO-MVPN 1-mvpn global task 2-BGP RT
Background
                AS path: I


1:100:1:7.0.0.4/240 (1 entry, 1 announced)
        *BGP    Preference: 170/-101
                Next hop type: Indirect
                Next-hop reference count: 8
                Source: 7.0.0.4
                Protocol next hop: 7.0.0.4
                Indirect next hop: 2 no-forward
                State: <Secondary Active Int Ext>
                Local AS:    100 Peer AS:    100
                Age: 14:53       Metric2: 1
                Task: BGP_100.7.0.0.4+64153
                Announcement bits (2): 0-PIM.FOO-MVPN 1-mvpn global task
                AS path: I
                Communities: target:100:1
                Import Accepted
                Localpref: 100
                Router ID: 7.0.0.4
                Primary Routing Table bgp.mvpn.0

1:100:1:7.0.0.5/240 (1 entry, 1 announced)
        *BGP    Preference: 170/-101
                Next hop type: Indirect
                Next-hop reference count: 4
                Source: 7.0.0.5
                Protocol next hop: 7.0.0.5
                Indirect next hop: 2 no-forward
                State: <Secondary Active Int Ext>
                Local AS:    100 Peer AS:    100
                Age: 14:53       Metric2: 1
                Task: BGP_100.7.0.0.5+54984
                Announcement bits (2): 0-PIM.FOO-MVPN 1-mvpn global task
                AS path: I
                Communities: target:100:1
                Import Accepted
                Localpref: 100
                Router ID: 7.0.0.5
                Primary Routing Table bgp.mvpn.0

3:100:1:32:192.168.1.9:32:238.1.1.1:7.0.0.1/240 (1 entry, 1 announced)
        *MVPN   Preference: 70
                Next hop type: Indirect
                Next-hop reference count: 4
```

Figure 2.194 Checking for BGP Routes – Detailed Outputs

```
                          Protocol next hop: 7.0.0.1
                          Indirect next hop: 0 -
                          State: <Active Int Ext>
                          Age: 5  Metric2: 1
                          Task: mvpn global task
Announcement bits (3): 0-PIM.FOO-MVPN 1-mvpn global task 2-BGP RT
Background
                          AS path: I


4:3:100:1:32:192.168.1.9:32:238.1.1.1:7.0.0.1:7.0.0.4/240 (1 entry, 1
announced)
         *BGP      Preference: 170/-101
                          Next hop type: Indirect
                          Next-hop reference count: 8
                          Source: 7.0.0.4
                          Protocol next hop: 7.0.0.4
                          Indirect next hop: 2 no-forward
                          State: <Secondary Active Int Ext>
                          Local AS:    100 Peer AS:    100
                          Age: 5  Metric2: 1
                          Task: BGP_100.7.0.0.4+64153
                          Announcement bits (2): 0-PIM.FOO-MVPN 1-mvpn global task
                          AS path: I
                          Communities: target:7.0.0.1:0
                          Import Accepted
                          Localpref: 100
                          Router ID: 7.0.0.4
                          Primary Routing Table bgp.mvpn.0


5:100:1:32:192.168.1.9:32:238.1.1.1/240 (1 entry, 1 announced)
         *PIM      Preference: 105
                          Next hop type: Multicast (IPv4)
                          Next-hop reference count: 7
                          State: <Active Int>
                          Age: 5
                          Task: PIM.FOO-MVPN
Announcement bits (3): 0-PIM.FOO-MVPN 1-mvpn global task 2-BGP RT
Background
                          AS path: I


5:100:1:32:192.168.1.9:32:239.1.1.1/240 (1 entry, 1 announced)
         *PIM      Preference: 105
                          Next hop type: Multicast (IPv4)
                          Next-hop reference count: 7
                          State: <Active Int>
                          Age: 8
                          Task: PIM.FOO-MVPN
Announcement bits (3): 0-PIM.FOO-MVPN 1-mvpn global task 2-BGP RT
Background
                          AS path: I


7:100:1:100:32:192.168.1.9:32:238.1.1.1/240 (2 entries, 2 announced)
         *PIM      Preference: 105
                          Next hop type: Multicast (IPv4)
                          Next-hop reference count: 7
```

Figure 2.194, cont'd

Continued

```
       State: <Active Int>
                       Age: 5
                       Task: PIM.FOO-MVPN
                       Announcement bits (2): 0-PIM.FOO-MVPN 1-mvpn global task
                       AS path: I
                       Communities: no-advertise target:7.0.0.1:5
              BGP      Preference: 170/-101
                       Next hop type: Indirect
                       Next-hop reference count: 8
                       Source: 7.0.0.4
                       Protocol next hop: 7.0.0.4
                       Indirect next hop: 2 no-forward
                       State: <Secondary Int Ext>
                       Inactive reason: Route Preference
                       Local AS:    100 Peer AS:    100
                       Age: 5 Metric2: 1
                       Task: BGP_100.7.0.0.4+64153
                       Announcement bits (2): 0-PIM.FOO-MVPN 1-mvpn global task
                       AS path: I
                       Communities: target:7.0.0.1:5
                       Import Accepted
                       Localpref: 100
                       Router ID: 7.0.0.4
                       Primary Routing Table bgp.mvpn.0

   7:100:1:100:32:192.168.1.9:32:239.1.1.1/240 (3 entries, 3 announced)
          *PIM      Preference: 105
                       Next hop type: Multicast (IPv4)
                       Next-hop reference count: 7
                       State: <Active Int>
                       Age: 8
                       Task: PIM.FOO-MVPN
                       Announcement bits (2): 0-PIM.FOO-MVPN 1-mvpn global task
                       AS path: I
                       Communities: no-advertise target:7.0.0.1:5
              BGP      Preference: 170/-101
                       Next hop type: Indirect
                       Next-hop reference count: 8
                       Source: 7.0.0.4
                       Protocol next hop: 7.0.0.4
                       Indirect next hop: 2 no-forward
                       State: <Secondary Int Ext>
                       Inactive reason: Route Preference
                       Local AS:    100 Peer AS:    100
                       Age: 8 Metric2: 1
                       Task: BGP_100.7.0.0.4+64153
                       Announcement bits (2): 0-PIM.FOO-MVPN 1-mvpn global task
                       AS path: I
                       Communities: target:7.0.0.1:5
                       Import Accepted
                       Localpref: 100
                       Router ID: 7.0.0.4
                       Primary Routing Table bgp.mvpn.0
```

Figure 2.194, cont'd

```
            BGP      Preference: 170/-101
                     Next hop type: Indirect
                     Next-hop reference count: 4
                     Source: 7.0.0.5
                     Protocol next hop: 7.0.0.5
                     Indirect next hop: 2 no-forward
                     State: <Secondary NotBest Int Ext>
                     Inactive reason: Not Best in its group - Router ID
                     Local AS:   100 Peer AS:   100
                     Age: 8  Metric2: 1
                     Task: BGP_100.7.0.0.5+54984
                     Announcement bits (2): 0-PIM.FOO-MVPN 1-mvpn global task
                     AS path: I
   Communities:      target:7.0.0.1:5
                     Import Accepted
                     Localpref: 100
                     Router ID: 7.0.0.5
                     Primary Routing Table bgp.mvpn.0
```

Figure 2.194, cont'd

```
operator@PE1# run show multicast route instance FOO-MVPN extensive
Family: INET
Group: 238.1.1.1
    Source: 192.168.1.9/32
    Upstream interface: ge-4/0/1.0
    Session description: Unknown
    Statistics: 29 kBps, 345 pps, 220507 packets
    Next-hop ID: 1048577
    Upstream protocol: MVPN
    Route state: Active
    Forwarding state: Forwarding
    Cache lifetime/timeout: forever
    Wrong incoming interface notifications: 0

Group: 239.1.1.1
    Source: 192.168.1.9/32
    Upstream interface: ge-4/0/1.0
    Session description: Administratively Scoped
    Statistics: 89 kBps, 1063 pps, 685281 packets -→ Traffic forwarded
    Next-hop ID: 1048576
    Upstream protocol: MVPN
    Route state: Active
    Forwarding state: Forwarding
    Cache lifetime/timeout: forever
    Wrong incoming interface notifications: 0
```

Figure 2.195 Checking the Multicast Forwarding Table

Validations at Egress PE Router PE2 For egress PE router PE2, we follow the same steps as performed for the I-PMSI validation of the same router, as shown in Figure 2.197. The first task is to check the MVPN routing table for Type 3 and Type 4 routing information, which is an indication of an S-PMSI signaling.

```
operator@PE1# run show mvpn instance
MVPN instance:
Legend for provider tunnel
I-P-tnl -- inclusive provider tunnel S-P-tnl -- selective provider tunnel
Legend for c-multicast routes properties (Pr)
DS -- derived from (*, c-g)          RM -- remote VPN route
Instance : FOO-MVPN
  MVPN Mode : SPT-ONLY
  Provider tunnel: I-P-tnl:RSVP-TE P2MP:7.0.0.1, 47053,7.0.0.1
  Neighbor                          I-P-tnl
  7.0.0.4
  7.0.0.5
C-mcast IPv4 (S:G)            Ptnl                                  St
192.168.1.9/32:238.1.1.1/32  S-RSVP-TE P2MP:7.0.0.1, 47055,7.0.0.1 RM
192.168.1.9/32:239.1.1.1/32  RSVP-TE P2MP:7.0.0.1,   47053,7.0.0.1 RM
```

Figure 2.196 Checking the Multicast Forwarding Table

We can check the detailed outputs for validating the S-PMSI attribute, which is advertised by ingress PE router PE1. In the output in Figure 2.198, the following information is attached to the Type 3 BGP announcement "PMSI: Flags 0x1: Label[0:0:0]: RSVP-TE: Session_13[7.0.0.1:0:47055:7.0.0.1]... "0x1" indicates an S-PMSI attribute.

We now check the multicast forwarding table, which indicates forwarding for two C-MCAST groups (238.1.1.1 and 239.1.1.1). See Figure 2.199.

We now check the MVPN instance for P-tunnel information on PE2. The output displays both the I-PMSI and S-PMSI information. See Figure 2.200.

Validations at Egress PE Router PE3 For egress PE router PE3, we follow the same steps as for the I-PMSI validation on the same router. The first task is to check the MVPN routing table for Type 3 and Type 4 routing information, which is an indication of an S-PMSI signaling. As shown in Figure 2.201, PE3 installs the Type 3 announcement from PE1; however, it does not respond with a corresponding Type 4 route, since there are no interested receivers for the group 238.1.1.1.

In Figure 2.202 we check the detailed outputs on PE3.

Next we verify the multicast forwarding state for the groups. In the output in Figure 2.203, we can verify the forwarding state for group "239.1.1.1" only.

Now we check the MVPN instance information. The output in Figure 2.204 shows only the I-PMSI information, since PE3 does not have an S-PMSI setup.

S-PMSI Configuration using a C-Source and C-Group with Traffic Threshold While configuring an S-PMSI for a source and

```
operator@PE2# run show route table FOO-MVPN.mvpn.0
FOO-MVPN.mvpn.0: 13 destinations, 15 routes (13 active, 0 holddown, 0
hidden)
+ = Active Route, - = Last Active, * = Both
1:100:1:7.0.0.1/240
                    *[BGP/170] 00:33:45, localpref 100, from 7.0.0.1
                      AS path: I
                   > to 172.16.1.6 via ge-4/0/3.0
1:100:1:7.0.0.4/240
                    *[MVPN/70] 1d 01:54:00, metric2 1
                      Indirect
1:100:1:7.0.0.5/240
                    *[BGP/170] 1d 01:53:47, localpref 100, from 7.0.0.5
                      AS path: I
                   > to 172.16.1.2 via ge-4/0/0.0
3:100:1:32:192.168.1.9:32:238.1.1.1:7.0.0.1/240   ---> From PE1
                    *[BGP/170] 00:18:57, localpref 100, from 7.0.0.1
                      AS path: I
                   > to 172.16.1.6 via ge-4/0/3.0
4:3:100:1:32:192.168.1.9:32:238.1.1.1:7.0.0.1:7.0.0.4/240 -> Originated
                    *[MVPN/70] 00:18:57, metric2 1
                      Indirect
5:100:1:32:192.168.1.9:32:238.1.1.1/240
                    *[BGP/170] 00:18:57, localpref 100, from 7.0.0.1
                      AS path: I
                   > to 172.16.1.6 via ge-4/0/3.0
5:100:1:32:192.168.1.9:32:239.1.1.1/240
                    *[BGP/170] 00:19:00, localpref 100, from 7.0.0.1
                      AS path: I
                   > to 172.16.1.6 via ge-4/0/3.0
6:100:1:100:32:7.0.0.1:32:238.1.1.1/240
                    *[PIM/105] 00:33:45
                      Multicast (IPv4)
6:100:1:100:32:7.0.0.1:32:239.1.1.1/240
                    *[PIM/105] 00:33:45
                      Multicast (IPv4)
7:100:1:100:32:192.168.1.9:32:238.1.1.1/240
                    *[MVPN/70] 00:18:57, metric2 1
                      Multicast (IPv4)
                     [PIM/105] 00:18:57
                      Multicast (IPv4)
7:100:1:100:32:192.168.1.9:32:239.1.1.1/240
                    *[MVPN/70] 00:19:00, metric2 1
                      Multicast (IPv4)
                     [PIM/105] 00:19:00
                      Multicast (IPv4)
```

Figure 2.197 Checking for BGP Routes

a group, we can also configure a threshold value. The threshold can be defined at a minimum rate of 10Kbps until 1000000Kbps. Traffic flows over an I-PMSI until the threshold is within the configured range. When it exceeds the rate, traffic is switched over to an S-PMSI. The relevant configuration is provided in Figure 2.205.

```
operator@PE2# run show route table FOO-MVPN.mvpn.0 detail
FOO-MVPN.mvpn.0: 13 destinations, 15 routes (13 active, 0 holddown, 0
hidden)
1:100:1:7.0.0.1/240 (1 entry, 1 announced)
        *BGP    Preference: 170/-101
PMSI: Flags 0x0: Label[0:0:0]: RSVP-TE: Session_13[7.0.0.1:0:47053:7.0.0.1]
                Next hop type: Indirect
                Next-hop reference count: 8
                Source: 7.0.0.1
                Protocol next hop: 7.0.0.1
                Indirect next hop: 2 no-forward
                State: <Secondary Active Int Ext>
                Local AS:   100 Peer AS:    100
                Age: 39:23      Metric2: 1
                Task: BGP_100.7.0.0.1+179
                Announcement bits (2): 0-PIM.FOO-MVPN 1-mvpn global task
                AS path: I
                Communities: target:100:1
                Import Accepted
                Localpref: 100
                Router ID: 7.0.0.1
                Primary Routing Table bgp.mvpn.0

1:100:1:7.0.0.4/240 (1 entry, 1 announced)
        *MVPN   Preference: 70
                Next hop type: Indirect
                Next-hop reference count: 4
                Protocol next hop: 7.0.0.4
                Indirect next hop: 0 -
                State: <Active Int Ext>
                Age: 1d 1:59:38          Metric2: 1
                Task: mvpn global task
Announcement bits (3): 0-PIM.FOO-MVPN 1-mvpn global task 2-BGP RT
Background
                AS path: I

1:100:1:7.0.0.5/240 (1 entry, 1 announced)
        *BGP    Preference: 170/-101
                Next hop type: Indirect
                Next-hop reference count: 2
                Source: 7.0.0.5
                Protocol next hop: 7.0.0.5
                Indirect next hop: 2 no-forward
                State: <Secondary Active Int Ext>
                Local AS:   100 Peer AS:    100
                Age: 1d 1:59:25         Metric2: 1
                Task: BGP_100.7.0.0.5+179
                Announcement bits (2): 0-PIM.FOO-MVPN 1-mvpn global task
                AS path: I
                Communities: target:100:1
                Import Accepted
                Localpref: 100
                Router ID: 7.0.0.5
                Primary Routing Table bgp.mvpn.0

3:100:1:32:192.168.1.9:32:238.1.1.1:7.0.0.1/240 (1 entry, 1 announced)
        *BGP    Preference: 170/-101
PMSI: Flags 0x1: Label[0:0:0]: RSVP-TE: Session_13[7.0.0.1:0:47055:7.0.0.1]
                Next hop type: Indirect
                Next-hop reference count: 8
```

Figure 2.198 Checking for BGP Routes – Detailed Outputs

Now we check the MVPN instance information and take note of the values within the P-tunnels on PE1. The tunnel ID information for the I-PMSI has a tag of "47053," while the S-PMSI has a value of "47056" attached, as shown in Figure 2.206.

```
                         Source: 7.0.0.1
                         Protocol next hop: 7.0.0.1
                         Indirect next hop: 2 no-forward
                         State: <Secondary Active Int Ext>
                         Local AS:    100 Peer AS:    100
                         Age: 24:35      Metric2: 1
                         Task: BGP_100.7.0.0.1+179
                         Announcement bits (2): 0-PIM.FOO-MVPN 1-mvpn global task
                         AS path: I
                         Communities: target:100:1
                         Import Accepted
                         Localpref: 100
                         Router ID: 7.0.0.1
                         Primary Routing Table bgp.mvpn.0

    4:3:100:1:32:192.168.1.9:32:238.1.1.1:7.0.0.1:7.0.0.4/240 (1 entry, 1
    announced)
            *MVPN    Preference: 70
                     Next hop type: Indirect
                     Next-hop reference count: 4
                     Protocol next hop: 7.0.0.4
                     Indirect next hop: 0 -
                     State: <Active Int Ext>
                     Age: 24:35      Metric2: 1
                     Task: mvpn global task
                     Announcement bits (3): 0-PIM.FOO-MVPN 1-mvpn global task 2-
    BGP RT Background
                     AS path: I
                     Communities: target:7.0.0.1:0

    5:100:1:32:192.168.1.9:32:238.1.1.1/240 (1 entry, 1 announced)
            *BGP     Preference: 170/-101
                     Next hop type: Indirect
                     Next-hop reference count: 8
                     Source: 7.0.0.1
                     Protocol next hop: 7.0.0.1
                     Indirect next hop: 2 no-forward
                     State: <Secondary Active Int Ext>
                     Local AS:    100 Peer AS:    100
                     Age: 24:35      Metric2: 1
                     Task: BGP_100.7.0.0.1+179
                     Announcement bits (2): 0-PIM.FOO-MVPN 1-mvpn global task
                     AS path: I
                     Communities: target:100:1
                     Import Accepted
                     Localpref: 100
                     Router ID: 7.0.0.1
                     Primary Routing Table bgp.mvpn.0

    5:100:1:32:192.168.1.9:32:239.1.1.1/240 (1 entry, 1 announced)
            *BGP     Preference: 170/-101
```

Figure 2.198, cont'd

```
                    Next hop type: Indirect
                    Next-hop reference count: 8
                    Source: 7.0.0.1
                    Protocol next hop: 7.0.0.1
                    Indirect next hop: 2 no-forward
                    State: <Secondary Active Int Ext>
                    Local AS:    100 Peer AS:    100
                    Age: 24:38      Metric2: 1
                    Task: BGP_100.7.0.0.1+179
                    Announcement bits (2): 0-PIM.FOO-MVPN 1-mvpn global task
                    AS path: I
                    Communities: target:100:1
                    Import Accepted
                    Localpref: 100
                    Router ID: 7.0.0.1
                    Primary Routing Table bgp.mvpn.0

6:100:1:100:32:7.0.0.1:32:238.1.1.1/240 (1 entry, 1 announced)
         *PIM    Preference: 105
                    Next hop type: Multicast (IPv4), Next hop index: 1048576
                    Next-hop reference count: 37
                    State: <Active Int>
                    Age: 39:23
                    Task: PIM.FOO-MVPN
                    Announcement bits (2): 0-PIM.FOO-MVPN 1-mvpn global task
                    AS path: I
                    Communities: no-advertise target:7.0.0.1:5

6:100:1:100:32:7.0.0.1:32:239.1.1.1/240 (1 entry, 1 announced)
         *PIM    Preference: 105
                    Next hop type: Multicast (IPv4), Next hop index: 1048576
                    Next-hop reference count: 37
                    State: <Active Int>
                    Age: 39:23

                    Task: PIM.FOO-MVPN
                    Announcement bits (2): 0-PIM.FOO-MVPN 1-mvpn global task
                    AS path: I
                    Communities: no-advertise target:7.0.0.1:5
7:100:1:100:32:192.168.1.9:32:238.1.1.1/240 (2 entries, 2 announced)
         *MVPN   Preference: 70
                    Next hop type: Multicast (IPv4), Next hop index: 1048576
                    Next-hop reference count: 37
                    State: <Active Int Ext>
                    Age: 24:35      Metric2: 1

                    Task: mvpn global task
Announcement bits (3): 0-PIM.FOO-MVPN 1-mvpn global task 2-BGP RT
Background
                    AS path: I
                    Communities: target:7.0.0.1:5
         PIM     Preference: 105
                    Next hop type: Multicast (IPv4), Next hop index: 1048576
                    Next-hop reference count: 37
                    State: <Int>
                    Inactive reason: Route Preference
                    Age: 24:35
                    Task: PIM.FOO-MVPN
                    Announcement bits (2): 0-PIM.FOO-MVPN 1-mvpn global task
                    AS path: I
                    Communities: target:7.0.0.1:5
```

Figure 2.198, cont'd

```
    7:100:1:100:32:192.168.1.9:32:239.1.1.1/240 (2 entries, 2 announced)
        *MVPN    Preference: 70
                 Next hop type: Multicast (IPv4), Next hop index: 1048576
                 Next-hop reference count: 37
                 State: <Active Int Ext>
                 Age: 24:38      Metric2: 1
                 Task: mvpn global task
Announcement bits (3): 0-PIM.FOO-MVPN 1-mvpn global task 2-BGP RT
Background
                 AS path: I
                 Communities: target:7.0.0.1:5
        PIM      Preference: 105
                 Next hop type: Multicast (IPv4), Next hop index: 1048576
                 Next-hop reference count: 37
                 State: <Int>
                 Inactive reason: Route Preference
                 Age: 24:38
                 Task: PIM.FOO-MVPN
                 Announcement bits (2): 0-PIM.FOO-MVPN 1-mvpn global task
                 AS path: I
                 Communities: target:7.0.0.1:5
```

Figure 2.198, cont'd

```
    operator@PE2# run show multicast route instance FOO-MVPN extensive
    Family: INET
    Group: 238.1.1.1
        Source: 192.168.1.9/32
        Upstream interface: lsi.21
        Downstream interface list:
            ge-4/0/2.100
        Session description: Unknown
        Statistics: 29 kBps, 342 pps, 717278 packets
        Next-hop ID: 1048576
        Upstream protocol: MVPN
        Route state: Active
        Forwarding state: Forwarding
        Cache lifetime/timeout: forever
        Wrong incoming interface notifications: 0

    Group: 239.1.1.1
        Source: 192.168.1.9/32
        Upstream interface: lsi.21
        Downstream interface list:
            ge-4/0/2.100
        Session description: Administratively Scoped
        Statistics: 97 kBps, 1154 pps, 2246202 packets
        Next-hop ID: 1048576
        Upstream protocol: MVPN
        Route state: Active
        Forwarding state: Forwarding
        Cache lifetime/timeout: forever
        Wrong incoming interface notifications: 0
```

Figure 2.199 Checking the Multicast Forwarding Table

```
operator@PE2# run show mvpn instance
MVPN instance:
Legend for provider tunnel
I-P-tnl -- inclusive provider tunnel S-P-tnl -- selective provider tunnel
Legend for c-multicast routes properties (Pr)
DS -- derived from (*, c-g)        RM -- remote VPN route
Instance : FOO-MVPN
  MVPN Mode : SPT-ONLY
  Provider tunnel: I-P-tnl:invalid:
  Neighbor                        I-P-tnl
  7.0.0.1                         RSVP-TE P2MP:7.0.0.1, 47053,7.0.0.1
  7.0.0.5
C-mcast IPv4 (S:G)            Ptnl                                    St
192.168.1.9/32:238.1.1.1/32  S-RSVP-TE P2MP:7.0.0.1, 47055,7.0.0.1   DS
192.168.1.9/32:239.1.1.1/32  RSVP-TE P2MP:7.0.0.1,   47053,7.0.0.1   DS
```

Figure 2.200 Checking the MVPN Instance

```
operator@PE3# run show route table FOO-MVPN.mvpn.0
FOO-MVPN.mvpn.0: 9 destinations, 10 routes (9 active, 0 holddown, 0 hidden)
+ = Active Route, - = Last Active, * = Both
1:100:1:7.0.0.1/240
                    *[BGP/170] 00:54:22, localpref 100, from 7.0.0.1
                      AS path: I
                     > to 172.16.1.1 via ge-1/0/1.0, Push 299856
1:100:1:7.0.0.4/240
                    *[BGP/170] 1d 02:14:37, localpref 100, from 7.0.0.4
                      AS path: I
                     > to 172.16.1.1 via ge-1/0/1.0
1:100:1:7.0.0.5/240
                    *[MVPN/70] 1d 02:14:24, metric2 1
                      Indirect
3:100:1:32:192.168.1.9:32:238.1.1.1:7.0.0.1/240
                    *[BGP/170] 00:39:34, localpref 100, from 7.0.0.1
                      AS path: I
                     > to 172.16.1.1 via ge-1/0/1.0, Push 299856
5:100:1:32:192.168.1.9:32:238.1.1.1/240
                    *[BGP/170] 00:39:34, localpref 100, from 7.0.0.1
                      AS path: I
                     > to 172.16.1.1 via ge-1/0/1.0, Push 299856
5:100:1:32:192.168.1.9:32:239.1.1.1/240
                    *[BGP/170] 00:39:37, localpref 100, from 7.0.0.1
                      AS path: I
                     > to 172.16.1.1 via ge-1/0/1.0, Push 299856
6:100:1:100:32:7.0.0.1:32:239.1.1.1/240
                    *[PIM/105] 00:54:22
                      Multicast (IPv4)
7:100:1:100:32:192.168.1.9:32:239.1.1.1/240
                    *[MVPN/70] 00:39:37, metric2 1
                      Multicast (IPv4)
                     [PIM/105] 00:39:37
                      Multicast (IPv4)
```

Figure 2.201 Checking for BGP Routes

```
operator@PE3# run show route table FOO-MVPN.mvpn.0 detail
FOO-MVPN.mvpn.0: 9 destinations, 10 routes (9 active, 0 holddown, 0 hidden)
1:100:1:7.0.0.1/240 (1 entry, 1 announced)
        *BGP    Preference: 170/-101
PMSI: Flags 0x0: Label[0:0:0]: RSVP-TE: Session_13[7.0.0.1:0:47053:7.0.0.1]
                Next hop type: Indirect
                Next-hop reference count: 8
                Source: 7.0.0.1
                Protocol next hop: 7.0.0.1
                Indirect next hop: 2 no-forward
                State: <Secondary Active Int Ext>
                Local AS:    100 Peer AS:    100
                Age: 1:01:01    Metric2: 1
                Task: BGP_100.7.0.0.1+179
                Announcement bits (2): 0-PIM.FOO-MVPN 1-mvpn global task
                AS path: I
                Communities: target:100:1
                Import Accepted
                Localpref: 100
                Router ID: 7.0.0.1
                Primary Routing Table bgp.mvpn.0

1:100:1:7.0.0.4/240 (1 entry, 1 announced)
        *BGP    Preference: 170/-101
                Next hop type: Indirect
                Next-hop reference count: 2
                Source: 7.0.0.4
                Protocol next hop: 7.0.0.4
                Indirect next hop: 2 no-forward
                State: <Secondary Active Int Ext>
                Local AS:    100 Peer AS:    100
                Age: 1d 2:21:16       Metric2: 1
                Task: BGP_100.7.0.0.4+63093
                Announcement bits (2): 0-PIM.FOO-MVPN 1-mvpn global task
                AS path: I
                Communities: target:100:1
                Import Accepted
                Localpref: 100
                Router ID: 7.0.0.4
                Primary Routing Table bgp.mvpn.0

1:100:1:7.0.0.5/240 (1 entry, 1 announced)
        *MVPN   Preference: 70
                Next hop type: Indirect
                Next-hop reference count: 3
                Protocol next hop: 7.0.0.5
                Indirect next hop: 0 -
                State: <Active Int Ext>
                Age: 1d 2:21:03          Metric2: 1
                Task: mvpn global task
Announcement bits (3): 0-PIM.FOO-MVPN 1-mvpn global task 2-BGP RT
Background
                AS path: I

3:100:1:32:192.168.1.9:32:238.1.1.1:7.0.0.1/240 (1 entry, 1 announced)
        *BGP    Preference: 170/-101
PMSI: Flags 0x1: Label[0:0:0]: RSVP-TE: Session_13[7.0.0.1:0:47055:7.0.0.1]
                Next hop type: Indirect
                Next-hop reference count: 8
```

Figure 2.202 Checking for BGP Routes – Detailed Outputs

Continued

In order to validate the S-PMSI setup, we can enable some debugging (traceoptions). Figure 2.207 shows the output of the traceoptions. Note that the I-PMSI gets un-bound from the C-MCAST Source and Group pair, when the traffic rate exceeds the threshold. Also visible is the exchange of Type 3 and Type 4

```
Source: 7.0.0.1
Protocol next hop: 7.0.0.1
Indirect next hop: 2 no-forward
State: <Secondary Active Int Ext>
Local AS:    100 Peer AS:    100
Age: 46:13      Metric2: 1
Task: BGP_100.7.0.0.1+179
Announcement bits (2): 0-PIM.FOO-MVPN 1-mvpn global task
AS path: I
Communities: target:100:1
Import Accepted
Localpref: 100
Router ID: 7.0.0.1
Primary Routing Table bgp.mvpn.0

5:100:1:32:192.168.1.9:32:238.1.1.1/240 (1 entry, 1 announced)
    *BGP    Preference: 170/-101
            Next hop type: Indirect
            Next-hop reference count: 8
            Source: 7.0.0.1
            Protocol next hop: 7.0.0.1
            Indirect next hop: 2 no-forward
            State: <Secondary Active Int Ext>
            Local AS:    100 Peer AS:    100
            Age: 46:13      Metric2: 1
            Task: BGP_100.7.0.0.1+179
            Announcement bits (2): 0-PIM.FOO-MVPN 1-mvpn global task
            AS path: I
            Communities: target:100:1
            Import Accepted
            Localpref: 100
            Router ID: 7.0.0.1
            Primary Routing Table bgp.mvpn.0

5:100:1:32:192.168.1.9:32:239.1.1.1/240 (1 entry, 1 announced)
    *BGP    Preference: 170/-101
            Next hop type: Indirect
            Next-hop reference count: 8
            Source: 7.0.0.1
            Protocol next hop: 7.0.0.1
            Indirect next hop: 2 no-forward
            State: <Secondary Active Int Ext>
            Local AS:    100 Peer AS:    100
            Age: 46:16      Metric2: 1
            Task: BGP_100.7.0.0.1+179
            Announcement bits (2): 0-PIM.FOO-MVPN 1-mvpn global task
            AS path: I
            Communities: target:100:1
            Import Accepted
            Localpref: 100
            Router ID: 7.0.0.1
            Primary Routing Table bgp.mvpn.0
```

Figure 2.202, cont'd

```
   6:100:1:100:32:7.0.0.1:32:224.2.127.254/240 (1 entry, 1 announced)
          *PIM     Preference: 105
                   Next hop type: Multicast (IPv4), Next hop index: 1048577
                   Next-hop reference count: 19
                   State: <Active Int>
                   Age: 1:01:01
                   Task: PIM.FOO-MVPN
                   Announcement bits (2): 0-PIM.FOO-MVPN 1-mvpn global task
                   AS path: I
                   Communities: no-advertise target:7.0.0.1:5

   6:100:1:100:32:7.0.0.1:32:239.1.1.1/240 (1 entry, 1 announced)
          *PIM     Preference: 105
                   Next hop type: Multicast (IPv4), Next hop index: 1048577
                   Next-hop reference count: 19
                   State: <Active Int>
                   Age: 1:01:01
                   Task: PIM.FOO-MVPN
                   Announcement bits (2): 0-PIM.FOO-MVPN 1-mvpn global task
                   AS path: I
                   Communities: no-advertise target:7.0.0.1:5


   7:100:1:100:32:192.168.1.9:32:239.1.1.1/240 (2 entries, 2 announced)

          *MVPN    Preference: 70
                   Next hop type: Multicast (IPv4), Next hop index: 1048577
                   Next-hop reference count: 19
                   State: <Active Int Ext>
                   Age: 46:16      Metric2: 1
                   Task: mvpn global task
Announcement bits (3): 0-PIM.FOO-MVPN 1-mvpn global task 2-BGP RT
Background
                   AS path: I
                   Communities: target:7.0.0.1:5
           PIM     Preference: 105
                   Next hop type: Multicast (IPv4), Next hop index: 1048577
                   Next-hop reference count: 19
                   State: <Int>
                   Inactive reason: Route Preference
                   Age: 46:16
                   Task: PIM.FOO-MVPN
                   Announcement bits (2): 0-PIM.FOO-MVPN 1-mvpn global task
                   AS path: I
                   Communities: target:7.0.0.1:5
```

Figure 2.202, cont'd

routing information between PE1 and PE2, indicated at the beginning of the output.

The last line of the output in Figure 2.207 indicates an RSVP-TE P-tunnel being setup, and a value of "47056" is visible. Compare this with the output above; this value will match the S-PMSI output displayed in the "MVPN instance."

S-PMSI Configuration Using Wild Cards Let us say we would like all C-MCAST traffic to use an S-PMSI instead of ever using an I-PMSI. This is akin to stating: use only a Data MDT and no Default MDT

```
operator@PE3# run show multicast route instance FOO-MVPN extensive
Family: INET
Group: 239.1.1.1
    Source: 192.168.1.9/32
    Upstream interface: lsi.1
    Downstream interface list:
        ge-1/0/2.0
    Session description: Administratively Scoped
    Statistics: 97 kBps, 1156 pps, 3375081 packets
    Next-hop ID: 1048577
    Upstream protocol: MVPN
    Route state: Active
    Forwarding state: Forwarding
    Cache lifetime/timeout: forever
    Wrong incoming interface notifications: 0
```

Figure 2.203 Checking the Multicast Forwarding Table

```
operator@PE3# run show mvpn instance
MVPN instance:
Legend for provider tunnel
I-P-tnl -- inclusive provider tunnel S-P-tnl -- selective provider tunnel
Legend for c-multicast routes properties (Pr)
DS -- derived from (*, c-g)          RM -- remote VPN route
Instance : FOO-MVPN
  MVPN Mode : SPT-ONLY
  Provider tunnel: I-P-tnl:invalid:
  Neighbor                           I-P-tnl
  7.0.0.1                            RSVP-TE P2MP:7.0.0.1, 47053,7.0.0.1
  7.0.0.4
C-mcast IPv4 (S:G)         Ptnl                                      St
192.168.1.9/32:239.1.1.1/32   RSVP-TE P2MP:7.0.0.1, 47053,7.0.0.1   DS
```

Figure 2.204 Checking the MVPN Instance

ever in the context of a Draft-Rosen implementation—which is not possible in Draft-Rosen MVPNs. However, this could be a requirement for operators who intend to save on bandwidth utilization and are not concerned about saving on additional state information. In this case, wild cards can be used. The relevant configuration is provided in Figure 2.208. A group entry "224.0.0.0/4" indicates all multicast groups, and a source entry of "0.0.0.0/0" indicates all sources or any source.

Validations at the Ingress PE Router – PE1 We can check the MVPN routing table to ensure that Type 3 and Type 4 announcements have been originated and received for groups (238.1.1.1 and 239.1.1.1). We notice two Type 4 route announcements from PE2 for groups (238.1.1.1 and 239.1.1.1), and just one Type 4 announcement from PE3 for group (239.1.1.1), since PE3 does not have an interested receiver for the group 238.1.1.1.

The output shown in Figure 2.209 validates the same. See some detailed outputs in Figure 2.210.

```
routing-instances {
FOO-MVPN {
    instance-type vrf;
    interface ge-4/0/1.0;
    interface lo0.1;
    route-distinguisher 100:1;
    provider-tunnel {
        rsvp-te {
            label-switched-path-template {
                P2MP-RSVP-TE;
            }
        }
        selective {
            group 238.1.1.1/32 {
                source 192.168.1.9/32 {
                    rsvp-te {
                        label-switched-path-template {
                            P2MP-RSVP-TE;
                        }
                    }
                    threshold-rate 10; ----> 10Kbps Threshold defined
                }
            }
        }
    }
    vrf-target target:100:1;
    vrf-table-label;
    protocols {
        bgp {
            family inet {
                unicast;
            }
            group peer {
                type external;
                export export;
                peer-as 65005;
                neighbor 192.168.1.9;
                neighbor 192.168.1.17 {
                    peer-as 65010;
                }
            }
        }
        pim {
            rp {
                local {
                    address 7.0.0.1;
                }
            }
            interface ge-4/0/1.0 {
                mode sparse;
                version 2;
            }
            interface lo0.1 {
                mode sparse;
                version 2;
            }
        }
        mvpn {
            traceoptions {
                file MVPN size 1m world-readable;
                flag all;
            }
        }
    }
}
}
```

Figure 2.205 Ingress PE Router Configuration – PE1

```
operator@PE1# run show mvpn instance
MVPN instance:
Legend for provider tunnel
I-P-tnl -- inclusive provider tunnel S-P-tnl -- selective provider tunnel
Legend for c-multicast routes properties (Pr)
DS -- derived from (*, c-g)          RM -- remote VPN route
Instance : FOO-MVPN
  MVPN Mode : SPT-ONLY
  Provider tunnel: I-P-tnl:RSVP-TE P2MP:7.0.0.1, 47053,7.0.0.1
  Neighbor                           I-P-tnl
  7.0.0.4
  7.0.0.5
  C-mcast IPv4 (S:G)              Ptnl                                  St
  192.168.1.9/32:238.1.1.1/32    S-RSVP-TE P2MP:7.0.0.1, 47056,7.0.0.1  RM
```

Figure 2.206 Checking the MVPN Instance

```
Sep 20 20:27:35.746064 Checking SPMSI bw: threshold=10, mc=1056
Sep 20 20:27:35.746163 Add SPMSI AD route for mvpn
3:100:1:32:192.168.1.9:32:238.1.1.1:7.0.0.1
Sep 20 20:27:35.746352 Flash call for MVPN from FOO-MVPN.MVPN.0
Sep 20 20:27:35.746361 Flash processing complete for MVPN from FOO-
MVPN.MVPN.0
Sep 20 20:27:35.758324 Flash call for MVPN from FOO-MVPN.MVPN.0
Sep 20 20:27:35.758337 Received LEAF-AD route from 4000007 for,
4:3:100:1:32:192.168.1.9:32:238.1.1.1:7.0.0.1:7.0.0.4 ----> PE2
Sep 20 20:27:35.758384 Flash processing complete for MVPN from FOO-
MVPN.MVPN.0
Sep 20 20:28:05.747471 Instance FOO-MVPN: unbind cmcast
238.1.1.1.192.168.1.9 from ptnl 0x8EAE900 flags 0x4001 refcnt 1 type 0 root
Flags 0x0: Label[0:0:0]: RSVP-TE: Session_13[7.0.0.1:0:47053:7.0.0.1]
Sep 20 20:28:05.747540 mvpn_fw_get_cmcast_nh Evaluating RD 0x64:1 for
cmcast 238.1.1.1.192.168.1.9 - fwd rt 0x900d8e8
Sep 20 20:28:05.747548 mvpn_fw_get_mcast_nh_source_rt done: add_ptnl (1/1),
nh empty 1
Sep 20 20:28:05.747554 mvpn_fw_get_mcast_nh_inherit_shrd_rt done: add_ptnl
(0/1), nh empty 1
Sep 20 20:28:05.747570 Instance FOO-MVPN: mvpn_ptnl_cmcast_fw_rt_upd for
238.1.1.1.192.168.1.9 on ptnl 0x8EAE900 flags 0x4001 refcnt 1 type 0 root
Flags 0x0: Label[0:0:0]: RSVP-TE: Session_13[7.0.0.1:0:47053:7.0.0.1]: nh
0x9007688
Sep 20 20:28:05.747580 Instance FOO-MVPN: mvpn_fw_rt_update for
238.1.1.1.192.168.1.9 on ptnl 0x8EAE900 flags 0x4001 refcnt 1 type 0 root
Flags 0x0: Label[0:0:0]: RSVP-TE: Session_13[7.0.0.1:0:47053:7.0.0.1]
Sep 20 20:28:05.747596 Instance FOO-MVPN: bind cmcast 238.1.1.1.192.168.1.9
to ptnl 0x8EAEB80 flags 0x8001 refcnt 1 type 0 root Flags 0x1:
Label[0:0:0]: RSVP-TE: Session_13[7.0.0.1:0:47056:7.0.0.1]
Sep 20 20:28:05.758441 mvpn_fw_get_cmcast_nh Evaluating RD 0x64:1 for
cmcast 238.1.1.1.192.168.1.9 - fwd rt 0x900d8e8
Sep 20 20:28:05.758448 mvpn_fw_get_mcast_nh_source_rt done: add_ptnl (1/1),
nh empty 1
Sep 20 20:28:05.758453 mvpn_fw_get_mcast_nh_inherit_shrd_rt done: add_ptnl
(0/1), nh empty 1
Sep 20 20:28:05.758464 Instance FOO-MVPN: mvpn_ptnl_cmcast_fw_rt_upd for
238.1.1.1.192.168.1.9 on ptnl 0x8EAEB80 flags 0x8021 refcnt 1 type 0 root
Flags 0x1: Label[0:0:0]: RSVP-TE: Session_13[7.0.0.1:0:47056:7.0.0.1]: nh
0x9007b08
Sep 20 20:28:05.758473 Instance FOO-MVPN: mvpn_fw_rt_update for
238.1.1.1.192.168.1.9 on ptnl 0x8EAEB80 flags 0x8021 refcnt 1 type 0 root
Flags 0x1: Label[0:0:0]: RSVP-TE: Session_13[7.0.0.1:0:47056:7.0.0.1]
```

Figure 2.207 Traceoptions Output

```
routing-instances {
FOO-MVPN {
    instance-type vrf;
    interface ge-4/0/1.0;
    interface lo0.1;
    route-distinguisher 100:1;
    provider-tunnel {
        rsvp-te {
            label-switched-path-template {
                P2MP-RSVP-TE;
            }
        }
        selective {
            group 224.0.0.0/4 {
                source 0.0.0.0/0 {
                    rsvp-te {
                        label-switched-path-template {
                            P2MP-RSVP-TE;
                        }
                    }
                }
            }
        }
    }
    vrf-target target:100:1;
    vrf-table-label;
    protocols {
        bgp {
            family inet {
                unicast;
            }
            group peer {
                type external;
                peer-as 65005;
                neighbor 192.168.1.9;
                neighbor 192.168.1.17 {
                    peer-as 65010;
                }
            }
        }
        pim {
            rp {
                local {
                    address 7.0.0.1;
                }
            }
            interface ge-4/0/1.0 {
                mode sparse;
                version 2;
            }
            interface lo0.1 {
                mode sparse;
                version 2;
            }
        }
        mvpn {
            traceoptions {
                file MVPN size 1m world-readable;
                flag all;
            }
        }
    }
  }
}
```

Figure 2.208 Ingress PE Router Configuration – PE1

```
operator@PE1# run show route table FOO-MVPN.mvpn.0
FOO-MVPN.mvpn.0: 12 destinations, 15 routes (12 active, 0 holddown, 0
hidden)
+ = Active Route, - = Last Active, * = Both
1:100:1:7.0.0.1/240
                      *[MVPN/70] 02:00:57, metric2 1
                         Indirect
1:100:1:7.0.0.4/240
                      *[BGP/170] 00:07:50, localpref 100, from 7.0.0.4
                         AS path: I
                       > to 172.16.1.5 via ge-4/0/0.0
1:100:1:7.0.0.5/240
                      *[BGP/170] 00:07:50, localpref 100, from 7.0.0.5
                         AS path: I
                       > to 172.16.1.5 via ge-4/0/0.0, Push 299792
3:100:1:32:192.168.1.9:32:238.1.1.1:7.0.0.1/240
                      *[MVPN/70] 00:06:49, metric2 1
                         Indirect
3:100:1:32:192.168.1.9:32:239.1.1.1:7.0.0.1/240
                      *[MVPN/70] 00:06:54, metric2 1
                         Indirect
4:3:100:1:32:192.168.1.9:32:238.1.1.1:7.0.0.1:7.0.0.4/240
                      *[BGP/170] 00:06:49, localpref 100, from 7.0.0.4
                         AS path: I
                       > to 172.16.1.5 via ge-4/0/0.0
4:3:100:1:32:192.168.1.9:32:239.1.1.1:7.0.0.1:7.0.0.4/240
                      *[BGP/170] 00:06:54, localpref 100, from 7.0.0.4
                         AS path: I
                       > to 172.16.1.5 via ge-4/0/0.0
4:3:100:1:32:192.168.1.9:32:239.1.1.1:7.0.0.1:7.0.0.5/240
                      *[BGP/170] 00:06:54, localpref 100, from 7.0.0.5
                         AS path: I
                       > to 172.16.1.5 via ge-4/0/0.0, Push 299792
5:100:1:32:192.168.1.9:32:238.1.1.1/240
                      *[PIM/105] 00:06:49
                         Multicast (IPv4)
5:100:1:32:192.168.1.9:32:239.1.1.1/240
                      *[PIM/105] 00:06:54
                         Multicast (IPv4)
7:100:1:100:32:192.168.1.9:32:238.1.1.1/240
                      *[PIM/105] 00:06:49
                         Multicast (IPv4)
                       [BGP/170] 00:06:49, localpref 100, from 7.0.0.4
                         AS path: I
                       > to 172.16.1.5 via ge-4/0/0.0
7:100:1:100:32:192.168.1.9:32:239.1.1.1/240
                      *[PIM/105] 00:06:54
                         Multicast (IPv4)
                       [BGP/170] 00:06:54, localpref 100, from 7.0.0.4
                         AS path: I
                       > to 172.16.1.5 via ge-4/0/0.0
                       [BGP/170] 00:06:54, localpref 100, from 7.0.0.5
                         AS path: I
                       > to 172.16.1.5 via ge-4/0/0.0, Push 299792
```

Figure 2.209 Checking the MVPN Routing Table

```
operator@PE1# run show route table FOO-MVPN.mvpn.0 detail
FOO-MVPN.mvpn.0: 12 destinations, 15 routes (12 active, 0 holddown, 0
hidden)
1:100:1:7.0.0.1/240 (1 entry, 1 announced)
        *MVPN   Preference: 70
                Next hop type: Indirect
                Next-hop reference count: 5
                Protocol next hop: 7.0.0.1
                Indirect next hop: 0 -
                State: <Active Int Ext>
                Age: 2:04:39    Metric2: 1
                Task: mvpn global task
                Announcement bits (3): 0-PIM.FOO-MVPN 1-mvpn global task 2-
BGP RT Background
                AS path: I


1:100:1:7.0.0.4/240 (1 entry, 1 announced)
        *BGP    Preference: 170/-101
                Next hop type: Indirect
                Next-hop reference count: 10
                Source: 7.0.0.4
                Protocol next hop: 7.0.0.4
                Indirect next hop: 2 no-forward
                State: <Secondary Active Int Ext>
                Local AS:   100 Peer AS:   100
                Age: 11:32    Metric2: 1
                Task: BGP_100.7.0.0.4+57844
                Announcement bits (2): 0-PIM.FOO-MVPN 1-mvpn global task
                AS path: I
                Communities: target:100:1
                Import Accepted
                Localpref: 100
                Router ID: 7.0.0.4
                Primary Routing Table bgp.mvpn.0


1:100:1:7.0.0.5/240 (1 entry, 1 announced)
        *BGP    Preference: 170/-101
                Next hop type: Indirect
                Next-hop reference count: 6
                Source: 7.0.0.5
                Protocol next hop: 7.0.0.5
                Indirect next hop: 2 no-forward
                State: <Secondary Active Int Ext>
                Local AS:   100 Peer AS:   100
                Age: 11:32     Metric2: 1
                Task: BGP_100.7.0.0.5+61278
                Announcement bits (2): 0-PIM.FOO-MVPN 1-mvpn global task
                AS path: I
                Communities: target:100:1
                Import Accepted
                Localpref: 100
                Router ID: 7.0.0.5
                Primary Routing Table bgp.mvpn.0


3:100:1:32:192.168.1.9:32:238.1.1.1:7.0.0.1/240 (1 entry, 1 announced)
        *MVPN   Preference: 70
                Next hop type: Indirect
                Next-hop reference count: 5
```

Figure 2.210 Checking the MVPN Routing Table

Continued

```
                        Protocol next hop: 7.0.0.1
                        Indirect next hop: 0 -
                        State: <Active Int Ext>
                        Age: 10:31      Metric2: 1
                        Task: mvpn global task
                        Announcement bits (3): 0-PIM.FOO-MVPN 1-mvpn global task 2-
BGP RT Background
                        AS path: I

3:100:1:32:192.168.1.9:32:239.1.1.1:7.0.0.1/240 (1 entry, 1 announced)
        *MVPN   Preference: 70
                        Next hop type: Indirect
                        Next-hop reference count: 5
                        Protocol next hop: 7.0.0.1
                        Indirect next hop: 0 -
                        State: <Active Int Ext>
                        Age: 10:36      Metric2: 1
                        Task: mvpn global task
                        Announcement bits (3): 0-PIM.FOO-MVPN 1-mvpn global task 2-
BGP RT Background
                        AS path: I

4:3:100:1:32:192.168.1.9:32:238.1.1.1:7.0.0.1:7.0.0.4/240 (1 entry, 1
announced)
        *BGP    Preference: 170/-101
                        Next hop type: Indirect
                        Next-hop reference count: 10
                        Source: 7.0.0.4
                        Protocol next hop: 7.0.0.4
                        Indirect next hop: 2 no-forward
                        State: <Secondary Active Int Ext>
                        Local AS:    100 Peer AS:    100
                        Age: 10:31      Metric2: 1
                        Task: BGP_100.7.0.0.4+57844
                        Announcement bits (2): 0-PIM.FOO-MVPN 1-mvpn global task
                        AS path: I
                        Communities: target:7.0.0.1:0
                        Import Accepted
                        Localpref: 100
                        Router ID: 7.0.0.4
                        Primary Routing Table bgp.mvpn.0

4:3:100:1:32:192.168.1.9:32:239.1.1.1:7.0.0.1:7.0.0.4/240 (1 entry, 1
announced)
        *BGP    Preference: 170/-101
                        Next hop type: Indirect
                        Next-hop reference count: 10
                        Source: 7.0.0.4
                        Protocol next hop: 7.0.0.4
                        Indirect next hop: 2 no-forward
                        State: <Secondary Active Int Ext>
                        Local AS:    100 Peer AS:    100
                        Age: 10:36      Metric2: 1
                        Task: BGP_100.7.0.0.4+57844
                        Announcement bits (2): 0-PIM.FOO-MVPN 1-mvpn global task
                        AS path: I
                        Communities: target:7.0.0.1:0
                        Import Accepted
                        Localpref: 100
```

Figure 2.210, cont'd

```
                        Router ID: 7.0.0.4
                        Primary Routing Table bgp.mvpn.0

4:3:100:1:32:192.168.1.9:32:239.1.1.1:7.0.0.1:7.0.0.5/240 (1 entry, 1
announced)
          *BGP       Preference: 170/-101
                     Next hop type: Indirect
                     Next-hop reference count: 6
                     Source: 7.0.0.5
                     Protocol next hop: 7.0.0.5
                     Indirect next hop: 2 no-forward
                     State: <Secondary Active Int Ext>
                     Local AS:    100 Peer AS:    100
                     Age: 10:36       Metric2: 1
                     Task: BGP_100.7.0.0.5+61278
                     Announcement bits (2): 0-PIM.FOO-MVPN 1-mvpn global task
                     AS path: I
                     Communities: target:7.0.0.1:0
                     Import Accepted
                     Localpref: 100
                     Router ID: 7.0.0.5
                     Primary Routing Table bgp.mvpn.0

5:100:1:32:192.168.1.9:32:238.1.1.1/240 (1 entry, 1 announced)
          *PIM       Preference: 105
                     Next hop type: Multicast (IPv4)
                     Next-hop reference count: 7
                     State: <Active Int>
                     Age: 10:31
                     Task: PIM.FOO-MVPN
                     Announcement bits (3): 0-PIM.FOO-MVPN 1-mvpn global task 2-
BGP RT Background
                     AS path: I

5:100:1:32:192.168.1.9:32:239.1.1.1/240 (1 entry, 1 announced)
          *PIM       Preference: 105
                     Next hop type: Multicast (IPv4)
                     Next-hop reference count: 7
                     State: <Active Int>
                     Age: 10:36
                     Task: PIM.FOO-MVPN
                     Announcement bits (3): 0-PIM.FOO-MVPN 1-mvpn global task 2-
BGP RT Background
                     AS path: I

7:100:1:100:32:192.168.1.9:32:238.1.1.1/240 (2 entries, 2 announced)
          *PIM       Preference: 105
                     Next hop type: Multicast (IPv4)
                     Next-hop reference count: 7
                     State: <Active Int>
                     Age: 10:31
                     Task: PIM.FOO-MVPN
                     Announcement bits (2): 0-PIM.FOO-MVPN 1-mvpn global task
                     AS path: I
                     Communities: no-advertise target:7.0.0.1:5
           BGP       Preference: 170/-101
                     Next hop type: Indirect
                     Next-hop reference count: 10
                     Source: 7.0.0.4
```

Figure 2.210, cont'd

Continued

```
                    Protocol next hop: 7.0.0.4
                    Indirect next hop: 2 no-forward
                    State: <Secondary Int Ext>
                    Inactive reason: Route Preference
                    Local AS:    100 Peer AS:    100
                    Age: 10:31      Metric2: 1
                    Task: BGP_100.7.0.0.4+57844
                    Announcement bits (2): 0-PIM.FOO-MVPN 1-mvpn global task
                    AS path: I
                    Communities: target:7.0.0.1:5
                    Import Accepted
                    Localpref: 100
                    Router ID: 7.0.0.4

                    Primary Routing Table bgp.mvpn.0

  7:100:1:100:32:192.168.1.9:32:239.1.1.1/240 (3 entries, 3 announced)
        *PIM        Preference: 105
                    Next hop type: Multicast (IPv4)
                    Next-hop reference count: 7
                    State: <Active Int>
                    Age: 10:36
                    Task: PIM.FOO-MVPN
                    Announcement bits (2): 0-PIM.FOO-MVPN 1-mvpn global task
                    AS path: I
                    Communities: no-advertise target:7.0.0.1:5
         BGP        Preference: 170/-101
                    Next hop type: Indirect
                    Next-hop reference count: 10
                    Source: 7.0.0.4
                    Protocol next hop: 7.0.0.4
                    Indirect next hop: 2 no-forward
                    State: <Secondary Int Ext>
                    Inactive reason: Route Preference
                    Local AS:    100 Peer AS:    100
                    Age: 10:36      Metric2: 1
                    Task: BGP_100.7.0.0.4+57844
                    Announcement bits (2): 0-PIM.FOO-MVPN 1-mvpn global task
                    AS path: I
                    Communities: target:7.0.0.1:5
                    Import Accepted
                    Localpref: 100
                    Router ID: 7.0.0.4
                    Primary Routing Table bgp.mvpn.0
         BGP        Preference: 170/-101
                    Next hop type: Indirect
                    Next-hop reference count: 6
                    Source: 7.0.0.5
                    Protocol next hop: 7.0.0.5
                    Indirect next hop: 2 no-forward
                    State: <Secondary NotBest Int Ext>
                    Inactive reason: Not Best in its group - Router ID
                    Local AS:    100 Peer AS:    100
                    Age: 10:36      Metric2: 1
                    Task: BGP_100.7.0.0.5+61278
                    Announcement bits (2): 0-PIM.FOO-MVPN 1-mvpn global task
                    AS path: I
                    Communities: target:7.0.0.1:5
                    Import Accepted
                    Localpref: 100
                    Router ID: 7.0.0.5
                    Primary Routing Table bgp.mvpn.0
```

Figure 2.210, cont'd

Figure 2.211 shows checking the multicast forwarding table.

Finally, we can check the MVPN instance, as shown in Figure 2.212.

Validations at Egress PE Router PE2 We can perform the same set of steps on PE2 and then on PE3. On PE2 we notice two Type 3 and corresponding Type 4 routes, since PE2 has interested receivers for groups (238.1.1.1 and 239.1.1.1). See Figure 2.213.

```
operator@PE1# run show multicast route instance FOO-MVPN extensive
Family: INET
Group: 238.1.1.1
    Source: 192.168.1.9/32
    Upstream interface: ge-4/0/1.0
    Session description: Unknown
    Statistics: 854 kBps, 615 pps, 474525 packets
    Next-hop ID: 1048576
    Upstream protocol: MVPN
    Route state: Active
    Forwarding state: Forwarding
    Cache lifetime/timeout: forever
    Wrong incoming interface notifications: 0

Group: 239.1.1.1
    Source: 192.168.1.9/32
    Upstream interface: ge-4/0/1.0
    Session description: Administratively Scoped
    Statistics: 1211 kBps, 872 pps, 674573 packets
    Next-hop ID: 1048577
    Upstream protocol: MVPN
    Route state: Active
    Forwarding state: Forwarding
    Cache lifetime/timeout: forever
    Wrong incoming interface notifications: 0
```

Figure 2.211 Checking the Multicast Forwarding Table

```
operator@PE1# run show mvpn instance
MVPN instance:
Legend for provider tunnel
I-P-tnl -- inclusive provider tunnel S-P-tnl -- selective provider tunnel
Legend for c-multicast routes properties (Pr)
DS -- derived from (*, c-g)          RM -- remote VPN route
Instance : FOO-MVPN
  MVPN Mode : SPT-ONLY
  Provider tunnel: I-P-tnl:invalid:
  Neighbor                           I-P-tnl
  7.0.0.4
  7.0.0.5
C-mcast IPv4 (S:G)          Ptnl                                    St
192.168.1.9/32:238.1.1.1/32  S-RSVP-TE P2MP:7.0.0.1, 47058,7.0.0.1  RM
192.168.1.9/32:239.1.1.1/32  S-RSVP-TE P2MP:7.0.0.1, 47057,7.0.0.1  RM
```

Figure 2.212 Checking the MVPN Instance

```
operator@PE2# run show route table FOO-MVPN.mvpn.0
FOO-MVPN.mvpn.0: 15 destinations, 17 routes (15 active, 1 holddown, 0
hidden)
+ = Active Route, - = Last Active, * = Both
1:100:1:7.0.0.1/240
                    *[BGP/170] 00:17:29, localpref 100, from 7.0.0.1
                     AS path: I
                    > to 172.16.1.6 via ge-4/0/3.0
1:100:1:7.0.0.4/240
                    *[MVPN/70] 1d 03:30:20, metric2 1
                     Indirect
1:100:1:7.0.0.5/240
                    *[BGP/170] 1d 03:30:07, localpref 100, from 7.0.0.5
                     AS path: I
                    > to 172.16.1.2 via ge-4/0/0.0
3:100:1:32:192.168.1.9:32:238.1.1.1:7.0.0.1/240
                    *[BGP/170] 00:16:28, localpref 100, from 7.0.0.1
                     AS path: I
                    > to 172.16.1.6 via ge-4/0/3.0
3:100:1:32:192.168.1.9:32:239.1.1.1:7.0.0.1/240
                    *[BGP/170] 00:16:33, localpref 100, from 7.0.0.1
                     AS path: I
                    > to 172.16.1.6 via ge-4/0/3.0
4:3:100:1:32:192.168.1.9:32:238.1.1.1:7.0.0.1:7.0.0.4/240
                    *[MVPN/70] 00:16:28, metric2 1
                     Indirect
4:3:100:1:32:192.168.1.9:32:239.1.1.1:7.0.0.1:7.0.0.4/240
                    *[MVPN/70] 00:16:33, metric2 1
                     Indirect
5:100:1:32:192.168.1.9:32:238.1.1.1/240
                    *[BGP/170] 00:16:28, localpref 100, from 7.0.0.1
                     AS path: I
                    > to 172.16.1.6 via ge-4/0/3.0
5:100:1:32:192.168.1.9:32:239.1.1.1/240
                    *[BGP/170] 00:16:33, localpref 100, from 7.0.0.1
                     AS path: I
                    > to 172.16.1.6 via ge-4/0/3.0
6:100:1:100:32:7.0.0.1:32:224.2.127.254/240
                    *[PIM/105] 00:17:29
                     Multicast (IPv4)
6:100:1:100:32:7.0.0.1:32:233.1.1.1/240
                    *[PIM/105] 00:17:29
                     Multicast (IPv4)
6:100:1:100:32:7.0.0.1:32:238.1.1.1/240
                    *[PIM/105] 00:17:29
                     Multicast (IPv4)
6:100:1:100:32:7.0.0.1:32:239.1.1.1/240
                    *[PIM/105] 00:17:29
                     Multicast (IPv4)
7:100:1:100:32:192.168.1.9:32:238.1.1.1/240
                    *[MVPN/70] 00:16:28, metric2 1
                     Multicast (IPv4)
                     [PIM/105] 00:16:28
                     Multicast (IPv4)
7:100:1:100:32:192.168.1.9:32:239.1.1.1/240
                    *[MVPN/70] 00:16:33, metric2 1
                     Multicast (IPv4)
                     [PIM/105] 00:16:32
                     Multicast (IPv4)
```

Figure 2.213 Checking the MVPN Routing Table

```
operator@PE2# run show route table FOO-MVPN.mvpn.0 detail
FOO-MVPN.mvpn.0: 15 destinations, 17 routes (15 active, 1 holddown, 0
hidden)
1:100:1:7.0.0.1/240 (1 entry, 1 announced)
        *BGP    Preference: 170/-101
                Next hop type: Indirect
                Next-hop reference count: 10
                Source: 7.0.0.1
                Protocol next hop: 7.0.0.1
                Indirect next hop: 2 no-forward
                State: <Secondary Active Int Ext>
                Local AS:    100 Peer AS:    100
                Age: 19:43      Metric2: 1
                Task: BGP_100.7.0.0.1+179
                Announcement bits (2): 0-PIM.FOO-MVPN 1-mvpn global task
                AS path: I
                Communities: target:100:1
                Import Accepted
                Localpref: 100
                Router ID: 7.0.0.1
                Primary Routing Table bgp.mvpn.0

    1:100:1:7.0.0.4/240 (1 entry, 1 announced)
        *MVPN   Preference: 70
                Next hop type: Indirect
                Next-hop reference count: 5
                Protocol next hop: 7.0.0.4
                Indirect next hop: 0 -
                State: <Active Int Ext>
                Age: 1d 3:32:34          Metric2: 1
                Task: mvpn global task
                Announcement bits (3): 0-PIM.FOO-MVPN 1-mvpn global task 2-
    BGP RT Background
                AS path: I

    1:100:1:7.0.0.5/240 (1 entry, 1 announced)
        *BGP    Preference: 170/-101
                Next hop type: Indirect
                Next-hop reference count: 2
                Source: 7.0.0.5
                Protocol next hop: 7.0.0.5
                Indirect next hop: 2 no-forward
                State: <Secondary Active Int Ext>
                Local AS:    100 Peer AS:    100
                Age: 1d 3:32:21         Metric2: 1
                Task: BGP_100.7.0.0.5+179
                Announcement bits (2): 0-PIM.FOO-MVPN 1-mvpn global task
                AS path: I
                Communities: target:100:1
                Import Accepted
                Localpref: 100
                Router ID: 7.0.0.5
                Primary Routing Table bgp.mvpn.0

3:100:1:32:192.168.1.9:32:238.1.1.1:7.0.0.1/240 (1 entry, 1 announced)
      *BGP      Preference: 170/-101
PMSI: Flags 0x1: Label[0:0:0]: RSVP-TE: Session_13[7.0.0.1:0:47058:7.0.0.1]
                Next hop type: Indirect
                Next-hop reference count: 10
                Source: 7.0.0.1
```

Figure 2.214 Checking the MVPN Routing Table – Detailed Outputs

Continued

```
                         Protocol next hop: 7.0.0.1
                         Indirect next hop: 2 no-forward
                         State: <Secondary Active Int Ext>
                         Local AS:    100 Peer AS:    100
                         Age: 18:42      Metric2: 1
                         Task: BGP_100.7.0.0.1+179
                         Announcement bits (2): 0-PIM.FOO-MVPN 1-mvpn global task
                         AS path: I
                         Communities: target:100:1
                         Import Accepted
                         Localpref: 100
                         Router ID: 7.0.0.1
                         Primary Routing Table bgp.mvpn.0

  3:100:1:32:192.168.1.9:32:239.1.1.1:7.0.0.1/240 (1 entry, 1 announced)
          *BGP     Preference: 170/-101
  PMSI: Flags 0x1: Label[0:0:0]: RSVP-TE: Session_13[7.0.0.1:0:47057:7.0.0.1]
                         Next hop type: Indirect
                         Next-hop reference count: 10
                         Source: 7.0.0.1
                         Protocol next hop: 7.0.0.1
                         Indirect next hop: 2 no-forward
                         State: <Secondary Active Int Ext>
                         Local AS:    100 Peer AS:    100
                         Age: 18:47      Metric2: 1
                         Task: BGP_100.7.0.0.1+179
                         Announcement bits (2): 0-PIM.FOO-MVPN 1-mvpn global task
                         AS path: I
                         Communities: target:100:1
                         Import Accepted
                         Localpref: 100
                         Router ID: 7.0.0.1
                         Primary Routing Table bgp.mvpn.0

  4:3:100:1:32:192.168.1.9:32:238.1.1.1:7.0.0.1:7.0.0.4/240 (1 entry, 1
  announced)
          *MVPN    Preference: 70
                         Next hop type: Indirect
                         Next-hop reference count: 5
                         Protocol next hop: 7.0.0.4
                         Indirect next hop: 0 -
                         State: <Active Int Ext>
                         Age: 18:42      Metric2: 1
                         Task: mvpn global task
                         Announcement bits (3): 0-PIM.FOO-MVPN 1-mvpn global task 2-
  BGP RT Background
                         AS path: I
                         Communities: target:7.0.0.1:0

  4:3:100:1:32:192.168.1.9:32:239.1.1.1:7.0.0.1:7.0.0.4/240 (1 entry, 1
  announced)
          *MVPN    Preference: 70
                         Next hop type: Indirect
                         Next-hop reference count: 5
                         Protocol next hop: 7.0.0.4
                         Indirect next hop: 0 -
                         State: <Active Int Ext>
                         Age: 18:47      Metric2: 1
                         Task: mvpn global task
                         Announcement bits (3): 0-PIM.FOO-MVPN 1-mvpn global task 2-
```

Figure 2.214, cont'd

```
BGP RT Background
                AS path: I
                Communities: target:7.0.0.1:0

5:100:1:32:192.168.1.9:32:238.1.1.1/240 (1 entry, 1 announced)
        *BGP    Preference: 170/-101
                Next hop type: Indirect
                Next-hop reference count: 10
                Source: 7.0.0.1
                Protocol next hop: 7.0.0.1
                Indirect next hop: 2 no-forward
                State: <Secondary Active Int Ext>
                Local AS:    100 Peer AS:    100
                Age: 18:42      Metric2: 1
                Task: BGP_100.7.0.0.1+179
                Announcement bits (2): 0-PIM.FOO-MVPN 1-mvpn global task
                AS path: I
                Communities: target:100:1
                Import Accepted
                Localpref: 100
                Router ID: 7.0.0.1
                Primary Routing Table bgp.mvpn.0

5:100:1:32:192.168.1.9:32:239.1.1.1/240 (1 entry, 1 announced)
        *BGP    Preference: 170/-101
                Next hop type: Indirect
                Next-hop reference count: 10
                Source: 7.0.0.1
                Protocol next hop: 7.0.0.1
                Indirect next hop: 2 no-forward
                State: <Secondary Active Int Ext>
                Local AS:    100 Peer AS:    100
                Age: 18:47      Metric2: 1
                Task: BGP_100.7.0.0.1+179
                Announcement bits (2): 0-PIM.FOO-MVPN 1-mvpn global task
                AS path: I
                Communities: target:100:1
                Import Accepted
                Localpref: 100
                Router ID: 7.0.0.1
                Primary Routing Table bgp.mvpn.0

6:100:1:100:32:7.0.0.1:32:224.2.127.254/240 (1 entry, 1 announced)
        *PIM    Preference: 105
                Next hop type: Multicast (IPv4), Next hop index: 1048576
                Next-hop reference count: 42
                State: <Active Int>
                Age: 19:43
                Task: PIM.FOO-MVPN
                Announcement bits (2): 0-PIM.FOO-MVPN 1-mvpn global task
                AS path: I
                Communities: no-advertise target:7.0.0.1:5

6:100:1:100:32:7.0.0.1:32:233.1.1.1/240 (1 entry, 1 announced)
        *PIM    Preference: 105
                Next hop type: Multicast (IPv4), Next hop index: 1048576
                Next-hop reference count: 42
```

Figure 2.214, cont'd

Continued

```
                    State: <Active Int>
                    Age: 19:43
                    Task: PIM.FOO-MVPN
                    Announcement bits (2): 0-PIM.FOO-MVPN 1-mvpn global task
                    AS path: I
                    Communities: no-advertise target:7.0.0.1:5

    6:100:1:100:32:7.0.0.1:32:238.1.1.1/240 (1 entry, 1 announced)
           *PIM     Preference: 105
                    Next hop type: Multicast (IPv4), Next hop index: 1048576
                    Next-hop reference count: 42
                    State: <Active Int>
                    Age: 19:43
                    Task: PIM.FOO-MVPN
                    Announcement bits (2): 0-PIM.FOO-MVPN 1-mvpn global task
                    AS path: I
                    Communities: no-advertise target:7.0.0.1:5

    6:100:1:100:32:7.0.0.1:32:239.1.1.1/240 (1 entry, 1 announced)
           *PIM     Preference: 105
                    Next hop type: Multicast (IPv4), Next hop index: 1048576
                    Next-hop reference count: 42
                    State: <Active Int>
                    Age: 19:43
                    Task: PIM.FOO-MVPN
                    Announcement bits (2): 0-PIM.FOO-MVPN 1-mvpn global task
                    AS path: I
                    Communities: no-advertise target:7.0.0.1:5

    7:100:1:100:32:192.168.1.9:32:238.1.1.1/240 (2 entries, 2 announced)
           *MVPN    Preference: 70
                    Next hop type: Multicast (IPv4), Next hop index: 1048576
                    Next-hop reference count: 42
                    State: <Active Int Ext>
                    Age: 18:42      Metric2: 1
                    Task: mvpn global task
                    Announcement bits (3): 0-PIM.FOO-MVPN 1-mvpn global task 2-
BGP RT Background
                    AS path: I
                    Communities: target:7.0.0.1:5
            PIM     Preference: 105
                    Next hop type: Multicast (IPv4), Next hop index: 1048576
                    Next-hop reference count: 42
                    State: <Int>
                    Inactive reason: Route Preference
                    Age: 18:42
                    Task: PIM.FOO-MVPN
                    Announcement bits (2): 0-PIM.FOO-MVPN 1-mvpn global task
                    AS path: I
                    Communities: target:7.0.0.1:5

    7:100:1:100:32:192.168.1.9:32:239.1.1.1/240 (2 entries, 2 announced)
           *MVPN    Preference: 70
                    Next hop type: Multicast (IPv4), Next hop index: 1048576
                    Next-hop reference count: 42
                    State: <Active Int Ext>
                    Age: 18:47      Metric2: 1
                    Task: mvpn global task
                    Announcement bits (3): 0-PIM.FOO-MVPN 1-mvpn global task 2-
```

Figure 2.214, cont'd

```
BGP RT Background
                AS path: I
                Communities: target:7.0.0.1:5
        PIM     Preference: 105
                Next hop type: Multicast (IPv4), Next hop index: 1048576
                Next-hop reference count: 42
                State: <Int>
                Inactive reason: Route Preference
                Age: 18:46
                Task: PIM.FOO-MVPN
                Announcement bits (2): 0-PIM.FOO-MVPN 1-mvpn global task
                AS path: I
                Communities: target:7.0.0.1:5
```

Figure 2.214, cont'd

```
operator@PE2# run show multicast route instance FOO-MVPN extensive
Family: INET
Group: 238.1.1.1
    Source: 192.168.1.9/32
    Upstream interface: lsi.21
    Downstream interface list:
        ge-4/0/2.100
    Session description: Unknown
    Statistics: 898 kBps, 1068 pps, 1313590 packets
    Next-hop ID: 1048576
    Upstream protocol: MVPN
    Route state: Active
    Forwarding state: Forwarding
    Cache lifetime/timeout: forever
    Wrong incoming interface notifications: 0

Group: 239.1.1.1
    Source: 192.168.1.9/32
    Upstream interface: lsi.21
    Downstream interface list:
        ge-4/0/2.100
    Session description: Administratively Scoped
    Statistics: 1223 kBps, 1454 pps, 1854674 packets
    Next-hop ID: 1048576
    Upstream protocol: MVPN
    Route state: Active
    Forwarding state: Forwarding
    Cache lifetime/timeout: forever
    Wrong incoming interface notifications: 0
```

Figure 2.215 Checking the MVPN Forwarding Table

Some detailed outputs are shown in Figure 2.214.

Now we can check the multicast forwarding table, as shown in Figure 2.215.

```
operator@PE2# run show mvpn instance
MVPN instance:
Legend for provider tunnel
I-P-tnl -- inclusive provider tunnel S-P-tnl -- selective provider tunnel
Legend for c-multicast routes properties (Pr)
DS -- derived from (*, c-g)        RM -- remote VPN route
Instance : FOO-MVPN
  MVPN Mode : SPT-ONLY
  Provider tunnel: I-P-tnl:invalid:
  Neighbor                         I-P-tnl
  7.0.0.1
  7.0.0.5
C-mcast IPv4 (S:G)          Ptnl                                      St
192.168.1.9/32:238.1.1.1/32  S-RSVP-TE P2MP:7.0.0.1, 47058,7.0.0.1 DS
192.168.1.9/32:239.1.1.1/32  S-RSVP-TE P2MP:7.0.0.1, 47057,7.0.0.1 DS
```

Figure 2.216 Checking the MVPN Forwarding Table

Now we can check the MVPN instance information, as shown in Figure 2.216.

Validations at Egress PE Router PE3 The same set of procedures for validation performed on PE 2 are now performed on PE3. See Figures 2.217, 2.218, 2.219, and 2.220.

MLDP Provider Tunnels

Let us move onto the details of using MLDP (Multicast LDP) as provider tunnels. This is defined in "draft-minei-mpls-ldp-p2mp.txt." In this section we discuss the setup and signaling of MLDP P2MP LSPs. From a functional standpoint, MLDP LSPs can be used for signaling both I-PMSI and S-PMSI tunnels. The difference between MLDP and RSVP-TE is that the former cannot provide any TE-specific features such as bandwidth guarantees, built-in link protection, or user-defined paths based on constraints.

The setup of I-PMSI and S-PMSI tunnels is the same as the process defined in the section titled "RSVP-TE P-tunnels," since the attributes are attached within the BGP MVPN routes. Hence there is no additional process involved.

An MLDP P2MP LSP allows traffic from a single root (or ingress) node to be delivered to a number of leaf (or egress) nodes. As with RSVP-TE, only a single copy of the packet is sent on any link traversed by the Multipoint (MP) LSP. This is accomplished without the use of a multicast protocol in the network. There can be several Multipoint LSPs rooted at a given ingress node, each with its own identifier. The leaf nodes (egress PEs) of the MP LSP come to know about the root node (ingress PE) and

```
operator@PE3# run show route table FOO-MVPN.mvpn.0
FOO-MVPN.mvpn.0: 11 destinations, 12 routes (11 active, 0 holddown, 0
hidden)
+ = Active Route, - = Last Active, * = Both

1:100:1:7.0.0.1/240
                      *[BGP/170] 00:25:04, localpref 100, from 7.0.0.1
                        AS path: I
                      > to 172.16.1.1 via ge-1/0/1.0, Push 299856
1:100:1:7.0.0.4/240
                      *[BGP/170] 1d 03:37:55, localpref 100, from 7.0.0.4
                        AS path: I
                      > to 172.16.1.1 via ge-1/0/1.0
1:100:1:7.0.0.5/240
                      *[MVPN/70] 1d 03:37:42, metric2 1
                        Indirect
3:100:1:32:192.168.1.9:32:238.1.1.1:7.0.0.1/240
                      *[BGP/170] 00:24:03, localpref 100, from 7.0.0.1
                        AS path: I
                      > to 172.16.1.1 via ge-1/0/1.0, Push 299856
3:100:1:32:192.168.1.9:32:239.1.1.1:7.0.0.1/240
                      *[BGP/170] 00:24:08, localpref 100, from 7.0.0.1
                        AS path: I
                      > to 172.16.1.1 via ge-1/0/1.0, Push 299856
4:3:100:1:32:192.168.1.9:32:239.1.1.1:7.0.0.1:7.0.0.5/240
                      *[MVPN/70] 00:24:08, metric2 1
                        Indirect
5:100:1:32:192.168.1.9:32:238.1.1.1/240
                      *[BGP/170] 00:24:03, localpref 100, from 7.0.0.1
                        AS path: I
                      > to 172.16.1.1 via ge-1/0/1.0, Push 299856
5:100:1:32:192.168.1.9:32:239.1.1.1/240
                      *[BGP/170] 00:24:08, localpref 100, from 7.0.0.1
                        AS path: I
                      > to 172.16.1.1 via ge-1/0/1.0, Push 299856
6:100:1:100:32:7.0.0.1:32:224.2.127.254/240
                      *[PIM/105] 00:25:04
                        Multicast (IPv4)
6:100:1:100:32:7.0.0.1:32:239.1.1.1/240
                      *[PIM/105] 00:25:04
                        Multicast (IPv4)
7:100:1:100:32:192.168.1.9:32:239.1.1.1/240
                      *[MVPN/70] 00:24:08, metric2 1
                        Multicast (IPv4)
                      [PIM/105] 00:24:07
                        Multicast (IPv4)
```

Figure 2.217 Checking the MVPN Routing Table

identifier of the MP LSP to which they belong via the BGP control
plane and routing announcements.

While discussing RSVP-TE we saw that the ingress PE initiates
the P2MP LSP using RSVP PATH messages, which egress PE
routers respond to with appropriate label information. In the case
of MLDP P2MP LSPs, the leaf nodes initiate P2MP LSP setup and

tear-down. For instance, if an egress PE router receives a BGP Type 1 route from an ingress PE router with an I-PMSI attribute, the leaf initiates the setup of the P2MP LSP and also installs forwarding state to deliver the traffic received on a P2MP LSP to wherever it needs to go. Transit nodes install MPLS forwarding state and propagate the P2MP LSP setup (and tear-down) toward the root, and the root node installs forwarding state to map traffic into the P2MP LSP. For the setup of a P2MP LSP with LDP, we define one new protocol entity, the P2MP FEC element to be used in the FEC

```
operator@PE3# run show route table FOO-MVPN.mvpn.0 detail
FOO-MVPN.mvpn.0: 11 destinations, 12 routes (11 active, 0 holddown, 0
hidden)
1:100:1:7.0.0.1/240 (1 entry, 1 announced)
        *BGP    Preference: 170/-101
                Next hop type: Indirect
                Next-hop reference count: 10
                Source: 7.0.0.1
                Protocol next hop: 7.0.0.1
                Indirect next hop: 2 no-forward
                State: <Secondary Active Int Ext>
                Local AS:    100 Peer AS:    100
                Age: 26:32       Metric2: 1
                Task: BGP_100.7.0.0.1+179
                Announcement bits (2): 0-PIM.FOO-MVPN 1-mvpn global task
                AS path: I
                Communities: target:100:1
                Import Accepted
                Localpref: 100
                Router ID: 7.0.0.1
                Primary Routing Table bgp.mvpn.0

1:100:1:7.0.0.4/240 (1 entry, 1 announced)
        *BGP    Preference: 170/-101
                Next hop type: Indirect
                Next-hop reference count: 2
                Source: 7.0.0.4
                Protocol next hop: 7.0.0.4
                Indirect next hop: 2 no-forward
                State: <Secondary Active Int Ext>
                Local AS:    100 Peer AS:    100
                Age: 1d 3:39:23          Metric2: 1
                Task: BGP_100.7.0.0.4+63093
                Announcement bits (2): 0-PIM.FOO-MVPN 1-mvpn global task
                AS path: I
                Communities: target:100:1
                Import Accepted
                Localpref: 100
                Router ID: 7.0.0.4
                Primary Routing Table bgp.mvpn.0
```

Figure 2.218 Checking the MVPN Routing Table – Detailed Outputs

```
    1:100:1:7.0.0.5/240 (1 entry, 1 announced)
          *MVPN    Preference: 70
                   Next hop type: Indirect
                   Next-hop reference count: 4
                   Protocol next hop: 7.0.0.5
                   Indirect next hop: 0 -
                   State: <Active Int Ext>
                   Age: 1d 3:39:10         Metric2: 1
                   Task: mvpn global task
                   Announcement bits (3): 0-PIM.FOO-MVPN 1-mvpn global task 2-
BGP RT Background
                   AS path: I

    3:100:1:32:192.168.1.9:32:238.1.1.1:7.0.0.1/240 (1 entry, 1 announced)
          *BGP     Preference: 170/-101
PMSI: Flags 0x1: Label[0:0:0]: RSVP-TE: Session_13[7.0.0.1:0:47058:7.0.0.1]
                   Next hop type: Indirect
                   Next-hop reference count: 10
                   Source: 7.0.0.1
                   Protocol next hop: 7.0.0.1
                   Indirect next hop: 2 no-forward
                   State: <Secondary Active Int Ext>
                   Local AS:    100 Peer AS:    100
                   Age: 25:31       Metric2: 1
                   Task: BGP_100.7.0.0.1+179
                   Announcement bits (2): 0-PIM.FOO-MVPN 1-mvpn global task
                   AS path: I
                   Communities: target:100:1
                   Import Accepted
                   Localpref: 100
                   Router ID: 7.0.0.1
                   Primary Routing Table bgp.mvpn.0

    3:100:1:32:192.168.1.9:32:239.1.1.1:7.0.0.1/240 (1 entry, 1 announced)
          *BGP     Preference: 170/-101
PMSI: Flags 0x1: Label[0:0:0]: RSVP-TE: Session_13[7.0.0.1:0:47057:7.0.0.1]
                   Next hop type: Indirect
                   Next-hop reference count: 10
                   Source: 7.0.0.1
                   Protocol next hop: 7.0.0.1
                   Indirect next hop: 2 no-forward
                   State: <Secondary Active Int Ext>
                   Local AS:    100 Peer AS:    100
                   Age: 25:36       Metric2: 1
                   Task: BGP_100.7.0.0.1+179
                   Announcement bits (2): 0-PIM.FOO-MVPN 1-mvpn global task
                   AS path: I
                   Communities: target:100:1
                   Import Accepted
                   Localpref: 100
                   Router ID: 7.0.0.1
                   Primary Routing Table bgp.mvpn.0

    4:3:100:1:32:192.168.1.9:32:239.1.1.1:7.0.0.1:7.0.0.5/240 (1 entry, 1
announced)
          *MVPN    Preference: 70
                   Next hop type: Indirect
```

Figure 2.218, cont'd

Continued

```
                    Next-hop reference count: 4
                    Protocol next hop: 7.0.0.5
                    Indirect next hop: 0 -
                    State: <Active Int Ext>
                    Age: 25:36      Metric2: 1
                    Task: mvpn global task
                    Announcement bits (3): 0-PIM.FOO-MVPN 1-mvpn global task 2-
        BGP RT Background
                    AS path: I
                    Communities: target:7.0.0.1:0


        5:100:1:32:192.168.1.9:32:238.1.1.1/240 (1 entry, 1 announced)
              *BGP    Preference: 170/-101
                      Next hop type: Indirect
                      Next-hop reference count: 10
                      Source: 7.0.0.1
                      Protocol next hop: 7.0.0.1
                      Indirect next hop: 2 no-forward
                      State: <Secondary Active Int Ext>
                      Local AS:    100 Peer AS:    100
                      Age: 25:31      Metric2: 1
                      Task: BGP_100.7.0.0.1+179
                      Announcement bits (2): 0-PIM.FOO-MVPN 1-mvpn global task
                      AS path: I
                      Communities: target:100:1
                      Import Accepted
                      Localpref: 100
                      Router ID: 7.0.0.1
                      Primary Routing Table bgp.mvpn.0


        5:100:1:32:192.168.1.9:32:239.1.1.1/240 (1 entry, 1 announced)
              *BGP    Preference: 170/-101
                      Next hop type: Indirect
                      Next-hop reference count: 10
                      Source: 7.0.0.1
                      Protocol next hop: 7.0.0.1
                      Indirect next hop: 2 no-forward
                      State: <Secondary Active Int Ext>
                      Local AS:    100 Peer AS:    100
                      Age: 25:36      Metric2: 1
                      Task: BGP_100.7.0.0.1+179
                      Announcement bits (2): 0-PIM.FOO-MVPN 1-mvpn global task
                      AS path: I
                      Communities: target:100:1
                      Import Accepted
                      Localpref: 100
                      Router ID: 7.0.0.1
                      Primary Routing Table bgp.mvpn.0


        6:100:1:100:32:7.0.0.1:32:224.2.127.254/240 (1 entry, 1 announced)
              *PIM    Preference: 105
                      Next hop type: Multicast (IPv4), Next hop index: 1048577
                      Next-hop reference count: 21
                      State: <Active Int>
                      Age: 26:32
                      Task: PIM.FOO-MVPN
                      Announcement bits (2): 0-PIM.FOO-MVPN 1-mvpn global task
                      AS path: I
                      Communities: no-advertise target:7.0.0.1:5
```

Figure 2.218, cont'd

```
6:100:1:100:32:7.0.0.1:32:239.1.1.1/240 (1 entry, 1 announced)
        *PIM    Preference: 105
                Next hop type: Multicast (IPv4), Next hop index: 1048577
                Next-hop reference count: 21
                State: <Active Int>
                Age: 26:32
                Task: PIM.FOO-MVPN
                Announcement bits (2): 0-PIM.FOO-MVPN 1-mvpn global task
                AS path: I
                Communities: no-advertise target:7.0.0.1:5

7:100:1:100:32:192.168.1.9:32:239.1.1.1/240 (2 entries, 2 announced)
        *MVPN   Preference: 70
                Next hop type: Multicast (IPv4), Next hop index: 1048577
                Next-hop reference count: 21
                State: <Active Int Ext>
                Age: 25:36       Metric2: 1
                Task: mvpn global task
                Announcement bits (3): 0-PIM.FOO-MVPN 1-mvpn global task 2-
BGP RT Background
                AS path: I
                Communities: target:7.0.0.1:5
        PIM     Preference: 105
                Next hop type: Multicast (IPv4), Next hop index: 1048577
                Next-hop reference count: 21
                State: <Int>
                Inactive reason: Route Preference
                Age: 25:35
                Task: PIM.FOO-MVPN
                Announcement bits (2): 0-PIM.FOO-MVPN 1-mvpn global task
                AS path: I
                Communities: target:7.0.0.1:5
```

Figure 2.218, cont'd

```
operator@PE3# run show multicast route instance FOO-MVPN extensive
Family: INET
Group: 239.1.1.1
    Source: 192.168.1.9/32
    Upstream interface: lsi.1
    Downstream interface list:
        ge-1/0/2.0
    Session description: Administratively Scoped
    Statistics: 1224 kBps, 1455 pps, 2359320 packets
    Next-hop ID: 1048577
    Upstream protocol: MVPN
    Route state: Active
    Forwarding state: Forwarding
    Cache lifetime/timeout: forever
    Wrong incoming interface notifications: 0
```

Figure 2.219 Checking the MVPN Forwarding Table

```
operator@PE3# run show mvpn instance
MVPN instance:
Legend for provider tunnel
I-P-tnl -- inclusive provider tunnel S-P-tnl -- selective provider tunnel

Legend for c-multicast routes properties (Pr)
DS -- derived from (*, c-g)          RM -- remote VPN route
Instance : FOO-MVPN
  MVPN Mode : SPT-ONLY
  Provider tunnel: I-P-tnl:invalid:
  Neighbor                              I-P-tnl
  7.0.0.1
  7.0.0.4
C-mcast IPv4 (S:G)            Ptnl                                 St
192.168.1.9/32:239.1.1.1/32   S-RSVP-TE P2MP:7.0.0.1, 47057,7.0.0.1 DS
```

Figure 2.220 Checking the MVPN Forwarding Table

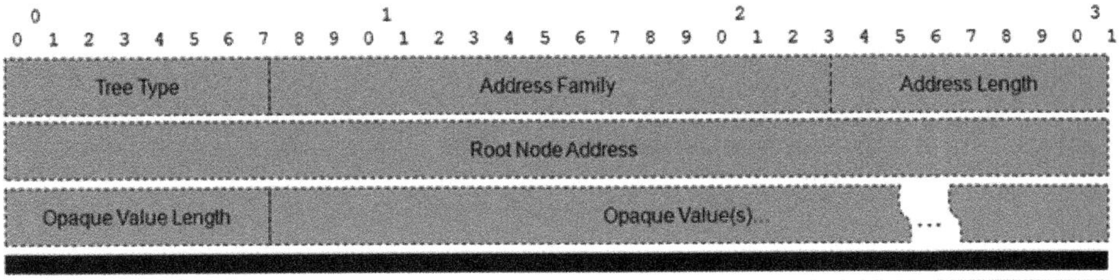

Parameters	Description
Tree Type	P2MP, MP2MP Up, MP2MP Down
Address Family	Root node address format (IPv4 =1 or IPv6 = 2)
Address Length	Number of octets in root address (IPv4 = 4, IPv6 = 16)
Root Node Address	Host address of MP LSP root (within MPLS core)
Opaque Value	One or more TLVs uniquely identifying MP LSP within the in context of the root

Figure 2.221

TLV. The description of the P2MP FEC element is as shown in Figure 2.221.

In the context of Next Generation MVPNs, the LDP Opaque Value Element is not used for any applications. However they are used in certain vendor (Non Next Generation Multicast VPN) MVPN implementations that also use MLDP as the forwarding plane. This is discussed in Chapter 7.

Now let us look at the setup of MLDP P2MP LSPs. As mentioned a bit earlier, an egress PE knows the next hop for the ingress PE connected to the multicast source, based on the BGP announcements. To receive the label switched packets, it needs to tell the upstream router what label it needs to use for this multicast stream. To advertise the label it sends a label mapping, containing the label to be used, to its upstream router for this multicast source. Since the upstream router does not need any knowledge of the source itself, it only contains a FEC to identify the P2MP tree. If the upstream router does not have any FEC state, it will create it and install the assigned downstream outgoing label. If the FEC state is created and this router is not the LSP-ingress of the P2MP tree, it needs to forward a label mapping upstream. This operation continues until the LSP ingress router is reached. This process is illustrated in Figure 2.222.

The same process is illustrated in Figure 2.223 from a forwarding point of view, that is, from the point of view of the ingress PE router.

Configurations

In this section we take a look at the I-PMSI and S-PMSI configurations needed for MLDP as the forwarding plane. The details on control-plane-specific outputs remain the same as detailed in the section on RSVP-TE, since the same BGP control plane infrastructure is used.

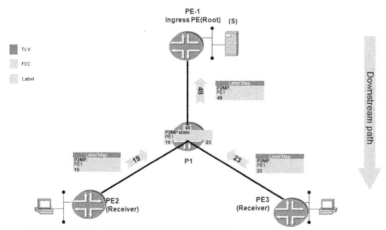

- Labels allocated from unicast label space
- Downstream on demand allocation method used

Figure 2.222

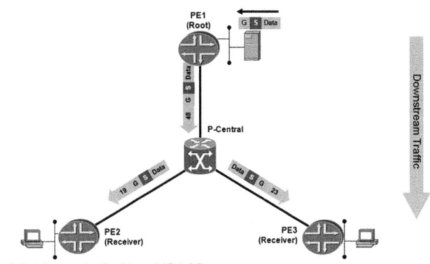

- PE-1 forwards (S, G) on MP-LSP
- Labels are swapped at each hop
  {48} → {19} and {23} at branching point

Figure 2.223

The only configuration needed for building an I-PMSI MLDP tunnel is the keyword "ldp-p2mp." See Figure 2.224.

Now we take a look at the S-PMSI configuration using MLDP. In this configuration we have defined an I-PMSI tunnel for all groups, and S-PMSI tunnel for the C-MCAST Source and Group pair (238.1.1.1 and 192.168.1.9). All possible options, including the use of wild-cards, as defined in the section on RSVP-TE P-tunnels, can be used with MLDP. An S-PMSI-only setup may also be used. This is possible since the BGP control plane is common for all the provider tunnel types. See Figure 2.225.

Now we move on to take a look at an MVPN P-tunnel specific output, as shown in Figure 2.226. The details here are similar to the details seen in the section on RSVP-TE.

PIM-SSM Provider Tunnels

In this section, we take a look at a network setup using PIM-SSM-based provider tunnels as the data plane along with the BGP control plane. The setup shown in Figure 2.227 will be used for demonstrating the functionality.

Configurations

In the configuration shown in Figure 2.228, we notice that the provider tunnel is now configured for PIM Source Specific Multicast with a group address "232.1.1.1". This group address is the PIM group address used in the provider network (think of the P-group address in Draft-Rosen Multicast VPNs), since we now

```
routing-instances {
FOO-MVPN {
    instance-type vrf;
    interface ge-4/0/1.0;
    interface lo0.1;
    route-distinguisher 100:1;
    provider-tunnel {
        ldp-p2mp;          -----------> P2MP I-PMSI Tunnel
        }
    vrf-target target:100:1;
    vrf-table-label;
    protocols {
        bgp {
            family inet {
                unicast;
            }
            group peer {
                type external;
                peer-as 65005;
                neighbor 192.168.1.9;
                neighbor 192.168.1.17 {
                    peer-as 65010;
                }
            }
        }
        pim {
            rp {
                local {
                    address 7.0.0.1;
                }
            }
            interface ge-4/0/1.0 {
                mode sparse;
                version 2;
            }
            interface lo0.1 {
                mode sparse;
                version 2;
            }
        }
        mvpn;
    }
}
}
```

Figure 2.224 I-PMSI Configuration Using MLDP Provider Tunnels

```
Routing-instances {
FOO-MVPN {
    instance-type vrf;
    interface ge-4/0/1.0;
    interface lo0.1;
    route-distinguisher 100:1;
    provider-tunnel {
       ldp-p2mp; ------------> I-PMSI Configuration
         selective { ----------> S-PMSI Configuration
             group 238.1.1.1/32 {
                 source 192.168.1.9/32 {
                     ldp-p2mp;

                         }
                     }
                 }
             }
    vrf-target target:100:1;
    vrf-table-label;
    protocols {
        bgp {
            family inet {
                unicast;
            }
            group peer {
                type external;
                peer-as 65005;
                neighbor 192.168.1.9;
                neighbor 192.168.1.17 {
                    peer-as 65010;
                }
            }
        }
        pim {
            rp {
                local {
                    address 7.0.0.1;
                }
            }
            interface ge-4/0/1.0 {
                mode sparse;
                version 2;
            }
            interface lo0.1 {
                mode sparse;
                version 2;
            }
        }
        mvpn;
    }
}
}
```

Figure 2.225 I-PMSI and S-PMSI Configuration

```
operator@PE1> show mvpn instance extensive
MVPN instance:
Legend for provider tunnel
I-P-tnl -- inclusive provider tunnel S-P-tnl -- selective provider tunnel
Legend for c-multicast routes properties (Pr)
DS -- derived from (*, c-g)          RM -- remote VPN route
Instance: FOO-MVPN
  Provider tunnel: I-P-tnl:LDP P2MP:7.0.0.1, lsp-id 1
  Neighbor                          I-P-tnl
  7.0.0.4
  7.0.0.5
  C-mcast IPv4 (S:G)               Ptnl                            St
  192.168.1.8/32:238.2.2.2/32      LDP P2MP:7.0.0.1, lsp-id 1      RM
```

Figure 2.226 Checking the MVPN Instance

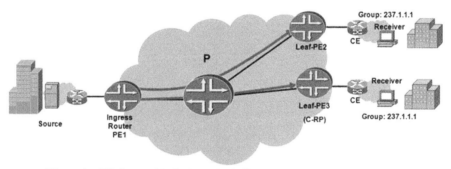

* The router "P" does not indicate a single Provider router, and indicates a
  Carrier Provider core, that may contain many devices. A single device is just
  given "ONLY" for illustrative reasons.

Figure 2.227

are using GRE-based SSM tunnels for creating the data plane infrastructure. To enable a PIM based infrastructure within the core, PIM has been enabled on the respective interfaces. However, notice that there is no RP configuration within the context of PIM in the master instance, since we are using SSM and not ASM or Spare Mode.

Now we move to the egress PE router configurations. Only the relevant portions of the configuration are displayed for the sake of simplicity. No P-tunnels are configured, since the egress PE routers only host receiver sites. See Figure 2.229 and Figure 2.230.

Validation of the Control Plane prior to Traffic Generation We start off by validating the control plane information on all the routers, prior to generating multicast traffic flows, as shown in Figures 2.231, 2.232, and 2.233.

```
protocols {
rsvp {
    interface ge-1/0/1.0;
}
mpls {
    interface ge-1/0/1.0;
    interface fe-1/1/0.0;
}
bgp {
    group PE {
        type internal;
        local-address 7.0.0.5;
        family inet-vpn {
            unicast;
        }
        family inet-mvpn {
            signaling;
        }
        neighbor 7.0.0.4 {
            peer-as 100;
        }
        neighbor 7.0.0.1 {
            peer-as 100;
        }
    }
}
ospf {
    area 0.0.0.0 {
        interface ge-1/0/1.0 {
            interface-type p2p;
        }
        interface lo0.0 {
            passive;
        }
        interface fe-1/1/0.0;
    }
}
ldp {
    interface ge-1/0/1.0;
    interface fe-1/1/0.0;
}
pim {
    interface all {
        version 2;
    }
}

routing-instances {
MVPN-FOO {
instance-type vrf;
interface ge-1/0/2.0;
interface lo0.1;
route-distinguisher 100:1;
provider-tunnel {
    pim-ssm {
        group-address 232.1.1.1;
    }
```

Figure 2.228 Ingress PE Router Configuration – PE1

Continued

```
        }
    vrf-target target:100:1;
    vrf-table-label;
    protocols {
        bgp {
            family inet {
                unicast;
            }
            group peer {
                type external;
                peer-as 65004;
                neighbor 192.168.1.5;
            }
        }
        pim {
            rp {
                static {
                    address 7.0.0.1;
                }
            }
            interface ge-1/0/2.0 {
                mode sparse-dense;
                version 2;
            }
            interface lo0.1 {
                mode sparse-dense;
                version 2;
            }
        }
        mvpn;
        }
    }
}
```

Figure 2.228, cont'd

Validation of the Control and Data Planes after Traffic Generation on PE1 Let us take a look at the respective outputs on PE1, after traffic has been generated from the C-MCAST source, connected behind PE1.

In the output shown in Figure 2.234, PE1 receives the Type 7 routes from PE2 and PE3, and also generates a Type 5 route. Another Type 5 route is received from PE3, which is the C-RP. Note that the customer multicast domain is still using ASM or PIM Sparse Mode.

Now we can check the multicast forwarding state on PE1, as shown in Figure 2.235. The downstream interface displays "MT," which means GRE-based Multicast Tunnel Interface.

Now we move on to checking the MVPN instance specific output. The display, represented in Figure 2.236, illustrates a PIM-SSM tunnel is being used, with associated C-MCAST Source

```
routing-instances {
MVPN-FOO {
instance-type vrf;
interface ge-4/0/2.100;
interface lo0.1;
route-distinguisher 100:1;
vrf-target target:100:1;
vrf-table-label;
protocols {
    bgp {
        family inet {
            unicast;
        }
        group peer {
            type external;
            peer-as 65003;
            neighbor 192.168.1.1;
        }
    }
    pim {
        rp {
            static {
                address 7.0.0.1;
            }
        }
        interface ge-4/0/2.100 {
            mode sparse-dense;
            version 2;
        }
        interface lo0.1 {
            mode sparse-dense;
            version 2;
        }
    }
    mvpn;
  }
 }
}
protocols {
 pim {
   interface all {
     version 2;
   }
 }
}
```

Figure 2.229 Egress PE Router Configuration – PE2

and Group Pairs. The P-tunnel also displays information on the PIM provider group being used in the core (232.1.1.1).

In the output in Figure 2.237, we check the PIM SSM specific information on the PIM Master instance. Note that we are using PIM-SSM in the core, and appropriate state information is created for the source (ingress PE) and provider multicast group address being used (232.1.1.1).

```
routing-instances {
MVPN-FOO {
instance-type vrf;
interface ge-4/0/2.100;
interface lo0.1;
route-distinguisher 100:1;
vrf-target target:100:1;
vrf-table-label;
protocols {
    bgp {
        family inet {
            unicast;
        }
        group peer {
            type external;
            peer-as 65003;
            neighbor 192.168.1.1;
        }
    }
    pim {
        rp {
            static {
                address 7.0.0.1;
            }
        }
        interface ge-4/0/2.100 {
            mode sparse-dense;
            version 2;
        }
        interface lo0.1 {
            mode sparse-dense;
            version 2;
        }
    }
    mvpn;
  }
 }
}
protocols {
 pim {
  interface all {
   version 2;
  }
 }
}
```

Figure 2.230 Egress PE Router Configuration – PE3

```
operator@PE1# run show route table MVPN-FOO.mvpn.0

1:100:1:7.0.0.1/240
                  *[BGP/170] 00:08:41, localpref 100, from 7.0.0.1
                    AS path: I
                  > to 172.16.1.1 via ge-1/0/1.0, Push 299808
1:100:1:7.0.0.4/240
                  *[BGP/170] 00:08:41, localpref 100, from 7.0.0.4
                    AS path: I
                  > to 172.16.1.1 via ge-1/0/1.0
1:100:1:7.0.0.5/240
                  *[MVPN/70] 00:00:22, metric2 1
                    Indirect
```

Figure 2.231 BGP MVPN Routing Information – PE1

```
operator@PE2# run show route table MVPN-FOO.mvpn.0
MVPN-FOO.mvpn.0: 5 destinations, 5 routes (5 active, 0 holddown, 0 hidden)
+ = Active Route, - = Last Active, * = Both
1:100:1:7.0.0.1/240
                    *[BGP/170] 00:30:07, localpref 100, from 7.0.0.1
                      AS path: I
                    > to 172.16.1.6 via ge-4/0/3.0
1:100:1:7.0.0.4/240
                    *[MVPN/70] 20:51:14, metric2 1
                      Indirect
1:100:1:7.0.0.5/240
                    *[BGP/170] 00:01:45, localpref 100, from 7.0.0.5
                      AS path: I
                    > to 172.16.1.2 via ge-4/0/0.0
6:100:1:100:32:7.0.0.1:32:237.1.1.1/240
                    *[PIM/105] 00:29:22
                      Multicast (IPv4)
```

Figure 2.232 BGP MVPN Routing Information – PE2

```
operator@PE3# run show route table MVPN-FOO.mvpn.0

1:100:1:7.0.0.1/240
                    *[MVPN/70] 00:31:50, metric2 1
                      Indirect
1:100:1:7.0.0.4/240
                    *[BGP/170] 20:47:15, localpref 100, from 7.0.0.4
                      AS path: I
                    > to 172.16.1.5 via ge-4/0/0.0
1:100:1:7.0.0.5/240
                    *[BGP/170] 00:03:27, localpref 100, from 7.0.0.5
                      AS path: I
                    > to 172.16.1.5 via ge-4/0/0.0, Push 299776
6:100:1:100:32:7.0.0.1:32:237.1.1.1/240
                    *[PIM/105] 00:00:08
                      Multicast (IPv4)
```

Figure 2.233 BGP MVPN Routing Information – PE3

Another interesting command, shown in Figure 2.238, can validate the control plane and data plane used. Here we see the data plane, control plane (NG-MVPN), and the associated routing instance.

Validation of the Control and Data Planes after Traffic Generation on PE2 Let us take a look at the respective outputs on PE2, which is an egress PE router, after traffic has been generated from the C-MCAST source, connected behind PE1. See Figure 2.239.

Now we can check the multicast forwarding state on PE2. As seen in Figure 2.240, the upstream interface displays "MT," which means GRE-based Multicast Tunnel Interface.

```
operator@PE1# run show route table MVPN-FOO.mvpn.0

1:100:1:7.0.0.1/240
                    *[BGP/170] 00:23:07, localpref 100, from 7.0.0.1
                      AS path: I
                    > to 172.16.1.1 via ge-1/0/1.0, Push 299808
1:100:1:7.0.0.4/240
                    *[BGP/170] 00:23:07, localpref 100, from 7.0.0.4
                      AS path: I
                    > to 172.16.1.1 via ge-1/0/1.0
1:100:1:7.0.0.5/240
                    *[MVPN/70] 00:14:48, metric2 1
                      Indirect
5:100:1:32:192.168.1.5:32:237.1.1.1/240
                    *[PIM/105] 00:00:03
                      Multicast (IPv4)
                     [BGP/170] 00:00:03, localpref 100, from 7.0.0.1
                      AS path: I
                    > to 172.16.1.1 via ge-1/0/1.0, Push 299808
7:100:1:100:32:192.168.1.5:32:237.1.1.1/240
                    *[PIM/105] 00:00:03
                      Multicast (IPv4)
                     [BGP/170] 00:00:03, localpref 100, from 7.0.0.1
                      AS path: I
                    > to 172.16.1.1 via ge-1/0/1.0, Push 299808
                     [BGP/170] 00:00:03, localpref 100, from 7.0.0.4
                      AS path: I
                    > to 172.16.1.1 via ge-1/0/1.0
```

Figure 2.234 BGP MVPN Routing Information – PE1

```
operator@PE1# run show multicast route instance MVPN-FOO extensive
Family: INET
Group: 237.1.1.1
    Source: 192.168.1.5/32
    Upstream interface: ge-1/0/2.0
    Downstream interface list:
        mt-0/3/0.32768 ------------> GRE interface
    Session description: Unknown
    Statistics: 75 kBps, 890 pps, 197055 packets
    Next-hop ID: 1048579
    Upstream protocol: MVPN
    Route state: Active
    Forwarding state: Forwarding
    Cache lifetime/timeout: forever
    Wrong incoming interface notifications: 0
```

Figure 2.235 Multicast Forwarding Information – PE1

Now we move on to checking the MVPN instance specific output, as shown in Figure 2.241.

In the output in Figure 2.242, we check the PIM SSM specific information on the PIM Master instance, Note that we are using PIM-SSM in the core, and appropriate state information is created

```
operator@PE1# run show mvpn instance extensive
MVPN instance:
Legend for provider tunnel
I-P-tnl -- inclusive provider tunnel S-P-tnl -- selective provider tunnel
Legend for c-multicast routes properties (Pr)
DS -- derived from (*, c-g)          RM -- remote VPN route
Instance : MVPN-FOO
  MVPN Mode : SPT-ONLY
  Provider tunnel: I-P-tnl:PIM-SSM:7.0.0.5, 232.1.1.1
  Neighbor                           I-P-tnl
  7.0.0.1
  7.0.0.4
  C-mcast IPv4 (S:G)            Ptnl                           St
  192.168.1.5/32:237.1.1.1/32  PIM-SSM:7.0.0.5, 232.1.1.1     RM
```

Figure 2.236 MVPN Instance Information – PE1

```
operator@PE1# run show pim source detail
Instance: PIM.master Family: INET
Source 7.0.0.5 --------> PE1
    Prefix 7.0.0.5/32
    Upstream interface Local
    Upstream neighbor Local
    Active groups:232.1.1.1 --> P-Group Address
Instance: PIM.master Family: INET6
```

Figure 2.237 PIM SSM State Information – PE1

```
operator@PE1# run show pim mvpn
Instance            VPN-Group            Mode            Tunnel
PIM.MVPN-FOO        232.1.1.1            NGEN-MVPN       PIM-SSM
```

Figure 2.238 MVPN Association

for the source (ingress PE) and provider multicast group address being used (232.1.1.1).

Validation of the Control and Data Planes after Traffic Generation on PE3 Let us now take a look at the respective outputs on PE3, which is an egress PE router, after traffic has been generated from the C-MCAST source, connected behind PE1. See Figure 2.243.

Now we can check the multicast forwarding state on PE2. The upstream interface shown in Figure 2.244 displays "MT," which means GRE-based Multicast Tunnel Interface.

```
operator@PE2# run show route table MVPN-FOO.mvpn.0

1:100:1:7.0.0.1/240
                    *[BGP/170] 01:01:20, localpref 100, from 7.0.0.1
                     AS path: I
                    > to 172.16.1.6 via ge-4/0/3.0
1:100:1:7.0.0.4/240
                    *[MVPN/70] 21:22:27, metric2 1
                     Indirect
1:100:1:7.0.0.5/240
                    *[BGP/170] 00:32:58, localpref 100, from 7.0.0.5
                     AS path: I
                    > to 172.16.1.2 via ge-4/0/0.0
5:100:1:32:192.168.1.5:32:237.1.1.1/240
                    *[BGP/170] 00:18:12, localpref 100, from 7.0.0.1
                     AS path: I
                    > to 172.16.1.6 via ge-4/0/3.0
                     [BGP/170] 00:18:12, localpref 100, from 7.0.0.5
                     AS path: I
                    > to 172.16.1.2 via ge-4/0/0.0
6:100:1:100:32:7.0.0.1:32:237.1.1.1/240
                    *[PIM/105] 01:00:35
                     Multicast (IPv4)
7:100:1:100:32:192.168.1.5:32:237.1.1.1/240
                    *[MVPN/70] 00:18:12, metric2 1
                     Multicast (IPv4)
                     [PIM/105] 00:18:12
                     Multicast (IPv4)
```

Figure 2.239 BGP MVPN Routing Information – PE2

```
operator@PE2# run show multicast route instance MVPN-FOO extensive
Family: INET
Group: 237.1.1.1
    Source: 192.168.1.5/32
    Upstream interface: mt-5/3/0.49152
    Downstream interface list:
        ge-4/0/2.100
    Session description: Unknown
    Statistics: 77 kBps, 916 pps, 31783 packets
    Next-hop ID: 1048577
    Upstream protocol: MVPN
    Route state: Active
    Forwarding state: Forwarding
    Cache lifetime/timeout: forever
    Wrong incoming interface notifications: 0
```

Figure 2.240 Multicast Forwarding Information – PE2

Now we move on to checking the MVPN instance specific output. See Figure 2.245.

In the output in Figure 2.246, we check the PIM SSM specific information on the PIM Master instance. Note that we are using PIM-SSM in the core, and appropriate state information is created

```
operator@PE2# run show mvpn instance
MVPN instance:
Legend for provider tunnel
I-P-tnl -- inclusive provider tunnel S-P-tnl -- selective provider tunnel
Legend for c-multicast routes properties (Pr)
DS -- derived from (*, c-g)          RM -- remote VPN route
Instance : MVPN-FOO
  MVPN Mode : SPT-ONLY
  Provider tunnel: I-P-tnl:invalid:
  Neighbor                           I-P-tnl
  7.0.0.1
  7.0.0.5                            PIM-SSM:7.0.0.5, 232.1.1.1
  C-mcast IPv4 (S:G)       Ptnl                            St
  192.168.1.5/32:237.1.1.1/32  PIM-SSM:7.0.0.5, 232.1.1.1  DS
```

Figure 2.241 MVPN Instance Information – PE2

```
operator@PE2# run show pim source detail
Instance: PIM.master Family: INET
Source 7.0.0.5 ------->  Ingress PE
    Prefix 7.0.0.5/32
    Upstream interface ge-4/0/0.0
    Upstream neighbor 172.16.1.2
    Active groups:232.1.1.1
```

Figure 2.242 PIM SSM State Information – PE2

```
operator@PE3# run show route table MVPN-FOO.mvpn.0

MVPN-FOO.mvpn.0: 7 destinations, 9 routes (7 active, 1 holddown, 0 hidden)
+ = Active Route, - = Last Active, * = Both

1:100:1:7.0.0.1/240
                *[MVPN/70] 01:33:53, metric2 1
                    Indirect
1:100:1:7.0.0.4/240
                *[BGP/170] 00:11:03, localpref 100, from 7.0.0.4
                  AS path: I
                 > to 172.16.1.5 via ge-4/0/0.0
1:100:1:7.0.0.5/240
                *[BGP/170] 00:11:03, localpref 100, from 7.0.0.5
                  AS path: I
                 > to 172.16.1.5 via ge-4/0/0.0, Push 299776
5:100:1:32:192.168.1.5:32:237.1.1.1/240
                *[PIM/105] 00:00:05
                  Multicast (IPv4)
                 [BGP/170] 00:00:05, localpref 100, from 7.0.0.5
                  AS path: I
                 > to 172.16.1.5 via ge-4/0/0.0, Push 299776
6:100:1:100:32:7.0.0.1:32:237.1.1.1/240
                *[PIM/105] 00:11:03
                  Multicast (IPv4)
7:100:1:100:32:192.168.1.5:32:237.1.1.1/240
                *[MVPN/70] 00:00:05, metric2 1
                  Multicast (IPv4)
                 [PIM/105] 00:00:05
                  Multicast (IPv4)
```

Figure 2.243 BGP MVPN Routing Information – PE3

```
operator@PE3# run show multicast route instance MVPN-FOO extensive
Family: INET
Group: 237.1.1.1
    Source: 192.168.1.5/32
    Upstream interface: mt-0/0/10.49152
    Downstream interface list:
        ge-4/0/1.0
    Session description: Unknown
    Statistics: 74 kBps, 877 pps, 462774 packets
    Next-hop ID: 1048576
    Upstream protocol: MVPN
    Route state: Active
    Forwarding state: Forwarding
    Cache lifetime/timeout: forever
    Wrong incoming interface notifications: 0
```

Figure 2.244 Multicast Forwarding Information – PE3

```
operator@PE2# run show mvpn instance
MVPN instance:
Legend for provider tunnel
I-P-tnl -- inclusive provider tunnel S-P-tnl -- selective provider tunnel
Legend for c-multicast routes properties (Pr)
DS -- derived from (*, c-g)          RM -- remote VPN route
Instance : MVPN-FOO
  MVPN Mode : SPT-ONLY
  Provider tunnel: I-P-tnl:invalid:
  Neighbor                          I-P-tnl
  7.0.0.4
  7.0.0.5                           PIM-SSM:7.0.0.5, 232.1.1.1
  C-mcast IPv4 (S:G)      Ptnl                          St
  192.168.1.5/32:237.1.1.1/32  PIM-SSM:7.0.0.5, 232.1.1.1   DS
```

Figure 2.245 MVPN Instance Information – PE3

```
operator@PE2# run show pim source detail
Instance: PIM.master Family: INET
Source 7.0.0.5
    Prefix 7.0.0.5/32
    Upstream interface ge-4/0/0.0
    Upstream neighbor 172.16.1.5
    Active groups:232.1.1.1
```

Figure 2.246 PIM SSM State Information – PE3

for the source (ingress PE) and provider multicast group address being used (232.1.1.1).

Case Study for a PIM-SSM-based Data Plane – S-PMSI Setup

In this section, we take a look at the actual configurations required for creating an S-PMSI based on PIM-SSM for certain

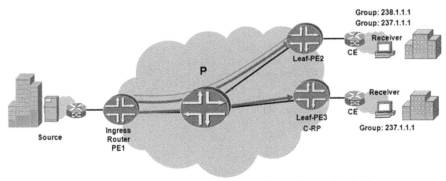

* The router "P" does not indicate a single Provider router, and indicates a
  Carrier Provider core, that may contain many devices. A single device is just
  given "ONLY" for illustrative reasons.

Figure 2.247

multicast groups. In this case study, we intend to have an S-PMSI created only for group "238.1.1.1" and source "192.168.1.5." This would be between ingress PE router PE1 and egress PE router PE2. Let us look at the relative configurations in Figure 2.247.

Configurations The S-PMSI configurations are required only on the ingress PE router. The C-MCAST Source and Group pairs are defined; the group-range for creating an appropriate P-group address similar to the Draft-Rosen Data MDTs also has to be defined. In our example, we use group (232.1.1.2). See Figure 2.248.

Validations on PE1 Let us look at the BGP MVPN routing information after traffic to both group "238.1.1.1" and "237.1.1.1" has been generated. There is one interesting observation in the output shown in Figure 2.249: PE1 does originate a Type 3 route for the specific (C-Source, C-Group) pair that has been configured to prompt creation of an S-PMSI infrastructure; however, a corresponding Type 4 route from PE2 has not been received. Non-MPLS-based S-PMSI infrastructures (GRE-based) will not have a Type 4 route sent by an interested receiver PE. Instead, the Type 7 route information (which indicates preference or interest in a given group) is used by the ingress PE to create the S-PMSI.

One may ask why an RSVP-TE P-tunnel (for instance) has the Type 4 response built in. The answer is: RSVP-TE-based P-tunnels support Type 4 announcements in order to support aggregation of multicast trees or S-PMSI tunnels; thus they rely on Type 4 routes, which provide more granularity in information. The topic of aggregation is discussed in Chapter 7.

```
Routing-instance {
MVPN-FOO {
    instance-type vrf;
    interface ge-1/0/2.0;
    interface lo0.1;
    route-distinguisher 100:1;
    provider-tunnel {
        pim-ssm {
            group-address 232.1.1.1;
        }
        selective {
            group 238.1.1.1/32 {
                source 192.168.1.5/32 {
                    pim-ssm {
                        group-range 232.1.1.2/32;
                    }
                }
            }
        }
    }
    vrf-target target:100:1;
    vrf-table-label;
    protocols {
        bgp {
            family inet {
                unicast;
            }
            group peer {
                type external;
                peer-as 65004;
                neighbor 192.168.1.5;
            }
        }
        pim {
            rp {
                static {
                    address 7.0.0.1;
                }
            }
            interface ge-1/0/2.0 {
                mode sparse-dense;
                version 2;
            }
            interface lo0.1 {
                mode sparse-dense;
                version 2;
            }
        }
        mvpn;
    }
}
}
```

Figure 2.248 S-PMSI Configuration on PE1

```
operator@PE1# run show route table MVPN-FOO.mvpn.0
1:100:1:7.0.0.1/240
                        *[BGP/170] 00:57:33, localpref 100, from 7.0.0.1
                           AS path: I
                        > to 172.16.1.1 via ge-1/0/1.0, Push 299808
1:100:1:7.0.0.4/240
                        *[BGP/170] 00:59:12, localpref 100, from 7.0.0.4
                           AS path: I
                        > to 172.16.1.1 via ge-1/0/1.0
1:100:1:7.0.0.5/240
                        *[MVPN/70] 00:41:44, metric2 1
                           Indirect
3:100:1:32:192.168.1.5:32:238.1.1.1:7.0.0.5/240
                        *[MVPN/70] 00:04:11, metric2 1
                           Indirect
5:100:1:32:192.168.1.5:32:237.1.1.1/240
                        *[PIM/105] 00:04:19
                           Multicast (IPv4)
                         [BGP/170] 00:04:19, localpref 100, from 7.0.0.1
                           AS path: I
                        > to 172.16.1.1 via ge-1/0/1.0, Push 299808
5:100:1:32:192.168.1.5:32:238.1.1.1/240
                        *[PIM/105] 00:04:11
                           Multicast (IPv4)
                         [BGP/170] 00:04:11, localpref 100, from 7.0.0.1
                           AS path: I
                        > to 172.16.1.1 via ge-1/0/1.0, Push 299808
7:100:1:100:32:192.168.1.5:32:237.1.1.1/240
                        *[PIM/105] 00:04:19
                           Multicast (IPv4)
                         [BGP/170] 00:04:19, localpref 100, from 7.0.0.1
                           AS path: I
                        > to 172.16.1.1 via ge-1/0/1.0, Push 299808
                         [BGP/170] 00:04:19, localpref 100, from 7.0.0.4
                           AS path: I
                        > to 172.16.1.1 via ge-1/0/1.0
7:100:1:100:32:192.168.1.5:32:238.1.1.1/240 -> Received only from PE2.
                        *[PIM/105] 00:04:11
                           Multicast (IPv4)
                         [BGP/170] 00:04:11, localpref 100, from 7.0.0.4
                           AS path: I
                        > to 172.16.1.1 via ge-1/0/1.0
```

Figure 2.249 BGP MVPN Routing Information – PE1

If a Type 4 route is not announced, how can we be sure that the specific (C-S, C-G) pair is indeed using an S-PMSI tunnel? The following output, shown in Figure 2.250, validates this. Note that traffic from source "192.168.1.5" destined for group "238.1.1.1" uses an S-PMSI (indicated as S-PIM-SSM), and traffic from the same source destined to group "237.1.1.1" uses an I-PMSI infrastructure.

We also check the multicast forwarding state for the groups "237.1.1.1" and "238.1.1.1," as seen in Figure 2.251.

```
operator@PE1# run show mvpn instance
MVPN instance:
Legend for provider tunnel
I-P-tnl -- inclusive provider tunnel S-P-tnl -- selective provider tunnel
Legend for c-multicast routes properties (Pr)
DS -- derived from (*, c-g)          RM -- remote VPN route
Instance : MVPN-FOO
  MVPN Mode : SPT-ONLY
  Provider tunnel: I-P-tnl:PIM-SSM:7.0.0.5, 232.1.1.1
  Neighbor                          I-P-tnl
  7.0.0.1
  7.0.0.4
  C-mcast IPv4 (S:G)              Ptnl                           St
  192.168.1.5/32:237.1.1.1/32    PIM-SSM:7.0.0.5, 232.1.1.1     RM
  192.168.1.5/32:238.1.1.1/32    S-PIM-SSM:7.0.0.5, 232.1.1.2   RM
```

Figure 2.250 Checking the MVPN Instance Information

```
operator@PE1# run show multicast route instance MVPN-FOO extensive
Family: INET
Group: 237.1.1.1
    Source: 192.168.1.5/32
    Upstream interface: ge-1/0/2.0
    Downstream interface list:
        mt-0/3/0.32769
    Session description: Unknown
    Statistics: 47 kBps, 561 pps, 35492 packets -> Traffic being forwarded
    Next-hop ID: 1048581
    Upstream protocol: MVPN
    Route state: Active
    Forwarding state: Forwarding
    Cache lifetime/timeout: forever
    Wrong incoming interface notifications: 0

Group: 238.1.1.1
    Source: 192.168.1.5/32
    Upstream interface: ge-1/0/2.0
    Downstream interface list:
        mt-0/3/0.32768
    Session description: Unknown
    Statistics: 14 kBps, 166 pps, 3765 packets -> Traffic being forwarded.
    Next-hop ID: 1048576
    Upstream protocol: MVPN
    Route state: Active
    Forwarding state: Forwarding
    Cache lifetime/timeout: forever
    Wrong incoming interface notifications: 0
```

Figure 2.251 Checking the MVPN Instance Information

Validations on PE2 Now we can check the outputs on egress PE
router PE2. In Figure 2.252, notice that PE2 has originated Type 7
routing information for both groups (237.1.1.1 and 238.1.1.1).

Now we can check the MVPN instance information. The output
in Figure 2.253 clearly validates an S-PMSI and I-PMSI being setup
to PE2.

```
operator@PE2# run show route table MVPN-FOO.mvpn.0
1:100:1:7.0.0.1/240
                        *[BGP/170] 18:59:03, localpref 100, from 7.0.0.1
                          AS path: I
                        > to 172.16.1.6 via ge-4/0/3.0
1:100:1:7.0.0.4/240
                        *[MVPN/70] 1d 16:42:59, metric2 1
                          Indirect
1:100:1:7.0.0.5/240
                        *[BGP/170] 00:07:10, localpref 100, from 7.0.0.5
                          AS path: I
                        > to 172.16.1.2 via ge-4/0/0.0
3:100:1:32:192.168.1.5:32:238.1.1.1:7.0.0.5/240
                        *[BGP/170] 00:07:10, localpref 100, from 7.0.0.5
                          AS path: I
                        > to 172.16.1.2 via ge-4/0/0.0
5:100:1:32:192.168.1.5:32:237.1.1.1/240
                        *[BGP/170] 00:03:53, localpref 100, from 7.0.0.1
                          AS path: I
                        > to 172.16.1.6 via ge-4/0/3.0
                         [BGP/170] 00:03:53, localpref 100, from 7.0.0.5
                          AS path: I
                        > to 172.16.1.2 via ge-4/0/0.0
5:100:1:32:192.168.1.5:32:238.1.1.1/240
                        *[BGP/170] 00:13:11, localpref 100, from 7.0.0.1
                          AS path: I
                        > to 172.16.1.6 via ge-4/0/3.0
                         [BGP/170] 00:07:10, localpref 100, from 7.0.0.5
                          AS path: I
                        > to 172.16.1.2 via ge-4/0/0.0
6:100:1:100:32:7.0.0.1:32:237.1.1.1/240
                        *[PIM/105] 18:55:42
                          Multicast (IPv4)
6:100:1:100:32:7.0.0.1:32:238.1.1.1/240
                        *[PIM/105] 18:10:45
                          Multicast (IPv4)
7:100:1:100:32:192.168.1.5:32:237.1.1.1/240
                        *[MVPN/70] 00:03:53, metric2 1
                          Multicast (IPv4)
                         [PIM/105] 00:03:53
                          Multicast (IPv4)
7:100:1:100:32:192.168.1.5:32:238.1.1.1/240
                        *[MVPN/70] 00:07:10, metric2 1
                          Multicast (IPv4)
                         [PIM/105] 00:03:10
                          Multicast (IPv4)
```

Figure 2.252 Checking the MVPN Instance Information

Finally the multicast forwarding state can be verified for both the C-MCAST groups (238.1.1.1 and 237.1.1.1), as shown in Figure 2.254.

Validations on PE3 Now we can check the outputs on the egress PE router PE3. In Figure 2.255, notice that PE3 has originated Type 7 routing information for only group (237.1.1.1).

```
operator@PE2# run show mvpn instance
MVPN instance:
Legend for provider tunnel
I-P-tnl -- inclusive provider tunnel S-P-tnl -- selective provider tunnel
Legend for c-multicast routes properties (Pr)
DS -- derived from (*, c-g)          RM -- remote VPN route
Instance : MVPN-FOO
  MVPN Mode : SPT-ONLY
  Provider tunnel: I-P-tnl:invalid:
  Neighbor                          I-P-tnl
  7.0.0.1
  7.0.0.5                           PIM-SSM:7.0.0.5, 232.1.1.1
  C-mcast IPv4 (S:G)      Ptnl                          St
  192.168.1.5/32:237.1.1.1/32  PIM-SSM:7.0.0.5, 232.1.1.1   DS
  192.168.1.5/32:238.1.1.1/32  S-PIM-SSM:7.0.0.5, 232.1.1.2 DS
```

Figure 2.253 Checking the MVPN Instance Information

```
operator@PE2# run show multicast route instance MVPN-FOO extensive
Family: INET
Group: 237.1.1.1
    Source: 192.168.1.5/32
    Upstream interface: mt-5/3/0.49152
    Downstream interface list:
        ge-4/0/2.100
    Session description: Unknown
    Statistics: 0 kBps, 0 pps, 35490 packets
    Next-hop ID: 1048577
    Upstream protocol: MVPN
    Route state: Active
    Forwarding state: Forwarding
    Cache lifetime/timeout: forever
    Wrong incoming interface notifications: 0

Group: 238.1.1.1
    Source: 192.168.1.5/32
    Upstream interface: mt-5/3/0.49152
    Downstream interface list:
        ge-4/0/2.100
    Session description: Unknown
    Statistics: 0 kBps, 0 pps, 74065 packets
    Next-hop ID: 1048577
    Upstream protocol: MVPN
    Route state: Active
    Forwarding state: Forwarding
    Cache lifetime/timeout: forever
    Wrong incoming interface notifications: 0
```

Figure 2.254 Checking the Multicast Forwarding Information

Then we can check the MVPN instance information. The output in Figure 2.256 clearly validates that only an I-PMSI has been setup to PE3.

Finally, the multicast forwarding state is checked. As Figure 2.257 shows, traffic is being forwarded only for group "237.1.1.1."

```
operator@PE3# run show route table MVPN-FOO.mvpn.0
1:100:1:7.0.0.1/240
                        *[MVPN/70] 20:27:48, metric2 1
                          Indirect
1:100:1:7.0.0.4/240
                        *[BGP/170] 19:04:58, localpref 100, from 7.0.0.4
                          AS path: I
                        > to 172.16.1.5 via ge-4/0/0.0
1:100:1:7.0.0.5/240
                        *[BGP/170] 00:13:06, localpref 100, from 7.0.0.5
                          AS path: I
                        > to 172.16.1.5 via ge-4/0/0.0, Push 299776
5:100:1:32:192.168.1.5:32:237.1.1.1/240
                        *[PIM/105] 00:00:03
                          Multicast (IPv4)
                         [BGP/170] 00:00:03, localpref 100, from 7.0.0.5
                          AS path: I
                        > to 172.16.1.5 via ge-4/0/0.0, Push 299776
6:100:1:100:32:7.0.0.1:32:237.1.1.1/240
                        *[PIM/105] 19:04:58
                          Multicast (IPv4)
7:100:1:100:32:192.168.1.5:32:237.1.1.1/240
                        *[MVPN/70] 00:00:03, metric2 1
                          Multicast (IPv4)
                         [PIM/105] 00:00:03
                          Multicast (IPv4)
```

Figure 2.255 Checking the MVPN Instance Information

```
operator@PE3# run show mvpn instance
MVPN instance:
Legend for provider tunnel
I-P-tnl -- inclusive provider tunnel S-P-tnl -- selective provider tunnel
Legend for c-multicast routes properties (Pr)
DS -- derived from (*, c-g)          RM -- remote VPN route
Instance : MVPN-FOO
  MVPN Mode : SPT-ONLY
  Provider tunnel: I-P-tnl:invalid:
  Neighbor                          I-P-tnl
  7.0.0.4
  7.0.0.5                           PIM-SSM:7.0.0.5, 232.1.1.1
  C-mcast IPv4 (S:G)       Ptnl                           St
  192.168.1.5/32:237.1.1.1/32  PIM-SSM:7.0.0.5, 232.1.1.1   DS
```

Figure 2.256 Checking the MVPN Instance Information

PIM-SM Provider Tunnels

In this section, we take a look at a network setup using PIM-SM-based provider tunnels as the data plane along with the BGP control plane. The setup in Figure 2.258 is used for demonstrating functionality. The setup is exactly the same as for the PIM-SSM P-tunnel illustration.

```
operator@PE3# run show multicast route instance MVPN-FOO extensive
Family: INET
Group: 237.1.1.1
    Source: 192.168.1.5/32
    Upstream interface: mt-0/0/10.49152
    Downstream interface list:
        ge-4/0/1.0
    Session description: Unknown
    Statistics: 0 kBps, 0 pps, 999 packets
    Next-hop ID: 1048576
    Upstream protocol: MVPN
    Route state: Active
    Forwarding state: Forwarding
    Cache lifetime/timeout: forever
    Wrong incoming interface notifications: 0
```

Figure 2.257 Checking the Multicast Forwarding Information

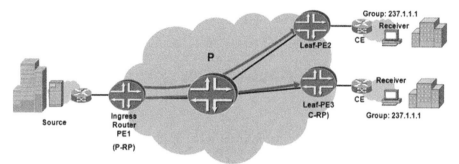

- The router "P" does not indicate a single Provider router, and indicates a Carrier Provider core, that may contain many devices. A single device is just given "ONLY" for illustrative reasons.

Figure 2.258

Configurations The P-tunnel configurations are only required on the ingress PE router. In this section we use an ASM or PIM-SM P-tunnel for the I-PMSI infrastructure; hence we need to configure an RP for the provider or master PIM instance. Note that PIM ASM relies on the RP for creating the required infrastructure. In our configuration, the PIM-provider group address used is (239.1.1.2). See Figure 2.259.

Now we move on to the configuration on egress PE router PE2. In our configuration, the PIM-provider group address used is (239.1.1.2), and this is identified by means of the P-tunnel configuration. Further PIM (master instance) is configured to statically point to PE1 as the provider RP. See Figure 2.260.

Now we move on to the configuration on egress PE router PE3. In our configuration, the PIM-provider group address used is

(239.1.1.2), and this is identified by means of the P-tunnel configuration. Further PIM (master instance) is configured to statically point to PE1 as the provider RP. See Figure 2.261.

Validations on PE1 We start off by checking the MVPN routing table on the ingress PE router PE1, as shown in Figure 2.262. We can see the Type 5 route being originated, and two Type 7 routes being received from PE2 and PE3.

We can also check the MVPN instance output and validate the P-tunnel information. In this case, the P-tunnel used is PIM-SM. See Figure 2.263.

Now we can check the multicast forwarding state for the group "237.1.1.1," as shown in Figure 2.264.

```
Protocols {
rsvp {
    interface ge-1/0/1.0;
}
mpls {
    interface ge-1/0/1.0;
    interface fe-1/1/0.0;
}
bgp {
    group PE {
        type internal;
        local-address 7.0.0.5;
        family inet-vpn {
            unicast;
        }
        family inet-mvpn {
            signaling;
        }
        neighbor 7.0.0.4 {
            peer-as 100;
        }
        neighbor 7.0.0.1 {
            peer-as 100;
        }
    }
}
ospf {
    area 0.0.0.0 {
        interface ge-1/0/1.0 {
            interface-type p2p;
        }
        interface lo0.0 {
            passive;
        }
    }
```

Figure 2.259 Configuration on PE1

```
    }
    ldp {
        interface ge-1/0/1.0;
        interface fe-1/1/0.0;
    }
    pim {
        rp {
            local {
                address 7.0.0.5; ->  Local router is RP for PIM master instance
            }
        }
        interface all {
            version 2;
        }
    }
    routing-instances {
    MVPN-FOO {
        instance-type vrf;
        interface ge-1/0/2.0;
        interface lo0.1;
        route-distinguisher 100:1;
        provider-tunnel {
            pim-asm { ---------->  PIM-ASM as the P-Tunnel
                group-address 239.1.1.2;
            }
        }
        vrf-target target:100:1;
        vrf-table-label;
        protocols {
            bgp {
                family inet {
                    unicast;
                }
                group peer {
                    type external;
                    peer-as 65004;
                    neighbor 192.168.1.5;
                }
            }
            pim {
                rp {
                    static {
                        address 7.0.0.1;
                    }
                }
                interface ge-1/0/2.0 {
                    mode sparse-dense;
                    version 2;
                }
                interface lo0.1 {
                    mode sparse-dense;
                    version 2;
                }
            }
            mvpn;
        }
    }
    }
}
```

Figure 2.259, cont'd

```
                            protocols {
                            rsvp {
                                interface so-4/1/0.0;


                                interface ge-4/0/3.0;
                                interface ge-4/0/0.0;
                                interface ge-4/0/7.0;
                            }
                            mpls {
                                interface ge-4/0/0.0;
                                interface ge-4/0/5.0;
                                interface ge-4/0/3.0;
                            }
                            bgp {
                                group PE {
                                    type internal;
                                    local-address 7.0.0.4;
                                    family inet-vpn {
                                        unicast;
                                    }
                                    family inet-mvpn {
                                        signaling;
                                    }
                                    neighbor 7.0.0.5 {
                                        peer-as 100;
                                    }
                                    neighbor 7.0.0.1 {
                                        peer-as 100;
                                    }
                                }
                            }
                            ospf {
                                area 0.0.0.0 {
                                    interface lo0.0 {
                                        passive;
                                    }
                                    interface ge-4/0/0.0 {
                                        interface-type p2p;
                                    }
                                    interface ge-4/0/5.0 {
                                        interface-type p2p;
                                    }
                                    interface ge-4/0/3.0 {
                                        interface-type p2p;
                                    }
                                }
                            }
                            ldp {
                                interface ge-4/0/0.0;
                                interface ge-4/0/3.0;
                                interface ge-4/0/5.0;
                                interface ge-4/0/7.0;
                            }
                            pim {
                                rp {
                                    static {
                                        address 7.0.0.5;
                                    }
                                }
                                interface all {
                                    version 2;
                                }
                            }
                        }
                        routing-instances {
                        MVPN-FOO {
                        instance-type vrf;
                        interface ge-4/0/2.100;
                        interface lo0.1;
                        route-distinguisher 100:1;
                        vrf-target target:100:1;
                        vrf-table-label;
                        protocols {
                            bgp {
```

Figure 2.260 Configuration on PE2

```
                                family inet {
                                    unicast;
                                }
                                group peer {
                                    type external;
                                    peer-as 65003;
                                    neighbor 192.168.1.1;
                                }
                            }
                            pim {
                                rp {
                                    static {
                                        address 7.0.0.1;
                                    }
                                }
                                interface ge-4/0/2.100 {
                                    mode sparse-dense;
                                    version 2;
                                }
                                interface lo0.1 {
                                    mode sparse-dense;
                                    version 2;
                                }
                            }
                            mvpn;
                        }
                    }
                }
```

Figure 2.260, cont'd

Validations on PE2 Next we check the outputs on egress PE
router PE2. In Figure 2.265 we can see that PE2 has originated
Type 7 routing information for group (237.1.1.1).

Now we check the MVPN instance information. The output
clearly validates an I-PMSI being setup to PE2. See Figure 2.266.

Finally the multicast forwarding state can be verified for the
C-MCAST group (237.1.1.1). See Figure 2.267.

Validations on PE3 Then we check the outputs on egress PE
router PE3. In Figure 2.268 we can see that PE3 has originated
Type 7 routing information for group (237.1.1.1).

Next we check the MVPN instance information. The output
shown in Figure 2.269 clearly validates that an I-PMSI has been
setup to PE3.

Finally, the multicast forwarding state is checked. As seen in
Figure 2.270, traffic is being forwarded for group "237.1.1.1."

S-PMSI PIM-ASM cannot provide S-PMSI tunnels, which are
source specific in nature; instead, they rely on PIM-SSM for this

```
protocols {
rsvp {
    interface ge-4/0/0.0;
    interface ge-0/1/0.0;
}
mpls {
    interface ge-4/0/0.0;
    interface ge-0/1/0.0;
}
bgp {
    group PE {
        type internal;
        local-address 7.0.0.1;
        family inet-vpn {
            unicast;
        }
        family inet-mvpn {
            signaling;
        }
        neighbor 7.0.0.5 {
            peer-as 100;
        }
        neighbor 7.0.0.4 {
            peer-as 100;
        }
    }
}
ospf {
    area 0.0.0.0 {
        interface lo0.0 {
            passive;
        }
        interface ge-4/0/0.0 {
            interface-type p2p;
        }
        interface ge-0/1/0.0 {
            interface-type p2p;
        }
    }
}
ldp {
    interface ge-0/1/0.0;
    interface ge-4/0/0.0;
}
pim {
    rp {
        static {
            address 7.0.0.5;
        }
    }
    interface all {
        version 2;
    }
}
}
routing-instances {
MVPN-FOO {
```

Figure 2.261 Configuration on PE3

```
instance-type vrf;
interface ge-4/0/1.0;
interface lo0.1;
route-distinguisher 100:1;
vrf-target target:100:1;
vrf-table-label;
protocols {
    bgp {
        family inet {
            unicast;
        }
        group peer {
            type external;
            export export;
            peer-as 65005;
            neighbor 192.168.1.9;
            neighbor 192.168.1.17 {
                peer-as 65010;
            }
        }
    }
    pim {
        rp {
            local {
                address 7.0.0.1;
            }
        }
        interface ge-4/0/1.0 {
            mode sparse;
            version 2;
        }
        interface lo0.1 {
            mode sparse;
            version 2;
        }
    }
    Mvpn ;
    }
  }
}
```

Figure 2.261—Cont'd

function. Therefore an ASM infrastructure can be used for the I-PMSI setup, and SSM tunnels, as illustrated in the PIM-SSM S-PMSI setup section, can be used for creating S-PMSI.

Migration from Draft-Rosen to NG-MVPNs

In this section we focus on the migration of a Draft-Rosen MVPN infrastructure to a Next Generation MVPN. By now we understand the various components of a Draft-Rosen MVPN setup, which essentially uses PIM for control plane signaling and GRE for the data plane. In comparison, NG-MVPNs use BGP for control plane, and offer a wide range of data plane options. Here we will examine the various steps involved in the

```
operator@PE1# run show route table MVPN-FOO.mvpn.0
1:100:1:7.0.0.1/240
                        *[BGP/170] 00:58:48, localpref 100, from 7.0.0.1
                          AS path: I
                        > to 172.16.1.1 via ge-1/0/1.0, Push 299808
1:100:1:7.0.0.4/240
                        *[BGP/170] 00:58:51, localpref 100, from 7.0.0.4
                          AS path: I
                        > to 172.16.1.1 via ge-1/0/1.0
1:100:1:7.0.0.5/240
                        *[MVPN/70] 00:36:57, metric2 1
                          Indirect
5:100:1:32:192.168.1.5:32:237.1.1.1/240
                        *[PIM/105] 00:02:07
                          Multicast (IPv4)
                         [BGP/170] 00:02:07, localpref 100, from 7.0.0.1
                          AS path: I
                        > to 172.16.1.1 via ge-1/0/1.0, Push 299808
7:100:1:100:32:192.168.1.5:32:237.1.1.1/240
                        *[PIM/105] 00:02:07
                          Multicast (IPv4)
                         [BGP/170] 00:02:07, localpref 100, from 7.0.0.1
                          AS path: I
                        > to 172.16.1.1 via ge-1/0/1.0, Push 299808
                         [BGP/170] 00:02:07, localpref 100, from 7.0.0.4
                          AS path: I
                        > to 172.16.1.1 via ge-1/0/1.0
```

Figure 2.262 BGP MVPN Routing Information – PE1

```
operator@PE1# run show mvpn instance
MVPN instance:
Legend for provider tunnel
I-P-tnl -- inclusive provider tunnel S-P-tnl -- selective provider tunnel
Legend for c-multicast routes properties (Pr)
DS -- derived from (*, c-g)          RM -- remote VPN route
Instance : MVPN-FOO
  MVPN Mode : SPT-ONLY
  Provider tunnel: I-P-tnl:PIM-SM:7.0.0.5, 239.1.1.2
  Neighbor                          I-P-tnl
  7.0.0.1
  7.0.0.4
  C-mcast IPv4 (S:G)        Ptnl                          St
  192.168.1.5/32:237.1.1.1/32  PIM-SM:7.0.0.5, 239.1.1.2   RM
```

Figure 2.263 Checking the MVPN Instance Information

```
operator@PE1# run show multicast route instance MVPN-FOO extensive
Family: INET

Group: 237.1.1.1
    Source: 192.168.1.5/32
    Upstream interface: ge-1/0/2.0
    Downstream interface list:
        mt-0/3/0.32768
    Session description: Unknown
    Statistics: 0 kBps, 0 pps, 882 packets
    Next-hop ID: 1048579
    Upstream protocol: MVPN
    Route state: Active
    Forwarding state: Forwarding
    Cache lifetime/timeout: forever
    Wrong incoming interface notifications: 0
```

Figure 2.264 Checking the MVPN Instance Information

```
operator@PE2# run show route table MVPN-FOO.mvpn.0
1:100:1:7.0.0.1/240
                        *[BGP/170] 19:54:43, localpref 100, from 7.0.0.1
                         AS path: I
                         > to 172.16.1.6 via ge-4/0/3.0
1:100:1:7.0.0.4/240
                        *[MVPN/70] 1d 17:38:39, metric2 1
                         Indirect
1:100:1:7.0.0.5/240
                        *[BGP/170] 00:41:09, localpref 100, from 7.0.0.5
                         AS path: I
                         > to 172.16.1.2 via ge-4/0/0.0
5:100:1:32:192.168.1.5:32:237.1.1.1/240
                        *[BGP/170] 00:06:19, localpref 100, from 7.0.0.1
                         AS path: I
                         > to 172.16.1.6 via ge-4/0/3.0
6:100:1:100:32:7.0.0.1:32:237.1.1.1/240
                        *[PIM/105] 19:51:22
                         Multicast (IPv4)
6:100:1:100:32:7.0.0.1:32:238.1.1.1/240
                        *[PIM/105] 19:06:25
                         Multicast (IPv4)
7:100:1:100:32:192.168.1.5:32:237.1.1.1/240
                        *[MVPN/70] 00:06:19, metric2 1
                         Multicast (IPv4)
```

Figure 2.265 Checking the MVPN Instance Information

```
operator@PE2# run show mvpn instance
MVPN instance:
Legend for provider tunnel
I-P-tnl -- inclusive provider tunnel S-P-tnl -- selective provider tunnel
Legend for c-multicast routes properties (Pr)
DS -- derived from (*, c-g)        RM -- remote VPN route
Instance : MVPN-FOO
  MVPN Mode : SPT-ONLY
  Provider tunnel: I-P-tnl:invalid:
  Neighbor                         I-P-tnl
  7.0.0.1
  7.0.0.5                          PIM-SM:7.0.0.5, 239.1.1.2
  C-mcast IPv4 (S:G)       Ptnl                         St
  192.168.1.5/32:237.1.1.1/32   PIM-SM:7.0.0.5, 239.1.1.2    DS
```

Figure 2.266 Checking the MVPN Instance Information

migration process, including the impact of the migration process on customer multicast traffic. We use the infrastructure in Figure 2.271 for illustrating the migration process, which can be broken down into three steps.

Step 1: Check the Existing Draft Rosen Infrastructure

Before starting the actual migration, we first examine the existing multicast routing tables and forwarding infrastructure, by

```
operator@PE2# run show multicast route instance MVPN-FOO extensive
Family: INET
Group: 237.1.1.1
    Source: 192.168.1.5/32
    Upstream interface: mt-5/3/0.49152
    Downstream interface list:
        ge-4/0/2.100
    Session description: Unknown
    Statistics: 0 kBps, 0 pps, 1896 packets
    Next-hop ID: 1048576
    Upstream protocol: MVPN
    Route state: Active
    Forwarding state: Forwarding
    Cache lifetime/timeout: forever
    Wrong incoming interface notifications:
```

Figure 2.267 Checking the Multicast Forwarding Information

```
operator@PE3# run show route table MVPN-FOO.mvpn.0
1:100:1:7.0.0.1/240
                    *[MVPN/70] 21:21:20, metric2 1
                       Indirect
1:100:1:7.0.0.4/240
                    *[BGP/170] 19:58:30, localpref 100, from 7.0.0.4
                       AS path: I
                    > to 172.16.1.5 via ge-4/0/0.0
1:100:1:7.0.0.5/240
                    *[BGP/170] 00:44:56, localpref 100, from 7.0.0.5
                       AS path: I
                    > to 172.16.1.5 via ge-4/0/0.0, Push 299776
5:100:1:32:192.168.1.5:32:237.1.1.1/240
                    *[PIM/105] 00:01:41
                       Multicast (IPv4)
                     [BGP/170] 00:01:41, localpref 100, from 7.0.0.5
                       AS path: I
                    > to 172.16.1.5 via ge-4/0/0.0, Push 299776
6:100:1:100:32:7.0.0.1:32:237.1.1.1/240
                    *[PIM/105] 19:58:30
                       Multicast (IPv4)
7:100:1:100:32:192.168.1.5:32:237.1.1.1/240
                    *[MVPN/70] 00:01:41, metric2 1
                       Multicast (IPv4)
                     [PIM/105] 00:01:41
                       Multicast (IPv4)
```

Figure 2.268 Checking the MVPN Instance Information

```
operator@PE3# run show mvpn instance
MVPN instance:
Legend for provider tunnel
I-P-tnl -- inclusive provider tunnel S-P-tnl -- selective provider tunnel
Legend for c-multicast routes properties (Pr)
DS -- derived from (*, c-g)          RM -- remote VPN route
Instance : MVPN-FOO
  MVPN Mode : SPT-ONLY
  Provider tunnel: I-P-tnl:invalid:
  Neighbor                          I-P-tnl
  7.0.0.4
  7.0.0.5                           PIM-SM:7.0.0.5, 239.1.1.2
  C-mcast IPv4 (S:G)       Ptnl                         St
  192.168.1.5/32:237.1.1.1/32  PIM-SM:7.0.0.5, 239.1.1.2    DS
```

Figure 2.269 Checking the MVPN Instance Information

```
operator@PE3# run show multicast route instance MVPN-FOO extensive
Family: INET
Group: 237.1.1.1
    Source: 192.168.1.5/32
    Upstream interface: mt-0/0/10.49152
    Downstream interface list:
        ge-4/0/1.0
    Session description: Unknown
    Statistics: 75 kBps, 890 pps, 184464 packets
    Next-hop ID: 1048576
    Upstream protocol: MVPN
    Route state: Active
    Forwarding state: Forwarding
    Cache lifetime/timeout: forever
    Wrong incoming interface notifications: 0
```

Figure 2.270 Checking the Multicast Forwarding Information

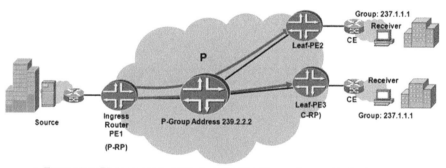

- The router "P" does not indicate a single Provider router, and indicates a Carrier Provider core, that may contain many devices. A single device is just given "ONLY" for illustrative reasons.

Figure 2.271

checking the "inet.1"multicast routing table and then the multicast forwarding state. We can take a look at PE1 as an example, as shown in Figure 2.272 and Figure 2.273.

The multicast forwarding state indicates the upstream protocol uses as "PIM," in contrast to "MVPN," which is used with NG-MVPNs.

Step 2: Enable the NG-MVPN Control and Forwarding Plane in the MVPN

Our objective is to minimize the disruption to customer traffic, and provide as optimal a migration as possible. In this step, we con the routing-instance or MVPN with the NGEN-Forwarding

```
operator@PE1# run show route table inet.1 detail
inet.1: 3 destinations, 3 routes (3 active, 0 holddown, 0 hidden)
239.2.2.2.7.0.0.1/64 (1 entry, 1 announced)
        *PIM     Preference: 105
                 Next hop type: Multicast (IPv4), Next hop index: 1048579
                 Next-hop reference count: 4
                 State: <Active Int>
                 Local AS:    100
                 Age: 11:02
                 Task: PIM.master
                 Announcement bits (1): 0-KRT
                 AS path: I

239.2.2.2.7.0.0.4/64 (1 entry, 1 announced)
        *PIM     Preference: 105
                 Next hop type: Multicast (IPv4), Next hop index: 1048579
                 Next-hop reference count: 4
                 State: <Active Int>
                 Local AS:    100
                 Age: 0
                 Task: PIM.master
                 Announcement bits (1): 0-KRT
                 AS path: I

239.2.2.2.7.0.0.5/64 (1 entry, 1 announced)
        *PIM     Preference: 105
                 Next hop type: Multicast (IPv4), Next hop index: 1048577
                 Next-hop reference count: 2
                 State: <Active Int>
                 Local AS:    100
                 Age: 11:15
                 Task: PIM.master
                 Announcement bits (1): 0-KRT
                 AS path: I
```

Figure 2.272 Checking the Multicast Routing Information

```
operator@PE1# run show multicast route instance MVPN-FOO extensive
Family: INET
Group: 237.1.1.1
    Source: 192.168.1.5/32
    Upstream interface: ge-1/0/2.0
    Downstream interface list:
        mt-0/3/0.32768
    Session description: Unknown
    Statistics: 70 kBps, 839 pps, 6257 packets
    Next-hop ID: 1048581
    Upstream protocol: PIM
    Route state: Active
    Forwarding state: Forwarding
    Cache lifetime/timeout: 360 seconds
    Wrong incoming interface notifications: 0
```

Figure 2.273 Checking the Multicast Forwarding Information

plane. In this example, we use P2MP-RSVP-TE tunnels. We also enable the support for NG-MVPN signaling—but within the context of the MVPN only. The configurations used are given in Figure 2.274. It is worth noting that a carrier may opt for an all-out migration, in which all MVPNs across the various PE routers are migrated within a single window, or a partial migration. A partial migration:

- Demonstrates the co-existence of Next Generation MVPNs with Draft-Rosen MVPNs within the same MVPN. Few sites use NG-MVPNs, and few other uses Draft-Rosen. The key is inter-operability across the two.
- Provides the carrier the ability to observe the behavior of the NG-framework and migrate sites in a phased manner.

We are using the phased migration approach, with the focus on migrating the sites connected to PE1 and PE2.

The configuration of the following parameters, shown in Figure 2.274 and Figure 2.275, does not disrupt any traffic. Additions to the existing configurations are highlighted in italics font.

At this stage, let us examine the multicast forwarding state for the MVPN. As can be seen in Figure 2.276 and Figure 2.277, the forwarding (upstream) protocol is still PIM.

Step 3: Enable BGP Support for the NG-MVPN Address Family

In step 3, we enable BGP to support the "mvpn" address family on PE1 and PE2. At this point, live C-MCAST traffic is flowing from a source connected to PE1 towards receivers connected via PE2 and PE3 over the Draft-Rosen Default MDT. Since the MVPN protocol under the "routing-instance" was enabled in step 2, the MVPN routing tables get created. However, these are not yet advertised between PE routers, since BGP has yet to be configured to support this signaling type.

Examining the MVPN routing infrastructure created on PE1 and PE2, as shown in Figure 2.278 and Figure 2.279, we can see that the MVPN routes are created, but no routes are yet advertised or received.

Now we can enable BGP support for the NG-MVPN control plane. This step causes the BGP neighbor to reset, since the support for a new address family (AF) needs to be negotiated. During this transition, we can look at the multicast forwarding table on PE1, PE2, and finally even PE3, as seen in Figures 2.280, 2.281, and 2.282. On PE1, the multicast forwarding state for the group is shown as "PRUNED," which indicates traffic outage for the given group. However, this outage is extremely minimal and, based on real-life tests, can be around a few seconds, depending on various factors.

```
protocols {
ospf {
    traffic-engineering;
    area 0.0.0.0 {
        interface ge-1/0/1.0 {
            interface-type p2p;
        }
        interface lo0.0 {
            passive;
        }
        interface fe-1/1/0.0;
    }
}
mpls {
label-switched-path P2MP-RSVP-TE {
    template;
    p2mp;
}
interface ge-1/0/1.0;
interface fe-1/1/0.0;
 }
}
routing-instances {
MVPN-FOO {
instance-type vrf;
interface ge-1/0/2.0;
interface lo0.1;
route-distinguisher 100:1;
provider-tunnel {
    rsvp-te {
        label-switched-path-template {
            P2MP-RSVP-TE;
        }
    }
}
vrf-target target:100:1;
vrf-table-label;
protocols {
    bgp {
        family inet {
            unicast;
        }
        group peer {
            type external;
            peer-as 65004;
            neighbor 192.168.1.5;
        }
    }
    pim {
        vpn-group-address 239.2.2.2;
        rp {
            static {
                address 7.0.0.1;
            }
        }
        interface ge-1/0/2.0 {
            mode sparse-dense;
            version 2;
        }
        interface lo0.1 {
            mode sparse-dense;
            version 2;
        }
    }
    mvpn;
  }
 }
}
```

Figure 2.274 Configuration on PE1

```
Protocols {
ospf {
    traffic-engineering;
    area 0.0.0.0 {
        interface lo0.0 {
            passive;
        }
        interface ge-4/0/0.0 {
            interface-type p2p;
        }
        interface ge-4/0/5.0 {
            interface-type p2p;
        }
        interface ge-4/0/3.0 {
            interface-type p2p;
        }
        interface ge-4/0/7.0 {
            interface-type p2p;
        }
    }
  }
}
routing-instances {
MVPN-FOO {
instance-type vrf;
interface ge-4/0/2.100;
interface lo0.1;
route-distinguisher 100:1;
vrf-target target:100:1;
vrf-table-label;
protocols {
    bgp {
        family inet {
            unicast;
        }
        group peer {
            type external;
            peer-as 65003;
            neighbor 192.168.1.1;
        }
    }
    pim {
        vpn-group-address 239.2.2.2;
        rp {
            static {
                address 7.0.0.1;
            }
        }
        interface ge-4/0/2.100 {
            mode sparse-dense;
            version 2;
        }
        interface lo0.1 {
            mode sparse-dense;
            version 2;
        }
    }
    mvpn;
  }
 }
}
```

Figure 2.275 Configuration on PE2

```
operator@PE1# run show multicast route instance MVPN-FOO extensive
Family: INET

Group: 237.1.1.1
    Source: 192.168.1.5/32
    Upstream interface: ge-1/0/2.0
    Downstream interface list:
        mt-0/3/0.32768
    Session description: Unknown
    Statistics: 75 kBps, 894 pps, 3554327 packets
    Next-hop ID: 1048581
    Upstream protocol: PIM
    Route state: Active
    Forwarding state: Forwarding
    Cache lifetime/timeout: 360 seconds
    Wrong incoming interface notifications: 0
```

Figure 2.276 Checking the Multicast Forwarding Information on PE1

```
operator@PE2# run show multicast route instance MVPN-FOO extensive
Family: INET

Group: 237.1.1.1
    Source: 192.168.1.5/32
    Upstream interface: mt-5/3/0.49152
    Downstream interface list:
        ge-4/0/2.100
    Session description: Unknown
    Statistics: 74 kBps, 885 pps, 4027320 packets
    Next-hop ID: 1048577
    Upstream protocol: PIM
    Route state: Active
    Forwarding state: Forwarding
    Cache lifetime/timeout: 360 seconds
    Wrong incoming interface notifications: 0
```

Figure 2.277 Checking the Multicast Forwarding Information on PE2

```
operator@PE1# run show route table MVPN-FOO.mvpn.0
MVPN-FOO.mvpn.0: 3 destinations, 3 routes (3 active, 0 holddown, 0 hidden)
+ = Active Route, - = Last Active, * = Both
1:100:1:7.0.0.5/240
                  *[MVPN/70] 01:51:21, metric2 1
                    Indirect
5:100:1:32:192.168.1.5:32:237.1.1.1/240
                  *[PIM/105] 01:51:21
                    Multicast (IPv4)
7:100:1:100:32:192.168.1.5:32:237.1.1.1/240
                  *[PIM/105] 01:51:21
                    Multicast (IPv4)
```

Figure 2.278 MVPN Routing Infrastructure on PE1

```
operator@PE2# run show route table MVPN-FOO.mvpn.0
MVPN-FOO.mvpn.0: 1 destinations, 1 routes (1 active, 0 holddown, 0 hidden)
+ = Active Route, - = Last Active, * = Both
1:100:1:7.0.0.4/240
                  *[MVPN/70] 01:54:54, metric2 1
                    Indirect
```

Figure 2.279 MVPN Routing Infrastructure on PE2

```
operator@PE1# run show multicast route instance MVPN-FOO extensive
Family: INET
Group: 237.1.1.1
    Source: 192.168.1.5/32
    Upstream interface: ge-1/0/2.0
    Session description: Unknown
    Statistics: 0 kBps, 2 pps, 56079 packets
    Next-hop ID: 0
    Upstream protocol: PIM
    Route state: Active
    Forwarding state: Pruned --> Forwarding PRUNED
    Cache lifetime/timeout: 360 seconds
    Wrong incoming interface notifications: 0
```

Figure 2.280 Multicast Forwarding State on PE1

```
operator@PE2# run show multicast route instance MVPN-FOO extensive
Family: INET
```

Figure 2.281 Multicast Forwarding State on PE2

```
operator@PE3# run show multicast route instance MVPN-FOO extensive
Family: INET
```

Figure 2.282 Multicast Forwarding State on PE3

```
operator@PE1# run show multicast route instance MVPN-FOO extensive
Family: INET
Group: 237.1.1.1
    Source: 192.168.1.5/32
    Upstream interface: ge-1/0/2.0
    Session description: Unknown
    Statistics: 74 kBps, 880 pps, 206802 packets
    Next-hop ID: 1048580
    Upstream protocol: MVPN --> Control Plane protocol is NGEN-MVPN.
    Route state: Active
    Forwarding state: Forwarding
    Cache lifetime/timeout: forever
    Wrong incoming interface notifications: 0
```

Figure 2.283 Multicast Forwarding State on PE1

After this minimal outage of traffic for a few seconds, we can again check the multicast forwarding state on all the PE routers. As shown in Figures 2.283, 2.284, and 2.285, the upstream protocol used on PE1 and PE2 has now changed to MVPN, indicating that the Next Generation infrastructure is being used, while PE3 still uses PIM + GRE.

```
operator@PE2# run show multicast route instance MVPN-FOO extensive
Family: INET
Group: 237.1.1.1
    Source: 192.168.1.5/32
    Upstream interface: lsi.21
    Downstream interface list:
        ge-4/0/2.100
    Session description: Unknown
    Statistics: 76 kBps, 901 pps, 176771 packets
    Next-hop ID: 1048575
    Upstream protocol: MVPN --➔ Control Plane protocol is NGEN-MVPN.
    Route state: Active
    Forwarding state: Forwarding
    Cache lifetime/timeout: forever
    Wrong incoming interface notifications: 0
```

Figure 2.284 Multicast Forwarding State on PE2

```
operator@PE3# run show multicast route instance MVPN-FOO extensive
Family: INET
Group: 237.1.1.1
    Source: 192.168.1.5/32
    Upstream interface: mt-0/0/10.49152
    Downstream interface list:
        ge-4/0/1.0
    Session description: Unknown
    Statistics: 74 kBps, 878 pps, 216899 packets
    Next-hop ID: 1048577
    Upstream protocol: PIM -➔ Still uses PIM+GRE
    Route state: Active
    Forwarding state: Forwarding
    Cache lifetime/timeout: 360 seconds
    Wrong incoming interface notifications: 0
```

Figure 2.285 Multicast Forwarding State on PE3

Now we finally activate NG-MVPN signaling at PE3. Then we can check the MVPN instance and routing tables on PE1, PE2, and PE3. As Figures 2.286, 2.287, and 2.288 show, the routing tables reflect the Type 5 and Type 7 routes being propagated between the PE routers.

Now we verify the multicast forwarding state on PE3. As shown in Figure 2.289, the upstream protocol is now "MVPN," indicating that the transition from PIM + GRE to NG-MVPN is complete.

Next-Generation MVPN Extranets

At the beginning of this chapter it was pointed out that building MVPN extranets within the context of NG-MVPNs is simplified by the fact that NG-MVPNs use the same model of extranet as BGP/MPLS Unicast VPNs. Use of the BGP control plane means

```
operator@PE1# run show route table MVPN-FOO.mvpn.0
1:100:1:7.0.0.1/240
                        *[BGP/170] 02:57:06, localpref 100, from 7.0.0.1
                          AS path: I
                        > to 172.16.1.1 via ge-1/0/1.0, Push 299776
1:100:1:7.0.0.4/240
                        *[BGP/170] 1d 16:00:05, localpref 100, from 7.0.0.4
                          AS path: I
                        > to 172.16.1.1 via ge-1/0/1.0
1:100:1:7.0.0.5/240
                        *[MVPN/70] 1d 16:14:06, metric2 1
                          Indirect
5:100:1:32:192.168.1.5:32:237.1.1.1/240
                        *[PIM/105] 00:00:12
                          Multicast (IPv4)
                         [BGP/170] 00:00:12, localpref 100, from 7.0.0.1
                          AS path: I
                        > to 172.16.1.1 via ge-1/0/1.0, Push 299776
7:100:1:100:32:192.168.1.5:32:237.1.1.1/240
                        *[PIM/105] 00:00:12
                          Multicast (IPv4)
                         [BGP/170] 00:00:12, localpref 100, from 7.0.0.1
                          AS path: I
                        > to 172.16.1.1 via ge-1/0/1.0, Push 299776
                         [BGP/170] 00:00:12, localpref 100, from 7.0.0.4
                          AS path: I
                        > to 172.16.1.1 via ge-1/0/1.0
```

Figure 2.286 Multicast Routing Information – PE1

```
operator@PE2# run show route table MVPN-FOO.mvpn.0
1:100:1:7.0.0.1/240
                        *[BGP/170] 02:58:57, localpref 100, from 7.0.0.1
                          AS path: I
                        > to 172.16.1.6 via ge-4/0/3.0
1:100:1:7.0.0.4/240
                        *[MVPN/70] 1d 16:01:57, metric2 1
                          Indirect
1:100:1:7.0.0.5/240
                        *[BGP/170] 1d 16:07:36, localpref 100, from 7.0.0.5
                          AS path: I
                        > to 172.16.1.2 via ge-4/0/0.0
5:100:1:32:192.168.1.5:32:237.1.1.1/240
                        *[BGP/170] 00:02:03, localpref 100, from 7.0.0.1
                          AS path: I
                        > to 172.16.1.6 via ge-4/0/3.0
                         [BGP/170] 00:02:03, localpref 100, from 7.0.0.5
                          AS path: I
                        > to 172.16.1.2 via ge-4/0/0.0
6:100:1:100:32:7.0.0.1:32:237.1.1.1/240
                        *[PIM/105] 1d 15:58:25
                          Multicast (IPv4)
7:100:1:100:32:192.168.1.5:32:237.1.1.1/240
                        *[MVPN/70] 00:02:03, metric2 1
                          Multicast (IPv4)
                         [PIM/105] 00:02:03
                          Multicast (IPv4)
```

Figure 2.287 Multicast Routing Information – PE2

```
operator@PE3# run show route table MVPN-FOO.mvpn.0
1:100:1:7.0.0.1/240
                       *[MVPN/70] 03:00:08, metric2 1
                         Indirect
1:100:1:7.0.0.4/240
                       *[BGP/170] 1d 15:59:36, localpref 100, from 7.0.0.4
                         AS path: I
                       > to 172.16.1.5 via ge-4/0/0.0
1:100:1:7.0.0.5/240
                       *[BGP/170] 1d 15:59:40, localpref 100, from 7.0.0.5
                         AS path: I
                       > to 172.16.1.5 via ge-4/0/0.0, Push 299792
5:100:1:32:192.168.1.5:32:237.1.1.1/240
                       *[PIM/105] 00:03:14
                         Multicast (IPv4)
                        [BGP/170] 00:03:14, localpref 100, from 7.0.0.5
                         AS path: I
                       > to 172.16.1.5 via ge-4/0/0.0, Push 299792
6:100:1:100:32:7.0.0.1:32:237.1.1.1/240
                       *[PIM/105] 00:03:28
                         Multicast (IPv4)
7:100:1:100:32:192.168.1.5:32:237.1.1.1/240
                       *[MVPN/70] 00:03:14, metric2 1
                         Multicast (IPv4)
                        [PIM/105] 00:03:14
                         Multicast (IPv4)
```

Figure 2.288 Multicast Routing Information – PE3

```
operator@PE3# run show multicast route instance MVPN-FOO extensive
Family: INET
Group: 237.1.1.1
    Source: 192.168.1.5/32
    Upstream interface: lsi.0
    Downstream interface list:
        ge-4/0/1.0
    Session description: Unknown
    Statistics: 77 kBps, 912 pps, 313607 packets
    Next-hop ID: 1048576
    Upstream protocol: MVPN -> MVPN being used.
    Route state: Active
    Forwarding state: Forwarding
    Cache lifetime/timeout: forever
    Wrong incoming interface notifications: 0
```

Figure 2.289 Multicast Forwarding State on PE3

that no additional configuration is required, apart from ensuring that Extranet connectivity is established within the Layer 3 VPN, using Unicast policies. In this section, we check the relevant portions of the configuration for the sample scenario illustrated in Figure 2.290.

In the illustration, VPN-RED has a set of receivers in each of its two sites. In VPN-BLUE, each department is interested in certain

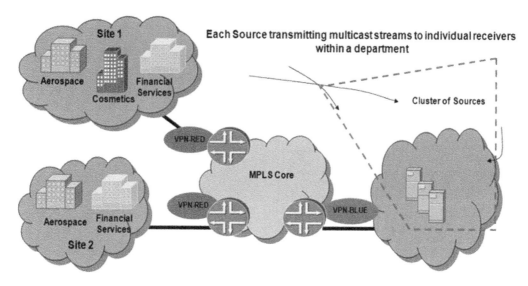

Figure 2.290

traffic, which is sent to a given C-MCAST group address, with sources centered at VPN-BLUE. VPN-BLUE has a set of multicast sources and hence is the sender site. To achieve multicast traffic flow across the two VPNs, extranet connectivity must be enabled. The relevant portions of the configurations are presented in Figures 2.291, 2.292, and 2.293.

PE Router Configurations

Looking at the configuration of the various PE routers, the only difference between MVPN intranets and extranets is the use of appropriate policies (two policies on each PE router) for ensuring that VPNv4 unicast routing information is available between VPNs. Once this reachability is ensured, multicast traffic flow between the VPNs is also established.

Outputs are not shown, since there is no difference in the MVPN route signaling between MVPN intranets and wxtranets.

Provider Router Configuration

A typical provider router configuration in the context of NG-MVPNs would comprise only configurations relevant to the infrastructure within the core, such as IGP, MPLS, LDP, RSVP-TE (if RSVP-TE P2MP LSPs are used), PIM (if PIM P-tunnels are used),

```
routing-instances {
VPN-BLUE {
instance-type vrf;
interface ge-4/0/2.100;
interface lo0.1;
route-distinguisher 200:1;
provider-tunnel {
    rsvp-te {
        label-switched-path-template {
            P2MP;
        }
    }
}
vrf-import import;
vrf-export export;
vrf-table-label;
protocols {
    bgp {
        family inet {
            unicast;
        }
        group peer {
            type external;
            peer-as 65003;
            neighbor 192.168.1.1;
        }
    }
    pim {
        rp {
            static {
                address 7.0.0.1;
            }
        }
        interface ge-4/0/2.100 {
            mode sparse-dense;
            version 2;
        }
        interface lo0.1 {
            mode sparse-dense;
            version 2;
        }
    }
    mvpn;
  }
 }
}
policy-options {
policy-statement export {
term 1 {
    then {
        community add BLUEVPN;
        accept;
    }
}
term 2 {
    then reject;
 }
}

policy-statement import {
term 1 {
    from community [ BLUEVPN REDVPN ];
    then accept;
}
term 2 {
    then reject;
 }
}
community BLUEVPN members target:200:1;
community REDVPN members target:100:1;
}
```

Figure 2.291 Configuration on PE1 – Source PE at VPN-BLUE

```
routing-instances {
VPN-RED {
instance-type vrf;
interface ge-4/0/1.0;
interface lo0.1;
route-distinguisher 100:1;
vrf-import import;
vrf-export export;
vrf-table-label;
protocols {
    bgp {
        family inet {
            unicast;
        }
        group peer {
            type external;
            export export;
            peer-as 65005;
            neighbor 192.168.1.9;
            neighbor 192.168.1.17 {
                peer-as 65010;
            }
        }
    }
    pim {
        rp {
            local {
                address 7.0.0.1;
            }
        }
        interface ge-4/0/1.0 {
            mode sparse;
            version 2;
        }
        interface lo0.1 {
            mode sparse;
            version 2;
        }
    }
    mvpn
  }
 }
}
policy-options {
policy-statement export {
term 1 {
    then {
        community add REDVPN;
        accept;
    }
}
term 2 {
    then reject;
 }
}

policy-statement import {
term 1 {
    from community [ REDVPN BLUEVPN ];
    then accept;
}
term 2 {
    then reject;
 }
}
community BLUEVPN members target:200:1;
community REDVPN members target:100:1;
}
```

Figure 2.292 Configuration on PE2 – Receiver PE at VPN-RED

```
routing-instances {
VPN-RED {
instance-type vrf;
interface ge-1/0/2.0;
interface lo0.1;
route-distinguisher 100:1;
vrf-import import;
vrf-export export;
vrf-table-label;
protocols {
    bgp {
        family inet {
            unicast;
        }
        group peer {
            type external;
            peer-as 65004;
            neighbor 192.168.1.5;
        }
    }
    pim {
        rp {
            static {
                address 7.0.0.1;
            }
        }
        interface ge-1/0/2.0 {
            mode sparse-dense;
            version 2;
        }
        interface lo0.1 {
            mode sparse-dense;
            version 2;
        }
    }
    mvpn
  }
 }
}
policy-options {
policy-statement export {
term 1 {
    then {
        community add REDVPN;
        accept;
    }
}
term 2 {
    then reject;
 }
}

policy-statement import {
term 1 {
    from community [ REDVPN BLUEVPN ];
    then accept;
}
term 2 {
    then reject;
 }
}
community BLUEVPN members target:200:1;
community REDVPN members target:100:1;
}
```

Figure 2.293 Configuration on PE3 – Receiver PE at VPN-RED

```
Protocols {
rsvp {
    interface ge-0/2/0.0;
    interface ge-0/0/0.0;
    interface ge-0/2/1.0;
    interface ge-0/0/1.0;
}
mpls {
    interface ge-0/2/0.0;
    interface ge-0/0/0.0;
    interface ge-0/2/1.0;
    interface ge-0/0/1.0;
}
ospf {
    traffic-engineering;
    area 0.0.0.0 {
        interface ge-0/2/0.0;
        interface ge-0/0/0.0;
        interface ge-0/2/1.0;
        interface ge-0/0/1.0;
        interface lo0.0;
    }
}
}
```

Figure 2.294 Provider Router Configuration

and MDLP (if P2MP LDP is used). No BGP-specific configuration is required. A sample configuration for a MPLS provider router supporting RSVP-TE P2MP LSPs is given in Figure 2.294.

Next-Generation MVPN – IPv6

This section examines some configurations for extending existing NG-MVPN functionality to transport multicast IPv6 customer traffic over the IPv4 core network. This feature does not require IPv6 support in the core. IPv6 is enabled only on PEs in VPN instance configuration. Figure 2.295 shows a configuration template for PIM-ASM P-tunnels.

Figure 2.296 shows a configuration template using RSVP-TE I-PMSI/S-PMSI tunnels.

Internet Multicast Using NG-BGP Control Plane

This section looks at deploying Internet multicast over MPLS. Assuming that a set of routers, running IP multicast, are connected by a MPLS network, the solution discussed here allows these IP routers to exchange multicast state and data. The solution is based on a BGP control plane between the border routers for

```
protocols {
    mld { --------------------> MLD version 2
### Only if MLD hosts are directly connected to PE.
### This is optional as MLD (version 1) is implicitedly enabled on
### all interfaces in the vpn instance
### You really need this only when version 2 is to be enabled.
        interface fe-1/3/0.0;
    }
    mpls {
        ipv6-tunneling;
        interface so-0/1/3.0;
        interface so-0/1/2.0;
    }
    bgp {
        group int {
            type internal;
            local-address 10.255.2.202;
            family inet-vpn {
                any;
            }
            family inet6-vpn {
                unicast;
            }
            family inet-mvpn {
                signaling;
            }
            family inet6-mvpn { -----> Support for IPv6 Multicast traffic
                signaling;
            }
            neighbor 10.255.2.204;
            neighbor 10.255.2.203;
        }
    }
    ospf {
        area 0.0.0.0 {
            interface so-0/1/3.0;
            interface so-0/1/2.0;
            interface lo0.0 {
                passive;
            }
        }
    }
    ldp {
        interface so-0/1/2.0;
        interface so-0/1/3.0;
    }
    pim {
        rp {
            static {
                address 10.255.2.203;
            }
        }
        interface lo0.0;
        interface so-0/1/3.0;
        interface so-0/1/2.0;
    }
}
routing-instances {
    vpn_blue {
        instance-type vrf;
        interface fe-1/3/0.0;
        interface lo0.1;
        provider-tunnel {
            pim-asm { -------------> PIM-ASM Provider Tunnel
                group-address 239.1.1.1;
            }
        }
        vrf-target target:100:200;
        vrf-table-label;
```

Figure 2.295 Provider Edge Router Configuration for IPv6 – Using PIM-ASM P-Tunnels

```
protocols {
    pim {
        rp {
            static {
                address 10.12.53.12;
                address ::10.12.53.12;
            }
        }
        interface lo0.1;
        interface fe-1/3/0.0 {
            priority 100;
        }
    }
    mvpn;
}
}
}
```

Figure 2.295, cont'd

carrying multicast routing and autodiscovery information, and an MPLS data plane between the border routers.

Assume that the IP network consists of edge routers that run the multicast protocol. A set of border routers connect to the edge routers downstream and run IP multicast on these interfaces. The border routers are connected to the MPLS core on the upstream, with each other. The border routers form a full-mesh iBGP session to exchange multicast control state, and a full-mesh P2P LSP for the data plane. The Internet multicast IP traffic is encapsulated by the border routers in MPLS and carried over MPLS LSPs to other border routers, and finally gets across to the edge routers.

To support IP multicast over an MPLS network, the existing JUNOS NG-MVPN infrastructure is used. A full-mesh iBGP session is run between all border routers to exchange multicast control state. The NLRI defined in [BGP-MVPN] is used to carry the multicast control state in BGP. Ingress replication tunnels are configured on all the border routers to form a full mesh of MPLS P2P LSPs. These MPLS P2P LSPs are triggered dynamically when the border routers autodiscover each other through the INET-MVPN autodiscovery route defined in the Next-Gen framework discussed in preceding sections. The procedures to exchange control messages and data are explained in the rest of this session.

A new routing instance type, called "Internet multicast," is defined to support Internet multicast over an MPLS network. Even though a new routing instance is defined, it merely leverages the existing infrastructure to provide support for multicast in the default instance (master instance). The Internet multicast instance does not have any forwarding entries.

```
protocols {
    rsvp {
        interface so-0/1/3.0;
        interface so-0/1/1.0;
    }
    mpls {
        ipv6-tunneling;
        label-switched-path lsp-to e {
            to 10.255.2.204;
            p2mp p2mp-to-e;
        }
        interface so-0/1/3.0;
        interface so-0/1/1.0;
    }
    bgp {
        group int {
            type internal;
            local-address 10.255.2.202;
            family inet-vpn {
                any;
            }
            family inet6-vpn {
                unicast;
            }
            family inet-mvpn {
                signaling;
            }
            family inet6-mvpn {
                signaling;
            }
            neighbor 10.255.2.204;
            neighbor 10.255.2.203;
        }
    }
    ospf {
        traffic-engineering;
        area 0.0.0.0 {
            interface so-0/1/3.0;
            interface so-0/1/1.0;
            interface lo0.0 {
                passive;
            }
        }
    }
    ldp {
        interface so-0/1/1.0;
        interface so-0/1/3.0;
    }
}
routing-instances {
    vpn_blue {
        instance-type vrf;
        interface fe-1/3/0.0;
        interface lo0.1;
        provider-tunnel {
            rsvp-te {
                label-switched-path-template {
                    default-template;
                }
            }
            selective { ------->S-PMSI Tunnel
                group ffff::/16 {
                    source ::192.168.90.0/120 {
```

Figure 2.296 Provider Edge Router Configuration for IPv6 – Using RSVP-TE P-Tunnels

```
                                    rsvp-te {
                                        static-lsp p2mp-to-e;
                                    }
                                    threshold-rate 12;
                                }
                            }
                        group 225.0.0.0/16 {
                            source 192.168.90.0/24 {
                                rsvp-te {
                                    static-lsp p2mp-to-e;
                                }
                                threshold-rate 12;
                            }
                        }
                    }
                }
                vrf-target target:100:200;
                vrf-table-label;
                protocols {
                    pim {
                        rp {
                            static {
                                address 10.12.53.12;
                                address ::10.12.53.12;
                            }
                        }
                        interface lo0.1;
                        interface fe-1/3/0.0 {
                            priority 100;
                        }

                    }
                    mvpn {

                    }
                }
            }
        }
    }
```

Figure 2.296, cont'd

The following attributes are defined for the Internet multicast instance:
- No interfaces can be configured in the instance.
- The interfaces running IP multicast on a border router will be associated with "inet.0," which is the global routing table and not the routing instance—the routing instance being primarily for control plane procedures.
- Only one instance of type Internet multicast can be defined.
- Currently, only MVPN protocol is supported under the instance.
- A provider tunnel can be configured in the instance for MVPN.

When the Internet multicast routing instance is configured, a VPN label is allocated to terminate the data received on the P2P

LSP in the default instance. Since data received on the LSP carry an inner VPN label, an lsi interface is created dynamically in the default instance to terminate the data. To accomplish this, packets arriving with the VPN label are mapped to the lsi interface, which in turn strips the VPN label and causes an IP lookup in the default instance's multicast RIB. These changes are summarized as follows:

- A VPN label is allocated for the default instance when the Internet multicast instance is configured.
- The VPN label maps to an lsi interface (which belongs to the master instance).
- The lsi interface is associated with the default instance's multicast RIB such that when the VPN label is popped, the next IP lookup is done in the default instance.

In order to associate the default instance's multicast protocol with the Internet multicast instance, a knob must be configured under the multicast protocol. Currently, this knob is supported for PIM.

When a border router receives a PIM join on its IP enabled interface, an RPF lookup is done to the source address. The following rule .is used to differentiate sources that are reachable through an IP interface (referred as local-source) and sources that are reachable through a different BR through the MPLS core (referred as remote-source):

> If the unicast route to the source has the vrf rt-import extended community and the source-as extended community, the source is treated as a remote-source reachable through a remote Border route. If these communities are not present, the source is treated as a local-source reachable through an IP interface.

Each border router participating in BGP/MPLS-based Internet multicast autodiscovers the other border routers that are participating in the same, using intra-AS AD routes. The P-tunnel attribute is used to signal whether a border router is configured to use ingress replication, i.e., P2P LSPs, for transporting Internet multicast traffic. The MVPN AD routes exchanged in the MPLS Internet multicast context differ from the VPN context in one aspect: Since the MPLS Internet multicast instance is not a VRF instance, the MVPN AD routes do not carry any target communites (in the VPN context they carry the import targets used for unicast inet-VPN routes). When a router receives such an AD route (without a target community), it accepts and imports the route if and only if the MPLS Internet multicast instance is configured.

In the MPLS Internet multicast context, PIM is configured only on the IP interfaces. Since the PIM relies on the MVPN infrastructure to carry control state between border routers, a new knob called "mpls-internet-multicast" is introduced under PIM to achieve this. When the knob is configured, a pseudo-interface is created in the master instance to be used as the RPF interface for all remote sources that are reachable through the MPLS core. When a border router receives a join for a remote source in the default instance, PIM:

- Uses the pseudo-interface as the upstream interface.
- Finds the MPLS Internet multicast instance.
- Installs a C-multicast route in the instance's MVPN TIB.

In addition, since the forwarding entries and control routes are maintained in different instances, PIM manages setting the correct instance based on the operation.

When MVPN is configured in an MPLS Internet multicast instance rather than a VRF instance, the following behaviors are changed:

- Unicast route lookup is done in the master instance.
- MVPN forwarding entries are always created in the master instance.
- RD value of 0:0 is used for MVPN routes, indicating that these routes are created by the MPLS Internet multicast instance.

When an egress border router receives a PIM-SSM or PIM-ASM (S, G) join, it discovers the Upstream Multicast Hop (UMH) for the S and generates a BGP source tree C-multicast route towards the UMH. Once the ingress BR receives a C-multicast route for an (S, G), it follows the procedures in [BGP-MVPN], which may generate a PIM join towards the source. Further, the ingress BR creates forwarding plane state to send packets for (S, G) to all egress BRs.

If the egress BR receives a PIM-ASM (*, G) join, then the BR discovers the UMH for the C-RP. It may or may not generate a BGP shared-tree C-multicast route towards the UMH, depending on whether PIM-ASM is configured using "only inter-site source trees" or "inter-site shared and source trees."

A border router creates (S, G) or (*, G) control plane state as a result of receiving a BGP C-multicast route originated by another border router. When ingress replication in configured as the provider tunnel, the ingress BR creates an (S,G) or (*,G) forwarding entry in the Internet IP forwarding table with the P2P LSPs to all other BRs downstream, along with IP enabled interfaces that have local receivers.

The inclusive ingress-replication tunnel results in a border router sending traffic, for which it has at least one remote receiver, to all the other border routers. When an ingress-replication-based selective P-tunnel is configured, the ingress BR forwards the data only on those LSPs that terminate at BRs that have sent C-multicast joins to the ingress BR. This ensure that the data is not flooded to BRs that are not interested in the data. It also ensures that a egress BR never receives duplicate data from multiple ingress BR.

A new provider tunnel called "ingress-replication" is implemented to support Internet multicast over the MPLS network and also as a new provider tunnel for multicast VPN. Ingress replication uses unicast tunnels between the border routers to create the multicast distribution tree.

A full mesh of unicast tunnels among the BRs (and PEs in the case of multicast VPNs) is required to ensure that the the inclusive provider tunnel rooted at all BRs can be established. When a BR needs to establish a multicast distribution tree to a set of egress BRs, the ingress BR replicates the data on all the unicast tunnels terminating at the egress BRs. The unicast tunnels from the ingress BR to all the egress BRs forms the ingress replication tunnel.

Ingress replication can be reached using different kinds of unicast tunnels, such as point-to-point LSP GRE tunnels. The version current at the time of this writing supports only point-to-point LSP-based ingress replication. The IR provider tunnel can be configured in two different modes:

- In the default "existing-unicast-tunnel" mode, when an application requests the addition of a destination to the IR tunnel, an existing unicast tunnel to the destination is used. If an unicast tunnel is not available, then the destination is not added to the IR tunnel. The IR module picks an existing tunnel to a destination through MPLS route lookup to the destination (in the inet.3 routing table). It also handles route changes to the destination and rebuilds the IR tunnel based on the changes in the MPLS route. The IR module assumes that the LSP routes in inet.3 are only for host addresses. The IR tunnel module cannot handle prefix routes currently.
- In the second mode, "create-new-ucast-tunnel," when an application requests the addition of destination to the IR tunnel, a new unicast tunnel is created to the destination and added to the IR tunnel. The unicast tunnel is deleted when the application requests deletion of the destination from the IR tunnel.

When ingress replication is used as the provider tunnel in MVPN, a downstream allocated MPLS label is advertised in the the intra-AS AD route. This downstream allocated label is used to de-multiplex the traffic arriving on the unicast tunnel to the correct MVPNs on the egress PE router. This is a requirement in

```
                     if1
           --        ---
          /             \      /
         /        if2 \       /
   BR1---- ...---- BR2 --- (IP interfaces)
         \          /     \
          \     if3/        \
           --        ---
```

Figure 2.297

the case of multicast VPN. However, in the case of MPLS Internet multicast, PHP results in IP packets reaching the egress BR. Since the traffic belongs to the default instance (and not a VPN), there is no need for the inner label to de-multiplex the traffic on the egress BR. But this presents a different problem. Consider the topology shown in Figure 2.297.

In this topology, BR2 has three MPLS core-facing interfaces: if1, if2, and if3. When the BR2 receives a join to a source connected to BR1 (remote source), BR2 must install an (S, G) forwarding entry to receive data from the MPLS core. Since multicast forwarding entries have RPF enabled, the MVPN module must compute the correct incoming interface for the forwarding entry. Since it is not possible to determine the incoming interface on the egress BR when a unicast tunnel delivers traffic (since the tunnelling protocol can compute its own path through the MPLS network), there are two options for mvpn handle RPF checks:

• Disable RPF check: The first option is to disable RPF check on routes for remote sources. This ensures that the traffic received on the unicast tunnel is accepted by the egress BR, irrespective of the incoming interface. This approach, however, breaks parts of the PIM functionality that depend on interface mismatch notification.

• Use lsi as iif: The second option is to add an inner MPLS label to the traffic sent on the unicast tunnel. The egress BR uses lsi interface to receive data on the unicast tunnel. This allows MVPNto use the lsi interface as the iif interface.

For the above-mentioned reason, an downstream allocated MPLS label is always used for traffic sent on the unicast tunnels, and the egress BR uses the lsi interface as the incoming interface for its forwarding entries to receive traffic from remote sources.

Configuring the MPLS Internet multicast instance automatically creates an lsi interface in the master instance. This interface is used by mvpn as the iif for the provider tunnel. See Figure 2.298.

```
routing-instances {
    <instance_name> {
+       instance-type mpls-internet-multicast;
        provider-tunnel {
+           ingress-replication {
+                   create-new-ucast-tunnel; /* trigger new ucast tunnel */
+               label-switched-path {      /* Use P2P unicast tunnel */
+                   label-swicthed-path-template { /* dynamic LSP */
+                       template <template name>; /* pre-defined template */
+                       default-template;          /* use default template */
+                   }
+               }
+           }
        }
        protocols {
            mvpn;
        }
    }
}
The following PIM configuration is necessary in order to work in a
mpls internet multicast context.

protocols {
    pim {
+       mpls-internet-multicast; /* Indicates mpls internet multicast instance is
used for PIM */
        ...
    }
}
admin@siluan> show ingress-replication mvpn
Ingress Tunnel: mvpn:1
  Application: MVPN
  Unicast tunnels
    Leaf Address        Tunnel-type      Mode        State
    10.255.245.2        P2P LSP          New         Up
```

Figure 2.298 Configuration Template for Internet Multicast

Considerations for Deploying Broadcast Video/IPTV

Traditionally, IPTV/Broadcast Video has been deployed both within the context of a MVPN and also in the global routing table also known as Internet multicast. A common question is: which is the better approach for deploying such traffic? The NG-MVPN framework based on BGP provides an operator with an excellent opportunity to deploy IPTV within a MVPN. Some of the benefits of this approach are as follows:

1. The BGP control plane with the various MVPN route types provides an opportunity to use autodiscovery of member sites and automates the provisioning of P-tunnels. This simplifies the provisioning aspect, compared with traditional Internet multicast schemes that rely mainly on static configurations.

2. The operator can choose to use either I-PMSI plus S-PMSI or S-PMSI tunnels only, depending on factors such as traffic thresholds, and source/group pairs.

3. An operator providing PIM-SSM transit services to smaller carriers and operators is always concerned about overlapping
   multicast groups causing undesirable effects on traffic and
   its users. Containing traffic within an MVPN provides a framework for ensuring individual privacy for multicast traffic on a
   per customer/carrier basis.
4. A wide range of tunnel types is available to choose from within
   the NG-MVPN framework.

Vendor Support for the NG-MVPN Framework

The industry, including vendors and carriers, has started moving towards the NG-MVPN framework due to the tremendous
benefits—including the paradigm shift in building multicast
infrastructures—it offers. A large, installed base of NG-MVPN
exists already, with some of the largest service providers deploying
it. Many customers who have used satellite infrastructures to offer
high definition video have successfully migrated their applications (such as Broadcast/Linear video) to a converged MPLS platform using NG-MVPNs, thus cutting costs on OPEX.

From a vendor standpoint, Alcatel-Lucent has been supporting
the NG-MVPN solution based on the BGP control plane for quite
some time, with some limitations on the support for the various
BGP route types. For instance, only autodiscovery (i.e., Type 1
BGP) routes are supported as of TiMOS release 7.0R5. Starting with
TiMOS release 8.0, Alcatel-Lucent supports a full-fledged version of
the NG-MVPN framework based on the BGP control plane, which is
completely inter-operable with the JUNOS-based implementation.

Summary

NG-MVPNs lay the foundation for a new dimension in delivery
multicast-enabled applications over a converged IP/MPLS infrastructure. They also define a paradigm shift in the delivery of applications that were once considered not optimal for delivery over an
IP core, for example, high definition video. The BGP-based control
plane provides an opportunity for creating new service types in the
form of MVPN routing information. The vendor and carrier community has expressed great interest and support for this framework, such that today this is not just an emerging solution but a
well-established and mature technology with many deployments
the world over. The following chapters examine the specific
nuances of implementation on Alcatel-Lucent and Cisco devices.

3

PROVIDER BACKBONE BRIDGING WITH VPLS

Introduction

Scaling VPLS to an extremely large number of instances in a service provider network has always been a topic of interest. In this chapter, we look at some of the issues involved in scaling P2P and MP2MP L2VPNs (VPLS) and provide some operational examples.

We look at one such mechanism, provider backbone bridging (PBB) integrated with VPLS, that attempts to address the scaling concerns, with a focus on limiting the scope of MAC flooding within a VPLS domain.

We also look at the PBB-VPLS architecture based on the Alcatel-Lucent implementation. The configuration snippets provided here are applicable to an Alcatel-Lucent TiMOS deployment.

Terminology

A service (like VPLS or VLL) on the Alcatel TiMOS consists of a customer ID, SAP, and SDP linked together. See Figure 3.1.

To provision a service, a customer ID must be associated with the service at the time of service creation.

A SAP identifies the customer interface point for a service. A SAP is a local entity and is uniquely identified by:
- The physical Ethernet port
- The encapsulation type (Ethernet-specific NULL, dot1q, or QinQ)
- The encapsulation identifier (ID)
  The SDPs can be subdivided into:
- Spoke SDP – A spoke SDP is treated like the equivalent of a traditional bridge port where flooded traffic received on the spoke SDP is replicated on all other "ports" (other spoke and mesh SDPs or SAPs) and not transmitted on the port it was received. This tunneling type is used for H-VPLS and Martini tunnels.

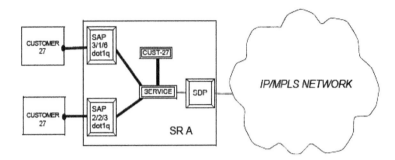

Figure 3.1

- Mesh SDP – All mesh SDPs bound to a service are logically treated like a single bridge port for flooded traffic, where flooded traffic received on any mesh SDP on the service is replicated to other "ports" (spoke SDPs and SAPs) and not transmitted on any mesh SDPs. This tunneling type is used for normal VPLS services and has split horizon capabilities.

We will see that it is important to know between which entities traffic can be forwarded in case of a VPLS service.

VPLS Scalability Factors

The way for VPLS to emulate IEEE 802.3-alike broadcast domains and to avoid loops at the same time is to (a) create a full mesh of PWEs among all the PEs and (b)to enforce the split horizon rule. As a consequence of the PWE full-mesh, the control and data planes are impacted by the so-called "N2" issue:

- From a control plane perspective, each PE node will require:
  - (N-1) TLDP sessions; N = the number of PEs in a particular network
  - (M-1) PWEs (mesh-SDP) per VPLS; M = number of PEs in a particular VPLS instance
  - (N-1)*2 initiated LSP tunnels assuming secondary LSPs; N = number of PEs in a particular VPLS network
  - (N-1)*2 terminated LSPs
  - (X) transit LSPs (if P function)

From a data plane standpoint, each PE node will require BUM replication: N-1 copies of the same BUM frame replicated at the ingress PE, even though all the copies may go over the same physical interface (ring topologies). This is inefficient and unnecessarily consumes bandwidth.

In a nutshell, we could state that the main scalability factors to take into account in VPLS networks are:

- TLDP sessions scaling
- PWE scaling

- MPLS tunnel scaling
- Replication efficiency

Scaling VPLS Using Hierarchical-VPLS

VPLS or "flat" VPLS establishes a full mesh of mesh SDPs (full mesh of PWs) among the PE nodes. H-VPLS partitions the control and data planes, providing a VPLS hierarchy that can scale much higher and reduces operational complexity. With H-VPLS we introduce a different type of PWE or SDP binding: the "spoke SDP." The main characteristic of a spoke SDP is that the split horizon rule is disabled on it; hence ingress traffic on a spoke SDP can be switched not only to a SAP but also to mesh SDPs or other spoke SDPs. This new type of PWE gives us the capacity to add a hierarchy to the "flat" VPLS domain, hence H-VPLS, as represented in Figure 3.2. According to RFC4762, the PE nodes with mesh SDPs are referred as PE-rs nodes, whereas the PE nodes connected by one (or two for redundancy) spoke SDP to the PE-rs are referred as MTU-s.

The table in Figure 3.3 outlines the default forwarding rules between the logical ports in a VPLS. The use of "split-horizon-groups" can influence this further.

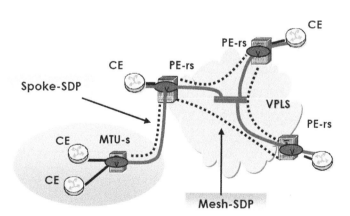

Figure 3.2

Source / Destination	SAP	Spoke SDP	Mesh SDP
SAP	Yes	Yes	Yes
Spoke SDP	Yes	Yes	Yes
Mesh SDP	Yes	Yes	No

Figure 3.3

As the RFC 4762 section 10.1.2 states, the spoke SDP connectivity offers several scaling and operational advantages for creating large-scale VPLS implementations while retaining the ability to offer all the functionality of the VPLS service:

- Eliminates the need for a full mesh of tunnels and mesh SDPs, thereby getting rid of the N2 problem.
- Minimizes signaling overhead, since fewer PWEs are required for the VPLS service (the MTU-s only requires one PWE to the higher VPLS level).
- Segments VPLS nodal discovery. MTU needs to be aware of only the PE-rs node, although it is participating in the VPLS service that spans multiple devices.
- Requires configuration of the new MTU-s with the addition of other sites but does not require any provisioning of the existing MTU-s devices or remote PE-rs nodes on that service. Hierarchical connections can be used to create VPLS service that spans multiple service provider domains.

See examples in Figure 3.4 and Figure 3.5.

The two examples defined in Figures 3.4 and 3.5 are illustrated in Figure 3.6.

Ultimately, we could scale in an unlimited way if we connect VPLS domains to each other through spoke SDPs, with approximately 50 peer nodes per domain. H-VPLS therefore overcomes the VPLS scaling limitations by partitioning the control and data

Example 1 Scaling factors	Values
Maximum number of PEs	215
Number of PE-rs nodes	10 (5 pairs)
Number of MTU-s nodes (dual-homed)	205 (41 per PE-rs pair)
Maximum number of VPLS	640 (32k PW / 50 PW/VPLS)
Maximum number of MACs per VPLS	300 (192k MACs / 640 VPLS)

Figure 3.4

Or if we increase the number of PE-rs nodes in the core:

Example 2 Scaling factors	Values
Maximum number of PEs	330
Number of PE-rs nodes	20 (10 pairs)
Number of MTU-s nodes (dual-homed)	310 (31 per PE-rs pair)
Maximum number of VPLS	640 (32k PW / 50 PW/VPLS)
Maximum number of MACs per VPLS	300 (192k MACs / 640 VPLS)

Figure 3.5

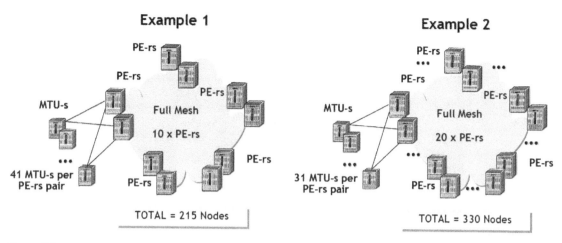

Figure 3.6

planes; however, H-VPLS introduces a new scaling factor or side effect: MAC scaling on the aggregation point, PE-rs.

In summary, H-VPLS offers:

- Efficient use of access network resources by restricting the replication to a limited set of PE's
- Minimal requirements on the L2PE device—scales linearly with the directly attached VPLS instances
- Minimizes the number of required PWs
- Site addition/deletion has local impact only
  Requirements on PE:
- PE needs to implement the VPLS/hierarchical VPLS model
- PE needs to be able to maintain a large number of VFIs

Redundancy with H-VPLS

We see that the previous H-VPLS indeed addresses the scalability requirements in terms of the number of pseudowires and replication; however, there is an obvious single point of failure in the network. The nodes connecting the spoke pseudowires are non-redundant so that if one of them fails, the traffic between the two metro segments is impacted. In order to resolve this, a second spoke pseudowire can be added to the network, as illustrated in Figure 3.7.

Because of the packet-forwarding behavior defined for a spoke pseudowire and the fact that VPLS is fundamentally a Layer 2 technology, an unbroken loop is created in the customer's VPN, as illustrated in Figure 3.8. The implementation may use a version of the VPLS called management VPLS (M-VPLS). The implementation of the M-VPLS has been optimized in an inter-operability fashion to improve the convergence times of the protocol in this application.

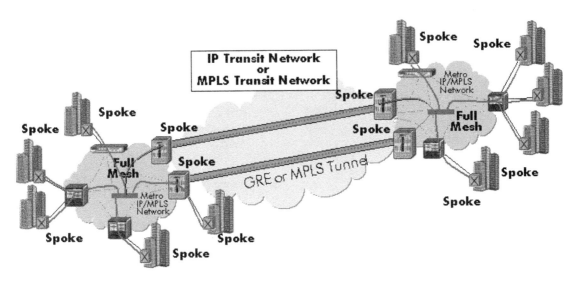

Figure 3.7

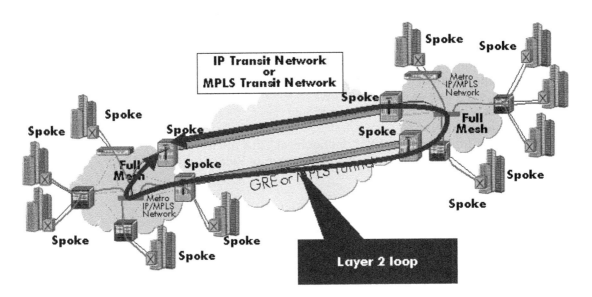

Figure 3.8

Spoke Redundancy Using M-VPLS

As shown in Figure 3.9, the management VPLS runs a control protocol to provide redundancy between the spoke pseudowires or SAPs. The sole purpose of the M-VPLS instances is to remove the loop in the network caused by the spoke pseudowires or

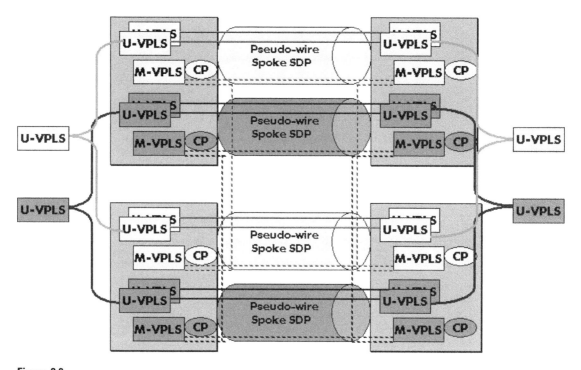

Figure 3.9

SAPs. An important note is that the M-VPLS instances do not carry customer traffic. The M-VPLS is protecting the data-VPLS instances with a control protocol such that the spoke pseudo-wires or SAPs are made redundant. Running the M-VPLS on the same SDPs as the data-VPLS instances it is protecting does this.

When the control protocol of the M-VPLS detects a loop, it puts the M-VPLS and all of the customer pseudowires that traverse the same transit tunnel LSP between the PE devices into a blocking state, thus breaking the loop, as shown in Figure 3.10. When a loop or a topology change is detected in the M-VPLS, all of its associated/affected pseudowires are informed such that the forwarding databases are flushed in order to facilitate transition of the traffic to the available pseudowires. The MAC withdraw mechanism that is described in the VPLS draft is the flush mechanism that is used.

As seen in Figure 3.10, the M-VPLS not only provides spoke pseudowire/SAP redundancy, it also allows for load balancing certain data VPLS traffic on the links between PE1-PE3 and traffic of other data-VPLS on the link between PE2 and PE4.

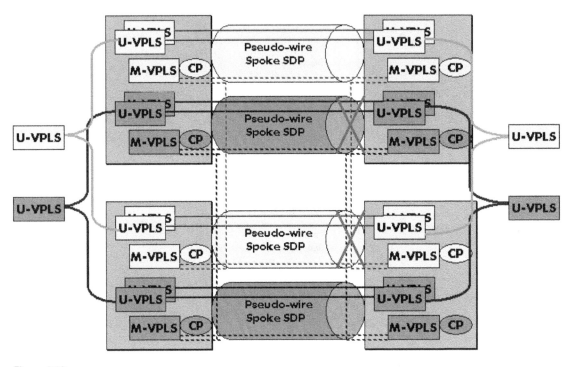

Figure 3.10

Operational Examples

The next section describes operational network models that show how to build L2VPN services in large networks. It explains how to scale the service, how to make it redundant, and so on. All the examples are shown with logical connections, so abstraction is made of the physical topology.

Scalable L2VPNs with Segmented Metro Networks

The illustration in Figure 3.11 shows a very widely deployed network. Metro segments are clearly segmented onto a core network that is connecting the different metro segments together. The metro segments are geographically split and connected to the backbone at various locations.

In this topology we see two scenarios: one where the core network consists of routers that do not have the M-VPLS capabilities and another whose core routers do have M-VPLS capabilities. In the following sections we discuss both models in more detail.

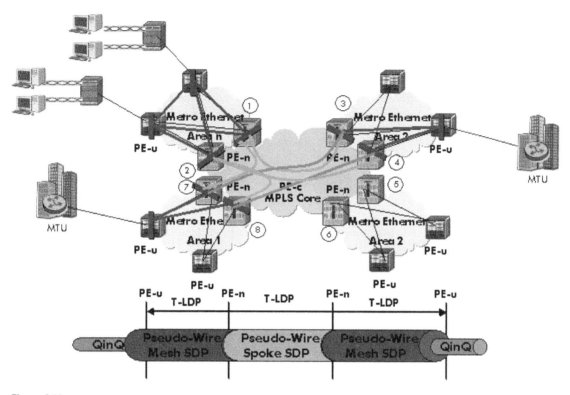

Figure 3.11

Metro Networks with P Routers without M-VPLS Capability

In this section we look at how to build a large L2VPN in a network where the core routers do not have M-VPLS capabilities. A simple diagram of this network is seen Figure 3.12, where only four routers, two PE-n nodes, and two PE-u nodes per metro segment are shown. The description is limited to three metro segments to simplify the diagram. Even in this simplified view, all the principles important to building a scalable L2VPN are shown.

Metro segment 1 consists of:

- PE-u11, PE-u12 – connecting to the PE-n of metro segment 1
- PE-n11, PE-n12 – connecting metro segment 1 to the core network

   Metro segment 2 consists of:

- PE-u21, PE-u22 – connecting to the PE-n of metro segment 2
- PE-n23, PE-n24 – connecting metro segment 2 to the core network

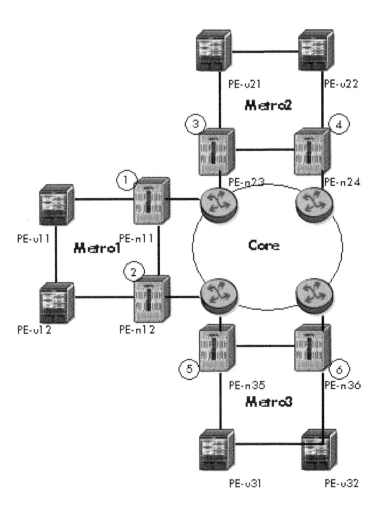

Figure 3.12

Metro segment 3 consists of:

- PE-u31, PE-u32 – connecting to the PE-n of metro segment 3
- PE-n35, PE-n36 – connecting metro segment 3 to the core network

Provisioning the Infrastructure

First the nodes onto which the M-VPLS will be enabled must be identified. In this example they would be PE-n11, PE-n12, PE-n23, PE-n24, PE-n35, and PE-n36. An M-VPLS is created between each pair of PE-n nodes of the metro segment. The M-VPLS consists of a spoke SDP between the even nodes of a metro segment and between the odd nodes of a metro segment, and a mesh SDP is created between the odd and even nodes of a metro segment. The following is then set up:

- An M-VPLS between nodes PE-n11, PE-n12, PE-n23, and PE-n24 with:
  - Spoke SDP between PE-n11 and PE-n23
  - Spoke SDP between PE-n12 and PE-n24
  - Mesh SDP between PE-n11 and PE-n12
  - Mesh SDP between PE-n23 and PE-n24
- An M-VPLS between nodes PE-n11, PE-n12, PE-n35, and PE-n36 with:
  - Spoke SDP between PE-n11 and PE-n35
  - Spoke SDP between PE-n12 and PE-n36
  - Mesh SDP between PE-n11 and PE-n12
  - Mesh SDP between PE-n35 and PE-n36
- An M-VPLS between nodes PE-n23, PE-n24, PE-n35, and PE-n36 with:
  - Spoke SDP between PE-n23 and PE-n35
  - Spoke SDP between PE-n24 and PE-n36
  - Mesh SDP between PE-n23 and PE-n24
  - Mesh SDP between PE-n35 and PE-n36

M-VPLS is created with spoke and mesh SDPs because a mesh SDP is never cut by the M-VPLS so that the spoke pseudowires are made redundant, as shown earlier. Figure 3.13 represents the configuration.

In this model, the number of M-VPLSs that have to be created in the network is $N \times (N-1)/2$, $N =$ number of metro segments.

The number of M-VPLSs per node is $N-1$, $N =$ number of metro segments.

In a network with three metro segments, the number of M-VPLSs in the network is $3 \times (3-1)/2 = 3$ and the number of M-VPLSs per node is $3-1 = 2$.

Provisioning the L2VPN Data Services

Once the infrastructure is set up we can start creating L2VPN data services that carry customer traffic The following section describes the provisioning of one service that has a customer on every metro node in order to simplify the diagrams. However, multiple services can be created where each L2VPN service can have different customers on different PEs.

An L2VPN that spans all PE nodes of all metro segments is created with:

- Fully meshed VPLS per metro segment
  - Fully meshed VPLS between PE-u11, PE-u12, PE-n11, and PE-n12

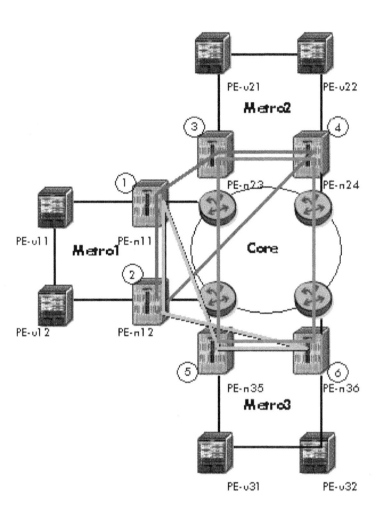

Figure 3.13

- Fully meshed VPLS between PE-u21, PE-u22, PE-n23, and PE-n24
- Fully meshed VPLS between PE-u31, PE-u32, PE-u35, and PE-u36
- A spoke SDP between every odd node of each metro segment and every even node of each metro segment using the same SDP as the M-VPLS:
  - Odd spoke SDPs
    - Spoke SDP between PE-n11 and PE-n23
    - Spoke SDP between PE-n11 and PE-n35
    - Spoke SDP between PE-n23 and PE-n35
  - Even spoke SDPs
    - Spoke SDP between PE-n12 and PE-n24
    - Spoke SDP between PE-n12 and PE-n36

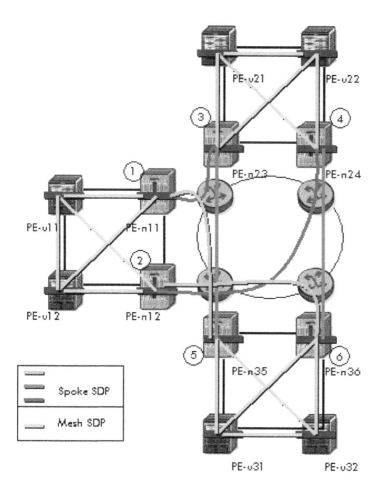

Figure 3.14

– Spoke SDP between PE-n24 and PE-n36

Once this is created, the service is up and running and can be used for data traffic. Figure 3.14 shows the configuration.

Packet Flow

In this section we assume that the M-VPLS disables the following spoke SDPs:

- Spoke SDP between PE-n12 and PE-n36
- Spoke SDP between PE-n23 and PE-n35
- Spoke SDP between PE-n12 and PE-n24

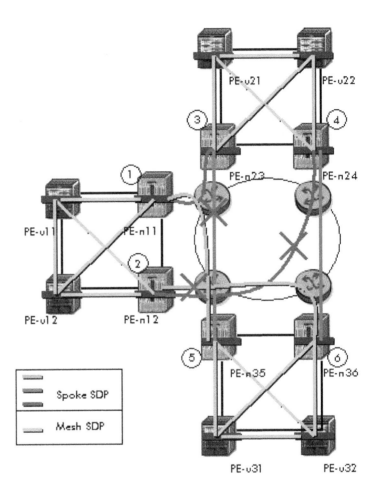

Figure 3.15

The diagram in Figure 3.15 illustrates this behavior.

To explain the loop-free topology that is created, let's examine how an unknown packet is forwarded entering the SAP on node PE-u31.

The packet that enters the SAP on PE-u31 of the VPLS service is forwarded to:

- Mesh SDP between PE-u31 and PE-n35
- Mesh SDP between PE-u31 and PE-n36
- Mesh SDP between PE-u31 and PE-n32

On node PE-u 32 the packet is forwarded to the SAPs connected to the VPLS service on PE-u32. The packet is not forwarded toward the mesh SDPs, as they have split horizon capabilities.

On node PE-n35 the packet is forwarded to the spoke SDP between PE-n35 and PE-n11 onto metro segment 1. The packet is not forwarded toward the mesh SDPs, as they have split horizon capabilities. The packet is not forwarded on the spoke SDP between PE-n35 and PE-n23, as this SDP is disabled by the M-VPLS.

On node PE-n36 the packet is forwarded to the spoke SDP between PE-n36 and PE-n24 onto metro segment 2. The packet is not forwarded toward the mesh SDPs, as they have split horizon capabilities. The packet is not forwarded on the spoke SDP between PE-n36 and PE-n12, as this SDP is disabled by the M-VPLS.

On metro segment 1 the packet enters node PE-n11 via spoke SDP PE-n35.

On node PE-n11 the packet is forwarded to:
- Mesh SDP between node PE-n11 and PE-u11
- Mesh SDP between node PE-n11 and PE-u12

The packet is not forwarded toward the spoke pseudowires PE-n11 and PE-n23 because the spoke SDPs are created with split horizon capabilities, as shown in the provisioning section.

On nodes PE-u11 and PE-u12 the packet is forwarded to the SAPs connected to the VPLS service on PE-u11/PE12. The packet is not forwarded toward the mesh SDPs, as they have split horizon capabilities.

On metro segment 2 the packet enters node PE-n24 via spoke SDP connected to PE-n36.

On node PE-n24 the packet is forwarded to:
- Mesh SDP between node PE-n24 and PE-u11
- Mesh SDP between node PE-n24 and PE-u12

The packet is not forwarded toward the spoke pseudowires PE-n24 and PE-n12 because the M-VPLS disabled that connection.

On nodes PE-u21 and PE-u22 the packet is forwarded to the SAPs connected to the VPLS service on PE-u21/PE22. The packet is not forwarded toward the mesh SDPs, as they have split horizon capabilities.

As shown in Figure 3.16, the VPLS service that is created across the different metro segments is completely loop-free. The MAC learning is not discussed here but works as in a normal bridge, meaning that a MAC address is learned based on the source MAC address of the packet. A packet sent to the source MAC address of the packet in Figure 3.16 will follow the reverse path to the destination on PE-u31.

Redundancy

Any link failure in the network will be protected via MPLS. In case of LDP, this protection is based on the IGP convergence, and in the case of RSVP, protection is based on MPLS FRR or

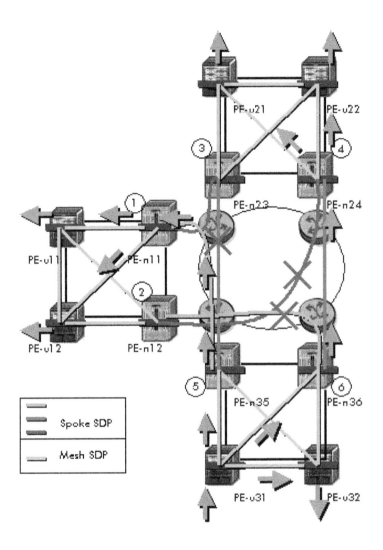

Figure 3.16

primary/backup features. In case of FRR, 50 ms convergence occurs.

In the event of a PE-n node failure the related M-VPLSs re-converge, resulting in a MAC withdraw so that the network re-converges quickly and is not dependent on MAC table timeouts, which typically take minutes.

For example, if PE-n23 fails, as shown in Figure 3.17, M-VPLS on node PE-n24 detects a topology change, which results in a MAC flush in the service and the opening of the spoke SDP between nodes PE-n24 and PE-n12. The other M-VPLS remains unchanged.

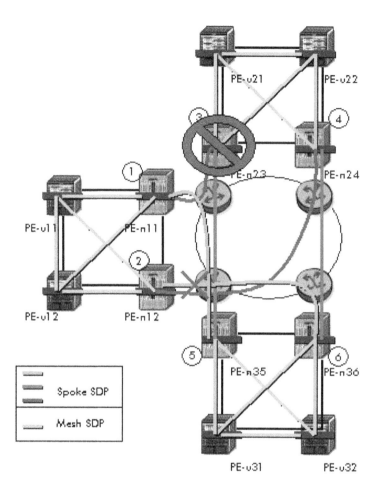

Figure 3.17

A complete loop-free topology is maintained, as shown in Figure 3.18. On the left side a packet is sent from PE-u31, and on the right side a packet is sent from PE-u11.

OAM

Troubleshooting the metro network service can be done using the following commands between the PE-u and PE-n nodes involved in the service:
• OAM LSP-ping: perform LSP ping
• OAM LSP-trace: perform LSP trace
• OAM MAC-ping: perform MAC ping
• OAM MAC-populate: populate a MAC

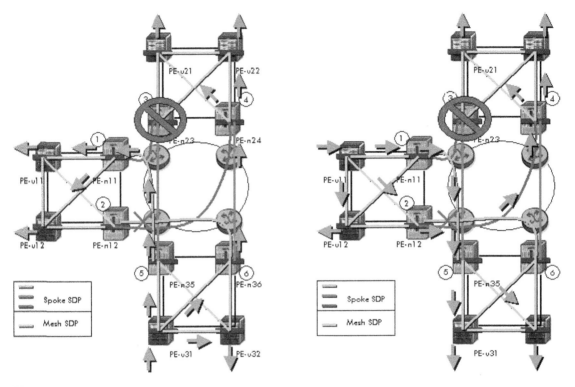

Figure 3.18

- OAM MAC-purge: perform MAC purge
- OAM MAC-trace: perform MAC trace
- OAM SDP-MTU: SDP MTU test
- OAM SDP-ping: SDP ping
- OAM SVC-ping: service ping—determines the existence and operative state of the SVC-ID on the far end ESR

The commands are specified in http://www.ietf.org/internet-drafts/draft-stokes-vkompella-l2vpn-hvpls-oam-00.txt and are based on the MPLS tool chain.

Conclusion

All aspects to create a fully redundant, loop–free, scalable L2VPN service can be created in the network topology outlined in this section.

The following design rules must be adhered to:

- Identify the PE-n nodes. These are the nodes that connect the metro segments to the core network.

- Create an M-VPLS between each pair of the PE-n nodes with spoke SDPs between the odd and even inter-metro PEs and a mesh SDP between each PE-n node of the metro segment.
- Create the data VPLS services with the following rules:
  - Full mesh between the metro segments
  - Spoke SDPs with split horizon capabilities between each odd/even node of the different metro segments

Metro Networks and P Routers with M-VPLS Capability

In this section we discuss how to build a large L2VPN in a network where the core routers have M-VPLS capabilities.

A simple diagram of this network is illustrated in Figure 3.19. Three routers, two PE-n nodes, and one PE-u node per metro segment are shown. Even in this simplified view, all the principles that are important to building a scalable L2VPN are included.

Metro segment 1 consists of:
- PE-u11: connecting to the PE-n of metro segment 1
- PE-n11, PE-n12: connecting the metro segment 1 to the core network

Metro segment 2 consists of:
- PE-u21: connecting to the PE-n of metro segment 2
- PE-n21, PE-n22: connecting metro segment 2 to the core network

Metro segment 3 consists of:
- PE-u31: connecting to the PE-n of metro segment 3
- PE-n31, PE-n32: connecting metro segment 3 to the core network

The core network consists of PE-c1, PE-c2, PE-c3, and PE-c4 connecting the three metro segments together.

Provisioning the Infrastructure

Identify the nodes onto which the M-VPLS will be enabled. In the example above, this is PE-n11, PE-n12, PE-n21, PE-n22, PE-n31, and PE-n32 together with PE-c1, PE-c2, PE-c3, and PE-c4. An M-VPLS is created between each pair of PE-n nodes of the metro segment and the core nodes connecting the metro segment onto the core network. The M-VPLS consists of a spoke SDP between the metro PE-n nodes of a metro segment and the core PE-c nodes connected to the metro segment. A mesh SDP is created between the PE-n of a metro segment and the PE-c of the core network. This results in:

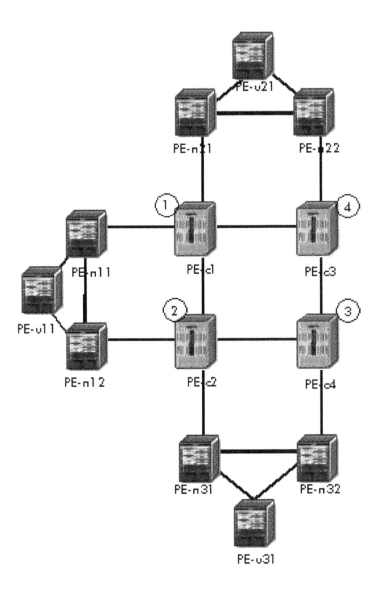

Figure 3.19

- An M-VPLS between nodes PE-n11, PE-n12, PE-c1, and PE-c2 with:
  - Spoke SDP between PE-n11 and PE-c1
  - Spoke SDP between PE-n12 and PE-c2
  - Mesh SDP between PE-n11 and PE-n12
  - Mesh SDP between PE-c1 and PE-c2
- An M-VPLS between nodes PE-n21, PE-n22, PE-c1, and PE-c3 with:
  - Spoke SDP between PE-n21 and PE-c1
  - Spoke SDP between PE-n22 and PE-c3

- Mesh SDP between PE-n21 and PE-n22
- Mesh SDP between PE-c1 and PE-c3
- An M-VPLS between nodes PE-n31, PE-n32, PE-c2, and PE-c4 with:
  - Spoke SDP between PE-n31 and PE-c2
  - Spoke SDP between PE-n32 and PE-c3
  - Mesh SDP between PE-n31 and PE-n32
  - Mesh SDP between PE-c2 and PE-c4

M-VPLS is created with spoke and mesh SDPs because a mesh SDP is never cut by the M-VPLS, so the spoke pseudowires are made redundant, as discussed in the previous chapter. Figure 3.20 illustrates the configuration.

In this model the number of M-VPLSs that have to be created in the network is Nx (N-1)/2, N = number of metro segments.

The number of M-VPLSs per node is M = number of metro segments connected.

In a network with three metro segments the number of M-VPLSs in the network is 3x(3-1)/2 = 3 and the number of M-VPLSs per node is either two or one, depending on how many metro networks are connected.

Provisioning the L2VPN Data Services

Once the infrastructure is set up we can start creating L2VPN data services that carry customer traffic. In the following section we describe the provisioning of one service that has a customer on every metro node in order to simplify the diagrams. However, multiple services can be created where each L2VPN service can have different customers on different PEs.

An L2VPN that spans all PE nodes of all metro segments is created with:

- Fully meshed VPLS per metro segment
  - Fully meshed VPLS between PE-u11, PE-n11, PE-n12
  - Fully meshed VPLS between PE-u21, PE-n21, PE-n22
  - Fully meshed VPLS between PE-u31, PE-u31, PE-u32
- Spoke SDP between every PE-n node of the metro segment and the connected PE-c node using the same SDP as the M-VPLS.
  - Spoke SDP between PE-n11 and PE-c1
  - Spoke SDP between PE-n12 and PE-c2
  - Spoke SDP between PE-n21 and PE-c1
  - Spoke SDP between PE-n22 and PE-c3
  - Spoke SDP between PE-n31 and PE-c2
  - Spoke SDP between PE-n32 and PE-c4

Once this is created the service is up and running and can be used for data traffic. The diagram in Figure 3.21 shows the configuration.

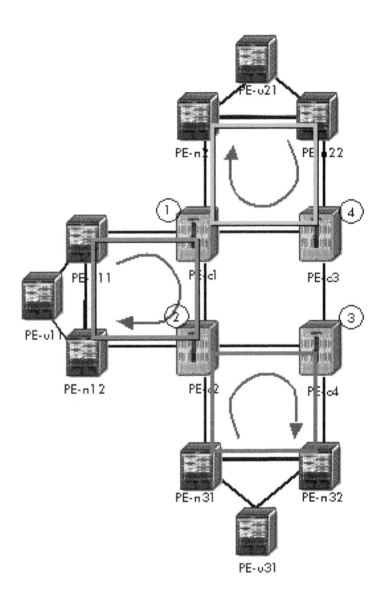

Figure 3.20

Packet Flow

In this section we assume that the M-VPLS disables the following spoke SDPs:

- Spoke SDP between PE-n12 and PE-c2
- Spoke SDP between PE-n22 and PE-c3
- Spoke SDP between PE-n32 and PE-c4

The diagram in Figure 3.22 illustrates this behavior.

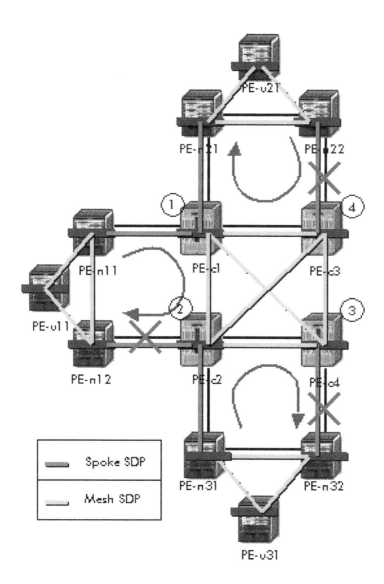

Figure 3.21

To explain the loop-free topology that is created, let's examine how an unknown packet is forwarded entering the SAP on node PE-u31.

The packet that enters the SAP on PE-u31 of the VPLS service is forwarded to:

- Mesh SDP between PE-u31 and PE-n31
- Mesh SDP between PE-u31 and PE-n32

On node PE-n31 the packet is forwarded to:

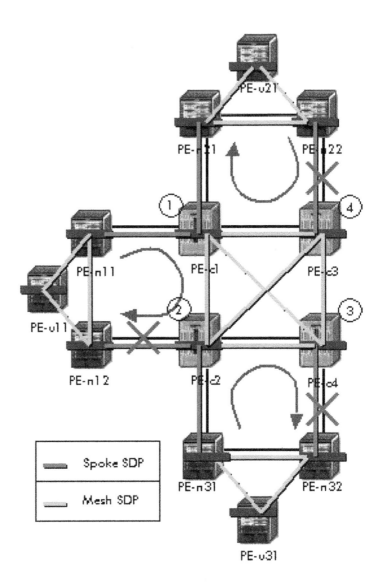

Figure 3.22

- SAPs connected to the VPLS service on PE-n31
- Spoke SDP between PE-n31 and PE-c2
  The packet is not forwarded toward the mesh SDPs as they have split horizon capabilities.
  The packet enters the core network via PE-c2. On node PE-c2 the packet is forwarded to:
- Mesh SDP between PE-c2 and PE-c1
- Mesh SDP between PE-c2 and PE-c3
- Mesh SDP between PE-c2 and PE-c4

The packet is not forwarded on the spoke SDP between PE-c2 and PE-n12, as this SDP is disabled by the M-VPLS.

On node PE-c1 the packet is forwarded to:
- Spoke SDP between PE-c1 and PE-n11 onto metro segment 1
- Spoke SDP between PE-c1 and PE-n21 onto metro segment 2

The packet is not forwarded toward the mesh SDPs, as they have split horizon capabilities.

On node PE-c3 the packet is forwarded to SAP connected to PE-c3 (potentially). The packet is not forwarded toward the mesh SDPs, as they have split horizon capabilities. The packet is not forwarded on the spoke SDP between PE-c3 and PE-n22, as this SDP is disabled by the M-VPLS.

On node PE-c4 the packet is forwarded to SAP connected to PE-c4 (potentially). The packet is not forwarded toward the mesh SDPs, as they have split horizon capabilities. The packet is not forwarded on the spoke SDP between PE-c4 and PE-n32, as this SDP is disabled by the M-VPLS.

On metro segment 1 the packet enters node PE-n11 via spoke SDP PE-c1.

On node PE-n11 the packet is forwarded to:
- SAPs connected to the VPLS service on PE-n11
- Mesh SDP between nodes PE-n11 and PE-u11
- Mesh SDP between nodes PE-n11 and PE-n12

On nodes PE-u11 and PE-n12 the packet is forwarded to SAPs connected to the VPLS service on PE-u11/PE-n12. The packet is not forwarded toward the mesh SDPs, as they have split horizon capabilities.

On metro segment 2 the packet enters node PE-n21 via spoke SDP connected to PE-c1.

On node PE-n21 the packet is forwarded to:
- SAPs connected to the VPLS service on PE-n21
- Mesh SDP between node PE-n21 and PE-u21
- Mesh SDP between node PE-n21 and PE-n22

On nodes PE-u21 and PE-n22 the packet is forwarded to SAPs connected to the VPLS service on PE-u21/PE-n22. The packet is not forwarded toward the mesh SDPs, as they have split horizon capabilities.

As shown in Figure 3.23, the VPLS service that is created across the different metro segments is completely loop-free. The MAC learning is not discussed here but works as in a normal bridge, meaning that a MAC address is learned based on the source MAC address of the packet. A packet sent to the source MAC address of the packet in Figure 3.23 will follow the reverse path to the destination on PE-u31.

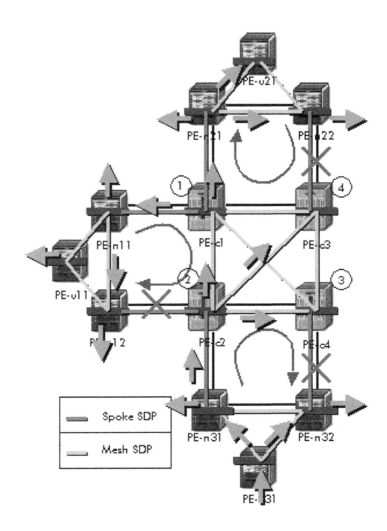

Figure 3.23

Redundancy

Any link failure in the network will be protected via MPLS. In case of LDP, this protection is based on the IGP convergence, and in case of RSVP, protection is based on MPLS FRR or primary/backup features. In case of FRR, 50 ms convergence is experienced.

In the event of a PE-n node failure the related M-VPLS re-converge, resulting in a MAC withdraw so that the network re-converges quickly and is not dependent on MAC table timeouts, which typically take minutes.

For example, if PE-c1 fails, as shown in Figure 3.24, M-VPLS on nodes PE-n22/PE-n12 detects a topology change, which results in a MAC flush in the service and the opening of the spoke SDPs between nodes PE-n12 and PE-c2 and nodes PE-n22 and PE-c3. The other M-VPLS remains unchanged.

In this example, a complete loop-free topology is maintained, as shown in Figure 3.25. On the left side a packet is sent from PE-u31, and on the right side a packet is sent from PE-u11.

OAM

Troubleshooting the metro network service can be done using the following commands between PE-u and PE-n nodes involved in the service:

- OAM LSP-ping: perform LSP ping
- OAM LSP-trace: perform LSP trace
- OAM MAC-ping: perform MAC ping
- OAM MAC-populate: populate a MAC
- OAM MAC-purge: perform MAC purge
- OAM MAC-trace: perform MAC trace
- OAM SDP-MTU: SDP MTU test
- OAM SDP-ping: SDP ping
- OAM SVC-ping: service ping—determines the existence and operative state of the svc-id on the far end ESR

The commands are specified in http://www.ietf.org/internet-drafts/draft-stokes-vkompella-l2vpn-hvpls-oam-00.txt and are based on the MPLS tool chain.

Conclusion

All aspects to create a fully redundant, loop-free, scalable L2VPN service can be created in the network topology outlined in this section.

The following design rules must be adhered to:

- Identify the PE-n/PE-c nodes. These are the nodes that connect the metro segments to the core network.
- Create an M-VPLS between each pair of the PE-n/PE-c nodes with spoke SDPs between the PE-n and PE-c nodes and a mesh SDP between each PE-n/PE-c node of the metro/core segment.
- Create the data VPLS services with the following rules:
  - Full mesh between the metro/core segments
  - Spoke SDPs between the PE-n nodes connected to the PE-c nodes.

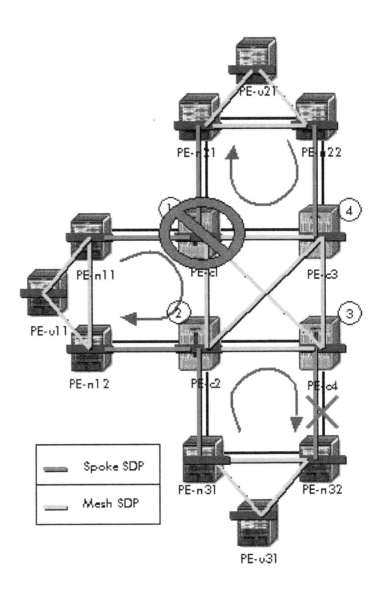

Figure 3.24

Provider Backbone Bridging (PBB)

This section describes the scalability factors identified in VPLS networks and how PBB-VPLS can help to scale in very large networks. Virtual private LAN service (RFC 4762) is a point-to-multipoint Layer 2 VPN service that provides separated broadcast domains (fully capable of learning and forwarding MAC addresses) closed to a given set of users over an IP/MPLS network. These broadcast domains are composed of bridging instances (virtual switching instances, or VSI) existing in each node that

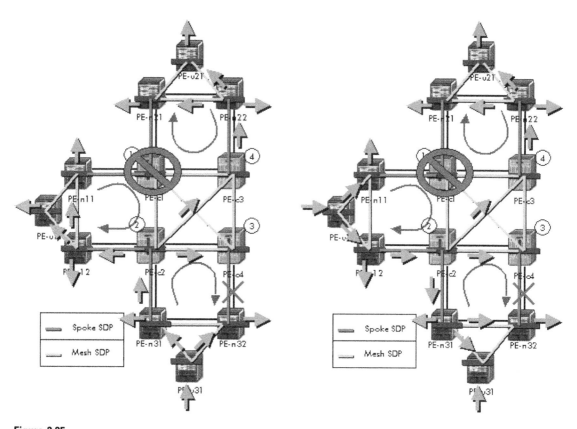

Figure 3.25

are connected to each other by a full mesh of pseudowires (PWE), also known as mesh SDP in the Alcatel-Lucent TiMOS terminology. The PWE full mesh is set up using TLDP in accordance with the RFC4447, martini signaling. The pseudowires, on the other hand, are transported over a full mesh of MPLS LSPs or GRE tunnels. Most of the VPLS implementations today use MPLS as a transport mechanism, being RSVP-TE or LDP used as label distribution protocol for the LSP setup. Sites that belong to the same broadcast domain or VPLS instance expect broadcast, multicast, and unicast traffic to be forwarded to the proper location(s), just like any Ethernet LAN. This expected behavior requires two functions:

- Broadcast/unknown unicast/multicast (BUM) packet replication. This happens at the ingress PE and requires a split horizon rule to break the loops. Split horizon prevents traffic coming from a PWE to be sent to another PWE.

- MAC address learning/aging on a per-pseudowire or access port basis. The PEs learns the valid source MAC addresses of all the packets entering into the VSI (VPLS instance) through a PWE or a SAP (attachment circuit). The MAC addresses age out when the aging time expires. These two functions allow each PE to build an FDB (forwarding data base) per VPLS instance in such a way that when a packet comes in, the destination MAC is looked up and the packet is forwarded to an SAP or a PW.

The MAC Scaling Issue and PBB

VPLS is a multipoint service for which MAC learning is required for traffic forwarding at the PEs. This is not generally an issue since not all the customers have presence in all the nodes. However, when introducing H-VPLS to address all the scaling issues discussed in the last section, the PE-rs nodes can potentially aggregate many MTU-s nodes and thereby aggregate many more VPLS instances and get exposure to many more MAC addresses. In a large scale or inter-domain deployment scenario the potential risk is twofold:

- We could exceed the FDB size on the PE-rs nodes and flood all the unknown destination packets.
- When a change of topology occurs (node/PWE failure), MAC flushing is propagated throughout the network; hence, massive learning must be performed at once on the PE-rs nodes.

The issue is outlined in Figure 3.26. The number of MAC addresses learned on the PE-rs nodes (in red) can be very high as a result of the aggregation of MTU-s nodes and services.

PBB, also known as MAC-in-MAC, "hides" the customer MAC addresses from the service provider core by encapsulating the customer frames into backbone frames at the ingress. These backbone frames are switched throughout the core using "backbone-MACs" (B-MAC). The source B-MAC (B-SA) identifies the source MTU-s node, whereas the destination B-MAC (B-DA) identifies the remote MTU-s where the customer is connected to. The PE-rs nodes learn only B-MACs, as many B-MACs as MTU-s nodes sending traffic (potentially up to 7 B-MACs in this particular example), as illustrated in Figure 3.26. Thousands of customer MAC addresses can reside behind an MTU-s and yet a PE-rs would only learn the MTU-s B-MAC. See Figure 3.27.

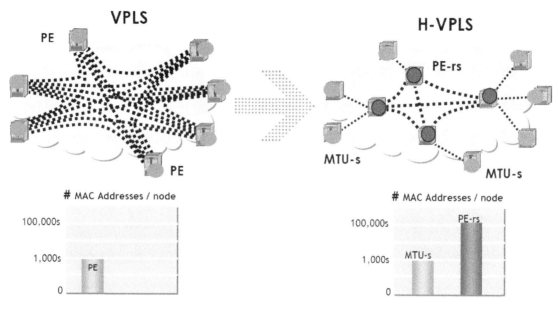

Figure 3.26

The Service/PW Aggregation and PBB

In addition to the dramatic decrease of MAC addresses being learned by the PE-rs nodes, PBB brings new benefits to the H-VPLS networks based on its aggregation capabilities. Figure 3.28 illustrates these benefits.

The hierarchy introduced by H-VPLS makes the PE-rs nodes aggregate many more services and PWs (left-hand diagram in Figure 3.28). PBB combined with H-VPLS in an M:1 model (this is explained later) reduces the number of services in the core and therefore the number of PW (right-hand diagram in Figure 3.28). Furthermore, the core is no longer "customer-aware" since the backbone services and PW are part of the service provider infrastructure and we don't need to create those resources on a per-customer basis any more.

In a nutshell, PBB reduces the backbone load in H-VPLS networks, not only in terms of MACs but also in terms of provisioning "touches"—we no longer need to provision the PE-rs nodes when new customer locations or services are added.

- Service instances – only backbone instances are needed in the core.
- Pseudowires – only the backbone instances require PWs in the core.

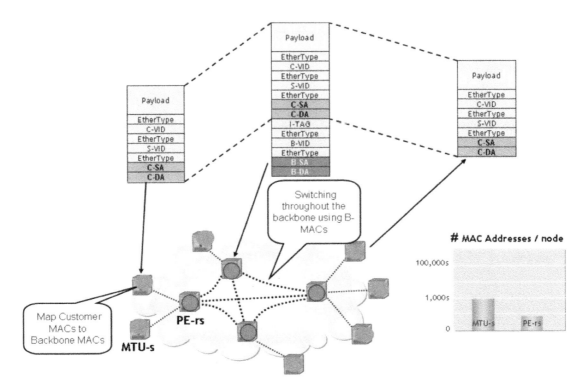

Figure 3.27

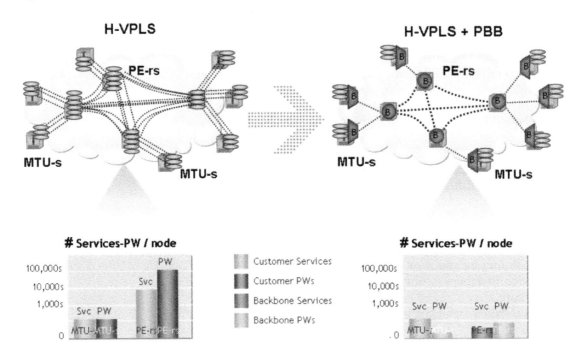

Figure 3.28

- MPLS tunnel topologies – only MPLS tunnels for the backbone PWs are required.
PBB protects the backbone from customer VPN instability.
- Customer addressing – the core becomes customer addressing "unaware."
- Topology changes, control plane, flooding, etc. – the core becomes customer service "unaware." We revisit these benefits throughout this document.

PBB with H-VPLS

In summary, we can conclude that H-VPLS takes VPLS to the next level of scalability. The table in Figure 3.29 justifies our conclusion.

Layer-2 multipoint networks are entering a new phase of deployment. Today many metro networks are being collected by regional hubs connecting to national and international backbones. As the node and service count grows, carriers are looking to enhance their H-VPLS networks, taking them to the next level. PBB complements H-VPLS networks and both technologies

Scaling Issue	Solution	Comments
TLDP sessions scaling	H-VPLS	H-VPLS keeps the TLDP full-mesh only in the core, growing by adding new domains connected through spoke-sdp.
PWE scaling	H-VPLS	H-VPLS keeps the mesh-sdp full-mesh only in the core, growing by adding spoke-sdps to other domains. However, although this is generally true, the PWE scaling issue could be shifted to the PE-rs since there are less PE-rs nodes and the number of PWEs is less distributed.
MPLS Tunnel scaling	H-VPLS / LDPoRSVP	VPLS domains can use different RSVP-TE domains too. Alternatively LDPoRSVP could also help to scale.
Replication Efficiency	H-VPLS	Replication is efficient using spoke-sdps to connect VPLS levels.

Figure 3.29

together—H-VPLS and PBB—overcome the scaling issues in large VPLS deployments. Probably the greatest understood advantage of using PBB is the MAC scalability. However, as already outlined, we will see that PBB-VPLS brings many more advantages forward, like PWE aggregation and further reduced operational complexity.

802.1ah PBB Architecture

This section describes PBB technology as set by the IEEE standard. Provider backbone bridging, or PBB (also known as Mac-in-Mac), is an IEEE technology currently being standardized by the IEEE802.1ah task group. It was conceived to interconnect provider bridge networks (PBN – IEEE 802.1ad or QinQ) in a scalable way, overcoming the two main scalability issues of QinQ in metropolitan deployments by:

- Avoiding the MAC explosion in the core, by adding a provider MAC header with provider MACs.
- Extending the service label from 12 to 24 bits, overcoming the 802.1ad service identifier shortage.

PBB is defined in IEEE as a connectionless technology based on multipoint VLAN tunnels. P-MSTP is used as the core control plane for loop avoidance and load balancing. As a result, the coverage of the solution is limited by STP scale in the core of large service provider networks. It is worth noting that PBB on its own still has the old Ethernet connectionless characteristics, which can be a drawback in most of the large service provider deployments:

- Connectionless forwarding based on MAC learning and forwarding, therefore no traffic engineering capabilities
- Loop avoidance based on STP technologies
- Continued use of a VLAN-ID for broadcast containment

IEEE Model for PBB

According to the model defined in the 802.1ah spec, at the edge of the service provider network (backbone edge bridge, or BEB), the customer Ethernet frame is encapsulated in a regular Ethernet header that we will call a backbone header. The header will, in principle, contain backbone MACs and a backbone q-tag; that is, B-DA and B-SA are the backbone destination and respectively source MACs; B-VID is the backbone VLAN. The loopback MACs or any other MAC addresses associated with the ingress and respective egress edge PEs (BEBs) may be used. A new extended

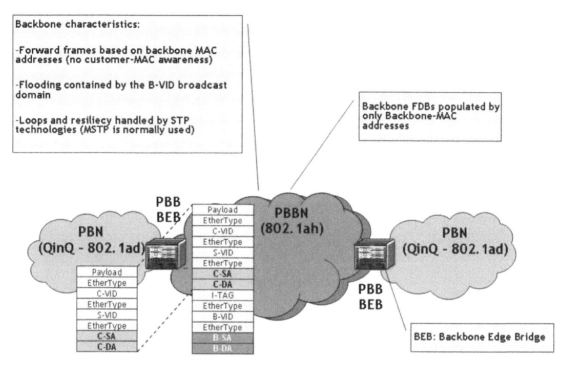

Figure 3.30

tag, I-TAG, is used to identify the service. See the following section for more details on the encapsulation.

The main characteristics of the PBBN, as outlined in Figure 3.30, are summarized as follows:

- Within the PBBN, frames are forwarded based on backbone destination MAC addresses (B-DA) and source backbone MACs are learned on the PBBN nodes' FDBs. No customer MAC addresses are learned.
- BUM traffic is flooded within the B-VID scope.
- Loops and resiliency are handled by STP protocols.

The IEEE PBB model also describes two components that must be present, at least on the BEB nodes:

- The B-component handles the provider backbone layer.
- The I-component is concerned with the mapping of customer/ provider bridge (QinQ) domain (i.e., C-MACs, C-VLANs) to the provider backbone (i.e., B-MACs, B-VLANs)

IEEE 802.1ah Frame Format

The 802.1ah frame format is illustrated in Figure 3.31 and Figure 3.32.

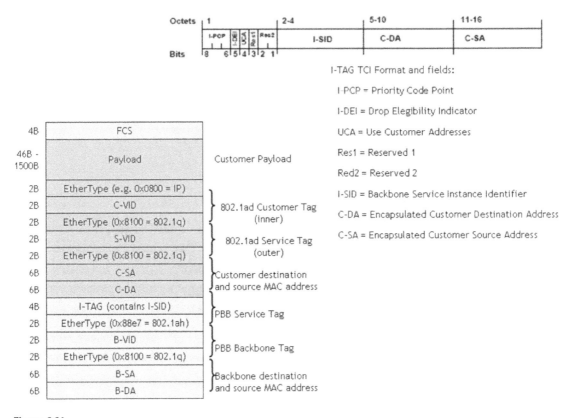

Figure 3.31

Ethertype	IEEE allocated value	SROS default value
Customer VLAN Tag (802.1q)	81-00	81-00 configurable
Service VLAN Tag (802.1ad)	88-a8	81-00 configurable
Backbone Service Instance Tag (802.1ah)	88-e7	88-e7 configurable

Figure 3.32

Regarding the rest of the PBB encapsulation fields: B-MACs, source, and destination (B-SA and B-DA respectively)—Eeach PBB node will be assigned one (or potentially more) Bbackbone MACs. For unicast traffic, B-SA and B-DA will identify the source and destination PEs. The backbone MAC for a specific BEB node can be locally assigned through configuration.

But how is customer BUM traffic handled within the PBBN? A special group MAC is used for the backbone destination MAC

(B-DA) when the customer frame is one of the following types: unknown unicast, multicast, or broadcast. According to the IEEEE 802.1ah spec (draft D4-2), this backbone group MAC ("a flooding MAC," in fact) is derived from the I-SID using the following rule: a standard-based group OUI with the multicast bit set followed by the 24-bit I-SID coded in the last three bytes of the MAC address. This is the only format supported and it isn't currently configurable.

The standard OUI defined as for IEEE 802.1ah with the multicast bit set is "01-1E-83." The resulting group MAC address used for flooding is "01-1E-83-xy-zw-rp," where "xy-zw-rp" is the encoding of the 24-bit I-SID.

- B-TAG (backbone TAG). The B-TAG field is a regular "dot1q" tag and has the role of controlling the size of the backbone broadcast domain by the use of the B-VID. Multiple PBB VPNs may share the same B-VID domain as long as their broadcast domains and communities of interest overlap. In some customer deployments B-VIDs will be deployed in a 1:1 relationship, whereas for some customers the B-VID can be shared among different I-SIDs in an M:1 fashion (I-SID to B-VID respectively).The B-TAG is composed of Ethertype and B-TAG TCI (tag control information), which contains:
  - Priority – 3 bits
  - Drop_eligible – 1 bit
  - B-VID – 12 bits
- I-TAG (extended service tag). Preceded by an Ethertype (standard value is 0x88E7), the I-TAG TCI encodes the following fields:
  - Priority - This 3-bit field carries the customer priority (I-PCP) associated with this frame. The provider network operates on the priority associated with the B-TAG.
  - Drop_eligible - This 1-bit field carries the customer drop eligibility (I-DEI) associated with this frame. The provider network operates on the drop eligibility associated with the B-TAG.
  - Use customer addresses (UCA) - This 1-bit field indicates whether the C-DA and C-SA fields of the tag contain valid addresses. A value of zero indicates the C-DA and C-SA fields contain valid addresses. A value of one indicates the C-DA and C-SA fields do not contain valid addresses; those address fields will contain all zeros. This may be used for PBB inserted service OAM levels. This new functionality (UCA bit was before Reserved1) was introduced in the later phases of the PBB specifications and it will most likely be required in later phases of the PBB deployment.

While the IEEE spec decides on the usage of the UCA bit, in the current implementation we will ignore the UCA indication. As a result, if the C-DA is all zeros, we will just flood it out. No MAC learning is performed on the C-SA of all zeros.

- Reserved 1 (Res1) - This 1-bit field is used for any future format variations. The Res1 field contains a value of zero when the tag is encoded and is ignored when the tag is decoded.
- Reserved 2 (Res2) - This 2-bit field is used for any future format variations. The Res2 field contains a value of zero when the tag is encoded. The frame will be discarded if this field contains a non-zero.
- Value when the tag is decoded.
- I-SID - This 24-bit field carries the service instance identifier associated with this frame. It is used at the destination PE as a demultiplex or field, similar to a VC-label in PWE. The table in Figure 3.33 lists the reserved values in the allocation for the I-SID field in the IEEE 802-1ah-D4-2.

PBB – Draft-Balus

Draft-balus (draft-balus-l2vpn-vpls-802.1ah-02.txt) discusses extensions to the VPLS model required to incorporate desirable PBB components while maintaining the service provider fit of the initial model. The PBB-VPLS model defined in draft-balus provides the following two main characteristics:

- Combines the best of both next-generation Ethernet technologies—PBB and H-VPLS
  - MPLS backbone is used (no need for MSTP), providing a common transport network over which PWE3 technologies can be used for multi-service virtual leased line services.

The following table summarizes the I-TAG field's information:

I-TAG field	Description
I-PCP	Backbone Service Instance Priority Code Point
I-DEI	Backbone Service Instance Drop Eligibility Indicator
UCA	Use Customer Address (0 = valid / 1 = no valid) used for PBB inserted service OAM
Res1 / Res2	Reserved for future use (encoded as zero)
I-SID	Backbone Service Instance Identifier (24 bits)

C-SA	Encapsulated Customer Source MAC Address
D-SA	Encapsulated Customer Destination MAC Address

Figure 3.33

- All MPLS benefits can be applied (sub-50 ms FRR, traffic engineering)
  - PBB is used for VPLS, resulting in MAC hiding in an H-VPLS environment, avoiding MAC scaling and operational issues.
  - PW aggregation in an M:1 model is possible, improving scalability and simplifying operations.
  - PBB can be used for ePipe (optional) without introducing MAC learning to a point-to-point VLL service. This option provides the following benefits:
    - A uniform provisioning model for VPLS and ePipe, using the same MPLS infrastructure
    - PW aggregation in an M:1 model
    - PBB and H-VPLS enable carrier-of-carrier VPLS

According to the model described in the draft and implemented, a PBB VPLS may be represented as one or more I-VPLSs interconnected via a backbone VPLS (B-VPLS) that may be seen as a multi-point tunnel. Figure 3.34 depicts this concept.

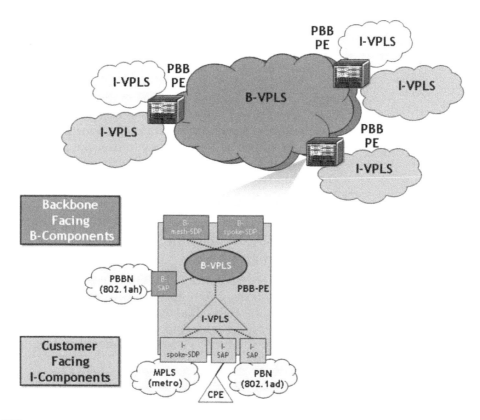

Figure 3.34

As shown in Figure 3.34, inside each edge PBB PE a "PBB VPLS instance" is modeled as an "I-VPLS instance" mapped to a "B-VPLS instance" operating at a customer and backbone MAC layer, respectively. The I-VPLS instance corresponds to the I-VSI component (draft-balus) or I-component (802.1ah), whereas the B-VPLS instance corresponds to the B-VSI component (draft-balus) or B-component (802.1ah). Each component, B and I, can have logical ports attached, which can be either Ethernet ports (dot1q, qinq, or port-based) or PWs (VC-type Ethernet or VLAN).

Other IETF Drafts Related to PBB

There are two additional PBB-related drafts in the IETF community:

- draft-sajassi-l2vpn-vpls-pbb-interop-02.txt
- draft-martini-pwe3-802.1ah-pw-01.txt

The draft-sajassi describes the framework and requirements for inter-operability between the IEEE 802.1ah and VPLS RFC4762 components, while draft-balus discusses the extensions to the VPLS model itself, which is required to incorporate the desirable PBB components. Draft-sajassi describes different inter-operability scenarios and H-VPLS models with PBB Ethernet access when other types of access networks are deployed, including existing MPLS and 802.1ad Ethernet access, in either single or multiple service domains. According to the draft-sajassi, some of those scenarios require new service interfaces based on an I-SID tag as well as a new PW type, different from the Ethernet and VLAN types. These additions allow to transport certain types of PBB encapsulated frames across a PW.

The proposed PW type is described in draft-martini-pwe3-802.1ah-pw, as seen in Figure 3.35.

PBB Mapping to Existing VPLS Constructs and Frame Formats

The PBB processing within the PBB PE is modeled as a chain of two VPLS contexts linked together by a "PIP" (the provider instance port, the I-component internal port connecting to the B-component); SAPs and SDPs will be tagged with an "I" or a "B" to indicate what VPLS type of instance they belong to; that

PW Type	Description
0x001F	Ethernet 802.1ah I-Tagged Mode

Figure 3.35

```
*A:PBB_PE1# configure service vpls 1 ?
  - vpls <service-id> [customer <customer-id>] [vpn <vpn-id>] [m-
vpls] [b-vpls|i-vpls] [create]  | no vpls <service-id>

<snip>

 <b-vpls|i-vpls>     : keyword - creates a backbone-vpls or ISID-vpls
 ...
<snip>
```

Figure 3.36

is, I-SAP, B-SAP, I-spoke-SDP, B-spoke-SDP, and B-mesh SDP. I and B VPLS instances are created just like any other VPLS instance but indicating—at creation time—whether the VPLS will be "I" or "B." Note that I and B VPLS instances can coexist without any problem with regular VPLS instances on the same node. See Figure 3.36.

The Service Component—I-VPLS

The I-VPLS operates in the customer domain and therefore participates in the customer MAC layer. The I-VPLS uses the customer MAC addresses the same way a standard learning switch would, learns on source MAC, and forwards based on destination when switching Ethernet frames. Each I-VPLS connects to maximum one B-VPLS.

I-VPLS characteristics:
- Operates using customer addressing
- Maintains a table used to map customer destination MACs to the appropriate backbone/provider MACs.
  I-SAP support:
- Regular VPLS SAP(s), connecting toward customer side: null, dot1q, qinq
  Local significant VLANs:
- Any service delimiting qtag used for service selection on the I-SAP is stripped before the PBB encapsulation is added. Appropriate qtags are added at the remote PBB PE when sending the packet out on the egress SAP.
  I-SDP support:
- Spoke SDPs only
- MPLS or GRE tunneling
- Split horizon groups supported
  I-VPLS does NOT support:
- Mesh SDPs (though the mesh SDP behavior can be emulated by the use of split horizon groups among spoke SDP)

The Backbone Component—B-VPLS

The B-VPLS operates in the backbone domain carrying one (1:1 mapping) or multiple (M:1) I-VPLS instances.

B-VPLS characteristics:

- Operates using the provider/backbone addressing (B-MACs)
- Provides backbone tunneling for one (1:1) or multiple (M:1) I-VPLS's

  B-SAP ("native" PBB) support:

- Accepts regular SAP(s) using PBB encapsulation for tunneling through an Ethernet-only network (PBB-enabled demarcation device): null, dot1q, qinq

  B-SDP support:

- Mesh or spoke SDPs
- MPLS tunneling only
- Split horizon groups are supported
- Same as for regular PW, the outgoing PBB frame on a B-SDP (i.e., B-PW) will contain a backbone VLAN-ID qtag only if the SDP VC-type = VLAN. If the SDP VC-type = ether, the backbone VLAN-ID qtag is stripped before the frame goes out. The PW type does not affect the I-SAP VLAN processing. All service delimiting VLANs as specified in the SAP definition will be removed before being passed to the B-component.

Frame Formats

Figure 3.37 shows the frame formats expected to be found at the ingress/egress SAP/SDP components (the format is shown next to its SAP/SDP). Note that customer VLAN tags are present in the frames depending on the encapsulation defined at the ingress I-SAP and hence determine whether they are stripped off at the ingress I-SAP, following regular rules existing for VPLS services. B-VID will be present at B-SAP depending on the ingress B-SAP encapsulation and at B-SDPs depending on the VC-type configured (Ethernet or VLAN).

PBB Packet Walkthrough

This section describes the packet behavior through the PBB components. Figure 3.38 depicts the reference diagram used in this section. Packet walk 1 (see the diagram) refers to those packets entering I-VPLS SAPs or SDPs. Packet walk 2 refers to packets entering B-VPLS SAPs or SDPs. See also Figure 3.39.

Packet Ingressing a B-VPLS SAP/SDP

The flow chart in Figure 3.40 describes the walkthrough followed by a packet that enters a B-VPLS SAP or an SDP. See also Figure 3.41.

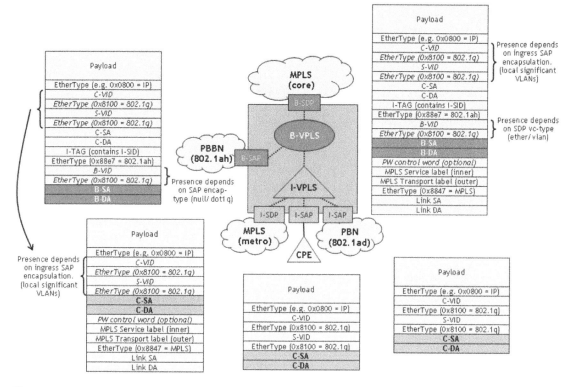

Figure 3.37

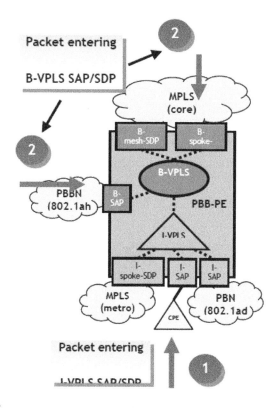

Figure 3.38

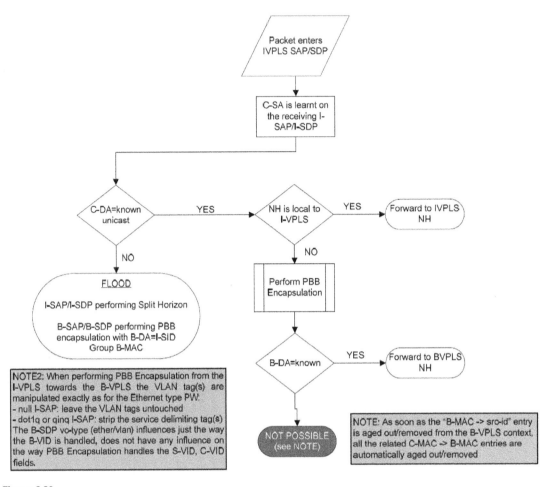

Figure 3.39

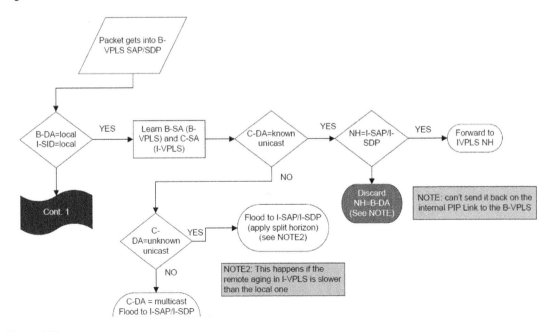

Figure 3.40

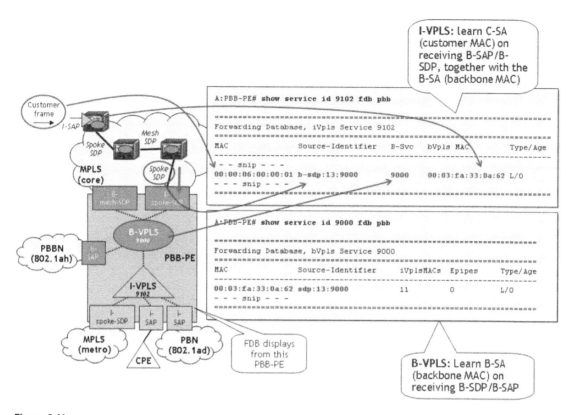

Figure 3.41

A continuation of the flow chart illustrated in this section is depicted in Figure 3.42.

A continuation of the flow chart is depicted in Figure 3.43.

I-VPLS and B-VPLS FDB Management

I-VPLS and B-VPLS FDBs look like regular VPLS FDBs, and they can be managed in the same way. Besides the usual FDB commands, additional CLI tools have been added. Figure 3.44 shows two examples.

When the "show service fdb pbb" command is executed for I-VPLS instances, it shows the associated remote backbone MAC addresses (the "bVpls MAC" field in Figure 3.44) for remote customer-MAC entries.

I-VPLS FDB Management Features

FDB management features per service:
- Configurable FIB size limit, FIB size alarms (low and high watermarks)

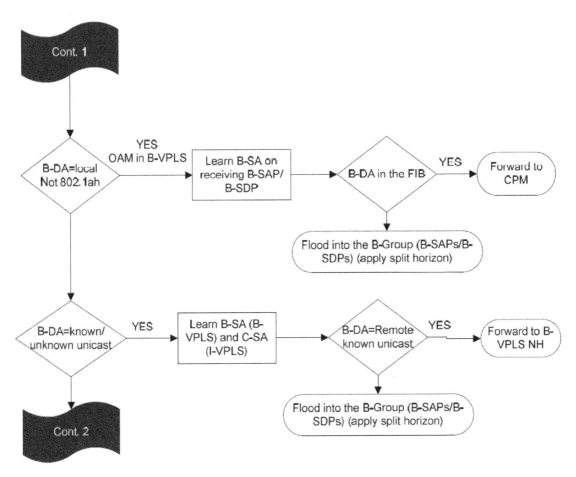

Figure 3.42

- Discard unknown
- MAC learning disable
- MAC aging disable
- Separate aging timers for locally and remotely learned MAC addresses
- MAC-move: loop avoidance between I-VPLS components—block the I-SAPs but not the uplink to B-VPLS (aka PIP), which is defined as non-blockable. This means that MAC Move configured in I-VPLS has no effect on B-VPLS components.
- MAC-protect: protect learning-dedicated MAC addresses
- Static-MAC configuration
  FDB management features per SAP/spoke SDP:
- Limit the amount of MAC addresses per SAP/spoke SDP
- Discard unknown

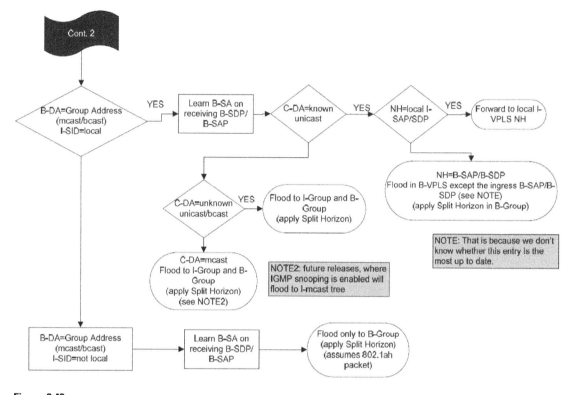

Figure 3.43

- MAC learning disable
- MAC aging disable

B-VPLS FDB Management Features

FDB management features per service:
- Configurable FIB size limit, FIB size alarms (low and high watermarks)
- Discard unknown
- MAC learning disable
- MAC aging disable
- Separate aging timers for locally (over B-SAP) and remotely (over B-SDPs) learned MAC addresses
- MAC-move: loop avoidance
- Static-MAC configuration
  FDB management features per SAP/spoke SDP:
- Discard unknown
- MAC learning disable

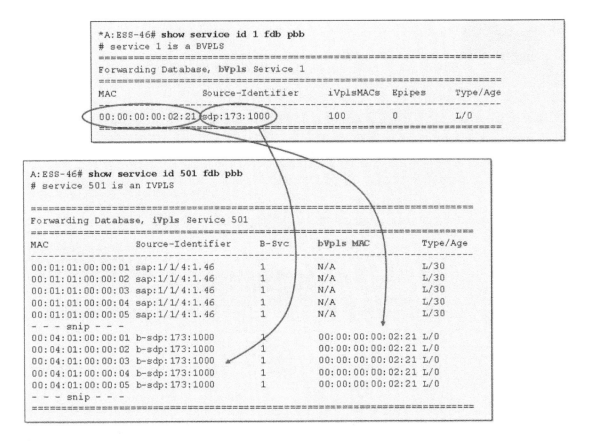

Figure 3.44

- MAC aging disable
- Ingress rate limiting for broadcast, multicast and destination unknown flooding per SAP (not spoke SDP)

Packet Walkthrough with "Discard-Unknown"

When the discard-unknown FDB feature is enabled at service level on I-VPLS or B-VPLS services (see the configuration output in Figure 3.45).

The behavior is as follows:

- I-VPLS – discard-unknown enabled:
  - Processing of this configuration option takes place in the Icomponent.
  - Unknown unicast packets arriving on an I-SAP/I-SDP are dropped.

```
service
      vpls 10000 customer 1 i-vpls create
             discard-unknown
<snip>
      vpls 1000 customer 1 b-vpls create
             service-mtu 1532
             discard-unknown
<snip>
```

Figure 3.45

- Unknown unicast (C-DA) packets arriving on an B-SAP/
  B-SDP that have an I-SID which maps to an I-VPLS with
  discard unknown enabled are also dropped in the local
  I-VPLS context and flooded in the B-VPLS only if the
  B-DA is a Group Mcast MAC.
- B-VPLS – discard-unknown enabled:
  - Processing of this configuration option takes place in the B
    component.
  - Unknown unicast (B-DA) packets arriving on a B-SAP/
    B-SDP are dropped.
  - Unknown unicast (C-DA) packets arriving on a B-SAP/
    B-SDP are processed normally in the I-VPLS if the B-DA
    is not unknown unicast.
  - Unknown unicast (C-DA) packets arriving on an I-SAP/
    I-SDP are not dropped and are flooded in the B-VPLS. This
    is because BDA=Group Mcast MAC is known.

Optimizing Flooding in the B-VPLS Domain: 802.1ak MRP

Based on the number of I-VPLS instances mapped to a single
B-VPLS instance, we can have two mapping models: 1:1 or M:1.
Figure 3.46 outlines the two mapping models in an MTU node,
where we normally have two core PW ports for core connectivity.

Both models provide the MAC scaling benefit given by the PBB
encapsulation. However, the M:1 model presents several advantages over the 1:1 model by reducing the following:
- the service awareness in the core, thereby simplifying provisioning and operations, as well as providing better scalability
  in terms of services
- the number of B-PWs in the MPLS core, since only a single service is needed, and therefore the number of PWs reduced by M
- the TLDP signaling overhead (as a direct consequence), since
  TLDP messages (Label Mapping, Address Withdrawal, MAC
  Address Withdrawal, etc.) are only required for the B-VPLS FEC

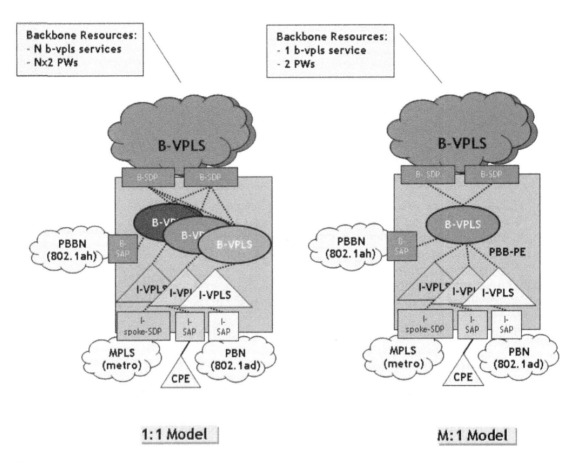

Figure 3.46

See the example in Figure 3.46. The M:1 model consumes only one VPLS service in the core and two PWs compared to M services and Mx2 PWs in the 1:1 model. The M:1 provides a significant saving in terms of services and PWs at the MTU-s level; these savings are even more important at the PE-rs nodes, which can potentially aggregate the traffic for thousands of services and PWs. Therefore, the M:1 model will be deployed on those networks where the number of services and PWs can be high. Although the M:1 model has notable advantages, in the absence of a broadcast containment mechanism, BUM traffic from all I-VPLS instances is flooded in the backbone VPLS instance to all other PBB-PEs.

Consider the M:1 model in Figure 3.47. BUM traffic being sent from PE-1 for the I-VPLS 1001 will be flooded throughout the

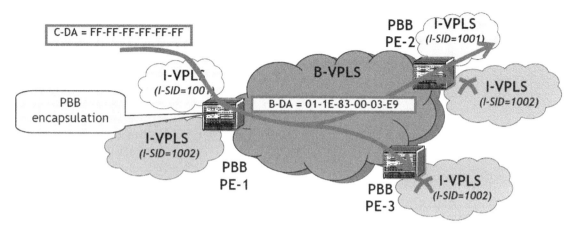

Figure 3.47

B-VPLS and will reach all the PE nodes and part of the B-VPLS, even though they don't have any I-VPLS 1001 endpoint configured, such as PE-3. In this example, PE-2 and PE-3 perform an I-SID lookup. If a local I-VPLS instance exists with I-SID matching the I-SID field in the I-TAG of the received frame, then the frame is flooded into this I-VPLS instance. Otherwise, the frame gets dropped (if no flooding is needed in the B-VPLS instance). When the service provider wants to generalize this scheme for all VPLS customers, regardless of the location of their sites, flood containment on a per I-VPLS basis becomes important. The flooded traffic originated in the I-VPLS with I-SID 1001 should be distributed to just the PBB PEs where I-VPLS instances with I-SID 1001 are present. This flooding optimization is implicitly achieved in the 1:1 model (there is one broadcast containment context or B-VPLS per IVPLS) but not in the M:1 model.

In the M:1 model, this may be achieved by creating per-I-VPLS flooding trees inside the B-VPLS. These trees use the related flooding B-MAC to replicate the traffic as required. Remember that PBB uses a Group B-MAC—built using a specific OUI (00-1E-83) with the multicast bit set and the I-SID value for the last 24 bits—to build these flooding trees (See Figure 3.48). Therefore a backbone bridge can easily identify the Group B-MAC and flood the frame over the corresponding flooding tree.

A protocol is required to build these trees inside the B-VPLS infrastructure by advertising the I-VPLS location as new instances are added. The protocol is 802.1ak—Multiple Registration Protocol.

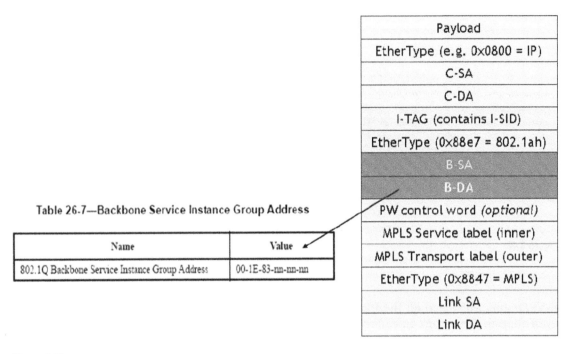

Table 26-7—Backbone Service Instance Group Address

Name	Value
802.1Q Backbone Service Instance Group Address	00-1E-83-nn-nn-nn

Figure 3.48

IEEE 802.1ak MRP Explained

IEEE Multiple Registration Protocol (MRP) allows participants in an MRP application to register attributes with other participants in a bridged local area network. MRP defines two applications:

• Registration of VLANs (Multiple VLAN Registration Protocol, or MVRP)
• Registration of Group MAC addresses (Multiple MAC Registration Protocol, or MMRP)

The protocols defined in 802.1ak replace other protocols defined in IEEE Std 802.1Q such as Generic Attribute Registration Protocol (GARP), GARP Multicast Registration Protocol (GMRP), and GARP VLAN Registration Protocol (GVRP). MRP is a simple, fully distributed, many-to-many protocol that supports efficient, reliable, and rapid declaration and registration of attributes by multiple participants on shared and virtual shared media. A full MRP participant maintains the following state machines:

• Registrar state machine
• Applicant state machine
• LeaveAll state machine
• PeriodicTransmission state machine

The first two state machines are maintained for each attribute in which the participant is interested, while the latter two are global to all the attributes. The job of the Registrar function is to record declarations of the attribute made by other participants on the LAN. A registrar does not send any protocol messages, as the applicant looks after the interests of all would-be participants. The job of the applicant is twofold: to ensure that this participant's declaration is correctly registered by other participants' registrars, and to prompt other participants to register again after one withdraws a declaration.

The MRP protocol is therefore based on a registration/declaration scheme that follows the active loop-free topology and makes a particular attribute to be propagated throughout the network, as depicted in Figure 3.49.

The participating bridges:
- Make or withdraw a declaration of attributes (which triggers the transmission of MRPDUs).
- Make registration or removal of registration of attributes (upon reception of MRPDUs).

MMRP is a specific application of MRP, where the attributes being declared (sent to others) or being registered (received from others) are MAC addresses. The operation of MMRP relies upon the services provided by MRP.

MRPDU Format and Decoding

All MRP applications (MMRP and MVRP) use the PDU format shown in Figure 3.50. The MRPDUs can be easily identified by their destination address (IEEE group MAC address 01-80-C2-00-00-20) and Ethertype (0x88f6 for MMRP), which identifies the protocol itself.

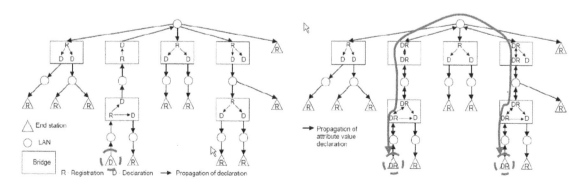

Figure 3.49

```
No.      Time        Source              Destination          Protocol Info
    459 244.896699  24:2e:ff:00:00:00   Ieee8021_00:00:20    0x88f6   Ethernet
        II

Frame 459 (60 bytes on wire, 60 bytes captured)
 Ethernet II, Src: 24:2e:ff:00:00:00 (24:2e:ff:00:00:00), Dst: Ieee8021_00:00:20
        (01:80:c2:00:00:20)
      Destination: Ieee8021_00:00:20 (01:80:c2:00:00:20)
      Source: 24:2e:ff:00:00:00 (24:2e:ff:00:00:00)
      Type: Unknown (0x88f6)      # MRRP
   Data (46 bytes)
      Data: 0002062003011E8300006481000000000000000000000000...

01 80 c2 00 00 20   # Destination address = MMRP address as defined in IEEE 802.1ak
24 2e ff 00 00 00   # Source address = system MAC address of originating node
88 f6               # Type = MMRP
00                  # Protocol Version = 0
02                  # MAC Vector Attribute Type
06                  # Attribute Length (of FirstValue field)= 6
20 03               # Vector header:
                    #    LeaveAllEvent  = 1
                    #    NumberOfValues (13bits) = 3
                    #       i.e. number of events encoded in the Vector
01 1e 83 00 00 64   # FirstValue = Backbone Group MAC address
81                  # Vector (ThreePackedEvent):
                    #    firstAttributeEvent  = 3
                    #    secondAttributeEvent = 3
                    #    thirdAttributeEvent  = 3
00 00               # End Marker
00 00               # End Marker
00 00               # Padding (min. Ethernet packet size)
0020   00 00 00 00 00 00 00 00 00 00 00 00 00 00 00 00  # Padding (min. Ethernet
       packet size)
0030   00 00 00 00 00 00 00 00 00 00 00 00             # Padding (min. Ethernet
       packet size)
```

LeaveAllEvent	
0:	NullLeaveAllEvent operator
1:	LeaveAll operator

Attribute	
0:	New operator
1:	JoinIn operator
2:	In operator
3:	JoinMt operator
4:	Mt operator
5:	Lv operator

Figure 3.50

The registration of group membership information makes the bridges aware of the fact that frames destined for the Group B-MAC address concerned should be forwarded only in the direction of the registered members of the group. Therefore, forwarding of frames destined for the address associated with that group occurs only on ports on which such membership registration has been received.

In the implementation for PBB, when an I-VPLS with a certain attribute (e.g., Group B-MAC) is added to a B-VPLS (I-VPLS must be "no shutdown"), a series of declarations and registrations for this attribute are propagated throughout the loop-free B-VPLS infrastructure. Transmitting ports (B-SAPs/BSDPs) declare the

Group B-MAC while receiving ports (B-SAPs/B-SDPs) register the Group B-MAC. Subsequent occurrences of the attribute (e.g., PIP additions on I-VPLS instances on other PEs for the same I-VPLS) will determine other declaration and registration throughout the B-VPLS context. When a certain virtual port sees both a declaration and a registration for a particular attribute propagated through it, the attribute is enabled on that virtual port.

Figure 3.51 depicts a simple example of broadcast trees created for some I-VPLS instances. I-VPLS 1000, 2000, and 3000 are mapped to the same B-VPLS, but only I-VPLS 1000 is present on MTU1, MTU2, and MTU3. PE1, PE2, and PE3 have only the green B-VPLS defined and no I-VPLS instances. The small, colored bubbles point to ports where the blue, red, and yellow Group B-MACs have been declared *and* registered; hence, they represent the flooding trees for each I-VPLS instance. The diagram also shows the I-SID lookup process occurring at every PBB PE where an I-VPLS is configured.

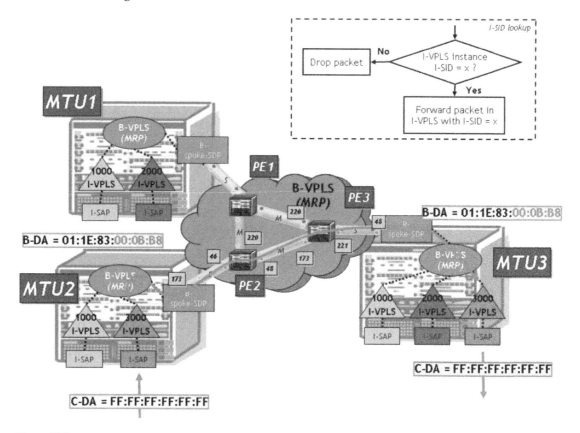

Figure 3.51

As depicted in Figure 3.51, a broadcast received on the blue I-SAP on MTU2 is only propagated through PE2_PE3_MTU3 (the blue line in the picture) and doesn't affect MTU1 or PE1. The following list describes the process followed by a broadcast customer frame received on the MTU2 blue I-SAP:

- The broadcast packet is received on the MTU2 ingress port and classified to I-VPLS 3000 (blue triangle).
- The customer packet is encapsulated into a PBB frame with B-DA the Group B-MAC for I-VPLS 3000 - 01:1e:83:00:0B:B8 (OUI:ISID), MPLS labels and an L2 header are added, and the packet is flooded through the flooding tree created for I-SID 3 (blue line).
- The flooded packet reaches MTU3. MTU3 performs a lookup based on the I-SID encoded in the I-TAG (see Figure 3.51)
- The packet is de-encapsulated and flooded in the blue I-VPLS. The command in Figure 3.52 shows the flooding tree for I-SID along the path. The BUM traffic for I-SID 3000 will be sent on all the ports where the Group B-MAC is registered and declared.

In the same way, the flooding trees for I-SID 1000 and 2000 would be established.

```
MTU2# show service id 1000 mmrp mac 01:1e:83:00:0B:B8
-----------------------------------------------------------
   SAP/SDP           MAC Address        Registered  Declared
-----------------------------------------------------------
   sdp:173:1000      01:1e:83:00:0B:B8 Yes          Yes
 .   .   .   .   .   .   .   .   .   .   .   .   .   .
PE2# show service id 1000 mmrp mac 01:1e:83:00:0B:B8
-----------------------------------------------------------
   SAP/SDP           MAC Address        Registered  Declared
-----------------------------------------------------------
   sdp:46:1000       01:1e:83:00:0B:B8 Yes          Yes
   sdp:48:1000       01:1e:83:00:0B:B8 Yes          Yes
   sdp:220:1000      01:1e:83:00:0B:B8 No           Yes
 .   .   .   .   .   .   .   .   .   .   .   .   .   .
PE3# show service id 1000 mmrp mac 01:1e:83:00:0B:B8
-----------------+-----------------------------------------
   SAP/SDP           MAC Address        Registered  Declared
-----------------------------------------------------------
   sdp:173:1000      01:1e:83:00:0B:B8 Yes          Yes
   sdp:220:1000      01:1e:83:00:0B:B8 No           Yes
   sdp:221:1000      01:1e:83:00:0B:B8 Yes          Yes
 .   .   .   .   .   .   .   .   .   .   .   .   .   .
MTU3# show service id 1000 mmrp mac 01:1e:83:00:0B:B8
-----------------------------------------------------------
   SAP/SDP           MAC Address        Registered  Declared
-----------------------------------------------------------
   sdp:48:1000       01:1e:83:00:0B:B8 Yes          Yes
```

Figure 3.52

There are other considerations related to MMRP and flooding. From the node perspective, the implementation creates an entry in the multicast forwarding information base (MFIB entry) when a particular attribute is registered on a port (B-SAP or B-SDP), regardless of the declaration state for that attribute on that port. The implementation allows the user to control the number of MMRP attributes (Group B-MACs) created on a per-B-VPLS basis; that is, the number of MFIB entries on a per-B-VPLS basis. This way, no B-VPLS can take up all the MFIB resources from the total pools. It is important to note that different control plane protocols might generate flooding in the B-VPLS context using a Group B-MAC that does not use the standard PBB OUI: e.g. 802.1ag CCM or LAG/P-MSTP in the B-VPLS space. In these cases, there are no MFIB entries created by MMRP for the associated Group B-MAC.

When MRP is enabled in a B-VPLS it is still necessary to accommodate the transmission of a packet with a multicast destination for a Group B-MAC under failure conditions. If a flooded PBB packet is received in a PE that has just a B-VPLS instance but there is no multicast tree (MFIB entry) for the Group B-MAC address used as a B-DA, we will revert to flooding in the B-VPLS context. Note: this situation should not occur under non-failure conditions at the PBB PE, as we will not allow the I-VPLS to flood into related B-VPLS until a registration from a remote PBB PE arrives. If the remote registration arrives, the B-VPLS PE on the path should at least have an MFIB entry for that Group B-MAC.

I-VPLS Changes and Related MMRP Behavior

The following section describes MMRP behavior for different changes in the I-VPLS. When an I-SID is set for a certain I-VPLS or the fully configured I-VPLS is activated, the Group B-MAC address is declared in the B-VPLS and is propagated to all active ports. When the I-SID is changed from one value to a different value, the old Group B-MAC address is undeclared on all active ports and the new Group B-MAC address is declared on all active ports in the B-VPLS.

When the I-VPLS is disassociated with the B-VPLS, the Group B-MAC is undeclared on all active ports in the B-VPLS. When an I-VPLS goes down operationally (either all SAPs or all SDPs are down) or the I-VPLS is shut down, the Group B-MAC is undeclared on all active ports in the B-VPLS. However, the I-SID is still considered to be local and the MFIB entries for any registration in the B-VPLS will be unchanged.

When the I-VPLS is deleted, the Group B-MAC should already be undeclared on all active ports in the B-VPLS because the I-VPLS has to be shut down to delete it. However, unlike the shutdown case, deleting the I-VPLS causes the I-SID to be considered non-local and MFIB entries are removed.

E-PIPE Service with PBB Encapsulation

For an Ethernet point-to-point service, it is important to be able to use the same operational model that would be in place for multipoint VPLS services that use a B-VPLS. If an I-VPLS service carrying only point-to-point services simply mapped to a B-VPLS, it would be treated like a regular VPLS and require MAC learning, flooding, etc. In order to ensure that the characteristics of the ePipe service remain transparent and do not require the MAC functions of a VPLS, an ePipe service can be directly mapped to a B-VPLS, specifying the remote B-MAC address. See Figure 3.53.

There is no need to perform any MAC switching, learning, or replication for the point-to-point service; that is, all the packets ingressing the I-SAP are PBB-encapsulated and forwarded to the PBB-tunnel; all the packets ingressing the B-VPLS destined for this I-SID are PBB de-encapsulated and forwarded to the I-SAP. A fully specified B-DA address must be provisioned for each PBB ePipe instance to be used for each incoming frame on the related I-SAP. Similar to the I-VPLS-to-B-VPLS service, the ePipe-to-B-VPLS service instance is built around B and I components:

- A point-to-point I-component or ePipe composed of an I-SAP and a PBB-tunnel end-point that points to the B-DA (see the required PBB-tunnel attributes in the CLI output in Figure 3.54).
- A multipoint B-component or B-VPLS to which the ePipe is mapped on a 1:1 or an M:1 basis. The B-VPLS can be shared among ePipes and I-VPLS instances.

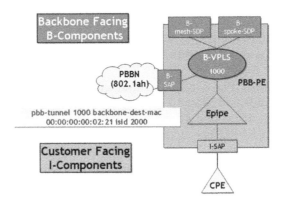

Figure 3.53

```
A:ESS-47# configure service epipe 2000 pbb-tunnel ?
 - no pbb-tunnel
 - pbb-tunnel <service-id> backbone-dest-mac <ieee-address> isid
<ISID>

 <service-id>           : [1..2147483647]
 <ieee-address>         : xx:xx:xx:xx:xx:xx or xx-xx-xx-xx-xx-xx
 <ISID>                 : [0..16777215]
```

Figure 3.54

All the ingress frames on the I-SAP are sent to the provisioned B-DA (backbone-dest-mac). See Figure 3.54. If the configured B-DA for the ePipe has not been learned beforehand, the PBB frame will be flooded throughout the B-VPLS domain. Periodic 802.1ag CCM messages can be generated at the remote PBB-PE so that the ePipe B-DA can be learned and maintained in the local FIB; hence, there is no need for flooding. All the supported B-VPLS constructs can be used, including the B-VPLS resiliency and OAM. All B-VPLS resiliency mechanisms for multipoint services are similarly supported on the point-to-point service (ePipe).

Use cases for PBB ePipe:

• To have a scalable solution for point-to-point services when native Ethernet (PBB) is used in the core
• To take advantage of the PW aggregation in the M:1 model
• To have a uniform provisioning model for both point-to-point (ePipe) and multipoint (VPLS) services.

Many ePipe services may use only a single service and set of PW over the backbone.

Using the PBB ePipe, the core MPLS/PW infrastructure does not need to be modified. The new ePipe inherits the existing PW and MPLS structures already configured on the B-VPLS and there is no need to configure new tunnels or PW switching instances at the core. Figure 3.55 illustrates this remark.

Figure 3.55 compares the PWE infrastructure required to build and operate an E-Line service (ePipe) in a multi-area environment for two cases: a regular ePipe and a PBB ePipe.

In the first case—regular ePipe—new PWs are required and new ePipe services on the intermediate nodes are needed (PW switching is needed on the PE nodes if the E-Line service is defined across different IGP areas/RSVP-TE domains over dynamic LSPs). However, as illustrated in the latter case—PBB ePipe—the ePipe services can be stitched to the existing B-VPLS services at the edge nodes, allowing the operator to easily define E-Line services without any provisioning in the intermediate nodes.

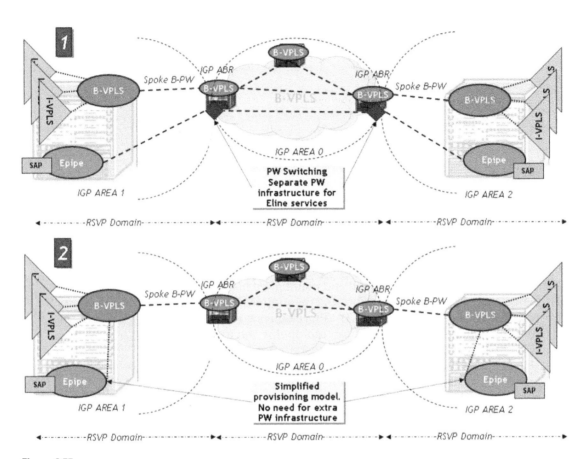

Figure 3.55

PBB ePipe Flooding Considerations

As discussed in the previous section, when provisioning a PBB ePipe, the remote backbone-dest-mac must be explicitly configured so that the ingress PBB PE can build the 802.1ah encapsulation. For instance, if we need to define a PBB ePipe between MTU1 and MTU2, the MTU2 backbone-dest-mac must be given when configuring the ePipe service on MTU1, as shown in Figure 3.56.

As discussed previously, if the configured remote backbone-destination MAC is not known in the local FIB, the ePipe customer frames will be 802.1ah encapsulated and flooded into the B-VPLS until the MAC is learned. Flooding could be indefinably prolonged in the following four cases:

- There is a configuration mistake of the backbone-destination-MAC. The operator will not detect the mistake since the customer traffic is not dropped. Every single frame is turned into an

```
*A:mtu1-R6>config>service>epipe# info
```

```
-------------------------------------------------
        pbb-tunnel 10000 backbone-dest-mac 00:03:fa:6e:e3:c0 isid 2010
        sap 1/1/8:2010 create          # MTU2 backbone MAC#
        exit
        no shutdown
-------------------------------------------------
```

Figure 3.56

unknown unicast PBB frame and flooded into the B-VPLS domain.

- There is only uni-directional traffic in the ePipe service. In this case, the backbone-dest-MAC won't ever be learned in the local FIB and the frames will always be flooded into the B-VPLS domain.
- The remote chassis is swapped out (the B-MAC is by default the chassis MAC). The ePipe connectivity would change to flooding because the B-DA would no longer exist in the network.
- The backbone-MAC in the remote PE B-VPLS instance is changed. MMRP does not help to avoid unnecessary flooding in PBB ePipes, since all the PBB ePipe traffic is unicast using the configured backbone destination MAC in the PBB encapsulation. MMRP builds flooding trees only for Group B-MACs, and not for unicast B-MACs.

The implementation does provide the operator with some tools to check whether a particular PBB ePipe is flooding the traffic into the B-VPLS domain, as well as OAM tools to generate the background traffic needed from the remote node in order to avoid flooding.

The "show service base" command shows a new flag that indicates when the configured backbone-dest-mac is not in the B-VPLS FIB and therefore whether a particular PBB ePipe service is flooding into the BVPLS. See Figure 3.57.

This is the Dot1ag (see Figure 3.58) UP MEP configuration in the B-VPLS on MTU2 (this MEP is sending messages every 10 seconds with the source MAC address that is needed). Note that the MEP is created in a bogus B-SAP that is part of the B-VPLS but can be shut down if its only purpose is to generate background traffic.

PBB E-Trees

PBB ePipes can be used in conjunction with I-VPLS to create E-Trees as is illustrated in Figure 3.59. A PBB E-Tree is a point-to-multi-point or hub-and-spoke service where the root instance

```
*A:mtu1-R6>show>service>id# base

===================================================================
Service Basic Information
===================================================================
Service Id          : 2010            Vpn Id             : 0
Service Type        : Epipe
```

```
Customer Id          : 1
Last Status Change: 02/29/2008 09:36:08
Last Mgmt Change  : 02/27/2008 20:11:26
Admin State          : Up              Oper State         : Up
MTU                  : 1514
Vc Switching         : False
SAP Count            : 1              SDP Bind Count     : 0

-------------------------------------------------------------------
Service Access & Destination Points
-------------------------------------------------------------------
Identifier                              Type       AdmMTU   OprMTU
Adm   Opr
-------------------------------------------------------------------
sap:1/1/8:2010                          q-tag        1570     1570
Up    Up
-------------------------------------------------------------------
[<sap-id>] indicates a Managed SAP

-------------------------------------------------------------------
PBB Tunnel Point
-------------------------------------------------------------------
B-vpls    Backbone-dest-MAC   Isid     AdmMTU  Adm  Opr  Backbone-
Flooding
-------------------------------------------------------------------
10000     00:03:fa:6e:e3:c0   2010      1532   Up   Up   Yes
===================================================================
```

- 802.1ag CCM (Continuity Check Messages) can be used to generate the background traffic needed to learn and keep the backbone-dest-mac in the local FIB. The following example shows the 802.1ag configuration needed at MTU2 so that MTU1 can immediately learn MTU backbone MAC and avoid unnecessary flooding:

```
*A:mtu2-R6>config>dot1ag# info
---------------------------------------------
        domain 2 name "bvpls" level 3
            association 1 format string name "bvpls"
                bridge-identifier 10000
                exit
                ccm-interval 10
                remote-mepid 2222
            exit
        exit
---------------------------------------------
```

Figure 3.57

```
*A:mtu2-R6>config>service>vpls# info
-----------------------------------------------
            service-mtu 1532
            stp
                shutdown
[snip]
            sap 1/1/8:4000 create
                shutdown
                dot1ag
                    mep 1111 domain 2 association 1 direction up
                        ccm-enable
                        mac-address 00:03:fa:6e:e3:c0
                        no shutdown
                    exit
                exit
            exit
```

Figure 3.58

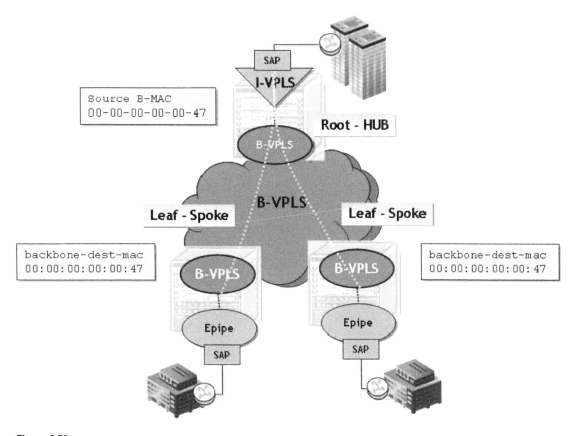

Figure 3.59

is based on an I-VPLS and the leaves are based on ePipes. The ePipes and hub I-VPLS share the same B-VPLS domain. Figure 3.59 depicts the concept.

The PBB E-Tree can be used for point-to-multipoint applications such as TV distribution and has the following characteristics:

- Traffic separation between spoke users, with traffic from one leaf never being transmitted to other leaves.
- Less provisioning than typical hub and spoke configuration using ePipes; spoke endpoints can easily be added without any provisioning touch on the hub node.
- All the leaves point to the root B-MAC address (00:00:00:00:00:47 in the example).
- Root-to-leaf flooding traffic uses Group B-MAC in the core.
- Leaf-to-root traffic always uses the root B-MAC, even for flooded traffic.

The relevant CLI output for the root and leaf nodes is shown in Figure 3.60.

PBB and OAM

All the VPLS OAM commands can be used in both I-VPLS and B-VPLS instances. The following OAM commands are only meaningful toward another I-VPLS service instance (spoke-SDP in I-VPLS): LSP-ping, LSP-trace, SDP-ping, and SDP-MTU.

The following I-VPLS OAM exchanges are transparently transported over the B-VPLS core: SVC-ping, MAC-ping, MAC-trace,

```
*A:Spoke-left>config>service>epipe# info
----------------------------------------------
        pbb-tunnel 10000 backbone-dest-mac 00:00:00:00:00:47 isid 2010
        sap 1/1/1:2010 create              # Hub backbone MAC#

*A:Spoke-right>config>service>epipe# info
----------------------------------------------
        pbb-tunnel 10000 backbone-dest-mac 00:00:00:00:00:47 isid 2010
        sap 1/1/8:2010 create              # Hub backbone MAC#

*A:Hub>config>service>vpls# info
----------------------------------------------
        backbone-vpls 10000:2010      # isid if id different from 2010#
        sap 1/1/5:2010 create
```

Figure 3.60

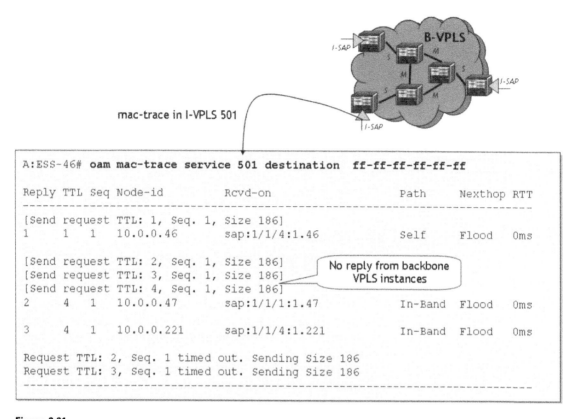

Figure 3.61

MAC-populate, MAC-purge, CPEping (towards customer CPE), 802.3ah EFM, and SAA.

For PBB uplinks using MPLS/SDP or native backbone Ethernet switching (B-SAP uplinks), there are no PBB specific OAM commands. Figure 3.61 shows an example using MAC-trace on the I-VPLS instance 501. As seen in the CLI output, there is no reply from the backbone VPLS instances, though the TTL is decremented on each hop.

There is no special 802.1ag connectivity fault management (CFM) support for PBB:

- B-component and I-component run their own maintenance domains and levels.
- CFM for I-components run transparently over the PBB network (they will appear as directly connected).

Figure 3.62 shows an example of 802.1ag application on a PBB scenario.

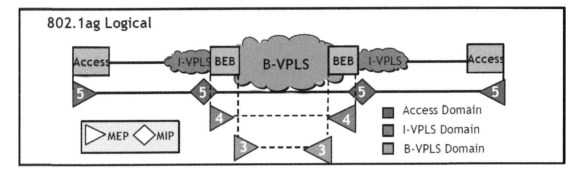

Figure 3.62

PBB and QoS

There are no QoS-related changes for I-VPLS compared with regular VPLS, therefore:

- I-SAP ingress
  - Use dot1p (from customer or qinq tag) and, optionally, the DE bit (802.1ad only), IP DSCP, or IP precedence bits to determine the internal forwarding class (FC) and priority.
- I-SAP egress
  - All the remarking is optional on a per-FC basis. The ingress profile is used to determine the dot1p/DE bits. This is the same behavior as an existing VPLS with dot1q SAPs.
- I-SDP ingress
  - Use EXP bits to determine the internal forwarding class (FC) and priority.
- I-SDP egress
  - Use the FC value to mark the EXP bits.

The forwarding class and profile determined for the packets originated from a related I-VPLS instance are used to set the related QoS fields from the PBB encapsulated packet; that is, backbone VLAN ID (B-VID) dot1p and DE bit or the MPLS EXP bits and the I-TAG dot1p and DE bit. PBB encapsulation provides the Ethernet QoS information (i.e., dot1p and DE bits) in two areas of the added header: the 802.1ad B-VID and the 802.1ah I-TAG. Figure 3.63 shows the QoS-related bits existing in the PBB header.

The QoS treatment specifics for the B-VPLS are described as follows:

- B-SAP ingress: Use this if the dot1p, DE-based classification is enabled through the related CLI commands. The B-TAG fields will be used by default to evaluate the FC and profile if there is a B-TAG field. The 802.1ah I-TAG will be used only if the B-TAG is absent (null SAP). If either one of the dot1p or DE-based

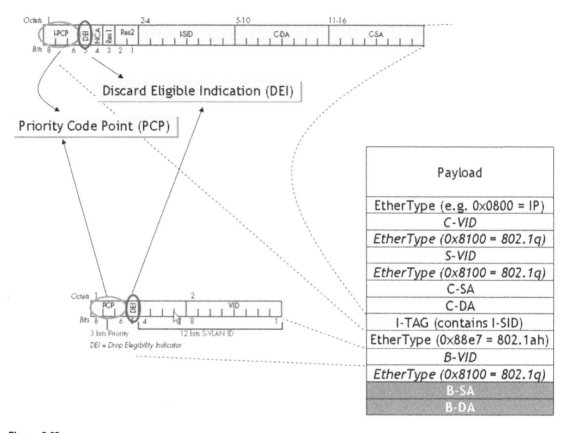

Figure 3.63

classifications is not explicitly enabled, or if the packets are untagged, then the default FC and profile are assigned.

- B-SAP egress: If the SAP-egress policy for the B-SAP contains a fc->dot1p/de mapping, this entry is used to set the dot1p and DE bits of the B-TAG for the frame going out from the B-SAP. The same applies for the I-TAG on frames originated locally from an I-VPLS. The mapping does not have any effect on the I-TAG of frames transiting the B-VPLS. If no explicit mapping exists, the related dot1p and DE bits are set to zero on both I-TAG and B-TAG if the frame is locally originated from an I-VPLS. If the frame is transiting the B-VPLS, the I-TAG stays unchanged. The B-TAG is set according to the type of ingress BSAP: if the ingress B-SAP is tagged the values of the dot1p, DE bits are preserved in the B-TAG going out on the egress BSAP. If the ingress B-SAP is untagged the dot1p, DE bits are set to zero in the B-TAG going out on the egress B-SAP.

- B-SDP ingress: QoS policies for dot1p and DE bits apply for just the outer VLAN ID; this is the VLAN ID associated with the link layer, not the PBB B-VID. As a result the dot1p, DE bits will be checked only if an outer VLAN ID exists in the packets ingressing the B-SDP. If that VLAN ID is absent, nothing above the PW service label will be checked; that is, no dot1p bits in the B-TAG or I-TAG will be checked. It is expected that the EXP bits will be used to transport QoS information across the MPLS backbone and into the PEs.
- B-SDP egress: When building PBB packets originated from a local I-VPLS the BTAG, I-TAG values (dot1p, DE bits) will be set according to the network egress policy. The same will apply for newly added B-VID (VLAN mode PWs) in a packet transiting the B-VPLS (B-SAP/BSDP->B-SDP). Note that if either one of the dot1p- or DE-based classifications is not explicitly enabled in the CLI, the values from the default FC->dot1p, DE mapping are assumed. Dot1p and DE bits for existing B-VIDs will remain unchanged; that is, they will remain applicable to packets transiting the B-VPLS and going out on B-SDP.

Conclusion

We have explored the options PBB provides in scaling VPLS infrastructures by reducing MAC addresses that need to be populated at each component in the network and via an I-VPLS and a B-VPLS component. However, the market really did not adopt PBB-VPLS on a large scale, given the complexity and lack of adoption among vendors and carriers alike. Alternate schemes such as seamless MPLS have become more popular in addressing scaling issues in carrier networks. Given that MPLS to the edge has become very popular in increasing service velocity for service providers, this topic is discussed further in following chapters.

4

SCALING PACKET
ETHERNET SERVICES
USING SEAMLESS MPLS

Introduction

Scaling packet (SP) business and operational models are challenged with the rapid developments of the telecom market increasingly dominated by IP packet services. Broadband developments with wireline optical access and optical 4G/LTE access enable much higher bandwidths to end users, quickly becoming key drivers for new service developments, and provide opportunity for SP innovation and differentiation in the marketplace. But proliferation of new high-bandwidth services and expectation of the same services being delivered over wireline and wireless access pose significant challenges to the present mode of operation for many SPs, due to increasing network and operation complexity, and resulting high costs. The desire to address these challenges has become the main driver for network and systems convergence as well as evolution to new network and service architecture.

This chapter describes a proposed converged packet network and service architecture based on IP/MPLS that addresses SP problems by providing required levels of flexibility, agility, and expandability, thereby allowing SPs to efficiently tackle rapidly evolving service mix and bandwidth growth. It is based on a simple principle of expanding the dynamic IP/MPLS network reach across core, metro, and access network infrastructure, enabling any-to-any packet connectivity and flexible service overlay.

State of the Mobile Transport Industry

The shift from mobile voice calls to mobile data as the dominant medium has led to a fundamental change in the mobile service mix. As mobile standards have evolved from 2G to 3G and

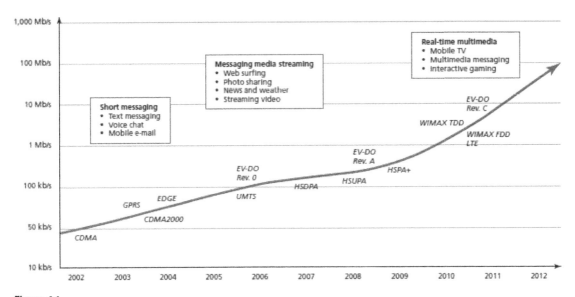

Figure 4.1

now to 4G, mobile operators are under constant pressure to improve mobile backhaul speed, scale, and QoS, while having the difficult task of controlling and reducing the cost per bit in the transport network. Legacy 2G and 3G transport is mostly synchronous digital hierarchy (SDH). based on using dedicated T1/E1 circuits for GSM (TDM) and Universal Mobile Telecommunications System (UMTS) (ATM) backhaul. Figure 4.1 illustrates the evolution of services and end user bandwidth in mobile networks.

The rollout of mobile broadband standards such as high speed packet access (HSPA) and evolution data-only optimized (EV-DO) made it clear that the underlying SDH infrastructure could no longer cost effectively scale at the increased traffic volumes, triggering the migration of mobile backhaul to packet networks. The debate between circuit transport versus packet transport has been laid to rest, as packet transport is now universally accepted as the better solution for next-generation mobile transport. As a result, all new 3G rollout has been based on IP transport over Ethernet interfaces, and mobile operators are transitioning their backhaul infrastructure to packet networks.

However, current industry solutions for RAN backhaul built on packet transport face several issues: operational complexity, the short reach of legacy RAN backhaul, and a lack of consideration for fixed mobile convergence. These are examined one by one.

Operational Complexity

Mobile standards have evolved over different transport technologies. While Layer 3 (L3) packet transport has been predominant in the core and to a large extent in the aggregation domains of the network, the access network build-out has largely been based on Layer 2 (L2) transport. Consequently, industry solutions for RAN backhaul have been based on mixed packet transport technologies across the access, aggregation, and core layers of the network. These solutions typically involve a combination of L2 and L3 transport, with an L2 access and aggregation interfacing with a L3 core, or an L2 access interfacing with an L3 aggregation and core. Such architectures intrinsically couple the transport and service layers of the network and are consequently plagued with both control and management plane translations at the boundaries of the following network domains:

- In mixed L2/L3 environments, increased complexity occurs in the control plane when MPLS RAN transport that uses pseudowire emulation (CESoPSN, SAToP, and ATM virtual channel and virtual path) for 2G/3G services is built over bridged infrastructures that rely solely on the L2 topology protection.
- Often interworking functions like multi-segment pseudowire (MSPW) stitching, VLAN to pseudowire (PW) XConnect, VLAN into VPLS VFI, spoke PW into H-VPLS VFI hub, or spoke PW into MPLS VPN virtual routing and forwarding (VRF) are required at the boundaries of these domains to provide the end-to-end services. These interworking entities are essentially touchpoints for the service that consume resources on the network device deployed at this boundary.
- These intermediate touchpoints introduce management complexity and require repeated provisioning as new services are added to the network.
- The intermediate touchpoints also complicate the operation and management of the service, since they do not allow for simple end-to-end service monitoring and require separate L2 and L3 OAM technologies to be used in the respective segments of the service.

Short Reach of Legacy RAN Backhaul

Existing industry solutions have been tailored to meet the immediate needs of 2G or 3G transport, which entails connectivity from the base transceiver station (BTS)/NodeB to the base station controller (BSC)/radio network controller (RNC). Therefore, the focus of backhaul thus far has been restricted to providing connectivity from the cell site to the controller located somewhere in the aggregation network, without considering implications for the mobile packet core (MPC).

While the limited reach of these backhaul designs suits the hierarchical nature of legacy 2G and 3G mobile standards, they have significant shortcomings for LTE deployments. The transition from a hierarchical 3G network architecture to a flat all-IP LTE/evolved packet core (EPC) network architecture has profound implications for the mobile transport network. LTE mandates reachability from the cell site all the way to the EPC gateways located deep in the core network. Extending the existing backhaul designs with interworking functions to provide reachability into the packet core will only introduce operational complexity and defeats the benefit that the flattened all-IP LTE/EPC architecture brings to mobile backhaul. These designs handicap the flexible placement of mobile gateways across the core network to address the gradual uptake in 4G scale as subscribers move from existing 2G and 3G services.

Lack of Consideration for Fixed Mobile Convergence

The biggest cost challenge facing mobile service providers (MSPs) today is the backhaul network. With circuit-to-packet migration being well under way, mobile operators are making huge investments in the rollout of packet-based networks. To this end, operators wanting to capitalize on their return on investment are looking to provide additional services on a converged network. In many cases, SPs are exploring the option of deploying fixed wireline services alongside 4G RAN backhaul in order to achieve fixed mobile convergence. The transport architecture plays a critical role in attaining this goal. However, existing industry solutions, which have been purpose built for legacy RAN backhaul with the transport architecture, essentially following the circuit-switched paradigm of hub-and-spoke connectivity from cell sites to centrally located radio controllers, are not conducive to meeting the active convergence of packet transport in fixed mobile operations.

Next Generation Mobile Transport Characteristics

The next generation mobile backhaul infrastructure has the following characteristics, which are discussed in the sections that follow:

- High-capacity requirements from edge to core
- Exponential increase in scale driven by LTE deployments
- Support for multiple and mixed topologies
- Seamless interworking with the mobile packet core
- Transport of multiple services from all locations

High-Capacity Requirements from Edge to Core

The mobile landscape is changing with consumer behavior. Powerful new mobile devices, increasing use of mobile Internet access, and a growing range of data-hungry applications for music, video, gaming, and social networking are driving huge increases in data traffic. A recent study forecast that mobile data traffic is set to increase 18-fold globally between 2011 and 2016, as pictured in Figure 4.2. These exploding bandwidth requirements are driving high-capacity requirements from the edge to the core with typical rates of 100Mbps per eNodeB, 1Gbps access, 10Gbps aggregation, and future 100Gbps core networks.

Exponential Increase in Scale Driven by LTE Deployments

LTE will drive ubiquitous mobile broadband with its quantum leap in uplink and downlink transmission speeds.

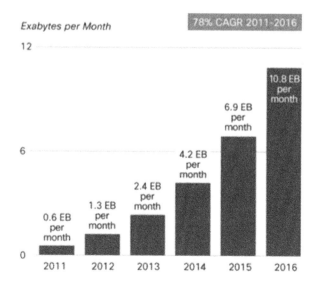

Figure 4.2

- In denser populations, the *increased data rates* delivered to each subscriber will force division of the cell capacity among fewer users. Because of this, cells must be much smaller than they are today.
- Another factor to consider is the *macro cell capacity*. The spectrum allotted to mobile networks has been increasing over the years, roughly doubling over a five-year period. With advancements in radio technology, a corresponding increase in average macro cell efficiency has occurred over the same period. As a result, the macro cell capacity, which is a product of these two entities, will see a four-fold increase over a five-year period. This increase, however, is nowhere close to the projected 26-fold increase in mobile data (as stated above) and will force mobile operators to deploy a small-cell network architecture.

These two factors will force operators to adopt small cell architectures, resulting in an exponential increase in cell sites deployed in the network. In large networks covering large geographies, the scale is expected to be in the order of several tens of thousands to a few hundred thousands of LTE NodeBs and associated CSGs.

Support for Multiple and Mixed Topologies

Many options exist for physical topologies in the RAN transport network, with hub-and-spoke and ring being the most prevalent. Capacity requirements driven by subscriber density, CAPEX of deploying fiber in large geographies, and physical link redundancy considerations could lead to a combination of fiber and microwave rings in access, fiber rings, and hub-and-spoke in aggregation and core networks, and so on. The transport technology that implements the RAN backhaul must be independent of the physical topology, or a combination thereof, used in various layers of the network, and must cost-effectively scale to accommodate the explosive increase in bandwidth requirements imposed by the mobile growth.

Seamless Interworking with the Mobile Packet Core

As mentioned a bit earlier, the flattened all-IP LTE/EPC architecture is a significant departure from previous generations of mobile standards and should be an important consideration in designing the RAN backhaul for 4G mobile transport.

The 2G/3G hierarchical architecture consists of a logical hub-and-spoke connectivity between BSC/RNC and the BTS/NodeBs, as shown in Figure 4.3. This hierarchical architecture lent itself

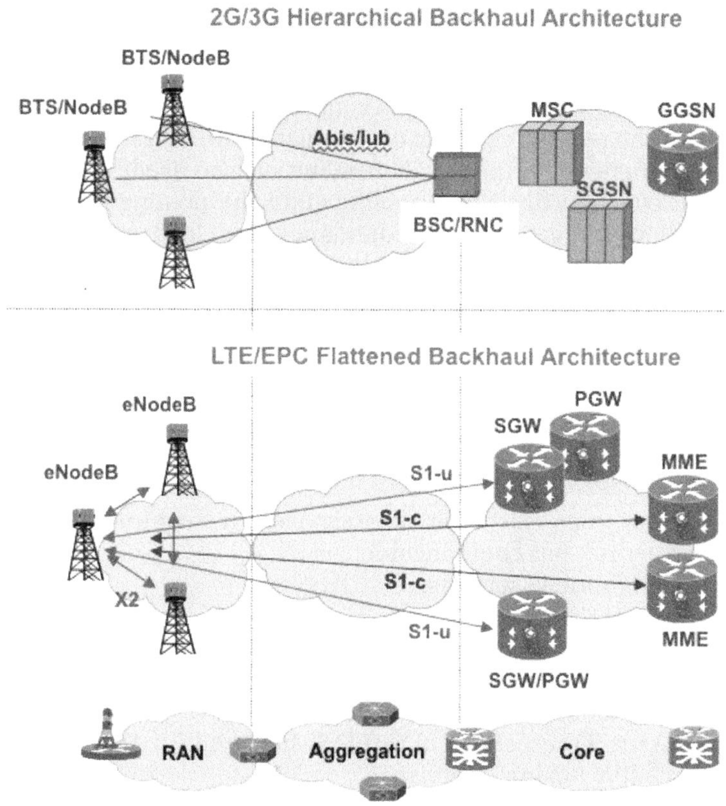

2G/3G Hierarchical Backhaul Architecture

LTE/EPC Flattened Backhaul Architecture

Figure 4.3

naturally to the circuit-switched paradigm of having point-to-point connectivity between the cell sites and controllers. However, the reach of the RAN backhaul was limited, in that it extended from the radio access network to the local aggregation/distribution location where the controllers are situated.

In contrast, the flat LTE architecture does away with the hierarchy by getting rid of the intermediate controller, like the BSC/RNC, and lets the eNodeB communicate directly with the EPC gateways, as shown in Figure 4.3. It also does away with the point-to-point relationship of 2G/3G architectures and imposes multipoint connectivity requirements at the cell site. This multipoint transport requirement from the cell site not only applies to the LTE X2 interface, which introduces direct communication between eNodeBs requiring any-to-any mesh network connectivity, but also applies to the LTE S1 interface, which requires a one-to-many relationship between the eNodeB and multiple EPC gateways. While the serving gateways (SGWs) may be deployed in a distributed manner closer to the aggregation network, the MMEs are usually fewer in number and centrally located in the core. This extends the reach of the RAN backhaul from the cell site deep into the core network. Important consideration also needs to be given to SAE concepts like MME pooling and SGW pooling in the EPC that allow for geographic redundancy and load sharing. The RAN backhaul service model must provide for eNodeB association to multiple gateways in the pool and migration of eNodeB across pools without having to re-architect the underlying transport architecture.

Transport of Multiple Services from All Locations

LTE has to co-exist with other services on a common network infrastructure that could include:

- Existing mobile services:
  - 3G UMTS IP/ATM
  - 2G GSM and SP WiFi in a mobile-only deployment
- A myriad of other services:
  - Residential broadband triple play
  - Metro Ethernet forum (MEF) E-Line and E-LAN
  - L3VPN business services
  - RAN sharing, wireline wholesale in a converged mobile and wireline deployment

In these scenarios, the network has to not only support multiple services concurrently, but also support all these services across disparate endpoints. Typical examples are:

- L3 transport for LTE and Internet high speed packet access (I-HSPA) controller-free architectures: from RAN to SAE gateways in the core network
- L3 transport for 3G UMTS/IP: from RAN to BSC in the aggregation network
- L2 transport for 2G GSM and 3G UMTS/ATM: from RAN to RNC/BSC in the aggregation network
- L2 transport for residential wireline: from access to broadband network gateways (BNG) in the aggregation network
- L3/L2 transport for business wireline: from access to remote access networks across the core network.
- L2 transport for wireline wholesale: from access to retail wireline SP peering point
- L3 transport for RAN sharing: from RAN to retail mobile SP peering point

The transport technology used in the RAN backhaul and the network architecture must be carefully engineered to be scalable and flexible enough to meet the requirements of various services being transported across a multitude of locations in the network.

System Concept

Seamless MPLS for mobile infrastructures provides the architectural baseline for creating a scalable, resilient, and manageable mobile backhaul infrastructure that is optimized to seamlessly interwork with the mobile packet core (MPC). The system is designed to concurrently support multiple generations (2G/3G/4G) of mobile services on a single converged network infrastructure. The system supports graceful introduction of LTE with existing 2G/3G services with support for pseudowire emulation (PWE) for 2G GSM and 3G UMTS/ATM transport, L2VPNs for 3G UMTS/IP, and L3VPNs for 3G UMTS/IP and 4G LTE transport.

It supports essential features like network synchronization (physical layer and packet based), HQoS, OAM, performance management, and fast convergence. It is optimized to cater to advanced 4G requirements like IPSec and authentication, direct eNodeB communication through the X2 interface, multicast for optimized video transport, virtualization for RAN sharing, capability of distributing the EPC gateways, and traffic offload.

The system meets the NGMN requirements for next-generation mobile backhaul, and it innovates on the broadband forum TR-221 specification for MPLS in mobile backhaul networks by unifying the MPLS transport across the access, aggregation, and core domains. The architecture is also extensible to a converged mobile and wireline deployment and supports wireline residential, business, retail/wholesale L2VPNs and L3VPNs, and IP services. The key aspects of the concept are described in this section.

Simplification of the End-to-End Mobile Transport and Service Architecture

A founding principle of seamless MPLS is the simplification of the mobile backhaul architecture by eliminating the control and management plane translations that are inherent in legacy designs. Traditional backhaul architectures relying on L2 transport are not optimized for 4G all-IP flat LTE architecture, and backhaul architectures built over mixed L2 and L3 transport are inherently complex to operate. The seamless MPLS architecture enables a unified L3 MPLS/IP transport extending end-to-end from the mobile core all the way to the RAN access. It simplifies the control plane by providing seamless MPLS LSPs across access, pre-aggregation, aggregation/distribution, and core domains of the network. In doing so, a fundamental attribute of decoupling the transport and service layers of the network and eliminating intermediate touchpoints in the backhaul is achieved. By eliminating intermediate touchpoints, it simplifies the operation and management of the service. Service provisioning is restricted only at the edges of the network where it is required: namely, at the CSGs in the access and the provider edge (PE) (hereby referred to as MTG) connecting the mobile gateways in the MPC. Simple carrier class operations with end-to-end OAM, performance monitoring of the GSM, UMTS, and LTE services are made possible.

Flexible Placement of L3 and L2 Transport Virtualization Functions for GMS, UMTS, LTE

The hierarchical RAN backhaul architecture of 2G and 3G releases involved an intermediate agent like the BSC/RNC, which mostly resided at the aggregation/distribution layer of the transport network. This simplified the requirements on the transport, in that it only required connectivity between the RAN access and the aggregation network layers. In comparison, 4G LTE imposes many new requirements on the backhaul:

- Because of the any-to-any relationship between eNodeBs for the X2 interface and the one-to many relationship between eNodeBs and EPC gateways (SGWs, MMEs) for the S1-u/c interface, the eNodeBs and associated CSGs in the RAN access need both local connectivity and direct connectivity to the EPC gateways in the MPC.
- The stringent latency requirements of the X2 interface requires a logical mesh connectivity among CSGs that introduces a minimum amount of delay in the order of 30 ms. The minimum delay is expected to be reduced further to around 10 ms for features such as collaborative multiple input multiple output (MIMO) in the future, with 3GPP LTE Release 10 and beyond.
- The Evolved Universal Terrestrial Radio Access Network (E-UTRAN)/EPC architecture supports MME pooling and SGW pooling to enable geographic redundancy, capacity increase, load sharing, and signaling optimization. This requires the transport infrastructure to provide connectivity from eNodeBs in the RAN access to multiple MME and SGWs within these pools in the core network.

- The introduction of LTE into a existing 2G/3G network has to be graceful, and the transition will take time. During the transition period, it is natural for a few centralized EPC gateways to be initially deployed and shared across different regions of the network. As capacity demands and subscriber densities increase, it is expected that new gateways will be added closer to the regions, and subscribers will have to be migrated. While the migration across gateways within the packet core could be done seamlessly based on gateway pooling, it is imperative that the underlying transport infrastructure require minimal to no provisioning changes for the migration.

In 2G and 3G releases, the hub-and-spoke connectivity requirement between the BSC/RNC and the BTS/NodeB makes L2 transport using Ethernet bridging with VLANs or P2P PWs with MPLS PWE3 appealing. In contrast, a L3 transport option is much better suited to meet the myriad of connectivity requirements of 4G LTE. The seamless MPLS architecture offers both L2 and L3 MPLS VPN transport options that provide the necessary virtualization functions to support the coexistence of LTE S1- u/c, X2, interfaces with GSM Abis TDM, and UMTS IuB ATM backhaul. The decoupling of the network infrastructure's transport and service layers and the seamless connectivity across network domains makes the system a natural fit for the flat all-IP LTE architecture. This is because it allows for the flexible placement of 2G/3G/4G gateways in any location of the network to meet all the advance backhaul requirements listed above.

Delivering of New Levels of Scale for MPLS with RFC-3107 Hierarchical-Labeled BGP LSPs

LTE deployments will introduce unprecedented levels of scale in terms of eNodeBs and associated network elements like CSGs into the network. However, while L2 and L3 MPLS VPNs are well suited to provide the required virtualization functions to transport 2G/3G/4G mobile services, LTE's requirement to have inter-domain connectivity from the RAN access all the way to the core network in order to reach the EPC gateways presents challenges of scale to the transport infrastructure. This is because the IP aggregation with route summarization usually performed between (access, aggregation, core) regions of the network does not work for MPLS. This is because MPLS is not capable of aggregating forwarding equivalency class (FEC). In MPLS deployments, the FEC is typically the PE's /32 loopback IP address. Exposing the loopback addresses of all the nodes (10 k to 100 k) across the network introduces two main challenges:

- Large flat-routing domains adversely affect the stability and convergence time of the IGP.
- The sheer size of the routing and MPLS label information control plane and forwarding plane state will easily overwhelm the technical scaling limits on the smaller nodes (CSGs, pre-aggregation nodes) involved in the network.

Seamless MPLS elegantly solves this problem with a divide-and-conquer strategy of isolating the access, aggregation, and core network layers into independent and isolated Interior Gateway Protocol (IGP) domains. Label Distribution Protocol (LDP) is used for setting up LSPs within these domains, and RFC-3107 BGP-labeled unicast is used for setting up LSPs across domains. This BGP-based inter-domain hierarchical LSP approach helps scale the network to hundreds of thousands of LTE cell sites without overwhelming any of the smaller nodes in the network. At the same time, the stability and fast convergence of the small, isolated IGP domains corresponding to various network layers are maintained.

Facilitation of Fixed Mobile Convergence

Seamless MPLS addresses all of the needs of next-generation mobile backhaul while concurrently supporting transport legacy 2G and 3G mobile services. The concept of seamless MPLS, however, is not restricted to mobile transport. By decoupling the transport and service layers on the network, seamless MPLS enables end-to-end MPLS transport for any service, at any scale. The architecture allows extensions for wireline residential, business, retail/wholesale L2 and L3 VPNs, and IP services on the common network infrastructure supporting mobile backhaul.

Transport Models

The ubiquitous mobile broadband adoption driven by LTE will introduce unprecedented levels of scale in terms of eNodeBs and CSGs into the RAN backhaul network. This factor, combined with the flattened LTE/EPC architecture requiring connectivity from the RAN access all the way to the core network, introduces challenges in scaling the MPLS network. The endpoint identifier in MPLS is the PE's /32 loopback IP address, and since MPLS is not capable of aggregating FEC, IP aggregation with route summarization cannot be performed between the access, aggregation, and core regions of the network. All network technologies meet a scale challenge at some point, and the solution is always some form of hierarchy to scale. Seamless MPLS uses this hierarchical approach to solve the scaling problem in MPLS-based LTE deployments.

Seamless MPLS adopts a divide-and-conquer strategy where the core, aggregation, and access networks are partitioned in different MPLS/IP domains. The network segmentation between the core and aggregation domains could be based on a single-AS multi-area design or on inter-AS organization. Regardless of the type of segmentation, the seamless transport concept involves partitioning the core, aggregation, and access layers of the network into isolated IGP/LDP domains. Partitioning these network layers into such independent and isolated IGP domains helps reduce the size of routing and forwarding tables on individual routers in these domains, which in turn leads to better stability and faster convergence. LDP is used for label distribution to build LSPs within each independent IGP domain. This enables a device inside an access, aggregation, or core domain to have reachability via intra-domain LDP LSPs to any other device in the same domain. Reachability across domains is achieved using RFC 3107 procedures, whereby BGP-labeled unicast is used as an inter-domain label distribution protocol to build hierarchical LSPs across domains. This allows the link state database of the IGP in each isolated domain to remain as small as possible while all external reachability information is carried via BGP, which is designed to scale to the order of millions of routes.In single-AS multi-area designs, interior Border Gateway Protocol (iBGP)-labeled unicast is used to build inter-domain LSPs. In inter-AS designs, iBGP-labeled unicast is used to build inter-domain LSPs inside the AS. and exterior Border Gateway Protocol (eBGP)-labeled unicast is used to extend the end-to-end LSP across the AS boundary. In both cases, the seamless MPLS transport across domains uses hierarchical LSPs that rely on a BGP-distributed label, used to transit the isolated MPLS domains, and on a LDP-distributed label, used within the AS to reach the inter-domain area border router (ABR) or autonomous system boundary router (ASBR) corresponding to the labeled BGP next-hop.

Seamless MPLS enables a comprehensive and flexible transport framework structured around the most common layers in SP networks: the radio access network, the aggregation network, and the core network. The transport architecture structuring takes into consideration the type of access and the size of the network.

The access types are as follows:
- MPLS Packet Access
  - MPLS-based packet access covers point-to-point links, rings, and hierarchical topologies.

- It applies to both fiber and newer Ethernet microwave-based access technologies with the MPLS access network enabled by the CSGs.
- The services include both mobile and wireline services and can be enabled by the CSGs in the access network and the pre-aggregation or aggregation nodes in the aggregation network.
- IP/Ethernet/TDM Access
  - IP/Ethernet/TDM access includes native IP or Ethernet links in point-to-point or ring topologies over fiber and newer Ethernet microwave-based access.
  - It covers point-to-point TDM + Ethernet links over hybrid microwave access.
  - The MPLS services are enabled by the aggregation network and includes GSM Abis, ATM IuB, IP IuB, and IP S1/X2 interfaces aggregated in MPLS pre-aggregation or aggregation nodes.

The network sizes are as follows:
- Small Network
  - Small networks are network infrastructures in small geographies where the core and aggregation network layers are integrated in a single domain.
  - The single IGP/LDP domain includes less than 1000 core and aggregation nodes.
- Large Network
  - Large networks are network infrastructures built over large geographies.
  - The core and aggregation network layers have hierarchical physical topologies that enable IGP/LDP segmentation.

This transport architecture structuring, based on access type and network size, leads to five architecture models that fit various customer deployments and operator preferences. These are:
- Flat LDP core and aggregation
- Labeled BGP access with flat LDP core and aggregation
- Labeled BGP core and aggregation
- Labeled BGP core access and aggregation
- Labeled BGP core and aggregation with redistribution into access network IGP

They are described in the sections below.

Flat LDP Core and Aggregation

The flat LDP core and aggregation architecture model applies to small geographies where core and aggregation networks may not have distinct physical topologies. They are integrated under common operations, and network segmentation is not required for availability reasons. This type of architecture assumes a non-MPLS IP/Ethernet or TDM access being aggregated in a small scale network.

The small scale aggregation network is assumed to be composed of core and aggregation nodes that are integrated in a single IGP/LDP domain consisting of less than 1000 nodes. Since no segmentation between network layers exists, a flat LDP LSP provides end-to-end reachability across the network. All mobile (and wireline) services are enabled by the aggregation nodes. The mobile access is based on TDM and packet microwave links aggregated in aggregation nodes that provide TDM/ATM/Ethernet VPWS and MPLS VPN transport. This architecture is presented in Figure 4.4.

Labeled BGP Access with Flat LDP Core and Aggregation

The labeled BGP access with flat LDP core and aggregation architecture model, illustrated in Figure 4.5, applies to small geographies. This type of architecture assumes an MPLS-enabled access network with fiber and packet microwave links being aggregated in a small scale network.

The small scale aggregation network is assumed to be composed of core and aggregation nodes that are integrated in a single IGP/LDP domain consisting of less than 1000 nodes. The RAN access network is comprised of a separate IGP domain. The separation can be enabled either by making the access network part of a different IGP area from the aggregation and core nodes, or by

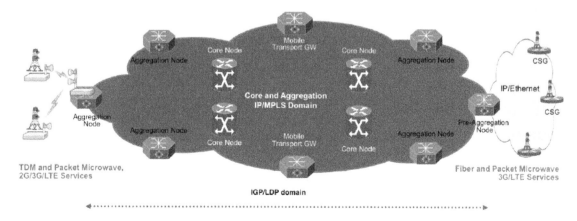

Figure 4.4

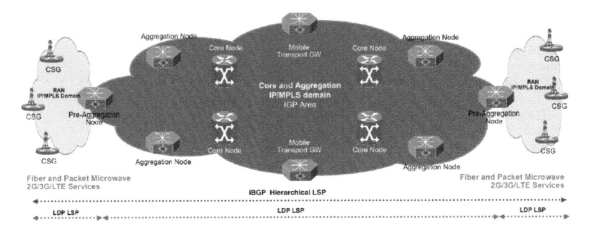

Figure 4.5

running a different IGP process on the pre-aggregation nodes corresponding to the aggregation/core and RAN access networks. LDP is use to build intra-area LSP within each segmented domain. The aggregation/core and RAN access networks are integrated with labeled BGP LSPs, with the pre-aggregation nodes acting as ABRs performing BGP next-hop-self (NHS) function to extend the iBGP hierarchical LSP across the two domains.

The mobile 2G/3G/LTE (and wireline) services can be enabled by the CSGs in the access as well as pre-aggregation/aggregation nodes. BGP community-based egress filtering is performed toward the RAN access at the pre-aggregation node ABRs so that the CSGs learn only the required remote destinations. All unwanted prefixes are dropped so as to keep their BGP labels small and prevent unnecessary updates.

Labeled BGP Core and Aggregation

The labeled BGP core and aggregation architecture model applies to networks deployed in medium-to-large geographies. This type of architecture assumes a non-MPLS IP/Ethernet or TDM access being aggregated in a relatively large scale network, as shown in Figure 4.6.

The network infrastructure is organized by segmenting the core and aggregation networks into independent IGP/LDP domains. The segmentation between the core and aggregation domains could be based on a single-AS multi-area design or an inter-AS organization. In the single-AS multi-area option, the separation can be enabled by making the aggregation network part of

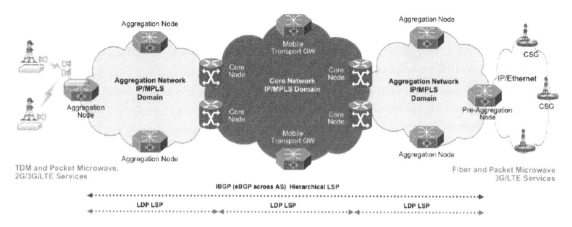

Figure 4.6

a different IGP area from the core network, or by running a different IGP process on the core ABR nodes corresponding to the aggregation and core networks. The mobile RAN access is based on native IP or Ethernet links in point-to-point or ring topologies over fiber and newer Ethernet microwave-based access, or point-to-point TDM + Ethernet links over hybrid microwave.

All mobile (and wireline) services are enabled by the aggregation nodes. LDP is used to build intra-area LSP within each segmented domain. The aggregation and core networks are integrated with labeled BGP LSPs. In the single-AS multi-area option, the core ABRs perform BGP NHS function to extend the iBGP hierarchical LSP across the aggregation and core domains. When the core and aggregation networks are organized in separate, autonomous systems, iBGP is used to build the hierarchical LSP from the pre-aggregation node to the ASBRs, and eBGP is used to extend the end-to-end LSP across the AS boundary. BGP community-based egress filtering is performed toward the aggregation networks at the core ABRs so that the pre-aggregation and aggregation nodes only learn required remote destinations and all unwanted prefixes are dropped. This helps reduce the size of the BGP tables on these nodes and also prevents unnecessary updates.

Labeled BGP Core Access and Aggregation

The labeled BGP core access and aggregation architecture model, shown in Figure 4.7, applies to networks deployed in large geographies. This type of architecture assumes an MPLS-enabled access network with fiber and packet microwave links being aggregated in a large-scale network. The network infrastructure is

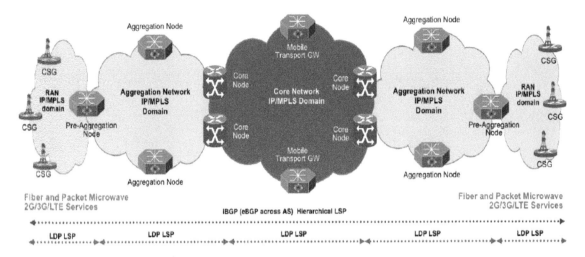

Figure 4.7

organized by segmenting the core, aggregation, and access networks into independent IGP/LDP domains. The segmentation between the core, aggregation, and access domains could be based on a single-AS multi-area design or an inter-AS organization.

In the single-AS multi-area option, the separation between core and aggregation networks can be enabled by making the aggregation network part of a different IGP area from the core network, or by running a different IGP process on the core ABR nodes corresponding to the aggregation and core networks. The separation between aggregation and access networks is enabled by running a different IGP process on the pre-aggregation nodes, corresponding to the aggregation and RAN access networks. In the inter-AS option, while the core and aggregation networks are in separate, autonomous systems, the separation between aggregation and access networks is enabled either by making the access network part of a different IGP area from the aggregation network, or by running a different IGP process on the pre-aggregation nodes, corresponding to the aggregation and RAN access networks.

The mobile 2G/3G/LTE (and wireline) services can be enabled by the CSGs in the access as well as by the pre-aggregation/aggregation nodes. LDP is use to build intra-area LSP within each segmented domain. The access, aggregation, and core networks are integrated with labeled BGP LSPs. In the single-AS multi-area option, the pre-aggregation nodes and core ABRs act as ABRs for their corresponding domains and extend the iBGP hierarchical LSP across the access, aggregation, and core domains. When the core and aggregation networks are organized in separate, autonomous systems, the pre-aggregation nodes act as ABRs performing BGP NHS function to extend the iBGP hierarchical LSP across the access and aggregation domains. At the ASBRs, eBGP is used to extend the end-to-end LSP across the AS boundary. BGP community-based egress filtering is performed toward the aggregation networks at the core ABRs, and toward the RAN access at the pre-aggregation node ABRs, so that the corresponding nodes in each domain only learn required remote destinations and all unwanted prefixes are dropped. This helps reduce the size of BGP tables on these nodes and also prevents unnecessary updates.

Labeled BGP Core and Aggregation with Redistribution into Access Network IGP

There is another labeled BGP core and aggregation model that includes redistribution into access network IGP. This architecture model applies to networks deployed in large geographies. It assumes an MPLS-enabled access network with fiber and packet microwave links being aggregated in a large-scale network. The network infrastructure organization in this architecture model is the same as the one described in the section titled "Labeled BGP Core, Aggregation, and Access," with options for both single-AS multi-area and inter-AS designs, as shown in Figure 4.8. The service options in this model are also the same, with support for mobile 2G/3G/LTE (and wireline) services that can be enabled by the CSGs in the access as well as the pre-aggregation/ aggregation nodes. This model, pictured below, differs from the

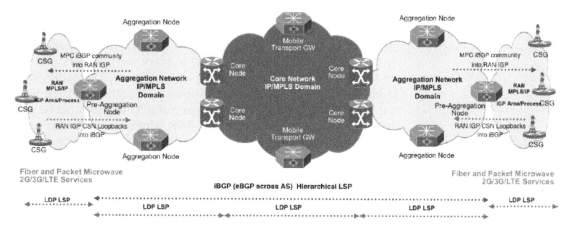

Figure 4.8

aforementioned one in that the hierarchical-labeled BGP LSP spans only the core and aggregation networks and does not extend to the RAN access. Instead of using BGP for inter-domain label distribution in the RAN, the end-to-end seamless MPLS LSP is extended into the RAN access using LDP with redistribution. The IGP scale in the RAN access is kept small by selective redistribution of required remote prefixes from iBGP based on communities.

Service Models

The fundamental goal of seamless MPLS is the simplification of the end-to-end mobile transport and service architecture. It achieves this goal by decoupling the transport and service layers of the network, thereby allowing these two distinct entities to be provisioned and managed independently. As described in the section titled "Transport Architecture Models," the architecture seamlessly interconnects the access, aggregation, and core MPLS domains of the network infrastructure with hierarchical LSPs at the transport layer. Once this seamless MPLS transport is established (a task that only needs to be undertaken once), a multitude of services can be deployed on top of it. These services can span any location in the network without restricting topological boundaries.

The decoupling of the transport and service layers makes it possible for the service architecture or service delivery model for any given service to be provisioned, managed, and changed independently, without the transport layer needing to be touched. It eliminates the unwanted complexity of having to provision and manage intermediate touchpoints, like the pre-aggregation, aggregation, and core ABRs for service delivery, and requires service provisioning only at the service endpoints.

Seamless MPLS is a comprehensive RAN backhaul solution that provides the foundation for LTE, legacy 2G GSM, and existing 3G UMTS transport services. The system proposes a highly scaled MPLS L3VPN-based service model to meet the immediate needs of LTE transport and accelerate its deployment. The MPLS VPN model provides the required transport virtualization for the graceful introduction of LTE into a existing 2G/3G network, while satisfying future requirements of RAN sharing in a wholesale scenario. It is well suited to meet the mesh connectivity and stringent latency requirements of the LTE X2 interface. Simple MPLS VPN route-target import/export mechanisms can be used to enable multipoint connectivity:

- Within the local RAN access for intra-RAN-access X2 handoff.
- With adjacent RAN access regions for inter-RAN-access region X2 handoff.

- With EPC gateways (SGWs, MMEs) in the MPC for the S1-u/c interface.
- With more than one MME and SGW for MME and SGW pooling scenarios.

The MPLS VPN-based service model allows for eNodeBs and associated CSGs to be added to the RAN at any location in the network, EPC gateways can be added in the MPC and have instant connectivity to each other without additional configuration overhead. It allows eNodeBs initially mapped to centralized EPC gateways to migrate seamlessly to more distributed ones to accommodate capacity and scale demands, without having to re-provision the transport infrastructure.

Service virtualization with MPLS-based L2 and L3 VPNs also allows legacy 2G GSM and existing 3G UMTS services to co-exist with LTE on the same transport infrastructure. The system supports MSPs with GSM- and ATM-based UMTS deployments wishing to remove, reduce, or cap investments in SONET/SDH and ATM transport infrastructure by using MPLS-based Circuit Emulation over Packet (CEoP) services.

- For mobile service providers who want to reduce SONET/SDH infrastructure used for GSM, seamless MPLS enables PWE3-based transport of emulated TDM circuits. Structured circuit emulation is achieved with CESoPSN, and unstructured emulation is achieved with SAToP. E1/T1 circuits from BTS equipment connected to the CSG or to the pre-aggregation node (PAN) are transported to MTG, where they are bundled into channelized STM1/OC-3 interfaces for handoff to the BSC.
- For mobile service providers who want to reduce the ATM infrastructure used for ATM-based UMTS, seamless MPLS enables ATM VC (AAL0 or AAL5) or VP (AAL0) PWE3-based transport. ATM E1/T1 or IMA interfaces from eNodeB equipment connected to the CSG or PAN can be transported to the MTG, where they are bundled into STM1 ATM interfaces for handoff to the RNC. Cell packing may be used to optimize the bandwidth used for this transport.

Large Network, Multi-Area IGP Design with IP/MPLS Access

This section details the system architecture for a transport model where the network organization between the core and aggregation domains is based on a single autonomous system, multi-area IGP design. This model, illustrated in Figure 4.9, follows the approach of enabling a seamless MPLSLSP using

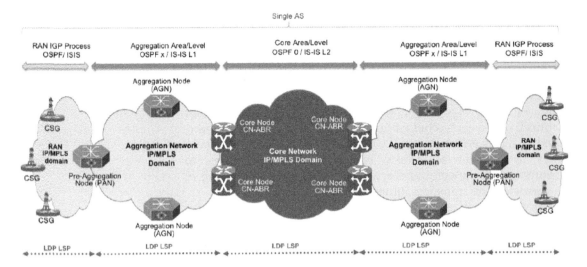

Figure 4.9

hierarchical-labeled BGP LSPs across the core and aggregation network, and presents two approaches for extending the seamless MPLSLSP into the mobile RAN access domain.

From a multi-area IGP organization perspective, the core network is either an intermediate system to intermediate system (IS-IS) Level 2 or an open shortest path first (OSPF) backbone area. The aggregation domains, in turn, are IS-IS Level 1 or OSPF non-backbone areas. No redistribution occurs between the core and aggregation IGP levels/areas, so the route scale in contained within each domain. The MPLS/IP mobile access networks subtending from aggregation or pre-aggregation nodes are based on a different IGP process, restricting their scale to the level of the local RAN. To accomplish this, the pre-aggregation nodes run two distinct IGP processes. The first process corresponds to core-aggregation network (IS-IS Level 1 or OSPF non-backbone area), and the second process corresponds to the mobile RAN access network. The second IGP process could be an OSPF backbone area or an IS-IS Level 2 domain. All CSGs that are part of the mobile RAN access network subtending from a pair of pre-aggregation nodes are part of this second IGP process.

Partitioning these network layers into such independent and isolated IGP domains helps reduce the size of routing and forwarding tables on individual routers in these domains, which, in turn, leads to better stability and faster convergence within each of these domains. LDP is used for label distribution to build intra-domain LSPs within each independent access, aggregation, and core IGP domain. Inter-domain reachability is enabled with hierarchical LSPs using BGP-labeled unicast as per RFC 3107 procedures, where iBGP is used to distribute labels in addition to remote prefixes, and LDP is used to reach the labeled BGP next hop. Two options for extending the seamless MPLSLSP into the mobile RAN access domain to accommodate different operator preferences are presented below.

Option 1: Multi-Area IGP Design with Labeled BGP Access

The Option 1 architecture model, illustrated in Figure 4.10, applies to networks deployed in large geographies. It assumes an MPLS-enabled access This option is based on the transport model described in the section "Labeled BGP Core, Aggregation, and Access."

In this option, the access, aggregation, and core networks are integrated with seamless MPLSLSPs by extending labeled BGP from the core all the way to the CSGs in the RAN access. Any node in the network that requires inter-domain LSPs to reach nodes in remote domain acts as a labeled BGP PE and runs iBGP IPv4 unicast + labels with their corresponding local RRs.

- The core PoP nodes (CN-ABR) are labeled BGP ABRs and act as inline RRs for their local aggregation network PAN clients. The CN-ABRs peer with other CN-ABRs using either an iBGP-labeled unicast in a full-mesh configuration, or a centralized core node route reflector (CNRR) within the core domain.

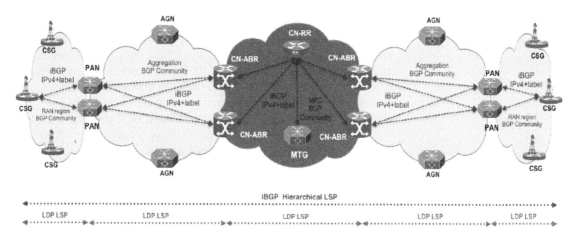

Figure 4.10

- The MTGs residing in the core network are labeled BGP PEs. They connect to the EPC gateways (SGW, PGW, MME) in the MPC. The MTGs peer either directly with the closest CN-ABR RRs, in the case of a CN-ABR full-mesh configuration, or with the CN-RR, depending on the deployment setting. The MTGs advertise their loopbacks into iBGP-labeled unicast with a common BGP community (MPC BGP community) representing the MPC.
- The PANs are labeled BGP PEs and act as inline RRs for their local access network CSG clients. All the PANs in the aggregation network that require inter-domain LSPs to reach remote PANs in another aggregation network or in the core network (to reach the MTGs, for example) run BGP-labeled unicast sessions with their local CN-ABR inline-RRs. The PANs advertise their loopbacks into BGP-labeled unicast with a common BGP community that represents the aggregation community. They learn labeled BGP prefixes marked with the aggregation BGP community and the MPC BGP community.
- The CSGs in the RAN access networks are labeled BGP PEs. They peer with iBGP-labeled unicast sessions to their local PAN inline-RRs. The CSGs advertise their loopbacks into BGP labeled unicast with a common BGP community that represents the RAN access community. They learn labeled BGP prefixes marked with the MPC BGP community for reachability to the MPC, or to the adjacent RAN access BGP community if inter-access X2 connectivity is desired.

Since routes between the core IS-IS Level 2 (or OSPF backbone) and aggregation IS-IS Level 1 (or OSPF non-backbone area) are not redistributed, the CN-ABRs have to reflect the labeled BGP prefixes with the next-hop changed to self in order to insert themselves into the data path to enable the inter-domain LSP switching and allow the aggregation and core IGP routing domains to remain isolated. This CN-ABR NHS function is symmetrically applied by the CN-ABRs toward its PAN clients in its local aggregation domain and the CN-RR in the core domain. Similarly, since the RAN access and aggregation networks are in different IGP processes, the PANs have to reflect the labeled BGP prefixes with the next-hop changed to self in order to insert themselves into the data path to enable the inter-domain LSP switching. This PAN NHS function is symmetrically applied by the PANs toward its CSG clients in its local RAN access domain, and the higher level CN-ABR inline-RR in the aggregation domain.

The MTGs in the core network are capable of handling large scale and will learn all BGP-labeled unicast prefixes, since they need connectivity to all the CGSs in the entire network. Simple prefix filtering based on BGP communities is performed on the CN-RRs in order to constrain IPv4+label routes from remote RAN access regions from proliferating into neighboring aggregation domains, where they are not needed. The PANs only learn labeled BGP prefixes marked with the aggregation BGP community and the MPC BGP community. This allows the PANs to enable inter-metro wireline services across the core, as well as reflect the MPC prefix to their local access networks. Using a separate IGP process for the RAN access enables the mobile access network to have limited control plane scale, since the CSGs only learn local IGP routes and labeled BGP prefixes marked with the MPC BGP community.

Option 2: Multi-Area IGP Design with IGP/LDP Access

The second option, pictured in Figure 4.11, is based on the transport model described in the section titled "Labeled BGP Core and Aggregation with Redistribution into Access Network IGP."

This option follows the approach of enabling labeled BGP across the core and aggregation networks and extends the seamless MPLS LSP to the access by redistribution between labeled BGP and the access domain IGP. All nodes in the core and aggregation network that require inter-domain LSPs to reach nodes in remote domains act as labeled BGP PEs and run iBGP IPv4 unicast+labels with their corresponding local RRs.

- The core PoP nodes (CN-ABR) are labeled BGP ABRs and act as inline RRs for their local aggregation network pre-aggregation node (PAN) clients. The CN-ABRs peer with other CNABRs,

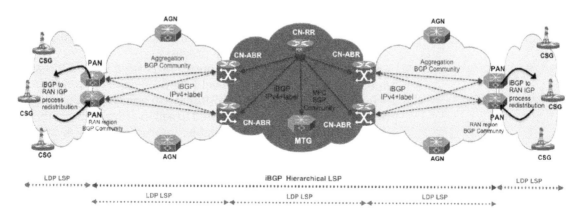

Figure 4.11

using iBGP-labeled unicast using either a full-mesh configuration or a centralized CNRR within the core domain.

- The MTGs residing in the core network are labeled BGP PEs. They connect to the EPC gateways (SGW, PGW, MME) in the MPC. The MTGs peer either directly with the closest CN-ABR RRs, in the case of a CN-ABR full-mesh configuration, or with the CN-RR, depending on the deployment setting. The MTGs advertise their loopbacks into iBGP-labeled unicast with a common BGP community (MPC BGP community) representing the MPC.
- All the PANs in the aggregation network that require inter-domain LSPs to reach remote PANs in another aggregation network, or in the core network (to reach the MTGs, for example), run BGP-labeled unicast sessions with their local CN-ABR inline RRs. The PANs advertise their loopbacks into BGP-labeled unicast with a common BGP community that represents the aggregation community. They learn labeled BGP prefixes marked with the aggregation BGP community and the MPC BGP community.
- The inter-domain LSPs are extended to the MPLS/IP RAN access with a controlled redistribution based on IGP tags and BGP communities. Each mobile access network subtending from a pair of PANs is based on a different IGP process. At the PANs, the inter-domain core and aggregation LSPs are extended to the RAN access by redistributing between iBGP and RAN IGP. In one direction, the RAN access node loopbacks (filtered based on IGP tags) are redistributed into iBGP-labeled unicast and tagged with RAN access BGP community that is unique to that RAN access region. In the other direction, the MPC prefixes that are filtered based on MPC-marked BGP communities, and optionally, adjacent RAN access prefixes that are filtered based on RAN-region-marked BGP communities (if inter-access X2 connectivity is desired), are redistributed into the RAN access IGP process.

Since routes between the core IS-IS Level 2 (or OSPF backbone) and aggregation IS-IS Level 1 (or OSPF non-backbone area) are not redistributed, the CN-ABRs have to reflect the labeled BGP prefixes with the next-hop changed to self in order to insert themselves into the data path. This enables inter-domain LSP switching and allows the aggregation and core IGP routing domains to remain isolated. This CN-ABR NHS function is symmetrically applied by the CN-ABRs toward its PAN clients in its local aggregation domain and the CN-RR in the core domain.

The MTGs in the core network are capable of handling large scale and will learn all BGP-labeled unicast prefixes, since they need connectivity to all the CGSs in the entire network. Simple prefix filtering based on BGP communities is performed on the CN-RRs, in order to constrain IPv4 + label routes from remote RAN access regions from proliferating into neighboring aggregation domains, where they are not needed. The PANs only learn labeled BGP prefixes marked with the aggregation BGP community and the MPC BGP community. This allows the PANs to enable inter-metro wireline services across the core, and also to redistribute the MPC prefix to their local access networks. Using a separate IGP process for the RAN access enables the mobile access network to have limited control plane scale, since the CSGs only learn local IGP routes and labeled BGP prefixes marked with the MPC BGP community.

Large Network, Inter-AS Design with IP/MPLS Access

This section details the system architecture for a transport model where the core and aggregation networks are organized as separate, autonomous systems. This model, shown in Figure 4.12, follows the approach of enabling a seamless MPLSLSP using hierarchical-labeled BGP LSPs based on iBGP-labeled unicast within each AS, and based on eBGP-labeled unicast to extend the LSP across AS boundaries. Two approaches are presented for extending the seamless MPLSLSP into the mobile RAN access domain.

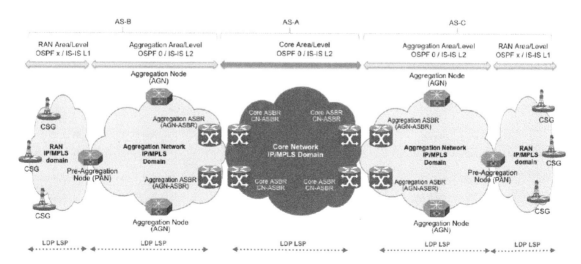

Figure 4.12

The core and aggregation networks are segmented into separate autonomous systems. Within each aggregation domain, the aggregation and access networks are segmented into different IGP areas or levels, where the aggregation network is either an IS-IS Level 2 or an OSPF backbone area, and subtending access networks are IS-IS Level 1 or OSPF non-backbone areas. No redistribution occurs between the aggregation and access IGP levels/areas, thereby containing the route scale within each domain. Partitioning these network layers into such independent and isolated IGP domains helps reduce the size of routing and forwarding tables on individual routers in these domains, which, in turn, leads to better stability and faster convergence in each domain. LDP is used for label distribution to build intra-domain LSPs within each independent access, aggregation, and core IGP domain.

Inter-domain reachability is enabled with hierarchical LSPs using BGP-labeled unicast as per RFC 3107 procedures. Within each AS, iBGP is used to distribute labels in addition to remote prefixes, and LDP is used to reach the labeled BGP next-hop. At the ASBRs, the seamless MPLSLSP is extended across the aggregation and core AS boundaries using eBGP-labeled unicast. The seamless MPLS LSP can be extended into the mobile RAN access using two different options as presented below to accommodate operator preference.

Option 1: Inter-AS Design with Labeled BGP Access

This option, shown in Figure 4.13, is based on the transport model described in the section titled "BGP Core, Aggregation, and Access."

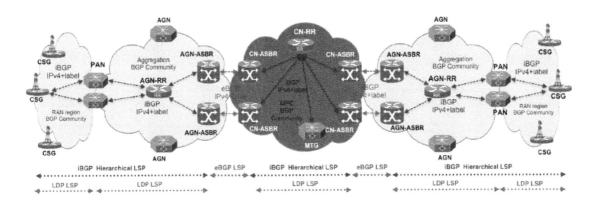

Figure 4.13

In this option, the access, aggregation, and core networks are integrated with seamless MPLS LSPs by extending labeled BGP from the core all the way to the CSGs in the RAN access. Any node in the network that requires inter-domain LSPs to reach nodes in remote domain acts as a labeled BGP PE and runs iBGP IPv4 unicast + labels with their corresponding local RRs.

The core PoP nodes are labeled BGP ASBRs (CN-ASBR). They peer with iBGP-labeled-unicast sessions with the centralized CN-RR within the core AS, and peer with eBGP-labeled unicast sessions with the neighboring aggregation ASBRs. The CN-ASBRs insert themselves into the data path to enable inter-domain LSPs by setting NHS on all iBGP updates toward their local CN-RRs and on all eBGP updates toward the neighboring aggregation ASBRs.

The mobile transport gateways (MTG) residing in the core network are labeled BGP PEs, which connect to the EPC gateways (SGW, PGW, MME) in the MPC. The MTGs peer with iBGP-labeled unicast sessions with the CN-RR and advertise their loopbacks into iBGP-labeled unicast with a common BGP community (MPC BGP community) representing the MPC.

- The aggregation PoP nodes act as labeled BGP ASBRs (AGN-ASBR) in the aggregation AS. They peer with iBGP-labeled unicast sessions with the centralized aggregation route reflector (AGN-RR) within the aggregation AS, and peer with eBGP-labeled unicast sessions to the CNASBR in the core AS. The AGN-ASBRs insert themselves into the data path to enable inter-domain LSPs by setting NHS on all iBGP updates toward their local AGN-RRs and on all Ebgp updates toward neighboring CN-ASBRs.

- All the PANs in the aggregation network that require inter-domain LSPs to reach remote PANs in another aggregation network, or in the core network (to reach the MTGs, for example), act as labeled BGP PEs and run BGP-labeled unicast sessions with their local AGN-RRs. The PANs advertise their loopbacks into BGP-labeled unicast with a common BGP community that represents the aggregation community. They learn labeled BGP prefixes marked with the aggregation BGP community and the MPC BGP community. In addition to being labeled BGP PEs, the PANs also act as inline RRs for their local access network Cell Site Gateway (CSG) clients. Each mobile access network subtending from a pair of PANs is part of a unique IS-IS Level 1 domain. All access rings/hub-spokes subtending from the same pair of PANs are part of the IS-IS Level 1 domain, where the CSGs are IS-IS L1 nodes and the PAN are L1/L2 nodes. Since routes between the aggregation IS-IS Level 2 (or OSPF backbone) and access IS-IS Level 1 (or OSPF non-backbone area) are not redistributed, the PANs have to reflect the labeled BGP prefixes with the next-hop changed to self in order to insert themselves into the data path to enable the inter-domain LSP switching and allow the aggregation and access IGP routing domains to remain isolated. This PAN NHS function is symmetrically applied by the PANs toward its CSG clients in its local RAN access domain, and toward the higher level AGN-RR in the aggregation domain.

- The CSGs in the RAN access networks are labeled BGP PEs. They peer with iBGP-labeled unicast sessions with their local PAN inline-RRs. The CSGs advertise their loopbacks into BGP labeled unicast with a common BGP community that represents the RAN access community. They learn labeled BGP prefixes marked with the MPC BGP community for reachability to the MPC, and marked with the adjacent RAN access BGP community if inter-access X2 connectivity is desired.

The MTGs in the core network are capable of handling large scale and will learn all BGP-labeled unicast prefixes, since they need connectivity to all the CGSs in the entire network. Simple prefix filtering based on BGP communities is performed on the CN-RRs in order to constrain IPv4 + label routes from remote RAN access regions from proliferating into neighboring aggregation domains, where they are not needed. The PANs only learn labeled BGP prefixes marked with the aggregation BGP community and the MPC BGP community. This allows the PANs to enable inter-metro wireline services across the core, and also to reflect the MPC prefix to their local access networks. Isolating the aggregation and RAN access domain by preventing the default redistribution enables the mobile access network to have limited route scale, since the CSGs only learn local IGP routes and labeled BGP prefixes marked with the MPC BGP community.

Option 2: Inter-AS Design with IGP/LDP Access

This option is based on the transport model described in the section titled "Labeled BGP Core and Aggregation with Redistribution into Access Network IGP."

It enables labeled BGP across the core and aggregation networks and extends the seamless MPLS LSP to the access by redistribution between labeled BGP and the access domain IGP, as shown in Figure 4.14. All nodes in the core and aggregation network that require inter-domain LSPs to reach nodes in remote domains act as labeled BGP PEs and run iBGP IPv4 unicast + labels with their corresponding local route reflectors (RR).

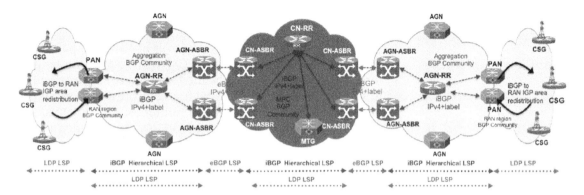

Figure 4.14

- The core PoP nodes are labeled BGP ASBRs (CN-ASBR). They peer with iBGP-labeled unicast sessions with the centralized CN-RR within the core AS, and peer with eBGP-labeled unicast sessions with the neighboring aggregation ASBRs. The CN-ASBRs insert themselves into the data path to enable inter-domain LSPs by setting NHS on all iBGP updates toward their local CN-RRs and on all eBGP updates toward the neighboring aggregation ASBRs.
- The MTGs residing in the core network are labeled BGP PEs, which connect to the EPC gateways (SGW, PGW, MME) in the MPC. The MTGs peer with iBGP-labeled unicast sessions with the CN-RR, and advertise their loopbacks into iBGP-labeled unicast with a common BGP community (MPC BGP community) representing the MPC.
- The aggregation PoP nodes act as labeled BGP ASBRs (AGN-ASBR) in the aggregation AS. They peer with iBGP-labeled unicast sessions with the centralized AGN-RR within the aggregation AS, and peer with eBGP-labeled unicast sessions to the CN-ASBR in the core AS. The AGN-ASBRs insert themselves into the data path to enable inter-domain LSPs by setting NHS on all iBGP updates toward their local AGN-RRs and on all eBGP updates toward neighboring CN-ASBRs.
- All the PANs in the aggregation network that require inter-domain LSPs to reach remote PANs in another aggregation network, or in the core network (to reach the MTGs, for example), act as labeled BGP PEs and run BGP-labeled unicast sessions with their local AGN-RRs. The PANs advertise their loopbacks into BGP-labeled unicast with a common BGP community that represents the aggregation community. They learn labeled BGP prefixes marked with the aggregation BGP community and the MPC BGP community.

• Each mobile access network subtending from a pair of PANs is part of a unique IS-IS Level 1 domain. All access rings/hub-spokes subtending from the same pair of PANs are part of an IS-IS Level 1 domain, where the CSGs are IS-IS L1 nodes and the PAN are L1/L2 nodes. The inter-domain LSPs are extended to the MPLS/IP RAN access with a controlled redistribution, based on IGP tags and BGP communities. At the PANs, the inter-domain core and aggregation LSPs are extended to the RAN access by redistributing between iBGP and RAN IGP levels/areas. In one direction, the RAN access node loopbacks (filtered based on IGP tags) are redistributed into iBGP-labeled unicast and tagged with RAN access BGP community that is unique to that RAN access region. In the other direction, the MPC prefixes filtered based on MPC-marked BGP communities, and optionally, adjacent RAN access prefixes filtered based on RAN-region-marked BGP communities (if inter-access X2 connectivity is desired), are redistributed into the RAN access IGP level/area.

The MTGs in the core network are capable of handling large scale and will learn all BGP-labeled unicast prefixes, since they need connectivity to all the CGSs in the entire network. Simple prefix filtering based on BGP communities is performed on the CN-RRs in order to constrain IPv4+label routes from remote RAN access regions from proliferating into neighboring aggregation domains, where they are not needed. The PANs only learn labeled BGP prefixes marked with the aggregation BGP community and the MPC BGP community. This allows the PANs to enable inter-metro wireline services across the core, and also reflect the MPC prefix to their local access networks. Using a separate IGP process for the RAN access enables the mobile access network to have limited control plane scale, since the CSGs only learn local IGP routes and labeled BGP prefixes marked with the MPC BGP community.

Large Network Inter-AS Design with Non-IP/MPLS Access

This section details the system architecture for the transport model described in the section titled "BGP Core and Aggregation," as illustrated in Figure 4.15. It assumes that the core and aggregation networks are organized as separate autonomous systems. It also assumes a non-MPLS IP/Ethernet or TDM access where all mobile and potentially wireline services are enabled by the aggregation nodes.

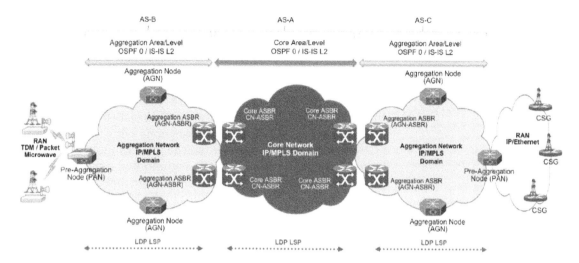

Figure 4.15

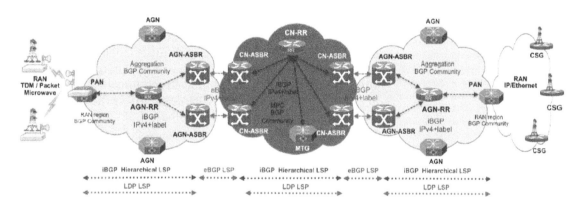

Figure 4.16

This model enables a seamless MPLSLSP using hierarchical-labeled BGP LSPs based on iBGP-labeled unicast within each AS, and using eBGP-labeled unicast to extend the LSP across AS boundaries, as shown in Figure 4.16. The core and aggregation networks are segmented into separate autonomous systems. LDP is used for label distribution to build intra-domain LSPs within each independent aggregation and core IGP domain. The access network is either based on native IP or Ethernet links over fiber or packet microwave integrated in point-to-point or ring topologies, or based on TDM+Ethernet links over hybrid microwave with point-to-point connectivity.

RFC 3107 procedures based on iBGP IPv4 unicast+label are used as an inter-domain LDP to build hierarchical LSPs across domains. All nodes in the core and aggregation network that require inter-domain LSPs act as labeled BGP PEs and run iBGP-labeled unicast peering with designated RRs, depending on their location in the network.

- The MTGs residing in the core network are labeled BGP PEs and peer with iBGP-labeled unicast sessions with the centralized CN-RR. The MTGs advertise their loopbacks into BGP-labeled unicast with a common BGP community representing the MPC. They learn all the labeled BGP prefixes and have reachability across the entire network down to the MPLS/IP RAN access.
- The core PoP nodes act as labeled BGP autonomous system boundary routers (CN-ASBR) in the core AS. They peer with iBGP-labeled unicast sessions with the CN-RR within the core AS, and peer with eBGP-labeled unicast sessions with the neighboring aggregation ASBRs. The CNASBRs insert themselves into the data path to enable inter-domain LSPs by setting NHS on all BGP updates toward their local CN-RRs and neighboring aggregation ASBRs.
- The aggregation PoP nodes act as labeled BGP AGN-ASBRs in the aggregation AS. They peer with iBGP-labeled unicast sessions to the centralized AGN-RR within the aggregation AS, and peer with eBGP-labeled unicast sessions to the CN-ASBR in the neighboring AS. The AGNASBRs insert themselves into the data path to enable inter-domain LSPs by setting NHS on all BGP updates toward their local AGN-RRs and neighboring core ASBRs.
- All PANs in the aggregation networks that require inter-domain LSPs either to reach nodes in another remote aggregation network or to cross the core network to reach the MTGs act as labeled BGP PEs, and peer with iBGP-labeled unicast sessions to the local AGN-RR. The PANs advertise their loopbacks into BGP-labeled unicast with a common BGP community that represents the aggregation community. They learn labeled BGP prefixes marked with the aggregation BGP community and the MPC BGP community.

All MPLS services are enabled by the PANs in the aggregation network. These include:

- GSM Abis, ATM IuB, IP IuB, and IP S1/X2 interfaces for 2G/3G/LTE services for RAN access domains with point-to-point connectivity over TDM or hybrid (TDM+Packet) microwave
- IP IuB, and IP S1/X2 interfaces for 3G/LTE services for RAN access domains with point-to-point or ring topologies over fiber or packet microwave.

Small Network, Integrated Core and Aggregation with IP/MPLS Access

This section details the system architecture for the transport model described in the section titled "Labeled BGP Access with Flat LDP Core and Aggregation." It assumes that the core and aggregation networks are integrated into a single IGP/LDP domain consisting of less than 1000 nodes. The aggregation nodes have subtending mobile RAN access networks that are MPLS enabled and part of the same AS as the integrated core+aggregation network. See Figure 4.17.

From a multi-area IGP organization perspective, the integrated core+aggregation networks and the access networks are segmented into different IGP areas or levels, where the integrated core+aggregation network is either an IS-IS Level 2 or an OSPF backbone area, and access networks subtending from the aggregation nodes are in IS-IS Level 1 or OSPF non-backbone areas. No redistribution occurs between the integrated core+aggregation and access IGP levels or areas, thereby containing the route scale within each domain. Partitioning these network layers into such independent and isolated IGP domains helps reduce the size of routing and forwarding tables on individual routers in these domains, which, in turn, leads to greater stability and faster convergence within each of these domains. See Figure 4.18.

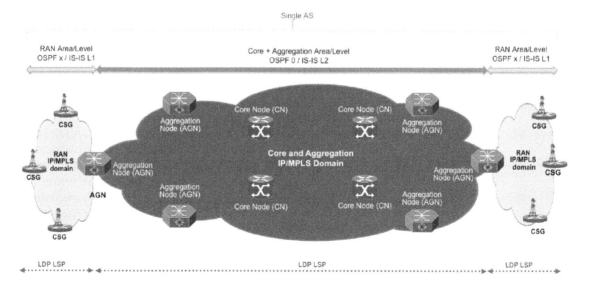

Figure 4.17

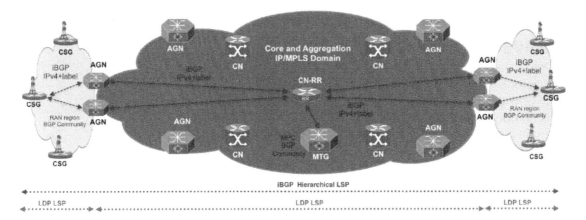

Figure 4.18

LDP is used for label distribution to build intra-domain LSPs within each independent IGP domain. Inter-domain reachability is enabled with hierarchical LSPs using BGP-labeled unicast according to RFC 3107 procedures, where iBGP is used to distribute labels in addition to remote prefixes, and LDP is used to reach the labeled BGP next-hop.

The collapsed core + aggregation and access networks are integrated with labeled BGP LSPs. Any node in the network that requires inter-domain LSPs to reach nodes in remote domains acts as a labeled BGP PE and runs iBGP IPv4 unicast + labels with their corresponding local route reflectors (RR).

- The MTGs residing in the core network are labeled BGP PEs. They connect to the EPC gateways (SGW, PGW, MME) in the MPC. The MTGs peer with iBGP-labeled unicast sessions with the CN-RR, and advertise their loopbacks into iBGP-labeled unicast with a common BGP community (MPC BGP community) representing the MPC.
- The aggregation nodes (AGN) act as inline-RRs for their local access network CSG clients. Each mobile access network subtending from a pair of AGNs is part of a unique IS-IS Level 1 domain. All access rings/hub-spokes subtending from the same pair of AGNs are part of ISIS Level 1 domain, where the CSGs are IS-IS L1 nodes and the AGN are L1/L2 nodes. Since routes between the integrated core + aggregation IS-IS Level 2 (or OSPF backbone) and access IS-IS Level 1 (or OSPF non-backbone area) are not redistributed, the AGNs have to reflect the labeled BGP prefixes with the next-hop changed to "self" in order to insert themselves into the data path to enable the inter-domain LSP switching and allow the two

IGP routing domains to remain isolated. This AGN NHS function is symmetrically applied by the AGNs toward its CSG clients in its local RAN access domain in and the higher level CN-RR in the integrated core + aggregation domain.

- The CSGs in the RAN access networks are labeled BGP PEs. They peer with iBGP-labeled unicast sessions with their local AGN inline-RRs. The CSGs advertise their loopbacks into BGP-labeled unicast, with a common BGP community that represents the RAN access community. They learn labeled BGP prefixes marked with the MPC BGP community for reachability to the MPC, and with the adjacent RAN access BGP community if inter-access X2 connectivity is desired.

The MTGs in the integrated core + aggregation network are capable of handling large scale and will learn all BGP-labeled unicast prefixes since they need connectivity to all the CGSs in the entire network. Simple prefix filtering based on BGP communities is performed on the CN-RRs for constraining IPv4 + label routes, from remote RAN access regions, from proliferating into other AGNs, where they are not needed. Since all the AGNs are part of the same IGP/LDP domain, they can enable wireline services across each other. The AGNs learn labeled BGP prefixes marked with the MPC BGP community and reflect the MPC prefixes to their local access networks. Isolating the integrated core + aggregation and RAN access domain by preventing the default redistribution enables the mobile access network to have limited route scale, since the CSGs only learn local IGP routes and labeled BGP prefixes marked with the MPC BGP community.

Small Network, Integrated Core, and Aggregation with Non-IP/MPLS Access

This section details the system architecture for the transport model described in the section titled "Flat LDP Core and Aggregation." This model assumes that the core and aggregation networks form a single IGP/LDP domain consisting of less than 1000 nodes. Since no segmentation between network layers exists, a flat LDP LSP provides end-to-end reachability across the network. The mobile access is based on TDM and packet microwave links aggregated in aggregation nodes that provide TDM/ATM/Ethernet VPWS and MPLS VPN transport.

All MPLS services are enabled by the aggregation nodes. These include:

- GSM Abis, ATM IuB, IP IuB, and IP S1/X2 interfaces for 2G/3G/LTE services for RAN access domains with point-to-point connectivity over TDM or hybrid (TDM + Packet) microwave.

- IP IuB, and IP S1/X2 interfaces for 3G/LTE services for RAN access domains with point-to-point or ring topologies over fiber or packet microwave.

Service Architecture

The seamless MPLS system design provides transport for both legacy and current mobile services. To accomplish this on a single network, MPLS service virtualization is employed, which provides emulated circuit services via L2VPN for 2G and 3G services and L3VPN services for IP-enabled 3G and 4G/LTE services.

L3VPN MPLS Service Model for LTE

The seamless MPLS system supports mobile SPs that are introducing 3G UMTS/IP and 4G LTE-based next-generation mobile access in order to scale their mobile subscribers and optimize their network infrastructure cost for the mobile broadband growth. To this end, the system proposes a highly scaled MPLS VPN-based service model to meet the immediate needs of LTE and to accelerate its deployment.

The mobile RAN includes cell sites with eNodeBs that are connected either:
- directly in a point-to-point fashion to the PANs utilizing Ethernet fiber or microwave *or*
- through CSGs connected in ring topologies using MPLS/IP packet transport over Ethernet fiber or microwave transmission.

The cell sites in the RAN access are collected in an MPLS/IP pre-aggregation/aggregation network that may be composed of a physical hub-and-spoke or ring connectivity that interfaces with the MPLS/IP core network that hosts the EPC gateways. From the E-UTRAN backhaul perspective, the most important LTE/SAE reference points are the X2 and S1 interfaces. The eNodeBs are interconnected with each other via the X2 interface and toward the EPC via the S1 interface.
- Either the S1-c or the S1-MME interface is the reference point for the control plane between E-UTRAN and MME. The S1-MME interface is based on the S1 Application Protocol (S1AP) and is transported over the Stream Control Transmission Protocol (SCTP). The EPC architecture supports MME pooling to enable geographic redundancy, capacity increase, and load sharing. This requires the eNodeB to connect to multiple MMEs. The L3 MPLS VPN service model defined by seamless MPLS allows eNodeBs in the RAN access to be connected

to multiple MMEs that may be distributed across regions of the core network for geographic redundancy.

- The S1-u interface is the reference point between E-UTRAN and SGW for the per-bearer user plane tunneling and inter-eNodeB path switching during handover. The application protocol used on this interface is GTPv1-U, transported over User Datagram Protocol (UDP). SGW locations affect u-plane latency, and the best practice for LTE is to place S/PGWs in regions closer to the aggregation networks that they serve so that the latency budget of the eNodeBs to which they connect is not compromised. The EPC architecture supports SGW pooling to enable load balancing, resiliency, and signaling optimization by reducing the handovers. This requires the eNodeB to connect to multiple SGWs. The L3 MPLS VPN service model allows eNodeBs in the RAN access to be connected to multiple SGWs, which include ones in the core close to the local aggregation network and SGWs that are part of the pool serving neighboring core PoPs.

- The X2 interface composed of the X1-c and X2-u reference points for control and bearer plane provides direct connectivity between eNodeBs. It is used to hand over a User Equipment (UE) from a source eNodeB to a target eNodeB during the inter-eNodeB's handover process. For the initial phase of LTE, the traffic passed over this interface is mostly control plane related to signaling during handover. This interface is also used to carry bearer traffic for a short period (<100 ms) between the eNodeBs during handovers. The stringent latency requirements of the X2 interface requires that the mesh connectivity between CSGs introduces a minimum amount of delay; that is, on the order of 30 ms. The L3 MPLS VPN service model provides shortest-path connectivity between eNodeBs so as not to introduce unnecessary latency.

- During initial deployments in regions with low uptake and smaller subscriber scale, MME and SGW/packet data network gateways (PGW) pooling can be used to reuse mobile gateways serving neighboring core PoPs. Gradually, as capacity demands and subscriber scale increase, newer gateways can be added closer to the region. The L3 MPLS VPN service model for LTE backhaul that is defined by the seamless MPLS system allows migrations to newer gateways to take place without any re-provisioning of the service model or re-architecting of the underlying transport network required.

- With the distribution of the new spectrum made available for 3G and 4G services, many new SPs have entered the mobility space. These new entrants would like to monetize the spectrum they have acquired, but lack the national infrastructure coverage owned by the incumbents. LTE E-UTRAN-sharing architecture allows different core network operators to connect to a shared radio access network. The sharing of cell site infrastructure could be based on:

- A shared eNodeB: a shared backhaul model where different operators are presented on different VLANs by the eNodeB to the CSG, *or*
- A different eNodeB: a shared backhaul model where the foreign operator's eNodeB is connected on a different interface to the CSG.

Regardless of the shared model, the seamless MPLS system provides per-mobile SP-based L3 MPLS VPNs that are able to identify, isolate, and provide secure backhaul for different operator traffic over a single converged network.

The system proposes a simple and efficient L3 service model that addresses the LTE backhaul requirements addressed above. The L3 service model is built over a seamless MPLS transport with a common highly scaled MPLS VPN that covers LTE S1 interfaces from all CSGs across the network and an LTE X2 interface per RAN access region, as seen in Figure 4.19. The single MPLS VPN per operator is built across the network, with VRFs on the MTGs connecting the EPC gateways (SGW, MME) in the MPC, down to the RAN access with VRFs on the CSGs connecting the eNodeBs. Prefix filtering across the VPN is done using simple MP-BGP route target (RT) import and export statements on the CSGs and MTGs.

A unique RT denoted as Common RT is assigned to the LTE backhaul MPLS VPN. It is either imported or exported at various

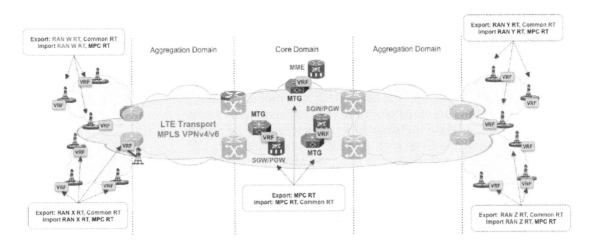

Figure 4.19

locations or at the VPN, depending on the role of the node implementing the VRF.

A unique RT denoted as MPC RT is assigned to the MTGs in the MPC.

Each RAN access region in the network is assigned a unique RT. These RTs are denoted as RAN X, RAN Y, and RAN Z RTs.

In every RAN access region, all CSGs import the MPC RT and the RAN x RT. The CSGs export the Common RT and the RAN x RT. Here, x denotes the unique RT assigned to that particular RAN access region. With this importing and exporting of RTs, the route scale in the VRF of the CSGs is kept to a minimum, since VPNv4 prefixes corresponding to CSGs in other RAN access regions—either in the local aggregation domain or RAN access regions in remote aggregation domains across the core—are not learned. The CSGs have reachability to every MTG and to the corresponding EPC gateways (SGW, MME) that they connect to anywhere in the MPC. They also have the shortest path mesh connectivity among themselves for the X2 interface.

In the MPC, the MTGs import the MPC RT and the Common RT. They export only the MPC RT. With this importing and exporting of RTs, the MTGs have connectivity to all other gateways in the MPC, as well as having connectivity to the CSGs in the RAN access regions across the entire network. The MTGs are capable of handling large scale and learn all of the VPNv4 prefixes in the LTE VPN. The rapid adoption of LTE and the massive increase in subscriber growth is leading to an exponential increase in cell sites being deployed in the network. This is introducing a crunch in the number of IP addresses that need to be assigned to the eNodeBs at the cell sites. For mobile SPs that are running out of public IPv4 addresses, or those that cannot obtain additional public IPv4 addresses from the registries for eNodeB assignment, the seamless MPLS system enables carrying IPv6 traffic over an IPv4 seamless MPLS transport infrastructure using 6VPE, as defined in RFC 4659. The eNodeBs and EPC gateways can be IPv6-only or can be dual-stack enabled to support IPv6 for S1 and X2 interfaces, while using IPv4 for network management functions, if desired. The dual-stack-enabled eNodeBs and EPC gateways connect to CSGs and MTGs configured with a dual-stack VRF carrying VPNv4 and VPNv6 routes for the LTE MPLS VPN service. The IPv6 reachability between the eNodeBs in the cell site and the EPC gateways in the MPC is exchanged between the CSGs and MTGs acting as MPLS VPN PEs using the BGP address family [AFI = 2, SAFI = 128]. See Figure 4.20.

In some cases, depending on the spread of the macro cell footprint, it might be desirable to provide X2 interfaces between CSGs

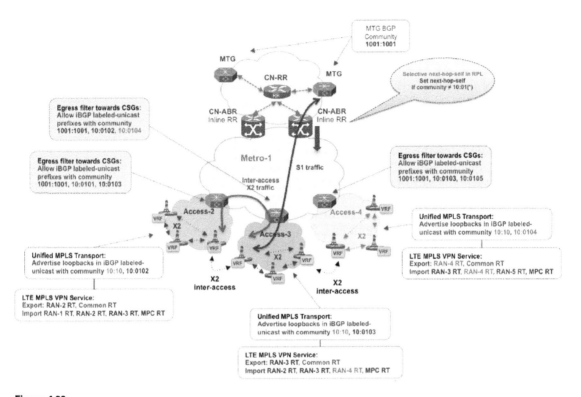

Figure 4.20

located in neighboring RAN access regions. This connectivity can easily be accomplished using the BGP community-based coloring of prefixes used in the seamless MPLS transport.

- As described in the section titled "Transport Architecture," the CSG loopbacks are colored in BGP labeled-unicast with a common BGP community that represents the RAN community and a BGP community that is unique to that RAN access region. This tagging can be done when the CSGs advertise their loopbacks in iBGP labeled-unicast if labeled BGP is extended to the access, or at the PANs when redistributing from the RAN IGP to iBGP when IGP/LDP is used in the RAN access using the redistribution approach.

- The adjacent RAN access domain CSG loopbacks can be identified at the PAN based on the unique RAN access region BGP community and can be selectively propagated into the access based on egress filtering—if labeled BGP is extended to the access—or be selectively redistributed into the RAN IGP if IGP/LDP is used in the RAN access using the redistribution approach.

It is important to note that X2 interfaces are based on eNB proximity, and therefore a given RAN access domain only requires connectivity to the ones immediately adjacent. This filtering approach allows for hierarchical-labeled BGP LSPs to be set up across neighboring access regions while preserving the low route scale in the access. At the service level, any CSG in a RAN access domain that needs to establish inter-access X2 connectivity will import its neighboring CSG access region RT in addition to its own RT, in the LTE MPLS VPN in Figure 4.20. The CN-ABR inline-RR applies selective NHS function using route policy in the egress direction toward its local PAN neighbor group in order to provide shortest-path connectivity for the X2 interface between CSGs across neighboring RAN access regions. The configuration logic involves changing the next-hop toward the PANs for only those prefixes that do not match the local RAN access regions based on a simple regular expression matching BGP communities. This allows for the CN-ABR to change the BGP next-hop and to insert itself in the data path for all prefixes that originate in the core corresponding to the S1 interface, while keeping the next-hop set by the PANs unchanged for all prefixes from local RAN regions. With this configuration, the inter-access X2 traffic flows across adjacent access regions along the shortest path interconnecting the two PANs without having to loop through the inline-RR CN-ABR node.

LVPN MPLS Service Model for 2G and 3G

The seamless MPLS system architecture allows MSPs with TDM-based 2G GSM and ATM-based 3G UMTS infrastructures to remove, reduce, or cap investments in SONET/SDH and ATM transport infrastructure through the use of MPLS-based CEoP services.

For the MSPs that want to reduce SONET/SDH infrastructure used for GSM, seamless MPLS enables PWE3-based transport of emulated TDM circuits. Structured circuit emulation is achieved with CESoPSN, and unstructured emulation is achieved with SAToP. E1/T1 circuits from BTS equipment connected to the CSG or to the PAN are transported to MTG, where they are bundled into channelized STM1/OC-3 interfaces for handoff to the BSC. Synchronization is derived from the BSC via TDM links, or from a primary reference clock (PRC), and transported across the core, aggregation, and access domains via SyncE, or via 1588 across domains where SyncE is not supported.

For the MSPs that want to reduce their ATM infrastructure used for ATM-based UMTS, seamless MPLS enables PWE3-based transport of ATM VC (AAL0 or AAL5) or VP (AAL0) circuits. ATM E1/T1 or IMA interfaces from NodeB equipment connected to the CSG or PAN are transported to the MTG, where they are bundled into STM1 ATM interfaces for handoff to the RNC. Cell packing may be used to optimize the bandwidth used for this transport. Synchronization is derived from the RNC via ATM links, or from a PRC, and transported across the core, aggregation, and access domains via SyncE, or via 1588 across domains where SyncE is not supported.

Typical GSM (2G) deployments will consist of cell sites that don't require a full E1/T1 for support. In such cell sites, a fractional E1/T1 is used. The operator can deploy these cell sites in a daisy chain fashion (i.e., down a highway) or aggregate them at the BSC location. To save in the CAPEX investment on the number of channelized STM-1/OC-3 ports required on the BSC, the operator can utilize a digital XConnect to merge multiple fractional E1/T1 links into a full E1/T1. This reduces the number of T1/E1s needed on the BSC, which results in fewer channelized STM-1/OC-3 ports being needed. Deploying CESoPSN PWs from the CSG to the RAN distribution node supports these fractional T1/E1s and the aggregation of them at the BSC site. In this type of deployment, the default behavior of CESoPSN for alarm sync needs to be changed. Typically, if a T1/E1 on the access nodes goes down, the PWs will forward the AIS alarm through the PW to the distribution node and then propagate the alarm indication signal (AIS) alarm to the BSC by taking the T1/E1 down. In this multiplexed scenario, TS alarming must be enabled on a CESoPSN PW to propagate only the AIS alarm on the affected time slots, thereby not affecting the other time slots (e.g., cell sites) on the same T1/E1.

The same BGP-based control plane and label distribution implemented for the L3VPN services is also used for circuit emulation services. For hub-and-spoke access topologies, BFD-protected static routes can be used to eliminate the need for an IGP at the cell site. The CSGs utilize MPLS/IP routing in this system release when deployed in a physical ring topology. TDM and ATM PWE3 can be overlaid in either deployment model.

The CSGs, PAN, aggregation nodes, and MTGs enforce the contracted ATM CoS SLA and mark the ATM and TDM PWE3 traffic with the corresponding PHB inside the access, aggregation, and core DiffServ domains. The MTG enables multi-router automatic protection switching (MR-APS) or single-router automatic protection switching (SR-APS) redundancy for the BSC or RNC interface, as well as pseudowire redundancy and two-way pseudowire redundancy for transport protection.

Fixed Mobile Convergence Use Case

This section describes how a wireline L2VPN service can be enabled in the access network to facilitate fixed-mobile converged deployments. This scenario assumes that the cell site is located in an urban area with fiber access from a business to a CSG. A CSG is used as a T-PE in this example, but the model is applicable to any MPLS-enabled access node subtending from the pre-aggregation.

Figure 4.21 shows a wireline VPWS such as an Ethernet Private Line (EPL) or an Ethernet Virtual Private Line (EVPL) business service, enabled using an EoMPLS pseudowire between two CSGs in the RAN access across the core network. The CSGs that enable the VPWS learn each others' loopbacks via BGP labeled-unicast, which is extended to the access network using the PANs as inline RR, as described in the section titled "BGP Core, Aggregation, and Access." As detailed in the section titled "Transport Architecture," the route scale in the RAN access is kept to a minimum by egress filtering on the PAN inline-RRs. The CSGs that enable mobile services advertise their loopbacks in iBGP labeled-unicast with a unique local RAN community and a common RAN community. The PANs acting as inline-RRs only reflect prefixes marked with the local RAN community (corresponding to local CSG loopbacks) and the MTG community (corresponding to MTG loopbacks) toward the RAN access. In this case, since we are enabling a new service, we need to use an additional BGP community.

The CSGs that also enable wireline services tag their loopbacks in iBGP labeled-unicast with a common wireline community in

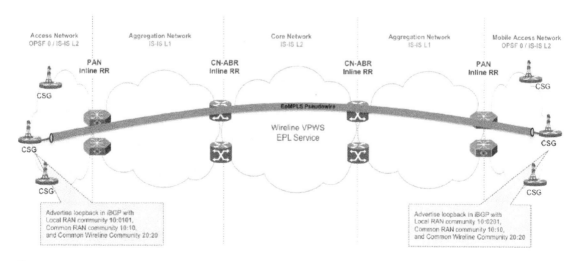

Figure 4.21

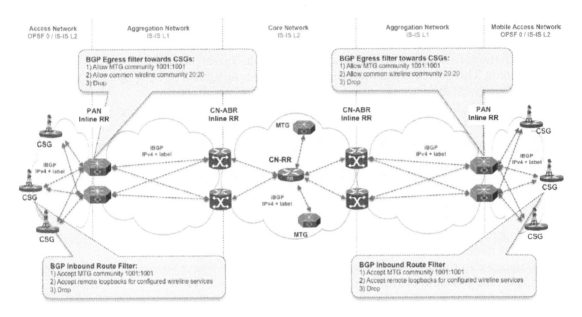

Figure 4.22

addition to the local RAN and common RAN community. Note that this common wireline community is only used on CSGs where wireline services are enabled. Figure 4.22 explains the filtering mechanism used to maintain the low route scale in the RAN while enabling this fixed-mobile deployment.

When reflecting labeled BGP routes toward their CSG clients, the PAN inline-RRs follow the logic of:

1. Allowing the MTG community.
2. Allowing the common wireline community.
3. Dropping all other prefixes.

The first rule enables the LTE S1 between the CSGs and the MPC. Reachability for VPN next-hops for LTE X2 interface between CSGs is available through LDP LSPs, since the CSGs are in same RAN IGP/LDP domain. The second rule enables wireline services to the access. All other prefixes are dropped to ensure that only required prefix updates are sent to the RAN access. This filtering logic is a one-time configuration that is performed on the PANs. The CSGs, on the other hand, perform inbound filtering on a per-PAN RR neighbor basis using a route map that:

1. Accepts the MTG community.
2. Accepts loopbacks of the remote destination to which wireline service(s) are configured on the device.
3. Drops all other prefixes.

When a wireline service is activated to a new destination, the route-map used for inbound filtering has to be updated. Since adding a new wireline service on the device results in a change in the routing policy of a BGP neighbor, the dynamic inbound soft reset function is used to initiate a non-disruptive dynamic exchange of route refresh requests between the CSG and the PAN. Note that both BGP peers must support the "route refresh" capability to use the dynamic inbound soft reset capability.

Inter-Domain Hierarchical LSPs

The seamless MPLS system uses hierarchical LSPs for inter-domain transport. The hierarchical LSP is based on a BGP-distributed label that is used to transit the isolated MPLS domains, and an LDP-distributed label that is used intra-domain to reach the labeled BGP next-hop. This section describes the different hierarchical LSPs that apply to various transport architecture options along with their corresponding service models.

Inter-Domain LSPs for Multi-Area IGP Design

This section describes inter-domain hierarchical LSPs that apply to large network, single-AS multi-area IGP designs, where the core and aggregation networks are part of the same autonomous system, but are segmented into isolated IGP areas.

Hierarchical LSPs for Remote PANs for Multi-Area IGP Design

This scenario applies to inter-domain LSPs between the loopback addresses of remote PANs connected across the core network. It is relevant to wireline L2/L3 MPLS VPN business services deployed between remote PANs across the core network that use the /32 loopback address of the remote PEs as the endpoint identifier for the t-LDP or MP-iBGP sessions. In Figure 4.23, the PANs are labeled BGP PEs and advertise their loopback using labeled IPv4 unicast address family (AFI/SAFI = 1/4).

The remote PANs learn each other's loopbacks through BGP-labeled unicast. For traffic flowing between the two PANs, the following sequence occurs:

1. The downstream PAN pushes the BGP label corresponding to the remote prefix, then pushes the LDP label that is used to reach the local core ABR (CN-ABR) that is the labeled BGP next-hop.

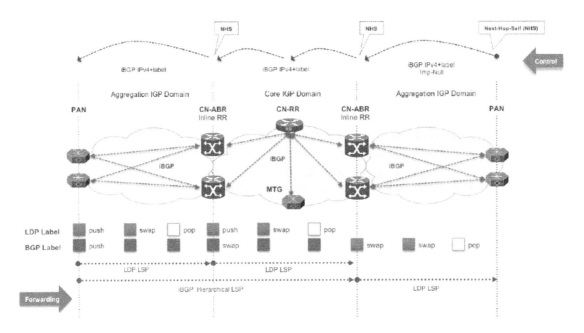

Figure 4.23

2. The aggregation nodes that transit the inter-domain LSP will swap the intra-domain LDP-based LSP label and perform a penultimate hop popping (PHP) before handing to the local CN-ABR.
3. The local CN-ABR will swap the BGP-based inter-domain LSP label and push the LDP label used to reach the remote CN-ABR that is the labeled BGP next-hop.
4. The core nodes that transit the inter-domain LSP will swap the intra-domain LDP-based LSP label and perform a PHP before handing off to the remote CN-ABR.
5. Since the remote CN-ABR has reachability to the destination PAN via IGP, it will swap the BGP label with an LDP label corresponding to the upstream PAN intra-domain LDP LSP.

Hierarchical LSPs between CSG and MTG for Multi-Area IGP Design with Labeled BGP Access

The inter-domain hierarchical LSP described here applies to the Option-1: Multi-Area IGP Design with Labeled BGP Access transport model described in the section titled "Large Network, Multi-Area IGP Design with IP/MPLS Access." This scenario applies to inter-domain LSPs between the loopback addresses

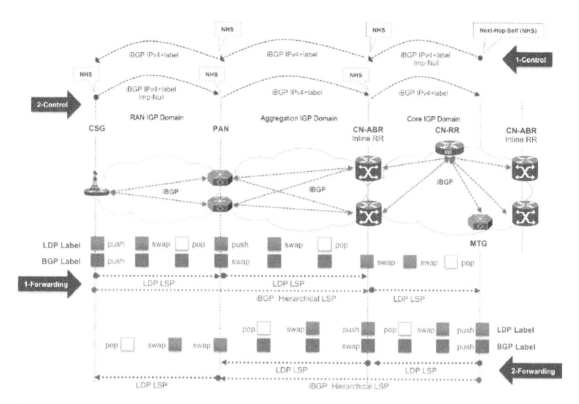

Figure 4.24

of CSGs in the RAN and the MTGs in the core network. It is relevant to 4G LTE and 3G UMTS/IP services deployed using MPLS L3 VPNs, or 2G GSM and 3G UMTS/ATM services deployed using MPLS L2 VPNs, that use the /32 loopback address of the remote PEs as the endpoint identifier for the t-LDP or the MP-iBGP sessions. The MTGs and CSGs are labeled BGP PEs and advertise their loopback using labeled IPv4 unicast address family (AFI/SAFI = 1/4), as seen in Figure 4.24.

The CSG in the RAN access learns the loopback address of the MTG through BGP-labeled unicast. For traffic flowing between the CSG in the RAN and the MTG in the MPC, the following sequence occurs:

1. The downstream CSG node will first push the BGP label corresponding to the remote prefix, then push the LDP label that is used to reach the PAN that is the labeled BGP next-hop.
2. The CSGs that transit the inter-domain LSP will swap the intra-domain LDP-based LSP label and perform a PHP before handing to the PAN.

3. The PAN will swap the BGP label corresponding to the remote prefix, then push the LDP label used to reach the CN-ABR that is the labeled BGP next-hop.
4. The aggregation nodes that transit the inter-domain LSP will swap the intra-domain LDP-based LSP label and perform a PHP before handing off to the local CN-ABR.
5. Since the local CN-ABR has reachability to the MTG via the core IGP, it will swap the BGP label with an LDP label corresponding to the upstream MTG intra-domain core LDP LSP.

The MTG in the MPC learns the loopback address of the remote RAN CSG through BGP-labeled unicast. For traffic flowing between the MTG and the CSG in the RAN, the following sequence occurs:

1. The downstream MTG node will first push the BGP label corresponding to the remote prefix, then push the LDP label that is used to reach the CN-ABR that is the labeled BGP next-hop.
2. The core nodes that transit the inter-domain LSP will swap the intra-domain LDP-based LSP label and perform a PHP before handing to the CN-ABR.
3. The CN-ABR will swap the BGP label corresponding to the remote prefix, then push the LDP label used to reach the PAN that is the labeled BGP next-hop.
4. The aggregation nodes that transit the inter-domain LSP will swap the intra-domain LDP-based LSP label and perform a PHP before handing off to the PAN.
5. Since the PAN has reachability to the CSG via the RAN IGP process, it will swap the BGP label with an LDP label corresponding to the upstream CSG intra-domain RAN LDP LSP

Hierarchical LSPs between CSG and MTG for Multi-Area IGP Design with IGP/LDP Access

The inter-domain hierarchical LSP described here applies to the Option-2: Multi-Area IGP Design with IGP/LDP Access transport model described in the section titled "Large Network, Multi-Area IGP Design with IP/MPLS Access." This scenario applies to inter-domain LSPs between the loopback addresses of CSGs in the RAN and the MTGs in the core network. It is relevant to 4G LTE and 3G UMTS/IP services deployed using MPLS L3 VPNs, or 2G GSM and 3G UMTS/ATM services deployed using MPLS L2 VPNs, that use the /32 loopback address of the remote PEs as the endpoint identifier for the t-LDP or the MP-iBGP sessions. The MTGs are labeled BGP PEs and advertise their loopback using labeled IPv4 unicast address family (AFI/SAFI = 1/4).

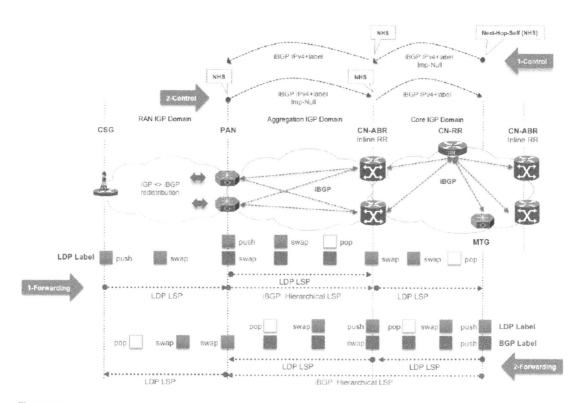

Figure 4.25

The CSGs do not run labeled BGP, but have connectivity to the MPC via the redistribution between RAN IGP and BGP-labeled unicast done at the local PANs, which are the labeled BGP PEs, as seen in Figure 4.25.

The CSG in the RAN access learns the loopback address of the MTG through the BGP-labeled unicast to RAN IGP redistribution done at the PAN. For traffic flowing between the CSG in the RAN and the MTG in the MPC, the following sequence occurs:

1. The downstream CSG will push the LDP label used to reach the PAN that redistributed the labeled BGP prefix into the RAN IGP.
2. The CSGs that transit the inter-domain LSP will swap the intra-domain LDP-based LSP label toward the PAN.
3. The PAN will first swap the LDP label with the BGP label corresponding to the remote prefix, then push the LDP label used to reach the local CN-ABR that is the labeled BGP next-hop.
4. The aggregation nodes that transit the inter-domain LSP will swap the intra-domain LDP-based LSP label and perform a PHP before handing off to the local CN-ABR.

5. Since the local CN-ABR has reachability to the MTG via the core IGP, it will swap the BGP label with an LDP label corresponding to the upstream MTG intra-domain core LDP LSP.

The MTG in the MPC learns the loopback address of the remote RAN CSG through BGP-labeled unicast. For traffic flowing between the MTG and the CSG in the RAN, the following sequence occurs:

1. The downstream MTG node will first push the BGP label corresponding to the remote prefix, then push the LDP label that is used to reach the CN-ABR that is the labeled BGP next-hop.
2. The core nodes that transit the inter-domain LSP will swap the intra-domain LDP-based LSP label and perform a PHP before handing to the CN-ABR.
3. The CN-ABR will swap the BGP label corresponding to the remote prefix, then push the LDP label used to reach the PAN that is the labeled BGP next-hop.
4. The aggregation nodes that transit the inter-domain LSP will swap the intra-domain LDP-based LSP label and perform a PHP before handing off to the PAN connecting the RAN.
5. The PAN will swap the locally-assigned BGP label and forward to the upstream CSG using the local RAN intra-domain LDP-based LSP label.

Inter-Domain LSPs for Inter-AS Design

This section describes inter-domain hierarchical LSPs that apply to inter-AS designs where the core and aggregation networks are segmented into separate autonomous systems.

Hierarchical LSPs between Remote PANs for Inter-AS Design

This scenario applies to inter-domain LSPs between the loopback addresses of remote PANs connected across the core network. It is relevant to wireline L2/L3 MPLS VPN business services, deployed between remote PANs across the core network, that use the /32 loopback address of the remote PEs as the endpoint identifier for the t-LDP or MP-iBGP sessions. The PANs are labeled BGP PEs and advertise their loopback using labeled IPv4 unicast address family (AFI/SAFI=1/4), as seen in Figure 4.26.

The remote PANs learn each other's loopbacks through BGP-labeled unicast. The iBGP-labeled unicast is used to build the inter-domain hierarchical LSP inside each autonomous system, and eBGP-labeled unicast is used to extend the LSP across the

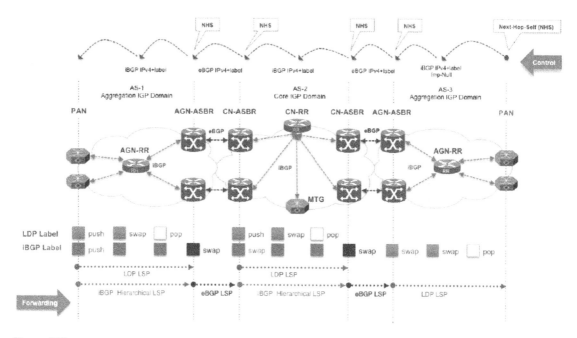

Figure 4.26

AS boundary. For traffic flowing between the two PANs, the following sequence occurs:

1. The downstream PAN pushes the iBGP label corresponding to the remote prefix, then pushes the LDP label that is used to reach the local AGN-ASBR that is the labeled BGP next-hop.

2. The aggregation nodes that transit the inter-domain LSP will swap the intra-domain LDP-based LSP label and perform a PHP before handing to the local AGN-ASBR.

3. The local AGN-ASBR will swap the iBGP-based inter-domain LSP label with the eBGP label assigned by the neighboring CN-ASBR.

4. The CN-ASBR will swap the eBGP label with the iBGP inter-domain LSP label, then push the LDP label that i used to reach the remote CN-ASBR that is the labeled BGP next-hop.

5. The core nodes that transit the inter-domain LSP will swap the intra-domain LDP-based LSP label and perform a PHP before handing off to the remote CN-ASBR.

6. The remote CN-ASBR will swap the iBGP-based inter-domain LSP label with the eBGP label assigned by the neighboring aggregation domain AGN-ASBR.

7. Since the remote AGN-ASBR has reachability to the destination PAN via IGP, it will swap the eBGP label with an LDP label corresponding to the upstream PAN intra-domain LDP LSP.

Hierarchical LSPs between CSG and MTG for Inter-AS Design with Labeled BGP Access

The inter-domain hierarchical LSP described here applies to the Option-1: Inter-AS Design with Labeled BGP Access transport model described in the section titled "Large Network, Inter-AS Design with IP/MPLS Access." This scenario applies to inter-domain LSPs between the loopback addresses of CSGs in the RAN and the MTGs in the core network. It is relevant to 4G LTE and 3G UMTS/IP services deployed using MPLS L3 VPNs, or 2G GSM and 3G UMTS/ATM services deployed using MPLS L2 VPNs, that use the /32 loopback address of the remote PEs as the end-point identifier for the t-LDP or the MP-iBGP sessions. The MTGs and CSGs are labeled BGP PEs and advertise their loopback using labeled IPv4 unicast address family (AFI/SAFI=1/4), as seen in Figure 4.27.

The CSG in the RAN access learns the loopback address of the MTG through BGP-labeled unicast. For traffic flowing between the

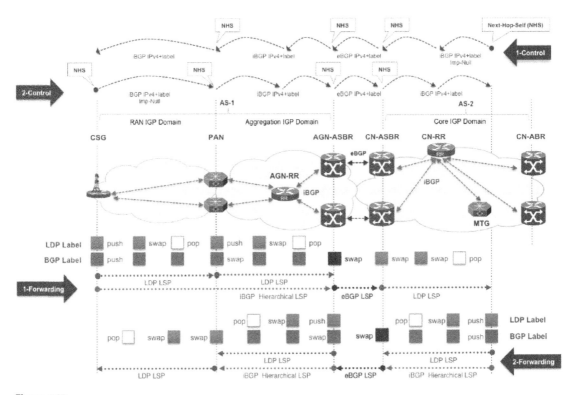

Figure 4.27

CSG in the RAN and the MTG in the MPC, the following sequence occurs:

1. The downstream CSG node will first push the BGP label corresponding to the remote prefix, then push the LDP label that is used to reach the PAN that is the labeled BGP next-hop.
2. The CSGs that transit the inter-domain LSP will swap the intra-domain LDP-based LSP label and perform a PHP before handing to the PAN.
3. The PAN will swap the BGP label corresponding to the remote prefix, then push the LDP label used to reach the AGN-ASBR that is the labeled BGP next-hop.
4. The aggregation nodes that transit the inter-domain LSP will swap the intra-domain LDP-based LSP label and perform a PHP before handing off to the local AGN-ASBR.
5. The local AGN-ASBR will swap the iBGP-based inter-domain LSP label with the eBGP label assigned by the neighboring CN-ASBR.
6. Since the CN-ASBR has reachability to the MTG via the core IGP, it will swap the eBGP label with an LDP label corresponding to the upstream MTG intra-domain core LDP LSP.

The MTG in the MPC learns the loopback address of the remote RAN CSG through BGP-labeled unicast. For traffic flowing between the MTG and the CSG in the RAN, the following sequence occurs:

1. The downstream MTG node will first push the iBGP label corresponding to the remote prefix, then push the LDP label that is used to reach the CN-ASBR that is the labeled BGP next-hop.
2. The core nodes that transit the inter-domain LSP will swap the intra-domain LDP-based LSP label and perform a PHP before handing to the CN-ASBR.
3. The CN-ASBR will swap the iBGP-based inter-domain LSP label with the eBGP label assigned by the neighboring aggregation domain AGN-ASBR.
4. The AGN-ASBR will swap the eBGP label with the iBGP inter-domain LSP label corresponding to the remote prefix, then push the LDP label that is used to reach the PAN that is the labeled BGP next-hop.
5. The aggregation nodes that transit the inter-domain LSP will swap the intra-domain LDP-based LSP label and perform a PHP before handing off to the PAN.
6. Since the PAN has reachability to the CSG via the RAN IGP area/level, it will swap the BGP label with an LDP label corresponding to the upstream CSG intra-domain RAN LDP LSP.

Hierarchical LSPs between CSG and MTG for Inter-AS Design with IGP/LDP Access

The inter-domain hierarchical LSP described here applies to the Option-2: Inter-AS Design with IGP/LDP Access transport model described in the section titled "Large Network, Inter-AS Design with IP/MPLS Access." This scenario applies to inter-domain LSPs between the loopback addresses of CSGs in the RAN and the MTGs in the core network. It is relevant to 4G LTE and 3G UMTS/IP services deployed using MPLS L3 VPNs, or 2G GSM and 3G UMTS/ATM services deployed using MPLS L2 VPNs, that use the /32 loopback address of the remote PEs as the end-point identifier for the t-LDP or the MP-iBGP sessions. The MTGs are labeled BGP PEs and advertise their loopback using labeled IPv4 unicast address family (AFI/SAFI = 1/4). The CSGs do not run labeled BGP, but have connectivity to the MPC via the redistribution between RAN IGP and BGP-labeled unicast done at the local PANs, which are the labeled BGP PEs, as seen in Figure 4.28.

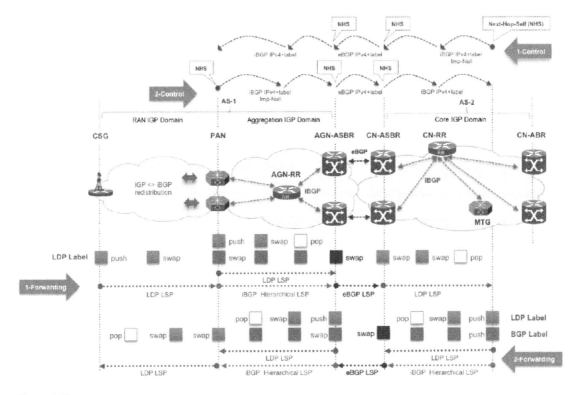

Figure 4.28

The CSG in the RAN access learns the loopback address of the MTG through the BGP-labeled unicast to RAN IGP redistribution done at the local PAN. For traffic flowing between the CSG in the RAN and the MTG in the MPC, the following sequence occurs:

1. The downstream CSG will push the LDP label used to reach the PAN that redistributed the labeled iBGP prefix into the RAN IGP.
2. The CSGs that transit the inter-domain LSP will swap the intra-domain LDP-based LSP label toward the PAN.
3. The PAN will first swap the LDP label with the iBGP label corresponding to the remote prefix, then push the LDP label used to reach the AGN-ASBR that is the labeled BGP next-hop.
4. The aggregation nodes that transit the inter-domain LSP will swap the intra-domain LDP-based LSP label and perform a PHP before handing off to the local AGN-ASBR.
5. The local AGN-ASBR will swap the iBGP-based inter-domain LSP label with the eBGP label assigned by the neighboring CN-ASBR.
6. Since the CN-ASBR has reachability to the MTG via the core IGP, it will swap the eBGP label with an LDP label corresponding to the upstream MTG intra-domain core LDP LSP.

The MTG in the MPC learns the loopback address of the remote RAN CSG through BGP-labeled unicast. For traffic flowing between the MTG and the CSG in the RAN, the following sequence occurs:

1. The downstream MTG node will first push the iBGP label corresponding to the remote prefix, then push the LDP label that is used to reach the CN-ASBR that is the labeled BGP next-hop.
2. The core nodes that transit the inter-domain LSP will swap the intra-domain LDP-based LSP label and perform a PHP before handing to the CN-ASBR.
3. The CN-ASBR will swap the iBGP-based inter-domain LSP label with the eBGP label assigned by the neighboring aggregation domain AGN-ASBR.
4. The AGN-ASBR will swap the eBGP label with the iBGP inter-domain LSP label corresponding to the remote prefix, then push the LDP label that is used to reach the PAN that is the labeled BGP next-hop.
5. The aggregation nodes that transit the inter-domain LSP will swap the intra-domain LDP-based LSP label and perform a PHP before handing off to the PAN connecting the RAN.
6. The PAN will swap the locally-assigned BGP label and forward to the upstream CSG using the local RAN intra-domain LDP-based LSP label.

Inter-Domain LSPs for Integrated Core and Aggregation Design

This section describes inter-domain hierarchical LSPs that apply to small network, integrated core, and aggregation designs where core and aggregation networks are integrated into a single IGP/LDP domain. The aggregation nodes have subtending mobile RAN access networks that are MPLS-enabled and part of the same AS.

Hierarchical LSPs between CSG and MTG for Integrated Core and Aggregation Design

This scenario applies to inter-domain LSPs between the loopback addresses of CSGs in the RAN and the MTGs in the integrated core and the aggregation network. It is relevant to 4G LTE and 3G UMTS/IP services deployed using MPLS L3 VPNs, or 2G GSM and 3G UMTS/ATM services deployed using MPLS L2 VPNs, that use the /32 loopback address of the remote PEs as the endpoint identifier for the t-LDP or MP-iBGP sessions. The MTGs and CSGs are labeled BGP PEs and advertise their loopback using labeled IPv4 unicast address family (AFI/SAFI = 1/4), as seen in Figure 4.29.

The CSG in the RAN access learns the loopback address of the MTG through BGP-labeled unicast. For traffic flowing between the CSG in the RAN and the MTG in the MPC, the following sequence occurs:

1. The downstream CSG node will first push the BGP label corresponding to the remote prefix, then push the LDP label that is used to reach the AGN that is the labeled BGP next-hop.
2. The CSGs that transit the inter-domain LSP will swap the intra-domain LDP-based LSP label and perform a PHP before handing to the AGN.
3. Since the AGN has reachability to the MTG via the aggregation IGP, it will swap the BGP label with an LDP label corresponding to the upstream MTG intra-domain aggregation LDP LSP.

The MTG in the MPC learns the loopback address of the remote RAN CSG through BGP-labeled unicast. For traffic flowing between the MTG and the CSG in the RAN, the following sequence occurs:

1. The downstream MTG node will first push the BGP label corresponding to the remote prefix, then push the LDP label that is used to reach the AGN that is the labeled BGP next-hop.
2. The CN and AGN nodes that transit the inter-domain LSP will swap the intra-domain LDP-based LSP label and perform a PHP before handing to the AGN connecting the RAN Access.

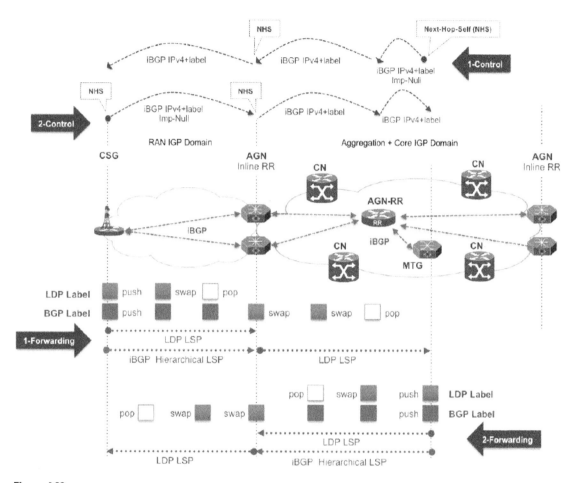

Figure 4.29

3. Since the AGN has reachability to the CSG via the RAN IGP area-x/level-1, it will swap the BGP label with an LDP label corresponding to the upstream CSG intra-domain RAN LDP LSP.

Transport and Service Control Plane

The seamless MPLS system proposes a hierarchical RR design for setting up the seamless MPLS transport and the LTE MPLS VPN service BGP control plane. The hierarchical RR approach is used to reduce the number of iBGP peering sessions on the RRs across different domains of the backhaul network. The following sections describe the BGP control plane aspects for network designs based on multi-area IGP and inter-AS organizations.

BGP Control Plane for Multi-Area IGP Design

This section details the hierarchical RR design to enable the BGP control plane for the seamless MPLS transport and the LTE MPLS VPN service in a single AS, multi-area IGP-based network. The need for standalone RRs in the lower layers of the network to support this hierarchy are eliminated by making use of the inline-RR functionality on the PANs and CN-ABRs, as seen in Figure 4.30. At the top level of the hierarchy, the CN-ABRs can either peer in a full mesh configuration across the core, or peer as RR clients to a centralized external CN-RR. In deployments with only a few PoPs, a full-mesh configuration between the CN-ABRs would suffice. In larger deployments, an external CN-RR to support the top level of the hierarchy helps simplify provisioning, as well as prefix filtering, across various PoPs.

BGP Control Plane for Seamless MPLS Transport

For the seamless MPLS transport layer, the PANs are inline-RRs to the CSG clients for the MP-iBGP IPv4-labeled-unicast address family:

They form iBGP session neighbor groups with the CSG RR-clients that are the labeled BGP PEs implementing the inter-domain iBGP hierarchical LSPs in the local RAN access network

They also form iBGP session neighbor groups toward the local CN-ABR inline RRs.

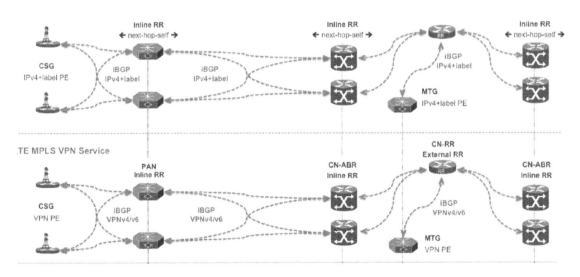

Figure 4.30

The PANs reflect the labeled BGP prefixes with the next-hop changed to "self" in order to insert themselves into the data path to enable the inter-domain LSP across the access and aggregation domains.

The CN-ABRs are inline-RRs to the PAN clients for the MP-iBGP IPv4-labeled unicast address family and form the next level of the RR hierarchy:

They form iBGP session neighbor groups with the PAN RR-clients that are the labeled BGP PEs implementing the inter-domain iBGP hierarchical LSPs in the local aggregation network. They either form neighbor groups toward other non-client ABRs in the core if a full-mesh configuration is used, or form neighbor groups toward higher level CN-RRs in the core network at the top level of the hierarchy.

If the full mesh option is used, the CN-ABRs also act as RRs serving the closest MTG RR clients in the core network that are labeled BGP PEs implementing the inter-domain iBGP hierarchical LSPs.

The CN-ABRs reflect the labeled BGP prefixes with the next-hop changed to "self" in order to insert themselves into the data path to enable the inter-domain LSP across the aggregation and core domains.

BGP Control Plane for LTE MPLS VPN Service

For the LTE MPLS VPN service, the PANs are inline-RRs to the CSG clients for the MP-iBGP VPNv4 and the VPNv6 address family:

They form iBGP session neighbor groups toward the local RAN access network to serve the CSG RR-clients that are the PEs implementing the LTE MPLS VPN.

They also form iBGP session neighbor groups toward the local CN-ABR inline RRs. The CN-ABRs are inline RRs for the MP-iBGP VPNv4 and the VPNv6 address family and form the next level of the RR hierarchy:

They form iBGP session neighbor groups toward the local aggregation network to serve the PAN RR clients.

They either form neighbor groups toward other non-client CN-ABRs in the core if a full-mesh configuration is used, or form neighbor groups toward higher level CN-RRs in the core network at the top level of the hierarchy.

If the full-mesh option is used, the core ABR RRs also form neighbor groups for the closest MTG RR clients in the core network that are the PEs implementing the LTE MPLS VPN. See Figure 4.31.

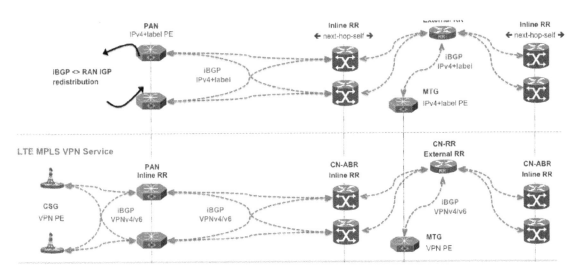

Figure 4.31

BGP Control Plane for Inter-AS Design

This section details the hierarchical RR design to enable the BGP control plane for the seamless MPLS transport and LTE MPLS VPN service in a network where the core and aggregation networks are organized as separate autonomous systems. The hierarchical RR approach is used to reduce the number of iBGP peering sessions on the RRs across different domains of the backhaul network. The need for standalone RRs in the access network to support this hierarchy is eliminated by making use of the inline-RR functionality on the PANs. See Figure 4.32.

BGP Control Plane for Seamless MPLS Transport

In the aggregation AS, the PANs are inline-RRs to the CSG clients for the MP-iBGP IPv4-labeled unicast address family:

They form iBGP session neighbor groups with the CSG RR-clients that are the labeled BGP PEs implementing the inter-domain iBGP hierarchical LSPs in the local RAN access network

They also form iBGP session neighbor groups toward the local AGN-RRs.

The PANs insert themselves into the data path to enable inter-domain LSPs by setting NHS on all iBGP updates toward their local AGN-RRs and CSG RR-clients. The AGN-RRs are external

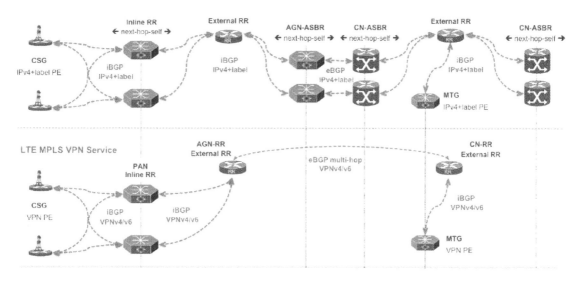

Figure 4.32

RRs for the MP-iBGP IPv4-labeled unicast address family and form the next level of the RR hierarchy:

They form iBGP session neighbor groups toward the AGN-ASBR and PAN RR-clients in the aggregation network.

The AGN-ASBRs insert themselves into the data path to enable inter-domain LSPs by setting NHS on all iBGP updates toward their local AGN-RRs and on all eBGP updates toward neighboring CN-ASBRs. In the core AS, the CN-RRs are external RRs for the MP-iBGP IPv4-labeled unicast address family:

They form iBGP session neighbor groups toward the MTG and CN-ASBR RR-clients in the core network.

The CN-ASBRs insert themselves into the data path to enable inter-domain LSPs by setting NHS on all iBGP updates toward their local CN-RRs and on all eBGP updates toward the neighboring aggregation ASBRs.

BGP Control Plane for LTE MPLS VPN Service

For the LTE MPLS VPN service, the PANs are inline RRs for the MP-iBGP VPNv4 and the VPNv6 address family:

They form iBGP session neighbor groups toward the local RAN access network to serve the CSG RR-clients that are the PEs implementing the LTE MPLS VPN.

They also form iBGP session neighbor groups toward the local aggregation network AGN-RR external RRs.

The AGN-RRs are external RRs for the MP-iBGP VPNv4 and the VPNv6 address family in the aggregation network and form the next level of the RR hierarchy:

They form iBGP session neighbor groups toward the local aggregation network to serve the PAN RR clients.

They enable the LTE VPN service with an eBGP multi-hop session toward the CN-RR in the core network to exchange VPNv4/v6 prefixes over the inter-domain transport LSP. The CN-RRs are external RRs for the MP-iBGP VPNv4 and the VPNv6 address family in the core network:

They form iBGP session neighbor groups in the core network to serve the MTG RR clients that are the PEs implementing the LTE MPLS VPN.

They enable the LTE VPN service with an eBGP multi-hop session toward the AGN-RRs in the neighboring aggregation network autonomous systems to exchange VPNv4/v6 prefixes over the inter-domain transport LSP. See Figure 4.33.

BGP Control Plane for Seamless MPLS Transport

At the top layers of the network, namely the core and aggregation domains, the BGP control plane for seamless MPLS transport is exactly the same as that in the inter-AS design with end-to-end-labeled BGP, as in the case described above. The only difference here is in the access domain of the network. In this case, since we are terminating labeled BGP at the PANs in the aggregation

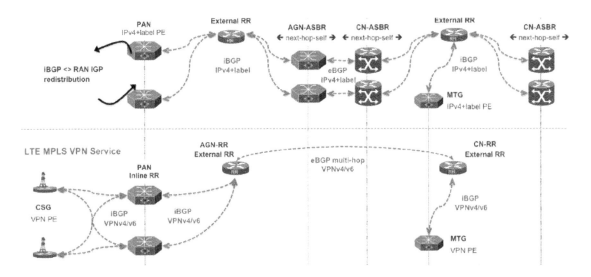

Figure 4.33

domain, the PANs are labeled BGP PEs and do not have to perform the inline-RR function to the CSGs in the RAN access. The end-to-end seamless MPLSLSP is extended into the RAN access using LDP with redistribution.

BGP Control Plane for Integrated Core and Aggregation Design

This section details the hierarchical RR design to enable the BGP control plane for the seamless MPLS transport and LTE MPLS VPN service in a network where the core and aggregation networks are integrated into a single IGP/LDP domain. The need for standalone RRs in the lower layers of the network to support this hierarchy are eliminated by making use of the inline-RR functionality on the AGNs. At the top level of the hierarchy, the AGNs peer as RR clients to a centralized external AGNRR. See Figure 4.34.

BGP Control Plane for Seamless MPLS Transport

For the seamless MPLS transport layer, the AGNs are inline-RRs to the CSG clients for the MP-iBGP IPv4-labeled unicast address family:

They form iBGP session neighbor groups with the CSG RR-clients that are the labeled BGP PEs implementing the inter-domain iBGP hierarchical LSPs in the local RAN access network

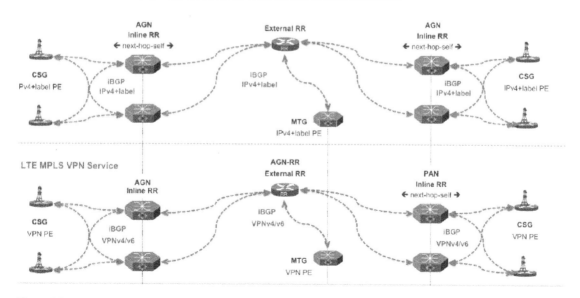

Figure 4.34

They also form iBGP session neighbor groups toward the local AGN-RRs.

The AGNs insert themselves into the data path to enable inter-domain LSPs by setting NHS on all iBGP updates toward their local CSG RR-clients and higher-level AGN-RR.

BGP Control Plane for LTE MPLS VPN Service

For the LTE MPLS VPN service, the AGNs are inline RRs for the MP-iBGP VPNv4 and the VPNv6 address family:

They form iBGP session neighbor groups toward the local RAN access network to serve the CSG RR-clients that are the PEs implementing the LTE MPLS VPN.

They also form iBGP session neighbor groups toward the higher level external AGN-RR in the aggregation network.

Quality of Service

The seamless MPLS system the IETF DiffServ Architecture (RFC 2475) across all network layers, utilizing classification mechanisms like MPLS EXP, IP DSCP, IEEE 802.1p, and ATM CoS for implementing the DiffServ PHBs in use. In a transport network, congestion can occur anywhere. However, congestion is more likely where statistical estimates of peak demand are conservative (i.e., under-provisioned), which happens more often on the design of access and aggregation bandwidth links. Congestion due to instantaneous ingress bandwidth to a node exceeding egress bandwidth (assuming the node can process all ingress bandwidth) therefore requires all nodes to be able to implement DiffServ scheduling functions.

The result is that the under-provisioning is unfairly distributed among the services transported. This redistribution with DiffServ can result in over-provisioning for higher quality services (like VoIP and video) and differing levels of under-provisioning for other services. This is in line with the functional requirements defined by standards bodies, such as the NGMN and Broadband Forum TR-221 specification for mobile backhaul.

Each network layer defines an administrative boundary, where traffic remarking may be required in order to correlate the PHBs between different administrative domains. A critical administrative and trust boundary is required for enforcing subscriber SLAs. Subscriber SLAs are enforced with sound capacity management techniques and functions, such as policing/shaping, marking, and hierarchical scheduling mechanisms. This administrative boundary is implemented by the CSG, NodeB equipment, or radio controllers—depending on the service model—for traffic received (upstream) from the subscribers and by the core nodes for traffic sent (downstream) to the subscribers.

In most administrative domains in the seamless MPLS system, a flat QoS policy with a single-level scheduler and shaper is sufficient for the required DiffServ functionality, as all links are capable of line rate transmission. The exception is in the case of microwave links in the access, where the connection to the equipment on either end of the link is GbE, but the wireless portion of the link is only capable of sub-gigabit speeds (typically 400Mbps sustained). In this case, the PAN interface facing the microwave access implements an H-QoS policy with a parent shaper equal to the sustained microwave link speed required for proper DiffServ functionality. If the microwave systems support DiffServ QoS and are able to synchronize the QoS classes used by the CSGs in the access to provide EF and AF guaranties, then flat QoS policies on the transit CSG NNIs are sufficient. On the other hand, if the microwave systems do not support DiffServ QoS, or are unable to synchronize the QoS classes used by the CSGs, the CSGs have to implement H-QoS policy with a parent shaper equal to the sustained microwave link speed on their network-to-network interface (NNI).

DiffServ QoS Domain

The traffic classification, marking, and DiffServ PHB behaviors considered in the system architecture, which are depicted in Figure 4.35, are targeted to fit the deployment of mobile services. PTP synchronization, GSM Abis, UMTS IuB control plane and voice user plane, LTE S1c, X2c, and the LTE GBR user plane are classified in a traffic class that requires an expedited forwarding (EF) PHB, as described in RFC 3246. This class will be serviced with a priority queue due to the stringent latency and delay variation requirements these services have.

The EF PHB defines a scheduling behavior that guarantees an upper limit on per hop delay variation that can be caused by packets from non-EF services. The UMTS IuB user plane that needs guaranteed bandwidth and the LTE MBR user plane are classified in traffic classes that use the advanced forwarding (AF) PHB behavior, as described in RFC 2597. The AF PHB guarantees a certain amount of bandwidth to an AF class while guaranteeing a certain limit of latency.

IuB and LTE S1 and X2 best effort (BE) traffic will use the BE PHB behavior. The system includes additional AF traffic classes,

Traffic Class	QCI	Resource	DiffServ PHB	Core, Aggregation, Access Network	Mobile Access UNI	
				MPLS/IP	IP NodeB, eNodeB	ATM NodeB
				MPLS EXP	DSCP	ATM
Network Management	7	Non-GBR	AF	7	56	VBR-nrt
Network Control Protocols	6	Non-GBR	AF	6	48	VBR-nrt
Network Sync (1588 PTP , ACR) Mobile Conversation (Voice & Video) Signaling (GSM Abis, UMTS Iub control, LTE S1c, X2c)	1 2 3	GBR	EF	5	46	CBR
Reserved	4	-	AF	4	32	VBR-nrt
Hosted Video	5	Non-GBR	AF	3	24	VBR-nrt
Reserved	8	-	AF	2 1	16 8	VBR-nrt
Internet Best Effort	9	Non-GBR	BE	0	0	UBR

Figure 4.35

used for network control protocols and network management traffic that will be serviced in the aggregation network by a weighted queue.

QoS Policy Enforcement

The QoS model described above is implemented via QoS service policies applied to the UNI interfaces at the edges of the network for classification and remarking and QoS service policies applied throughout the intermediate nodes within the network to provide proper queuing and scheduling of those traffic classes.

For Ethernet UNI interfaces, traffic classification is based on IP DSCP or 802.1P CoS markings. The ingress QoS service policy will match on these markings and map them to the corresponding MPLS EXP value based on the DiffServ QoS Domain table shown in Figure 4.35. IP DSCP markings are preserved within the MPLS transport, and thus the egress QoS policy may use DSCP markings for queuing and scheduling. In the case of 802.1P, an ingress service policy on the CSG or MTG will map the MPLS EXP values back to 802.1P, and the egress service policy can thus use the 802.1P CoS for queuing and scheduling.

For TDM UNI interfaces to be transported via CEoPs pseudowires, both for SAToP and CESoPSN, all traffic is classified as real-time and requires EF PHB. The ingress QoS policy matches all traffic inbound to the interface, and applies an MPLS EXP value of 5. There is no egress service policy required for TDM UNI interfaces. For ATM UNI interfaces to be transported via CEoPs pseudowires, traffic is classified according to the ATM CoS on a particular VC. The ingress QoS policy is applied to the ATM PVC sub-interface and imposes an MPLS EXP value that corresponds to the type of traffic carried on the VC and proper ATM CoS according to the table in Figure 4.35.

For further distinction, the ingress QoS policy also has the ability to match on the Cell Loss Priority bit of the incoming ATM traffic and can map to two different MPLS EXP values based on this. For egress treatment, the PVC interface is configured with the proper ATM CoS. If the CLP to EXP mapping is being used, then an egress QoS policy applied to the ATM PVC sub-interface can map an EXP value back to a CLP value for proper egress treatment of the ATM cells.

The core, aggregation, and access network traffic marking is based on MPLS EXP. The core network may use different traffic marking and simplified PHB behaviors, or it may be transporting services in addition to mobile backhaul, therefore requiring traffic remarking in between the aggregation and core networks.

More details on QoS for mobile IP networks are provided in the next chapter.

Synchronization Distribution

Synchronization distribution for both frequency and phase is a fundamental functional component of the access and aggregation areas of the seamless MPLS system. The primary target for the current system release is to provide frequency synchronization using the Ethernet physical layer (SyncE) and phase synchronization using IEEE 1588-2008 PTP. SyncE operates on a link-by-link basis and will provide a high quality frequency reference equal to SONET and SDH networks. SyncE supports an ESMC, which provides a communications channel for transmitting synchronization status message (SSM)-quality levels over SyncE-enabled links. This allows the SyncE node to derive timing from the most reliable source and detect timing loops, which is essential for deployment of SyncE in ring topologies.

Because not all links on the network may be SyncE-capable or have synchronization distribution at the physical layer, the IEEE 1588 packet-based mechanism may also be used for frequency distribution. IEEE 1588-based synchronization distribution is overlaid across the entire system infrastructure; third-party master and third-party IP-NodeB client equipment are considered outside the scope of the system.

The mechanism is standards-based and provides frequency and phase distribution and relies on unicast or multicast packet-based transport. As with any packet-based mechanism, IEEE 1588 PTP traffic is subject to packet loss, packet delay, and packet delay variation. To minimize the effects of these factors and meet the requirements for synchronization delivery utilizing IEEE 1588, EF PHB treatment across the network is required. The seamless MPLS system also supports a combination of SyncE and 1588v2 in a hybrid synchronization architecture, aiming to improve the stability and accuracy of the phase and frequency synchronization delivered to the client for deployments such as TDD-LTE eNodeBs. In such architecture, the packet network infrastructure is frequency-synchronized by SyncE with ESMC/SSM support. The phase is delivered by 1588v2 PTP. The CSG, acting as a PTP ordinary client clock or BC, combines the two synchronization methods, using the SyncE frequency as a reference clock for the 1588v2 PTP engine. The combined frequency plus phase is delivered to the client via 1pps, BITS timing interface, or SyncE for clients that support these physical synchronization interfaces, or 1588 PTP for clients that support packet synchronization based on PTP. For access networks that don't support SyncE, the hybrid 1588 BC function may be moved to the PANs. See Figure 4.36.

The timing source for the mobile backhaul network is the primary reference clock (PRC), which sources timing via a global navigational satellite system receiver or other primary reference time clock (PRTC). This PRC then distributes frequency and phase synchronization, via building integrated timing supply (BITS) interfaces, to the aggregation nodes, and if required by the architecture, the 1588 Primary Master Clock (PMC). From this point, three models of synchronization distribution are supported:

1. For mobile services that require only frequency synchronization, where all network nodes support SyncE, then frequency is carried to NodeB via SyncE. The ESMC provides transport of synchronization messages between nodes, and SSM prevents timing loops in Ethernet ring topologies.

2. For mobile services that require synchronization over an infrastructure that does not support SyncE, 1588v2 PTP is utilized for all synchronization distribution. The PMC generates a 1588v2 PTP stream that is routed globally by the regional MTG to the CSG, which then provides sync to the eNodeB. The network design should ensure that the PTP streams do

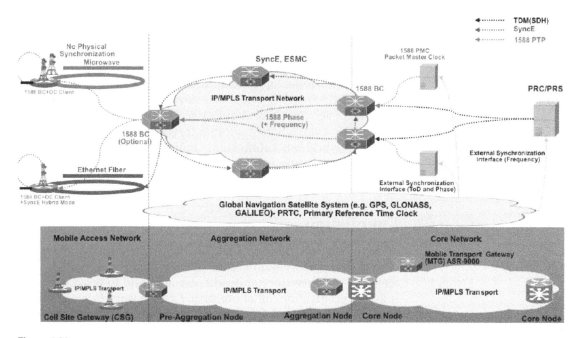

Figure 4.36

not traverse more than 20 network hops en-route to NodeB without resynchronization via another frequency source (see the 1588 BC description below).

3. For mobile services that require frequency and phase and/or time of day (ToD) synchronization, IEEE 1588v2 PTP is used in conjunction with SyncE to provide a hybrid synchronization solution, where SyncE provides frequency distribution, and 1588v2 is used for phase and/or ToD distribution. Again, the 1588v2 PTP streams are routed globally from the regional MTG to the CSG, which then provides sync to the eNodeBs.

In general, a packet-based timing mechanism such as 1588v2 PTP has strict packet delay variation requirements, which limits the number of hops over which the recovered timing from the source is still valid. Even with strict priority queuing of the PTP streams, it is generally not acceptable to have more than 20 hops from the PMC to NodeB, thus placing an upper limit on the distance between the PMC and NodeB. This limit can be increased through the use of 1588v2 BC functionality.

Scalability and reliability of 1588v2 in the seamless MPLS system is enhanced by enabling BC in some or all of the following: the aggregation node, the PAN, and CSG. Implementing BC functionality in these nodes serves two purposes:

1. It increases scaling of 1588v2 phase/frequency distribution by replicating a single stream from the PMC to multiple destinations, thus reducing the number of PTP streams needed from the PMC.

2. It improves the phase stability of 1588v2 by re-synchronizing the PTP from SyncE or another frequency source as described in the hybrid synchronization architecture, thus increasing the number of hops and distance supported between the PMC and NodeB.

Conclusion

As illustrated and explained in depth, seamless MPLS gives operators a proven architecture, platforms, and solutions to stay ahead of the curve for bandwidth demand and to provide operational simplification, all at optimized cost points. It is a comprehensive RAN backhaul solution that supports LTE, 3G, and 2G service deployment. It provides flexible cell site connectivity options, including integration of third-party microwave vendors. It supports both retail and wholesale backhaul options and concurrent transport for residential and business services traffic over the same infrastructure.

5

QoS IN MOBILE IP NETWORKS

Introduction

This chapter explores the quality of service framework required for mobile networks over an NGN infrastructure.

There is no question that the advent of mobile broadband speeds and native IP communications for voice and data, courtesy of 3G technology, are one of the important drivers for the NGN story among providers. Developments in WiMAX, often referred to as 4G, are further fueling the converged NGN vision.

An introduction to mobile network evolution is explored, with emphasis on the 3G standards and transport options through the various releases. Recent work in the area of legacy radio access network transport to the cell sites is also discussed. Finally, a framework for QoS is developed for 2.5G GSM, 3G Release 99, Release 4 and Release 5. For specific CLI commands please refer to the MPLS VPN and Multicast QoS chapters.

The First Generation Mobile Network

The concept of cellular handheld devices was conceived by Bell Labs in the late 1950s. The framework was based on optimizing the use of frequency bands into geographic regions referred to as cells, hence the term "cellular network."

Bell Labs groups frequency bands into clusters of seven cells, allowing reuse of frequencies while ensuring enough separation to avoid overlap between base stations, as shown in Figure 5.1.

The late 1970s and early 1980s saw the first real mobile network implementations across the US and Japan (using AMPS: advanced mobile phone service), northern Europe (using NMT: Nordic mobile telephony) and Britain (using TACS: total access communication system).

The Second Generation Mobile Network

As technology improved and customer expectations grew, the functionality and services on the mobile network infrastructure

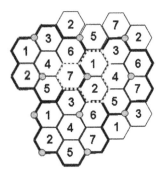

Figure 5.1

evolved. The second generation networks delivered superior, more efficient voice as well as basic data capabilities from 2.5G onwards.

The second generation of mobile networks are digital-transmission based. Although there were many standards in the 2G space, of most interest was the emergence of the two most prolific technologies in the mobile space today;

- Code Division Multiple Access (CDMA)-based IS-95
- Time Division Multiple Access-based Global System for Mobile (GSM)

Given that GSM is by far the most dominant technology in the mobile space, currently considered to carry up to 90 percent of mobile traffic today, this chapter will explore GSM network evolution toward 3G and the transport over an IP/MPLS infrastructure.

The initial 2G networks for GSM were voice-only with no data services. Digital transmission techniques led to superior voice quality, improved spectrum efficiency, and reliability over the analogue first generation networks, driving mobile providers to upgrade infrastructure to second generation.

The reference model for GSM 2G is shown in Figure 5.2.

The user equipment (UE) is used by the subscriber to access services. The UE connects to the nearest base transmission station (BTS) over an air interface. The BTS connects to a base station

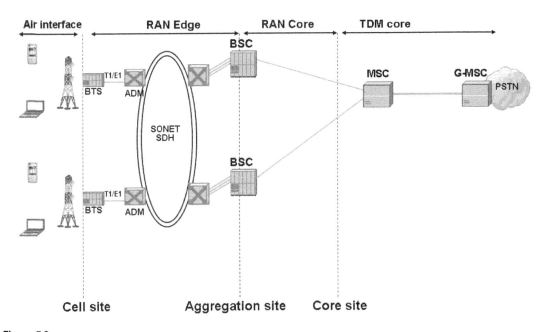

Figure 5.2

controller (BSC) through a TDM network via point-to-point transport such as E1/T1 or microwave via SONET/SDH rings. The BTS and BSC combined are often referred to as the base station subsystem (BSS).

The BSCs are aggregated at the mobile switching center (MSC) once again over TDM infrastructure. The MSC is the node that resides between the access network, including the RAN core, the RAN edge and air interface, and other networks such as partner mobile vendors and the PSTN. The MSC is responsible for keeping track of where users are located at any given point in time and for setting up and tearing down calls to and from mobile terminals, among other duties. Mobile telephone calls originating in, or destined for, the PSTN traverse a purpose-built device called Gateway MSC (G-MSC).

In terms of traffic flow in the 2G network, Figure 5.3 shows the call signaling and voice flow as well as an overview of the responsibilities of major components in the call path.

Voice traffic enters the mobile network at the BTS in the RAN edge, then flows through to a designated regional BSC on a circuit-switched 64 K bps channel within the bundled E1/T1 transmission link. The voice traffic then moves through the BSC to an MSC, which will route the call to other users in the mobile network or via the gateway MSC (GMSC) to the public-switched telephone network (PSTN), or other mobile vendors, as required. All voice calls and signaling are circuit-switched over a TDM-based T1/E1 or microwave infrastructure typically supported by an underlying SONET/SDH layer in the RAN edge, RAN core, and network core where the GMSC is required.

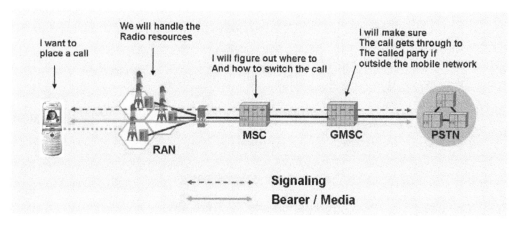

Figure 5.3

The 2.5G Mobile Network

The requirement for data services rapidly emerged as handsets and users became more sophisticated, particularly given that the competing standard CDMA had data capabilities from the outset of deployment. The additional of general packet radio service (GPRS) gave the data service capabilities required, albeit at relatively slow data rates and typically through cumbersome gateways. This step in GSM evolution was referred to as enhanced GSM or 2.5G and had a data transfer capability of up to 115 kbps. Enhanced GSM was deployed in the mid-1990s and represents the most widely deployed GSM standard today.

The 2.5G technology was a step between 2G and 3G mobile technologies, enabling data without any true multimedia capabilities. The GPRS concept was developed by the ITU and would ultimately be continued through the 3GPP standards. The 2.5G term actually describes 2G systems that have implemented a packet-switched domain for data in addition to the circuit-switched domain for voice; however, it should be noted that "2.5G" is a marketing term rather than an officially defined standard.

A commonly implemented architecture for 2.5G is shown in Figure 5.4.

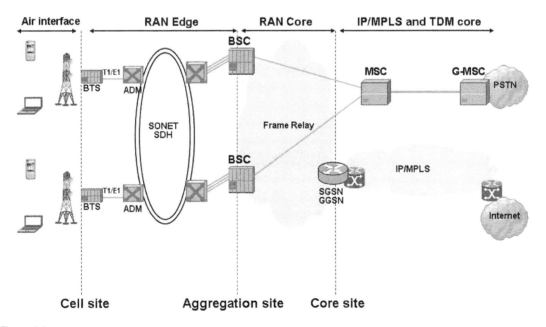

Figure 5.4

The introduction of the serving GPRS support node (SGSN) and the gateway GPRS support node (GGSN) connected to the BSC via frame relay enabled the data packet capabilities in the GSM network by the addition of a packet-switched (PS) domain.

A serving GPRS support node (SGSN) is responsible for the delivery of data packets to and from mobile devices. The SGSN is generally specific to a geographical region. The SGSN is responsible for packet routing, mobility management, logical link management, authentication, and charging functions. The SGSN includes a location register for connected users, which stores information such as current cell, current VLR, and user profiles.

A gateway GPRS support node (GGSN) is a gateway between a wireless data network user and other data networks such as the Internet or private networks. The GGSN is the data anchor point enabling the mobility of the user terminal in the GPRS networks. The GGSN is effectively the GPRS equivalent of a home agent in mobile IP. It maintains routing necessary to tunnel the protocol data units (PDUs) to the SGSN that service a particular mobile subscriber (MS).

Other functions include subscriber screening, IP pool management, address mapping, QoS, and PDP context enforcement.

The air interface standards did not change to the UE with the introduction of GPRS; instead, slices of spectrum could be allocated to data traffic as well as voice.

The Third Generation Mobile Vision

The standards for the third generation network are governed by the International Telecommunication Union (ITU). The ITU umbrella name for 3G standards is IMT-2000, which stands for International Mobile Telecommunications 2000. In Europe, IMT-2000 is typically referred to as universal mobile telephone service (UMTS).

Wideband CDMA is the standard for universal mobile telephone service. UMTS is the committed standard for Europe and is the likely migration path for other GSM operators globally. UMTS leverages GSM's dominant position as the preferred mobile standard by building on the 2.5G standard architecture for the access aggregation and core; however, it requires substantial new spectrum and significant investment at the base station level, as the radio standards are CDMA-based.

There are two specific groups aligned with the dominant mobile technologies of GSM and CMDA. The 3rd Generation Partnership Project (3GPP) is focused on GSM and UMTS evolution.

The 3rd Generation Partnership Project 2 (3GPP2) is a separate organization focused on the evolution of CMDA toward the 3G vision. The goal of an ultimate merger (3GPP + 3GPP2) remains a priority and a talking point in the ITU, although an exact framework has not been formalized.

National and regional standards bodies across the globe, such as ARIB, TIA, TTA, TTC, CWTS, T1, and ETSI, are collaborating with ITU in the 3G Partnership Projects, as shown in Figure 5.5.

Note that, although there are groups aligned with GSM and CDMA, with GSM being the dominant technology, the accepted 3G radio standards (CDMA2000, W-CDMA, and TD-SCDMA) are all CDMA-based. As such, the migration of GSM to W-CDMA requires extensive forklift upgrades at the radio access layer, whereas CDMA to CMDA2000 can be achieved with additions to the existing infrastructure.

The IMT-2000 framework envisions coverage provided by a combination of cell sizes ranging from "in building" pico/femto cells to global cells provided by satellite, giving service to the more remote regions of the world.

According to the ITU, "The IMT-2000 third generation mobile standard enables mobile users to harness the full power of the Internet through efficient high-speed radio transmission, optimized for multimedia communications."

The overall IM-2000 vision is shown in the Figure 5.6.

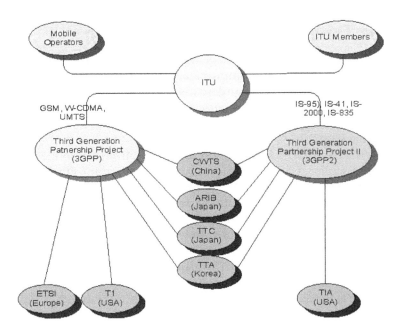

Figure 5.5

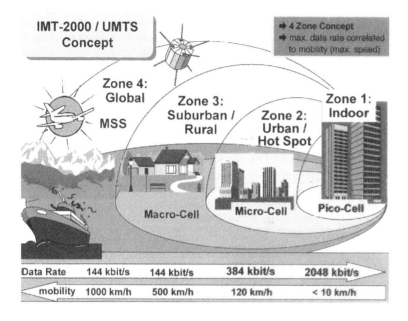

Figure 5.6

Some stated goals for the third generation network are as follows:
- Universal global roaming
- Genuine multimedia support for voice, data, and video
- Increased data rates up to broadband speeds, 384 kbps while moving, and two Mbps when stationary at specific locations
- Increased capacity over the same frequency spectrum, so it is more spectrally efficient
- A native IP architecture

The Evolution toward 3G

As shown in the Figure 5.7, the path toward the third generation network vision is complex and must take into account the dominant mobile technologies, GSM and CDMA, as well as a variety of less popular standards deployed in different regions around the globe. The various evolutionary steps within the dominant technologies, 2.5G and 2.75G (commonly referred as EGDE, enhanced data rates for GSM evolution), adds further challenge to the convergence toward a 3G standard.

The Third Generation Evolution for GSM

The 3G Partnership Project (3GPP) has defined specific releases for GSM within the third generation framework. The

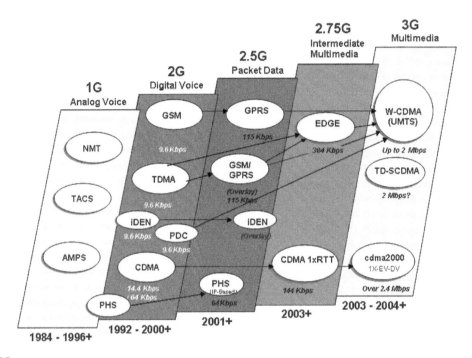

Figure 5.7

intention is to define a smooth migration path from GSM to UMTS (W-CDMA) with allowances for 2G infrastructure and for handsets to remain active, given the investment in this technology by providers all over the globe.

The GSM release high-level roadmap is defined below:

- 3GPP Release 99: Adds 3G radio devices, voice services, emergency call capability, short message service, and Internet access
- 3GPP Release 4: Adds softswitch/ voice gateways, optimization of UTRAN, removal of legacy MSC, quality of service, and preparation for all IP packet core
- 3GPP Release 5: All IP multimedia services (IMS) with SIP and QoS, all IP UTRAN, open systems architecture, and high speed downlink packet access phase 1
- 3GPP Release 6: "All IP" network, HSDPA phase 2

The following section gives a complete description of the terminology used for the 3G network. Briefly, UMTS terrestrial radio access network (UTRAN) refers to the Node B base stations and radio network controllers that make up the UMTS radio access network. The UTRAN allows connectivity between the user equipment (UE) and the core network carrying voice and data traffic. Within the UTRAN, the RNC and its corresponding Node Bs are called the radio network subsystem (RNS). There can be more than one RNS present in a UTRAN.

Another common term in the radio access layer is the GSM EDGE radio access network (GERAN). GERAN is a key part of GSM and of combined UMTS/GSM networks existing during the evolution from GSM to 3G. GERAN is the radio part of GSM/EDGE together with the circuit-switched network that joins the base stations and the base station controllers. A mobile phone operator's network may be composed of one or more GERANs, together with UTRANs in the case of a UMTS/GSM hybrid network.

The IP multimedia subsystem (IMS) is an architectural framework for delivering Internet protocol (IP) multimedia to mobile users. The IMS concept is defined by the 3rd Generation Partnership Project (3GPP) as part of the vision for evolving mobile networks beyond GSM. The original specification (3GPP R5) represented an approach to delivering Internet services over GPRS.

The 3G standards rely on two important technologies in the evolution of the radio network, from narrowband data services to true broadband capabilities. High speed data packet access (HSDPA) and CDMA 1x evolution-data optimized (EV-DO) are the standards that will achieve this transformation.

HSDPA is a critical feature of R5/6 in the 3G standards. There are three phases, increasing in speed and ability, to support real-time applications that all rely on IP as the converged transport. The first phase, specified in 3GPP Release 5, will see the introduction of several new basic functions, with the objective of achieving a peak data rate of 10.8 Mbps. The second phase, specified in 3GPP Release 6, will introduce antenna array processing technologies to optimize the air interfaces and enhance the potential peak data rate to around 30 Mbps. The third phase is intended to encompass additional access technologies beyond radio-based mobile.

The advent of "all IP" from Release 5 onward refers to handsets and user equipment that rely on IP for data and voice applications. The 3GPP has positioned IP as the converged network layer that will ultimately meet the IMT2000 vision across all access technologies. Using IP for data and voice will allow consistent service delivery across any device type and any transport media. Note that the original standards for IMS were IPV6-based only; however, industry pressure forced the ITU to allow IPV4 and/or IPV6 in the IMS standards.

Converged NGN Infrastructure for Mobile Transport

As discuss in Chapter 1, network operators are consolidating disparate networks to reduce their capital expenses (CapEx) and operating expenses (OpEx). Mobile networks evolving toward 3G standards are perfect candidates for this convergence. The drive toward a consolidated IP/MPLS NGN framework is changing the mobile operator's approach to the 3G evolution roadmap, including R99 onward and the RAN.

The 3G technology standards implementation is by far the easiest part of the evolution story. The challenge facing operators is to support the evolving standards in a cost-effective manner. The transport network infrastructure from the edge cellular base station through the aggregation network is the greatest expense facing operators when considering upgrades to support 3G. Current backhaul networks for 2G were designed using narrowband, point-to-point TDM technologies such as leased lines or microwave.

Upgrading the existing TDM-based backhaul infrastructure to support capacity demanded by 3G with multimedia capabilities is prohibitively expensive. Hence, operators must find alternative approaches. Operators are seeking to take advantage of cost-effective IP transport prior to the full IP Release 5 implementation. Furthermore, operators recognize that their networks will spend a large amount of time on the transition to the final goal, hence, converging the transport first will extend their investment return in radio equipment.

Operators have taken steps to introduce the GPRS network for data handling; now they are deploying packet-based technology in the voice core, such as softswitches and media gateway nodes as defined in 3GPP standards. Clearly, for these operators, the path to optimizing CAPEX and OPEX is to extend the IP packetization into the backhaul network. As discussed in Chapter 1, this goal is driven by the NGN vision of convergence across all packet-based services onto a single IP/MPLS infrastructure.

The 3G standards intend to ultimately achieve the goal of IP packetization from the handset through the RAN to the core, starting with ATM-defined interfaces in R99. Clearly, the optimum path lies in an IP interface at the base station to realize an IP radio access network (IPRAN), which is a goal of the 3GPP standards. One possible interim solution, while evolving toward 3G IMS, is the mobile transport over pseudowire (MTOP). The overall position of IP in the mobile operator network is defined in the following section.

The Cisco IP Next-Generation Network (IP NGN) architecture for mobile operators is a roadmap to realizing the vision of next-generation mobile services—the delivery of data, voice, and video anywhere and any time across virtually any access or core transport technology. The Cisco IP NGN provides mobile operators a migration path to an IP foundation prior to the implementation of the all-IP 3G IMS vision starting in Release 5. This IP foundation can reduce OPEX and allow operators, and indeed handset owners, additional time to depreciate their investment in technology that implements 3G Release 4 or earlier.

The NGN framework also allows inter-operability with different radio access technologies and vendors. This is possible with convergence at application, service control, and network layers, as shown in the Figure 5.8.

Mobile operators need an application layer that interfaces with the customer device; a network layer that creates and delivers the services; and a service layer enabling the delivery, operations, features, and billing of the services portfolio across all access types. The service layer is known as the Cisco Service Exchange Framework (SEF). Please refer to Chapter 1 for a full description of the NGN framework.

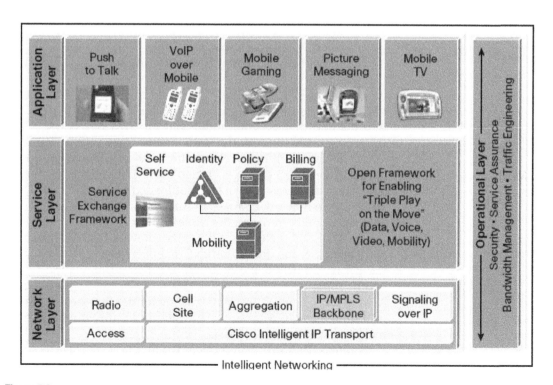

Figure 5.8

Third Generation Release 99 Overview

In the introduction of 3G specifications for GSM, ATM has figured prominently starting from the Release 99 specifications. ATM was the obvious choice given the relatively high speed and class of service capabilities at the time of drafting the standards in the 1990s.

The introduction of ATM into the mobile standards was intended to be a solution for integrated voice, data, and video for speed and differentiation of service types. However scalability and management of ATM transport quickly became concerns under increasing expected IP data traffic loads on mobile networks. As identified in chapter 1, quality of service capabilities in native IP environments across faster, cheaper layer 2 technologies such as Ethernet, were also maturing putting further pressure on the ATM approach for mobile network. Although ATM represented a cost effective solution compared to upgrading existing 2G point to point, E1/T1 TDM links, it cannot compete with a converged IP infrastructure over more cost effective media running the providers full services suite which is the goal of NGN. Had the standards been drafted some 5 years later the adoption of IP as a converged network layer would have been very likely and in fact the standards for Release 4 onwards clearly defined a roadmap towards this concept.

The reference architecture for 3G Release 99 is shown in Figure 5.9.

The Release 99 specifications started the path towards multimedia and broadband data speeds to the end user through the introduction of new equipment and an ATM based RAN. The RAN must still support the 2.5G architecture with voice over TDM and data over frame relay to the SGSN as it shown in the diagram. 3G Release 99 voice is carried over ATM as far as the media gateway in this release, then being offloaded to the MSC over TDM to minimize network changes in this step.

ATM extends from the 3G Node-B through the 3G radio network controller (RNC) to the media gateway (MGW) for voice and the SGSN for data. The RNC is effectively a 3G version of the 2G BSC, responsible for routing calls and regulating bandwidth. The media gateway (MGW) is introduced to do voice over ATM to TDM conversion and signaling for the first step of the 3G evolution. The MGW takes on a greater role in subsequent releases including retiring the 2G MSC.

Figure 5.10 shows the interfaces within the 3G Release 99 specified RAN. 2G interfaces are also shown for reference.

As mentioned previously, the new interfaces for the 3G Release 99 RAN are ATM based. The data capabilities of GPRS through the

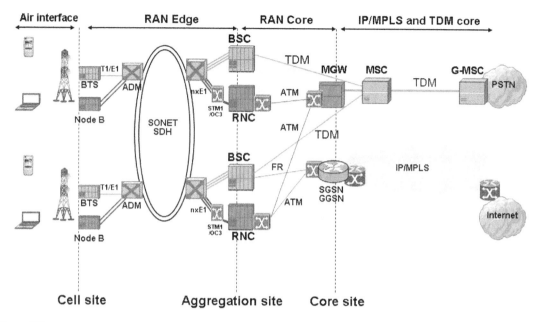

Figure 5.9

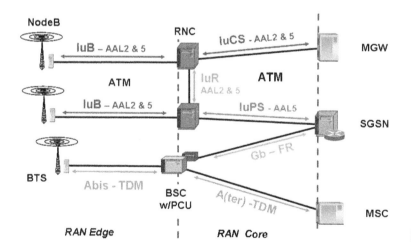

Figure 5.10

SGSN are still used by Release 99 hence an additional ATM interface in the SGSN router is required from the BSC or alternatively a dedicated 3G SGSN/GGSN pair can be implemented, which tended to be the most common approach by providers adopting Release 99 standards.

The intention of the Release 99 specifications is to position the mobile network for the subsequent Release 4, and beyond, evolution. Careful consideration is given to maintaining the providers investment in the 2G infrastructure when the 3G standards and releases were conceived.

Third Generation Release 99 Convergence over IP/MPLS

The intention of introducing the ATM interfaces in the 3G standards was to allow providers to leverage more cost-effective ATM backhaul rather than expand existing costly and inefficient TDM-based E1/T1 transport. In fact, the majority of mobile providers had expansive ATM networks for enterprise customers and backhaul of broadband Internet traffic already using ADSL. Contributors drafting the 3G standards saw this ATM network as the obvious evolutionary step for faster data rates and more efficient bandwidth usage for voice and signaling.

Ultimately, with the drive toward a consolidated IP/MPLS infrastructure, converging voice and data over a single packet-switched IP/MPLS network as early as possible is the preferred option for providers. This requires multiple gigabit speeds, enhanced availability in the IP infrastructure, and QoS to match ATM to ensure that strict requirements are met for mobile network traffic including multimedia, voice, and signaling. Leveraging IP/MPLS for transport of the ATM links would achieve this goal with the necessary requirements across transport and QoS.

A network with 2G and 3G R99, with IP/MPLS extending to the RAN core network for the 3G services including voice and data, is as shown in the Figure 5.11. This is the logical first step towards network consolidation of the RAN and packet-switched data networks for the mobile provider.

The IP/MPLS cloud is effectively extended to include the RAN core ATM interfaces north from the 3G RNC toward the network core. Cisco Any Transport over MPLS (AToM), specifically ATM over MPLS, is used to transport the cells with the required QoS over the IP infrastructure. Interfaces transported over AtoM are IuCS for voice, IuPS for data, and IuR, which carries both voice and data. The existing 2G TDM infrastructure is not carried by the IP/MPLS network at this stage in the evolution; however, mobile transport over pseudowire (MToP) can be used. The 2.5G frame relay interface between the BSC and the SGSN will also be transported over IP/MPLS at this stage in the convergence, if required.

The goal of converging to an NGN infrastructure is to carry all traffic over IP/MPLS in a single network infrastructure. This would ultimately include the RAN access layer from the BTS or the Node

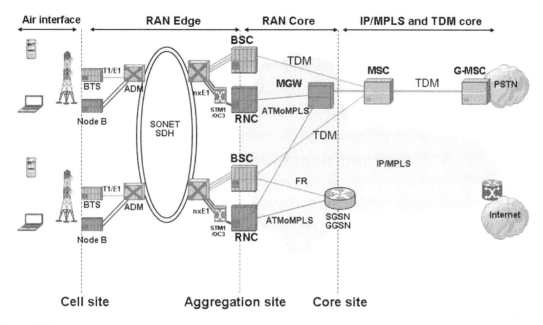

Figure 5.11

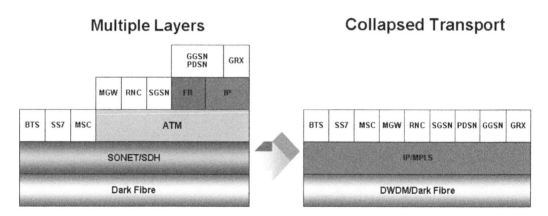

Figure 5.12

B toward the provider core network. True convergence would see all aspects of the mobile network infrastructure using IP/MPLS as the transport technology. The introduction of ATM-based 3G into the existing 2G network builds a complex stack of protocols, including SONET/SDH, ATM, frame relay, and IP.

Figure 5.12 depicts the network with 2G/3G in the existing protocol stack evolving into the converged NGN vision.

As shown in the diagram, the IP/MPLS network can run over DWDM or directly over fiber. Given IP/MPLS as the converged communications layer, any physical infrastructure can potential be used for the transport, including Ethernet, POS, ADSL, cable, or metro Ethernet, assuming that the necessary traffic requirements for delay, jitter, and packet loss can be implemented adequately.

Third Generation Release 4 Overview

The 3GPP Release 4 framework (R4) introduces two new key architectural changes: the split architecture and removal of the MSC.

From a mobile voice-switching point of view, the split framework, commonly referred to as the bearer-independent circuit-switched architecture, means that the centralized TDM mobile switching center (MSC) responsible for signaling and voice switching in 2G are now being decommissioned, with the functions decoupled and separated into two new devices: the existing MGW from the Release 99 deployment and a new MSC server installed as part of Release 4. Similarly, the gateway MSC (GMSC) is split into a GMSC server coupled with one or more CS-MGW devices. The GMSC handles the mobility and call control duties and the CS-MGW manages the bearer plane.

An overview of the evolution to split architecture is shown in Figure 5.13.

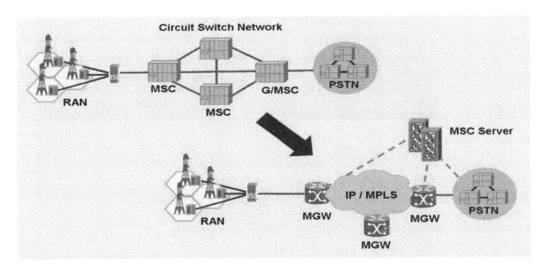

Figure 5.13

With this split architecture, the voice services are no longer handled by the MSC and G-MSC. Interest in this split architecture for voice is based on the desire of mobile operators to retire their traditional TDM-based MSCs. In some cases, the circuit-switched infrastructure is approaching end of life and often entails very high OpEx. Few mobile operators want to invest further in what is seen as the legacy circuit-switched technology, which is difficult to scale to the demands of 3G services. VoIP is also considered much less expensive when mobile operators use a converged IP/MPLS network instead of traditional transport over T1/E1 lines. Introduction of VoIP in the core at this stage positioned the network for IP voice to the handset as part of IMS in Release 5.

The MSC server and MGW combined basically perform the same functions as the legacy MSC. The separation of these functions allows greater scalability, support of legacy 2G services, the introduction of VoIP, support of new 3G services, and a graceful evolution toward the ultimate 3G vision, with multimedia over IP transport.

Note that the R4 evolution to a split architecture does not entail changes to the radio access network from the Release 99 phase. This ensures minimum changes to the mobile network in the 3G R4 evolution step. The CS-MGW (CS for circuit-switched domain) provides the physical interfacing between the radio access network and the core network for voice and related signaling. It is also responsible for processing—and converting, if required—bearer traffic, that in some cases traverse different networks running different technologies (ATM for 3G and TDM for 2G).

Figure 5.14 shows the resulting separation of the signaling and voice traffic in the 3G R4 split architecture framework.

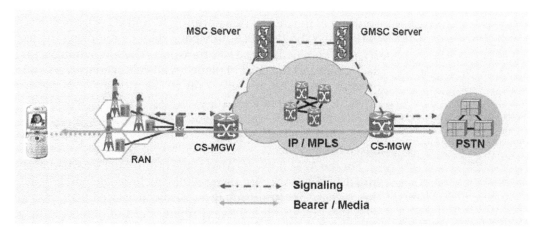

Figure 5.14

The 3GPP Release 4 framework defines the ATM as the transport of circuit switch domain traffic, the same as the Release 99 specifications. This essentially means that, according to the standards, both signaling and bearer traffic going between MSC servers, GMSC servers, and CS-MGW nodes must be transported using ATM. The signaling traffic leverages SCTP transport and the bearer is transported using AAL2/ATM. Some radio vendors preferred to move to IP-based protocol stacks from the Release 5 standards rather than stay with Release 99 and Release 4 ATM options.

Third Generation Release 4 Convergence over IP/MPLS

The 3G Release 4 standard introduces the concept of a split architecture. For 3G voice traffic, the connection between the MGWs has a control plane and a user plane. The control plane is IP-based Signaling System 7 (SS7), as defined by SIGTRAN, enabled through the MSC server. The user plane must handle TDM for 2G and ATM or IP for 3G R4.

SIGTRAN is the Internet Engineering Task Force (IETF) working group responsible for producing protocol specifications that provide reliable datagram service and user layer adaptations for SS7 and ISDN communications protocols. SIGTRAN is an extension of the SS7 protocol supporting the same application and call management standards as SS7, using an IP transport called Stream Control Transmission Protocol (SCTP). In the mobile network, SCTP is used to carry PSTN signaling over IP.

The real savings and simplicity for the mobile operators come courtesy of the MGWs transforming 3G and 2G voice services into VoIP across the IP/MPLS RAN core, thereby removing the legacy 2G MSC and inefficient TDM transport. The interconnects for the user plane and the control plane for all voice services, 2G and 3G, beyond the MGW are based on IP technology from Release 4 onward. Some operators are even deploying the Release 4 split architecture for 2G-only network solutions to retire the existing TDM infrastructure in the core and make use of converged IP-based interconnects.

For the ATM RAN, 3G ATM voice traffic can be carried over IP/MPLS in the RAN core using AToM technologies exactly as per the Release 99 approach previously discussed. For providers who have taken the R99 step (many did not, choosing instead to move directly to R5), transporting the mobile traffic over an IP/MPLS core using AToM in the R4 step required no additional

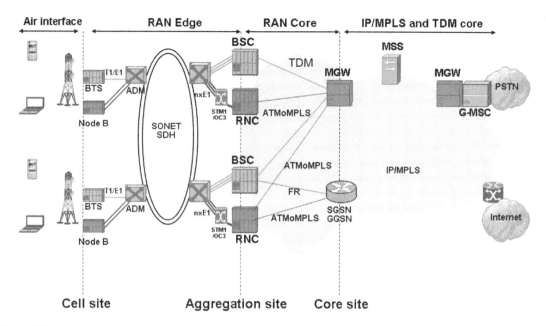

Figure 5.15

effort. Note that from 3G R99, GTP tunnels for data are terminated to the RNC, which actually means the interface for packet-switched data (Iu-PS) is IP-transported over ATM from the RNC.

Figure 5.15 shows the connectivity and transport in the 3G Release 4 standards mobile network. Note the absence of the legacy MSC device. The MSS is the MSC server, as previously defined.

Once again, note that the frame relay connection between the 2G BSC and the SGSN can converge over the IP/MPLS core if the providers choose this option.

Figure 5.16 shows the interface type in the 3G R4 network with the 2G co-existence.

As can be seen, the legacy BSC now connects to the MGW with the retirement of the MSC. The interface remains TDM-based, as upgrading the BSC to packet-based is not seen as cost effective by providers.

Third Generation Release 5/6 Overview

Release 5 and Release 6 were defined with the concept of the IP multimedia subsystem (IMS). The IP multimedia subsystem (IMS) is an architectural framework for delivering multimedia to mobile users, including voice, data, and video, over Internet

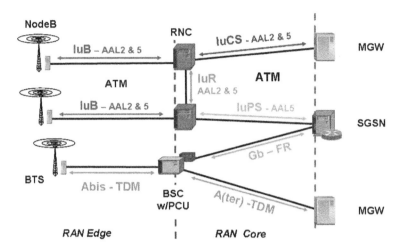

Figure 5.16

Protocol (IP). The original specifications were drafted by the wireless standards body 3rd Generation Partnership Project (3GPP) as part of the vision for evolving mobile networks beyond 2.5G.

In the standards original form, known as 3G R5, IMS represented an approach to delivering multimedia services over GPRS. Later standards by 3GPP, 3GPP2, and TISPAN expanded to networks other than GPRS, such as wireless LAN, CDMA2000, and fixed line, which leveraged the move to IP and SIP protocols.

With the move to IMS based on IP, the 3GPP opted for the IETF protocol, Session Initiation Protocol (SIP). The IMS standard is not intended to define applications, but instead addresses the access of multimedia and voice applications across wireless and wireline terminals, with a view to fixed mobile convergence (FMC). As with the Cisco NGN vision, this is achieved by using a horizontal control layer between the access network and the service layer to allow any media.

The uptake of IMS has thus far been slow in the mobile operator community. Handsets are being developed utilizing SIP; however, the current 3G handsets not yet enabled with SIP already include Internet capabilities around messaging and multimedia, which meet consumer demands. Ultimately, the consumer will not be aware if the voice call is IP-based or not; the introduction of native IP is of benefit to the mobile provider.

A disruptive new standard such as WiMAX, requiring development of a new handset anyway, may drive the 3G IMS vision with the handset and radio vendors.

The reference architecture for the 3G IMS includes R5 and R6 is shown in Figure 5.17.

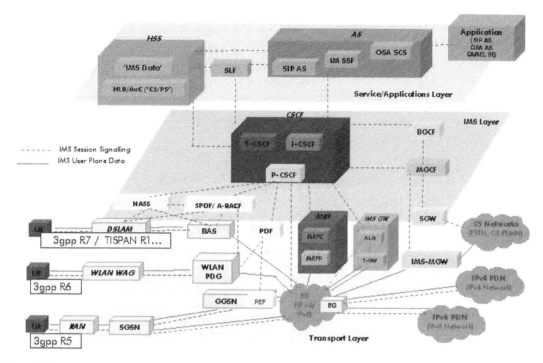

Figure 5.17

The evolution from Release 5 onward saw the introduction of additional functionality and media types. Of more relevance to this chapter is the RAN convergence toward IP for the mobile network RAN.

The UTRAN specifications up to Release 4 define ATM as the transport method in the RAN access. Within 3GPP Release 5, the radio access transport can be IP or ATM. Release 5 specifications allow IP from Node B, which enables any data link layer in the RAN access, including ATM if preferred. Note that ATM is still an option in the standards if desired by the provider.

The interface definitions and options for Release 5 in the RAN access and core are shown in Figure 5.18.

Third Generation Release 5/6 Convergence over IP/MPLS

Increased use of IP/MPLS to the RAN access with 3G Release 5 and beyond will simplify and accelerate the introduction of VoIP over the converged IP network end to end, which is one of the stated goals of IMS. As seen in Figure 5.19, eventually IP/MPLS

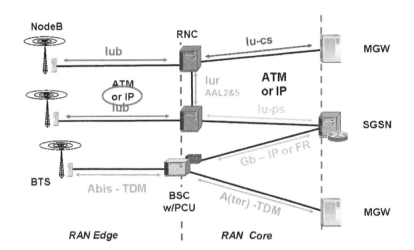

Figure 5.18

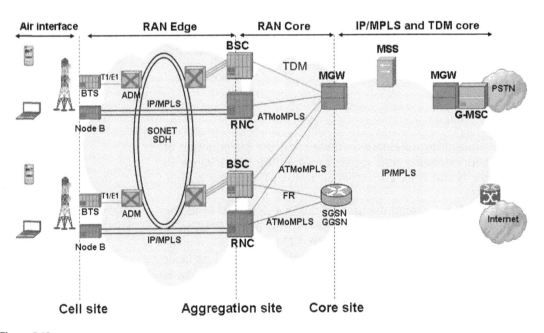

Figure 5.19

will become the transport technology in the RAN access and core infrastructure. With an IP/MPLS-based RAN and core, mobile operators will be able to reap cost savings, simplify network operations, and accelerate time to market for new services.

Figure 5.19 shows a converged network for the 3G Release 5 and onward infrastructure. Note that the 2G will remain TDM-based through the RAN, leaving MToP as the only option for converging this network over IP/MPLS.

The introduction of the packet-based Node B capabilities makes extending the IP/MPLS cloud to the edge a relatively simple technical task. Any technology at the access layer can be used, assuming the strict SLAs as defined by 3GPP can be met. Some common access technologies considered by mobile providers so far include metro Ethernet.

Mobile Network RAN Access

The 3G goal of IP convergence in the mobile core network drove providers and vendors to consider extending this vision beyond the RNC into the access. With the advent of standards allowing higher data speeds to the user equipment, more and more of the costly E1 access transmission would be utilized by IP-based data applications. Providers saw the value in transporting the access layer for 3G, which is ATM over E1/T1, and legacy 2G, which is TDM using E1/T1, over IP/MPLS.

To achieve the access layer convergence goal, vendors realized that new interface cards and standards would be required. Networking vendors and providers alike could safely assume that aging equipment in the 2G network, such as the BTS and BSC, would not be natively upgraded to allow packet-based connectivity. As such, the fastest path to convergence was equipment capable of interfacing to the BTS and BSC and converting from cells to packets.

The technology for transport at the RAN layer is mobile transport over pseudowire (MToP). MToP relies on circuit emulation over packet (CEoP) standards to convert TDM or ATM traffic into packets, as the name suggests. These packets are sent across an IP network in MPLS pseudowires to the selected destination. Importantly, this technology is designed to transport both TDM for 2G and ATM for 3G to optimize the benefits to the provider. MToP gives significant benefits in terms of availability in the access layer as well, allowing rerouting of pseudowires in the event of layer device failure in the IP network.

The existing RAN structure for a 2G and 3G infrastructure is shown in Figure 5.20.

As previously discussed, the backhaul for the legacy BTS for 2G is TDM using E1/T1 transport. The TDM links are terminated at the BSC, which connects through to the core using TDM over SDH.

The new generation Node Bs for 3G rely on ATM encapsulation, still over E1/T1 transmission. For the 3G transmission,

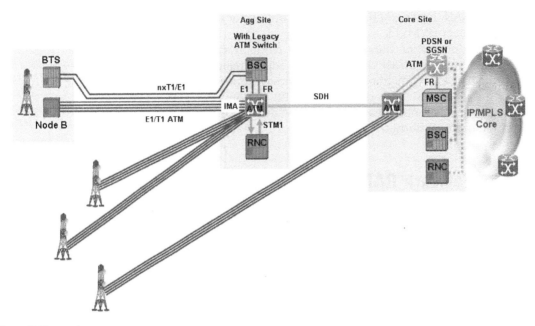

Figure 5.20

ATM switches were required to terminate and aggregate the connection to the RNC. Likewise, ATM was used from the RNC to the core mobile network over the SDH transmission. Remember that the 3GPP evolution sought to reduce new infrastructure investment as much as possible; hence, the SDH transmission into the MGW in the core network remained.

Figure 5.21 shows the extension of MPLS to the network edge. The Node B sites can be connected at strategically located aggregation sites to optimize the backhaul without placing IP transport equipment at every base station site.

Multiple Node Bs are transporting over traditional E1/T1 TDM links to the pre-aggregation site, which connects to the MPLS network.

Given that the capability for transporting the mobile access over IP/MPLS was now in place, providers realized the potential for further savings. The QoS requirements for the voice, signaling, and data were vastly different, giving an opportunity to use more cost-effective transport options for the less important traffic.

The voice and signaling traffic is very sensitive to any packets loss, delay, or jitter. If received traffic strays outside the strict parameters, user experience can be severely impacted. Effectively all of the traffic in these categories can be considered as requiring the highest possible forwarding priority.

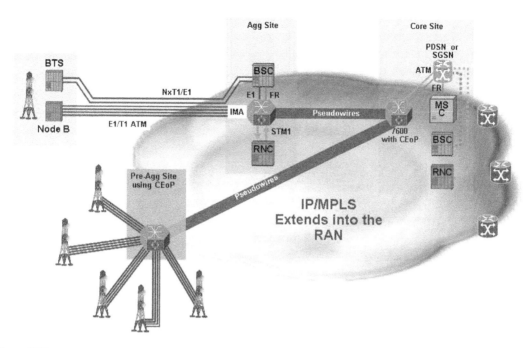

Figure 5.21

The data traffic, however, is generally of much lower priority. Some of the traffic may be video, which has similar requirements to the voice and signaling; however, the vast majority of data is not sensitive to delay, loss, and jitter parameters. As such, sending this traffic over more cost-effective transport could greatly reduce transmission costs for the provider while still meeting customer expectations.

Vendors implementing the Node B and RNC have standard PVC mappings for the signaling, voice, and data, making separation technically possible by mapping to the VC/VP identifiers. The ATM interfacing device simply needs to route a given VC/VP over the alternative transport paths based on the vendors' mapping standards.

The data path can utilize standard broadband access types such as metro Ethernet or xDSL to provide a cost-effective, high capacity channel for the less sensitive traffic traversing the access layer. If video is a data service implemented by the provider, this traffic can be sent through the data path with higher priority to other traffic. If the data path does not support the necessary QoS for the video traffic, the provider can choose to forward the video over the voice and signaling path to ensure that QoS parameters are met. See Figure 5.22.

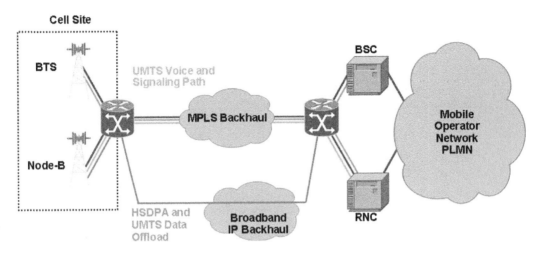

Figure 5.22

IPV6 in 3G Networks

The 3G working groups are encouraging the adoption of Internet Protocol Version 6 (IPv6) within the mobile community. Given the IP capabilities to the handset envisioned by IMS, the number of IP-addressable devices could potentially explode as 3G gains momentum beyond Release 4.

Support for IPv6 in IP backbones, and eventually the radio access network (RAN), is a clear direction stated in 3GPP specifications. An MPLS-enabled IP network provides a simple path for support of IPv4, IPv6, and ATM protocols, which will all be required as mobile operators evolve their infrastructures from the initial Release 99 step. The IPv6 provider edge router (6PE) approach is a straightforward method of integrating IPv6 into an IP/MPLS infrastructure.

Compelling reasons for using IPv6 include the expansion of the address space required to enable the growth of mobile multimedia applications. IPv6 has been proposed as a primary technology enabler for wide-scale adoption of IMS. Even with commercial deployment of IMS as per the standards being slowed, the drivers for IPv6 remain.

One strategy for service providers is to insert IPv6 support only at the edge of their current IP networks where feasible to minimize changes to the core of the network. It is likely that IPv6 traffic will grow slowly, which is one reason why the previous 3GPP mandate of IMS as exclusively using IPv6 is no longer the case. MPLS 6PE is

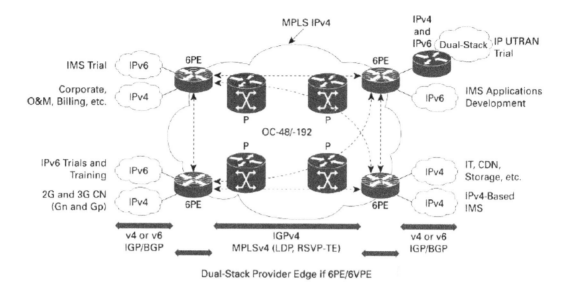

Figure 5.23

the simplest solution for mobile network operators requiring IPv6 support.

The 6PE approach allows existing IP/MPLS networks to carry the IPv6 packets using MPLS labels; hence, only the provider edge (PE) device needs to support the IPv6 protocol and addressing. As shown in Figure 5.23, the core transport remains IPv4 with MPLS labeling, while the 6PE at the edge of the network labels the traffic.

3GPP Specifications for IPv6

The wireless mobile market is only one of the factors for IPv6 adoption. In many regions, including the Asia Pacific, there is currently a lack of IPv4 address space, which will only increase into the future. Growing Internet adoption in emerging countries such as China and India, and the adoption of new Internet-connected appliances, is fueling the IPv6 drive.

According to the 3GPP IMS standards, IPv6 can be used in any area where IPv4 is currently the protocol of choice. As shown in Figure 5.24, IPv6 can be adopted at the data-bearer level for user applications and transport-bearer level for user data transport.

At the user layer, IPv6 may be used for GPRS data for some or all applications. Clearly, to support IPv6 at the user layer, all network elements including mobile station, SGSN recognizing the IP address field for charging purposes, GGSN, address provisioning, and name services, such as Domain Name System (DNS), must

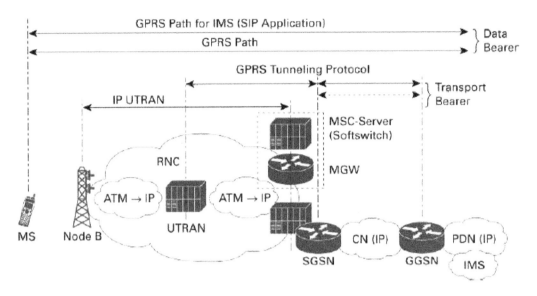

Figure 5.24

support IPv6. As of this writing, the main focus area is in the delivery of commercial IPv6 services at the two endpoints—the user equipment and the applications. Internetworking beyond the mobile provider network will also be a prerequisite for applications if services are to span outside the local provider domain or if complex gateways are to be avoided.

The concept of IMS was not an application but rather a framework to offer Session Initiation Protocol (SIP)-based applications on a GPRS bearer. This capability is based on three primary technologies:

- SIP as the control plane for the establishment of IMS sessions
- IPv6 as the transport
- Authentication, authorization, accounting (AAA), and billing

Examples of IMS-based applications include Push-To-Talk over cellular or rich voice applications based on voice over IP (VoIP). New messaging capabilities far beyond current handset functionality is also an example of SIP implementation. Other aspects of IMS are QoS enforcement at Layer 2 (radio bearer) and Layer 3 (IP), authentication and security, and charging and support of multiple types of devices.

Mobile operators quickly realized the advantages of developing new applications using SIP; however, they remained concerned about the IMS mandate for IPV6. Clearly, despite its limited scalability in the future, IPv4 was widely deployed from

2.5G onward and technically could be used within the initial 3GPP IMS model for SIP deployments. In response to mobile operator and radio vendor pressure, 3GPP modified the exclusive statement of IPv6 to allow IPv4. The 3GPP TS23.221 specification states: "3GPP specifications design the IM CN subsystem elements and interfaces to exclusively support IPv6. However, early IMS implementations and deployments may use IPv4." This statement reinforced the discussions and the work on SIP, IPv6, and IPv4 and IPv6 internetworking.

Currently, most IP traffic from the mobile station is IPv4 with the exception of some experimental work by selected vendors. Adoption of IPv6 will probably take a few more years because of multiple factors, including availability of IPv6 mass-market handsets, applications for IMS based on an SIP framework supported by both 3GPP and IETF, and the IMS and GPRS support-node infrastructure.

Ultimately, in the context of QoS, the specifications for IPv6 and IPv4 will be identical in an MPLS-labeled network. Please refer to later sections in this document for details on the QoS framework in 3G networks.

Overview of QoS and the 3GPP Standards

There are many documents arising from the 3GPP working groups regarding the issue of quality of service. The foundation standard is Quality of Service (QoS) Concept and Architecture (3GPP TS 23.107), which defines the overall framework for QoS within the 3G mobile network.

Quality of Service (QoS) Concept and Architecture (3GPP TS 23.107)

This section gives an overview of the QoS framework to be adopted in the 3G network infrastructure. The definitions are across all traffic types in the UMTS, including voice, signaling, and data. The parameters for QoS are given in specific terms, albeit not commonly understood ATM or IP network terms; hence, a mapping is required.

General requirements for QoS are identified as follows:

- QoS attributes (or mapping of them) should not be restricted to one or few external QoS control mechanisms, but the QoS concept should be capable of providing different levels of QoS by using UMTS-specific control mechanisms (not related to QoS mechanisms in the external networks).

- All attributes must have unambiguous meaning.
- The QoS mechanism must allow efficient use of radio capacity.
- It must allow independent evolution of core and access networks.
- It must allow evolution of UMTS network (i.e., eliminate or minimize the impact of evolution of transport technologies in the wireline world).
- All attribute combinations must have unambiguous meaning.

In terms of general high-level technical requirements for the UMTS, QoS will be defined with a set of generic attributes. The attributes should meet the following criteria:

- UMTS QoS control mechanisms shall provide QoS attribute control on a peer-to-peer basis between UE and 3G gateway node;
- the UMTS QoS mechanisms shall provide a mapping between application requirements and UMTS services;
- the UMTS QoS control mechanisms shall be able to efficiently interwork with current QoS schemes. Further, the QoS concept should be capable of providing different levels of QoS by using UMTS-specific control mechanisms (not related to QoS mechanisms in the external networks);
- a session-based approach needs to be adopted for all packet mode communication within the 3G serving node with which UMTS QoS approach shall be intimately linked; essential features are multiple QoS streams per address;
- the UMTS shall provide a finite set of QoS definitions;
- the overhead and additional complexity caused by the QoS scheme should be kept reasonably low, as well as the amount of state information transmitted and stored in the network;
- QoS shall support efficient resource utilization;
- the QoS attributes are needed to support asymmetric bearers;
- applications (or special software in UE or 3G gateway node) should be able to indicate QoS values for their data transmissions;
- QoS behavior should be dynamic; that is, it shall be possible to modify QoS attributes during an active session;
- the number of attributes should be kept reasonably low (increasing number of attributes increase system complexity); and
- user QoS requirements shall be satisfied by the system, including when change of SGSN within the core network occurs.

As can be seen, these attributes are high level at best, with generic statements giving no indication of methods or measurable criteria.

The network architecture presented is end to end from terminal equipment (TE) to the remote TE for all services. The reference mode defined in the standard is shown in Figure 5.25.

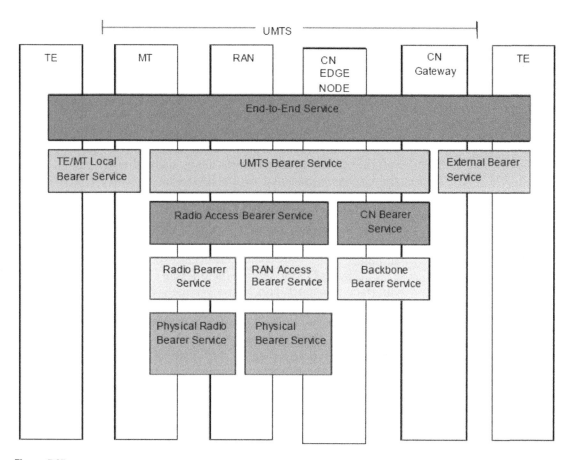

Figure 5.25

Traffic flowing from TE to TE traverses different bearer services of the network. By 3GPP definition, a TE is connected to the UMTS network through a mobile termination (MT) device. The end-to-end service on the application level uses the bearer services of the underlying network.

The end-to-end service used by the TE will traverse a TE/MT local bearer service, a UMTS bearer service, and an external bearer service, as shown in Figure 5.25. The TE/MT local bearer service is actually outside the 3G network and is not discussed further in the standards. An example may be an Ethernet or a USB connection to some sort of mobile network modem or even a communications card in a computer PC card slot.

The UMTS bearer service is within the boundaries of the operator and it is this bearer service that provides the QoS for traffic.

By definition, as shown in Figure 5.25, the UMTS bearer service consists of two parts: the radio access bearer service and the core network bearer service.

The radio access bearer service provides secure transport of signaling and user data between MT and CN edge node, with QoS enforced to meet the negotiated UMTS bearer service or with the default QoS for signaling

The core network bearer service of the UMTS core network connects the UMTS CN edge node with the CN gateway, which interfaces to external networks. Once again, this layer must honor the QoS as contracted to the UMTS bearer service. The UMTS packet core network must support different backbone bearer services for a variety of QoS parameters.

The radio access bearer service is further broken down into a radio bearer service and an RAN access-bearer service, as shown in Figure 5.25.

The radio bearer service includes all the aspects of the radio interface transport. This bearer service is provided by the UTRAN FDD/TDD or the GERAN. QoS at this level requires honoring requirements per user subflow, equating to an application the TE is using, typically belonging to a flow.

The RAN access bearer service, together with the physical bearer service, provides the transport between RAN and CN. RAN access bearer services for packet traffic shall provide different bearer services for a variety of QoS. The RAN access bearer service is provided by the Iu or the Gb bearer service.

The core network bearer service uses a generic backbone network service according to the standard. The backbone network service provides transport functionality, and although it must fulfill the QoS requirements of the core network bearer service, no further details are given in the standard as to how this will happen. According to 3GPP 23.107, "Backbone Network Service is not specific to UMTS but may reuse an existing standard," further reinforcing the fact that QoS enforcement is up to the mobile network operator.

3G Traffic Classes

One challenge facing the drafters of the 3G standards was enforcement of QoS over the air interface. Any complexity in the standards would lead to problems in application to the air interface, hence potentially jeopardizing the end-to-end QoS goal. As such, the standards were kept as simple as possible to ensure seamless QoS from user to user.

	Conversational Class	Streaming Class	Interactive Class	Background Class
Characteristics	Preserve time relation (variation) between information entities of the stream Conversational pattern (very low delay and jitter)	Preserve time relation (variation) between information entities of the stream Delay and jitter requirements not as stringent as conversational	Request response pattern Retransmission of payload content in route	Destination is not expecting the data within a stringent time Retransmission of payload content in route may occur
Example of application	Voice over ip	Streaming Video	Web browsing	Email download

Figure 5.26

The 3rd Generation Partnership Program (3GPP) has four different classes of QoS as follows:
- Conversational
- Streaming
- Interactive
- Background

Figure 5.26 shows the class definitions, characteristics of each class, and an example of the traffic types that can be expected in each class.

The most notable difference between these QoS classes is the delay parameter. Conversational class is intended for traffic that is extremely delay sensitive. Background class is the most delay-insensitive traffic class.

Conversational and Streaming classes are intended to be used for real-time traffic. Once again, the difference between these classes is delay sensitivity. Conversational real-time services, such as video telephony, are highly delay-sensitive and should be classified as Conversational.

Interactive and Background classes are intended for traditional Internet applications like WWW, Email, Telnet, and FTP. The Interactive class is used by interactive applications such as interactive Email or interactive Web browsing. The Background class is intended for background traffic, as the name suggests; that is, download of emails or files. As would be expected, traffic in the Interactive class has higher priority to Background class traffic, so background applications use transmission resources only when the other traffic classes are not.

Bearer Service Attributes

Bearer service attributes describe the service provided by the network to the end user. A set of QoS attributes are used to specify a given service. At bearer service establishment for a user application, QoS profiles mapping to the application needs must be classified and subsequently enforced.

These attributes are as follows:

- Traffic class
- Maximum bit rate
- Guaranteed bit rate
- Delivery order
- Maximum service data unit (SDU) size
- SDU format information
- SDU error ratio
- Residual bit error ratio
- Delivery of erroneous SDUs
- Transfer delay
- Traffic handling priority (THP)
- Allocation and retention priority
- Source statistics descriptor
- Signaling indication

Details of these attributes are not given here; however, the specifications give an exhaustive view of recommendations for each attribute to each service class at each layer of the reference model.

Mobile Network Protocol Stacks

To understand the QoS requirements in a mobile network, it is important to understand the traffic and protocols in detail that must be transported across the network infrastructure.

The General Protocol Model is described in standard 3G TS 25.401. The UTRAN interface consists of a set of horizontal and vertical layers, as shown in Figure 5.27. The UTRAN requirements are addressed in the horizontal radio network layer across different types of control and user planes.

Control planes are used to control a link or a connection, as the name suggests. User planes are used to transparently transmit user data from the higher layer applications.

Five major protocol blocks are shown in Figure 5.27 as follows:

- Signaling bearers are used to transmit higher layers' signaling and control information.
- Data bearers are the frame protocols used to transport user data streams generated from higher layer applications.

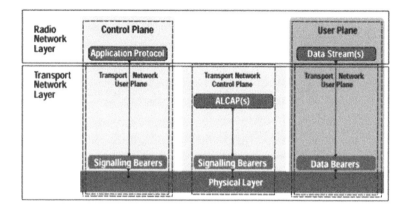

Figure 5.27

- Application protocols refer to UMTS—specific signaling and control within UTRAN rather than user applications. An example is establishing bearers in the radio network layer.
- Data streams contain the user data that is transparently transmitted between the network elements. User data is composed of the subscriber's personal data and mobility management information that are exchanged between the peer entities MGW/MSC and UE.
- Access link control application part (ALCAP) protocol layers are provided in the transport network control plane (TN–CP). ALCAP manages the radio network layer's demands to set up, maintain, and release data bearers. The primary objective of introducing the TN–CP was to totally separate the selection of the data bearer technology from the control plane where the UTRAN-specific application protocols are located. The TN–CP is present in the Iu–CS, Iur, and Iub interfaces.

In 3GPP R99, ATM is the dominant transport technology from Node B through the CN. With Release 5, both ATM and IP are equally valid transport technologies, with IP as the converged network layer.

For 3G Release 99 and Release 4, transport is either AAl2 or AAL5. AAL2 offers synchronous mode, connection-oriented connections with VBR (e.g., voice traffic). AAL5 offers asynchronous mode, connection-oriented VBR (e.g., packet data). Currently, within the UTRAN, AAL5 carries all control data, as well as user data, over the Iu-PS interface to the SGSN. AAL2 carries user voice data in the circuit-switched domain over Iu-CS. However, since 3GPP Release 5, IP is the converged transport for all data, including control and Iu-PS user data.

Figure 5.28 shows an overview of the protocol stacks in the UMTS network with both ATM and IP options at the relevant

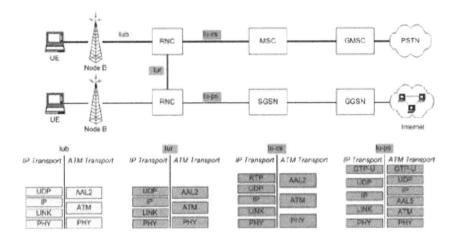

Figure 5.28

network interface reference points. A detailed view of the protocol stacks transported for both GSM and 3G per release will is discussed in the rest of this section.

Packet-Switched Domain Network Protocol Stacks

The GPRS sub-network is responsible for user application data transport. As discussed in the previous sections, there must be connectivity for 2.5G and 3G services in the mobile operator's network. Figure 5.29 gives a high level overview of the GPRS sub-network for the GSM legacy users and the 3G UMTS RAN.

A detailed diagram of the converged GSM 2.5G and 3G GPRS sub-network as per the specification 3GPP TS123060 is as follows: note that the reference interfaces in the data path do not change

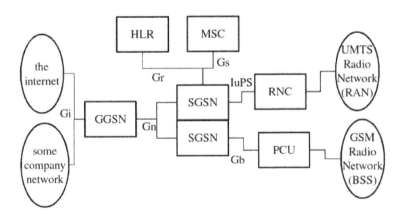

Figure 5.29

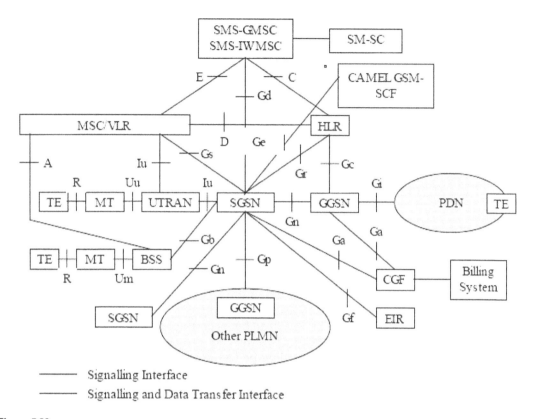

Figure 5.30

through to Release 5; only the underlying transport protocol changes from ATM to IP. See Figure 5.30.

There are many interfaces required within the data packet-switched domain. These interfaces span the UTRAN and GSM BSS connectivity. However, the majority are after the SGSN, which is the same for either 2.5G or 3G.

A complete list of reference interfaces in the GPRS network is as follows;

- Gb – Interface between the base station subsystem and the SGSN the transmission protocol could be frame relay or IP.
- Gn – IP-based interface between SGSN and other SGSNs and (internal) GGSNs. DNS also shares this interface. Uses the GTP Protocol.
- Gp – IP-based interface between internal SGSN and external GGSNs. Between the SGSN and the external GGSN, there is the border gateway (which is essentially a firewall). Also uses the GTP Protocol.

- Ga – The interface servers the CDRs (accounting records), which are written in the GSN and sent to the charging gateway (CG). This interface uses a GTP-based protocol, with modifications that support CDRs (Called GTP' or GTP prime).
- Gr – Interface between the SGSN and the HLR. Messages going through this interface use the MAP3 Protocol.
- Gd – Interface between the SGSN and the SMS gateway. Can use MAP1, MAP2, or MAP3.
- Gs – Interface between the SGSN and the MSC (VLR). Uses the BSSAP+ Protocol. This interface allows paging and station availability when it performs data transfer. When the station is attached to the GPRS network, the SGSN keeps track of which routing area (RA) the station is attached to. An RA is a part of a larger location area (LA). When a station is paged, this information is used to conserve network resources. When the station performs a PDP Context, the SGSN has the exact BTS the station is using.
- Gi – The interface between the GGSN and a public data network (PDN), either directly to the Internet or through a WAP gateway. Uses the IP protocol.
- Ge – The interface between the SGSN and the service control point (SCP). Uses the CAP Protocol.
- Gx – The on-line policy interface between the GGSN and the charging rules function (CRF). It is used for provisioning service data flow-based charging rules. Uses the Diameter Protocol.
- Gy – The on-line charging interface between the GGSN and the online charging system (OCS). Uses the Diameter Protocol (DCCA application).
- Gz – The off-line (CDR-based) charging interface between the GSN and the charging gateway (CG). Uses GTP'.
- Gmb – The interface between the GGSN and the Broadcast-multicast service center (BM-SC), used for controlling MBMS bearers.

Not all of these interfaces are of interest in the context of QoS within the mobile provider's infrastructure. The following section identifies the interfaces in the GPRS sub-network that require QoS enforcement.

GSM 2.5G GPRS Protocol Stacks

Figure 5.31 shows the protocol stack for the 2.5G GPRS traffic flow from the end user terminal to the GGSN gateway. The first diagram shows the user plane while the second diagram shows the control plane.

Note that the network service interface for Gb between the BSC in the BSS and the SGSN is generally frame relay.

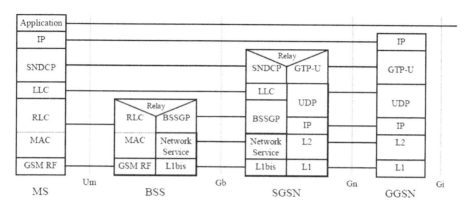

Figure 5.31

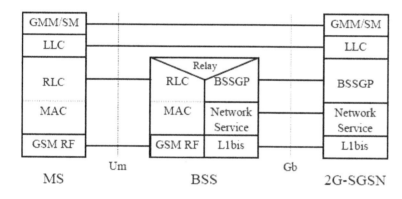

Figure 5.32

Figure 5.32 shows the protocol stack for the control plane. Note that the protocol stack for the control plane is identical to the user plane up to the SGSN.

Once again, as for the data bearer plane, the network service for the Gn connection typically uses frame relay.

Note that the control plane data only extends as far as the SGSN in Figure 5.32. Control and signaling for connections is handled exclusively by the SGSN device. The GGSN accepts tunneled data and forwards as requested by the SGSN. This is the case for all the 3G releases, as can be seen from the subsequent control protocol stack figures.

3G Release 99 and Release 4 GPRS Protocol Stacks

The 3G Release 99 and Release 4 protocol stacks for GPRS are identical. Both these releases rely on ATM for the transport, as shown in Figure 5.33 and Figure 5.34, for the user and control planes.

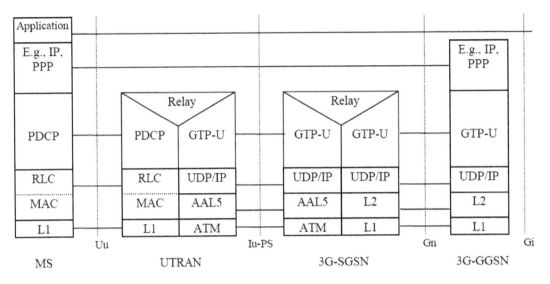

Figure 5.33

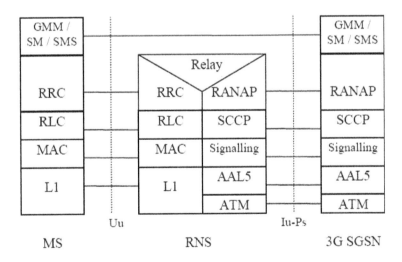

Figure 5.34

The connection from the UTRAN RNC through to the SGSN for both user and control data utilizes the AAL5 adaption layer for both the control and user planes. Also worthy of note is the extension of the GPRS Tunneling Protocol (GTP-U) through to the RNC. In the GSM network, the GTP protocol is exclusively between the SGSN and the GGSN.

3G Release 5 GPRS Protocol Stacks

Release 5 introduces IP as an option in the transport from the RNC. Although IP becomes the converged network layer, providers with ATM investment may still use this technology as the Layer 2 network if desired.

The protocol stack for 3G Release 5, GPRS in the user and control planes, is shown in Figure 5.35 and Figure 5.36.

With IP as the converged Layer 3 from the UTRAN RNC through to the GGSN, any Layer 1 and Layer 2 transport technology can be used. This is an important step on the path to IP-enabled multimedia applications. Once again, note that

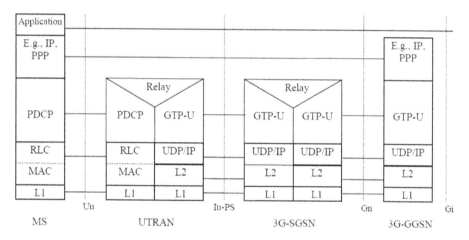

Figure 5.35

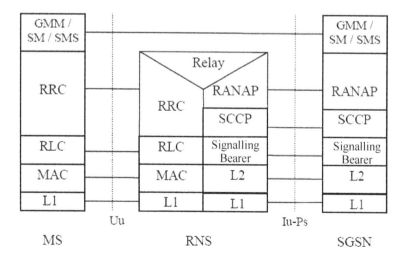

Figure 5.36

throughout the evolution of 3G releases, the SGSN to GGSN Gn interface remains unchanged.

In practice, many mobile providers have opted to implement dedicated 3G SGSN/GGSN pairs in parallel with the existing GSM pairs. Additionally, many providers preferred to move to the Release 5 standards directly, rather than implement the Release 99 and Release 4 specifications using ATM.

As shown in the Iu-PS figures, the protocol stack on the interface supports radio access network application part (RANAP) in the control plane. RANAP is the radio network layer signaling protocol for the Iu interface, including Iu-PS and Iu-CS. It manages the signaling and GTP connections between RNC and 3G-SGSN. It also manages signaling and circuit-switched connections between RNC and 3G MGW on the Iu interface.

RANAP also provides a signaling channel to transparently pass messages between UE and the core network. HSS RANAP protocol implementation provides the elementary procedures for accomplishing radio access bearer management, serving RNS relocation, transport of NAS information between UE and CN, paging UE, and release of Iu resources.

RANAP gives three types of services:
- General control services
- Notification services
- Dedicated control services

Circuit-Switched Domain Network Protocol Stacks

The circuit-switched domain contains protocols specifically for voice signaling and transport. In the Release 99 specifications, the MGW is placed between the RNC and the legacy MSC connected via TDM. This is to allow a graceful evolution to bearer-independent infrastructure from Release 4 onwards.

With the introduction of Release 4, the MSC and GMSC are retired in favor of the MGW plus MSC server and GMSC server. The reference model used by the 3GPP for the Release 4 circuit-switched domain is shown in Figure 5.37.

According to the standards, "The Mc reference point in the present document considers the aspects of the interface between the (G)MSC server and the MGW. The H.248 protocol [5] together with 3GPP specific extensions/packages shall be used over the Mc interface. The Network-Network based call control is used over the Nc interface. Any suitable call control protocol may be used over the Nc interface (e.g. BICC). The bearer control signaling and transport are carried over the Nb interface."

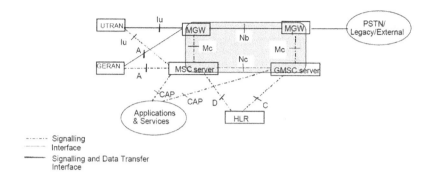

Signalling
Interface
Signalling and Data Transfer
Interface

Figure 5.37

AAL-2 SAR SSCS (I.366.1)
AAL2 (I.363.2)
ATM

Figure 5.38

AAL2 connection signalling (Q.2630.2)
AAL2 Signalling Transport Converter for MTP3b (Q.2150.1)
MTP3b
SSCF-NNI
SSCOP
AAL5
ATM

Figure 5.39

The Nb interface user plane protocol stack can be ATM- or IP-based. Figure 5.38 and Figure 5.39 show the ATM options for user plane and control plane.

The IP option for the Nb interface for control and user plane is shown in Figure 5.40.

Note that IPV4 or IPV6 are valid options for the transport. Also note that Layer 1 and Layer 2 protocols are not shown, since IP is

RTP
UDP
IPv4 or IPv6

Figure 5.40

the converged Layer 3, making the choice of transport at lower layers irrelevant. In the case of the control path, the upper layer protocol will be RCTP; otherwise the protocol stack is identical to the user plane.

For the remainder of this chapter, IP is assumed as the chosen transport option for the Nb, Nc, and Mc interfaces.

The Iu Interface in the Circuit-Switched Domain

The Iu interface toward the circuit-switched domain is Iu-CS. This interface is between the 3G RNC and the MGW. This interface services the voice traffic and signaling to and from the core network. In the Release 99 specification, the interface from the RNC into the MGW is ATM, which the MGW then converts to TDM for connection to the legacy MSC. In Release 4, VoIP is introduced and the MSC is retired. However, the Iu-CS interface remains ATM and unchanged from Release 99.

Figure 5.41 shows a detailed breakdown of the Iu-CS protocol stack for the control and user planes in the Release 99 and Release 4 specifications.

Note that in the user plane for the circuit-switched domain traffic, the transport is ATM AAL2. The control and network planes rely on AAL5.

As was the case with the Iu-CS protocol stack, from Release 5 the option exists for IP transport on the Iu-CS interface for both the control and the user plane. Figure 5.42 shows the Iu-CS protocol stack for Release 5 onward.

Note that, in Release 5, both ATM and IP are valid transport options to support legacy equipment from Release 99 and Release 4.

The IuR interface connects the 3G RNCs together for both control and user planes. The protocol stack for IuR is shown in Figure 5.43.

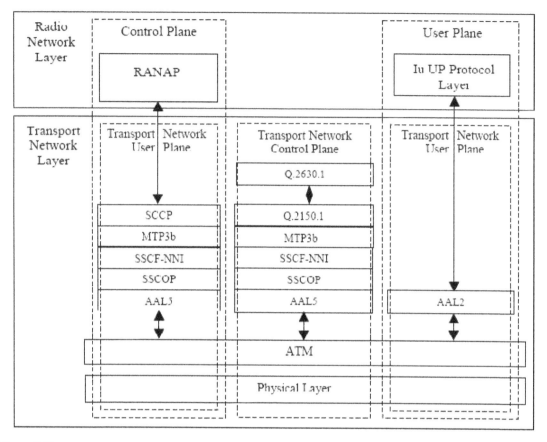

Figure 5.41

The control plane relies on AAL5, whereas the user plane relies on AAL2. This is the same as the Iu-CS interface.

Mobile Network Transport Framework

This section covers the transport of mobile traffic through the provider network. Layer 3 VPN-based transport is the preferred option for mobile traffic. The recommended structure for VPNs are outlined. The QoS framework and requirements are defined for the mobile network supporting legacy 2G data and 3G Release 99 through to Release 5 connectivity. For specific details of the QoS configurations, please refer to the later MPLS VPN and Multicast QoS chapters.

Note that in the Release 99 specification the legacy MSC remains; however, since it is TDM-connected, no reference is

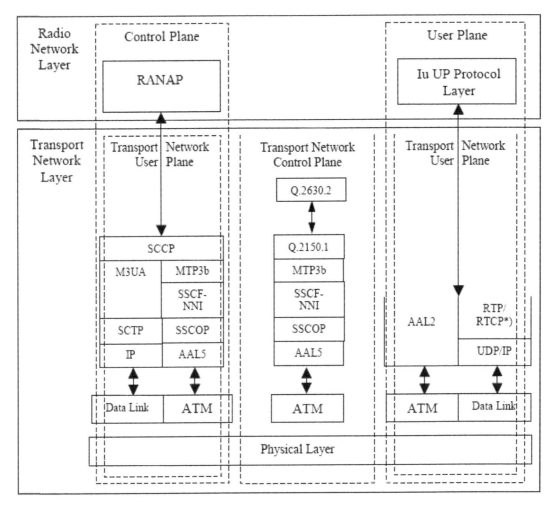

Figure 5.42

made to the MSC in the QoS framework. Also note that the MSC server and GMSC servers are shown in the diagram in Figure 5.44 with reference to Release 4 and beyond. These devices are not included in the Release 99 specifications.

Figure 5.45 gives a more detailed view of the connections from each of the devices to the edge PE router.

The interface names and associated types are shown in Table 5.1. Building on the previous sections, the mobile network infrastructure must support the following interfaces within a mobile network on the evolutionary path to 3G. Entries for 2.5G and 3G Releases 99, 4, and 5 are shown.

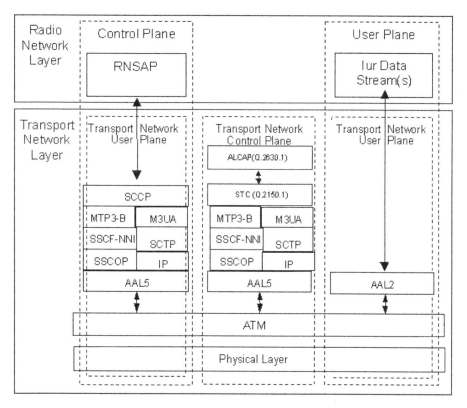

Figure 5.43

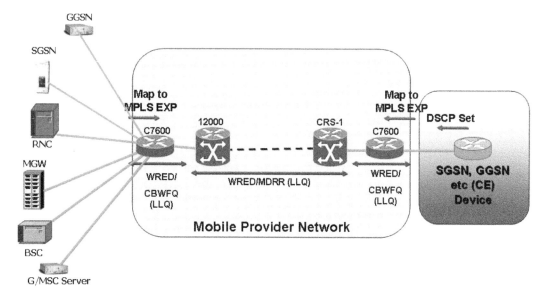

Figure 5.44

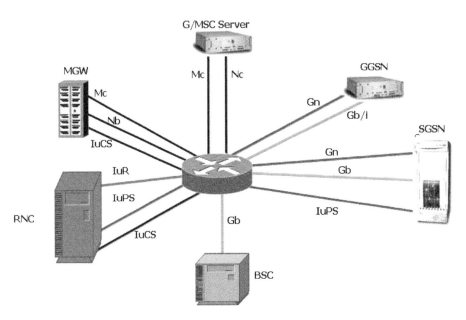

Figure 5.45

MPLS layer 2 VPN for ATM traffic and layer 3 VPN for all IP traffic are accepted as leading practice for transporting of mobile traffic through the provider network. All traffic for the

Quality of Service Framework

Throughout these discussions, we prefer to use the Cisco-modified informational RFC4594 recommendations as the baseline for classification. Figure 5.46 lists the classification guidelines.

Vendors of the mobile network equipment must classify the traffic prior to transport across the core network. This is the only option available within the network, particularly for the data transport, as there is no scalable way of the edge PE implementing a classification policy. When the data context is initiated, the mobile equipment marks the traffic with the appropriate DiffServ fields.

Figure 5.47 shows a mapping of DSCP bits to the four data classes as defined by 3GPP. This gives a reference for the typical QoS model that may be used by a mobile equipment vendor in the GGSN and SGSN.

Table 5.1   Mobile Network Interfaces for 2.5G and 3G Releases 99, 4, and 5

Mobile Generation	Interface Name	Interface Type
2.5G GSM	Um	Air/Radio
	Abis	TDM
	A	TDM
	Gb	Frame Relay
	Gn	IP
	Gi	IP
3G Release 99	Uu	Air/Radio
	Iub	ATM AAL2/5 E1
	A	TDM
	IuCS	ATM AAL2/5
	IuPS	ATM AAL5
	IuR	ATM AAL2/5
	Gn	IP
	Gi	IP
3G Release 4	Uu	Air/Radio
	Iub	ATM AAL2/5 E1
	A	TDM
	IuCS	ATM AAL2/5
	IuPS	ATM AAL5
	IuR	ATM AAL2/5
	Gn	IP
	Gi	IP
	Nb	IP
	Nc	IP
	Mc	IP
3G R5	Uu	Air/Radio
	Iub	ATM AAL2/5 E1
	A	TDM
	IuCS	IP
	IuPS	IP
	IuR	ATM AAL2/5
	Gb	Frame Relay or IP
	Gn	IP
	Gi	IP
	Nb	IP
	Nc	IP
	Mc	IP

Application	L3 Classification		IETF
	PHB	DSCP	RFC
Network Control	CS6	48	RFC 2474
VoIP Telephony	EF	46	RFC 3246
Broadcast Video	CS5	40	RFC 2474
Multimedia Conferencing	AF41	34	RFC 2597
Real-Time Interactive	CS4	32	RFC 2474
Multimedia Streaming	AF31	26	RFC 2597
Call Signaling	CS3	24	RFC 2474
Low-Latency Data	AF21	18	RFC 2597
OAM	CS2	16	RFC 2474
High-Troughput Data	AF11	10	RFC 2597
Best Effort	DF	0	RFC 2474
Low-Priority Data	CS1	8	RFC 3662

Figure 5.46

3GPP QoS Information		DiffServ PHB	DSCP	QoS Requirement on GRX				Service Example
Traffic Class	THP			Max Delay	Max Jitter	Packet Loss	SDU Error Ratio	
Conversational	N/A	EF	101110	20ms	5ms	0.5%	10^{-6}	VoIP, Video Conferencing
Streaming	N/A	$AF4_1$	100010	40ms	5ms	0.5%	10^{-6}	Audio/Video Streaming
Interactive	1	$AF3_1$	011010	250ms	N/A	0.1%	10^{-8}	Transactional Services
	2	$AF2_1$	010010	300ms	N/A	0.1%	10^{-8}	Web Browsing
	3	$AF1_1$	001010	350ms	N/A	0.1%	10^{-8}	Telnet
Background	N/A	BE	000000	400ms	N/A	0.1%	10^{-8}	E-mail Download

Figure 5.47

According to the GSMA PRD IR.34 recommendations, six classes of service are strictly required; however, the Interactive class contains three-subclasses, which can be aggregated into a single class if required by the provider. Hence, the minimum requirement is for four classes to carry the 3GPP data classes. The provider may have a converged network carrying many services, including mobile traffic and hence the QoS framework must be in the context of the network as a whole.

QoS Traffic Management for Mobile

With the classification established for the traffic, important aspects of the traffic management must now be agreed:

- Mapping of data DiffServ classes to MPLS EXP bits for enforcement through the provider network
- Clearly defining the treatment for out-of-contract traffic in each class
- Clearly understanding the requirement for WRED to further optimize traffic patterns

Traffic levels that are beyond what has been agreed to are referred to as out-of-contract traffic and should be defined for each class to make sure that all traffic uses the same out-of-contract behavior in that class. If the traffic in one class exceeds what the GPRS/UMTS operator has allocated in the CoS traffic contract, there are various options that can be performed.

Conversational Class

The conversational traffic class will be marked as DiffServ expedited forwarding. To preserve the low-latency queuing behavior, out-of-contract conversational class is defined to be dropped. To accommodate the burst nature of conversational traffic, metering with token bucket algorithms can be used to determine whether traffic is out-of-contract.

The proposed marking is as follows:

- EF—in-contract conversational traffic class
- Out-of-contract conversational traffic is dropped

The expedited forwarding behavior aggregate makes use of low latency queuing (LLQ), as described in Chapter 2. Strict-priority queuing allows delay-sensitive data such as voice to be sent in preference to other queued traffic, effectively giving delay-sensitive data preferential treatment. This can lead to a situation where the LLQ traffic can starve other queues of bandwidth, potentially impacting other services. Typically, the LLQ is limited to a maximum of 30 percent of the total link capacity for this reason. Configuration of traffic management includes a bandwidth argument that gives *maximum* bandwidth for this behavior aggregate. If congestion occurs, when the allocated bandwidth for the strict-priority queue is exceeded, policing is used to drop packets.

Given that the traffic in the conversational class is UDP-based and there is a hard out-of-contract policy enforced, WRED is not used.

Streaming Class

As recommended by GSM Association PRD IR.34, streaming traffic class is marked as Assured Forwarding (AF4x). Video traffic, because of its usually limited burst behavior and large packet size, is typically more complex to manage than voice.

As with conversational traffic, in the event of exceeded traffic in this class, the allocated bandwidth packets are dropped rather than remarked.

- AF41—in-contract streaming class is passed
- Out-of-contract streaming traffic class is dropped

Given that the majority of traffic in the streaming class is UDP-based and there is a hard out-of-contract policy enforced, WRED is not used.

Interactive Class

Interactive traffic classes use the remaining Assured Forwarding classifications. According to GSM Association PRD IR.34, the differences between AF3x, AF2x, and AF1x traffic classes are the priority of the queuing behavior and the maximum buffer size, which is defined to accommodate the high delay possibilities for the lower-priority traffic.

- AFx1—In-contract Interactive traffic class
- AFx2—Exceeded-contract Interactive traffic class
- AFx3—Violated-contract Interactive traffic class

The provider may choose to map each of these interactive subclasses into a single class within the IP/MPLS core or they may keep them separate. Both these options are explored in the following sections.

Interactive traffic class mainly contains TCP traffic. TCP congestion-avoidance techniques can therefore be used. WRED is recommended to manage traffic in this class.

Background Class

The background class is recommended to be marked as "best effort" by the standards document by GSM. Given that the traffic in this class has traversed the radio interface in the case of ingress traffic from the UE, marking this class as best effort has caused the use of valuable resources to possibly see the data dropped.

The provider may choose to give the background class priority through the network beyond best effort if they determine other network traffic is of lower priority.

Alternative QoS Models

There are many alternative models for the QoS framework. Figure 5.48 gives an example of a five class QoS model.

Note that the Interactive classes are all configured as a single IP precedence and MPLS EXP class for management in the provider network. This gives fewer classes to manage in the network, making issues such as capacity planning less complex for the network operator. The disadvantage is that the delay differences between the Interactive classes are combined, giving a single profile for transactional services and general web browsing.

A more granular QoS class approach also gives the provider greater visibility into the network bandwidth usage. This enables more effective understanding of the traffic profiles and hence more accurate capacity planning.

Ultimately, the parameters for the Interactive classes are identical except for delay parameters, leading many providers to the five-class model.

Where the provider prefers a more granular model, the Interactive class can be split into separate classes, as shown in Figure 5.49.

3GPP Class	Diffserv	DSCP	IP Prec	MPLS Exp
Routing/signalling	AF	48	6	6
Conversational	EF	40	5	5
Streaming	AF	32	4	4
Interactive Gold	AF	24	2	2
Interactive Silver	AF	16	2	2
Interactive Bronze	AF	8	2	2
Background	BE	0	0	0

Figure 5.48

3GPP Class	Diffserv	DSCP	IP Prec	MPLS Exp
Routing/signalling	AF	48	6	6
Conversational	EF	40	5	5
Streaming	AF	32	4	4
Interactive Gold	AF	24	3	3
Interactive Silver	AF	16	2	2
Interactive Bronze	AF	8	1	1
Background	BE	0	0	0

Figure 5.49

As mentioned before, the chosen scheme will depend on:
- The implementation of classes from the vendor equipment, such as the GGSN and RNC
- The QoS framework adopted by the provider in the context of all services carried through the network

Given the recommendations in GSMA PRD IR.34, the seven class scheme supporting the 3GPP QoS framework is preferred where possible. As noted, many providers consider the five class model adequate, given the close alignment of requirements in the three Interactive category sub-classes.

The QoS scheme extends beyond the 3GPP QoS framework for the provider. The network must also support traffic for the Iu interface types being transported. The QoS framework for all traffic in the provider network for 3G Release 99 through to Release 5/6 is discussed in the following sections.

Quality of Service Mapping for 2.5G and 3G Release 99

The interface mappings in Figure 5.50 and Table 5.2 give examples of how a provider may map the IP precedence and MPLS EXP bits at the edge of the network for the 2.5G and 3G Release 99 mobile standards.

Note that the 2.5G and 3G GGSN may be the same device; however, separating these devices is common practice with providers implementing the 3G roadmap.

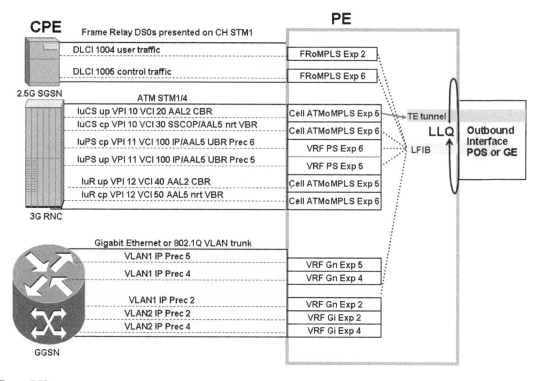

Figure 5.50

For simplicity, the Gb interface between the SGSN and the BSC is represented in the diagram on the SGSN only. Likewise, the Gn interface between the SGSN and the GGSN is shown on the GGSN only. The MGW is not shown, as the Iu-CS interface is represented on the RNC device and the interface from the MGW to the MSC is TDM; hence, QoS is not required.

The Gn and Gi VRF show multiple VLANs and IP precedence or DSCP settings. This is vendor-dependent and is shown only an example. Likewise the mapping for VPI and VCI from the RNC, and the frame relay DCLIs from the 2.5 GGSN is only to illustrate the QoS principle.

Note that the seven class model from the previous section is used for the QoS mapping.

Quality of Service Mapping for 3G Release 4

The following interface mappings in Figure 5.51 and Table 5.3 give examples of how a provider may map the IP Precedence and MPLS EXP bits at the edge of the network for the 3G Release 4 mobile standards.

Table 5.2 QoS Mapping for 2.5G and 3G Release 99

Release	Interface Name	Interface Type	QoS Requirement	IP Prec/MPLS EXP
2.5G GSM	Um	Air/Radio	N/A	
	Abis	TDM	N/A	
	A	TDM	N/A	
	Gb	Frame Relay	User Traffic	2
			Control Traffic	6
	Gn	IP	User Traffic	2
	Gi	IP	User Traffic	2
3G Release 99	Uu	Air/Radio	N/A	
	Iub	ATM AAL2/5 E1	MTOP N/A	
	A	TDM	N/A	
	IuCS	ATM AAL5	Control Plane	6
		ATM AAL2	User Plane	5
	IuPS	ATM AAL5	Control Plane	6
			User Plane	5
	IuR	ATM AAL5	Control Plane	6
		ATM AAL2	User Plane	5
	Gn	IP	Conversational	5
			Streaming	4
			Interactive 1	3
			Interactive 2	2
			Interactive 3	1
			background	0
	Gi	IP	Conversational	5
			Streaming	4
			Interactive 1	3
			Interactive 2	2
			Interactive 3	1
			background	0

The RNC, GGSN, and SGSN interfaces are identical to those in the previous section. The MGW requires ATM and Ethernet interface types for the Release 4 specifications. The Nc interface between the MGW and the MSC Server is shown on the MSC server only.

Quality of Service Mapping for 3G Release 5

The following interface mappings in Figure 5.52 and Table 5.4 give examples of how a provider may map the IP precedence and MPLS EXP bits at the edge of the network for the 3G Release 5 mobile standards.

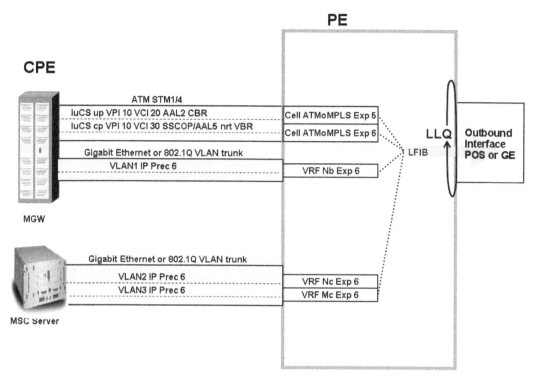

Figure 5.51

Table 5.3 QoS Mapping for 2.5G and 3G Release 4

Release	Interface Name	Interface Type	QoS Requirement	IP Prec/MPLS EXP
3G Release 4	Uu	Air/Radio	N/A	
	Iub	ATM AAL2/5 E1	MTOP N/A	
	A	TDM	N/A	
	IuCS	ATM AAL5	Control Plane	6
		ATM AAL2	User Plane	5
	IuPS	ATM AAL5	Control Plane	6
			User Plane	5
	IuR	ATM AAL5	Control Plane	6
		ATM AAL2	User Plane	5
	Gn	IP	Conversational	5
			Streaming	4
			Interactive 1	3

Continued

Table 5.3 QoS Mapping for 2.5G and 3G Release 4—cont'd

Release	Interface Name	Interface Type	QoS Requirement	IP Prec/MPLS EXP
			Interactive 2	2
			Interactive 3	1
			background	0
	Gi	IP	Conversational	5
			Streaming	4
			Interactive 1	3
			Interactive 2	2
			Interactive 3	1
			background	0
	Nb	IP	Signaling	6
	Nc	IP	Signaling	6
	Mc	IP	Signaling	6

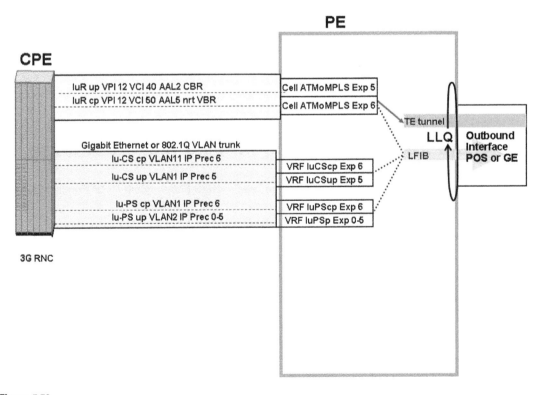

Figure 5.52

Table 5.4 QoS Mapping for 2.5G and 3G Release 5

Release	Interface Name	Interface Type	QoS Requirement	IP Prec/MPLS EXP
3G Release 5	Uu	Air/Radio	N/A	
	Iub	ATM AAL2/5 E1	MTOP N/A	
	A	TDM	N/A	
	IuCS	IP	Control Plane	6
		IP	User Plane	5
	IuPS	IP	Control Plane	6
			Conversational	5
			Streaming	4
			Interactive 1	3
			Interactive 2	2
			Interactive 3	1
			background	0
	IuR	ATM AAL5	Control Plane	6
		ATM AAL2	User Plane	5
	Gn	IP	Conversational	5
			Streaming	4
			Interactive 1	3
			Interactive 2	2
			Interactive 3	1
			background	0
	Gi	IP	Conversational	5
			Streaming	4
			Interactive 1	3
			Interactive 2	2
			Interactive 3	1
			background	0
	Nb	IP	Signaling	6
	Nc	IP	Signaling	6
	Mc	IP	Signaling	6

The GGSN, SGSN, and MSC server interfaces are identical to those in the previous sections. The 3G RNC Iu-PS and Iu-CS interfaces are IP-based over Ethernet interfaces. The IuR interface is shown as IP; however, it may be ATM or IP according to the standards.

The Iu-PS user plane interface now carries the traffic based on 3GPP classification based on conversational, streaming, interactive, and background. The DSCP or IP precedence markings are applied by the RNC.

Conclusion

The mobile provider network is rapidly evolving toward an end-to-end IP infrastructure. The mobile network is an important aspect of the NGN vision, driving toward a single converged infrastructure.

6

EMERGING TRENDS IN PACKET OPTICAL CONVERGENCE

Introduction

Packet-optical transport has been a major trend in optical networking over the past 18 months. New products have emerged that combine WDM transport, ROADMs, SONET/SDH ADMs, and centralized-carrier Ethernet-switching in a single converged device. These products are known as packet-optical transport systems (P-OTS).

To date, the P-OTS evolution has been all about the metro, but now we're seeing P-OTS move into the core of the network. Part of the reason core P-OTS is emerging now is that the core transport network has largely been ignored for a couple of years while the industry has focused on rebuilding access, metro, and aggregation networks for packets and IP. In reality, growth in Ethernet and IP, Internet data and video, and mobile data and video affect core as well as metro access networks. The migration from SONET/SDH circuits to packets is not just a metro issue.

While metro networks are moving toward converged transport and switching, the core network today consists primarily of stand-alone DWDM elements, optical cross-connects, SONET/SDH ADMs, and overlay carrier Ethernet-switched networks. First-generation optical cross-connects, which are widely installed worldwide, pose significant challenges for operators. They are based on SONET/SDH switching fabrics. They are effective in networks that are primarily SONET/SDH with some Ethernet, but were not designed for networks that are primarily based on Ethernet and IP. Limited Ethernet functionality has been added to optical cross-connects over time, allowing for Ethernet over SONET/SDH transport or for a small amount of Ethernet switching. But optical cross-connects remain TDM devices.

The other key shortcoming of optical cross-connect elements is that they never really migrated out of the network core. Metro/regional networks to date have mostly been populated with

SONET/SDH multiplexers and WDM multiplexers based on traditional ring topologies, not mesh topologies. Thus, operational and bandwidth-saving benefits enabled by core mesh networks haven't been extended beyond the core. Also, the benefits of rapid service provisioning have been largely isolated to the core, preventing the emergence of true end-to-end service provisioning.

Today, as operators have begun their transition from TDM to packet networking, they are faced with a hodgepodge of different networks and different types of networks elements. The network backbone/core is populated with specialized long-haul DWDM equipment and separate optical cross-connect elements for switching. These DWDM and optical cross-connect elements interface with core routers that handle the IP layer. Metro networks are populated with specialized metro WDM equipment and multiservice SONET/SDH equipment. Meanwhile, separate Ethernet-switched networks are also in the metro mix for handling switched Ethernet services. These metro Ethernet networks are overlay networks. Across all of these disparate elements and disparate networks, there is no unified control plane for tying them all together. The bottom line is that some of problems of the past decade have been solved, as operators are able to offer packet-based services to their customers. However, the solution has resulted in CapEx and OpEx levels that simply cannot scale as the network transition shifts from TDM-centric with some packet-to-packet-centric with some TDM and, ultimately, to all packet networking.

Increasingly, operators see core packet-optical transport as the solution to the challenges facing the core evolution. In short, this new class of network element takes many of the functions being put into metro/regional P-OTS (such as WDM, Ethernet, and SONET/SDH integration) with greater capacity and scale—and with some key differences, such as high-capacity optical transport network (OTN) switching and an automatically switched optical network (ASON)/generalized MPLS (GMPLS) control plane. In this chapter we discuss the integration aspects between the packet and optical domains.

Basics about Optical Networks

In order to understand the design requirements for packet optical networking, called IPoDWDM in this chapter, and the evolution from traditional DWDM systems, an understanding of the DWDM technology is required. The following section gives an overview of the DWDM technology and the components that comprise DWDM.

Figure 6.1

DWDM Basics

Dense wavelength division multiplexing (DWDM) is a fiber-optic transmission technique. It involves the process of multiplexing many different wavelength signals onto a single fiber. Each fiber has a set of parallel optical channels and each one uses slightly different light wavelengths. The fibers employ light wavelengths to transmit data parallel-by-bit or serial-by-character. DWDM is a very crucial component of optical networks that will allow the transmission of data: voice, video-IP, ATM, and SONET/SDH respectively, over the optical layer. Figure 6.1 shows this technique at its most basic representation.

DWDM System

As mentioned earlier, optical networks use dense wavelength multiplexing as the underlying carrier. The most important components of any DWDM system are transmitters, receivers, Erbium-doped fiber amplifiers (EDFA), optical add and drop multiplexors (OADM), DWDM multiplexors, and DWDM de-multiplexors. Figure 6.2 gives the structure of a typical DWDM system.

Optical Transmission Principles

The DWDM system has an important photonic layer, which is responsible for transmission of the optical data through the network. Some basic principles concerning the optical transmission are explained in this section. These are necessary for the proper operation of the system.

Channel Spacing

The minimum frequency separation between two different signals multiplexed is known as the "channel spacing." Since the wavelength of operation is inversely proportional to the

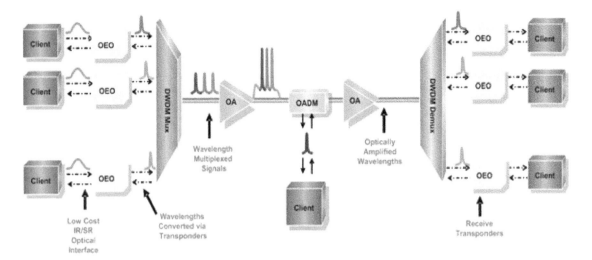

Figure 6.2

frequency, a corresponding difference is introduced in the wavelength of each signal. The factors controlling channel spacing are the optical amplifier's bandwidth and the capability of the receiver in identifying two close wavelengths sets the lower bound on the channel spacing. Both factors ultimately restrict the number of unique wavelengths passing through the amplifier.

Signal Direction

An optical fiber helps transmit signal in both directions. Based on this feature, a DWDM system can be implemented in two ways:
- Unidirectional: All wavelengths travel in the same direction within the fiber. It is similar to a simplex case. This calls in for laying one another parallel fiber for supporting transmission on the other side.
- Bi-directional: The channels in the DWDM fiber are split into two separate bands, one for each direction. This removes the need for the second fiber, but it reduces the capacity or transmission bandwidth.

DWDM Transponders

Transponders are devices that, in DWDM networks, receive an optical signal (data-stream) from short-reach optics at one wavelength; for example, 1310 nm. This is used to modulate the light output from a laser source operating on a different wavelength; for example, 15xx nm used for long-reach optics.

- One transponder has to be used for every input or output channel, as it is only capable of operating one specific wavelength out of the ITU grid.
- On the receive side, there is a long-haul receiver optimized to handle the presence of noise, dispersion and other complexities of long-haul DWDM systems.
- Finally, the signal is driven onto a short-reach, low-cost transmitter to connect optically to the terminal equipment.

DWDM systems use transponders at both the transmit side and the receive side of the link, providing a clear demarcation between the long-haul transmission system and the terminal equipment. It provides, for example, performance monitoring at the transponder interface to determine if errors have been generated outside the DWDM system or within it.

Transponders provide the 3R regeneration functions, re-amplify, reshape, and retime, as they are realized in electronics.

Multiplexers and De-Multiplexers

Because DWDM systems send signals from several sources over a single fiber, they must include some means to combine the incoming signals. This is done with a multiplexer, which takes optical wavelengths from multiple fibers and converges them into one beam. At the receiving end the system must be able to separate out the components of the light so that they can be discreetly detected. See Figure 6.3.

De-multiplexers perform this function by separating the received beam into its wavelength components and coupling them to individual fibers. De-multiplexing must be done before the light is detected, because photodetectors are inherently broadband devices that cannot selectively detect a single wavelength.

Optical Add/Drop Multiplexers

Between multiplexing and de-multiplexing points in a DWDM system, as shown in Figure 6.4, there is an area in which multiple wavelengths exist. It is often desirable to be able to remove or insert one or more wavelengths at some point along this span. An optical add/drop multiplexer (OADM) performs this function.

Rather than combining or separating all wavelengths, the OADM can remove some while passing others on. Figure 6.5 shows the flexibility of OADMs in adding and removing channels.

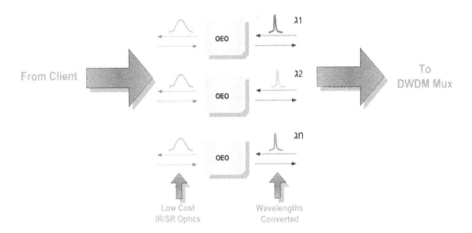

Figure 6.3

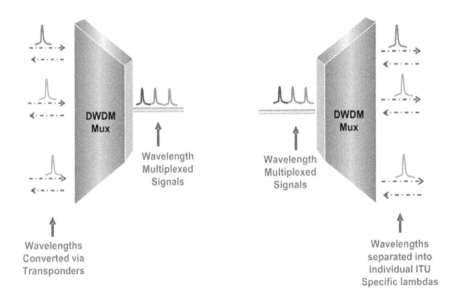

Figure 6.4

Overview of Fixed OADM & ROADM Technology

First- and second-generation DWDM networks were built with fixed optical add/drop multiplexer (OADM) technology. While these systems have enormous capacity and are in wide use worldwide, they are complex systems to design, configure, and install.

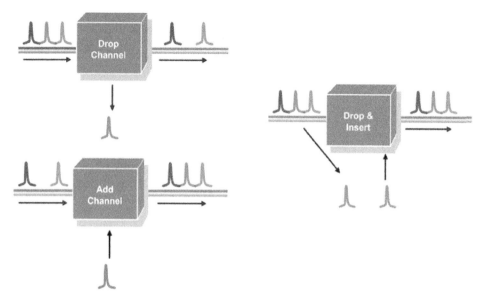

Figure 6.5

Fixed OADM systems are also extremely complex to change. More recently, reconfigurable OADM (ROADM) technologies have been introduced to the market, allowing service providers much greater flexibility in network design and installation and, most importantly, have allowed for flexibility in moves, adds, and changes.

Fixed OADM Technology

While there are many different DWDM vendors and system architectures, there are some basic components that are used in all fixed OADM systems. These components are depicted in Figure 6.6. In a fixed OADM system, multiple optical wavelengths are used to create separate optical transport channels. Terminal filters are used at the end points of a linear (point-to-point) network or at the hub of a ring to originate or terminate optical channels. The terminal filters operate at fixed wavelengths and can only originate or terminate optical channels operating at those *fixed wavelengths*. At any point along the ring, channels can be added or dropped by an optical OADM. These OADMs are also *fixed to specific wavelengths* and typically allow add/drop of a *fixed number* of channels.

Electrical-optical transponders are used to convert standard service interfaces to ITU DWDM optical signals for transport on

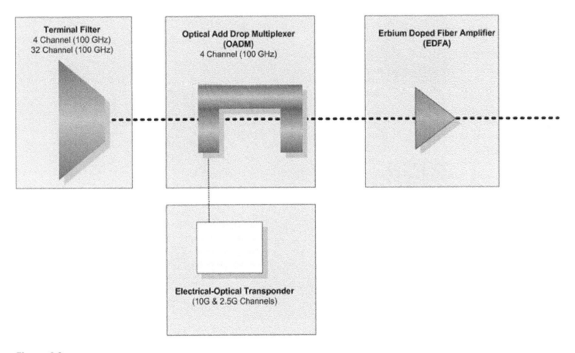

Figure 6.6

the DWDM network. Transponders have many service interfaces (gigabit Ethernet [GbE], 10 GbE, OCn, Fiber Channel, etc.) and come in two fundamental data rates: 2.5 gigabit and 10 gigabit transponders. Another fundamental component of all DWDM systems is the erbium-doped fiber amplifier (EFDA), which is used to amplify the optical signal for medium to long-haul fiber links.

In fixed OADM systems, EFDAs need to be manually adjusted so that the amplification accounts correctly for the number of channels that are added or dropped at a particular site. Manual adjustments need to be made on all EDFAs in the network as new channels are added or dropped.

An example of a fixed OADM network is illustrated in Figure 6.7. In the fixed OADM network, channels are interconnected using fixed filters/OADMs. Because all channels and wavelengths in the network are fixed, it is essential that network planning and engineering account for traffic growth and changes as the network evolves. Adding capacity and/or making changes to the network is difficult and can cause service outages because there is very little flexibility in a fixed OADM system.

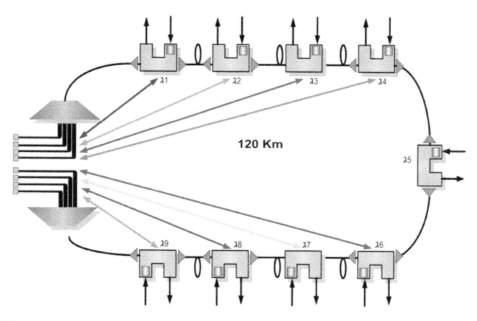

Figure 6.7

The characteristics of a Legacy DWDM, as shown in Figure 6.7, are as follows:
- Fixed channel filters require specific part numbers.
- Current functionality does not support dynamic traffic management.
- Optical span power management is a manual process.
- Channel balancing is a manual process.
- Adding additional wavelength channels is intrusive.
- There is inefficient sparing.
- Wavelength drop locations are configuration-specific.

ROADM Technology

Many of the weaknesses of fixed OADM technology are addressed in the development of reconfigurable optical add/drop multiplexers (ROADMs). While there are several different technology implementations of ROADMs such as microelectronic mirrors (MEM) and planar lightwave circuit (PLC), they all provide a similar capability.

ROADMs enable flexible network transport design by allowing add/drop of any channel at any ROADM node. ROADMs also automatically adjust the power in the network as channels are dropped or inserted in ROADM nodes. Some ROADMs can also

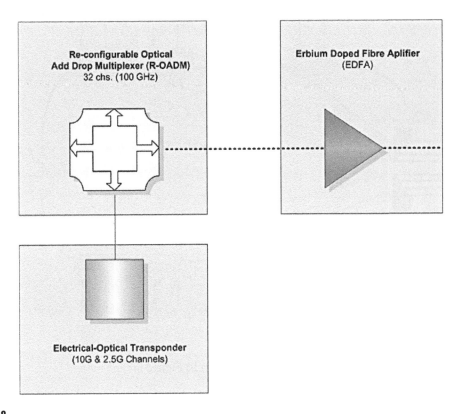

Figure 6.8

provide the ability to switch wavelengths from one path to another, but that is beyond the scope of this book.

The basic components of the ROADM are depicted in Figure 6.8.

The fundamental component of a ROADM DWDM system is the reconfigurable OADM. It typically allows 32–40 channels to be dropped or inserted at any node. As demand in the network changes, additional channels can be dropped or inserted, creating a flexible provisioning system. The ROADM also uses or works with a transponder that is similar in nature to the transponder in the fixed OADM system. One difference, however, is that they are tunable and use pluggable optics (SFPs or XFPs) for client (customer-facing) interfaces. This allows for more flexibility in inventory management and more efficient sparing. ROADM nodes also use EDFAs for optical amplification.

One of the differences in ROADM networks is that all EDFAs in the network are automatically adjusted to provide the correct transmission power across fiber links. As channels are dropped

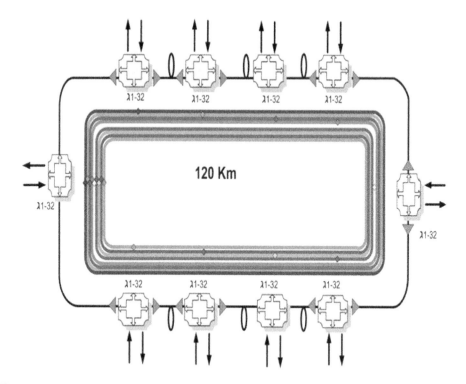

Figure 6.9

or inserted, power requirements change. In the fixed network this is accomplished manually, while in the ROADM network power is adjusted automatically.

The ROADM network also provides per-channel power monitoring for troubleshooting at all sites. This allows technicians to monitor power levels via the management tool. This capability is not available with a fixed OADM system. A ROADM DWDM network is represented in Figure 6.9

A ROADM-based network has the following characteristics:
- Provides drop tuning and lambda blocking
- Is software-selectable between add and pass path
- Has per-channel equalization and power monitoring
- Enables dynamic allocation of ITU paths
- Scales from one to 32 lambda services
- Enables ability to pre-deploy ITU interfaces without predetermined lambda path (source to destination)
- Lessens Txpdr-ROADM re-cabling
- Reduces sparing costs
- Has enhanced flexibility
- Allows any lambda to any drop

The Optical Transport Network (OTN)

The aim of the optical transport network (OTN) is to combine the benefits of SONET/SDH technology with the bandwidth expandability of DWDM. In short, OTNs will apply the operations, administration, maintenance and provisioning (OAM&P) functionality of SONET/SDH to DWDM optical networks. The OTN is specified in ITU-T G.709 Network Node Interface for the Optical Transport Network (OTN).

This recommendation, sometimes referred to as digital wrapper (DW), takes single wavelength SONET/SDH technology a step farther, enabling transparent, wavelength-manageable multi-wavelength networks. Forward error correction (FEC) adds an additional feature to the OTN by offering the potential for network operators to reduce the number of regenerators used, leading to reduced network costs.

ITU-T G.709 Standards for OTNs

The ITU-T G.709 standard, Network Node Interface for the Optical Transport Network (OTN), defines the OTN IrDI (inter-domain interface) in the following ways:
- Functionality of the overhead in preparing the multi-wavelength optical network
- Optical Transport Unit framing structure
- Bit rates and formats permitted for mapping of the clients

Two types of interface are described in the ITU-T G.872 recommendation, Architecture of the Optical Transport Networks, the locations of which are illustrated in Figure 6.10.

Inter-Domain Interfaces (IrDI)

Inter-domain interfaces define:
- the location between the networks of two operators;
- the location between the sub-networks of two vendors in the same operator domain; and
- the location within the sub-network of one vendor.

Intra-Domain Interfaces (IaDI)

Intra-domain interfaces define the location of an individual manufacturer's sub-network between the equipment.

As with SONET/SDH, the OTN has a layered structure design.

The basic OTN layers are visible in the OTN transport structure and consist of the optical channel (OCh), the optical multiplex

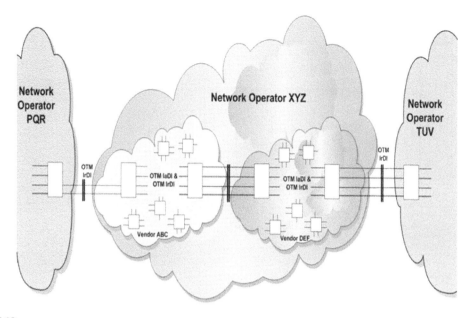

Figure 6.10

section (OMS), and the optical transmission section (OTS), as shown in Figure 6.11.

The aim of the OTN is to enable the multi-service transport of packet-based data and legacy traffic, while DW technology accommodates non-intrusive management and monitoring of each optical channel assigned to a particular wavelength. The "wrapped" overhead (OH) would therefore make it possible to manage and control client signal information. Figure 6.12 illustrates how the OTN's management capabilities are achieved with the addition of OH at several positions during the transport of the client signal.

The steps are as follows:
- OH is added to the client signal to form the optical channel payload unit (OPU).
- OH is then added to the OPU, thus forming the optical channel data unit (ODU).
- Additional OH plus FEC are added to form the optical channel transport unit (OTU).
- Adding further OH creates an optical channel (Och), which is carried by one color.
- Additional OH may be added to the OCh to enable the management of multiple colors in the OTN.
- The OMS and the OTS are then constructed.

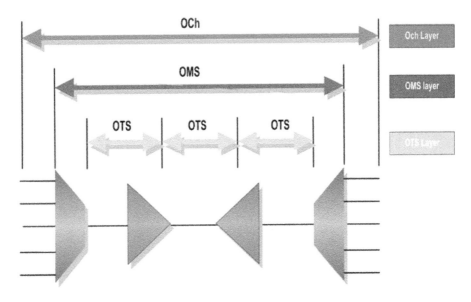

Figure 6.11

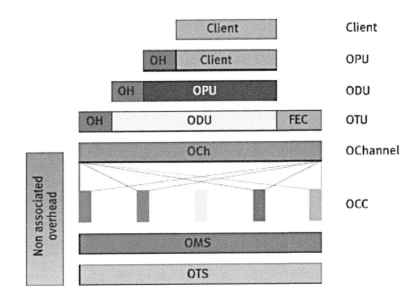

Figure 6.12

The result is an optical channel comprising an OH section, a client signal, and an FEC segment, as shown in Figure 6.13.

The OCh OH, which offers the OTN management functionality, contains four substructures:

- Optical channel payload unit (OPU)
- Optical channel data unit (ODU)

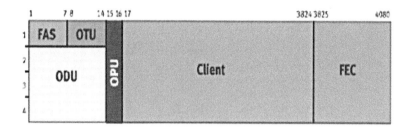

Figure 6.13

- Optical channel transport unit (OTU)
- Frame alignment signal (FAS)
  The client signal or actual payload to be transported could be
of any existing protocol such as SONET/SDH, GFP, IP, and GbE.

The optical channel payload unit (OPU): OH is added to the
OPU payload and is used to support the various client signals.
It regulates the mapping of the many client signals and pro-
vides information on the type of signal transported. The
ITU-T G.709 currently supports asynchronous as well as syn-
chronous mappings of client signals into the payload.

The optical channel data unit (ODU): OH allows the user to
support tandem connection monitoring (TCM), path monitoring (PM), and APS. End-to-end path supervision and client
adaptation via the OPU (as previously described) are also
made possible.

The optical channel transport unit (OTU): OTU is used in the
OTN to support transport via one or more optical channel connections. It also specifies both frame alignment and FEC.

Forward error correction (FEC): In conjunction with the
OCh OH of the digital wrapper "envelope," additional
bandwidth—in this case FEC—is added. The implemented
algorithm/FEC enables the correction and detection of errors
in an optical link.

The FEC implementation defined in the G.709 recommendation uses the so-called "Reed-Solomon" code RS(255/239). An
OTU row is split into 16 sub-rows, each consisting of 255 bytes.
The sub-rows are formed byte interleaved, meaning that the first
sub-row consists of both the first OH byte and the first payload
byte. The first FEC byte is inserted into byte 240 of the first sub-
row, as shown in Figure 6.14. This is true for all 16 sub-rows.

Of these 255 bytes, 239 are used to calculate the FEC parity
check, the result of which is transmitted in bytes 240 to 255 of
the same sub-row. See Figure 6.15.

The Reed-Solomon code detects 16-bit errors or corrects 8-bit
errors in a sub-row. The FEC RS(255,239) is specified for the fully

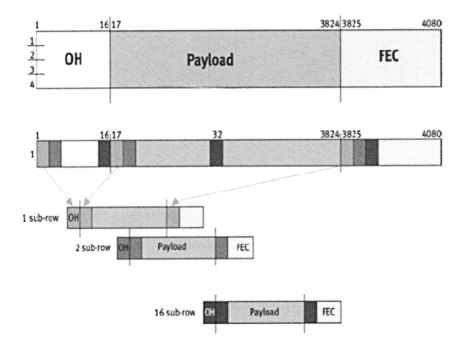

Figure 6.14

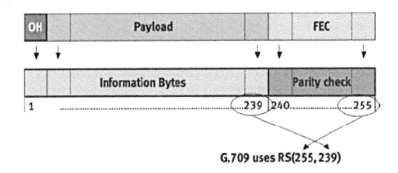

Figure 6.15

standardized IrDI interface. Other OTUkV interfaces (eg; IaDI), which are only functionally standardized, may use other FEC codes.

FEC in Optical Networks

FEC enables the detection and correction of bit errors caused by physical impairments in the transmission medium. These impairments are categorized into linear (attenuation, noise, and dispersion) and nonlinear (four-wave mixing, self-phase modulation, cross-phase modulation) effects.

When FEC is used in a network link, the network operator can accept a lower quality signal in the link so that potential errors can be corrected.

Advantages of FEC

The quality of a fiber optic link is determined by a variety of parameters. The span of a link is typically determined by the optical power budget, which is the difference in power between what the optical transmitter can produce and what the optical receiver can detect. Within the link, the attenuation from every kilometer of fiber and every connector or coupler adds together to consume this budget. To create links with large spans, system designers can choose to use amplifiers or repeaters. A system with a larger optical power budget preserves the link's bit error rate (BER) and has less need for amplifiers and repeaters. Designers typically achieve this increased optical power budget by using higher-quality, higher-cost optical components.

FEC effectively adds a significant gain to the link's optical power budget, while keeping the BER as low as possible.

Because FEC systems must detect an error before correcting it, using FEC across a link lets the designer measure performance and allows early identification of link degradation.

FEC provides the following benefits for fiber optic communications links:

- Improves performance of an existing link between two points
- Increases the maximum span of the link in systems without repeaters
- Increases the distance between repeaters in optically amplified systems or relaxes the specifications of the optical components or fiber
- Improves the overall quality of the link by early diagnosis of degradation and link problems

Once the optical channel is formed, additional non-associated OH is added to individual OCh wavelengths, which then form the optical multiplexing sections (OMS) and the optical transmission sections (OTS), as shown in Figure 6.16.

In the optical multiplex section (OMS) layer, both the OMS payload and non-associated overhead (OMS OH) are transported. The OMS payload consists of multiplexed OChs. The OMS-OH, although undefined at this point, is intended to support the connection monitoring and assist service providers in troubleshooting and fault isolation in the OTN.

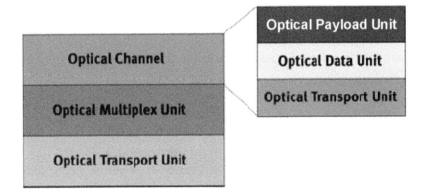

Figure 6.16

The optical transmission section (OTS) layer transports the OTS payload as well as the OTS overhead (OTS-OH). Similar to the OMS, the OTS transports the optically multiplexed sections described above. The OTS OH, although not fully defined, is used for maintenance and operational functions. The OTS layer allows the network operator to perform monitoring and maintenance tasks between the Nes, which include: OADMs, multiplexers, de-multiplexers, and optical switches.

Design Constraints and Initial Design Considerations for Fiber Optic Networks

Optical networks should be engineered for a maximum anticipated capacity. Careful planning for future requirements is imperative, since subsequent changes will have an impact on all of the variables outlined below.

Designing DWDM networks has always been a complex task because of the intrinsic nature of optical transmission, which is based on analog technology despite the transport of digital signals. A number of different parameters have to be taken into account because of linear and nonlinear effects. Linear effects include noise accumulation, optical power budget, and chromatic dispersion effects; nonlinear effects include cross-phase modulation, self-phase modulation, and four-wave mixing. Metro and metro-regional DWDM networks, which usually require many add/drop locations, have an additional layer of complexity because the same network supports different optical paths that must use the same common optical units (such as optical amplifiers and dispersion compensation units).

Before an individual transport technology is selected, the following factors, which impact optical transmission, must be evaluated:

- Fiber
- Optical power budget
- Amplification
- Attenuation/loss
- Dispersion
- Non-linearities

Fiber

Any network design using fiber optics must take into account the condition and the type of fiber. The actual fiber used is a critical factor. It is imperative that the condition of the dark fiber be known prior to any network design. It is important that an actual analysis of the fiber be done and estimates or rules of thumb not be used; otherwise, issues can arise if the estimates turn out to be incorrect. Tools such as an optical time domain reflectometer (OTDR) should be used to test fiber and verify specifications.

Light breaks up into multiple paths called modes. There is multi-mode fiber and single-mode fiber. Single-mode fiber is used for the longer distances of a long-haul optical network and has the ability to support higher data rates.

It is very important to make sure the fiber is clean. Just briefly touching a fiber with the oil or dirt present on a finger can result in imperfections sufficient to impact performance. The customer should have fiber-cleaning devices available.

Single-mode fiber falls into two broad categories: dispersion-shifted (DSF) and non-dispersion-shifted (NDSF).

For the purpose of this design, all fiber considered is G.652 SMF standard.

Transmitter Power

Transmitter power, sometimes called "launch power," is the actual power of the laser and is one determinant of the maximum possible distance between endpoints. It is typically specified as a unit of measure called a dBm. This parameter is available on the data specification sheets of the STM card interfaces.

Receiver Sensitivity and Overload (Saturation)

Receiver sensitivity is the minimum power level at which the receiving node is able to clearly receive the bits being transmitted. This, too, is measured in dBm and is also available on the interface data specification sheets. To simplify, if the distance between nodes results in a loss of transmit power that falls below the receiver sensitivity, amplification somewhere in the path to the receiver would be required to boost the signal above this threshold.

Overload or saturation is the maximum power level at which the receiving node is able to clearly receive the bits being transmitted. When the power threshold is exceeded, the saturation point of the receiver is reached and attenuation (inserting a loss between the transmitter and receiver) is required.

Power Budget

Power budget is the difference between the transmitter power and the receiver sensitivity. The allowed power budget must be greater than the net power loss (from fiber splices, connectors, distance, fiber used, etc.) between CPE end points. In addition, a safety margin should also be applied.

The following describes a simple example:

- Tx power = +7dBm
- Rx sensitivity = -10 dBm
- The power budget is +7dBm – (-19dBm), or 26 dB
- Losses due to fiber distance, connectors, splices, patch panels, etc. should not exceed this value; therefore, optical communications between transmit and receive are unattainable. Other factors such as latency are not considered.

Attenuation

One of the factors that affects the quality of a transmitted signal is attenuation, or weakening of signal power. This is measured in dB/km. There are different contributors to attenuation such as connector loss, splice loss, fiber bends, fiber loss over the distance between end points, absorption of signal by the fiber, multiplexing and de-multiplexing of signals, patch panel connections, etc. Deliberate attenuation may also need to be applied when the power of a signal is too strong.

Amplification

The first step in any design is to attempt to design an unamplified solution. However, this may not be possible because of path distances and/or signal loss along the path. Optical amplifiers would then be used to boost a signal. The key performance parameters for an amplifier are:

- gain (signal boost)

- gain flatness (with DWDM—all wavelengths should have the same power)
- noise level (amplifiers themselves introduce noise)
- output power

It is important to know that noise, along with the signal, is amplified. In general, noise consists of any undesired signal in a telecommunications circuit. This sets a limit as to how much amplification can be done, since eventually the noise level will exceed the tolerance of the receiver. Amplification does not perform what is known as the 3R function (reshape, retime, retransmit) of a device known as an optical signal regenerator.

Optical Signal-to-Noise Ratio Tolerance

The optical signal-to-noise ratio (OSNR) is the relative measure of the strength of the optical signal to the noise. The optical signal must meet a minimum strength so a receiver can distinguish the bits received. This measure is relevant when amplification is used and is a limiting factor in the number of amplifiers that can be concatenated in practice.

Dispersion Tolerance

Dispersion is the spreading out of a light pulse as it travels down the fiber. If there is too great a spread, the receiver cannot differentiate between the different pulses of light and hence the bits being received.

This spreading of a light pulse is called "chromatic dispersion." Dispersion is measured in picoseconds per nanometer kilometer (ps/nm km), or the degree of spread over a distance. This typically is a measure of the physical fiber quality. Dispersion tolerance, as the name implies, is the maximum amount of spread that can be tolerated. Dispersion tolerance is measured in picoseconds per nanometer (ps/nm) and is defined by the transmitter and receiver. This parameter is available on the data sheet specifications for the device laser.

Here is a simple example for illustrative purposes: If the dispersion tolerance is 1800 ps/nm for the path between a transmitter and a receiver, and the fiber dispersion is 18 ps/nm km, then the maximum distance between end nodes would be 100 km (1800/18). The dispersion tolerance, or limitation, is inversely proportional to the data rate and is typically not an issue at speeds below STM-64 (10Gbps). Dispersion compensation units or optical signal regenerators can be used if chromatic dispersion is an issue.

Non-Linear Effects

Factors that pose challenges for optical transmission fall into two general categories: linear effects and non-linear effects. Linear effects increase in proportion to the length of the fiber. The major linear effects mentioned above are attenuation (signal loss) and dispersion (signal spread). Linear effects can be compensated for through the use of amplifiers, dispersion compensation units, and optical signal regenerators.

Non-linear effects change in proportion to the signal's power, not the distance, and become the limiting factor in optical design as bandwidth capacity increases, requiring higher power for transmission.

IPoDWDM

IP over DWDM (IPoDWDM) enables the convergence of service providers' IP and DWDM core networks, increasing service flexibility and reliability while lowering operating expenses (OpEx) and capital expenditures (CapEx).

IPoDWDM provides the features, benefits, and function of a DWDM transponder on a router interface. This network architecture provides both CapEx and OpEx savings by eliminating the transponders and associated shelves forming the network. Eliminating this optoelectronic equipment not only reduces CapEx and OpEx but also enhances reliability by removing additional components.

In typical networks, a short-reach interface is used on the router and connects it to an L1 transponder, which readies the signal for DWDM transport. This transponder monitors the health of the DWDM (L1 system) by utilizing G.709 performance monitors (PMs), which provide SONET-like PMs. These PMs terminate on the transponders, leaving the router interfaces blind to the actual health of the L1 system, so they must be reactive rather than proactive to L1 issues.

By providing the transponder functionality on the router interface, we actually move the performance monitoring capabilities of the transponder that utilizes G.709 and forward error correction (FEC) from the L1 transponder to the router interface so the router can make decisions based on real-time L1 network data.

Requirements for IPoDWDM

To meet the demands for converged packet infrastructures, networks are moving toward an IP NGN-based architecture. This shift is driven by the need to reduce OpEx and CapEx while offering new revenue-generating services over a single, converged infrastructure. IP NGNs can enable convergence at the application, service, and network layers. This document focuses on the network layer and specifically on the convergence of two important technologies within service providers' core networks: IP and DWDM.

Core Network Infrastructure Evolution

The recent core network trend is the consolidation of multiple Layer 2/3 networks into a single IP/multiprotocol label-switching (IP/MPLS) infrastructure. In spite of this Layer 2/3 convergence, however, the underlying transport layer (Layer 1) of many core networks has continued to use SONET/SDH, an infrastructure that was introduced in the early 1990s to support traditional time-division multiplexing (TDM)-based data and voice services. The SONET/SDH infrastructure was implemented to support three critical functions: grooming, protection, restoration, and thorough operational support (such as alarming and performance monitoring).

When it was introduced, SONET/SDH allowed the efficient multiplexing of lower-speed TDM circuits such as T1/E1 and T3/E3 to higher-speed OC-3 and OC-12 trunks for transport across service providers' core networks. Because of their synchronous nature, the trunk connections could be switched independently when needed without the need for complex de-multiplexing, as is demanded by TDM-based data and voice services. The infrastructure also allowed the growth to faster aggregate links such as OC-48 and higher while supporting the emerging IP networks of the day. This "grooming" function allowed the bandwidth efficiency and automation that was required to support multiple switched TDM services in the core of networks by using SONET/SDH add/drop multiplexers (ADMs) and cross-connect equipment.

The SONET/SDH infrastructure, which typically uses a ring-based topology within the core, also allowed for protection and fast restoration (50 ms) during a failure on one part of the ring to maximize the availability of the overall network. With the advent of SONET/SDH standardization, a separate, standardized, message-based channel was used for alarms, control, monitoring, and administration of the links from a centralized location.

In the latter part of the 1990s, DWDM emerged as a way to significantly increase the efficiency of the installed fiber plant by allowing transmission of multiple wavelengths over a single physical fiber. This function introduced another level of multiplexing and de-multiplexing at the optical level to support greatly increased bandwidth at the core of the network, which followed the dramatic rise of IP-based networks fueled by the explosion of the Web. The SONET/SDH layer, which now handled increasing amounts of IP traffic, was mapped into wavelengths at the DWDM transport layer to be carried across the core long-haul networks spanning regions and, in many cases, countries. This has remained largely the case in many networks globally today.

The IP Explosion

The volumes of IP traffic on these core networks have, however, continued to increase steadily, to the point where today the primary use of these core long-haul networks is to carry massive amounts of transient IP traffic, significantly outpacing the traffic volumes of traditional voice and data services. Over the next five years alone, global monthly IP traffic is expected to rise to *26 exabytes*, accelerated by the application convergence of all video, voice, and data traffic to IP, resulting in a compound annual growth rate (CAGR) in excess of 56 percent globally. The convergence of traditional applications such as broadcast television, video on demand, and voice to new distribution models over IP, as well as the explosion of new applications such as music and video podcasting and peer-to-peer (P2P) file sharing, will only continue to fuel this tremendous growth of core IP traffic.

Multiple Transport Layer Elements

Some network inefficiencies result from the way core transport networks are currently built out to support the IP layer over the SONET/SDH layer, supported by an underlying DWDM infrastructure. Consider the paths of two types of traffic entering and exiting a typical network point of presence (POP). The first scenario is IP traffic that needs a Layer 3 lookup at the POP and therefore is riding a wavelength that will terminate on a router. The second is called "pass-through" (or transient) traffic, which stays in the transport domain and bypasses the router to travel on to an adjacent POP in the core network.

Router-Terminated Traffic

Currently, the IP traffic typically comes into the POP through 10-Gbps SONET/SDH OC-192/STM-64 circuits or 10/100Gbps Ethernet interfaces, which are composed of colored wavelengths multiplexed through DWDM onto a physical fiber. This fiber is fed into a DWDM de-multiplexer, which splits out the individual colored wavelengths. These individual wavelengths that are to be terminated on the router are then fed into transponders, which convert them from optical (colored) to electrical and then to a standard short-reach wavelength ("grey light"). This optical-to-electrical-to-optical (OEO) conversion is used because, historically, short-reach optics have been used for connectivity inside the POP environment.

The grey light is then typically fed into a short-reach interface on a SONET/SDH cross-connect, which recovers the SONET/SDH clocking, performs any grooming necessary, checks for errors, and monitors for loss of signal (LOS) so that it can perform SONET/SDH-level restoration if needed. However, in most cases today, no grooming is actually needed because the full 10 Gbps is being connected to the router (rather than 2.5 Gbps or lower speed links in the past). Therefore, from a connectivity perspective, the cross-connect is essentially serving as a patch panel. The SONET/SDH cross-connect then feeds the 10 Gbps to the router, which performs performance monitoring at Layer 1 through Layer 3, monitors for LOS so it can perform MPLS fast reroute (FRR) restoration, and performs a Layer 3 and above lookup to route the packet to its destination.

On the aggregation side, the core router is typically aggregating multiple lower-speed links and grooming the IP traffic into well-used 10-Gbps links to present back into the core transport network.

Pass-Through Traffic

As traffic patterns in the core have become more distributed, the amount of traffic passing through a given POP purely at the transport layer (as opposed to terminating on a IP router) has tended to increase and can sometimes be as high as 70 to 80 percent of the overall traffic that the POP handles. In this case, the incoming DWDM link goes through a similar method of interconnections through the DWDM de-multiplexer and transponders to the SONET/SDH cross-connect through short-reach optics. It checks for errors and monitors for LOS so that it can perform SONET/SDH restoration. Again, the grooming function that would have occurred here previously is no longer required because typically full 10-Gbps links are being passed through the POP. Hence the cross-connect is again serving as a patch panel from a connectivity perspective. A similar process of interconnections occurs for outgoing traffic from the POP.

These OEO conversions and the associated electrical processing result in an additional cost in terms of space, because many racks of shelves may be required in a service provider POP, as well as additional power and cooling that is necessary because of the active electronics components that they contain. Furthermore, in this core network scenario, the SONET/SDH functions are redundant because of the capabilities that have been integrated into the router.

- Grooming: Because most traffic has moved to IP, the router now performs the grooming function by aggregating IP traffic and presenting it to the core transport layer within well-used 10-Gbps links.
- Operational support: The router and its associated interfaces can measure errors at Layers 1 through 3, collect performance statistics, generate appropriate alarms, etc.
- Protection and restoration: Using MPLS FRR, the router can provide 50-ms protection or better and do so much more efficiently than the traditional SONET/SDH protection schemes (such as BLSR), which waste up to 50 percent of the bandwidth for protection purposes.

For these reasons, the use of manual patching in place of the cross-connect is being implemented to save cost.

Benefits of an IPoDWDM Architecture

In order to show the benefits of IPoDWDM, it is important to first show the traditional core architecture.

Traditional Core Architecture

In a traditional core architecture, the layers in the network perform different functions. These functions are detailed below and shown in Figure 6.17.

- Routers are responsible for aggregating IP traffic to 10G, fast restoration at Layer 3, and performance monitoring at Layer 2 and Layer 3.
- TDM cross-connects groom low speed circuits, fast restoration at Layer 1, and performance monitoring at Layer 1.
- Transponders are responsible for conversion of short-reach optics to colored optics
- The DWDM layer multiplexes lambdas onto fiber.

The characteristics of a traditional core network architecture are:

- distinct IP and DWDM management planes;
- distinct IP and DWDM control planes;

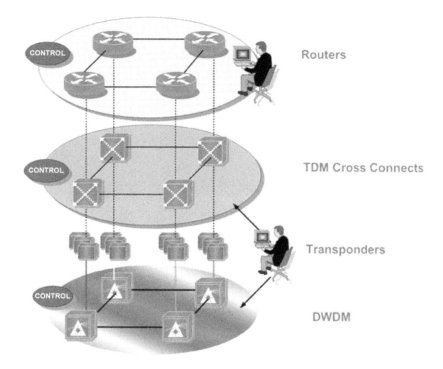

Figure 6.17

- expensive electrical cross-connects (OEO);
- multiple transponders per wavelength (OEO); and
- truck rolls for reconfiguration.

IPoDWDM Architecture

In an IPoDWDM architecture, the network is split into two distinct networks. The main features of these networks are listed below and a graphical representation of the two networks is shown in Figure 6.18.

- The IP network performs efficient interconnection directly at 10/40G and provides performance monitoring and fast L3 protection.
- The DWDM network provides transparent multi-service transport and WDM automation (hiding complexity of fiber transmission).

The benefits of the IPoDWDM Architecture are listed below:

- The complexities of the TDM cross-connects have been removed.

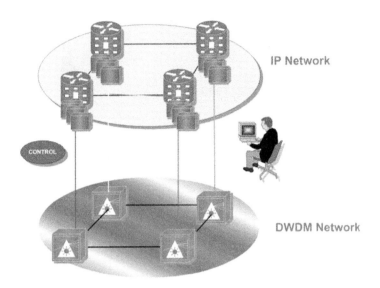

Figure 6.18

- There is less electrical processing (OEO).
- The transponder layer has been integrated into the routing platforms.
- There is management and control-plane coordination.

7

MPLS TRANSPORT PROFILE

Introduction

The trends have been clear for some time: the growth of IP and mobile data traffic, low-cost Ethernet ports, the revenue shift from voice to data, and the packet video explosion. Network convergence, a topic of conversation for over two decades, is finally a reality. Or is it? True, these days it's mostly all packets, all the time, but we're still shy of the finish line. Most voice, mobile data, and video are now inside packets, but in many cases, they are still running over TDM transport such as SDH, SONET, or OTN. Taking the last step means clearing away a few hurdles. The most recent focus of this convergence is the effort to bring the strengths of legacy transport networks to the new packet world—strengths like path-level monitoring and fault detection, simple provisioning, fast protection switching, and robust timing and synchronization. And the solution in the spotlight is MPLS Transport Profile (MPLS-TP), the result of a joint effort of the ITU-T and the IETF to simplify an existing label-switching protocol to address those capabilities. This section explores why MPLS-TP is emerging at this stage in the convergence journey, the applicability of MPLS-TP in the mobile backhaul and access networks, and the importance of testing new MPLS-TP deployments.

Why MPLS-TP? Why Now?

In 2011, after years of joint development between the ITU-T and IETF, MPLS-TP has emerged as the technology of choice for next-generation transport networks and is being put to the test in multi-vendor inter-operability trials. Why is a transport protocol the focus of attention at this stage in the converged network game?

The Problem with TDM and SONET/SDH Transport

The current TDM transport has a lot going for it. It provides operators the ability to provision bi-directional connections with guaranteed bandwidth, supports OAM procedures, and enforces service level agreements (SLAs). However, the disadvantages far outweigh the advantages. Driven by smartphones and new services, global mobile data traffic nearly tripled in 2010 and global IP traffic will have quadrupled between 2009 and 2014. Such a dramatic increase in mobile backhaul traffic is stretching the traditional TDM transport beyond its capabilities. The T1/E1 and SONET/SDH circuits are not only inefficient for transporting packet-based traffic, they are also significantly more expensive (per port and per bit) than packet-based alternatives such as Ethernet. In the long run, persisting with TDM is untenable for operators. The answer is to define a set of protocols and procedures that inherit all the efficiencies of the packet networks and at the same time can be extended to meet the OAM requirements of the transport world.

MPLS-TP

MPLS has been running over Ethernet for over a decade. It is a creature of the packet network, designed to optimize packet transport through tunnels via label switching. There was no question that it would work well in a packet-based environment. In addition, MPLS was designed to set up end-to-end circuits in large-scale networks. It knew about discovering and recovering from path failure. It knew about QoS. It was already well on its way to satisfying necessary requirements. And perhaps best of all, MPLS is a mature, standards-based technology deployed in almost every service provider network worldwide. Adapting it for use in the transport network meant developing a simplified version of IP/MPLS—a subset of the existing capabilities—and tuning it to support additional capabilities.

What are the needed additional capabilities? MPLS had to be enhanced to support static provisioning, in-band OAM, fault detection and switchover to backup path within 50 ms, and a network management system (NMS) interface to configure and manage the network. By adapting MPLS to handle the special needs of transport networks, designers ensured seamless integration between layers in existing production networks, making possible a single end-to-end OAM architecture across the OSI model. See Figure 7.1.

The work actually began in the ITU in Study Group 15 under the project name T-MPLS, and in 2008 the IEFT joined forces with the ITU and took the lead. In the IETF, the project was renamed MPLS-TP.

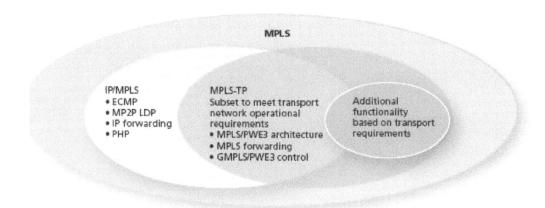

Figure 7.1

How MPLS-TP Works

RFC 5654 defines 115 requirements for MPLS-TP in the areas of layering, data plane, control plane, recovery, and QoS. It also references requirements for network management, OAM, performance monitoring, and security in other documents. This document specifies the required behavior, not a required implementation.

The most basic element for implementing MPLS-TP is use of the associated channel header (ACH), previously limited to pseudowires, to create a generic associated channel (G-ACh) by assigning one of the reserved MPLS label values (13) to the generic associated channel label (GAL), as defined in RFC 5586. The G-ACh does not carry user traffic.

RFC 5586 generalizes the ACH to apply to LSPs and sections to create a label-based exception mechanism to address the requirements in RFC 5654 for transport-network performance monitoring, automatic protection switching, and support for management and signaling communication channels. It is an in-band management channel on a PW or LSP that does not rely on routing, user traffic, or dynamic control plane functions.

The GAL provides an alert-based exception mechanism to differentiate G-ACh packets from others such as user-plane packets, and to indicate that the ACH appears immediately after the bottom of the label stack. The GAL is used only where both of these purposes apply. See Figure 7.2.
*   For LSPs, the GAL is at the bottom of the label stack and identifies the packet as belonging to the G-Ach.

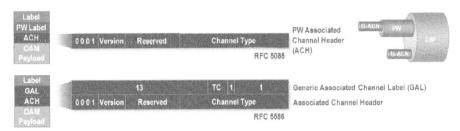

Figure 7.2

- OAM capabilities extended using a generic associated channel (G-ACh) based on RFC 5085 (VCCV)

- A G-ACh Label (GAL) acts as exception mechanism to identify maintenance packets

- GAL not required for pseudowires (first nibble as exception mechanism)

- G-ACh used to implement FCAPS (OAM, automatic protection switching (APS), signaling communication channel, management communication channel, etc)

- For PWs, the PWE3 control word, as defined in RFC 4385, is used to identify a packet belonging to the G-ACh with a value of 1 in the first four bits. The first 32 bits following the bottom of the stack label carries the GAL.

  The essential features of MPLS-TP defined by IETF and ITU-T are:
- MPLS forwarding plane with restrictions
- PWE3 pseudowire architecture
- Control plane: static or dynamic generalized MPLS (G-MPLS)
- Enhanced OAM functionality
- OAM monitors and drives protection switching
- Use of a generic associated channel (G-ACh) to support fault, configuration, accounting, performance, and security (FCAPS) functions

  Multicasting is under further study.

MPLS-TP Supports Both Static and Dynamic Signaling

MPLS-TP can operate in two modes:
- Through a network management system for static provisioning of primary and backup connections with fast protection switching. Provisioning a static MPLS-TP connection typically

involves selecting the port and VLAN (if the interface is Ethernet) and manually assigning incoming and outgoing labels for the connection. This action is independently performed on both ends of the connection.

• Through a G-MPLS control plane for dynamic provisioning of primary and recovery paths with fast reroute.

To meet transport-network compatibility requirements, MPLS-TP restricts LSPs to bi-directional paths that are co-routed, meaning both directions follow the same path.

MPLS-TP OAM Procedures

MPLS-TP provides mechanisms to support in-band OAM functions such as continuity check, connectivity verification, loss measurement, delay measurement, remote defect indication, and alarm indication signal. Like legacy transport networks, these mechanisms allow for fault localization, performance monitoring, remote indications, and alarm suppression. Rather than define new OAM protocols, the MPLS-TP IETF drafts specify mechanisms (via G-Al/G-Ach) to reuse traditional MPLS and carrier Ethernet OAM procedures such as BFD and Y.1731.

The BFD and Y.1731 procedures can be used to monitor LSPs, sections, or PWs. In addition, recent IETF drafts also define Fault OAMs (AIS, RDI, and LKR) for signal failure detection, for propagation of the signal fail condition across layers, and for alarm suppression. MPLS-TP provides mechanisms to support in-band OAM functions such as continuity check, connectivity verification, loss measurement, delay measurement, remote defect indication, and alarm indication signal.

MPLS-TP Protection Switching and Restoration

An operator typically provisions the primary and backup paths (LSPs) of an MPLS-TP connection statically. OAM protocols running at either end of the MPLS-TP connection monitor its liveliness and quickly detect the presence of faults. Upon loss of connectivity or fault detection, both ends of the MPLS-TP connection switch over to the backup LSP (either independently or by being coordinated by a per-hop-behavior scheduling class) and bi-directional traffic is exchanged on the backup LSP as soon as the switchover is complete. The high frequency of the OAM heartbeats (for example, BFD messages are exchanged as frequently as once every 3.3 ms) ensures failure detection within 10–15 ms and switchover within 50 ms.

Differences between MPLS and MPLS-TP

The following list describes the major differences between MPLS and MPLS-TP (see also Figure 7.3):

Bi-directional Label Switched Paths (LSPs). MPLS is based on the traditional IP routing paradigm—traffic from A to B can flow over different paths than can traffic from B to A. But transport networks commonly use bi-directional circuits, and MPLS-TP also mandates the support of bi-directional LSPs (a path through an MPLS network). In addition, MPLS-TP must support point-to-multipoint paths.

Management plane LSP setup. Paths across MPLS networks are set up with control-plane protocols (IP routing protocols or Resource Reservation Protocol (RSVP) for MPLS Traffic Engineering (MPLS-TE). MPLS-TP could use the same path setup mechanisms as MPLS (control plane-based LSP setup) or the traditional transport network approach, where the paths are configured from the central network management system (management plane LSP setup).

Control plane is not mandatory. Going a step farther, MPLS-TP nodes should be able to work with no control plane, with paths across the network computed solely by the network management system and downloaded into the network elements.

Out-of-band management. MPLS nodes usually use in-band management or at least in-band exchange of control-plane messages. MPLS-TP network elements have to support out-of-band management over a dedicated management network (similar to the way some transport networks are managed today).

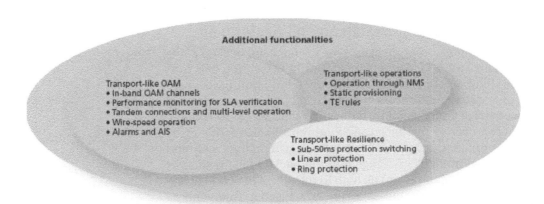

Figure 7.3

Total separation of management/control and data plane. Data forwarding within an MPLS-TP network element must continue even if its management or control plane fails. High-end routers provide similar functionality with non-stop forwarding, but this kind of functionality was never mandatory in traditional MPLS.

No IP in the forwarding plane. MPLS nodes usually run IP on all interfaces because they have to support the in-band exchange of control-plane messages. MPLS-TP network elements must be able to run without IP in the forwarding plane.

Explicit support of ring topologies. Many transport networks use ring topologies to reduce complexity. MPLS-TP thus includes mandatory support for numerous ring-specific mechanisms.

Why Is It Important to Test MPLS-TP?

NEMs from all over the world have been racing to incorporate MPLS-TP functionality into their devices and to keep up with the rapidly evolving IETF drafts and RFCs. For service providers, it is not a matter of if, but when, they will replace the aging TDM backhaul with MPLS-TP-based Ethernet backhaul. The pace of deployment of MPLS-TP will ultimately depend on the reliability and completeness of the MPLS-TP implementations. Without TDM-like reliability, service providers will not risk the migration to MPLS-TP and will not risk customer churn owing to quality issues. Establishing the reliability and completeness of an MPLS-TP implementation can only be accomplished by thorough testing of the following aspects of MPLS-TP:

1. IP/MPLS and MPLS-TP inter-operability
    a. Static provisioning of PW in the MPLS-TP domain and LDP signaled PW in the IP/MPLS domain
    b. Forwarding across MS-PW
2. OAM procedures and fault detection
3. Protection switching

IP/MPLS and MPLS-TP Inter-operability

With superior reliability and flexible ETE service deployment, IP/MPLS firmly dominates bearer networks. Most operators use IP/MPLS for their core networks, while MPLS-TP shows more and more powerful service-bearing capability in mobile backhaul networks as a result of complete OAM and protection mechanisms.

Figure 7.4

Figure 7.4 depicts the development trend of MPLS-TP and IP/MPLS application scenarios and shows MPLS-TP and IP/MPLS will coexist for a long time. MPLS-TP is applied to the metro network and is inevitably connected to the core-layer MPLS network, so the interconnection between MPLS-TP and MPLS is the focus all parties are concerned about. If MPLS-TP and IP/MPLS inter-operability is achieved and is combined with their positioning in existing networks, they can meet service development demands and reduce technical risks and TCO. This section introduces major technologies in combination with two models of MPLS-TP and IP/MPLS inter-operability.

MPLS-TP and IP/MPLS Inter-operability Models

MPLS and MPLS-TP inter-operability has no IETF JWT draft, but it has a personal draft, "draft-martinotti-mpls-tp-interworking-02," which describes the models of the inter-operability. Generally, two inter-operability models are available: "Overlay" and "Peer."

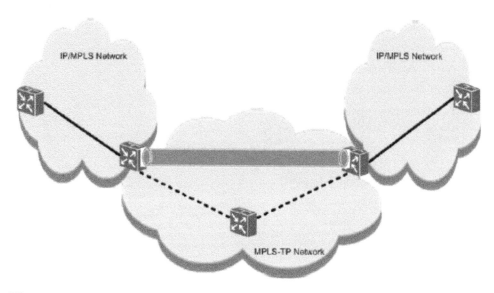

Figure 7.5

As shown in Figure 7.5, the overlay is the service layer of one network (e.g., MPLS-TP) for the other network (e.g., IP/MPLS). After being encapsulated properly at a network boundary node, client-layer data (including control-plane data and transport-plane data) is transparently transmitted to the corresponding service-layer network boundary node via a service-layer channel (e.g., TP LSP). A service-layer network is just a hop of a client-layer network; namely, two boundary nodes in the service-layer network are considered as adjacent nodes in the client-layer network.

As shown in Figure 7.6, two networks are peer in the model and independently process data in their own networks, while network boundary nodes map information between two networks to transmit data.

Overlay Model

MPLS-TP and IP/MPLS have two overlay interconnection modes: IP/MPLS over MPLS-TP and MPLS-TP over IP/MPLS.

IP/MPLS over MPLS-TP

LSP is created in two ways in IP/MPLS over MPLS-TP. One way is to create MPLS-TP LSP, and notify the IP/MPLS network in FA (forwarding adjacent) mode. When IP/MPLS LSP is created, the created TP LSP can be considered as a direct link to participate

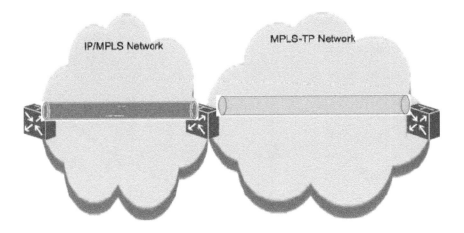

Figure 7.6

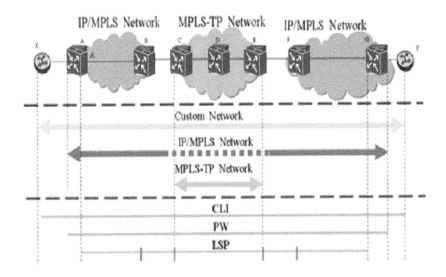

Figure 7.7

in the routing. The other way is to create the signaling via IP/MPLS LSP to trigger TP LSP creation through RSVP-TE at the TP domain edge, transparently transport IP/MPLS LSP signaling information via the created TP LSP, and finally to create IP/MPLS LSP.

As shown in Figure 7.7, the entire TP LSP is just a hop of IP/MPLS, and IP/MPLS data and information are transparently transmitted via TP LSP.

Forwarding Adjacent (FA)

Forwarding adjacent (FA) means calculating the route via the bi-directional TE tunnel interface in IGP/IGP-TE. The bi-directional TE tunnel works as a link for notification in IGP/IGP-TE. Thus the TE tunnel interface participates in route calculation and works as an egress interface of a specific route in the forwarding table so that a packet is forwarded via MPLS/nested MPLS rather than via IP/MPLS.

As shown in Figure 7.8, when the regular IGP route is calculated, the route from A to T is A—B—C—T, and the egress interface is the interface of B. If the bi-directional TE tunnel from A to C starts FA, namely, take the TE tunnel as a link of the overhead 10 and notify IGP, A thinks the overhead from A to C is 10, and the TE tunnel interface is selected as the egress interface. It is mentioned above that the bi-directional TE tunnel participates in IGP or IGP-TE route selection in the FA mode. If the TE tunnel working as a link is notified in IGP, the TE tunnel interface participates in IP route calculation and works as an egress interface of a specific route in the IP forwarding table so that a packet is forwarded via MPLS rather than via IP. If the TE tunnel working as a TE link is notified in IGP-TE, the TE tunnel interface participates in MPLS-TE route calculation and works as an egress interface of a specific route in the MPLS forwarding table, namely, create a nested LSP. The IP/MPLS over MPLS-TP mentioned here is the latter.

Encapsulation

In "draft-martinotti-mpls-tp-interworking-02," two overlapping interconnection encapsulations are mentioned: ETH overlapping encapsulation and IP/MPLS overlapping encapsulation.

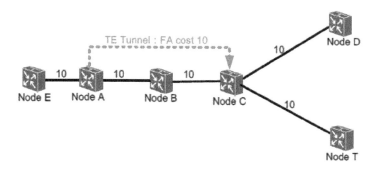

Figure 7.8

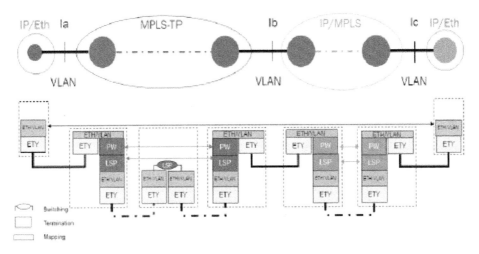

Figure 7.9

1. ETH overlapping encapsulation: In this scenario, MPLS-TP works as the service layer of IP/MPLS. IP/MPLS packets are first encapsulated in ETH, then ETH packets are encapsulated in pseudowire of MPLS-TP as shown in Figure 7.9.
2. IP/MPLS overlapping encapsulation: In this scenario, as the service layer of IP/MPLS, MPLS-TP is connected to the IP/MPLS device by UNI. IP/MPLS packets are directly encapsulated into LSP in MPLS-TP (by label stack). The MPLS-TP domain edge device takes processing of IP/MPLS MPLS-TP at the same time as shown in Figure 7.10.

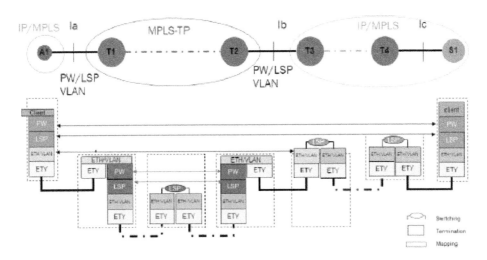

Figure 7.10

In Figure 7.10, the ETH/VLAN field (in yellow) at the network edge node is used for packet encapsulation and mapping. In practical application, the field may be deleted together with the ETY field. In the illustration, two IP/MPLS networks are connected by an MPLS-TP network. The overlapping model is adopted to complete inter-operation of the IP/MPLS and MPLS-TP network. The MPLS-TP network is considered the service layer of the IP/MPLS network, and the IP/MPLS network is considered the customer layer of the MPLS-TP network.

If using Ethernet encapsulation, the physical layer is Ethernet. Nodes C and E receive the Ethernet packets from nodes B and F and transport the data based on Ethernet service simulation. In this way, the interconnection protocol between IP/MPLS and MPLS-TP is not needed. MPLS-TP doesn't need to implement IP/MPLS, but its encapsulation is the poorest. Using unified L3 (ETH) encapsulation, MPLS-TP and the MPLS network don't need any connection, though they are considered independent PSNs with low encapsulation efficiency.

If using IP/MPLS encapsulation, two IP/MPLS networks are connected by MPLS-TP. The MPLS-TP network is considered the service layer of IP/MPLS network, while the IP/MPLS network is considered the customer layer of MPLS-TP layer. IP/MPLS is directly encapsulated into LSP of MPLS-TP (label stack). In this way, interconnection protocol is not needed for the IP/MPLS device or the MPLS-TP device, but the MPLS-TP device will implement IP/MPLS functions with poor encapsulation efficiency. In other words, MPLS-TP is considered as the service layer of MPLS. MPLS packets sent by the IP/MPLS network are taken as the customer layer and encapsulated into MPLS-TP PSN.

OAM

The overlapping inter-operation model of MPLS-TP and IP/MPLS has OAM of the following layers:
- Directly connected link layer OAM. OAM on this layer could be many types. It could be a physical layer OAM but more than it and link layer OAM mechanism.
- OAM of the LSP layer in an MPLS-TP network.
- OAM of the PW layer in an MPLS-TP network.
- OAM of the sectional LSP layer in an IP/MPLS network, which is OAM on the section of LSP between the two domain edge nodes of IP/MPLS crossing the TP network.
- OAM of the E2E LSP layer in an IP/MPLS network.

The OAMs on each layer can interact with each other. For example, when the TP LSP layer detects a failure, it will send an AIS message to notify the failure to the TP PW layer (the OAM customer layer of TP LSP). But there's no related research result in standards in notification to the IP/MPLS network by OAM in the TP network.

In the overlapping model, the implementation steps of IP/MPLS over MPLS-TP are as follows:

- Create LSP: When MPLS-TP bears the IP/MPLS network, there are two LSP establishing methods: one is to establish MPLS-TP LSP first, send notification to the IP/MPLS network by FA (forwarding adjacent), and get the established TP LSP participated in pathing as a directly-connected link when establishing IP/MPLS LSP. The other is to establish signaling by LSP of IP/MPLS to trigger establishment of TP LSP at the TP domain edge by RSVP-TE, so as to transparently transport the signaling message of IP/MPLS LSP through the established TP LSP, and finally to establish IP/MPLS LSP.

- Create PW: Configure the VLAN message manually at the network domain edge node, and configure the corresponding relationship between VLAN and PW at the edge node of the MPLS-TP network. That is to say, encapsulate the IP/MPLS packet into a PWE3 Ethernet frame at the TP network edge incoming node based on the mapping relationship of VLAN and PW, then transport it from the TP network to the IP/MPLS network. Restore the PWE3 Ethernet frame to the IP/MPLS packet at the edge incoming node of the TP network based on the mapping relationship of VLAN and PW, and transport it to the IP/MPLS network domain edge node.

- Configure OAM and protection: Establish OAM and the protection relationship of the corresponding layer based on the needs. The routine fast route convergence and FRR system are inherited for protection in the overlapping model.

MPLS-TP over IP/MPLS Model

Currently, L2 technology is usually adopted to deploy in MPLS-TP. When two MPLS-TP network services cross an IP/MPLS network, the L2/L3 VPN bridging can be used to take inter-operation between the MPLS-TP and the IP/MPLS networks.

L2/L3 VPN Bridging

L2/L3 VPN bridging is to integrate L2VPN and L3VPN on one device in order to implement logic separation and interconnection of L2 and L3 VPN in one virtual group, which is the

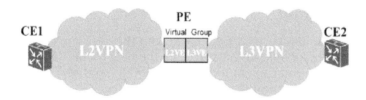

Figure 7.11

implementation of L2VPN termination and L3VPN forwarding. Actually, it's a kind of gateway bridge of L2/L3VPN by which the connection between VPNs can be realized.

As shown in Figure 7.11, the PE device can be divided into two parts: one corresponds to L2VPN, which is called L2 Virtual Entity (L2VE). The other corresponds to L3VPN, which is called L3 Virtual Entity (L3VE). The two are integrated as a virtual group, which has the features of both L2VPN and L3VPN.

When L2VPN packets arrive, the corresponding L2VPN information is found by port and by VLAN information (CIP access) or PW incoming label information (PW access). If L3 forwarding is needed (MAC of the packets are local host MAC), the corresponding L3VPN information should be obtained based on the L2/L3 VPN binding relationship in the virtual group to start the L3 forwarding procedure.

When L3VPN packets arrive, if the egress of L3 forwarding is an L3VE with an L2VE bound, the packets will be transmitted to the L2VE and start the L2VPN forwarding procedure. See Figure 7.12.

After L2/L3 VPN bridging deployment, the services all carry an MPLS label during the whole process of transmission so that E2E QoS features and integrated protection switching strategy can be easily deployed, network complexity can be dramatically reduced, and network construction costs can be saved.

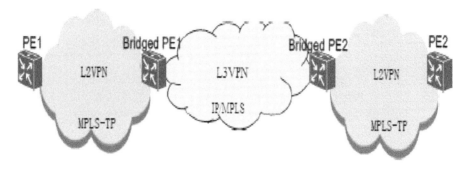

Figure 7.12

Peer Model

As seen in Figure 7.13, MPLS-TP and IP/MPLS are connected by a section of link. In this situation, the peer model can be used to complete inter-operation of the IP/MPLS and MPLS-TP networks. MPLS-TP and IP/MPLS are in one layer.

At present, the MPLS-TP and IP/MPLS peer interconnection model has two interconnection systems: one is the MS-PW system in which PW inside the network domain is established respectively in each network. The network domain edge node works as SPE to take the PW in the network domain as sub-PW so as to establish an E2E MS-PW crossing MPLS-TP and an IP/MPLS network. The other is an SS-PW+LSP stitching system in which PW inside the network domain is established respectively in each network. These LSPs are stitched at the network domain edge node to compose an E2E-stitched LSP crossing MPLS-TP and IP/MPLS. The stitched LSP is used to bear PW (a common PW, which is SS-PW).

MS-PW

Here we introduce several concepts first: PWE3, SS-PW, and MS-PW. Pseudowire Emulation Edge-to-Edge (PWE3) is an L2 service-bearing technology that tries to emulate as much as possible the basic behaviors and features of ATM, frame relay, Ethernet, low-speed TDM (time division multiplexing) circuit, and SONET/SDH. In PE of PSN, PWE3 takes LDP/RSVP as a signaling protocol. It emulates various L2 services (such as L2 data packets and bit flows) at the customer edge (CE) by tunnel (which could be

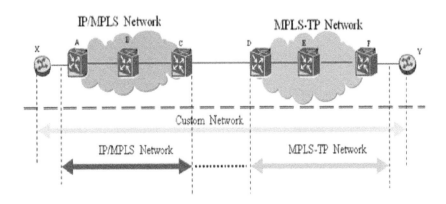

Figure 7.13

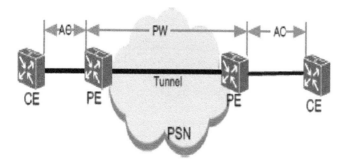

Figure 7.14

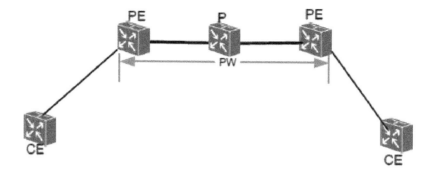

Figure 7.15

an MPLS tunnel, a GRE, an L2TPV3, or others), and transparently transmits L2 data of the CE end.

The basic diagram of PWE3 is shown in Figure 7.14.

PWE3 can be divided into SS-PW and MS-PW based on networking type: Single-segment pseudowire is a PW directly established between T-PE and T-PE without label switching of the PW label as shown in Figure 7.15.

Multi-segment pseudowire is multiple PW segments between T-PE and T-PE as shown in Figure 7.16. The forwarding system for T-PE in multiple segments is the same as that for T-PE in a single segment, except that multi-segment PW needs to connect the single-segment PW on two sides by the PW switching device S-PE, and complete PW label switching at S-PE.

MS-PW is usually used in the following scenarios:

As the source and destination PEs are not in the same service area, signaling connection or tunnels cannot be built between the two PEs. The signaling on the source and destination PEs are different. Although the access device can run MPLS, it can't build

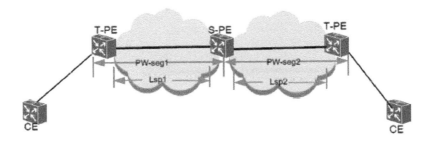

Figure 7.16

many LDP sessions. In other words, it cannot realize a full-mesh LDP session. At this moment, the access device can be used as T-PE, and the high-performance device S-PE is used as the switching point of the LDP session. Then set more PW S-PEs (switching PE) as the switching point of the LDP to converge with the bearer PW in the tunnel.

The multi-segment pseudowire allows multiple PWs between the source and the destination PEs. The PW switching device S-PE is used to connect the single PW at both sides together and to implement the PW-layer label switching at the S-PE site. Helping the user out of the scenario in which single-end PW cannot be built between the source and destination PEs, the multi-segment pseudowire technology satisfies different application requirements in cross-local network, cross-operator, and cross-control platform scenarios.

In addition, this technology can meet the requirements of deploying the network in a static, dynamic, or hybrid way. In the peer-to-peer scenario, if the multi-segment pseudowire is used, that is, one tunnel is built in the two networks respectively, the boundary node message will first pop up tunnel labels for PW label switching, then the labels will be encapsulated to another network tunnel. In this process, the IP/MPLS boundary node and the MPLS boundary node need to implement PW label switching.

LSP Stitching

As shown in Figure 7.17, the LSP stitching means there are multiple-segment LSPs between the T-PEs. Each section of LSP in the LSP stitching is an average LSP. The only task is to connect the single LSP at both sides via the LSP S-PE in the LSP stitching and implement the LSP-layer label switching at the S-PE.

LSP stitching differs from MS-PW only in different levels. The LSP stitching connects the single LSPs at both sides on the S-PE.

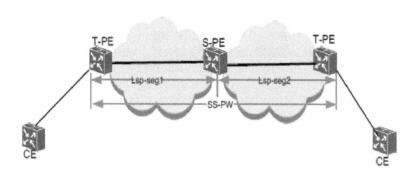

Figure 7.17

However, the MS-PW connects the single PW at both sides on the S-PE. As shown in the peer-to-peer scenario, if LSP stitching is used, which means one tunnel passes through two networks at the same time, then the boundary node is used only for tunnel label switching. In this method, the IP/MPLS boundary node, the MPLS boundary node, and the service X/Y should interconnect their protocols. The encapsulation efficiency is great.

The entire process equates to an independent SS-PW process with a changing PSN tunnel. Besides, the tunnel label switching is required at the two PSN network boundary nodes.

OAM

When using MS-PW and LSP stitching in the peer-to-peer operating models of MPLS-TP and IP/MPLS, the definitions of OAM are different.

When using the MS-PW peer-to-peer operating model, OAM refers to:

Direct-connected OAM. There can be many sorts of OAM, including but not limited to the physical layer OAM and the link layer OAM mechanisms.

The end-to-end OAM on the LSP layer, including end-to-end LSP OAM on the MPLS-TP network and end-to-end LSP OAM on the IP/MPLS network.

The end-to-end OAM on the PW layer; that is, MS-PW OAM in the MPLS-TP and IP/MPLS networks.

When using the LSP stitching peer-to-peer operating model, OAM refers to:

Direct-connected OAM. There can be many sorts of OAM, including but not limited to the physical layer OAM and the link layer OAM mechanisms.

The end-to-end OAM on each sub-LSP layer, including the OAM on the end-to-end LSP of the MPLS-TP network and the OAM on the end-to-end LSP of the IP/MPLS network.

The end-to-end OAM on the LSP layer; that is, the LSP stitching OAM crossing the MPLS-TP and IP/MPLS networks.

The end-to-end OAM on the PW layer.

The OAMs on different layers may interact with each other. But the standards of the announcement from the LSP OAM to the PW OAM in the MS-PW mechanism and the announcement from the sub-LSP layer OAM to the LSP stitching OAM in the LSP stitching mechanism are still under research.

In the peer-to-peer model, the interaction between the MPLS-TP network and the IP/MPLS network includes the following steps:

Create LSP: First, build intra-segment LSP in the networks respectively. If the LSP stitching mechanism is used, the administrator should stitch two LSPs (sub-LSP) at both networks to one LSP manually at the network boundary node (SPE); that is, build an LSP stitching relationship on the SPE. In this way, the end-to-end LSP stitching crossing the MPLS-TP network and the IP/MPLS network can be built.

Create PW: If the MS-PW mechanism is used, the administrator should stitch two PWs (PW fragment) at both networks to one PW manually at the network boundary node (SPE); that is, build a PW stitching relationship on the SPE. In this way, the end-to-end MS-PW crossing the MPLS-TP network and the IP/MPLS network can be built. If the LSP stitching mechanism is used, the administrator can keep using this LSP stitching to build the end-to-end PW crossing the MPLS-TP network and the IP/MPLS network. Besides, this PW is a single-segment PW. Configure OAM and protection: Build the proper OAM and the protection relationship according to the requirements. The protection in the peer-to-peer model usually keeps the regular fast route convergence mechanism and the FRR mechanism. In addition, to avoid S-PE single-point failure, one PW/LSP for protection can be configured. This protection PW/LSP does not pass the S-PE mentioned above.

Application Scenario: The Overlapping Interconnection Scenario of the L2/L3 VPN Bridging in the LTE Environment

In most LTE scenarios, the access aggregation deploys the MPLS-TP and the core layer deploys the IP/MPLS. The L2/L3 VPN bridging mode can be used to realize the interconnection of two networks.

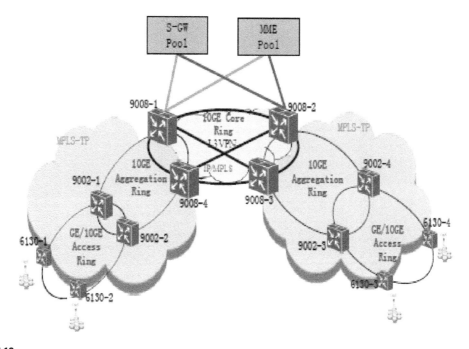

Figure 7.18

As Figure 7.18 shows, the access layer and the aggregation layer use EVPL service to access and converge the S1 and X2 services to the core node (9008-N in the figure). Then core layer devices use the L2/L3 VPN bridging technology to map the EVPL service to one VRF entity. At the same time, the L3VPN in the core layer is used to realize flexible scheduling of the S1 and X2 services to satisfy the LTE bearer requirements.

In the entire forwarding process, the message encapsulation format is as shown in Figure 7.19. The access convergence services are encapsulated via the L2VPN PW. They are forwarded via the L3VPN. Implement the L2/L3 bridging on the aggregation core boundary node 9008-N, and finish the interconnection between MPLS-TP and IP/MPLS.

Application Scenario: The Peer-to-Peer Interconnection Scenario in the MS-PW Environment

If MS-PW is used for implementing the MPLS-TP and the IP/MPLS network interconnection, the ZTE MS-PW mechanism includes a DHI PW 3-point bridge solution and an MS-PW

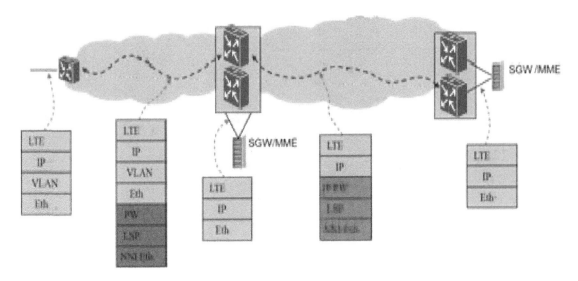

Figure 7.19

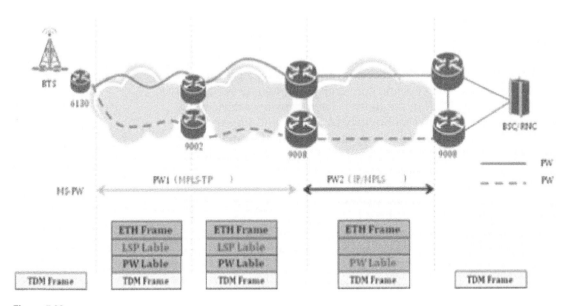

Figure 7.20

all-connection redundant protection solution. It gives comprehensive support to the dynamic, static, and hybrid application scenarios.

As Figure 7.20 shows, the access convergence layer deploys MPLS-TP, the core layer deploys IP/MPLS, and MS-PW is used to interconnect the two networks. In other words, build the corresponding PW fragment in the MPLS-TP and the IP/MPLS networks respectively. Use the aggregation core boundary node 9008 as S-PE to stitch the PW fragments at both sides of the S-PW to one MS-PW. In the PW fragment, the messages can only be sent according to the outer LSP label.

On the S-PE, the inner PW label is distributed to the next PW fragment. Check the corresponding LSP information. In this way, the messages are transferred by another network after implementing two-layer label switching on the S-PE.

In the dynamic MS-PW and redundant protection scenarios, MC-APS/MC-LAG, ICCP, and MC-PW APS protocols can be configured on the corresponding devices.

INDEX

Note: Page numbers followed by *f* indicate figures and *t* indicate tables.

Printed and bound by CPI Group (UK) Ltd, Croydon, CR0 4YY

03/10/2024

01040327-0008